Sideshow

Dubcek:
Dubcek and Czechoslovakia 1968-1990

Crime and Compromise:
Janos Kadar and the Politics of Hungary
since Revolution

The Quality of Mercy:
Cambodia, Holocaust and Modern Conscience

Watergate: The Full Inside Story
(co-author)

The Shah's Last Ride:
The Story of the Exile,
Misadventures and Death of the Emperor

Kowtow! After Tiananmen Square:
A Plea on Behalf of Hong Kong

Rupert Murdoch:
Ringmaster of the Information Circus

Sideshow

Kissinger, Nixon and
the Destruction of Cambodia

WILLIAM SHAWCROSS

The Hogarth Press
LONDON

Published in 1991 by
The Hogarth Press
An imprint of
Chatto and Windus
20 Vauxhall Bridge Road
London SW1V 2SA

Reprinted 1993

First published in Great Britain by André Deutsch Ltd 1979
New edition published with additional material in Great Britain
1986

'Sideswipe: Kissinger, Shawcross and the Responsibility for
Cambodia', 'Shawcross Swipes Again' and 'Rodman responds'
from *The American Spectator*, vol. 14, nos. 3 and 7, and their
reprint 'William Shawcross vs. Peter Rodman' © *The American
Spectator* 1981. Reproduced by kind permission of *The American
Spectator*.

A CIP catalogue record for this book is available from the
British Library

ISBN 0 7012 0944 5

Printed in Finland by
Werner Söderström Oy

For Conrad and all my family

Contents

Sideshow

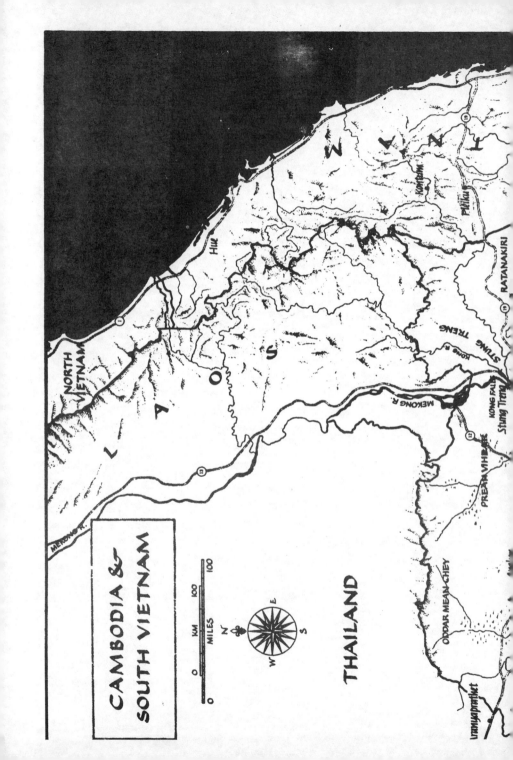

CAMBODIA &
SOUTH VIETNAM

KM
MILES
0   100
0   100

N
W   E
S

THAILAND

LAOS

NORTH
VIETNAM

MEKONG R.

MEKONG R.

KONG R.

STUNG TRENG

RATANAKIRI

PREAH VIHEAR

KONG FALLS
Stung Treng

ODDAR MEAN-CHEY

Kontom

Pleiku

Hue

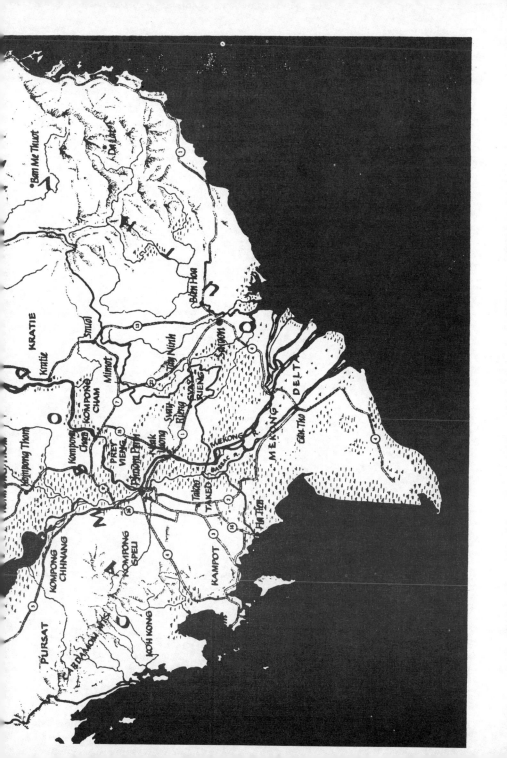

Foreword

THIS BOOK is an attempt to examine the Nixon administration's uses of power. It tries to demonstrate how decisions made in Washington affected the lives of one particular and distant people. It is, in some ways, a look at the foreign-policy side of Watergate.

During the early seventies Cambodia was often referred to as a "sideshow." Journalists who covered the war there used the term with irony; in Washington some officials employed it almost as a matter of policy. It was apt enough. The main arena was Vietnam, and it was there that attention was concentrated. Cambodia was always off stage, away from the light. Many of the decisions regarding the country were made in secret, others were presented inaccurately; inquiry was discouraged and exactly what was happening remained obscure.

From 1970 onward I reported the war in Indochina for *The Sunday Times* of London and other papers. I regret that I too saw Cambodia as peripheral and was there for only one week; those who knew the country well may find that aspects that they loved are missing from these pages. In 1972 I covered the North Vietnamese offensive in South Vietnam, and then the Harkness Foundation gave me a scholarship to go and learn something about the United States. I became a Congressional Fellow of the American Political Science Association and worked on Capitol Hill through much of 1973. I also wrote for *The Sunday Times*, was the Washington correspondent of the *New Statesman* and of the *Far Eastern Eco-*

nomic Review, and co-authored a book on Watergate. I felt then that unusual events were taking place in Cambodia, and I began to write on its war from Washington. In April 1975, I covered the end of the American effort, from Saigon and then from Washington. Soon after that, reports of brutal behavior by the Communist victors in Cambodia began to reach the West. I wanted to find out whether they were true and, if so, why; I started the research that ended in this book.

In the course of my research I worked in the United States, China, Thailand, France, Hong Kong, Germany and Britain. I interviewed more than three hundred people and corresponded with many others. They included American, Cambodian, Vietnamese and French cabinet ministers, generals and other military men, civil servants, journalists, and refugees. Dr. Kissinger declined to see me. I have quoted extensively from U.S. Government documents. Some of these have already been published, others I have obtained under the Freedom of Information Act. The Department of Defense, the State Department, the Central Intelligence Agency, the National Security Council and the Agency for International Development released to me several thousand pages of memoranda, cables and internal histories. Their classification ranged from "Confidential" to "Top-Secret-Sensitive-Eyes of Addressee Only-No Forn" (no foreigners).

The Freedom of Information Act is a tribute to the self-confidence of American society; it recognizes rights of citizens that are hardly to be conceived anywhere else in the world. It creates, however, problems for the historian. Departmental files are almost boundless. Every cable or memorandum refers to previous messages; one, ten, even fifty cables do not necessarily complete a story. The costs of pursuing every single relevant paper are prohibitive.

In many cases the agency concerned denied me documents or deleted material on receiving my original request. Under the terms of the Act, I appealed most such denials. (I did not do so if, for example, the material was withheld on the grounds that an individual's life would be endangered by its release.) In making my appeals I stressed that I had no wish to damage the national security of the United States or to harm any agency of the U.S. Government, but was concerned only to tell a story as fully as I could. (For this same reason I have not identified by name CIA officials who served in Phnom Penh during the war.) In response to my appeals a great deal, though not all, of the denied material was given to me. I did not take legal action, as the Act allows, to try and compel the release of the material that was withheld on appeal.

Despite such provisions, I am confident that my research offers a coherent history. In cases where the documentation may be incomplete I have tried to advise the reader, either in the text or in the notes at the end of the book. I have used the notes to elaborate on specific points and I have also identified there, when possible, the sources of my information. This was not always possible because, although I tried to conduct every interview on the record, there were some people who wished to aid me but were only able to do so if it were not for attribution. I hope I have respected their confidences.

There are many people whom I wish to thank for different kinds of help and encouragement: my friend Anthony Smith, with whom I first visited Indochina; my wife, Marina, with whom I returned there and with whom I went to America; Robert Johnston and Martha English of the Harkness Foundation, for the opportunity to begin to appreciate the United States; Stephen Fitzgerald, the Australian ambassador in Peking, who related to me a story that convinced me I should begin this project; Bruce Page, the features editor of *The Sunday Times*, who encouraged my research; John Barry, his successor, who saw the preliminary results into the paper; Charles W. Hinkle and the staff of the Pentagon's Freedom of Information bureaus (particularly of the Air Force), who responded to my requests patiently and as promptly as possible; and my colleagues in the American press who knew more about Cambodia and Washington than I did and were very generous with their time—in particular, Elizabeth Becker.

While I was writing the book I was appointed Visiting Research Fellow at Merton College, Oxford; my thanks especially to Dr. John Roberts, the Acting Warden, and to Judith Roberts. I was also given a grant from the Field Foundation through the Center for National Security Studies in Washington; I am grateful to the Director of the Center, Robert Borosage. Among all those who gave me time, experience, criticism or hospitality are Harry and Anne-Douglas Atherton, Christiane and Tony Besse, David Chandler, Dan Davidson, Derek Davies, Robert Ducas, Fred Emery, David Esterly, Elaine Greene, Stanley Karnow, Phillip Knightley, Edith Lenart, Michael Leifer, Michael Levin, Magnus and Veronica Linklater, Dan Morgan, Anne Norman, Peter Pringle, Robert Silvers, Carine Slade, Brooke Shearer and Strobe Talbott, Lloyd and Marva Shearer, Laurence Stern, Judy Stowe, Angela and Tiziano Terzani, Kathy Vignos. Lek Tan's generosity in sharing his own knowledge and

13

feeling for Cambodia with me was invaluable. I wrote most of the book in London, where my editor at André Deutsch, Faith Evans, gave me unstinting encouragement and criticism throughout. The final stages were completed in New York. At Simon and Schuster I was given great help by Gwen Edelman, Wayne Kirn, Ed Schneider, Sophie Sorkin and Vincent Virga; my editor, Alice Mayhew, was a constant inspiration and a marvelous guide.

I give my thanks to all of these and to everyone else who has aided in any way—especially to my mother and my father, whom I thank for years of understanding.

This book deals in detail with Cambodia, but I hope it suggests, in a general way, the consequences that other countries face when the world's most powerful nation and, in my opinion, the world's most vital democracy, is governed as it was after Richard Nixon and Henry Kissinger moved into the White House in January 1969.

London, January 1979 w.s.

Cast of Characters

Abrams, General Creighton. Commander, U.S. Forces, Vietnam, 1968–72.

Cleland, General John. Chief, Military Equipment Delivery Team, Cambodia, 1972–74.

Dean, John Gunther. U.S. Ambassador to Cambodia, 1974–75.

Enders, Thomas Ostrom. Deputy Chief of Mission, U.S. Embassy, Phnom Penh, 1971–74.

Green, Marshall. Assistant Secretary of State for East Asian and Pacific Affairs, 1970.

Halperin, Morton. Assistant to Dr. Henry Kissinger on the National Security Council staff, 1969.

Haig, Alexander. Military assistant and then chief deputy to Henry Kissinger, 1969–73.

Hou Yuon. Cambodian Marxist who fled Phnom Penh for the *maquis*, 1967.

Hu Nim. Cambodian Marxist who fled Phnom Penh for the *maquis*, 1967.

Ieng Sary. Cambodian Marxist who fled Phnom Penh for the *maquis*,

15

Sideshow

1963; Deputy Prime Minister charged with foreign affairs in the government of Democratic Kampuchea, 1975–78.

Keeley, Robert. Deputy Chief of Mission, U.S. Embassy, Phnom Penh, 1974–75.

Khieu Samphan. Cambodian Marxist who fled Phnom Penh for the *maquis*, 1967; Minister of Defense in Royal Government of National Union of Kampuchea, 1970–75; Minister of Defense and Commander in Chief, Chairman of the State Presidium and Head of State of Democratic Kampuchea, 1976–78.

Khmer Rouge. Left-wing *maquis* in the Cambodian countryside, so called by Prince Sihanouk.

Khmer Serei. Right-wing guerrillas, based in Thailand and South Vietnam, led by Son Ngoc Thanh.

Kissinger, Henry A. Assistant to the President for National Security Affairs, 1969–75; Secretary of State, 1973–77.

Ladd, Jonathan "Fred." Political-Military Counselor, U.S. Embassy Phnom Penh, 1970–72.

Laird, Melvin. Secretary of Defense, 1969–73.

Le Duc Tho. North Vietnam's chief negotiator with Henry Kissinger at the Paris Peace Talks on Vietnam.

Lon Nol, General. Minister of Defense and Prime Minister of Cambodia before 1970. Co-author of the coup that overthrew Prince Norodom Sihanouk, March 1970; Prime Minister, Commander in Chief and Head of State of the Khmer Republic, 1970–75. Fled to Hawaii, April 1975.

Lon Non, Colonel. Lon Nol's younger brother. Executed by the Khmer Rouge, April 1975.

Manac'h, Etienne, French Ambassador to China, 1969–75.

Mataxis, General Theodore. Chief, Military Equipment Delivery Team, Cambodia, 1971–72.

McCain, Admiral John. Commander in Chief, Pacific Forces (CINCPAC), 1968–72.

Palmer, General William. Chief of Military Equipment Delivery Team, Cambodia, 1974–75.

16

Penn Nouth. Prime Minister in various Sihanouk governments during the 1950s and 1960s; Prime Minister in the Royal Government of National Union of Kampuchea, 1970–75.

Pol Pot. *See* Saloth Sar.

Pursley, Colonel Robert. Military Assistant to Melvin Laird, Secretary of Defense, 1969–71.

Rives, Lloyd "Mike." Chargé d'affaires, U.S. Embassy, Phnom Penh, 1969–70.

Rogers, William. U.S. Secretary of State, 1969–73.

Saloth Sar (later known as Pol Pot). Cambodian Marxist who fled Phnom Penh for the *maquis*, 1963. Secretary General, Central Committee of the Communist Party of Kampuchea, 1963–1978; Prime Minister of Democratic Kampuchea 1976–78.

Sihanouk, Prince Norodom. Crowned King of Cambodia 1941; abdicated in favor of father 1955; ruled Cambodia as prince until deposed in 1970; head of government in exile, Royal Government of National Union of Kampuchea, 1970–75; returned to Phnom Penh under Khmer Rouge rule, as nominal head of state, 1975; forced into retirement 1976.

Sirik Matak, Prince. Leader of the Cambodian business community; co-author of the coup that overthrew Prince Norodom Sihanouk, March 1970; Prime Minister during the Khmer Republic, 1970–75; executed by the Khmer Rouge, April 1975.

Son Ngoc Thanh. Leader of the right-wing guerrillas, Khmer Serei, 1945–70; Prime Minister during the Khmer Republic, 1972; disappeared in Vietnam after April 1975.

Swank, Emory Coblentz "Coby." U.S. Ambassador to Cambodia, 1970–73.

We had fed the heart on fantasies,
The heart's grown brutal from the fare;
More substance in our enmities
Than in our love

W. B. Yeats
"Meditations in Time of Civil War"
1923

CHAPTER 1

The Secret

THE FIRST request was unpretentious. On February 9, 1969, less than a month after the inauguration of Richard Nixon, General Creighton Abrams, commander of United States forces in South Vietnam, cabled General Earle G. Wheeler, Chairman of the Joint Chiefs of Staff, to inform him that "recent information, developed from photo reconnaissance and a rallier gives us hard intelligence on COSVN HQ facilities in Base Area 353."

COSVN HQ was the acronym for the elusive headquarters—"Central Office for South Vietnam"—from which, according to the United States military, the North Vietnamese and Viet Cong were directing their war effort in South Vietnam. Until then, Abrams remarked, the military had placed COSVN in Laos. Now he was certain the headquarters was much farther south, in one of neutral Cambodia's border states which were being used by the Communists as bases and sanctuaries from the fighting in Vietnam. Abrams wanted to attack it.

The area is covered by thick canopy jungle. Source reports there are no concrete structures in this area. Usually reliable sources report that COSVN and COSVN-associated elements consistently remain in the same general area along the border. All our information, generally confirmed by imagery interpretation, provides us with a firm basis for targeting COSVN HQs.

Already Abrams had been instructed by the new administration to discuss United States troop withdrawals with the South Vietnamese. Now he reminded Wheeler that he had predicted a large-scale enemy offensive around Saigon in the near future. An attack on COSVN, he argued, "will have an immediate effect on the offensive and will also have its effect on future military offensives which COSVN may desire to undertake." An appropriate form of assault would be "a short-duration, concentrated B-52 attack of up to 60 sorties, compressing the time interval between strikes to the minimum. This is more than we would normally use to cover a target this size, but in this case it would be wise to insure complete destruction."

Abrams seems to have understood some of the implications of this request. Prince Norodom Sihanouk, Cambodia's ruler, had long been trying to keep his country out of the war in Vietnam. Abrams assured Wheeler that "there is little likelihood of involving Cambodian nationals if the target boxes are placed carefully. Total bomber exposure over Cambodian territory would be less than one minute per sortie." (Put another way, sixty sorties would take about one hour.) The general also thought it necessary to point out that "the successful destruction of COSVN HQs in a single blow would, I believe, have a very significant impact on enemy operations throughout South Vietnam." He asked for authority for the attack.

The Joint Chiefs sent Abrams' memo up to Melvin R. Laird, a former Wisconsin Republican Congressman, who was the new Secretary of Defense. Laird passed it to the White House, where it received the immediate attention of the new President and his National Security Affairs adviser, Dr. Henry Kissinger.

Two days later General John P. McConnell, the acting chairman in Wheeler's absence, sent a reply that must have cheered Abrams; it indicated that Washington was taking the idea even more seriously than Abrams himself. His request to Wheeler had not been highly classified, but simply headed "Personal for Addressees." McConnell's answer, however, was routed so that almost no one but he and Abrams could see it and was plastered with classifications: "Top Secret"—"Sensitive"— "Eyes Only"—"Delivery During Waking Hours"—"Personal for Addressee's Eyes Only."

McConnell told Abrams that his request had been presented to "the highest authority." In the conventions of cable language, this meant that President Nixon himself had seen it. The President had not rejected the idea; Abrams was told that "this matter will be further considered." The cable went on:

2. The highest authority desires that this matter be held as closely as possible in all channels and in all agencies which have had access to it.

3. The highest authority also wants your estimate on the number of Cambodian civilians who might become casualties of such an attack.

4. It will not, repeat not, be necessary for you to send a briefing team to Washington. However, it will be important for you to keep me informed on any further developments from your viewpoint. Warm regards.

Despite McConnell's advice, Abrams did send a briefing team to Washington. Two colonels arrived at the Pentagon, and a special breakfast meeting was arranged at which they could explain Abrams' proposals to a number of senior officials. These included Melvin Laird, General Wheeler, Colonel Robert Pursley, Laird's military assistant, and Lieutenant General John Vogt, then the Air Force's Assistant Deputy Chief of Staff for Plans and Operations. The meeting was also attended by a representative from Dr. Kissinger's National Security Council staff, Colonel Alexander Haig.

The colonels outlined their argument with conviction. This time, they claimed, it really was true: Viet Cong and North Vietnamese headquarters had been located. Base Area 353 was in the so-called Fish Hook, a corner of Cambodia that jutted into South Vietnam, northwest of Saigon. Even without COSVN, it was considered one of the most important Communist sanctuaries in Cambodia. Several regiments were based there and it also contained military hospitals and large caches of food and arms.

Over the next five weeks Abrams' request was frequently discussed by the National Security Council staff and at Presidential meetings in the Oval Office of the White House. Understandably perhaps, the Joint Chiefs were enthusiastic in support of the proposal. Melvin Laird was more skeptical. But he acknowledged that if COSVN had really been discovered it should be destroyed and argued that it could be publicly justified as an essential precondition to troop withdrawal. Nixon and Kissinger, however, were adamant that if it were done, it had to be done in total secrecy. Normal "Top Secret" reporting channels were not enough. Later General Wheeler recalled that the President said—"not just once, but either to me or in my presence at least half a dozen times"—that nothing whatsoever about the proposal must ever be disclosed.

Before a final decision was made, the Chiefs cabled Abrams to tell him that he could make tentative plans for launching the strike on the early morning of March 18. He was told of the demands for secrecy and was given a code name for the operation—"Breakfast," after the Pentagon briefing.

The cable set out in detail the way in which the raids were to be concealed. The planes would be prepared for a normal mission against targets in Vietnam. If the Joint Chiefs sent the signal "Execute repeat Execute Operation Breakfast," they would then be diverted to attack the Cambodian base area. No announcement would be made. "Due to sensitivity of this operation addressees insure that personnel are informed only on a strict need-to-know basis and at the latest feasible time which permits the operation to be conducted effectively."

Abrams made the necessary dispositions, and on March 17 Wheeler cabled him: "Strike on COSVN headquarters is approved. Forty-eight sorties will be flown against COSVN headquarters. Twelve strikes will be flown against *legitimate* targets of your choice in SVN not repeat not near the Cambodian border." (Emphasis added)

The strikes were to take place almost at once, between three o'clock and seven o'clock on the morning of March 18, unless Abrams received a priority "Red Rocket" message "Cancel repeat Cancel Operation Breakfast."

The cable described how the press was to be handled. When the command in Saigon published its daily bombing summary, it should state that, "B-52 missions in six strikes early this morning bombed these targets: QUOTE Enemy activity, base camps, and bunker and tunnel complexes 45 kilometers north-east of Tay Ninh City. UNQUOTE. Following the above, list two or more other B-52 targets struck (12 sorties)."

Wheeler continued:

> In the event press inquiries are received following the execution of the Breakfast Plan as to whether or not U.S. B-52s have struck in Cambodia, U.S. spokesman will confirm that B-52s did strike on routine missions adjacent to the Cambodian border but state that he has no details and will look into this question. Should the press persist in its inquiries or in the event of a Cambodian protest concerning U.S. strikes in Cambodia, U.S. spokesman will neither confirm nor deny reports of attacks on Cambodia but state it will be investigated. After delivering a reply to any Cambodian protest, Washington will inform the press that we have apologized and offered compensation.

Finally, Wheeler reminded Abrams and the B-52 commanders, "Due to the sensitivity of this operation all persons who know of it, who partic-

ipate in its planning, preparation or execution should be warned not repeat not to discuss it with unauthorized individuals."

Many of the B-52s used in Indochina were based at Anderson Air Force
Base in Guam. The planes had been built in the 1950s as an integral part
of the United States' nuclear deterrent, but since 1965 more than a
hundred of them had been adapted to carry dozens of conventional 750-
lb. bombs in their bellies and under their wings. They were still controlled
by Strategic Air Command but were at the disposition of the Commander
of U.S. Forces in South Vietnam. Abrams could call upon sixty planes a
day. Each plane could carry a load of approximately thirty tons of bombs.

Before takeoff, the crews of the B-52s were always briefed on the
location of their targets in South Vietnam. After Wheeler's March 17
"Execute Operation Breakfast" order was received, the pilots and navigators of the planes to be diverted were taken aside by their commanding
officer and told to expect the ground controllers in Vietnam to give them
the coordinates of new targets—they would be bombing Cambodia.

That evening the heavily laden planes rumbled off the long runway,
rose slowly over the Russian trawlers, which almost always seemed to be
on station just off the island, and climbed to 30,000 feet for the monoto-
nous five-hour cruise to Indochina. There was little for the six-man crew
to do—except watch for storm clouds over the Philippines and refuel in
mid-air—until they were above the South China Sea approaching the dark
line of the Vietnamese coast.

At this point they entered the war zone and came under control of the
ground radar sites in South Vietnam. But even now there was little reason
for concern. There were no enemy fighter planes to harass and chivvy
them, no antiaircraft fire, no ground-to-air missiles. A ground radar controller gave the navigator the coordinates of the final bomb run. Then the
controller watched on his radar screen as the planes, in cells of three,
approached the target; as they did so he counted down the bombardiers
with the words "Five—four—three—two—one—hack."

Twenty times that night the ground controllers, sitting in their air-con-
ditioned "hootches" in South Vietnam, cans of Coke or 7-Up by their
elbows, called out hack. Sixty long strings of bombs spread through the
dark and fell to the earth faster than the speed of sound. Each plane load
dropped into an area, or "box," about half a mile wide by two miles long,
and as each bomb fell, it threw up a fountain of earth, trees and bodies,
until the air above the targets was thick with dust and debris, and the

ground itself flashed with explosions and fire. For the first time in the war, so far as is known, forty-eight of such boxes were stamped upon neutral Cambodia by the express order of the President.

One group of men was especially delighted by the event. Since May 1967, when the U.S. Military Command in Saigon became concerned at the way the North Vietnamese and Viet Cong were evading American "search and destroy" and air attacks in Vietnam by making more use of bases in Laos and Cambodia, the U.S. Special Forces had been running special, highly classified missions into the two countries. Their code name was Daniel Boone.

The Daniel Boone teams entered Cambodia all along its 500-mile frontier with South Vietnam from the lonely, craggy, impenetrable mountain forests in the north, down to the well-populated and thickly reeded waterways along the Mekong river. There was a quality of fantasy about the missions. They usually contained two or three Americans and up to ten local mercenaries, often recruited from the hill tribes of the area. All the Americans were volunteers, and they were enjoined to the strictest secrecy: the release they had to sign subjected them to a $10,000 fine and up to ten years' imprisonment for disclosing details of the forays. Because the missions were supposed to be what the Army called "sterile," the Americans either wore uniforms that could not be traced to any American unit or were disguised in the black pajamas of the Viet Cong. They carried what had become by the middle '60s the universal symbol of revolution, the Soviet-designed AK-47 automatic rifle made in China. Deaths were reported to relatives as having occurred "along the border."

These and other precautions helped conceal the work from the American press and the Congress. But black pajamas do not really hide wellfed Caucasians prowling around Southeast Asian jungles. Teams often found that, within two hours of being "inserted" by helicopter (parachutes were not used, because the Americans fell so much faster than the Vietnamese), their opponents had put trackers onto them. Their reconnaissance mission abandoned, they had to flee through the jungle or crawl through the thick fifteen-foot grass, evading their stalkers until they could find a suitable clearing to call helicopter support for rescue.

Randolph Harrison, who saw himself then as a "gung-ho lieutenant," arrived at the Special Forces headquarters in Ban Me Thuot, in the Central Highlands, in August 1968. He was given command of one of the reconnaissance companies, and he made his first mission into Cambodia on November 17, 1968, just after the American people, in the hope of peace, narrowly elected Nixon. At this time there was no consensus within the United States' intelligence establishment on the extent to which the North Vietnamese and Viet Cong were using Cambodia as a sanctuary or as a supply route, but Harrison was shocked by the evidence he saw of the enemy's insouciance just across the border from his own camp.

"There were hard-surface roads, those concrete reinforced bunkers. I personally found some abandoned base camps that were acres in size . . ." he said later. "When you get an opportunity to see that blatant an example of their presence there, you scream and beg and do everything you can to get somebody to come in there and blast them." What he and his friends wanted most of all, he said, were B-52 "Arclight" strikes— "We had been told, as had everybody . . . that those carpet bombing attacks by B-52s [were] totally devastating, that nothing could survive, and if they had a troop concentration there it would be annihilated." They were enthusiastic when, on the morning of March 18, Major Michael Eiland, the Daniel Boone Operations officer, came up from Saigon to tell them of Operation Breakfast. He ordered a reconnaissance team into Area 353 by helicopter to pick up any possible Communist survivors. "We were told that . . . if there was anybody still alive out there they would be so stunned that all [we would] have to do [was] walk over and lead him by the arm to the helicopter."

Captain Bill Orthman was chosen to lead this team; he was given a radio operator named Barry Murphy and eleven Vietnamese. All were confident and rather excited. They were flown over the border and landed in rubble and craters. After the helicopters had taken off, the Daniel Boone men moved toward the tree line in search of their dead or dazed enemy. But within moments they were, in Harrison's words, "slaughtered."

The B-52 raid had not wiped out all the Communists as the Special Forces men had been promised. Instead, its effect, as Harrison said, had been "the same as taking a beehive the size of a basketball and poking it with a stick. They were mad."

The Communists fired at them from behind the trees on three sides. Three of the Vietnamese soldiers were immediately hit and Orthman himself was shot both in the leg and in the stomach. The group split apart and Orthman stumbled toward a bomb crater. Then a C.S. gas grenade in his rucksack burst into flames, searing the flesh off his back and his left arm. Barry Murphy threw himself into another crater and radioed frantically for the helicopters to return. Back at base they heard his call, "This is

25

Bullet. We've got four wounded and are taking fire from all directions. We don't . . . Oh God! I'm hit!, hit! I'm hit! My leg! Ow! I'm . . . again! My back ahh can't move!" His last scream was indecipherable.

Eventually one helicopter managed to come back down through the automatic-weapons fire to pick up the survivors. Orthman was saved because a friend jumped out and rushed across the ground to carry him aboard. Three of the Vietnamese made it to the helicopter; Barry Murphy's body was not recovered.

Despite the setback, another reconnaissance team was immediately ordered to take off for Cambodia to gather "dazed" Viet Cong. Their earlier enthusiasm for the mission was now gone and in a rare breach of discipline the Daniel Boone men refused. Three of them were arrested. "You can't be courtmartialled for refusing to violate the neutrality of Cambodia," Randolph Harrison reassured them. They were not.

As that night fell over Indochina, day was beginning in Washington. In his basement office in the White House, Henry Kissinger was discussing a point of policy with Morton Halperin, a young political scientist who had worked in the Pentagon during the previous administration and was now Kissinger's assistant for planning.

As the two men were talking, Colonel Alexander Haig came into the room and handed Kissinger a paper. As he read it, Halperin noticed, Kissinger smiled. He turned to Halperin and said that the United States had bombed a base in Cambodia and the first bomb-damage assessment showed that the attack had set off many secondary explosions. What did Halperin think of that? Halperin, who knew nothing of Breakfast, made a noncommittal answer. Kissinger told him that he was placing great trust in him and he must respect the confidence; almost no one else knew about the attack and no one else must know.

In his February 9 cable, Abrams had asked for a single attack to destroy COSVN headquarters. But once the decision had been made in principle that Communist violations of Cambodia's neutrality justified aggressive reciprocal action, it was not difficult to repeat the performance. The first mission had not been discovered by the press, nor had Cambodia protested. Indeed, it would now have been hard for the White House to insist on only one attack: Base Area 353 was, according to Abrams' headquarters, the Military Assistance Command, Vietnam (MACV), only one of fifteen Communist sanctuaries.

COMMUNIST LOGISTICS
IN CAMBODIA
1969–70

VC Base Areas
"Menu" Targets
Sea-land Supply Lines
Ho Chi Minh Trail Supply Lines

LAOS

CAMBODIA

SOUTH
VIETNAM

Siem Reap

Stung Treng

Kompong Thom

Kratie

Kompong Cham

Phnom Penh

Prey Veng

Takeo

Ha Tien

Can Tho

Tay Ninh

Bien Hoa

Saigon

PARROT'S
BEAK

GULF OF
THAILAND

SOUTH CHINA SEA

609   LUNCH
702
701
740   SUPPER
351   SNACK
350   DESSERT
353   DINNER
707
352
354   BREAKFAST
706
704   367

MEKONG RIVER

TONLE SAP

BASSAC R.

MILES

Sideshow

Over the next fourteen months 3,630 B-52 raids were flown against suspected Communist bases along different areas of Cambodia's border. Breakfast was followed by "Lunch," Lunch by "Snack," Snack by "Dinner," Dinner by "Dessert," Dessert by "Supper," as the program expanded to cover one "sanctuary" after another. Collectively, the operation was known as "Menu."

In 1973, after the bombing was finally discovered, both Nixon and Kissinger maintained, and still maintain, that the secrecy was necessary to protect Sihanouk, who was variously described as "acquiescing in," "approving," "allowing" or even "encouraging" the raids, so long as they were covert. They maintained that the areas were unpopulated and that only Vietnamese Communist troops, legitimate targets, were there. When he was confirmed as Secretary of State in 1973, for example, Kissinger declared that "It was not a bombing of Cambodia, but it was a bombing of North Vietnamese in Cambodia," and "the Prince as a minimum acquiesced in the bombing of unpopulated border areas." In 1976 he stated that "the government concerned [Sihanouk's] never once protested, and indeed told us that if we bombed unpopulated areas they would not notice." In fact, the evidence of Sihanouk's "acquiescence" is at least questionable, and the assertion that no Cambodians lived in these areas not only was untrue, but was known to be untrue at the time. The Joint Chiefs themselves informed the administration as early as April 1969 that many of the sanctuary areas were populated by Cambodians who might be endangered by bombing raids. The White House was to ignore this reservation.

The Chiefs' description of the bases is contained in a memorandum of April 9, 1969, written for the Secretary of Defense, in which they advocated invasion as well as bombing of Cambodia. Its conclusions were based on "Giant Dragon" high-altitude overflights, "Dorsal Fin" low-level aerial surveys and the Daniel Boone ground forays, among other evidence. It described the military purpose as well as the nature of each of the fifteen bases they had identified, and went on to estimate the number of Cambodians they contained. The figures are worth considering.

Base Area 353, Breakfast, covered 25 square kilometers and had a total population of approximately 1,640 Cambodians, of whom the Joint Chiefs reckoned 1,000 to be peasants. There were, according to the Chiefs, thirteen Cambodian towns in the area. (Villages would be a more accurate description.)

Base Area 609, Lunch, was north, near the Laotian border, in wild country without any towns. The Chiefs asserted that there were an estimated 198 Cambodians there, all of them peasants.

Base Area 351, Snack, covered 101 square kilometers and had an estimated 383 Cambodians, of whom 303 were considered peasants. There was one town in the area.

Base Area 352, Dinner, had an estimated Cambodian population of 770, of whom 700 were peasants. It contained one town.

Base Area 350, Dessert, had an estimated Cambodian population of 120, all peasants.

The Chiefs believed that all these "sanctuaries" should be attacked. They attempted to estimate how many Cambodians would be killed; they maintained that, as the Cambodians lived apart from the Vietnamese troops, their casualties would be "minimal." But they conceded that such calculations depended on many variables and were "tenuous at best." There was no pretense that the raids could occur without danger to the Cambodians—"some Cambodian casualties would be sustained in the operation." And they agreed that "the surprise effect of attacks could tend to increase casualties, as could the probable lack of protective shelters around Cambodian homes to the extent that exists in South Vietnam." Cambodian peasants, unlike the Vietnamese, had little experience of being bombed.

Some scruples, however, were brought to bear. Three of the fifteen sanctuaries—base areas 704, 354 and 707, which had "sizeable concentrations of Cambodian civilian or military population" in or around them—were not recommended for attack at all. (The definition of "sizeable" is not known; presumably it was higher than the 1,640 Cambodians living in the Breakfast site, which they had approved.) Base Area 740, Supper, had an estimated Cambodian population of 1,136.

Because of Nixon's repeated insistence on total secrecy, few senior officials were told about Menu. The Secretary of the Air Force, Dr. Robert Seamans, was kept in ignorance; since he is not in the chain of command, this was not illegal, but General Wheeler later said that, if necessary, he would have lied to him and denied that the raids were taking place. The Chief of Staff of the Air Force, General John Ryan, was not informed; nor were the Cambodian desk officers on Abrams' intelligence arm in Saigon, the Office of Strategic Research and Analysis. None of the Congressional committees, whose duty it is to recommend appropriations and thus enable the Congress to fulfill its constitutional function of authorizing and funding war, was notified that the President had decided to carry war into a third country, whose neutrality the United States professed to respect. Instead, only a few sympathetic members of Congress, who had no constitutional authority to approve this extension of war, were quietly informed.

Sideshow

But if Congress and the public were easily kept in ignorance, the official record-keeping system required more sophisticated treatment. The Pentagon's computers demanded, for purposes of logistics, a complete record of hours flown, fuel expended, ordnance dropped, spare parts procured. In response to Nixon's demands for total and unassailable secrecy, the military devised an ingenious system that the Joint Chiefs liked to describe as "dual reporting."

Whether they flew from Guam, from Okinawa, or from Thailand, most B-52 missions over South Vietnam were guided to their targets by the "Skyspot" ground radar controllers at one of four radar sites in the country. The controllers received details—known as the "frag"—of the proposed strike after it had been approved in Washington. From the "frag," they calculated the range and bearing of the target from the radar site and the altitude, airspeed and ballistics of the bomb load. They then guided the planes down a narrow radar beam to target.

After missions were completed, B-52 crews reported what primary or secondary explosions they had seen to their debriefing officer at base, and the ground controllers sent their own poststrike reports to Saigon. Both reports entered the Pentagon computers and the official history of the war.

The procedures for Menu were modeled on Operation Breakfast. After a normal briefing on targets in Vietnam, the pilots and navigators of the planes that were to be diverted that night were told privately to expect the ground controllers to direct them to drop their bombs on a set of coordinates that were different from those they had just received. It was not a wide diversion; the South Vietnamese cover targets were usually selected so that the planes could simply fly another few kilometers beyond, until they were over the Cambodian target.

Major Hal Knight of Memphis was, for much of 1969, supervisor of the radar crews for the region of Vietnam that lay between Saigon and the Cambodian border. Every afternoon before a Menu mission, a special Strategic Air Command courier flight came to Bien Hoa airbase, where he worked, and he was handed a plain manila envelope containing an ordinary poststrike report form on which target coordinates had already been filled in. He locked it in his desk until evening and then, when the shift had assembled, gave the coordinates to his radar crew. They fed them through their Olivetti 101 computers to produce the details of the final bombing run for the new Cambodian target. These were called to the navigators when the B-52s arrived on station overhead in the early-morning dark.

After the bombs were released, the plane's radio operator—who was not supposed to know of the diversion—called his base by high-frequency radio to say that the mission had been accomplished. At base, the intelligence division, which also knew nothing of the change, entered the original South Vietnamese coordinates on the poststrike report. When the crews landed and were debriefed they were asked routine questions about malfunction, bomb damage and weather. The pilots and navigators were to make no mention of the new target—they had, after all, been forewarned, so it did not really count as a diversion.

At Bien Hoa itself Knight was under instructions to gather up every scrap of paper and tape with which the bombing had been plotted and lock them in his desk until daybreak. Only then (his superiors were afraid that pieces of paper might be dropped in the dark) was he to take the documents to an incinerator behind the hut and very carefully burn them. He was then to call a Saigon number he had been given—it was at Strategic Air Command Advanced Echelon—in order to tell the unidentified man who answered the telephone that "the ball game is over." The normal poststrike reports from the radar site were filled out with the coordinates of the original South Vietnamese cover target and sent, in the ordinary way, to Saigon by security mail. The night's mission over Cambodia entered the records as having taken place in Vietnam. The bombing was not merely concealed; the official, *secret* records showed that it had never happened.

The system worked well by the book, but it took no account of the attitudes of the men who were expected to implement it. Hal Knight, for example, accepted the military logic of bombing Cambodia but intensely disliked this procedure. Strategic Air Command is responsible for the nation's nuclear defense, and falsification of its reporting process was, for him, alarming; Knight had been trained to believe that accurate reporting was "pretty near sacred." He was especially concerned that he was violating Article 107 of the Military Code of Justice, which provides that any one "who, with intent to deceive, signs any false record, return, regulation, order or other official document, knowing the same to be false . . . shall be punished as a court martial may direct."

Red tape protects as well as restricts, and Knight feared that the institutional safeguards and controls that are integral to the maintenance of discipline and of a loyal, law-abiding army were being discarded. He did not know at what level the bombing had been authorized or whom these unprecedented procedures were supposed to deceive; but he did appreciate, to his dismay, that the practice gave him horrifying license.

A normal target was known to many people at the radar site, to the entire B-52 crew, to the intelligence unit at the plane's base and to dozens of Pentagon officials; a Menu mission was known only to him and a very few others. There was nothing to stop him from choosing the coordinates of a town in South Vietnam or Cambodia and having it bombed. Indeed, "if someone could have punched the right number into the right spot they could have had us bombing China," he observed later.

Knight discussed the falsification with other radar operators on other sites; they too found it hard to explain. If confidentiality were so important, why not simply raise the classification from "Secret" to "Top Secret"? He asked his commanding officer, Lieutenant Colonel David Patterson, about it; he was told not to do so.

"So I said, well, what is the purpose of it?"

Patterson replied "Well, the purpose is to hide these raids."

"Who from?" asked Knight.

He was apparently told, "Well, I guess the Foreign Relations Committee."

The Foreign Relations Committee did not find out about the unauthorized and illegal extension of the war into a neutral country until 1973, when Knight himself wrote to Congress to complain. But even under the restrictions imposed, the campaign was, to paraphrase Dean Rusk, known to the President, two members of the NSC, a couple of State Department officials and three hundred colonels in the Pentagon.

One evening soon after the raids began, the pilot of a Forward Air Control plane (FAC), which guided fighter bombers to their targets in South Vietnam, was sitting outside his hootch at An Loc, a few miles from the Cambodian border. "We saw beacons going overhead to the West," said Captain Gerald Greven later. "We saw the flames in the distance and the trembling of the ground from what appeared to be B-52 strikes." He was surprised, because he knew of no targets in that area. The next morning he flew to find the craters, and "to my astonishment they were on the West side of the river separating the borders of South Vietnam and Cambodia."

Greven was impressed by the amount of destruction the raids had caused, but puzzled. "I went back to my commander and he said he had no knowledge of the strike and why it had taken place." He spoke to the regional commander for the Forward Air Controllers—"he also declared to have no knowledge." He then went on to Air Support headquarters at Bien Hoa and spoke to the commanding officer. "I was told, with a slight smile, that obviously my 'maps were in error.' " Greven correctly took that to mean that he "did not have a need to know." He asked no more questions. But eventually he, too, contacted Congress.

William Beecher was *The New York Times* Pentagon correspondent, a diligent reporter. After Nixon's victory in November 1968, Beecher asked his contacts in the Defense Department how they would advise the new President to extricate American troops from Vietnam. He was told that one possible way of "buying time" would be to bomb the sanctuaries. Beecher noted this hypothesis and by April 1969 began to suspect that it was being carried out. The Pentagon was reporting its bombing strikes in South Vietnam near the Cambodian border, but he knew that no targets were there. And, despite the special "security precautions," information began to leak almost at once. On March 26, one week after the Breakfast mission, *The New York Times* reported briefly but accurately that Abrams had requested B-52 strikes against the sanctuaries. Ronald Ziegler, the White House Press Secretary, was quoted as giving a "qualified denial" to the reports. "He said that to his knowledge no request had reached the President's desk." This story was followed by comments—in *U.S. News & World Report* and by columnist C. L. Sulzberger in *The New York Times*—urging that Nixon do what he had in fact already begun. But only Beecher took the trouble to follow the obvious lead that any "qualified denial" offers. He revisited those to whom he had talked at the end of 1968, and on May 9 he revealed in the *Times* that "American B-52 bombers have raided several Viet Cong and North Vietnamese supply dumps and base camps in Cambodia for the first time, according to Nixon Administration sources, but Cambodia has not made any protest."

Beecher wrote that the bombing had started because of the increase in supplies reaching South Vietnam by sea and through Cambodia, supplies that "never have to run any sort of bombing gauntlet before they enter South Vietnam." He claimed that Prince Sihanouk had dropped hints that he would not oppose American pursuit of Communist forces which he was himself unable to dislodge. Perhaps most important, Beecher stated that the bombing was intended "to signal" Hanoi that the Nixon admin-

33

istration, "while pressing for peace in Paris, is willing to take some military risks avoided by the previous Administration . . . to demonstrate that the Nixon Administration is different and 'tougher.'. . ."

The revelation aroused no public interest. Four years later, this same account was to cause at least a short-lived uproar and spark demands for impeachment, but at the time it had little obvious effect. There was no press follow-up, and no members of the Senate Foreign Relations Committee, the Senate Armed Services Committee or the Appropriations committees voiced concern. In Key Biscayne, however, where Nixon and Kissinger and their staffs were working on the first of Nixon's major Vietnam speeches, the article provoked reactions that verged on hysteria.

After reading the story with Nixon, Kissinger spent much of his morning on the telephone with FBI Director J. Edgar Hoover. According to Hoover's detailed memoranda of the conversations, Kissinger asked him, in his first call at 10:35 A.M., to make "a major effort to find out where [the story] came from." A half hour later Kissinger telephoned again to say that while the FBI was about it they should try to find the sources of previous Beecher stories as well. Hoover replied that he would call back the next day with any information they had managed to gather. But within two hours Kissinger was on the line again, this time to ask Hoover to be sure he was discreet "so no stories will get out." Just how the Director liked being told how to protect his beloved FBI is not recorded, but Hoover assured Kissinger that discretion would be maintained; he had decided, he said, not to contact Beecher directly but to try to divine the source of the story from other reporters.

That afternoon, relaxing by the swimming pool with other members of the National Security Council staff, Kissinger invited his aide Morton Halperin to walk with him down the beach. Strolling along the sand, Kissinger told him of the great concern he felt over the Beecher leak. Halperin knew Kissinger well; they had been together at Harvard. He recalls that Kissinger assured him of his personal trust in him but reminded him that there were others in the Nixon administration who were suspicious of Halperin's New York and Harvard background and the fact that he had worked in McNamara's Pentagon. It was he who was suspected of leaking to Beecher. Halperin replied that he could not have been the source; after all, it was only by chance (and Kissinger's indiscretion) that he knew anything about the bombing. Kissinger apparently agreed that this was so, but said that he was under great pressure from other members of the administration and the White House.

Kissinger now proposed an ingenious way of justifying his confidence in Halperin to the others. So that he could not possibly be held responsible for any future leaks, Kissinger suggested that he be taken off the distribution list for highly classified material. Then, when a leak next occurred, he would be above suspicion and also retroactively cleared.

Halperin did not find the arrangement amusing; he had been dealing with classified materials for years and had never been asked to prove his loyalty. But Kissinger was such an old friend and presented his case with such charm and solicitousness, Halperin recalls, that he agreed to the proposal.

Kissinger and Hoover talked once more that day. At 5:05 P.M. the FBI director telephoned to report his progress. To judge by Hoover's memo, it was a bizarre conversation.

Hoover told Kissinger that Beecher "frequented" the Pentagon press office (hardly a surprising piece of information, in view of the fact that he was a Pentagon correspondent). There were still many pro-Kennedy people in the Pentagon, Hoover remarked, and they all fed Beecher with information. But on this occasion he was convinced that Morton Halperin was the culprit. According to FBI files, Halperin believed the United States had "erred in the Vietnam commitment"; moreover, the Canadian Mounted Police had discovered that he was on the mailing list of a Communist publication, "Problems of Peace and Socialism." Both Halperin and Beecher were members of the "Harvard clique" (as, of course, was Kissinger), and it was clear where the blame must lie. At the end of his memo Hoover noted, in words which resonate down the years, "Dr. Kissinger said he appreciated this very much and he hoped I would follow it up as far as we can take it, and they will destroy whoever did this if we can find him, no matter where he is."

That same afternoon the FBI placed a wiretap on Halperin's home in Bethesda, a bedroom suburb of Washington. This tap was immediately followed by others. In important, specific detail, these taps infringed the limits of the law.* They marked the first of the domestic abuses of power now known as Watergate.

Night after night through the summer, fall and winter of 1969 and into the early months of 1970 the eight-engined planes passed west over South Vietnam and on to Cambodia. Peasants were killed—no one knows how many—and Communist logistics were somewhat disrupted. To avoid the attacks, the North Vietnamese and Viet Cong pushed their sanctuaries and supply bases deeper into the country, and the area that the B-52s bombarded expanded as the year passed. The war spread.

* For a brief statement of the law, see footnote to p. 107.

CHAPTER 2

The Land

CAMBODIA HAS held a special appeal for foreigners. Many of the journalists, tourists and diplomats who visited it in the 1950s and '60s wrote of an idyllic, antique land unsullied by the brutalities of the modern world. Phnom Penh was, it is true, an exquisite riverine city, and its fine white and yellow-ocher buildings, charming squares and cafés lent it a French provincial charm that gave it a considerable edge over its tawdry neighbors Bangkok and Saigon. It had not been overwhelmed by the pressures of trade and war; its population was only about 600,000, and there was little sign of the shanty towns of Coca-Cola-can slums in which Thai and Vietnamese peasants eked out a miserable existence. The huge covered market was stacked high with local produce—vegetables, rice and dozens of kinds of fish caught in the many waters of the land. And the countryside, where 90 percent of the people lived in villages built around their Buddhist temples seemed, if anything, even more attractive than the capital.

The Cambodian people were taller, darker, more sensuous and apparently more friendly than the Thais or the Vietnamese; visitors took to them immediately. There were no strategic hamlets, no refugee camps, no State Department men with M-16 rifles and earnest smiles explaining the logic of rural development, and neither were there any Soviet or Chinese B-40 rockets firing indiscriminately from the tree line into the villages.

The country is about the same size as Missouri, or of England and Wales. Thick tropical forests cover much of the land, and two great rivers flow across and fertilize the central plains, where most of the people have always lived. The overriding impression was of fecundity and greenness, and of chocolate-brown waterways where buffalo and sometimes elephants steamed gently in the heat, with small brown boys or large white birds perched on their backs.

Not all of the country was easily accessible. Bandits operated out of the Cardamom mountains in the southwest, and troupes of pirates sped along many of the waterways. In the mountains of the northeast, the hill tribes people, the Khmer Loeu, lived outside government control, and the Viet Cong and North Vietnamese moved among them. A few groups of indigenous Communist guerrillas, the Khmer Rouge, operated deep in the forests, but their influence was small in a conservative, religious country where most land was owned by the tiller, where even the most relaxed could usually be assured enough rice, and where fish were to be had for the drop of a net. Such was the illusion—bucolic plenty, Buddhist serenity, neutralist peace. It was, however, an oversimplification. Like any other country, Cambodia was the complex product of geographical, social and political experience that provides precedent and warning for future history. It was never quite the smiling, gentle land that foreigners liked to see.

Water has fashioned Cambodia. In prehistory the central plain of the country was under the sea, and waves broke against the Dangrek mountains of Southern Laos. The Mekong river fell through the narrow Laotian ranges and over the Khong Falls into the sea. Gradually the river built up the soil and filled the gulf to form present-day Cambodia and southern Vietnam. Today only the Great Lake (Tonle Sap) in the center of Cambodia marks the original line of the seacoast. The lake is shaped like an upside-down violin from northwest to southeast across the country, its stem leading into the Tonle Sap river to join the Mekong at the watershed on which the city of Phnom Penh was eventually built. The rivers meet briefly and divide again, as the Mekong and the Bassac, and flow on in two streams through fertile, red, muddy fields into the great fanlike Delta of the Mekong, and so to the South China Sea.

In late spring the rivers begin to swell as torrents flow from the Himalayas over the Khong Falls and into the central plains. The great clouds that have been lowering over the Indian Ocean are driven toward the

37

Asian land mass by the southwest trades. They break over the cracked plains and for four months Cambodia is inundated. The Mekong and the Bassac cannot contain the mass of silt-laden water that pours down toward the sea, and it backs up in the Tonle Sap. In what should constitute a wonder of the world, the waters are actually reversed; they rush swirling back up the Tonle Sap river and burst into the Great Lake, which instantly spills over its shores and drowns thousands of acres of trees and fields. For most of the summer months the land remains under water to be refertilized and reinvigorated, and all of Cambodia is, in Rimbaud's words, "filled with ochrous skies and drowned forests." By November, the Himalayan snows have melted, prevailing winds are reversed, the clouds are driven away, the torrents of the monsoon cease, and the pressure on the Tonle Sap eases. The waters slip off the land and, filled with millions of fish, sweep down the rivers and into the sea.

As a result, parts of Cambodia are potentially among the most fertile of the tropical zones. But in its raw state the area is hostile; the damp atmosphere is draining and oppressive, the animal life is unfriendly, and the receding waters leave stagnant swamps as well as fertilized soil. Only extensive irrigation ensures a crop necessary for an expanding population. Civilizations have flourished in the plains when the water has been brought under control, but—as elsewhere in Southeast Asia—there has always been tension between the people in the plains and the nomadic groups who have lived in the forests or the mountains.

The precise origins of the plains people are not known, but the shores of the South China Sea were originally populated by people very closely resembling those found in the islands of the Pacific. Soon after the birth of Christ, the culture of India began to influence the area that is now Cambodia, and contact with China then followed. Most of what we know of those times comes from Chinese dynastic annals. The Chinese name for the state that occupied the Mekong Delta from the second to sixth century A.D. was "Funan." Funan was the crucible in which Indian culture and the local people fused to produce a new civilization, the Khmers. It was a major stop on the sea trade routes to China; excavations have uncovered Indian-influenced art and trade goods from China, India and the Roman Empire.

Funan was expansionist, and according to Chinese texts, one of its first leaders, Fan Man, "attacked and conquered the neighboring kingdoms; all gave allegiance to him." But just to the north a more clearly Khmer state appears in Chinese texts as "Chenla." It too was heavily under the influence of Indian cultures.

By the middle of the sixth century Funan fell into decline, and the state was unable to repair the ravages of catastrophic floods that swept away the canals and the dikes, and forced the inhabitants to withdraw northward, abandoning the Mekong Delta once more to the mud. Then, it seems, Funan was annexed by Chenla, and from the combination of these two states Cambodia evolved.

It was not an easy association, and Chinese texts of the next two centuries refer to endless disputes and civil wars. Capital cities were evacuated and abandoned as kingdoms crumbled; it was not until the end of the eighth century that any kind of unity was achieved. Then the extraordinary civilization of Angkor, based on slavery, on worship of the God-King and on control of the waters, began.

King Yasorvarman I, who reigned from 889 to 900 A.D., built the first city of Angkor northwest of the Great Lake and harnessed the Siem Reap river. Using slave labor, subsequent kings went on to build enormous reservoirs, or "barays," intricate canals and careful dams. Year by year the canals stretched farther and farther out into the country, linking every town in the land. The big ships sailed up the Mekong into the Great Lake and transferred their cargoes to smaller barques, which could reach even the least accessible areas. The waterworks provided an everlasting and totally controlled source of irrigation, and the Khmers managed to produce three or four harvests a year.

This strong economic base enabled the kings of Angkor to pursue an expansionist foreign policy and to extend their suzerainty over vast areas of Southeast Asia, from the Mekong Delta across what is now Laos and Thailand, west into Burma, and down the isthmus toward Malaya. Water also provided the hydraulic power and the transport for the construction of huge "temple-mountains," which each king erected to his own glory. The most famous of them, Angkor Wat, was built in the twelfth century by Suryavarman II, a militant ruler (contemporary of Frederick Barbarossa) who waged war on all his neighbors. It was a stupendous creation; the main structure stood 130 feet high within square walls inside a moat that encompassed an area of almost one square mile. The temple rose in three successive tiers, and each terrace was surrounded by a carved gallery interrupted by pavilions, corner towers, stairways.

Suryavarman II's creation was not unassailed for long. The Chams invaded Angkor crossing the Great Lake from the south, sacking it and driving out the people. The empire never really regained its strength, but its decline was arrested for a time at the end of the twelfth century by King Jayavarman VII, who routed the Chams in a great naval battle and extended the country's frontiers southward.

Jayavarman was a Buddhist, a follower of Mahayana, the Greater Vehicle. But during his reign the influence of Theravada Buddhism, the Hinayana or Lesser Vehicle, began to spread from Siam. Unlike almost all the previous religions of the country, its doctrines were not imposed from above but were preached to the people. It was simple, required no expensive priesthood or temples and little ceremonial. Its missionaries practiced austerity, solitude, humility and poverty. Their example and their direct contact with the people started to undermine the old state religion and the monarchy which rested upon it. Theravada Buddhism remained the great belief and comfort of the Khmer people until 1975.

Only one eyewitness account of life in Angkor remains. It comes from Kubla Khan's envoy, Chou Ta-kuan, who spent a year there at the end of the thirteenth century. He reported that for the mass of the people life still revolved around the palace and the temples. Thousands were conscripted into the armies of laborers, masons, sculptors and decorators who built the temples. Thousands more served these shrines once they had been constructed; one such sanctuary contained 18 high priests, 2,740 officiants, 2,202 servers and 615 dancing girls.

The little houses along the canals of the city were dominated by the pagodas and by the green and gold tiles of the palace roof. The king's family held almost all the important posts of state, and if any commoner weçe chosen for office he offered his daughter as a royal concubine. The people could, however, approach the king; he frequently held audiences in a marvelous pillared hall hung with mirrors.

Chou Ta-kuan was not uncritical of life in Angkor. Slaves were treated badly and chained by the neck. Capital offenses were invariably punished by burial alive; lesser offenses by the removal of fingers, hands, feet, nose. If a dead man was found lying in the street, he would simply be dragged into the fields to be eaten by wild animals.

Eventually, perhaps inevitably, the extravagant building program and foreign policy of the God-Kings led to the destruction of Angkor. No society could sustain such enormous undertakings indefinitely; it is a tribute to the power of the irrigation system that it lasted as long and created as much as it did. No one knows exactly what happened, but it appears that through the thirteenth and fourteenth centuries the spirit of the empire dissipated. The waterways were no longer properly tended, the barays began to leak, and the canals became clogged. Rice fields reverted to swamp or savannah, food production fell and so did the population. As the Siamese (Thais) expanded their kingdom to the West they began, with the encouragement of Kubla Khan to the north, to lay waste to Angkor. They annexed province after province and finally seized and sacked the capital itself. In 1431 the Khmers were driven out; thousands were carried off to Siam as slaves. Conscious of the power of the waterworks, the Siamese destroyed them. They stripped the temples and palaces of their rich adornments; the gray stones were left naked to face an encroaching jungle.

Cambodia became a vassal of Siam, unnoticed and almost unmentioned. Occasional attempts were made by her kings to reassert themselves, and Angkor was briefly reoccupied, but the efforts never lasted long. For the next several centuries the Siamese and Vietnamese kingdoms grew and Cambodia waned. Siamese armies moved back and forth across the western part of the unproductive land, and to the east the Vietnamese moved southward into the Mekong Delta. The capital shifted from site to site, including Phnom Penh, as different dynasties occupied the throne. Successive princes sought support from either the Vietnamese or the Siamese and became beholden to either one or the other.

The Khmers' fear of their more populous neighbors increased as more and more of the old empire was annexed. But there was a vital difference in the relationships. The Siamese and the Khmers shared the same religion and similar cultural patterns; this mitigated the effects of occupation by Siam. Relations with Vietnam by contrast involved a sharp cultural clash between Indian-influenced and Chinese-dominated views of society; they were much more brutal and bitter. Unlike the Siamese, the Vietnamese regarded the Cambodians as "barbarians" and attempted to eradicate Cambodian customs in the areas they seized.

By the early nineteenth century, the king received his crown from the Siamese and paid tribute to the Vietnamese. Cambodia was reduced to a sliver between the two countries; Angkor, largely lost from view, was well inside Siam. As one scholar has noted, thousands of Khmers were being "killed and uprooted in a series of ruinous wars, carried on inside [their] territory by the Thai, the Vietnamese and local factions." The Thais burned down the Khmer capital three times in the first half of the century; Vietnamese advisers kept the Cambodian monarch a prisoner for fifteen years; the chronicles are filled with references to plagues, famines and floods. It was a dark period.

In 1840 the Cambodians mounted a rebellion against the increasing Vietnamese domination of Khmer life. The Vietnamese emperor, Minh Mang, characterized Vietnam's attitude to the Khmers in a letter to his general, Truong Minh Giang: "Sometimes the Cambodians are loyal; at other times they betray us. We helped them when they were suffering, and lifted them out of the mud . . . Now they are rebellious: I am so angry that my hair stands upright . . . Hundreds of knives should be used against them, to chop them up, to dismember them. . . ." Elsewhere he ordered that they be "crushed to powder." The Cambodian view was expressed by an official who said simply, "We are happy killing Vietnamese. We no longer fear them." On this occasion the Khmer rebels used hit-and-run tactics against the better-armed Vietnamese, who were forced to withdraw from around Phnom Penh to the Delta. Even so, by the middle of the century the country was on the verge of disappearing altogether into the grasp of its neighbors; it would have happened had the French not intervened and imposed a protectorate.

At the end of the 1850s Henri Mouhot, a French naturalist, made a long tour of Siam, Cambodia and Laos. Cambodia he found rather pitiful, the people conceited, poor and terrified of the king. Mouhot traveled widely through the country, spending time with the "savages" in the hills and then journeying by boat up the Great Lake. The fish were so incredibly abundant that even when the water was high "they are actually crushed under the boats and the ply of the oars is frequently impeded by them." He passed the pole in the middle of the Lake which marked the Siamese-Khmer boundary, and which the Siamese had constantly pushed further into Cambodia, and landed on the northern shore. His destination was the ruined city of "Ongcor," of which almost nothing was then known.

It had vanished so completely that earlier in the nineteenth century, when Chinese texts mentioning Angkor were translated, no one believed it still existed at all. With his servants and his bearers Mouhot cut his way through the woods, and all of a sudden he came upon Angkor Wat stretching up and out before him. He was overcome, and he wrote in his diary that the sight made the traveler "forget all the fatigues of the journey, filling him with admiration and delight, such as would be experienced in finding a verdant oasis in the sandy desert. Suddenly, and as if by enchantment, he seems to be transported from barbarism to civilization, from profound darkness to light." He could not understand how the temples could possibly have been built, and no one in Cambodia was able to explain. He heard, "It is the work of giants"; "It was built by the leprous king"; "It made itself"; "It is the work of Pra-Wun, the king of the angels."

He was startled by the contrast between the traces of splendid civilization and the deplorable state of the country he was visiting. He saw only one hope for the future: "European conquest, abolition of slavery, wise and protecting laws, and experience, fidelity and scrupulous rectitude in those who administer them." Since France was about to subject Cochin China to her sway she should take Cambodia as well; the country would be "a magnificent jewel in her crown."

French officials shared his views. Through the 1850s they had become increasingly alarmed by the difficulty of maintaining security in Saigon when Vietnamese rebels and bandits could swoop on the city and then rush back into sanctuaries in Cambodia only forty miles away across flat woodlands. Furthermore, they saw the Mekong as a road to China. In 1861 Admiral Charner, the French commander in Saigon, traveled to the Cambodian capital, Oudong, to tell King Norodom that the French were determined to occupy Indochina permanently and would like to help Cambodia maintain its freedom. The king, who was now under the control of the Siamese resident in the capital, replied that his country owed its existence to the Siamese, who had saved it from Vietnamese dominance. He welcomed the French offer of help but was concerned lest, after he had defied his neighbors, the French would withdraw from the area leaving him at their mercy. Eventually, however, French pressure overcame his doubts. Despite the anger of the Siamese, a protectorate was established over Cambodia in 1864.

It was not long before the king realized that the interests of the French resident differed little from those of his Siamese predecessor. In 1867 the French ceded to the Siamese the provinces of Battambang and Angkor, which were already in their hands, in return for their renunciation of sovereignty over Cambodia as a whole. The king protested in vain. The French did manage to preserve the country from the worst encroachments of its old enemies—in 1907 the two provinces were returned, thanks in part to the wisdom of an American adviser to the Thai monarchy, Edward H. Strobel. But, because Cochin China was a full colony and Cambodia merely a protectorate, the French tended to push the Vietnamese borders northward and westward at the expense of Cambodia. Constant minor changes in the frontier took place; maps were always out of date, or ambiguously drawn, or both. Such alterations remain a source of bitterness and warfare.

French concern lay much more in erecting a buffer between Vietnam and Siam, where the British had established strong trading interests, and in securing the upper reaches of the Mekong, than in developing Cambodia. The country was treated, in some ways, as a granary for Cochin

China. The French found, however, that it was not the placid indolent place that some of them had anticipated, and a series of revolts broke out in the provinces. The king's semidivinity helped the French, but his own feelings about the protectorate became more and more hostile. In 1884 the French tried to take full control, forcing Norodom to sign a convention relinquishing all power to the French resident and making Cambodia, in effect, a colony. The king was furious, and with at least his tacit support an insurrection spread.

As ninety years later, the rebels were based principally in the mountains and forests in the east of the country, they had the support of local officials and feudal chiefs, and they acted in the name of their king. The French failed to subdue them. In January 1886, the French resident in Kompong Cham reported that with few exceptions "the uprising is master of the whole region. Everywhere, bands of insurgents circulate in the countryside . . . the people . . . all foresee the possibility of our evacuation of the country. The entire Cambodian population acquiesces in the revolt."

Eventually the French had to concede. They withdrew their more humiliating demands, and the king called for an end to the revolt. Afterward they applied their control more carefully. In order to diminish the power of the king, they denigrated Norodom as a bumbling, clownish figure of fun and paid court to the rival branch of the royal family, the Sisowaths, who were more amenable to their control. When Norodom died in 1904 the French discounted his heir and forced the Crown Council to choose his half brother, Prince Sisowath, to succeed him.

Throughout the early part of this century the country remained undeveloped and heavily taxed. There was sporadic violence, but little political activity. The Indochinese Communist Party, formed in 1930, was almost wholly Vietnamese, and it was not until the end of the 1930s that nationalism really began to stir in Cambodia. It was led by Son Ngoc Thanh, a man who was to exercise a vital, if mainly symbolic influence over Cambodian politics during the next forty years. He was a Khmer Krom, an ethnic Khmer from Vietnam's Mekong Delta area. In 1937, he founded the first Cambodian-language newspaper, *Nagaravatta (Angkor Wat)*, and he soon gathered around him groups of Buddhist monks, sons of rich families who resented the way in which the French gave preferment to Vietnamese in the civil service, and some of those few young Cambodians whose intellectual and political aspirations had been sharpened in France. As Secretary of the Buddhist Institute, he disseminated anti-French, anticolonialist and republican ideas.

The French, meanwhile, decided that their best protection against nationalism was to switch royal families once again. When Sisowath's son Monivong died in 1941, they dropped the Sisowaths and reverted to the Norodoms. The Sisowaths were as dismayed as the Norodoms had been at their own arbitrary exclusion from power in 1904 and few more so than Prince Sisowath Sirik Matak, who had expected his family to retain power all his life. He was now forced to watch as his nineteen-year-old cousin, Prince Norodom Sihanouk, whom the French had selected because of his pliable youthfulness, was crowned king.

CHAPTER 3

The Prince

NORODOM SIHANOUK presided feudally over Cambodia from 1941 to 1970, as King, Chief of State, Prince, Prime Minister, head of the main political movement, jazz-band leader, magazine editor, film director and gambling concessionaire, attempting to unite in his rule the unfamiliar concepts of Buddhism, socialism and democracy. His exercise of power was so astonishing and so individual that he came to personify his country and its policies abroad as well as at home. He was vain, a petulant show-man who enjoyed boasting of his sexual successes. He would not tolerate criticism or dissent, and he treated his aides as flunkies. He could be generous with those who served him well, but everyone feared his tem-per. His speech was high-pitched and idiosyncratic, and his comments were often ambiguous.

At the same time he had enormous political skill, charm, tenacity and intelligence. After an uncertain beginning he exploited all these qualities in the interests of one overriding cause—the preservation of Cambodia's peace and its independence from further encroachment by its neighbors. This concern inevitably won him enemies abroad just as his autocracy created them at home. Indeed, his relations with his own people and with foreign powers—in particular with the United States as it came to replace France as the dominant power in Indochina—are an essential part of the history of Cambodia's destruction.

The Japanese occupied much of Southeast Asia in 1941. In Cambodia they left Sihanouk on the throne and the Vichy French in nominal control, but they insisted that the provinces of Battambang and Angkor (now Siem Reap), which the Cambodians had regained in 1907, revert once more to Thailand. There the Thais encouraged the growth of an anti-French Cambodian guerrilla movement known as the Khmer Issarak ("Free Khmer"). The Japanese also supported Son Ngoc Thanh; he spent most of the war in Tokyo. Sihanouk spent the time in Phnom Penh, offering no visible resistance to either Vichy French or Japanese interests.

In March 1945, as the Allies approached Indochina, the Japanese took full control from the French in order to block moves by French officers to overthrow them. They declared that the colonialist era was over and ordered the Emperor of Vietnam (Bao Dai), the King of Laos and Sihanouk to declare independence. In Vietnam, Ho Chi Minh, the leader of the Communist resistance, the Viet Minh, refused to accept Bao Dai's declaration and seized Hanoi.

In Cambodia, the more docile Sihanouk appointed Son Ngoc Thanh Foreign Minister and then Prime Minister, at the request of the Japanese. The war years had somewhat radicalized Phnom Penh's tiny educated class, and in spite of his Japanese associations, Thanh's republicanism contrasted well with Sihanouk's apparent acquiescence to any form of foreign control and with the inbred, corrupt elitism of the monarchy. But "independence" and Thanh's incumbency were short-lived. When Japan surrendered, Thanh tried to seize power and declare a republic and *de facto* independence of France, but he was arrested by the French with the help of the British and, to Sihanouk's relief, was exiled to France.

For the next fifteen years Thanh conducted his republican fight from Thailand, South Vietnam and the forests along Cambodia's peripheries, where he first joined the Khmer Issarak and then formed his own guerrilla group, the Khmer Serei, which also means Free Khmer. He became important as a symbol of consistent opposition to Sihanouk, and over the years he attracted at least emotional support from some sections of Cambodian society. His conviction that only armed struggle against France and an end to the monarchy could liberate Cambodia was shared by the Viet Minh, and in the late forties Thanh was prepared to collaborate with them. Gradually, however, as the United States became the dominant power in both South Vietnam and Thailand, he came to look to the Americans for support against Sihanouk.

In 1946 the French secured the return of the Battambang and Siem Reap provinces. Cambodia's prewar borders were more or less restored, though neither the Thais nor the Vietnamese respected them. The haziness of the maps led to bitter disputes, which continue even today. The French then induced Sihanouk to agree to a quasi-French constitution, similar to that of the Fourth Republic, whose main effect was to legitimize new political parties. Almost all of these were run by various princes, yet Sihanouk complained that the monarch's power had been handed over to politicians. This was the start of a long conflict between him and the elite of Phnom Penh.

Sihanouk soon began to understand that the only way to preserve his own position against parliamentary democratic sentiment was to identify himself more completely with the nation; independence alone could guarantee his rule. In 1949, he negotiated partial freedom from the French, and then in 1952 he emerged as a real national leader by conducting a brilliant anti-French campaign in Phnom Penh and around the world, employing all the tricks of threat, bombast, arrogance and ultimatum, which later became his trademark. The French, hard-pressed by the war in Vietnam, were anxious to be rid of this minor concern; in November 1953 Sihanouk returned to Phnom Penh from self-imposed exile, claiming independence from France.

In 1954 the Geneva Peace Conference on Indochina agreed to the temporary division of Vietnam into North and South. It also recognized Cambodia's neutrality and territorial integrity, and it guaranteed that the Viet Minh would withdraw from the country's eastern areas that they had used in their war against the French. Those Cambodian Communists who were operating in the jungles of their country were required to unite with the national community. Some stayed in the bush, and several thousand were taken north to Hanoi. Those who remained in the *maquis* and those who joined them later came to regard this as an outright betrayal by Hanoi, done in Vietnam's national interest with no regard for proletarian solidarity. This concession by Hanoi, under Soviet and Chinese pressure, at Geneva had considerable impact on the development of Cambodian Communism.

Geneva also committed Cambodia to elections based on universal suffrage and supervised by the International Control Commission. Despite Sihanouk's new standing, it seemed clear that the election would be won by the Democratic Party, which in the last two elections had won most seats and whose members, many of them republican-minded civil servants sympathetic to Son Ngoc Thanh, had little time for the monarchy. Sihanouk had refused Thanh's offer that he return from the forests and run openly, but there seemed to be no way to prevent further erosion of his power in favor of the politicians. The Control Commission rejected

Sihanouk's suggestion that the suffrage should be limited, and so he abdicated his throne in favor of his father. As Prince but no longer Monarch, he announced that he was now a politician. It was deftly done.

He claimed that he wished only to establish a truly democratic government, end the rule of privilege, and cut out the "whole hierarchy of court mandarins amongst whom slide the intriguers, like bloodsucking leeches that fasten themselves on the feet of elephants." He formed a movement, the Sangkum Reastr Niyum (People's Socialist Community), which cut across party lines and took as its themes loyalty to Nation, Buddhism and Monarchy.

The new electoral process was quite unable to withstand the attraction of a charismatic former king. His appeal was irresistible to the mass of the peasantry, and several parties immediately merged with the Sangkum. The others were almost all eliminated by Sihanouk's victory at the polls; only the Democrats and the left-wing Pracheachon group, which had links to the Viet Minh, survived at all. But despite his sweeping victory, the way in which Sihanouk had used his status to isolate the political elite from power and bypass the country's new institutions was bitterly resented by, perhaps, a few hundred people in Phnom Penh—as well as by Son Ngoc Thanh and those few Cambodian Communists, or as Sihanouk later called them, "Khmers Rouges," who remained in the forests.

From now on Sihanouk would tolerate no intermediaries. He took his mandate from the vote of 1955, renewed it by regular elections and referenda, and continued for the next fifteen years to assume that legitimacy derived uniquely from his communion with the peasantry. The communion did exist, and Sihanouk guarded it well. Like the kings of Angkor, he held popular audiences at which the people could present their grievances personally; he would stand in the courtyard of the palace in Phnom Penh shouting shrilly above the din of the eager villagers, "Water shortage in Mondolkiri, corruption in Kompong Cham? I'll deal with it. Where is the Minister?" If the unfortunate man was not at hand, another courtier would be ordered to fetch him and he would have to stand and listen while the Prince gave a high-pitched peroration of abuse against corrupt and inefficient officials, food prices and the "imperialists."

Other times Sihanouk would fling himself around the country with ferocious energy, scattering bales of cloth and sacks of food in remote hamlets of Ratanakiri, standing in village squares and mopping the sweat from his face as he swapped raucous jokes with the delighted peasantry, exploiting both his semidivinity and his obvious humanity in a unique brand of personal populism. His thoughts he delivered, not like Mao, in pithy aphorisms, but in speeches, several hours long, which he shouted into the microphone of Radio Phnom Penh. These rambling, disjointed harangues were vigorous and often quite unrestrained. When Sukarno was deposed in Indonesia, Sihanouk declared that he was a "scatter-brained old man fond of virgins" who had been destroyed by his Japanese wife.

Through the 1960s, Sihanouk gradually came to dominate radio and all other means of communication; he would express himself only slightly more subtly in the magazine *Etudes Cambodgiennes*, which he edited. He also conducted his relationship with the foreign press on an entirely personal basis. A visiting correspondent so bold as to ask for an interview as soon as he arrived in Phnom Penh might be answered by a tirade on the radio. He denounced critical articles and banned authors from the country; and he sent long, warm telegrams of praise to reporters whose observations he approved.

He loved to upset the diplomatic corps and once insisted that all am-bassadors take part in digging a new railroad track; the discomfort this caused the men from the Quai d'Orsay, Foggy Bottom, Gorky Street and Whitehall was only slightly mitigated by the fine lunch and vintage cham-pagne with which he later refreshed them. Sometimes he would fly home from abroad, not to Phnom Penh but to Siem Reap near Angkor Wat. The entire corps had to drive there; at the ferry long lines of ambassadorial limousines stretched away in the heat, their occupants mopping them-selves.

It was an adroit performance, but Sihanouk, believing that only his relationship with the populace assured the stability of the country, never fully succeeded in unifying Cambodia. It remained a feudal kingdom in which various barons, war lords and landowners ruled in their own fief-doms, paying him varying tributes and recognition. His political organi-zation, the Sangkum, was little more than a loose coalition of powerful families and cliques of different ideologies, which remained subservient to Sihanouk partly because there was no alternative, and partly because he genuinely enjoyed real popularity.

His control over such political life as he tolerated was total; there was no real role for other classes or sections of the community. Above all, there was no place for a middle class. After independence, education was expanded and a Cambodian civil service slowly developed, but nothing was done to encourage ambition or professional pride. To obtain a job of influence in Phnom Penh meant, in effect, being a member of Sihanouk's court, and that was not a prospect that all university graduates, particularly those educated abroad, relished. Sihanouk made no bones about his contempt for the political elite and the educated class. "I have never accepted political defeat in my life. You can do as you wish, but you must not think that you can defeat me, for I am the kind of man who never accepts defeat. I will only accept punishment from the people, for you are not the people. You belong to a special category, another class, for you are neither prince nor people."

This became increasingly hard to bear. Students returning from France were jailed for venturing thoughts that they had been encouraged to debate at college. Skepticism could mean criticism, criticism *lèse majesté, lèse majesté* prison, sometimes death. Throughout the sixties Sihanouk's autocracy became increasingly unpredictable and a trickle of young men and women both on the right and on the left retired to Paris or faded into the forests to join either Son Ngoc Thanh's Khmer Serei or the few Communists who had remained after 1954. Even so, most Cambodians acknowledged that in his central ambition, to preserve the country's independence, Sihanouk, the God-King, fared remarkably well. Until 1970 he managed to prevent the Vietnam war from spilling very far inside Cambodia's frontiers.

In Cambodia, as in few other countries (Israel provides something of an analogy), the very survival of the nation was a major political issue. From the start of his rule Sihanouk devised methods of playing his neighbors off against one another, exploiting both their ambitions and their weaknesses. He called this policy "extreme neutrality," and for a time it worked well, though it pleased few people outside Cambodia. In particular the United States never found Sihanouk or his Cambodia easy to appreciate. Richard Nixon, as Vice-President of the United States, visited the country in 1953, and twenty-five years later wrote in his memoirs that Sihanouk was "vain and flighty. He seemed prouder of his musical talents than of his political leadership, and he appeared to me to be totally unrealistic about the problems his country faced." American anxiety over Sihanouk's neutralism, particularly his accommodation of Hanoi, grew in direct proportion to United States involvement in Vietnam and, to a lesser extent, Thailand.

In the 1950s and '60s history repeated itself in Cambodia. After the United States began to increase its political and military commitment to the anti-Communist regime in Saigon, American officials found that Cambodia posed for them the same sort of problems as it had for the French a century earlier. Sihanouk's refusal to cooperate became all the more irksome as the difficulties of controlling South Vietnam became manifest. The Prince had been disappointed in America's leaders when, on his world crusade for independence in 1952, he had visited Washington. He felt both snubbed and rebuked by John Foster Dulles, who lectured him that French protection was essential if Cambodia was to be saved from the Communists. (Dulles could not accept Sihanouk's contention that French control was feeding the Communists' basic support.) Shortly after independence, Sihanouk's Prime Minister Penn Nouth announced, "Although we are not Communists we do not oppose Communism as long as the latter is not imposed on our people from outside." Such expressions of neutralism did not accord well with Dulles' own attitude, although Sihanouk was at this time himself virulently anti-Communist. Throughout 1953 and 1954 he threatened to bomb Viet Minh-controlled villages whether or not any Cambodians lived there, and in 1954 he requested United States aid after the Viet Minh launched a probe into northeast Cambodia from Southern Laos. At Geneva, Cambodia had established the right to enter foreign alliances in certain circumstances. The United States then pressed Sihanouk to associate himself with SEATO, the Southeast Asia Treaty Organization, which was formed under American influence in 1954 and which included the United States, Britain, France, Pakistan, Thailand, Australia and New Zealand. Dulles saw SEATO as a critical chain that would contain China; a protocol committed it to protect Indochina. Sihanouk, however, refused to recognize it. Although he requested military aid from Washington he also sought assurances of non-interference from both Peking and Hanoi.

Dulles considered that his attitude weakened SEATO. A National Security Council study of September 1956 asserted that United States policy toward Cambodia itself must be to "maintain Cambodia's independence and to reverse the drift towards pro-communist neutrality, encourage individuals and groups in Cambodia who oppose dealing with the communist bloc and who serve to broaden the political power base in Cambodia."

The policy was not pursued subtly. In 1956, after Sihanouk attacked SEATO while visiting Peking, his army suddenly had to cope with a number of incidents on the Thai border; the South Vietnamese Air Force began to violate Cambodian airspace; Cambodian fishing boats were harassed when both the Thais and Vietnamese closed their Cambodian frontiers, and supply convoys up the Mekong, the country's main artery—it had no deep-water port on the sea—were stopped in South Vietnam.

These measures were temporary, but their effect was long-lasting and counterproductive. Sihanouk exploited the role of nationalist patriot to the full, established relations with the Soviet Union and Poland, accepted aid from China, and repeated his denunciations of SEATO. In May 1957 the National Security Council acknowledged that "the United States has been unable to influence Cambodia in the direction of a stable government and non-involvement with the communist bloc."

The Prince's relationship with Washington was in part a casualty of Senator Joseph McCarthy's manhandling of the State Department. Its Bureau of Far Eastern Affairs had recently been purged of the men who had "lost China," and sympathy for a nonaligned Prince who was wedged strategically south of China and between Thailand and Vietnam could not be eagerly expressed by those who survived. There were never many foreign-service officers who displayed enthusiasm for Sihanouk; even those who tolerated his neutralism claimed to find his jokes, his high-pitched voice and his grasping mother-in-law offensive. A pattern of mis-understanding between the United States and Sihanouk was established with the arrival of the first American Ambassador after the Geneva Conference. Robert McClintock was one of those individuals who prosper on a reputation for brilliance that travels before and, somehow, even after them. His most obvious characteristic was an overweening arrogance. He considered that the posting was beneath his talents, and he treated both the country and Sihanouk with disdain, making it clear that he found the Prince's extravagant gestures, his five-hour harangues and his unpredictable reactions evidence of an essential triviality. His visits to the palace were made more for the purposes of lecturing than for diplomatic inquiry or advice, and he openly displayed his contempt by arriving in shorts or, on other occasions, with a walking stick and his Irish setter. It was not the way to treat the ruler of a newly independent country, but McClintock could not abide Sihanouk's brand of neutralism. He would protest extravagantly when the Cambodian press lavished praise on the Soviet Union for the gift of a modest fire engine and ignored more handsome American bounty. At the opening of an American-equipped maternity clinic the Ambassador, according to Sihanouk, strutted about praising the material and said, "Ah, Prince Sihanouk, this should particularly interest you as a great one-man manufacturer of babies."

McClintock's successor, Carl Strom, was more tactful, but he infuri-ated Sihanouk in 1958, after the South Vietnamese attacked across the Cambodian border, when he warned that no arms supplied under the United States aid program could be used against them. That the United

States should have sided with its clients Saigon or Bangkok in the endless border disputes is not surprising. Neither was Sihanouk's response. To fill the void, he promptly began to negotiate full diplomatic relations with Peking. In Washington a Presidential study by the Operations Coordinating Board warned that this meant "a net loss to the free world's position in Cambodia." Strom was called to Washington and was told that Sihanouk would now have to go and that United States aid would be cut off to precipitate his fall. He managed to convince the State Department this was not wise, but Washington's displeasure was evident; relations between Bangkok and Phnom Penh completely broke down. NSC papers of the period cited in the Pentagon papers confirm that Washington saw Thai and Vietnamese pressure across the borders as one of the principal weapons to be used in an effort to move Sihanouk toward a more pro-American position. Sihanouk later claimed that the CIA also then began to give consistent support, through the South Vietnamese, to Son Ngoc Thanh's Khmer Serei.

Relations between Phnom Penh and Washington deteriorated after the following year, 1959, when Sihanouk proclaimed that he had discovered a plot by which the Khmer Serei was to terrorize several provinces while his right-wing enemies fomented dissatisfaction in the capital. He claimed that French and Chinese intelligence services had warned him that the military governor of Siem Reap province, Dap Chhuon, would secede with Khmer Serei support. The plan, said Sihanouk's paper, *Réalités Cambodgiennes*, was to topple him so that "the present monarchistic, neutral and independent Khmer state would be replaced by a republic adopting a pro-Western stance." Dap Chhuon was shot, and Victor Matsui, a member of the CIA station in Phnom Penh, hurriedly left the country after Sihanouk accused him of being party to the plot.

William Colby, who was then in the CIA in Saigon, claims now that the CIA was not plotting with Dap Chhuon. But he agrees that Matsui had contacts with him. He says, "The Thais and the South Vietnamese were in league with Dap Chhuon and we had links with them. So Sihanouk assumed that we were *behind* them. In fact, we were urging them to desist, but as part of our intelligence coverage we developed an agent in the Dap Chhuon entourage. We gave him a radio to keep us informed, not to encourage Dap Chhuon."

The explanation seems somewhat disingenuous, and Colby admits that "Sihanouk's misapprehension was understandable." In the United States press, the Prince's allegations were virtually dismissed, just like many others he had made over the years. *Time* magazine reported that Dap

54

Chhuon had given Sihanouk "something to chew on." Dap Chhuon was a great patriot and the "saxophone tootling" Prince who "tries to play it real cool at both ends of the scale" had been duped by the Communists. According to *Time*, Washington was not the least hostile to the Prince, but considered him "as a likeable but volatile fellow whose popularity among his 5,000,000 people is undisputed."

Sihanouk's charges of American interference are worth considering in the light of a study that was commissioned by the Pentagon in 1959. The document, "Psychological Operations: Cambodia," is 471 pages long, and it is of significance today because it was probably a fairly accurate reflection of the official American view of Sihanouk's regime.

The report was intended to discover which social groups in Cambodia were both "effective" in the society and "susceptible" to American pressure; the groups which most interested the planners were those who scored high in both categories. Of the country as a whole, the report noted that almost all Cambodians were fishermen or farmers, whose prowess did not impress their neighbors. "From the French, Chinese and Vietnamese points of view, Khmer are indifferent farmers, incapable traders, uninspired fishermen, unreliable laborers." Soldiers were little better; they lacked stamina, did not understand machinery, behaved arrogantly and had poor officers. The police were untrained, under-equipped, extortionists, "the most corrupt group in Cambodia."

The report shared the conventional belief that the Cambodians were "by and large a docile passive people." As such they were disappointing material from the American point of view. They could not be easily panicked, their horizons were limited to village, pagoda and forest, they respected their government, they knew of no other countries, they feared ghosts and, in short, "they cannot be counted on to act in any positive way for the benefit of U.S. aims and policies."

But if the United States could not woo the society, it could disrupt it and encourage the spread of "privatization (the preoccupation of the individual with his personal rather than his social situation), discouragement, defeatism and apathy." There were two groups in Cambodia that could be counted upon to further American aims: the middle-class urban elite and the officer corps. (It was the coalition of these two groups that in 1970 overthrew Sihanouk and brought Cambodia into the American camp.)

In 1959 the report noted that the older elite was "rapidly becoming susceptible to exploitation by the United States," because of the way Sihanouk forced it either to collaborate with him or to "languish in frustration and bitterness." The younger generation was equally valuable because it was "crass and materialistic . . . bribed thus compromised . . . a weak spot in the Cambodian government and social structure." Neutralism made them all nervous, and they were frightened by the Prince's "mercurial" temper. There was one problem—"until the popular image of Sihanouk is tarnished they will not resist or rebel"—but it was not insuperable.

The report stressed the necessity for Americans to behave correctly in Cambodia. They should dwell upon Angkor and the glorious past rather than upon present weaknesses; they should eat all food offered to them, "even if it does not look appetizing." Typical American "locker-room language" must be avoided, because "courtesy to the point of formality, gentleness and dignity" were essential forms of address in Cambodia; and they must never "show anger under any circumstances, because anger is synonymous with madness in the Cambodian language." Photographs should be carefully used. "Candid shots" of the political elite must not do them discredit, "unless such is intended." More importantly, they should recognize that "the prototype of the successful American might be objectionable because of the connotation of disparate wealth. The economic gap is so great that Cambodians have no understanding of the typical American version of 'play.' " Nonetheless, the report said, Cambodians were a jolly people who loved to laugh; humor could be an effective weapon. But care should be taken; "jokes about Texas or income taxes will not strike the Khmer as funny even if they are explained—they have no base in Cambodian experience."

A large part of the report was made up of 207 different "appeal ideas" to be directed at different sections of the population—peasants, Chinese, Vietnamese, the police—in the attempt to win them to the free world. Enlisted men in the Cambodian army were to be persuaded that they were fighting only for Peking, while Chinese merchants seduced their wives and venal politicians sat at ease in Phnom Penh. They must be convinced that their officers were corrupt and were appointed on the basis of nepotism; if they deserted, "your family will consider you a hero . . . it will also be a joke on your officers."

The Buddhist monks were another target. They could not, unfortunately, be aroused to violence—"this would be asking the clergy to be non-Buddhist"—but "psy-warriors" could play on the fact that "the monks are also human" and try to persuade them that they were hated by the intelligentsia.

Great stress was placed on the importance of American aid in winning over the military and the elite—and in frightening the mass of the people. The officer corps would, by its very nature, be grateful for military aid. Its effect on the soldier would be different: "Soldier, you have seen the power of American equipment. You have seen the power of the American army. You cannot win." The report noted that there was one problem with such a slogan: "For this appeal—as in others which treat of American power—effectiveness would depend upon the extent to which Cambodian soldiers would have felt that power."

But once extended, United States aid could be used in many mysterious ways. One "appeal idea" in the study was a leaflet showing Phnom Penh railway station blown up, with the bodies of dead monks and women all around. This was an exceptionally good idea, because "the railway station is one of the finest public buildings in Cambodia and a source of great pride to the people. (Note: upon completion, the port of Kompong Som and the road to it, now under construction with U.S. money, will be important objectives.)"

There were ideas that placed the blame for rice shortages on the elite, on the Chinese merchants, on the Peking government (to whom the merchants were said to owe allegiance), on neutralism, on loss of United States imports, on broken promises of the government. Panic was to be encouraged by illustrations of young men being carried off into the distance on Chinese trucks. Whole sections of the study were devoted to trying to convince the people that the United States alone wanted freedom, peace, happiness and independence for Cambodia. Others sought to persuade Cambodians that an American victory was inevitable, come what may.

The analysts appreciated, at times, the contradictions of their work. One suggested picture of an American and a Cambodian embracing has the American saying that when the war is over "I'd like to come back and work in Cambodia. I know something about animals and perhaps could help you." A word of caution is added: "Some Cambodians might not relish the idea of Americans in their land even if they were there only to assist." Another appeal idea suggests showing a map of the United States dotted with Buddhist temples. But the comment points out that "Those Cambodians who have been in the United States know the difficulty in locating a Theravada Buddhist temple. Those who know only Cambodia would not recognize a makeshift location such as a converted storeroom as a 'temple.'"

As a satire on the way in which the military-sociological complex might have set about subverting a society in the late 1950s the report's language, assumptions and cautions are droll. It was, however, a serious exercise and not unique to Cambodia; within the same series similar studies were made of Burma, Egypt, China, Iran, Iraq, Laos, Syria, Thailand and Vietnam. The report helps to explain the paranoia that many smaller nations, especially nonaligned countries of the Third World, have long felt about the real purpose of American military and economic aid. And, in the case of Cambodia, the "special audiences" considered most likely to work for United States interests—the officer corps and the elite—were just those who did so and who eventually replaced Sihanouk.

United States aid, which Sihanouk at first encouraged, had some obvious effects on the country. Throughout the fifties and sixties Cambodia remained an overwhelmingly rural society, and the vast majority of peasants worked their own land. But by 1963 American aid provided about 14 percent of its annual revenue and accounted for around 30 percent of the military budget. The sums involved were not enormous, but they did have an impact, particularly in Phnom Penh, where the American presence helped to create a large new servant class—waiters, bartenders, auto and air-conditioner mechanics, clerks, messengers, drivers, prostitutes. (Khieu Samphan, who became the Khmer Rouge commander in chief after 1970, bitterly described the development of this service sector even before the Americans arrived, in a thesis on the Cambodian economy, written in 1959.)

The effects on the middle class were also marked. For many of the graduates disillusioned with Sihanouk's system, American power and aid offered the one hope of economic and social progress. Because the Americans' standard of living was high (and more conspicuous than that of the French) their presence also encouraged greed and envy among the rich, who spent much of their time building villas to rent to foreign officials at high prices and trying to emulate their life style.

All this was inevitable in such a tiny society, but the way the American embassy was constituted created further problems. It prefigured, to some extent, the military and aid missions that were sent to Phnom Penh after 1970. Many officials who were stationed there considered Phnom Penh a delightful provincial town, but professionally it was a backwater; a high-flier in the State Department or Army would prefer Bangkok or Saigon. Phnom Penh was rated a hardship post; few officials remained there more than two years, almost none of them knew Khmer, and an extraordinarily high number could not even speak French.

The military mission faced an added problem. After independence, Cambodia's relations with France improved considerably, and the French had left their own military-training cadre behind. The traditions of the Cambodian army were French, and the Americans found it difficult to change them. Although the official purpose of the American military group was to help Cambodia's tiny army "to maintain internal security against Communist subversion and insurgency and to encourage a pro-Western orientation," many officers spent more time worrying about their French counterparts than about the Viet Minh. They stressed that the French had lost the Indochina war, that American aid and methods were now the only hope. But since they were allowed to give advice only, not training, to the Khmers, and since Cambodian officers generally were looking forward to periods of study in France, it was a difficult task. No command or staff relationship was set up between the two missions. French officers strolled down one side of the boulevards and Americans strolled up the other, the French saluting laconically as they passed. Sihanouk, it must be said, delighted in the mutual distrust and did all he could to provoke it.

The French had encouraged the Cambodians to base their defense on hundreds of police posts that stretched out along the borders and the lines of communication. It was a sensible enough idea since it enabled the army to mix with the population. But the Americans, inculcated with the idea of an army as a heavily equipped expeditionary force, tried to persuade the Cambodians to concentrate their troops in a brigade structure. It was exactly not the way to cope with small guerrilla attacks in isolated parts of the country. But it was what U.S. Army field manuals advised.

Through the late fifties and early sixties, the United States military mission began to provide more and more equipment, much of it surplus material that had been destined for the French before their surrender and much of it unsuitable. Some was distributed to units, but a great deal piled up in Phnom Penh warehouses.

Under United States law it was (and is) the responsibility of the military mission to inspect the "end-use" of all equipment supplied by the United States, to ensure *inter alia* that it is not being sold to the Communists (as happened after 1970) or simply misused. Sihanouk, and a good many of his officers, found these inspections humiliating and often canceled them at the last minute with explanations that troops or vehicles were suddenly *"en mission."* The American embassy renamed the inspections "technical visits" and tried to make them social occasions. They would ask the Cambodians to arrange lunches or dinners and send the bill to the embassy. The Cambodians very quickly understood the possibilities

Sideshow

and produced great quantities of champagne and cognac; Brigadier General Robert Taber, head of the United States military mission till 1964, complained in his after-action report that "many unit commanders exhibited not only lavish tastes but a shameless propensity for padding the bill. Discreet requests for less opulent hospitality were generally ignored." Attempting to explain the phenomenon to the Pentagon in terms of a Khmer tradition of hospitality, he admitted, "It is also possible that FARK [Royal Khmer Armed Forces] felt that the more the visits cost, the fewer [we] would be able to afford."

American Air Force officers were the most frustrated of all. The Cambodians did not take the idea of the maintenance of equipment very seriously and hated to retire planes. The Americans felt as if they were flying an "aerial museum," and they intensely disliked the Air Force Chief of Staff, Major General Ngo Hou, who was also Sihanouk's pilot and one of his favorite medical advisers. Taber's report refers to the general as "a sycophant and a toady" with "dubious business interests."

But there were many Cambodian officers, of course, who accepted American equipment and American advice in the way the 1959 survey had hoped they would—with friendship and gratitude. American aid, in particular military aid, began to create a new focus of loyalty that was quite separate from the government and might have been even stronger but for French competition.

By 1963 Sihanouk suspected that too many of his more conservative generals and ministers were becoming dependent upon both American aid and American attitudes. He also believed, at that time, that Hanoi would eventually win the growing war in South Vietnam. He shifted leftward. Just after the assassination of President Diem in November 1963, he commenced a broad program of economic reform, nationalizing foreign trade and the banks. At the same time he made a crucial decision—he renounced the American economic and military aid program that he had accepted since 1955. He demanded that the United States embassy close down its aid missions and that their personnel leave the country.

In explaining this new policy, he denounced the United States for continuing to support Son Ngoc Thanh, whose Khmer Serei troops were being trained in South Vietnam and whose radio was beaming vituperative broadcasts into Cambodia. He also complained about the corrupting effects of the American missions on Cambodian attitudes.

The head of the United States military mission, General Taber, paid his final call on the Minister of Defense, General Lon Nol, on January 4, 1964. It was a warm encounter, Taber recorded. Lon Nol

60

displayed a friendly attitude and expressed appreciation for the help given by MAAG [Military Assistance Advisory Group] to the Cambodian Armed Forces. He remarked on the great friendship that had been built up between the Cambodian and American officers and between the people of the two countries as well. He then made the following statements which may have significance as indicators of the present attitude of Sihanouk's ministers: 1) the departure of the MAAG had not been brought about by "the Government" (this was interpreted as implying that Sihanouk alone was responsible); 2) Cambodia would never join the Communist bloc unless militarily overcome by the communists; 3) at some unspecified time in the future "the U.S. might wish to furnish aid to Cambodia without preconditions, perhaps as in Burma or Indonesia"; and 4) the Cambodians cannot understand the inability of the U.S. to stop the Khmer Serei broadcasts.

Taber was delighted with his visit and wrote, shrewdly:

Lon Nol's friendliness was apparently genuine and his indirect placing of responsibility on Sihanouk for the termination of U.S. aid, as well as his assurance that Cambodia will never voluntarily become a communist country imply the possibility that there is a point beyond which the military will refuse to support the Chief of State. It is obvious that Lon Nol regrets the present turn of events and it is safe to say that he is not the only Cambodian official who is already anticipating a time when political factors will permit the RKG [Royal Khmer Government] to make a request for renewed military assistance.

General Taber was correct, though it took six years for that time to come.

After he threw out the American aid missions, the Prince continued to try to play off Chinese, Soviet and American interests, describing the superpowers as "depraved" and insisting that he had no wish to see Cambodia turn Communist. He ordered his police and army brutally to suppress the tiny groups of Khmer Rouge in the countryside. At the same time he was edging toward Hanoi. In 1965, after *Newsweek* had published an article that scorned him and accused his family of running the profitable Phnom Penh brothel business, he broke off diplomatic relations with Washington altogether. He cited the article as an intolerable intrusion— but a more important reason for the break was that the first American combat troops had just splashed ashore at Danang in South Vietnam.

Relations with the United States now began to deteriorate further. Nonetheless, Sihanouk still tried to remain detached; he wrote to *The New York Times* to acknowledge that "after the disappearance of the U.S.A. from our region and the victory of the communist camp, I myself and the People's Socialist Community I have created would inevitably disappear from the scene."

CHAPTER 4

The War

IT WAS to be the expansion of the United States involvement in the region that precipitated Sihanouk's disappearance. If Sihanouk had been walking a tightrope, then as the interests of the superpowers and the tensions within Vietnam grew, the pole of studied neutralism with which he tried to balance himself and his country shortened; his step, as a result, became less and less steady.

Through 1965 the American advisers and ‚ecial Forces, who had, till then, borne the brunt of the American commitment to South Vietnam, were superseded by main-force units and air power committed to military victory over the Viet Cong. The new American strategy in Vietnam began to affect Cambodia almost at once. The commander of United States forces in Vietnam, General William C. Westmoreland, believed that the infantry's unalterable task was to conduct "Search and Destroy" missions against its enemy. The vast majority of the Vietnamese population live along the eastern coastline of the country and in the Mekong Delta. But Westmoreland's purpose was not so much to create coastal enclaves as to pursue and eliminate the Communists in the intractable Central Highlands, which run like a backbone parallel to the Laotian and Cambodian borders. "Search and Destroy," together with the extensive use of air power, did not protect the people of South Vietnam. It did help to inflict heavy casualties on both sides, and it also encouraged the Communists to move westward out of range, thus creating a new dilemma for Sihanouk.

Like most of his compatriots, Sihanouk distrusted and disliked his Vietnamese neighbors. He recognized, however, the power of Hanoi. Although he realized that Cambodia would be far more vulnerable to a united Marxist Vietnam than to a divided nation at war, he believed that he had no alternative to reaching an ambiguous *modus vivendi* with the Communists. In 1965 he allowed them to come across the ill-defined border and build semipermanent base camps in areas of the eastern provinces of his country. These "sanctuaries" were to become a source of increasing frustration to Westmoreland.

The American coastal blockade of Vietnam forced the Communists to find new supply routes. At first they began to make more use of the Ho Chi Minh Trail down through Laos, into northeastern Cambodia and so to Vietnam. Then, in 1966 Chou En-lai personally asked Sihanouk to allow supplies to be brought into the port of Sihanoukville. Sihanouk was unhappy with the idea, but he had little alternative. "Two thirds for the Viet Cong, one third for yourself. At that rate one sells oneself," he later complained. From now until 1970 supplies landed at the port were handled by the Cambodian army and a Chinese firm called Haklee. The goods were trucked by night up the "Friendship Highway" that United States aid had built, through Phnom Penh and eastward to the border areas. This transport business and the Communists' straightforward purchase of food and medicine on the Phnom Penh market, were extremely profitable. Members of the royal family and many senior Cambodian army officers— including those who, like Lon Nol, were correctly considered pro-American—were involved in the traffic.

Within the United States intelligence establishment there was a sharp dispute over the significance of the Sihanoukville connection. The CIA thought it almost irrelevant; but the military and the Saigon embassy considered it such a vital source of supply for Hanoi and the Viet Cong that it should at all costs be destroyed. (In the first study of the war that Nixon and Kissinger commissioned in 1969, the military estimate of the supplies coming through Sihanoukville was five times as high as that of the CIA. The CIA, as events were to establish, was wrong.)

It was not only the Communists who romped across Cambodia's borders. The Americans conducted secret forays as well. In Vietnam the U.S. Special Forces and the CIA recruited mercenaries, called Civilian Irregular Defense Groups (CIDG), from the mountain tribes people and from the Cambodians who had lived in the Mekong Delta since the kingdom of Chenla embraced the whole area. They were under the command of Special Forces Colonel Jonathan "Fred" Ladd, an affable man well known to journalists for his acerbic comments on the way in which Westmoreland was fighting the war. Ladd—who was to play a prominent part in Cambodian events after the fall of Sihanouk—says that among these recruits, known as Khmer Krom, were many members of the Khmer Serei who had signed up both for training and in order to convert others to the anti-Sihanouk cause. Officially the United States always denied any connection at all with the Khmer Serei or its leader, Son Ngoc Thanh. In fact, whenever Thanh wished to visit the CIDG camps spaced along the Cambodian border, he was flown there by U.S. helicopter. "He was used as a recruiter," says William Colby. "This certainly gave him the mark of U.S. approval."

The Khmer Serei were also recruited into another branch of the Special Forces, the Studies and Operations Group, which was responsible for clandestine reconnaissance and sabotage missions into Cambodia and Laos. Throughout the sixties these Special Forces teams secretly slipped across the Vietnamese border in search of Communist trails, hospitals, bases, villages. (Ethnic Khmers were not supposed to go on the missions into Cambodia.) In 1967, without the knowledge of Congress, these operations were institutionalized under the name Salem House (later changed to Daniel Boone). The teams were allowed to delve up to 30 kilometers inside Cambodia and were authorized to place "sanitized self-destruct antipersonnel" land mines as they went. Their primary purpose was supposed to be intelligence gathering; in 1,835 missions over four years they captured 24 prisoners.

Despite the Salem House forays, and in spite of fairly constant, though haphazard artillery and tactical air attacks across the border, the Vietnamese Communists enjoyed relative security inside Cambodia through the Johnson years. As the failure of "Search and Destroy" became ever more evident, Cambodia became a scapegoat for Westmoreland and the Joint Chiefs. "No guerrilla war in history was ever won without sanctuaries" was a favorite phrase. Helped by press reporting that was often both careless and gullible, the United States military began by 1968 to build up an image of a Pentagon East and several Fort Braggs just across the ill-defined frontier. No one command headquarters of "COSVN" was ever found, but, as we have seen, in the late sixties air reconnaissance and the Salem House/Daniel Boone missions had identified along the length of the frontier about fifteen areas in which the Communists were thought to have bases.

Some of these were in the wild Northeast, where the Ho Chi Minh Trail emerged from the mountains of Laos. It was a sparsely populated area in which there were only a few settlements of hill people who were in almost constant revolt against Phnom Penh. As the border twists its way southward, the land becomes more fertile and more populous. The territory that the Pentagon called Base Area 353 (the target of the first Breakfast B-52 mission) was in the Fish Hook area, which juts into South Vietnam just north of Tay Ninh (where the cohesive Cao Dai sect had a magnificent temple in which they revered Sun Yat-sen, Victor Hugo and Winston Churchill). The Joint Chiefs considered this "the most important" of the base areas in Cambodia, but they also knew it to be surrounded by Cambodian villages.

Here and farther south, where the bases stretched into the Parrot's Beak—only about forty miles from Saigon—and then down into the thickly reeded waterways of the Mekong Delta, the Vietnamese Communists were in constant touch with the local population. At the beginning, their relations were good; they cultivated the bonzes and brought a great deal of commerce. There was a flourishing black market in stolen American supplies all along the more populated areas of the frontier. Rice, C-rations, M-16 rifles, cameras, watches, ammunition and even, it was said, Cadillacs could be bought.

Westmoreland recounts in his memoirs his exasperation that Lyndon Johnson always rejected requests for massive retaliations by air or ground across the frontier. The President was intrigued by Sihanouk—"Everything I hear about the Prince suggests we ought to get on well with him," he told his National Security Council staff early in 1966. He tried to send Averell Harriman to visit Phnom Penh; Sihanouk refused to see him. But under the pressure of the war, which was sharpening the internal political contradictions of Cambodia, the Prince was about to change his policy and move back toward the United States.

Sihanouk's quixotic government had not entirely succeeded. The economic reforms of 1963 had not vitiated the functional corruption in the capital; they had simply introduced the state more enthusiastically into the business. Corruption could have been eliminated only by structural reforms that Sihanouk was not prepared to make. During the period of American bounty many rough and smooth palms had been crossed; after 1963, with the money supply shrunken, it was only the rich who benefited, and even they found the return on capital invested in villas and import licenses vastly reduced. Minor civil servants, for whom bribes had been an essential supplement to meager salaries, joined the unemployed graduates and the officer corps in bitter resentment of the expulsion of the Americans and the socialization of the economy.

The pressure from the bourgeois—both the middle and the upper—was more voluble than that from the left. The pro-Communist Pracheachon group had been driven underground. Sihanouk had, nonetheless, tried to incorporate left-wing views and personalities into the Sangkum and the cabinet, but after 1963 the flow of disillusioned left-wing intellectuals to Paris and, less often, to the forests had increased. In 1966 Sihanouk allowed the election of a far more conservative government than before, and the following year he authorized his new Prime Minister, General Lon Nol, to repress savagely a peasant revolt in Battambang, a prosperous western province. Sihanouk was badly frightened by the rebellion, and publicly he blamed both Peking and those leftists who remained in the Sangkum for inciting it. In Phnom Penh it was clear to such left-wing former cabinet members as Khieu Samphan, Hu Nim and Hou Yuon that the relative tolerance with which the Prince had viewed their activities was ended. By October 1967 they had separately melted away into the forests; many people in Phnom Penh were convinced that Sihanouk's police had murdered them. In fact, they returned to sight as leading members of the Khmer Rouge after 1970.

From now on, Sihanouk's control over domestic politics diminished. He spent more and more time playing jazz and making melodramatic films; stories about the corruption of his wife, Monique, and her rapacious mother became increasingly scandalous, and the Phnom Penh court degenerated. Sihanouk started a casino to raise money and to pander to the nation's obsession with gambling; he seemed unaware of the extent of the domestic crisis. In his long speeches he enumerated meaningless sets of statistics about primary and secondary education, and ignored the nation's structural malaise.

But Sihanouk's interest in playing the Americans off against the Communists remained consuming. He was distressed by the Chinese Cultural Revolution and was becoming aware that the increasing use by the North Vietnamese of his border areas might provoke stronger American retaliation than the random shelling, bombing and small-unit ground attacks now taking place. At first, the sanctuaries had been tolerable; the personal and the institutional profits that his generals had made out of trade with the Communists had offset patriotic irritation at the way in which the country's neutrality was being abused. But in 1967 massive American operations in "War Zone C," close to Saigon, pushed more and more Communist troops across the border, and their presence became increasingly irksome. There was almost nothing Sihanouk could do.

His army's equipment and condition had deteriorated since he rejected American military aid in 1963. A trickle of supplies came from France and the USSR, but much of it was of poor quality or out of date. General Nhiek Thioulong, Sihanouk's commander in chief, now living in Paris, believes that by the end of the decade only about 11,000 of Cambodia's 30,000 troops could even hypothetically be called on to fight. Battalions and companies, operating at half strength, were scattered in villages throughout the provinces. In the northeast some border posts were prudently set 100 kilometers back from Vietnam. The precise boundaries often were unknown, almost always disputed. In the whole of Mondolkiri province, opposite Ban Me Thuot in the Central Highlands of South Vietnam, there was a single battalion of 320 men organized into three companies. If a serious skirmish with the Vietnamese, North or South, occurred, reinforcements would take two or three days to arrive from Phnom Penh, and then the capital would be left virtually undefended. "We were less effective than the Paris police," says Nhiek Thioulong.

Sihanouk's solution was to make gestures of friendliness toward Washington. They were reciprocated. First, Jacqueline Kennedy was allowed to make a much-publicized visit to the ruins of Angkor that was intended, she claimed, "to fulfill a childhood dream." Cambodian officials began to drop hints of rapprochement, even of allowing American "hot pursuit" into some sanctuaries. After discussions that took place through the Australian ambassador, who represented American interests in Phnom Penh, the Cambodian government agreed to accept American evidence of VC/NVA use of the border areas. Known by the code name "Vesuvius," this highly secret project was intended to provide the Prince with irrefutable documentation of the Communists' violations of Cambodia's territory so that he might somehow act against them. The first package was delivered by the Australian Ambassador Noel St. Clair Deschamps in December 1967. A few weeks later the American ambassador to New Delhi, Chester Bowles, came to Phnom Penh on an official mission.

Even at the time this was an important initiative, but Bowles's mission subsequently assumed even greater significance; years later the sustained Menu bombing by B-52s would be defended on the grounds that Sihanouk had told Bowles he could not object to it. The State Department's own contemporary account of the visit, written by an officer who accompanied Bowles, together with the ambassador's own reports to Washington, suggest that this is not so. They cannot be used as conclusive evidence, because, before they were declassified under the Freedom of Information Act, certain sections were excised by the State Department. On appeal, some—but not all—of the deleted passages were restored.

Bowles had long been a critic of American involvement in the war, and he arrived in Cambodia well disposed toward Sihanouk. As his plane began its descent toward Phnom Penh, he rehearsed his talking paper for their meeting; the paper makes clear that his mission was to convince the Prince that growing Communist use of the border areas threatened a wider war. If this was, as Washington hoped, to be avoided, then there was "a need to develop measures which are practical and useful to inhibit VC/NVA unauthorized use of Cambodian territory." The United States was keen to see the International Control Commission—a relic of the 1954 Geneva Agreement—strengthened, but this was not enough. Cambodian forces, though limited, could do rather more, and so might the United States. In this regard, his talking paper continued,

We have noted Cambodian statements on the possibility of U.S. Forces operating in Cambodia to defend themselves against VC/NVA. 2. We do not regard so-called "hot pursuit" as desirable remedy. 3. If Cambodia, with I.C.C. [International Control Commission] support, can prevent enemy presence, question of U.S. action in Cambodia does not arise. This is what we prefer and what we seek. 4. Present situation may provoke cross border actions such as a) reconnaissance by very limited forces to guard against attacks, b) returning hostile fire from Cambodia, c) tactical maneuvers to defend against hostile enemy action from within Cambodia. 5. There could be no secrecy about such defensive moves by U.S. forces. 6. We have noted possibility (deleted) about U.S. cross border action against VC/NVA forces. 7. We have noted distinction between inhabited and uninhabited areas. 8. Honoring this distinction would depend on effective measures being taken by RKG or ICC in inhabited areas. 9. Wish to re-emphasize that U.S. prefers such actions not be necessary.

When Bowles met Sihanouk, the Prince immediately began to criticize America's presence in Vietnam. He could not understand why the United States was attacking North Vietnam and other small countries while avoiding confrontation with Moscow and Peking, who were really to blame for the conflict. Ho Chi Minh was a nationalist, yet American intervention was pushing him into China's arms. He asserted that Cambodia had to maintain good relations with the Vietnamese Communists because the future of Southeast Asia was "red." But he wanted to keep the Vietnamese out of Cambodian territory, and he hoped the Control Commission would get off the cocktail circuit and into the border areas. He asked that the United States continue to inform him about VC/NVA presence in Eastern Cambodia.

At the end of the discussion Bowles emphasized that the United States had "absolutely no desire" to carry out military operations in Cambodia. "We prefer that other measures be taken to prevent VC/NVA use of Cambodian territory," he told the Prince. Sihanouk, according to the State Department report, "rejoined by saying he understood why we did not wish to become involved in military operations on Cambodian soil."

Sihanouk asked that Washington publicly recognize Cambodia's borders, promising Bowles that when relations were restored the United States military attaché would be free to roam the country and see anything he wished. Later in the visit, Prime Minister Son Sann returned to this theme. According to the State Department memo, "He wanted the U.S. to offer a guarantee against U.S. bombing or firing on Cambodian villages and frontier posts. General Nhiek Thioulong joined in, citing statistics on the number of killed and wounded in the US/SVN provoked incidents. Ambassador Bowles again assured the Cambodian delegation that the United States had no aggressive intentions. He acknowledged, however, that, given the prevailing situation, accidents might occasionally occur."

Whether Sihanouk actually told Bowles that the United States was free to bomb the sanctuaries cannot be definitely determined from the sanitized State Department papers, and Bowles himself was too ill to give an interview when this book was written. Charles Meyer, Sihanouk's long-time French aide, recalls that the Prince did tell Bowles that just as he could not prevent the Vietnamese from usurping Cambodian territory, so he could not object to the United States attacking them there. But Meyer insists—and this is crucial—that Sihanouk meant to allow only isolated small-scale attacks, not a vast B-52 campaign along the length of the border. "There was no question of B-52s," Meyer says.

Certainly neither Bowles nor those who were with him seem to have believed that the achievement of the visit was to allow the United States to extend the war into Cambodia. The State Department report notes that by the end of the visit the Bowles party believed that "there seemed little doubt that on the Cambodian side fears of 'hot pursuit' had been allayed. The Americans, for their part, sensed that a catastrophic widening of the war had been averted and that the Bowles mission had succeeded in overcoming many of the problems which had embittered United States-Cambodian relations."*

Bowles cabled his own analysis to Washington on his return to New Delhi; it was astute. "I came away deeply convinced, as on previous visits to Cambodia, that Sihanouk's decisions and attitudes, however bizarre, are shaped by intense and deeply rooted nationalism in which ideology has little or no part." He also considered that the talks represented a very important shift of Cambodia's foreign policy toward the United States; he was all in favor of trying to find a formula by which Washington could give Cambodia the public assurances on the borders that Sihanouk required, without unduly offending the Thais or Vietnamese.

Bowles wrote that he was "fully conscious of mercurial and unpredictable characteristics of the Prince. In any dealings with Cambodia we must expect sudden switches and caustic and unfair criticism. However, we should not let Sihanouk's intemperate . . . outbursts deter us from the main business at hand: to keep Cambodia neutral, to keep the Viet Cong and NVA out of its territory and, with an eye to the future, to improve our relations with this small but important country."

After Bowles's visit, the Vietnamese Communists launched their February 1968 Tet offensive in South Vietnam. Sihanouk appears to have been more impressed by the casualties the Communists sustained than by the political impact within the United States. In March he sent a letter to *Le Monde* in which he complained that Peking and Hanoi were conspiring to overthrow him. "It is perfectly clear that Asian communism does not permit us any longer to remain neutral," he wrote. Elsewhere he publicly affirmed—as he had said to Bowles—that he was ready to restore relations with Washington if only the Americans would recognize the inviolability of Cambodia's existing borders.

The Prince's attempts at rapprochement caused a furious debate in the State Department. Chester Bowles and Arthur Goldberg, Ambassador to the U.N., both urged that the United States recognize Cambodia's bor-

---

* The State Department's contemporary, eyewitness summary on "hot pursuit" should be compared with Kissinger's statements on the same matter. For example, in a written response to questions submitted by Senator Harold Hughes at the time of Kissinger's confirmation as Secretary of State in September 1973, Kissinger wrote, under oath, "In a January 10, 1968, meeting with U.S. emissary Chester Bowles, Sihanouk stated that he did not want any North Vietnamese in Cambodia, and further stated that while he could not say so officially, he wanted the United States to retaliate against these North Vietnamese forces with 'hot pursuit' or bombing in the unpopulated border areas of Cambodia."

ders. On March 18, Bowles sent Secretary of State Dean Rusk a cable saying that restored relations would help, "both in terms of improving our understanding of what is going on in that country and in reversing a deteriorating trend in our whole relationship with South East Asia."

Many diplomats tend to defend the interests of the country to which they are accredited, and Bowles's proposal was attacked, as he knew it would be, by the embassies in both Saigon and Bangkok. In Saigon Robert Komer, a deputy ambassador, wrote an angry memo to his superior, Ambassador Ellsworth Bunker; his language is revealing of the way many American diplomats thought Sihanouk should be treated. "We want to make Sihanouk nervous rather than give him reason to believe we are moving his way. That can come later if the preliminary softening up process works. Hence, why not actively enter the lists against Bowles by filing a demurrer?" Bunker followed this advice. Dean Rusk decided, nonetheless, to go ahead with exploratory talks. The Saigon embassy went on complaining.

Throughout the year the United States continued to provide Sihanouk with Vesuvius packages detailing Communist violations of Cambodian neutrality; but, to the disgust of the embassy in Saigon and the Joint Chiefs in Washington, the Cambodians took little action. They lacked the means. In September Eugene Black came to Phnom Penh as the personal envoy of Lyndon Johnson on another conciliatory visit. He told the new Prime Minister, Penn Nouth, of American concern. Penn Nouth replied that he would speak "with brutal frankness" and, according to Black's report, he assured the American party that Cambodia was even more uneasy about the North Vietnamese than the United States government, that the Khmers had historical reasons to distrust all Vietnamese. (He also complained about continued United States support for the Khmer Serei, and one of Black's entourage, General Charles Corcoran, denied brazenly that there was any such thing.)

That was where matters rested in early 1969, when Nixon and Kissinger entered the White House and General Abrams sent his request for permission to bomb Base Area 353. Talks had begun but were not completed. Sihanouk's domestic position had deteriorated because of the war and because of his failure either to deal effectively with the economy or to satisfy middle-class aspirations. But he was still in power, and the vast majority of his people were at peace.

Sihanouk's role has been examined critically here because an understanding of Cambodia is not helped by idealizing his role. His shortcomings must, however, be related to the context. By the beginning of 1969,

Vietnam and Laos were torn apart by war, their people driven into camps, their societies already irrevocably destroyed. Thailand had endured no fighting, but it too had been corrupted by the commerce of war and now, under a repressive military dictatorship, served as a "land-based aircraft carrier" for the B-52 bombers that daily pounded the grounds of its Indochinese neighbors. Only Cambodia was unassailed. Her neutrailism was vulnerable and abused by all parties to the conflict, particularly by the Vietnamese Communists, but the policy had managed to allow the vast majority of her people to live around their pagodas, work their fields and fish their streams. There was, in 1969, a small insurgent movement, the Khmer Rouge, numbering about four thousand. It was able to hit isolated military posts and assassinate village officials, but it had no prospects of success. The honest illusion of plenty, peace and security was enough to convince most of the population. For this, almost all credit—save that which was due to the relative self-restraint displayed by Lyndon Johnson—must go to Prince Norodom Sihanouk. Despite his many failures, domestic and foreign, he alone had seen how the Cambodian people could be protected, and he alone had accomplished it.

It was not enough. The White House was now occupied by men who were prepared to take risks that Johnson had rejected and to ignore limits that he had recognized.

CHAPTER 5

The Adviser

LONG AFTER President Nixon's taping system was discovered, it was revealed that Henry Kissinger recorded his telephone calls as a matter of course. Robert Keatley, the *Wall Street Journal*'s diplomatic correspondent, obtained the transcripts of one series of calls that Kissinger had made in March 1976, eighteen months after Nixon resigned from office. They referred to a report that Nixon had just written for President Ford on his recent trip to China, and they serve to illustrate the extraordinary relationship that existed between the former President and his principal adviser.

In one call, Kissinger was talking to Nixon himself and, in another, to the current Vice-President, Nelson Rockefeller.

"Mr. President," the Secretary began in the first call, "I wanted you to know I have read the report and I find it very fascinating."

"As I said, there is a lot of things that are repetitive," replied Nixon.

"But that too is interesting. The fact there is repetition is interesting," Kissinger said.

". . . I'm not sure that maybe some of your other people saw it, but you could see the subtlety of the analysis I was making."

"I thought you were very, very clever."

Nixon recounted what he had told the Chinese about Taiwan.

"I thought you were very, very good on this," Kissinger replied.

Nixon mentioned his discussions on SALT. Kissinger responded, "I thought that was very clever."

A short time later Kissinger was on the telephone to Nelson Rockefeller, for whom he had once worked.

". . . I have read the Nixon report on his trip now," said Kissinger to his patron. "He is such an egomaniac. All he wrote was—"

"—his memoirs," interjected Rockefeller.

"Just what he said. Nothing what the Chinese said. Practically nothing. A fascinating account of himself," agreed Kissinger.

"I love it. . . ." the Vice-President responded.

Kissinger's remarkable career has frequently been described since he came to general attention in 1969: a Bavarian-Jewish childhood, flight from the Nazis at age fifteen, escape from the Bronx into Army Counter-intelligence during World War II, return to Germany to administer a district in Hesse, Government School at Harvard, academic success, and control of the Harvard International Seminar at which young highfliers from around the world debated. Denied tenure at Harvard, he moved to two other citadels of the Establishment, the Council on Foreign Relations and the Rockefeller Brothers Fund. He gained academic respectability with an interesting and revealing work on Metternich and Castlereagh, and unexpected fame with a treatise that rejected the Dulles doctrine of "massive retaliation" in favor of "limited nuclear war." Another book, more work for Rockefeller, a short unhappy stint on McGeorge Bundy's National Security Council, back to Harvard, adviser to Rockefeller in the 1964 Republican campaign, a fourth book, on the Atlantic Alliance, then off with Rockefeller again on the 1968 Presidential campaign around the nation—and an invitation from President-elect Richard Nixon to become his National Security Assistant.

Why Kissinger should have been so swift to reverse his well-publicized judgment in 1968 that Nixon was "unfit to be President" is clear enough. It is more rewarding to examine what Nixon saw in him. Whatever contempt Kissinger displayed for Nixon before he worked for him and—behind his back—in the White House, the terms in which they had both always seen the world and the manner in which they perceived their own roles were remarkably similar.

Nixon had risen from the House to the Senate to the Vice-Presidency on anti-Communism. Kissinger was not among the academics who questioned the conventions of the Cold War. His International Seminar at

Harvard was an anti-Soviet forum in which the leaders of tomorrow could articulate and refine the notions of Iron Curtain, containment, and rollback. Nixon favored the use of American bombers to rescue the French at Dien Bien Phu and asserted that "tactical atomic explosives are now conventional and will be used against the targets of any aggressive force." It was Kissinger's book *Nuclear Weapons and Foreign Policy* which made the notion of limited nuclear war respectable. He advanced the premise that "the problem is to apply graduated amounts of destruction for limited objectives and also to permit the necessary breathing spaces for political contacts." The idea that nuclear war could be controlled by good sense was novel and optimistic for a man who also believed that statesmen must have the freedom to act with "credible irrationality." But it coincided with the realization at the end of the fifties that the doctrine of massive retaliation was inhibiting.

Kissinger's political assessments also fitted the times. He argued that the Communists simply exploited Americans' desire for peace and fear of all-out nuclear war by playing with skill their "strategy of ambiguity"— alternating force, as in Hungary, subtle infiltration, as in the Middle East, and "peaceful coexistence." He dismissed the hundreds of thousands who marched to ban the bomb as tools of Soviet propaganda. Moscow's intent was "to undermine the will to use it by a world-wide campaign against the horrors of nuclear warfare. [Their campaign was a] tour de force, masterful in its comprehension of psychological factors, brutal in its consistency, and ruthless in its sense of direction. With cold-blooded effrontery, as if no version of reality other than its own were even conceivable, through all the media and organizations at its disposal, the Kremlin . . ." pursued its ends.

By the beginning of the sixties, Kissinger had exchanged limited nuclear war for limited conventional war, a notion that was finding support within the Kennedy White House. Even so, he did not last long as a consultant on Kennedy's National Security Council, and it was said by those who imagined that it reflected poorly on him that his style was not Camelot. A story went around that when Kissinger decided to call a press conference to announce his resignation, Kennedy's press aide, Pierre Salinger, remarked, "I didn't know he was a consultant in the first place." The experience must have shown him how the national security adviser can protect a President from others' views, and how essential access is to influence.

In *The Necessity for Choice*, Kissinger endorsed the idea that a missile gap existed between the United States and the USSR. He also developed the theme expressed in *Nuclear Weapons and Foreign Policy,* that leadership is only for the very exceptional and that one of its prices is to be alone and misunderstood by the masses and by most politicians whose vision is narrowed by their "preoccupation with domestic development." Kissinger later insisted that any statesman who "wish[ed] to affect events must be opportunistic to some extent," and he suggested that "the real distinction is between those who adapt their purposes to reality and those who seek to mould reality in the light of their purposes."

His writings might suggest that Kissinger was more moved by the statesman's freedom of action than by the needs and dynamics of democratic restraint. It has been said that his early experience of the Weimar republic and then fascism impressed him with the irreducible will and purpose of totalitarianism. Certainly he appeared to believe that democracy seemed an ineffective David against dictatorship.

The Soviet achievements were due to "greater moral toughness, to a greater readiness to run risks both physical and moral." The Russians were "iron-nerved," they analyzed events with a ruthless objectivity, they conceptualized the world more subtly than Western politicians. They were cold-blooded, logical, without compunction, steadfast. American methods of policy making were inadequate to confront them. Kissinger argued that no coherent purpose governed America's actions and decisions; far too much was done on a random basis outside a philosophical framework. Problems should not be disposed of individually on their merits, for that was "as if, in commissioning a painting, a patron would ask one artist to draw the face, another the body, another the hands, and still another the feet, simply because each artist was particularly good in one category." Kissinger's demand that each problem be dealt with only in the context of an over-all ideology was an early statement of his subsequent notion of "linkage," a concept that wishes to impose a framework upon an untidy world.

One of his proffered solutions to the problems of policy making involved the identification of a new class. This was separate from the businessmen, lawyers and bureaucrats who traditionally ran United States foreign policy, but it was still part of the foreign-policy cadre. It consisted of "intellectuals" whom Kissinger appeared to see as men with a specific calling. Unlike lawyers or businessmen or even many "policymakers," they have "addressed themselves to acquiring substantive knowledge"; this was something that the policymakers should be eager to acquire. But too often the intellectual's value, his investment in himself, was squandered by policymakers who asked him "to solve problems, not to contribute to the definition of goals" and to provide "not ideas but endorsement." Because, perhaps, the policymaker has not had the advantages of reflection that distinguish an intellectual, "his problem is that he does not know the nature of the help he requires."

The intellectual, Kissinger wrote, must deal with the policymaker "from a position of independence"; he should guard his "distinctive" and "most crucial qualities." These were "the pursuit of knowledge rather than administrative ends and the perspective supplied by a nonbureaucratic vantage point." Kissinger did not seem to raise the question of whether the intellectual could find himself unable to associate with certain policies and still retain his integrity. In certain respects, his "intellectual" was a mercenary.

Among Kissinger's qualities are charm and persuasiveness. At Harvard he was as sincere as he was serious. To talk to Kissinger was for many a pleasure; to be consulted was considered a privilege; "brilliant" was the commonly used word. There is reason to believe that Nelson Rockefeller and those men whose earlier patronage was helpful to his career felt honored by his company. Kissinger is a true diplomat; he can make anyone feel grateful and flattered. Some colleagues also detected other aspects of his personality. Stanley Hoffmann, professor of government at Harvard, once said that part of Kissinger's philosophy of life was always that "goodwill won't help you defend yourself on the docks of Marseilles." One distinguished Harvard economist now claims (not for attribution) that Kissinger appeared at Harvard to be "terribly inconsiderate, terribly self-centered, the most single-mindedly self-serving ambitious individual, who cultivated people only for the good they could do him." Another colleague has suggested that he was capable of experiencing shame and not allowing it to hamper him. Certainly he could be unkind as well as charming; secretaries were frequently brought to tears by his tantrums. And he engaged in terrible feuds; the longest was with Robert Bowie, Director of Harvard's Center for International Affairs, who had helped Kissinger eventually to get tenure at Harvard in 1957 and felt that Kissinger had not since repaid the kindness. For a time their offices were in the same suite, and each sent his secretary out to see that the coast was clear rather than risk meeting the other. The nearest thing to a go-between was Thomas Schelling, professor of economics at Harvard. He might have found the role wearisome anyway: Kissinger made it a little harder. Once, when Kissinger heard that Schelling had said something critical of him, he expressed outrage and injury in a letter in which he said also that his whole concept of friendship had now been changed.

Despite the mauling of Nelson Rockefeller by the Republican right in 1964, Kissinger continued to expand his areas of political interest and attempted in the middle sixties to come to terms with the developing war in Vietnam. Visiting Saigon, he impressed Daniel Ellsberg with a certain openness of mind. But his views were unexceptional; he agreed with most of Johnson's administration officials (and with Richard Nixon) that however unfortunate the Vietnam commitment had been, it now had to be met.

What Kissinger hoped for in 1968 is not clear. He had been a Rockefeller family counselor for almost a decade; this was his second Presidential campaign for Nelson. From early in the year he obviously doubted its chances of success and he accepted a fellowship at All Souls, Oxford.

When Rockefeller lost the Republican nomination to Nixon, Kissinger told Dean Brown, an American diplomat, that he would have to abstain. "I could never vote for Nixon, of course, and that clown Humphrey would never make a President." Publicly he called Nixon "the most dangerous" of the candidates. But he began to reconsider, and soon All Souls was receiving diplomatic messages that he might not arrive at the beginning of the term in October. Nixon records in his memoirs that in the weeks before the election Kissinger used his "entrée" with the Johnson administration to uncover foreign-policy information that he passed on to help Nixon's campaign. This was done in complete secrecy, and when the columnist Joseph Kraft told him that Nixon was considering him as national security adviser, Kissinger reacted, in Kraft's words, "like a totally scared rabbit" and called several times begging Kraft not to tell *anyone*. He was apparently anxious to keep his options open and appear uncommitted throughout the campaign. His discreet advice impressed Nixon, and at the end of November the President-elect summoned him to his transition headquarters in the Hotel Pierre in New York. Kissinger was asked to become National Security Assistant. Encouraged by Nelson Rockefeller, Kissinger went to the White House.

Even those of whom he had been most critical and had sought—at least in his writings—to displace were delighted by his appointment. In Wall Street, in big law firms, in academe and in the press, his selection was praised, most especially by those who had been apprehensive about Nixon. Did Kissinger's appointment not prove that there was "a new Nixon"? "Excellent . . . very encouraging," said Arthur Schlesinger. "I'll sleep better with Henry Kissinger in Washington" said Adam Yarmolinsky. The Establishment was relieved, wrote Henry Brandon of *The Sunday Times* of London. ("Establishment relief" was what Brandon again praised in 1976, when another outsider, Jimmy Carter, chose Cyrus Vance as Secretary of State.) James Reston of *The New York Times* wrote that it was "significant that Kissinger has the respect of most of the foreign-policy experts who have served the last three Presidents." Reston noted that Nixon had chosen his White House adviser before he chose the Secretaries of State or Defense. "This may lead to some friction," he suggested. But, after Nixon's friend William Rogers, a New York lawyer with scarcely any experience in foreign affairs, was appointed Secretary of State, Reston wrote that rumors that Nixon wanted to be his own Secretary were wrong. "Indeed the Nixon-Rogers relationship is likely to be a much more equal relationship than the Johnson-Rusk relationship."

When the staff members of the National Security Council and the senior officials in State, Defense and CIA returned to their desks after watching the Inauguration on January 20, 1969, each found a stack of memoranda. On top was a four-page paper headed NSDM 1—National Security Decision Memorandum One—and signed by Nixon. They were informed that the President was reorganizing the National Security Council system. The effects of the reorganization were to be critical in many areas of foreign policy, particularly Cambodia.

The new structure relocated *de facto* and *de jure* power over foreign decision making. It was the work of Kissinger and Morton Halperin, who had known Kissinger at Harvard and had become a critic of the war working in the Pentagon for Robert McNamara and Clark Clifford, Johnson's last Secretary of Defense.

Kissinger called Halperin to the Pierre soon after he arrived there himself. Before the cabinet had been selected, Halperin began devising new procedures by which the President could make foreign policy. There were excellent reasons for reorganization. Under Johnson, many vital decisions had been reached at Tuesday lunches, where the discussions were inadequately recorded and the participants often were unclear as to what decisions had been reached. Moreover, bureaucrats have a vested interest in protecting the policies of the past, however unsuccessful, and an organization like the State Department, disparate in its views but united in self-regard, can prove a serious barrier to new ideas.

Halperin wanted the President to have real power of decision among genuine options. The bureaucracies were to be denied the traditional technique of presenting three choices: you can blow up the world, do as we say, or surrender to the Kremlin. "It was the B-1 and B-2 options we were after," says Halperin.

In theory, the main instrument of foreign-policy making was now to be the National Security Council (NSC) founded by Truman in 1947 as "the place in the government where the military, diplomatic and resources problems could be studied and continually appraised." Eisenhower had used it as a rather loose discussion group for reaching what Dean Acheson called "agreement by exhaustion." Both Kennedy and Johnson had disregarded it in favor of more informal methods. Halperin and Kissinger reestablished it as the principal forum for decision making. Its membership now included the President, the Vice-President, the Secretaries of State and Defense, the Director of the Office of Emergency Preparedness and as advisers, the Director of the CIA and the Chairman of the Joint Chiefs. But it was soon clear that the Council itself was to be less influential than its committees and its staff.

Nixon was anxious to keep meetings of the NSC to a minimum; the agenda were to be set by Kissinger's office, and discussion was to be limited. In the past, officials as humble as cabinet secretaries could occasionally gain personal access to the President. Now anything of importance and any memos to the President had to pass through an elaborate process. The first filter was a subcommittee called the Review Group. This was chaired by Kissinger and included representation of the Director of the CIA, the Chairman of the Joint Chiefs of Staff, the Deputy Secretary of Defense and the Under Secretary of State. The group's task was to determine whether a specific issue merited the attention of the full Council. If it decided not, the matter was referred to a new Under-Secretaries Committee representing the departments. Halperin's plan also preserved the NSC's existing interagency groups of Assistant Secretaries whose purpose was to prepare papers for the NSC, and it allowed the President to set up an ad hoc working group on any specific subject.

Two new series of memoranda were now created: National Security Study Memoranda and National Security Decision Memoranda. The Study Memoranda, to be signed usually by Kissinger, sometimes by Nixon, would direct the agencies to review particular problems or situations for the President by a certain date. Decision Memoranda informed the bureaucracies of Presidential decisions "when," in the words of the original Halperin-Kissinger memo, "the President wants the agencies concerned clearly to understand what he desires and the reasons for his decision."

When confronted with a policy problem the system enabled Kissinger to send a two- or three-page study memorandum, the NSSM (pronounced Nisim), to the appropriate interagency group requesting all views by a certain date. Each member of the group would have officials in his agency submit papers, and these would be collated to be passed on to the Review Group. This body, controlled by Kissinger, worked as what Halperin called a "traffic cop." It could pass the study up to the National Security Council and the President, or it could send it back to the agencies for further work. Eventually, after the Study Memorandum had been discussed by the NSC, the President made his decision, and a Decision Memorandum, also signed by Kissinger, was issued to the departments. To make sure there was no backsliding, its implementation was monitored by the Under-Secretaries Committee, of which Kissinger was the most important member.

On paper, the system gave the President real choice of genuine alternatives for policy making. But even on paper it conferred exceptional powers on the National Security adviser. Access to the President was through him; it was he who, in the President's name, informed the bureaucracies what they were to examine; his staff sat through the entire development of the studies, and when these reached the Review Group he could either accept them, reject them or demand changes in whatever had so far been accomplished. Final papers for the President had his covering memo on top of them. Subsequently, many more NSC committees were created to coordinate different aspects of foreign policy; Kissinger was made their chairman.

Halperin finished the draft of the memo before Christmas 1968, and Kissinger gave it, without telling him, to another new aide, Lawrence S. Eagleburger. Eagleburger's reaction was, "Whatever happened to the Secretary of State?" The way in which Kissinger then managed, in very few days, to have the plan accepted by Nixon reflects considerable bureaucratic skill, even at a time when he was still uncertain of his relationship with his employer.

Among the members of the transition team at the Pierre was General Andrew Goodpaster, Eisenhower's staff assistant during World War II, and then defense liaison officer and staff secretary in his White House. Nixon had liked him in the fifties, and in 1968 he asked him to advise on how the NSC should be reformed. Kissinger, who apparently did not relish the prospect of Nixon hiring such an independent figure as Goodpaster as his military adviser, handed the Halperin memo to the General for his advice. The General had none. Probably unconscious of how useful he was being, he gave the scheme his imprimatur. When Kissinger sent the memo to Nixon he included a cover note: "The attached memo outlines my ideas for organizing the NSC and my own staff. It is based on extensive conversations with a number of people—particularly General Goodpaster, who agrees with my recommendations. I apologize for its length, but the decisions you make on the issues raised here will have an important effect on how we function in the field of foreign affairs in the years ahead. I thought, therefore, that it would be best for you to have as full a description as possible of what General Goodpaster and I have in mind."

Just after Christmas the President agreed to it all. But then he apparently gave Kissinger a surprise. Nixon insisted that Kissinger secure the approval of both Rogers and the new Secretary of Defense, Melvin Laird. Evidently, he was not willing himself to present them with a scheme that deprived them of power. But another Kissinger aide, Roger Morris, has reported that he told Kissinger not to worry about Rogers—he would not object. And he did not. Despite the protests of some career State Department officers around him, Rogers airily endorsed the plan, dismissing the importance of "all these committees." His officials made a wretched attempt to recoup something, and one of them came up to the Pierre to suggest to Kissinger that perhaps a role for the Secretary of State could be worked in somewhere. Kissinger suggested he take any problems he had straight to Nixon.

Melvin Laird should have proved a more formidable obstacle. He was tough, rather brash, and for fifteen years he had represented a Wisconsin district in Congress. He had served on the Defense Appropriations Subcommittee in the House and knew something about the Pentagon. More importantly, he was an acute judge of the political mood of parts of the United States into which Kissinger had never ventured and of which Nixon, despite his later talk of the "silent majority," understood little. Nonetheless, Laird also seems to have been impressed by the Goodpaster connection; he too accepted the reorganization. He realized his mistake sooner than Rogers and he subsequently began to react.

But he lost an important first battle when he tried to have Nixon abolish the liaison office that had existed between the Joint Chiefs of Staff and the White House since 1950. He argued that it encouraged the two organizations to deal directly with each other behind the back of the Secretary of Defense, who is required by law to exert complete authority over the military. Kissinger, however, insisted that this channel between the White House and the President's principal military advisers be kept open. In the event, Laird's misgivings were justified—Kissinger did create a close relationship with the Chiefs that, in some important ways, excluded Laird. But even Laird could not suspect to what extent the use made of the liaison office would later reveal the mistrust and paranoia in the White House.

The new NSC procedures went into effect immediately after the Inauguration. The departments found themselves inundated with study memoranda demanding surveys of dozens of different international situations and problems, many to be completed in haste. Some useful material undoubtedly derived from the surveys, and some Presidential decisions were certainly improved by all the research, the compilations, the reviews, the submissions, the re-reviews, the re-submissions. But it soon became evident to Laird and others that one purpose of the many NSSM's was to keep the departments occupied and under the illusion that they were participating in the policy-making process while decisions were actually made in the White House.

Kissinger's intentions were, in fact, fairly clear. Nothing in his academic writings had suggested that he was concerned to involve the bureaucracies in policy making. In 1968 he had said, "The only way secrecy can be kept is to exclude from the making of the decisions all those who are theoretically charged with carrying it out." Early in the administration he acknowledged what he considered to be one of the most serious organizational problems he faced: "There are twenty thousand people in the State Department and fifty thousand in Defense. They all need each other's clearances in order to move . . . and they all want to do what I'm doing. So the problem becomes: how do you get them to push papers around, spin their wheels, so that you can get your work done?"

Kissinger devised the NSSM process but few of the most important decisions that he and Nixon made were subjected to it. There were no NSSMs to discuss whether Cambodia should be bombed or invaded, whether Allende's government should be subverted, whether Kissinger should conduct secret talks with the North Vietnamese, or to plan his first flight to China. Indeed many of those policies that are most characteristic of the Nixon administration's record in foreign policy were subjected to no formal debate at all.

CHAPTER 6

The Problem

IT WAS in expectation of peace that Nixon was narrowly elected President in November 1968. His inheritance was not enviable. There were 536,000 American soldiers in Vietnam in January 1969 (the peak, to be reached that April, was 543,000). Every week about three hundred bodies were flown back to the States in "reusable metal transfer cases." Domestic opposition to the war had mounted and had exploded in the melodrama of 1968. General Westmoreland's attrition strategy, which sent recruits to the perimeters of Vietnam to find Communists, had failed. By the Pentagon's estimates, Communist combat forces had grown from 56,000 in 1964 to at least 150,000 in 1968. South Vietnamese forces had also been increased by the American effort and now numbered about 819,000 men, but their performance was poor and their leadership inadequate.

By the end of 1968 Nixon had managed to obscure the record of his views on Indochina. He had consistently favored escalation. In 1954 he had advocated sending American troops and bombers to help the French. In 1962 he had encouraged Kennedy to "step up the buildup." In 1964 he had advised that the enemy be pursued into Laos and North Vietnam. In August 1966 he had demanded that half a million American men be sent to Saigon. Throughout he had contributed significantly to the public impression that the war was essential to restrain Peking. Just as Dean Rusk claimed that the war kept "a billion Chinese armed with nuclear weapons" at bay, so Nixon campaigned in New Hampshire in February

85

1968 on grounds that the Vietnam effort was "the cork in the bottle of Chinese expansion in Asia."

After the impact on American opinion of the Viet Cong's Tet offensive, and when his prospects of victory were increased by Johnson's abdication, Nixon became more cautious. Throughout the summer of 1968 he refused to discuss the war; he claimed that it was too important to be introduced into partisan politics. The Democrats were in disarray, and he was able to evade the issue almost completely. But rumors that Nixon had "a secret plan to end the war" were encouraged, and at the Republican National Convention he promised that "the long dark night for America was almost over." For the Republicans and for about half the American electorate it was enough.

Blame for many of the errors of judgment over Vietnam has been ascribed to the "Munich mentality." Horror of the consequences of appeasement had led to a post-World War II determination to stand firm anywhere, anytime. For both Nixon and Kissinger, the memory of the Korean War was also influential. To Nixon it proved that only coercion could succeed. "How do you bring a war to a successful conclusion?" he asked a group of Southern delegates at the 1968 Republican Convention. "I'll tell you how Korea was ended. We got in there and had this messy war on our hands, Eisenhower let the word go out—let the word go out diplomatically—to the Chinese and the North Koreans that we would not tolerate this continued war of attrition. And within a matter of months they negotiated. . . . Well, as far as the negotiation [in Vietnam] is concerned that should be our position. We'll be militarily strong and diplomatically strong. . . . We need a massive training program so that the South Vietnamese can be trained to take over the fighting—that they can be phased in as we phase out."

To Kissinger, Korea had shown the limits imposed by contemporary strategic thinking. The United States had been far too concerned lest it frighten its European allies and provoke the USSR. "We thought we could not win in Korea despite our strategic superiority, because Russia could not afford to lose," he had written. Similarly, in 1954 the idea of sending United States troops to help the French in Vietnam was dismissed because the British were against it and the risk of provoking the Soviets seemed too great. It was from such considerations that he came to oppose the doctrine of "massive retaliation"—he considered that its fearsomeness discouraged intervention. Hence, his notion first of limited nuclear war and then of limited conventional wars in which each side could test its own mettle and the other's resolve. That notion had been applied to Vietnam.

A serious problem of such war is that much more is at stake than the battleground or its inhabitants. The fight is more for myth than for reality, more for credibility than for territory, and the prospect of loss is therefore more disconcerting than the "limited" nature of the war might be thought to imply. McGeorge Bundy wrote in 1965 that a sustained policy of reprisal against North Vietnam was worthwhile as a demonstration of American resolve, even if it failed militarily. Walt Rostow's dictum, "We are the greatest power in the world—if we behave like it" was expressed a little more delicately by Kissinger.

Kissinger had serious misgivings about Vietnam as a battleground. When he went there in 1965 and 1966 he moved away from the platitudinous embassy and military hierarchy, to talk to local Vietnamese officials and to the Americans stationed in the boondocks. He decided that Westmoreland's tactics were abysmal and that the South Vietnamese establishment was as inept as it was corrupt. But he did not conclude that the United States should extricate itself as quickly as possible. He knew that negotiations were "inevitable," but he held that "withdrawal would be disastrous"; a "victory by a third-class Communist peasant state over the United States" would "strengthen the most bellicose factions in the internecine Communist struggle around the world," and "demoralize" America's friends in Southeast Asia; and it might encourage Japan or India to move toward Moscow or Peking. "A demonstration of American impotence in Asia cannot fail to lessen the credibility of American pledges in other fields. . . . We are no longer fighting in Vietnam only for the Vietnamese; we are also fighting for ourselves and for international stability," he wrote, in terms hardly different from the famous statement that year of the Assistant Secretary of Defense, John McNaughton, that, "The present U.S. objective in Vietnam is to avoid humiliation" and at risk was not a "friend" (Vietnam), but above all "our reputation as a guarantor."

There was little that distinguished Kissinger's views from the Washington consensus, except perhaps a greater reservation about the capacity of the South Vietnamese. His most intriguing contribution to the Vietnam debate before he assumed office was an article written in 1968 for *Foreign Affairs*, published as he and Nixon moved to Washington. His analysis of American policy mistakes was cogent, but it would be ignored over the years to come. The basic error, Kissinger argued, was that "we fought a military war; our opponents fought a political one. We sought physical attrition; our opponents aimed for psychological exhaustion. In the process we lost sight of one of the cardinal maxims of guerrilla war; the guerrilla wins if he does not lose; the conventional army loses if it does not win." He recognized that Tet 1968 had been a political defeat for Washington, even if the Viet Cong infrastructure had been badly mauled.

There was talk in Washington in 1968 of a coalition government as a solution to Vietnam's problems. Kissinger wanted none of it. He thought that it made "as much sense as to attempt to overcome the problems of Mississippi through a coalition between the SDS and the Ku Klux Klan. . . . It is beyond imagination that parties that have been murdering and betraying each other for twenty-five years could work together as a team giving joint instructions to the entire country." He was also opposed to any American involvement in political discussions between the two sides lest "our pressure may wind up being directed against Saigon as the seeming obstacle to an accommodation." After he came to office these two sensible warnings were forgotten.

Kissinger proposed parallel talks in which political and military affairs would be strictly separated. The North Vietnamese and the Americans would discuss military matters; the South Vietnamese government and the NLF would negotiate political changes. The American objective would be to avoid military defeat "or a change in the political structure of South Vietnam brought about by external military force." Washington must try to effect a staged withdrawal of both North Vietnamese and American forces; any discussion of the future political composition of South Vietnam must be left to the Vietnamese.

As a new idea to break the Paris deadlock this may have sounded eminently reasonable in Washington, but it ignored the fact that to the Vietnamese Communists this was a revolutionary struggle in which military and political ends can rarely be separated. The Chinese had acceded to such a separation at Geneva in 1954, but Hanoi was not grateful for the way its allies had then imposed a moratorium on its revolution. (Nor were the Cambodian Communists.) And although the idea of mutual withdrawal might seem an advance on Lyndon Johnson's 1966 offer to withdraw American troops six months after a cease-fire, it disregarded the fact that, for the Vietnamese, this was a *civil* war.

While he was still at the Hotel Pierre in December 1968, Kissinger had asked Daniel Ellsberg, who had returned from Vietnam to the Rand Corporation, to help draw up a paper discussing the options available to the United States in Vietnam. Ellsberg suggested that the possibility of unilateral withdrawal should be among the ideas considered. Kissinger deleted it from the list. In 1975, after the war was lost, he said he had thought from the beginning that it was a "disaster." But in 1968 he was not prepared to consider whether America's world position, its "honor," might better be served by an immediate end to it; all the options to be considered involved remaining in Vietnam.

At the Pierre, Kissinger's staff posed questions to be presented to departments as National Security Study Memorandum One. The replies, when they came, were not encouraging; the only point of agreement was pessimism. The Secretary of Defense's office concluded that the South Vietnamese armed forces were unlikely ever to be a match for the Viet Cong. The Joint Chiefs stated that Thieu could not hold out for the whole of the first Nixon term if all United States troops were withdrawn in that time; they said both United States troops and United States air power were needed until at least 1972. And the embassy reported that Saigon's "political system, as it now is, is probably inadequate for a political confrontation with the enemy."

But both Nixon and Kissinger believed that the war could quickly be brought to a conclusion that was satisfactory to them. Nixon thought Vietnam only a "short-term problem"; what was needed was a policy that would create political stalemate at home and at least military stalemate on the battlefield. Their plan involved complementary but contradictory features: domestic opposition must be reduced, but at the same time Hanoi must be convinced that this administration was willing to sustain the war and even widen it beyond anything that Johnson had considered. "A prolonged, even if ultimately victorious, war might leave Vietnam so exhausted as to jeopardize the purpose of decades of struggle," Kissinger wrote in *Foreign Affairs*. The important point was that whatever errors America had made "we are so powerful that Hanoi is simply unable to defeat us militarily" and must therefore eventually be forced to compromise.

The first of the two aims seemed the easier to achieve. Both Kissinger and Nixon were convinced that it was the draft, not the long bleeding of Indochina, that was arousing most of the domestic opposition. If American combat troops could be withdrawn as Vietnamese battalions were developed, an appearance of progress toward peace could be created.

But while the American people were being persuaded that the war was being wound down, plausible threats of escalation would have to be made, and the threats would have to be impressive not only to Hanoi but to Moscow. At the Republican National Convention Nixon told the Southern delegates that "critical to the settlement of Vietnam is relations with the Soviet Union . . . you've got to broaden the canvas, because in Vietnam they have no reason to end that war. It's hurting us more than it's hurting them."

The United States embassy in Saigon reported in January 1969 that there was no evidence that either Moscow or Peking had so far applied any pressure on Hanoi to settle the conflict. But it also concluded that the Sino-Soviet dispute foreclosed the possibility of either nation urging settlement for fear of being seen as "betraying" its socialist ally. This view was widely shared. Nixon and Kissinger believed, however, that the Soviets could be persuaded to place their own national interests before those of revolutionary solidarity. This belief underestimated the extent to which maintaining at least the façade of such solidarity is in itself a Soviet national interest. At his early press conferences as well as privately, Nixon began to hint at the possibility of talks on strategic arms, on Berlin, and on a European Security Conference, if the Russians were helpful on Vietnam. On March 4, 1969, he introduced the first of many public threats to escalate the war if progress toward a settlement were not made. "I believe at this time that the Soviet Union shares the concern of many other nations . . . about the extension of the war in Vietnam. . . . They recognize that if it continues over a long period of time, the possibility of escalation increases."

The over-all concept was given, by Melvin Laird, the ugly and only partially accurate name "Vietnamization." On one level it was an extension of Lyndon Johnson's demand that "Asian boys fight Asian wars," involving the rapid development of Vietnamese combat battalions and the redeployment of American ones. In the theater of the war it also envisaged the extension of another form of American power, bombing, to be used not only to give tactical help to the South Vietnamese but also in a wider strategic sense—to impress Washington's determination upon the enemy.

The use of threats in international affairs is not novel. For Nixon and Kissinger, however, it had a special purpose. Each believed in the value of unpredictability, of appearing "irrational" to one's enemy. Nixon publicly declared that "the real possibility of irrational U.S. action is essential to the U.S.-Soviet relationship." Privately he was more explicit. H. R. Haldeman records that in 1969 Nixon explained to him that "the threat was the key . . . Nixon coined a phrase for his theory which I'm sure will bring smiles of delight to Nixon haters everywhere. . . . He said, 'I call it the Madman Theory, Bob. I want the North Vietnamese to believe I've reached the point where I might do *anything* to stop the war. We'll just slip the word to them that "for God's sake, you know Nixon is obsessed about Communism. We can't restrain him when he's angry—and he has his hand on the nuclear button"—and Ho Chi Minh himself will be in Paris in two days begging for peace.' "

A problem with this theory is that reputations for irrationality have to be established, and that can be done only by irrational actions.

The idea of invading Cambodia arose not, as Nixon and Kissinger later claimed, after the removal of Sihanouk in March 1970, but at the very beginning of the administration. At this stage, they had decided to embark on what they called a "two-track" policy toward Cambodia. The United States would respond to the overtures to resume relations that Sihanouk had made through 1968, but it would insist that a test of his seriousness be the extent to which he dealt with the Communist "sanctuaries"—or allowed the United States to do so.

On his first day in office, Nixon asked the Pentagon how the United States could "quarantine" Cambodia. The Joint Chiefs forwarded the President's quarantine request to Saigon for Creighton Abrams' advice. It was at that point that the General cabled his own proposal for a single B-52 raid against "COSVN headquarters" in Base Area 353. He knew from the "quarantine" memorandum that his idea would have a sympathetic hearing in the new Washington.

On February 15, as Abrams' request was being considered by "highest authority," the ambassadors in Saigon, Bangkok and Vientiane received a highly classified cable from William Rogers informing them that "the President has authorized a diplomatic course of action which envisages responding to recent Cambodian initiatives by proceeding gradually, with full control and possibility of reversal at all stages, toward resumption of diplomatic relations with Cambodia." At the same time Nixon sent a personal message to Sihanouk, through the Australians, assuring him that the United States would now formally recognize Cambodia's existing borders.

The Chiefs' study on how to quarantine Cambodia was finished in late February. Their conclusions are helpful in interpreting the events of the next fourteen months. They argued that Sihanouk's good faith in his diplomatic overtures toward the United States "can be most easily and profitably put to test and use by a series of steps towards normalization in the border areas," including "acquiescence in the undertaking of short term preemptive operations by U.S. forces."

They thought that a blockade of all Cambodian ports and airports would be feasible, and that it might prevent supplies from getting through to the Viet Cong and North Vietnamese. But they understood that it would have to be sustained over a long period and would be widely criticized abroad. Bombing raids and limited invasions of the border areas would be more practical. The Chiefs admitted that such "temporary encroachment on Cambodian territory would carry the same implications of an overt hostile act as blockade operations"—a fact that was subsequently denied by the administration—but they considered that the surprise and speed of such attacks would make them politically much more acceptable. Any protests would come after the event, not simultaneously as they would during a blockade, and "confrontation with other nations would be unlikely." They asked approval for "preemptive operations" by land and air.

General Westmoreland had asked for similar permission to attack the sanctuaries as they began to grow in late 1967 and then a few months later in 1968. Subsequently, the Pentagon explained that "in the light of the prevailing political and diplomatic environment, the President did not approve the operation for execution at that time." This bureaucratic euphemism indicates that Johnson considered the advantages of such an attack to be more than offset by the domestic upheaval it would cause (he did not contemplate doing it in total secrecy) and the damage it might inflict on Cambodia's fragile neutrality.

On April 8 Kissinger sent Laird a reply to the Chiefs' quarantine proposals. He said that they should be held in abeyance to see if Sihanouk would now "adopt more positive policies and practices concerning the illegal use of his country by Communist forces." In fact, however, only one of the "preemptive operations" was being held back; following Abrams' request for an attack on COSVN, bombing of the sanctuaries had already begun with the Breakfast attack on March 18. The records had been falsified, and Sihanouk had made no protest.

In his memoirs Nixon claims that the next attack—code-named Lunch—was mounted in lieu of retaliating against North Korea for the way in which it had just shot down an American EC-121 spy plane. Nixon says he intended it "to impress the Communist leaders of both North Korea and North Vietnam with our resolve to support our allies and resist aggression." The military situation in Cambodia or Vietnam is not mentioned. Lunch was then followed by all the other meals.

Nixon's desire to demonstrate toughness by bombing Cambodia coincided with the organizational requirements of the Armed Services. Many of the sorties flown in Indochina, by both tactical aircraft and B-52s, were flown because the services responsible for the aircraft needed to justify their existence on station. One senior Pentagon analyst, Thomas Thayer, wrote a classified study in which he likened the use of air power in Indochina to a fire hose "running under full pressure most of the time and pointed with the same intensity at whichever area is allowed, regardless of its relative importance in the scheme of things.'' When Lyndon Johnson decided to cut back the bombing of North Vietnam in November 1968, the Joint Chiefs reluctantly agreed after Secretary of Defense Clark Clifford assured them that the strikes could be redirected against Laos. The statistics help tell the story. In 1968, 172,000 sorties were flown against North Vietnam and 136,000 against Laos. In 1969 the bombing halt reduced sorties against the North to 37,000—the attacks in Laos rose to 242,000. In January 1969, when Nixon and Kissinger arrived in the White House there was capacity to spare for Cambodia.

Kissinger's subsequent claim that the areas bombed under the Menu program contained no Cambodians was untrue, as the figures and the memoranda produced at the time by the Joint Chiefs clearly showed. One such memorandum has already been quoted. There are others. Laird, as has been noted, was opposed to concealing the bombing of Cambodia from Congress, but (as he often was to do during the war) he accepted a policy that he thought incorrect. At the same time, he attempted to control the enthusiasm of the Chiefs and frequently sent them questions about the Menu operations. In one such memorandum he asked, ''Are steps being taken, on a continuing basis, to *minimize* the risk of striking Cambodian people and structures? If so, what are the steps? Are we *reasonably* sure such steps are effective?'' (emphasis added). The Chiefs replied that everything was under control, citing only one attack in which Cambodians were known to have been killed. Their response did, however, indicate how extensively the Communists mingled with the villagers. ''If identified as an area of Cambodian habitation, no target boxes are placed closer than one kilometer to this area.'' In Vietnam, except in extreme emergency, B-52 boxes were not allowed nearer than three kilometers from American positions. The Chiefs nonetheless considered that their concern for Cambodian lives had forfeited them ''lucrative targets.'' Later, however, they admitted publicly that they had had no way whatsoever of assessing Cambodian casualties.

After the bombing became public in 1973, both Kissinger and Nixon frequently maintained that it was encouraged by Sihanouk as long as it was kept secret. As evidence, Kissinger cited the visit by Chester Bowles in 1968, a talk between Senator Mansfield and Sihanouk in 1969, a 1969 press conference in which Sihanouk said that he had control over what happened in the border areas, and a series of letters between Nixon and Sihanouk during 1969. These letters (reproduced in the Notes) dealt with restoring diplomatic relations; Kissinger said that had Sihanouk wished to protest about Menu he could have done so in this context.

Sideshow

It is possible that Prince Sihanouk was indeed a party to the conspiracy. It would have fitted in with his policy of playing enemies off against one another, with his dislike of the Vietnamese and with his move back toward Washington. It is certainly true that while Phnom Penh continued to denounce American defoliant attacks, artillery barrages and tactical airstrikes against Cambodian villages throughout 1969, it made no public protest that specifically mentioned B-52 strikes. Furthermore, in July 1969, after Washington publicly recognized Cambodia's "territorial integrity," diplomatic relations were restored, and Sihanouk allowed an American embassy, a small mission run by a chargé d'affaires named Lloyd "Mike" Rives, to be opened again in Phnom Penh.

But several points about Sihanouk's role need to be repeated. First, as has been noted, his aide Charles Meyer maintains that although (like any other Cambodian) he was happy to see Vietnamese bombed, he was never asked to approve a vast B-52 campaign and never did so. Secondly, if he did indicate his compliance to Washington, it was not regarded as very certain. Throughout Menu, the Joint Chiefs considered each of Abrams' bombing requests individually, and in their replies they always reminded him what to do if the Cambodians made trouble: "After delivering a reply to any Cambodian protest Washington will inform the press that we have apologized and offered compensation." Thirdly, Sihanouk had no alternative. American violations of Cambodian neutrality were as impossible to prevent as Vietnamese. Each had to be tolerated in the hope that the war could at least be contained and a fullscale invasion by the United States—which, Sihanouk knew, would have a devastating impact on Cambodia—could be prevented.

Most important of all in American terms, the issue that Kissinger has consistently failed to address is that in the context of United States law Sihanouk's attitude was irrelevant. The whims of, and the constraints upon, a foreign prince are not grounds for the President to wage war. The Constitution gives the power to declare war, to make appropriations and to raise and support armies to Congress. By informing only a few sympathetic legislators in a general way of the bombing, the White House was deliberately usurping the Congress' constitutional rights and responsibilities.

The evidence indicates that "the Sihanouk excuse" was merely that; the secrecy, the wiretaps, the burning and falsification of reports, were principally intended to conceal the administration's widening of the war from the American people. Even after 1970 when Menu had ended and Sihanouk, exiled, no longer needed protection, Nixon, Kissinger, Rogers,

Laird, Elliot L. Richardson and other officials all continued to assure
Congress, press and public, without equivocation, that the United States
had scrupulously declined to attack Communist positions in Cambodia
before spring 1970. Official, highly classified Pentagon computer print-
outs of the bombing of Indochina continued to show "Nil" for Cambodia
in 1969.

In 1973, when some of the truth was established, these same officials
denied all responsibility for the falsification. Some of them claimed that,
as all those with a "need to know" did know about Menu, no deception
had taken place. Others expressed outrage that the procedures, which
contravened the United States Military Code of Justice, had been allowed
to develop. But no one in the United States government or in the armed
services would admit having authorized them. Eventually, unidentified
junior officers in the field were blamed for being "overzealous." In fact,
the falsifications were the result of Nixon and Kissinger's repeated insistence to General Wheeler that total secrecy must be preserved at all cost.
Memoranda from the period show that there was never any question
about that. General Brent Scowcroft, who became Kissinger's deputy
and then his successor as National Security Adviser, states that the falsification was done on direct White House orders. In his memoirs Nixon
admitted that one reason for the secrecy "was the problem of domestic
antiwar protestors. My administration was only two months old, and I
wanted to provoke as little public outcry as possible at the outset."

Kissinger's attitude is probably accurately summed up by Marvin and
Bernard Kalb in their admiring biography, written with his full cooperation: "Kissinger had no trouble justifying the deception. He felt that if it
became known that the United States was widening the war geographi-
cally, extending the bombing into Cambodia, this would prompt a wave
of angry denunciations from an increasingly disillusioned Congress and
antiwar critics across the country. This kind of nationwide uproar would
only complicate the Administration's plans for peace in Vietnam."

These "plans for peace" did not prevent the Communists from attacking South Vietnam, but in Cambodia, as the Chiefs reported, it forced
them to "disperse over a greater area than before." The raids spread the
fighting out from the border areas, where it had been contained, and
diminished the main claim that Sihanouk still had to legitimacy—that he
had kept his country out of Vietnam's conflict. The "Madman Theory of
War" was being put into practice.

CHAPTER 7
The Bridges

THE PERSONAL and intellectual inclinations of Richard Nixon and Henry Kissinger probably had a greater impact on the policymaking process than those of their immediate predecessors because they strove more vigorously to subordinate the bureaucracy's perceptions and interests. To a large extent they succeeded, and the manner in which they did so is of crucial importance. Most credit must go to Kissinger; from early 1969, he built bridges and barricades all across Washington.

The highest barricades were erected against William Rogers and Melvin Laird and the departments of State and Defense. The principal bridges were to Nixon, to his principal aides, H. R. Haldeman and John Ehrlichman, to carefully chosen leaders of Congress, to the Joint Chiefs of Staff, and to a certain section of the press. Of these the most enduring was the one to the press. It was a fine and careful structure, thrown with confidence across the gap that separated the new White House from the liberal denizens of Georgetown in Washington.

Washington is the only capital city in the world where information is so freely available that political and diplomatic reporting can be done without the gift of "access." But paradoxically, Washington is also the city where "access" is both most easily obtained and most treasured. Kissinger understood from the start that many of the town's best-known journalists consider themselves essential to the business of government.

When they are critical, it is in the most intimate sense; their comments are not intended to disrupt their relations with the men at the center whose opinions they seek to interpret and convey. In the easy, uncomplicated days before Watergate, younger men modeled their careers and styles on the town's dozen or so columnists. It was only afterward that "investigative reporting" became fashionable.

Kissinger knew some of these journalists before he came to Washington. He seems to have appreciated that they could provide him with the constituency that he, unlike the heads of great departments, lacked. Soon after the Inauguration he told his staff that he alone would leak information to reporters. He made one exception: anyone could talk to *Time* magazine for a cover story that was being planned on him. He began to cultivate some journalists socially and others privately.

The lavishly furnished house of Joseph Alsop in Dumbarton Avenue in Georgetown epitomized the nature of the journalistic elite. Alsop's views on the war were straightforward; he supported coercion. Although an abrupt man, he was cultured and he served fine food and wine; his invitations were prized. Kissinger was soon a frequent guest, invited far more often than Melvin Laird or William Rogers. His wit, his apparently modest and self-deprecating irony, his exquisite charm, a willingness to discuss high matters of state after dinner, and the apparent confidences that he entrusted—all this made him irresistible. He was quickly recognized throughout Georgetown as the one oasis in this dour, rather hostile and boring administration of bond salesmen, advertising executives and zoning lawyers.

Behind their backs, Kissinger was often contemptuous of individual journalists—he regaled his staff with accounts of their ignorance and their willingness to have information spoon-fed to them—but to their faces he was delightful, and he had a highly developed way of persuading each one, whatever his views, that he respected him enormously and agreed with him. Few reporters were able to resist the flattery of the discreet murmur, "I wouldn't trust this information with anyone else but . . ."; or the unexpected phone call, "I would like you alone to know that . . ." Each was convinced that he and Kissinger had a special relationship. Joseph Kraft (who was wiretapped by Ehrlichman) said later, "He would always deal with me as though I was responsible and all the rest of the colleagues in the press were irresponsible." Henry Brandon, of the *Sunday Times* of London, said: "Henry used to tell me that I was the one correspondent in this town that he doesn't try to manipulate." Kissinger had Brandon wire-tapped.

Ordinary reporters saw less of him socially than columnists, but those covering the State Department or the White House were both amazed and grateful for the access they had to him. It had never before happened that a national security adviser met them or returned their phone calls so often; few wished to upset their source. And that, they soon learned, was easy to do. Even the slightest criticism would send him into a rage and result in angry calls either to the reporter himself or, worse still, to his editor—who might well have had dinner with Kissinger only the night before. If there was a story in the first edition of the *Washington Post* that he disliked, Kissinger might call the paper's publisher, Katherine Graham, that same evening to denounce it. Such likelihood made many reporters understandably wary when writing about Kissinger.

He used his position both to obtain public attention and to shield himself from it. He would talk to Congressmen and to Senators as he would talk to journalists—for their ears only. He would not testify before Congress, on grounds of executive privilege, and he would give few interviews for the record. In this way his views simply seeped into the public consciousness. Kissinger's leaks became editorials, newspapers took up the issues in which he was interested and, in Washington, a good many attitudes to the war were altered. Many journalists believed, and helped their readers to believe, that this administration was full of new foreign-policy ideas and, above all, was really withdrawing from Indochina. Few of the reporters who had Kissinger's confidence produced stories which showed unusual journalistic endeavor. Those whose work did have this quality were reporters who refused to play by his rules—men like I. F. Stone, Jack Anderson, Laurence Stern and Seymour Hersh. It was their stories—on the Indo-Pakistan War, My Lai, Cyprus or Chile—that revealed the truth and helped somewhat to change policy.

But their efforts and even the force of the Watergate investigation, which showed the links between the foreign policy of Kissinger and Nixon and the abuses of power at home, did little to weaken Kissinger's bridge to the press. By mid-1973, when the Watergate story began to emerge, too many journalists and editors had invested too much in "Henry" as "Super-K" to allow the image to be destroyed by his unfortunate association with Richard Nixon. As Nixon sank, Kissinger began to look like the only hope of the Republic. It is true that by the end of 1975 press inquiries and Congressional committees had uncovered several misuses of American power·in Greece, Chile, Southwest Africa, the Middle East and Italy, quite apart from Indochina. As a result, there was a short period when some of the facing of the bridge crumbled and Jimmy

Carter gingerly criticized Kissinger in his Presidential campaign. But no
serious harm was done to Kissinger's relationship with the media.

The bridge to the press served Kissinger best and longest, but more
crucial was the one to Nixon. The precise nature of their personal and
intellectual collaboration is unclear. Which of them conceived strategy
and which tactics, who first suggested the trip to China, who formulated
the "Nixon Doctrine" for the defense and self-defense of Asia, who
insisted on extensive covert use of the CIA to subvert and destroy foreign
politicians they considered hostile to their cause—these questions have
not in all cases been answered. The uncertainty lies in part in the ambiguous way in which they have treated each other publicly. The mutual
praise of the early years of euphoria gave way after 1974 to a tendency by
each to deprecate the other's accomplishments.

In January 1969, Kissinger's access to Nixon was dependent upon H. R.
Haldeman and, to a lesser extent, on John Ehrlichman. Each had served
Nixon loyally for years, and each regarded Kissinger with the suspicion
due a man who had so quickly somersaulted from public contempt for
their mentor into a position of privilege. It is a tribute to Kissinger's
charm and willingness to adapt himself to their mores, that he quickly
won their confidence, and was therefore able to spend more and more
time with a President whose attitudes and concerns he understood very
well.

Nixon hated to be rushed. Any official who came into the Oval Office
with the request that the President make a decision there and then, rarely
passed Haldeman again. Kissinger knew that Nixon's enjoyment of foreign policy stemmed in part from the fact that it enabled him to ramble
around the world every day of the week. In the first months of 1969 their
morning meetings were like seminars in which each saw himself as the
teacher. Kissinger never forced an issue; he deferred to Nixon's solilo-
quies and reminiscences while gently inserting his own views and positions.

In front of the President or with Haldeman and Ehrlichman, Kissinger's
deference to Nixon was often obsequious. William Safire, a Nixon
speechwriter, excused this because "he was the newcomer to the group,
had never called Nixon by his first name or been made to feel needed by
a man struggling to come back." The habit endured after the group accepted him. But in the privacy of his own office Kissinger often denigrated the President. He would gossip about Nixon's instability, his lone-

Sideshow

liness and his "meatball mind," and he encouraged his aides to listen in on his rambling telephone calls. Some of Kissinger's staff found the President puzzling. The comments that he scribbled on interoffice memoranda were of uneven quality. The authors of *The Final Days* have noted occasions when he wrote, "This man is a goddamn fool," or "Bomb them," on memos and when he ticked all three of mutually exclusive options offered him.

Larry Lynn, a systems analyst who had been at the Pentagon, remembers that in one discussion of the budget in 1969 Nixon's eyes glazed, he gripped his chair and launched into a soliloquy on the need for more assassination squads in Vietnam. Lynn was embarrassed. So was the wife of the British ambassador when she sat next to Nixon at a White House dinner early in the administration.

"I understand you are a very good friend of Henry Kissinger," he said.

"Yes."

"He's a remarkable and much misunderstood man."

"Oh you mean by the press?"

"No," said Nixon, turning to her. "I mean by his wife. Women like that should be shot."

Despite this incident, she did not entirely believe Kissinger when he assured her that he had agonized before accepting his job and that he had only done so "because I would never have forgiven myself if some unbelievable disaster had happened to the world." Others accepted his explanation; his mellifluous, intimate expositions of the nature of power were hard to reject.

Kissinger's concept of office life caused tensions on his staff. Personally he was disorganized and untidy, incapable of setting a schedule and maintaining it. He believed that people do not produce their best work if treated gently and that the lash of the tongue is by far the best incentive. His own was often cruel and sarcastic, but some people did respond to it and his methods of exacting work had their own rewards; he could be just as generous in his praise. He would often attempt to make up for an attack with a little kindness. One young woman whom he had loudly scorned for making a mistake about ballet found two tickets on her desk next week. Such behavior inspired loyalty in some; others found it intolerable, and throughout 1969 some of the more sensitive recruits gradually disappeared.

Kissinger realized that he needed the help of a competent manager for the office. The man he took on, Colonel Alexander Haig, later played a

100

large part in determining the conduct of the war in Cambodia. Haig was a West Point man, forty-five years old, had served Douglas MacArthur in Korea and had done a tour in Vietnam on Search-and-Destroy operations. Most of his career had been in the Army bureaucracy, where he had often been a "horse-holder," an aide to a senior official. After working for both Robert McNamara and Cyrus Vance in the Pentagon he became Deputy Commander of West Point, where he had insisted that the cadets march with their fingers cocked at the second knuckle, their thumbs pointed straight at the ground, their elbows locked. He was quoted as explaining, "If they can get that hand straight, that elbow stiff, then all the rest of it falls into place. Every directive becomes second nature. It's my way of putting a signature on a unit."

Haig had at first no policy responsibilities on the NSC; but, industrious as he was efficient, he gradually became indispensable to Kissinger. "Stalin to Henry's Lenin," one aide suggested unkindly. He was one of the few people who were able to withstand the abuse and the complex demands Kissinger would extend; within a few months he had started his rise to a prominent policy position on the staff. But even Haig sometimes came out of Kissinger's office gritting his teeth and clenching his fists.

Occasionally Haig would gossip with other members of the staff about the madness of the two men for whom they all worked, but he bristled at anything he saw as weakness toward the war. His attitude to Indochina was that of a narrow soldier; he considered Kissinger was often too soft on the enemy. Haig believed in his commander in chief, right or wrong, and his loyalty to the Army was such that Kissinger used to joke, "I'm going to call the Pentagon to ask them to release you for a day's work on my staff," or "There's no point in your coming, Al, the Army doesn't have anything at stake in this meeting."

By the summer of 1969, Haig was virtually running the staff. He attempted to instill a sense of discipline and hierarchy, and he took upon himself the moral as well as the organizational problems of the office. (He had one girl removed because he disapproved of her love life.) He was known as an intellectual soldier, but some of his peers from the Pentagon doubt the extent of his independent thought. In the Lenin-Stalin analogy, he was the adjutant who saw that Kissinger's plans and theories were implemented as effectively as possible. He was enormously diligent about it and soon became known as the last man to leave the office. While Kissinger was building bridges in Georgetown, Haig worked quietly in the basement. So it happened that the lonely President, wandering around

101

at night with little or nothing to do, first came to know him and then to recognize that he had qualities that "Henry" lacked.

Kissinger did not consolidate his control over foreign policy until the invasion of Cambodia. But it became clear through 1969 that much of the new National Security Council structure, which itself greatly favored his own position, was to be cosmetic. It did have important functions. In the first four months of 1969 about fifty-five National Security Study memoranda were issued and the bureaucracies became buried in paper work. At the same time, power was removed elsewhere. After the North Koreans shot down the EC-121 spy plane (an event to which Kissinger, unlike Laird, wanted to respond with force), a special crisis committee, the Washington Special Action Group, was set up. Kissinger chaired it. The other NSC groups that he ran included the Verification Panel, which directed arms-control strategy; the Vietnam Special Studies Group, which monitored the conduct of the war; the Defense Program Review Committee, which oversaw the Pentagon's budget; and the 40 Committee, which was to plan all foreign covert intelligence activities (such as the prolonged and successful campaign to destroy President Salvador Allende of Chile).

Despite such early bureaucratic successes, Kissinger continued to take the competition between him and both Rogers and Laird seriously. It was easy for the President to make a distinction between him and Rogers. The Secretary of State was affable but idle; he refused to go into detail and would arrive at White House meetings with a short memo on the subject in hand. Kissinger would come with a huge briefing book and, sometimes, aides to check facts and lend dignity. It was soon evident that Nixon paid more attention to Kissinger, but Kissinger was not reassured. "It's like the Arabs and the Israelis. I'll win all the battles and he'll win the war. He only has to beat me once," he said to William Safire. In fact, it took Rogers a long time to realize even that battle had been joined, let alone that war had been declared.

Safire describes how Kissinger used the transcripts of his telephone calls as a secret weapon in the war. "Complaining to a correspondent about the perfidy of his arch rival, Secretary of State Rogers, Henry then edited [a] transcript, changing words to reflect stronger support of the President by Kissinger, and sent the revised version along to Haldeman— an act of dishonor to the unsuspecting reporter and an act of disloyalty to the President." On foreign trips Kissinger seemed always anxious to keep the State Department ignorant of the substance of the most important conversations. He refused to use embassy secretarial help; everything had to be done by the staff he brought with him. Many of Rogers' aides were from the American U.N. delegation and were oblivious to the scheming, but Nixon understood the battle between the two men. He told Safire, "I'm sorry about how Henry and Bill go for each other. Henry thinks Bill isn't very deep and Bill thinks that Henry is power crazy. In a sense they are both right." In his memoirs he wrote: "Rogers felt that Kissinger was Machiavellian, deceitful, egotistical, arrogant, and insulting. Kissinger felt that Rogers was vain, uninformed, unable to keep a secret and hopelessly dominated by the State Department bureaucracy." Nixon said that Haldeman had to act as a "demilitarized zone" between the two men and that he needed to include Attorney General John Mitchell in many foreign policy discussions as a stabilizing influence.

Kissinger paid as much, perhaps greater, attention to Melvin Laird, and in the case of Cambodia this competition was more important. The Department of Defense houses more different interest groups than the State Department. The overriding tension is between the military, headed by the Joint Chiefs of Staff and their civilian controllers, led by the Secretary. The Secretary is empowered to represent the vast bureaucracy, and the Chiefs are not supposed to transmit orders or advice without his authority. Laird found that Kissinger frequently attempted to deal directly with the Chiefs.

In the late sixties, when Robert McNamara became disillusioned by the military's enthusiastic analyses of the war, he had attempted to assert civilian control over the Chiefs more effectively. The Chiefs had resisted McNamara and invoked the help of their Congressional allies. At the end of 1967, for example, the Preparedness Investigating Subcommittee of the Senate Armed Services Committee held hearings on the dispute between McNamara and the Chiefs on the efficacy of bombing. It declared, "It is high time, we believe, to allow the military voice to be heard in connection with the tactical details of military operations." The Chiefs were especially infuriated by the inquisitive and skeptical nature of the Office of Systems Analysis, which subjected to rather scathing criticisms such programs as the bombing of trucks in Laos and the whole of the B-52 bombing operations.

Melvin Laird made some early mistakes and lost some ground won from the military by McNamara.

He refused a military request that he close the Systems Analysis Office, but he downgraded the Office of International Security Affairs, ISA, the

Pentagon's mini-State Department, which was supposed to evaluate the political and diplomatic consequences of military moves. In the Kennedy and Johnson administrations Paul Nitze, William Bundy, John Mc-Naughton and Paul Warnke had made ISA into a powerful institution; now it was placed in the hands of Warren Nutter, a rather ineffective right-wing academic from the University of Virginia. At one NSC meeting on Vietnam, early in 1969, Nutter simply repeated as every topic came up, "ISA's views are already represented; we agree with the Joint Chiefs." Mort Halperin recalls that after the meeting he and other NSC aides said to Kissinger "ISA just died. You'll regret it." "No I won't," said Kissinger.

About Indochina, the Chiefs soon perceived that the reality, as opposed to popular belief, was that Kissinger almost always took a tougher line than Laird. Laird wanted to complete Vietnamization and withdraw American troops as fast as possible. Kissinger still insisted either that victory could be achieved by force, or that, if it could not, then force must nonetheless be applied to demonstrate toughness and determination. Whenever Laird attempted to cut back the rate of bombing, Kissinger resisted.*

General Westmoreland, the former Commander of U.S. forces in Vietnam, who was back in Washington as Army Chief of Staff, later said that by April 1969 he and his colleagues saw Kissinger as "the architect" of Vietnam policy. Kissinger treated Westmoreland cleverly; though he despised the General for his intellectual and military limitations, he always carefully deferred to him when they met. Westmoreland described Kissinger as "a diplomat and a historian with a feel for power," whereas Laird had an "overly superficial feel for things"; he was "a secret dove" who would often agree with Congress against the military. Kissinger, on the other hand, thought so little of Congress that he proposed a moratorium on all debates about the administration's Vietnam policies. That was how the Chiefs liked to see business conducted.

Kissinger had several direct connections with the Chiefs. Haig was one, and another was Air Force General John Vogt, the Air Force's Assistant Deputy Chief of Staff for Plans and Operations. Vogt was a former student of Kissinger's and an unrestrained advocate of bombing.

---

* Laird held a daily Vietnamization meeting with his staff at the Pentagon. A detailed memorandum of record of each meeting was kept by Philip Odeen, Deputy Assistant Secretary of Defense for Regional Programs. These memoranda are very useful in documenting the tensions and disagreements between Laird and the White House. Many of the positions and opinions ascribed to Laird in this book are based on the evidence of these memoranda.

Kissinger used to ask Westmoreland to come over to the White House "to touch base," as well. In the summer of 1969, Laird tried to stop such conclaves, but the two men evaded his supervision by being more discreet, often using Alexander Haig as a courier. Another link was, of course, the liaison office between the NSC and the Joint Chiefs, which Laird had tried unsuccessfully to have Kissinger close down. What he had feared happened: the Chiefs and Kissinger used the office to communicate about matters on which they considered Laird's views "unnecessary."

The wiretaps were used as yet another way to isolate Laird and Rogers. On May 9, 1969, the day William Beecher broke his story on the secret bombing of Cambodia, Laird was playing golf outside Washington. He was summoned to the telephone; it was Nixon and Kissinger in Key Biscayne. "It was a hell of a go-round," Laird recalls. "They were furious and accused me of leaking the information to prove that secrecy was not important, that Sihanouk didn't care." Laird denied he had done any such thing, but Kissinger did not seem reassured. It was later that day that Kissinger walked along the beach with Mort Halperin and told him that Laird had accused him of being the leaker. Laird denies this. The tap that was placed on Halperin's telephone that evening was to remain there for twenty-one months, despite the fact that Halperin agreed not to receive secret documents and even though he left the staff later in the year, disillusioned by the nature of his employer.

Beecher's story was not the first leak to disturb Kissinger and Nixon. A fairly precise account of their approach to SALT had been published, and Beecher himself had written about the administration's ideas for retaliating against North Korea over the EC-121 plane. Such leaks, Kissinger said later, were of enormous importance to a novice like himself. He had already met with Nixon and Mitchell and Hoover to discuss how leaks could be plugged. Hoover and Kissinger had already agreed that their aides, Haig and William Sullivan, should stay in touch on the matter. Beecher's story on the secret bombing pushed them into action

On May 10, Kissinger sent Haig over to the FBI with the names of Halperin and three more "suspected leakers." They were all tapped. Two, Helmut Sonnenfeldt and Daniel Davidson, were on the NSC staff. Within weeks Davidson was asked by Haig to leave; his tap had apparently shown that he talked to journalists, but not that he leaked classified information. Davidson was not unduly upset; he too was beginning to find Kissinger's methods distasteful.

The third man, Colonel Robert E. Pursley, was an Air Force officer who had worked as military assistant to secretaries McNamara, Clark Clifford, and, now, Laird, and who had won the admiration of all three. He was often spoken of as a future Chairman of the Joint Chiefs. Laird relied greatly on Pursley and frequently called him at home in the evening to discuss the business of the day. His record suggested that he was highly unlikely to have leaked information. The explanation for tapping him, Laird and Pursley are certain, was to enable Kissinger to know what was in Laird's mind. (Personal animus may also have been involved. Pursley had made his opposition to Menu clear; he had written Laird's periodic questions to the Chiefs; he had been opposed to armed retaliation against North Korea. He and Haig disliked each other.)

The FBI produced transcripts and summaries of the taps, and on May 20, 1969, Kissinger and Haig went over to Sullivan's office in the FBI to read them. Sullivan wrote Hoover a memorandum about the meeting that same day; Haig and Kissinger later had "no recollection" of its having taken place. According to Sullivan's memo, "Dr. Kissinger read all the logs. On doing this he said, 'It is clear that I do not have anybody in my office that I can trust except Colonel Haig here.' " Haig submitted two more members of the NSC staff to be tapped. They were Richard Sneider and Richard Moose. Moose was the staff secretary of the NSC. Like Davidson, Moose was already dispirited by the atmosphere in Kissinger's office and was about to go to work for Senator J. William Fulbright, Chairman of the Senate Foreign Relations Committee. (In that capacity he later undertook several missions to Cambodia and produced pessimistic reports that conflicted with Haig's official enthusiasm and helped turn the Congress against the war. Haig once told Moose that Fulbright was a "traitor.")

Altogether, seventeen people were tapped over a period of eighteen months; they included other members of Kissinger's staff, White House aides, several journalists (some of whom regarded themselves as close confidants of Kissinger), and officials from State and Defense. Apart from Pursley, whose tap was removed and then replaced, probably the most significant was Richard Pedersen, the Counselor at State and one of William Rogers' principal aides.

The full story of the wiretap program is still unknown. Neither Kissinger nor Haig was able to remember many of the details after its outline was revealed in 1973.

Since then, Kissinger has tried to minimize his role, admitting some of his meetings with Hoover but forgetting the details. The sole purpose was to plug leaks, he has asserted; and he went along with it because he was assured by men more schooled in government that it was standard practice. He did not "originate" names, but "supplied" them on instruction, reluctantly; he found the whole process "distasteful."

The record shows that Kissinger participated fully in the process. He was, in Nixon's word, "outraged" by the Beecher story. Anxious to "destroy whoever did this," he met with Hoover at least three times in that period, talked with him by telephone several times, sent Haig to the FBI with the names of fourteen of the seventeen people to be wiretapped, actually picked some of the names himself (certainly Colonel Pursley's), was aware when Haig went over to read the transcripts and went with him at least once, and received thirty-seven summaries of the taps from the FBI. There is no evidence that Kissinger felt any qualms until publicly confronted. In 1969, the taps were useful not only in discovering a good deal about his own staff and Laird's and Rogers', but also in demonstrating to Nixon, Haldeman and Ehrlichman that he was one of them. They were important blocks in his bridge to the President and his closest aides. They produced no evidence of leaking; in his memoirs Nixon wrote wistfully, "Unfortunately none of these wiretaps turned up any proof linking anyone in the government to a specific national-security leak."

After the tapes were revealed in 1973, Halperin began a lawsuit against Nixon, Kissinger, Haig, Haldeman, Mitchell and others for invading his privacy. When a deposition was taken from Kissinger, Halperin was in the room. The lawyers commented on the fact that, although he had professed his "distaste," Kissinger did not apologize to Halperin. The lawyers could not have known that Kissinger had just spoken to Nixon on the telephone. Nixon had referred to Halperin, "He is obviously smart but hung up on this thing. We treated him too well." Kissinger had replied, "Too well. That is the only mistake I made." *

---

* The law on wiretapping is complex. The Fourth Amendment to the Constitution provides: "The right of the people to be secure in their persons, houses, papers, and effects, against unreasonable searches and seizures, shall not be violated, and no Warrants shall issue, but upon probable cause, supported by Oath or affirmation, and particularly describing the place to be searched, and the persons or things to be seized." Title III of the Omnibus Crime Control and Safe Streets Act authorized the use of wiretaps and bugs in cases of domestic crimes, but only after the issuance of a judicial warrant based on probable cause that one of certain specified crimes had been or was likely to be committed. Various safeguards were imposed, including a thirty-day limit on the duration of each wiretap without reauthorization by the judge. At the same time, however, Title III of the Act specifically refrained from legislating in the area of "national security" wiretaps or bugs.

Halperin and his family argued in their case against Henry Kissinger et al. that the wiretaps had violated their First and Fourth Amendment rights and had also violated Title

"Give us six months," Kissinger urged liberal critics of the war when he arrived in Washington in January 1969. Eight months later there was no obvious sign of progress in Vietnam and the antiwar movement was girding itself for another mass protest. There had, however, been developments in Indochina. Relations with Sihanouk had been restored, and Cambodia was being secretly bombed. Nixon had outlined in Guam the basis of what he was to call the "Nixon Doctrine": in the future Washington would provide only matériel, instead of men, to any Asian friend in need of help. Kissinger had had a secret meeting with the North Vietnamese in Paris, and Nixon had announced the first withdrawal of 25,000 American combat troops. He maintained that his policy—which limited the removal of American combat troops to the pace at which Vietnamese soldiers were trained—was the only alternative to "precipitous withdrawal" that would result in "defeat and humiliation." There was, how-

III of the Safe Streets Act. On December 16, 1976, Judge John Lewis Smith, Jr., of the District Court in the District of Columbia found that Richard Nixon, H. R. Haldeman and John Mitchell had indeed violated the Halperin family's Fourth Amendment rights:

> At no time were there any reviews or evaluation of the material obtained through the electronic surveillance. No attempt was made to minimize the interception of plaintiff's conversations, either as regards individuals intercepted or information gathered. . . . No further investigation or questioning of Mr. Halperin took place during this period. In addition, the tap continued after he left the National Security Council to engage in various antiwar efforts, and long after many of the other national security wiretaps were removed. Numerous summary letters in the later course of the surveillance relate solely to Halperin's political activities and beliefs.
> The wiretap thus appears to have developed into a dragnet which lacked temporal and spatial limitation. It represents the antithesis of the "particular, precise, and discriminate" procedures required by the Supreme Court in numerous Fourth Amendment cases. . . . The surveillance constituted an invasion of plaintiff's privacy and freedom of expression. For these reasons, even granting the inapplicability of the general warrant requirement, the Court finds the wiretap per se unreasonable under the Fourth Amendment and unjustified by any possible exception thereto.

At the same time the Court also ruled that Kissinger was not liable for these violations on grounds of his "inactive role and lack of oversight authority." Halperin immediately appealed this ruling. In their statement of the case for the appeal, Halperin's lawyers (from the American Civil Liberties Union) noted that "documentary evidence and the Nixon and Mitchell testimony [in the case] indicates that Kissinger was responsible not only for suggesting names for the surveillance program but also for recommending the termination of particular surveillances. According to FBI memoranda, Kissinger exercised this authority to terminate other surveillances and to order the continuation of the Halperin surveillance, despite observations from the FBI that it was not yielding any information about leaks and should be terminated. These documents also show that the FBI viewed Kissinger, acting through Haig, as responsible for beginning and terminating the surveillances. Indeed [William] Sullivan [Assistant Director of the FBI] confirmed this was his impression at his deposition."

ever, a third option. Hanoi was demanding a fixed timetable for the withdrawal of *all* American forces, not just combat troops. Nixon rejected this on the grounds that it "would completely remove any incentive for the enemy to negotiate." What was not clear was how much incentive Nixon's terms gave Hanoi. The North Vietnamese realized that Nixon's principal domestic concern was to reduce American casualties; in the absence of a timetable it was in Hanoi's interests to maintain, if not step up, military attacks to keep the pressure on Washington.

The Pentagon's Systems Analysis Office reported throughout 1969 that the Communists were now stressing the importance of inflicting a high rate of American casualties, and that they were, in effect, able to determine the rate at which Americans died. One enemy document, captured in late April 1969, noted that the spring offensive "was a significant tactical and a great strategic victory . . . we killed more Americans than we did in the 1968 spring offensive. [It] upset Nixon's plan, because U.S. forces were heavily hit and their weakening puppet army could no longer provide support for the implementation of neocolonialism. The antiwar movement in the U.S. flared up again strongly demanding the withdrawal of U.S. troops. . . . For each additional day's stay the U.S. must sustain more casualties . . ." In the same spirit, the Vietnamese Communists dismissed the announcement of the first troop withdrawals as "tokenism," and as "only a grain of sand [that] in no way affects the continuation and intensification of the war."

At his first meeting with the North Vietnamese on August 4, Kissinger warned that if progress had not been made by November 1, "we will be compelled—with great reluctance—to take measures of the greatest consequences." Hanoi showed no flexibility. The administration was already being entrapped in the logic of its own methods. Threats have to be followed through if they are to carry weight in the future. Neither the bombing of Cambodia, nor Nixon's public warnings to Moscow, nor Kissinger's remark to Soviet Ambassador Anatoly Dobrynin that "the train has left the station and is now headed down the track" had shown results. In his memoirs, Nixon says that he realized "I had to prepare myself for the tremendous criticism and pressure that would come with stepping up the war." In September, while the antiwar movement was preparing for a nationwide protest and demanding a moratorium, Kissinger ordered a few members of his staff to work with the Joint Chiefs to produce plans for a "savage, punishing blow" against this "third-rate power," North Vietnam.

The proposals of the "September Group" on the NSC staff included an invasion of Laos, the mining of Haiphong harbor, and more widespread bombing of North Vietnam—including Hanoi—than ever before. According to Roger Morris, a member of Kissinger's staff at the time, the group also considered bombing the dikes that hold back the waters that irrigate North Vietnam. In Tad Szulc's account of the Nixon foreign policy, *The Illusion of Peace*, Szulc maintains that Kissinger also considered using a nuclear device to block the railroad pass from China to North Vietnam. The important thing, Kissinger repeatedly told his staff, was to find Hanoi's "breaking point."

Rogers and Laird were opposed to escalation. Laird argued fiercely that it would divert resources from Vietnamization and be vastly counterproductive at home; it was all that the antiwar movement needed, he thought—a shot in the arm. Nixon was not impressed by arguments about public opinion. At a breakfast meeting on September 25, he cheered General Westmoreland by dismissing the Secretary of Defense's concerns— public opinion, he noted, should follow the President, not the other way around. Kissinger was of a similar mind. "What we do in Vietnam," he said once, "has to be measured in terms larger than Vietnam itself. And history teaches us that people do not easily forgive their leaders for producing disaster, even if they do seem to reflect their immediate desires."

As for the specific proposals, Kissinger's opinions were at this time, as they often were, hard to discern. When William Watts, who had replaced Moose as the staff secretary on the National Security Council, saw the plans he was horrified, and he wrote Kissinger a long memo setting out his objections. Like Laird he warned of the dangers of domestic unrest. Such arguments did not seem to impress Kissinger, but he gave the plans to Larry Lynn. As a Systems Analyst, Lynn subjected the plans to strict criticism and concluded that even in the narrowest military sense they were unsound. It was his analysis, rather than Laird's concerns about public protest, still less any consideration of "morality," that did the proposals most damage. They were not now implemented. Instead, Nixon made an effective appeal to "the silent majority," and Vice-President Spiro Agnew was sent around the nation to combat the press.

But the "September Group" was significant. Only eight months into his administration, when no Communist offensive had been launched, Nixon's policies had brought him close to raising the stakes in Vietnam over the objections of the Secretaries of Defense and State. For a time the whole exercise became something of a joke among those NSC staff members who knew of it. They would repeat the first line of the draft speech with which Nixon was to have announced the escalation: "Tonight pursuant to my orders . . ." adding to it such phrases as "Strategic Air Command has launched a defensive attack on Moscow." In the end, however, it was only the package that was rejected. Many of the components of the September 1969 strategy were implemented as Nixon and Kissinger attempted step by step to increase the pressure on Hanoi and on Moscow. Cambodia was also used.

CHAPTER 8

The Coup

SIHANOUK WAS overthrown by his Prime Minister, General Lon Nol, and by his cousin, Prince Sirik Matak, in March 1970. Ever since then, allegations of American complicity in the coup have persisted.

Such allegations of United States involvement in right-wing takeovers have often proved justified, and the use that Nixon and Kissinger are known to have made of the CIA has helped to legitimize paranoia. It is true, however, that suspicions of this nature can reflect not only an exaggerated view of the Agency's own powers but also a slightly contemptuous belief that other societies have no political strengths or issues of their own. There were, inside Cambodia, persuasive reasons for removing Sihanouk; the hostility of two of the most powerful groups—the urban elite and the officer corps—toward him could itself provide an adequate motive. Nonetheless, it is also true that to some extent external interests, especially those of the United States, coincided with and supported those who plotted against the Prince inside the country.

No direct link between the United States government and Sihanouk's usurpers before the coup has been established. Nixon and Kissinger have maintained in public that there was no United States involvement whatsoever, that the coup came as a shocking surprise to the White House, and that the first reaction was dismay, since relations with Sihanouk had been improving steadily. Later, when the secret Menu bombing was revealed, the Prince's alleged "acquiescence" (or at least his failure to protest) was used to demonstrate how amenable he had become by March 1970. What was denied, in other words, was not only foreknowledge of Sihanouk's fall and complicity in it but also any motives for seeking it. However, when the coup is considered in the light of contemporary documents and post-factum interviews with Cambodian, French and American officials, two things become clear. There was ample American motive for Sihanouk's removal, and if the administration was, as Kissinger and Nixon claimed, surprised by the coup, then its most senior members cannot have been reading their own intelligence reports.

By fall 1969, General Creighton Abrams and the Joint Chiefs had accepted that the Menu bombing had failed in its primary military purpose; neither COSVN headquarters nor the sanctuaries themselves were destroyed. But it was having another effect. To escape the bombardment, the Vietnamese Communists had begun to move deeper into Cambodia—"thus," as Abrams later acknowledged to the Senate, "bringing them into increasing conflict with the Cambodian authorities." More and more reports of serious clashes between the Communists and Cambodian villagers and troops reached Phnom Penh. The effect was inevitable (especially when it coincided with a deepening economic crisis); Sihanouk's balance of right against left became more precarious. The bombing was destabilizing him.

Abrams had no problems with this—"I did not like what was happening in Sihanouk's Cambodia." Nor, presumably, did the White House. Nixon and Kissinger had embarked on a "two-track" policy toward the country whose purpose, by one track or another, was to clean out the sanctuaries. Although the Chiefs' request for invasion had been deferred, the bombing had been expanded while diplomatic relations with Sihanouk were restored. The hope was that either Sihanouk would take effective action against the Vietnamese Communists himself or that changed circumstances would allow the United States to do so.

In August 1969 Sihanouk appointed a "Gouvernement de Sauvetage" that was far to the right of the previous "Gouvernement de la Dernière Chance." His new Prime Minister was General Lon Nol—the man who had told General Taber back in 1963 how much he hoped that United States military aid would soon be restored to Cambodia. For some time now Lon Nol, as Minister of Defense, had been the principal scourge of the Vietnamese Communists while privately profiting from the thriving covert business that they brought through Sihanoukville. Now, however, the Vietnamese presence was becoming less easy to tolerate. Lon Nol claimed that they had between 35,000 and 40,000 troops in the country.

He published maps of their bases and supply lines, and he pointed out that their spread was due to flooding and to "the operational pressure exerted by their adversary," that is, to "clearing operations by American and South Vietnamese troops." At Ho Chi Minh's funeral in September Sihanouk apparently asked Hanoi's leaders to try to restrict their use of his country. When this had little effect, he seems to have begun complaining privately even to North Korean officials. Publicly he announced that in the provinces of Mondolkiri and Ratanakiri "a vast part of our territory has been occupied by the North Vietnamese." Phnom Penh complained that "Cambodia is not in a position to prevent these infiltrators with its restricted and poorly equipped forces"; but the new government, with Sihanouk's compliance, began to harass the intruders in several of the eastern provinces.

Toward the end of 1969, Lon Nol flew to France for medical treatment, leaving Prince Sisowath Sirik Matak as acting premier. It was Sirik Matak's family that had been passed over by the French when Sihanouk was crowned king in 1941. Sirik Matak had resented the Prince's unexpected accession to power then, and his differences with Sihanouk had grown ever since. He was now the most important Cambodian in the business community, he opposed Sihanouk's attempts to collectivize the economy, and he was a fervent supporter of American policies in Southeast Asia. He had always despised Sihanouk's tolerance of the Vietnamese Communists. Some Cambodians suspected that his links with the United States were not merely informal; a profile compiled by the Defense Intelligence Agency in Washington noted that, "he had been a friend of the West and was co-operative with U.S. officials during the 1950s." During the 1970s, CIA officials had ready access to him and his entourage. Now he and Sihanouk clashed over the speed with which the economy should be denationalized to spur recovery. The row led to speculation in Phnom Penh chanceries that a government crisis was at hand. But it did not develop, and in early January 1970, Sihanouk himself left for one of his periodic rest cures at a clinic in the South of France. His health was not that poor, and presumably he felt that the political situation was containable. He was mistaken. A few weeks later he was overthrown. It was more than five years before he returned to Phnom Penh.

In assessing how the coup took place, the testimony of two former CIA agents must be considered. The first is Frank Snepp,* who in 1970 was a

---

* In 1978 Snepp published a book, *Decent Interval*, detailing the way in which inadequate preparations by Kissinger and the embassy in Saigon caused thousands of Vietnamese employees of the United States to be abandoned when Saigon fell to the Communists in

strategic analyst in the CIA station in Saigon. At that time many CIA operations in Cambodia were being run out of South Vietnam. The Agency had in the Saigon embassy a Cambodian reports division that handled the processing, hiring of agents, debriefing and instructions. Snepp maintains that in early 1970 both MACV and the Agency believed that if Sihanouk was replaced by Lon Nol, "He would welcome the United States with open arms and we would accomplish everything." At the same time, he says, "there was a lot of speculation amongst my colleagues that we were cultivating Son Ngoc Thanh [the leader of the Khmer Serei rebels based in South Vietnam] as a possible replacement for Sihanouk. At the beginning of 1970 we were encouraging both him and Lon Nol."

The other agent is Drew Sawin whose own account for his role is mysterious. The son of missionaries, Sawin had lived in Indochina since 1947 and had worked for the CIA since 1960, largely in the Central Highlands of South Vietnam. His superior was Gilbert Layton, the Chief of Combined Studies of the CIA in South Vietnam.

Sawin says that he resigned from the CIA at the end of 1968; but he continued to report to Layton at CIA headquarters in Langley, Virginia. In 1969 Sawin moved from South Vietnam to Phnom Penh in an attempt, he says, to secure the release of American missionaries captured by the Communists in the Central Highlands. He says he thought that neutral Phnom Penh, with its North Vietnamese and Viet Cong embassies, would be a good place for an individual to do such work in, on a private basis, and that Sihanouk, whom he claims to have known well, would help him.

Sihanouk arrived in France in January 1970. He met there with Lon Nol, who had completed his own medical treatment. One version of the conspiracy theory alleges, without much evidence, that Lon Nol and representatives of the CIA had already plotted Sihanouk's removal around Lon Nol's hospital bed at Neuilly-sur-Seine, in late 1969. Other stories, recounted by many Cambodian sources and by Sawin, claim that together the Prince and the Prime Minister now devised a method of trying to enlist Soviet and/or Chinese help in persuading the North Vietnamese to moderate their use of Cambodia.

Sihanouk was planning to return to Phnom Penh via Moscow and Peking. While he was there, Lon Nol—so the accounts go—was to stage anti-Vietnamese demonstrations in Phnom Penh to drive home the extent

---

April 1975. The book was published without permission of the Agency, which then took Snepp to court for violating the oath of secrecy that all its members sign.

of Cambodian anger over the way in which their territory was being abused. Sihanouk would then implore the Soviet and Chinese leaders to exert pressure on their Vietnamese ally to withdraw from Cambodia.

It is certainly true that by early 1970 Sihanouk appeared more and more alarmed by the way in which the war was intruding into Cambodia and was directing most of his public anger against the Communists, and such a plan might well have appealed to his agile mind. Drew Sawin makes the remarkable claim that he met Sihanouk in France at this time and that the Prince told him he had ordered Lon Nol to stage such demonstrations. Sawin says he questioned the wisdom of this and suggested that Sihanouk discuss the whole range of his concerns with someone from the CIA. In previous anti-American outbursts Sihanouk had often blamed his troubles on the Agency, and after his overthrow he published a rather tendentious memoir, *My War with the CIA*, which laid almost every Cambodian problem at the door of that organization. But Sawin asserts that early in 1970 the Prince asked him to arrange such a meeting. Given Sihanouk's deviousness, this is not impossible; to the Prince the preservation of Cambodia's peace was always far more important than political consistency. He was secretly receiving the Vesuvius intelligence packages—there is no *a priori* reason why he should not have had contacts with the CIA.

Sawin says he went at once to CIA headquarters at Langley, Virginia. He informed Gilbert Layton and others of his talks with Sihanouk, but, he claims, their superiors decided against closer involvement with the Prince; if Sihanouk wanted to make contact he shou'ld speak to the United States ambassador in Paris. Layton confirms this account. Sawin relayed this suggestion to Sihanouk, who, he says, was disappointed and rejected it. Sawin then flew back to Phnom Penh.

In February Lon Nol called a meeting of provincial governors in Phnom Penh to discuss the Vietnamese situation. Apparently the governors painted a dismal picture of the high-handed manner in which the Viet Cong and North Vietnamese were behaving in several provinces. Lon Nol then closed Sihanoukville to Communist supplies and shipments as Sihanouk had done for a time in the spring of 1969. A report on Communist infiltration, designed to stir up public anger, was presented to the Assembly; there were now alleged to be 60,000 Communist troops in the country—20,000 more than Lon Nol had estimated in September.

Meanwhile, in Saigon, General Abrams was pressing Secretary Laird to agree to an invasion of the sanctuaries. Such an invasion would have little long-term military effect. But the arguments of American commanders shifted to accommodate failures. A new cause was sought for each new setback, and a hitherto denied target that had compromised the entire war effort had to be located. A year before, the military had argued that the destruction of COSVN in one "surgical" B-52 strike would cripple the Communist war effort. When that failed they urged a sustained bombardment of the sanctuaries. Now a ground attack assumed major significance in the mouths and the memos, if not truly in the minds, of the military.

For his part, Melvin Laird considered that poor economic performance and leadership were now the most pressing issues in Vietnam. In a report to the President on his trip there in February 1970, he made absolutely no mention of the risks posed by the Cambodian sanctuaries. But he authorized clandestine South Vietnamese ground attacks across the border to begin at once. A full-scale invasion was still ruled out, because of the certain opposition of Sihanouk. Later, Abrams told *The New York Times* that "the ouster of Prince Sihanouk and the change in Phnom Penh really did an awful lot to assist the orderly withdrawal [of American troops]." Elliot Richardson told Congressmen privately that it was only Sihanouk's overthrow that allowed the invasion even to be "considered."

The last ten days of Sihanouk's rule were a period of uncertainty. What was intended by whom, and even what happened, are still unclear. The motives of Lon Nol and Sihanouk themselves are obscure. On March 8 Lon Nol staged anti-Vietnamese demonstrations in the border provinces, particularly in the Parrot's Beak, where infiltration and bombing had been especially heavy. In Paris, however, Sihanouk publicly declared that relations with North Vietnam were reasonable now, and that the number of Communist troops in the country had been dropping. North Vietnamese Premier Pham Van Dong, he announced, would visit Cambodia in two months' time. (At a private dinner party, by contrast, he complained that since 1954 the North Vietnamese had always ignored his requests to withdraw from Cambodia.) If any rebuke or warning was implicit in his public remarks, it was lost on Phnom Penh. On March 11 several thousand students, soldiers, Buddhist monks and bystanders gathered at the Independence Monument and began to march toward the embassy of the Provisional Revolutionary Government of South Vietnam.

To begin with the crowd was peaceful as it strolled down Norodom Avenue in the sunshine. When it reached the Viet Cong embassy, cheerleaders began to whip up angry shouting. The embassy and then the North Vietnamese mission were assaulted by teams of raiders, said to have been organized by Lon Nol's aggressive younger brother, Lon Non. To the delight of the onlookers, furniture was flung through windows, cars were overturned and burned, and the Cambodian flag was run up on both buildings. There was little doubt among the few journalists there that the violence had been organized. An American official, Robert Blackburn, watched part of the attack and then retreated to his embassy. The chargé d'affaires, Mike Rives, cabled the State Department: "Knowing propensity for Cambodians to balance attitudes in maintaining 'neutrality,' embassy personnel keeping out of sight."

Now, in Paris, Sihanouk angrily denounced the demonstrations, saying they were "organized by personalities aiming at destroying beyond repair Cambodia's friendship with the socialist camp and at throwing our country into the arms of a capitalist, imperialist power." He cabled his mother to say he was canceling his trip to Moscow and Peking and returning home at once to prevent his country from becoming a second Laos. In Phnom Penh, the bunting was laid out for his arrival, but his ministers continued their anti-Communist policies. On March 12, Sirik Matak canceled the trade agreement that allowed the Vietnamese to use Sihanoukville port and purchase supplies in Cambodia. Lon Nol formally apologized for the attacks on the Vietnamese embassies, but he also issued an ultimatum that their troops must leave the country in seventy-two hours. This was a crucial event for Cambodia. It was a ludicrous demand, one that could only be made by a man who had a tenuous grasp on reality, or had promises of external support.

Up to this moment Sihanouk's ministers in Phnom Penh do not seem to have been united in an attempt to remove him. In fact Lon Nol may well, as suggested, have discussed the demonstrations with the Prince. If accounts of Cambodians close to Lon Nol are to be believed, his original intention was not to overthrow Sihanouk but to wrest executive authority from him and force him to adopt a more aggressive attitude toward the Vietnamese Communists. Sirik Matak, on the other hand, seems to have been determined from the start to remove his cousin.

On the twelfth of March, the CIA received a report entitled, "Indications of Possible Coup in Phnom Penh." (It appears that this and other reports about the political crisis in Phnom Penh were not distributed at once through Washington.) The report informed Washington that the demonstrations the previous day were planned by Sirik Matak with Lon Nol's support. "Sirik Matak decided to adopt a showdown policy against Sihanouk's followers. The demonstration had support from all the anti-Sihanouk elements who had been without a leader for the past few years," and the army had been put on alert, "to prepare . . . for a coup against Sihanouk if Sihanouk refused to support the current government or exerted pressure upon the government." It seems to have been Sihanouk's attempts to do that which encouraged Lon Nol to move to the right, to Sirik Matak's position.

The Prince now made a series of uncharacteristic misjudgments which were to prove fatal. Although his welcome-home plans were proceeding, he decided after all to continue to Moscow and Peking. He refused to meet two envoys sent by the Queen Mother and Lon Nol to show him documents, seized from the North Vietnamese embassy which revealed the extent of Communist designs upon his kingdom. Instead, in the Cambodian embassy in Paris, Sihanouk ranted about his turbulent ministers, threatening them with imprisonment, even death. Reported back to Phnom Penh by embassy staff, the threats aroused, as might be expected, considerable fear among his cabinet. Sihanouk in a rage was not predictable. A few days after the coup, Lon Nol told *The Times* of London that it was the Prince's angry behavior in Paris that transformed the idea of a constitutional amendment to limit his royal powers into a *coup d'état*.

Why Sihanouk reacted thus is unknown; had he returned quickly and calmly to Phnom Penh he would most likely have been able to avert disaster. Frank Snepp, observing from Saigon, asserts that the CIA can claim some credit. "We exacerbated the crisis by throwing up misinformation." He says, for example, that the CIA persuaded the Queen Mother to reassure Sihanouk that the situation was not so serious as to require his return. This cannot be proved, but it is certain that she did send such a message.

Throughout this period, Snepp and others assert, various United States agencies were in touch with Lon Nol and Sirik Matak and their associates. One link was through Son Ngoc Thanh and his Khmer Serei. At the end of 1969 several units of Khmer Serei ostentatiously "defected" from South Vietnam to Cambodia; they were incorporated into Sihanouk's armed forces. The Prince later claimed that their defection was a ruse and that they were a Trojan Horse. Snepp does not disagree; he says that the Agency was assuring Lon Nol, through the defectors, that he had American support for a hard line against the Communists. Again, specific allegations are hard to prove. But it is certain that the United States had links to Son Ngoc Thanh and that he had links to Phnom Penh during the coup. To preserve its "deniability," the station in Saigon maintained contact with him through South Vietnamese intelligence. One CIA report from Saigon quoted him as assuring a South Vietnamese officer that he had kept in close touch with Sirik Matak by courier throughout the crisis, and that Lon Nol had approved a plan he had submitted to use the Khmer Serei to attack the sanctuaries. He did not, however, plan to return to Phnom Penh, because, according to the report, "he feels his presence . . . would only cause embarrassment to Lon Nol" (because of his known connections with the United States) "and would serve the Viet Cong with a major target for propaganda exploitation." (A few weeks later he did, in fact, return to Cambodia and in 1972 he became Prime Minister.)

Son Ngoc Thanh was only one channel between American officials and men around Lon Nol or Sirik Matak. Snepp says there were links between the Defense Intelligence Agency in Saigon and Lon Nol. General William Rosson, Creighton Abrams' deputy, confirms that United States commanders were informed several days beforehand that a coup was being planned; he says that American support was solicited. A further channel used by the Agency was the Indonesian embassy in Phnom Penh. This was a two-way street. The Indonesians were giving tactical advice to Lon Nol and reporting to the Agency his plans and other diplomatic intelligence from Phnom Penh.*

On March 15, three days after the demonstrations, Lon Nol's ultimatum to the Communists expired. They were still on Cambodian territory, and the Cambodians asked the South Vietnamese to provide artillery support against the sanctuaries. The request was granted. Nonetheless, the next day Viet Cong, North Vietnamese and Cambodian officials met in Phnom Penh to discuss Lon Nol's demands. It was now, according to Son Ngoc Thanh, that Lon Nol finally decided to go along with Sirik Matak's proposed coup.

On the seventeenth of March two cabinet members loyal to Sihanouk attempted to have Lon Nol arrested. They were detained along with other supporters of the Prince, while Lon Nol placed the army on alert. More anti-Vietnamese demonstrations were organized, the airport was closed, and troops and armored cars took up positions around the ministries, the radio station and the Assembly. But Sihanouk's usurpers had still not determined to abandon his policy of accommodation with the Commu-

---

* During this period American public attention fixed on Cambodia only when the *Columbia Eagle*, an American munitions ship en route to Thailand, was hijacked by two American hippies in the Gulf of Thailand and brought into Sihanoukville on March 13. Some left-wingers have assumed that the hijacking was part of a CIA plot to furnish arms to Lon Nol. They have discovered no evidence. The two hijackers were arrested by the Cambodians. One escaped and disappeared; the other was repatriated and was imprisoned in the United States.

nists. On the morning of March 18, the first anniversary of the Breakfast attack on "COSVN HQ," the American chargé Mike Rives was summoned to the Ministry of Defense, where a colonel carefully read him a prepared statement informing the United States government that, despite rumors, Cambodian neutrality would continue. He repeated the message several times. Rives cabled the State Department: "I believe that this move may be a special effort by [the government] to inform [the United States] that if *coup d'état* should occur it will not alter policy . . ." and to discourage speculation in South Vietnam that "a new ball game" was beginning. Rives urged that Washington make "every effort to avoid official comment and speculation events Cambodia until situation clarified." Soon after this message was transmitted, most communications between Phnom Penh and the outside world were severed.

Some hours later a telex was received in the White House Situation Room. It was a message from the CIA Operations Center: "According to monitored broadcasts of Radio Phnom Penh, both houses of the Cambodian legislature met in special closed session on March 18 at the request of the government. The legislature then voted unanimously to withdraw its confidence in Sihanouk as Chief of State." The message then cited a supposedly "reliable" source, who said that the March 11 demonstrations had "involved a behind-the-scenes struggle between pro- and anti-Sihanouk elements" and that Sirik Matak, with Lon Nol's support, had decided to stage a showdown with Sihanouk." Between March 11 and 17, Sirik Matak had controlled the government. The coup "represents a reversal of the slow nibbling-away at [Sihanouk's] power that had been underway for the past six months. . . . Lon Nol apparently believed that Sihanouk had decided, while he was in Paris, to overthrow the government." He therefore agreed with Sirik Matak that "the time was propitious for the move against Sihanouk."

The message concluded:

> If the army is as loyal to the new government as it now appears and if Sirik Matak and Lon Nol are as determined to have their way, Sihanouk faces a rough road. The question then becomes whether the Prince's enormous vanity will get the better of his usually astute judgment and cause him to embark on a course that could bring a period of prolonged instability in Cambodia.

Sihanouk did embark on such a course but what caused him to do so is less clear than the Agency's analysts have suggested. Across the world, says Frank Snepp, the CIA began to put out more "misinformation"—this time assuring the Prince that there was absolutely no chance of his return. United States recognition was immediately conferred upon the men who overthrew him.

This account of the coup is neither complete nor conclusive; the extent of American complicity (if any) could probably only be uncovered by Congressional investigation. Privately Henry Kissinger has raised the possibility of United States intervention. At a lunch in January 1977 with a group of European journalists, he defended his role in the whole Cambodian drama and said that the United States had not been involved in Sihanouk's overthrow, "at least not at the top level." Nobody pursued this qualification. But whatever individual agents did in the final days of Sihanouk's rule there is a more general and important sense in which some responsibility should be assumed by Washington.

The United States had always found the Sihanouk regime inadequate. Eleven years before the coup the Pentagon had identified the political elite and the officer corps as the groups that would best serve United States interests. Represented by Prince Sirik Matak and General Lon Nol, these two groups had no reason now to doubt that their removal of Sihanouk would be acceptable to Washington. For the past decade the Cambodian organization with which American officials had had the closest contact was the Khmer Serei, an illegal armed force of exiles dedicated to Sihanouk's overthrow. Even tacit support by the United States for Son Ngoc Thanh inevitably enlarged the extent of opposition in Cambodia. Prom Thos, an opponent of Sihanouk, who was Lon Nol's Minister of Industry and is now in exile in Paris, says that whether Lon Nol had specific promises of United States help before he overthrew Sihanouk in March 1970 is unimportant. "We all just knew that the United States would help us; there had been many stories of CIA approaches and offers before then."

William Colby, the former Director of the CIA agrees—"Lon Nol may well have been encouraged by the fact that the U.S. was working with Son Ngoc Thanh. I don't know of any specific assurances he was given but the obvious conclusion for him, given the political situation in South Vietnam and Laos, was that he would be given United States support." Laird, confirming that there were contacts between Lon Nol and Son Ngoc Thanh before the coup, says "I have no direct knowledge that the approval of Sihanouk's overthrow was made." When finally they made their move, says Frank Snepp, "We were in a position to rub our hands and take advantage of it."

The fabric of Sihanouk's Cambodia, already patchy, disintegrated very fast after his removal. It became clear how artfully he had preserved some peace in his isolated country and how hopelessly ill-equipped was his court to rule without him.

At first Lon Nol promised to pursue the same policy of ardent neutralism as had Sihanouk—just more effectively. But the interests of others, if not his own inclinations, precluded that.

In Washington the administration's initial response was low key. The South Vietnamese ambassador told the State Department that, although the coup put the North Vietnamese in a very embarrassing position, "any public enthusiasm about Cambodian events would be contrary to our interests and might harmfully affect the outcome in Cambodia." The State Department accepted his warning and Secretary Rogers forwarded it to the Saigon and Phnom Penh embassies, adding, "All elements of U.S. mission should similarly be directed to avoid comments on events in Cambodia."

In Saigon, President Thieu, who apparently had advance warning of the coup, was obviously delighted. He remarked that he expected excellent cooperation along the border now, and thought that together the two countries would "drive the Communists out." South Vietnamese troops and air force began to attack the border areas and following their own contingency plans the Communists soon dispersed even farther west than the Menu strikes had already driven them.

Prince Sihanouk heard the news of the coup in Moscow on March 18 as Premier Alexei Kosygin was driving him to the airport for his flight to Peking. The Russians were clearly unsympathetic to him, as Washington had known they would be. Recent CIA reports from Bangkok and Vientiane had quoted Soviet officials as calling Sihanouk "a blundering fool," "finagler," "a spoiled child" who would not be able to blackmail them into pressuring Hanoi. Kosygin thrust the Prince onto the plane without any offers of help. In *My War with the CIA*, Sihanouk claims that his immediate response was to fight. On the flight to Peking, he writes, he rejected the advice of his wife, Monique, to retire to France and declared

Of all times this is not the moment to hide ourselves. We would be condemned by history if we permitted Cambodia to become not only a military dictatorship but once more a colony. All my life I have dreamed and fought for my country's independence. I did not win it from France in order to abandon it now . . . The Americans will be beaten by the Vietnamese and by our own Khmer Rouge, together with us. And the Pathet Lao will win in Laos. It is the duty of the monarchy to remain with the people.

It is a splendid speech, and it is attractive to think of the little Prince standing in his Soviet plane high above Mongolia, en route from one Communist capital to the next, proudly proclaiming his independence and his solidarity with his former enemies. But although his memoirs have charm and contain some useful material, they are not always an accurate record. In fact, Sihanouk arrived in Peking uncertain as to what he would do next, but tending toward exile in France.

The Chinese too were undecided. The initial Chinese reaction to the demonstrations in Phnom Penh had apparently been to try to arrange Sihanouk's return. On March 15, the day before the Prince was originally due to arrive from Moscow, the French Ambassador Etienne Manac'h was summoned to the Chinese Foreign Ministry and asked if an Air France plane could fly the Prince to Phnom Penh as soon as he arrived in Peking. Why no, Manac'h replied, Air France had been refused landing rights in Peking on the grounds that the runway was inadequate. Chinese officials conferred briefly. Improvements had been made; the runway was now quite suitable. The French began to make the arrangements. But Sihanouk did not leave Moscow until March 18, the day of the coup, and the plan was abandoned.

Peking's immediate priority appears to have been to try to persuade Lon Nol to leave the sanctuaries alone. When Sihanouk arrived at Peking airport on March 19 he was greeted by Chou En-lai with the honors due a head of state. But the Chinese Premier was, at first, noncommittal. In Phnom Penh the Chinese Ambassador Kang Mang-chao was negotiating with Lon Nol to renew the agreement for the use of the sanctuaries and Sihanoukville.

The uncertainties of the situation were outlined in a March 21 CIA report, which pointed out that Lon Nol had ordered Cambodian border units "to avoid friction with VC/NVA forces and to take no action at this time as talks are continuing with VC/NVA representatives in Phnom Penh." It added that the Communists were equally circumspect:

COSVN has not issued any order to VC/NVA forces in Cambodia to either withdraw or to fight. COSVN is currently trying to resolve its differences with the Cambodian government through negotiations in Phnom Penh. COSVN attributes the recent coup to U.S. backing. . . . In the event that negotiations with the Lon Nol government are unsuccessful, the VC/NVA will support the red Khmer in launching a guerrilla war against the Cambodian government similar to the one in Laos.

In Peking Sihanouk's first reaction also appears to have been to extricate himself. He sent for Ambassador Etienne Manac'h. Manac'h is a highly intelligent diplomat who had known Sihanouk for years. The two men understood one another. (Kissinger was to claim that Washington was initially interested in securing Sihanouk's immediate return home. If Kissinger had seriously wanted to be in touch with the Prince, Manac'h would have been a crucial intermediary. No approach was made to him.) Sihanouk wished to know whether he would be able to return to his house at Mougins in the South of France. Manac'h responded that the French would be glad to give him asylum.

But plans for retirement were short-lived. Although it was still negotiating with the Communists, the new Phnom Penh regime unleashed furious attacks on Sihanouk and his family, denigrating his policies and their corruption. One newspaper published a picture purporting to show him with a naked woman, and the government radio harped on "the abuses, *gaffes* and monumental errors he has committed." His pictures were ordered out of shop windows and off office walls, and streets that were named after him were renamed. Frank Snepp maintains that the CIA encouraged this iconoclasm. Its predictable effect was to drive Sihanouk into a rage and a desire for revenge.

On March 21 the Prime Minister of North Vietnam, Pham Van Dong, flew secretly to Peking and, after further conversation with Chou En-lai, Sihanouk agreed to swallow his distaste for the North Vietnamese, stay in China, and accept leadership of the Cambodian Communists he had bitterly fought. It was a fateful decision, and his motives may have mixed injured pride and fury at his usurpers, genuine dislike of the prospect of atrophying like Vietnam's former emperor Bao Dai on the Riviera, and, perhaps, distaste for what he perceived as the American role in his removal. A few weeks later he said, "I had chosen not to be with either the Americans or the Communists, because I considered that there were two dangers, American imperialism and Asian Communism. It was Lon Nol who obliged me to choose between them."

On the twenty-third of March the Prince issued his first public call to arms, castigated his "unpardonable naïveté" in trusting Lon Nol, "irrevocably" dissolved the government in Phnom Penh and announced that he would soon establish his own new administration. In the meantime he established a National United Front of Kampuchea (FUNK), whose task was "to liberate our motherland." Sihanouk called upon all those who had the stomach "to engage in guerrilla warfare in the jungles against our enemies." The North Vietnamese, the Viet Cong and the Pathet Lao immediately pledged their support to the new Front, and in Hanoi a statement of support was issued in the name of the Khmer Rouge. In Phnom Penh, the Vietnamese Communists canceled a meeting with Lon Nol officials that was to have made another attempt to accommodate Communist supply needs to the new government's policy. But the Communists still did not break off relations with Lon Nol. Most of their diplomats flew out of Phnom Penh, but a skeleton North Vietnamese staff remained throughout April. The Chinese also stayed and in the coming weeks attempted to negotiate agreement with Lon Nol on the use of the sanctuaries. It took the United States invasion at the end of April to bring the final break. Only then did Lon Nol finally tell the Chinese that there was no possibility of tolerating the sanctuaries longer. On May 5 Sihanouk announced the formation of his government, the Royal Government of National Union of Kampuchea (GRUNK). Peking recognized it.

Sihanouk's appeal had little effect in Phnom Penh. His removal had been welcomed by the middle class, and many diplomats and foreign journalists were also infected by the enthusiasm with which educated Khmers now talked of their future. Lon Nol released political prisoners on both the right and the left, a committee of intellectuals was formed to support him and the mass of students, wearied by the fear of imprisonment for criticizing Sihanouk, applauded. "We were bored with him and humiliated by him. His damn film shows and endless radio speeches in that singsong voice. If he tries to come back I hope they shoot him at the airport," said one rich young man. The middle class was promised that the economic stagnation of recent years was over; that industry would be denationalized; that interest rates would rise; and that tourists and capital would flow into Phnom Penh. The army was behind Lon Nol; the change in regime suggested a resumption of American military aid. When he made a call to arms it was popular in the capital for its offer of employment and the prospect of killing Vietnamese.

But in much of the Cambodian countryside, where Sihanouk's corruption had been less visible and his autocracy less painful, the Prince's overthrow seemed an act of sacrilege. Rioting broke out in several provinces; opposition was strongest in the market town of Kompong Cham,

Cambodia's second city, fifty miles northeast of Phnom Penh. After Sihanouk's radio broadcast, the town filled with peasants, fishermen and rice farmers from the neighborhood. The townspeople refused the government's orders to remove the Prince's portrait, and they burned down the house of the new governor whom Lon Nol had appointed. Demonstrators gathered in buses and trucks to march on Phnom Penh. They were halted by an army roadblock, and after that "it was very rapid, very calm," said the governor; "three salvos of repression and then—*fini.*" About ninety people were killed or wounded.

The violence spread to other towns. In Skoun, an important crossroads north of Phnom Penh, police and troops opened fire on a crowd that the government said was, like all hostile crowds, Viet Cong. Over six hundred arrests of other demonstrators were made around Phnom Penh. The most vivid display of anger against Lon Nol occurred, again in Kompong Cham, when peasants seized his brother Lon Nil, killed him and tore his liver from his stomach. The trophy was taken into a Chinese restaurant, where the owner was ordered to cook and slice it. Morsels were handed to everyone in the streets around.

Some years earlier Bernard-Philippe Groslier, the French archaeologist, had noted that in Cambodia "beneath a carefree surface there slumber savage forces and disconcerting cruelties which may blaze up in outbreaks of passionate brutality." In March 1970, those forces were aroused, and for years to come they simmered and shifted as war spread.

In a cable describing "atmospherics" Mike Rives reported to the State Department the story his servants were whispering in dismay. The Queen Mother (who had fainted on hearing news of the coup) had held a special ceremony at the palace to determine whether or not her son would return. The climax required the Queen to draw a sacred sword from its scabbard. Usually the sword was gleaming and burnished, but when Queen Kossomak now withdrew it she and her courtiers were horrified to see that the blade was a filthy black. The story was around the city within hours, and Rives reported with the understatement of cablese that the event "portends negative answer and trouble ahead."

CHAPTER 9

The Invasion

LON NOL was an unlikely war leader. Most of his life had been spent in the armed services, and he had been a minister in several of Sihanouk's cabinets, Prime Minister in the last. But he was more used to taking orders than giving them and, a believer in hierarchy, he had prostrated himself at the Queen Mother's feet after Sihanouk was deposed, to ask her forgiveness. Lon Nol had long been in favor of an American role in Southeast Asia and in Cambodia, and although he had profited from the cross-country trade with the Vietnamese Communists, as a devout Buddhist, he considered fighting Communism a holy duty. In financial matters he may have been worldly, but at moments of crisis a strain of mysticism, never far from the surface, overwhelmed him.

Almost nothing was known of him in the White House at the time of the coup. One American cartoonist aptly drew Kissinger saying to Nixon "All we know about Lon Nol is that his name spelled backwards makes Lon Nol." But immediately after Sihanouk's deposition the staff of the National Security Council found their "in" trays clogged with memoranda, questions and demands from the Oval Office. Roger Morris, who resigned over the invasion, believes these "stream-of-consciousness excursions into courage and aggression" will make extraordinary reading for historians—if they survive. Their message was that the United States must act somehow and decisively, and that this man Lon Nol must be helped at all costs. There was to be no pause to see whether Sihanouk might return or even whether the new government was at all competent. "From Day One," says Marshall Green, the Assistant Secretary of State for East Asian and Pacific Affairs and State's representative on WASSAG—the White House's crisis management body—"Nixon was insistent on building up Lon Nol." It was a decision that disturbed many officials in both State and Defense Departments. It led to the invasion and the five-year war.

On March 24, Mike Rives cabled from Phnom Penh that "one of greatest dangers present situation exists in possible clashes between Cambodia and NVN/VC troops, whether initiated by former or latter. Once serious fighting starts there would appear very serious chance escalation not only through possible calls for help by one side or other but because of good possibility that Khmer people would rise or be encouraged rise against resident Vietnamese and Chinese."

Rives was exactly right, and his views were endorsed by Marshall Green, who was unwise enough to send a memo on his reservations to both Kissinger and Rogers on the twenty-eighth, arguing that the United States should try to work through the French and the Algerians to find a diplomatic solution to Cambodia's new problems. The French had proposed an international conference on Indochina. "It would be very risky to try to solve the North Vietnamese problem in Cambodia by force," he wrote. "I would consider our best action to be to wait on events, saying little." Green believed that the only hope for Cambodia lay in continuing Sihanouk's policies if not actually helping to restore Sihanouk himself. But the White House declined to give public support to France's call for a conference, and lukewarm private agreement was inadequate.

In another memo dealing with the problems of aid Green pointed out the paradox that "without massive U.S. support the Government of Cambodia cannot rebuild its position . . . but U.S. support could restrict its neutrality, which is its greatest resource." He argued, moreover, that Congress would see aid to Lon Nol as widening the war and might therefore impose further restrictions on aid to Vietnam. Helping Cambodia could hinder Vietnamization. This is exactly what happened.

Green reflected the opinion of many members of Congress. Fears of America being drawn into another "quagmire" were now being frequently expressed on Capitol Hill.* But Green's pleas for caution were

---

* The "quagmire myth" which stated that the United States was drawn unwillingly deeper and deeper into the Vietnam commitment had not yet been effectively destroyed in April 1970. It took the publication of the Pentagon Papers in 1971 to show how consciously and willingly most of the decisions to escalate had been made.

futile, and they were ruinous to his career. His dissent infuriated the White House, and as a result he was subsequently denied the one job for which he had trained himself for years, ambassador to Japan.

By the end of March little or no attempt was being made to restrain the South Vietnamese from crashing across the border when they wished. Simultaneously, the North Vietnamese moved westward into Cambodia with the apparent intention of securing their lines of communication. In Washington, Press Secretary Ronald Ziegler suggested that United States troops might move after them. Even the Lon Nol government deplored this and repeated that it sought only to protect Cambodia's neutrality with United Nations support. But Robert Pursley, Laird's military assistant, was receiving constant calls from Alexander Haig and others on Kissinger's staff, stressing the need for a coordinated assault on the sanctuaries. The options under consideration were heavy artillery attacks, the use of South Vietnamese troops with or without United States air and artillery support, and at the outside, a combined US-ARVN ground operation. Pursley reacted cautiously to Haig's calls. He was instructed that the State Department was to know nothing of the discussions. "We were told to keep everything, particularly cables between Abrams and the JCS, on a very close-held basis" says Pursley. "State got very little information, except when the White House decided to bring them in."

Melvin Laird was alarmed by the White House's truculence and, despite Haig's command to exclude State, he kept in touch with Rogers. On March 31 he wrote Rogers that, although Lon Nol's replacement by a "Communist-oriented" government would undermine the United States position in Vietnam, "We will be in a difficult position if Cambodia asks the U.S. government to become militarily involved in that country." He suggested the United States should do all it could, short of direct involvement, to strengthen Lon Nol; for example, Washington could see that both South Vietnam and Thailand unilaterally dropped their border claims and other suits against Cambodia. (By suggesting this, Laird implicitly acknowledged that the United States had previously encouraged those pressures to harass Sihanouk.) He thought also that the Australians should be encouraged to send military advisers and give economic aid to Lon Nol.

By the beginning of April Lon Nol was clearly alarmed at his inability to stop the march of the war westward. At steamy briefings in Phnom Penh, government spokesmen were vaguer than usual, and on April 3, journalists were surprised to find that the official transcript of the press conference Lon Nol had just given them included questions and answers that had not been asked or answered. For example, "Question 10: But can we insist on this question—will American troops be called in? Answer: My opinion is that I am thinking of the possible intervention of all friendly countries, for example, Indonesia or others."

By mid-April, 70,000 volunteers had enlisted in the army. This was 60,000 more than the government had called for, twice as many as the old regular army. Their induction was cursory, their training on a golf course outside Phnom Penh was erratic, and their equipment was nonexistent. Every day they could be seen setting out from the city, hanging on the sides of Coca-Cola trucks or brightly painted buses, wearing shower clogs or sandals, shorts or blue jeans, parts of very old French uniforms or oversized American fatigues, some empty-handed, some carrying French, Russian, East German, American, Chinese weapons, AK-47s, M-16s, rifles, pistols, and submachine guns, laughing as they headed for the war in the plains. "We cannot just send these men armed with sticks to face an enemy armed to the teeth and with twenty years' fighting experience," said one officer. Lon Nol made an international appeal for arms.

The White House had already secretly decided that they would be provided. In Saigon, Abrams ordered that all captured AK-47 rifles be sent to Phnom Penh. "I don't want to see any hanging on officers' club walls," he said. The White House instructed the Pentagon to devise surreptitious ways of delivering these and other weapons. The Chiefs were doubtful that this could work, but General Westmoreland cabled Abrams in Saigon to suggest that "it would appear that we might consider delivering arms by sea to Vung Tau and then by air to Phnom Penh. We would want delivery to be covert if possible; however, this may not be feasible over a long period or if large quantities are involved."

The White House also ordered that the Khmer units that had for years been trained in Vietnam finally be launched on a grand scale into Cambodia. The order covered not only ordinary ethnic Khmer battalions, known as Khmer Krom, but also Son Ngoc Thanh's Khmer Serei. In late March and early April Son Ngoc Thanh was flown around Vietnam on a recruiting drive, and Abrams cabled the Chiefs to say, "Three battalions of Khmer Serei with a total strength of about 1,500 are available now . . . if these units are urgently needed to support the Lon Nol government they should be inserted by air at Phnom Penh."

More and more Khmer Serei and Khmer Krom were flown into Cambodia over the coming months. They were far better trained than the

Cambodian troops and, as an elite corps, seemed to Lon Nol a political threat. They were subsequently thrust into all the worst meat-grinder battles, and few survived.

Inevitably, news of Nixon's decision to assist Lon Nol leaked out in Washington. The administration assured the Senate Foreign Relations Committee that the amounts were insignificant. But the first step is always the hardest, and here it had been taken without any consultation with Congress and with no consideration of the long-term implications. Lon Nol immediately asked for more. Within weeks he said he needed full infantry equipment for 400 battalions, massive communications gear, 2,500 military trucks, 1,000 jeeps, 30 helicopters, 30 fighters, 12 transport aircraft. By the end of the war this was small beer.

Throughout the first part of April the new government demonstrated its ability to rule Cambodia without Sihanouk in a way that should have given the administration cause for reflection. Lon Nol was being advised by Indonesian officers. Rather as Suharto had unleashed hatred of the Chinese population after the coup against Sukarno, so Lon Nol tried to compensate for lack of peasant support by exploiting the Khmers' traditional fear of the Vietnamese. After the division of French Indochina, some 400,000 Vietnamese had remained in Cambodia; many of them were merchants, and a good number of them had, like Lon Nol himself, profited from the trade with the Vietnamese Communists. Sihanouk had made a point of controlling the violent racial antipathies that existed between his subjects, but now the government propaganda machinery was geared to persuade the Cambodians that all Vietnamese residents were members of the Viet Cong. The radio screamed abuse and in Phnom Penh the government staged a pageant at which the brilliant, beautiful Khmers were seen liquidating their knavish neighbors.

The real killings of Vietnamese began in the village of Prasaut, in the Parrot's Beak; the government blamed their deaths on crossfire. Journalists there insisted that Khmer troops had simply shot them. Then about 800 Vietnamese men were taken from their riverside village of Chrui Changwar. Their hands were tied behind their backs, they were pushed into boats, shot and thrown into the Mekong. More and more were executed in this way, and for days their swollen bodies floated downstream, getting caught in the ferries and in fishermen's nets, staining the muddy water the color of rust.

When journalists arrived at a schoolyard in the town of Takeo, it looked like an abattoir, with flies buzzing through the classrooms and over the pools of coagulating blood. Dozens of wounded Vietnamese lay on the ground, gasping and writhing in the sun, watched by young Cambodian soldiers who lounged against the walls with spent cartridge cases around their feet. The soldiers had come the night before: "They shot and shot and shot," wept one teen-age boy. One man, lying on his back in his own blood, had stuffed his clothes into his gaping stomach. There was a hospital only one hundred yards away, but no help had been given. Some of the wounded Vietnamese begged the reporters for help: they were sure they would be killed off that night. The journalists went to the province chief, who blandly assured them that the crossfire in the vicinity was really shocking. One reporter lost his temper and angrily abused the surprised official, and they were then allowed to bundle as many of the wounded as they could into their hired cars. As the sun was setting they raced them back through roadblocks to hospitals in Phnom Penh. Later the car-rental firm complained about blood on the seats.

Protests by diplomats and the press, and also the White House, eventually led Lon Nol to admit that the murder of Vietnamese civilians was not essential to his revolution. Nonetheless he ordered a band of Vietnamese detainees taken from a camp in Phnom Penh to help relieve the town of Saang, southwest of the capital. The detainees were told, as they were driven in trucks toward the town, that they were "volunteers" and that their role was simply to persuade the Communists to leave. They were dropped on a country road about two miles outside Saang; one nervous man was given a white flag to lead the procession and Cambodian officers brought up the rear, prodding with sticks. From over a mile away two women were ordered to read the government's message through megaphones: the Viet Cong must leave, respect the 1954 Geneva Accords and recognize that Sihanouk's overthrow was an internal matter. One senior Cambodian officer explained to Kevin Buckley of *Newsweek:* "This is a new tactic of ours. It's psychological warfare." After the pitiful procession shuffled round the last bend in the road, a rapid exchange of automatic-weapon fire began: bullets snapped across and along the road and Lon Nol's "volunteers" fell howling to the tarmac. The town was not captured.

The next day the Cambodians attacked Saang themselves. Their order of battle on this occasion was not untypical of the way in which they then went to war. The troops took three hours to edge up the last 500 yards into town. They were nervous and moved only because of the accuracy with which one of their colonels flung rocks at them from behind. As they inched forward they blasted the houses and shops in front with small arms, mortars and recoilless rifles. There was no response. When they reached the wreckage of the center of the town they found it empty except for an old Buddhist monk who sat by the road, laughing. "We are going to win now," exulted one young soldier, "the Viet Cong didn't stay to fight."

Ever since 1970, Nixon and his associates have claimed that the invasion of Cambodia at the end of April was a great success. This assessment has been widely accepted. It is not accurate. The invasion not only was disastrous for Cambodia, but it also had serious long-term effects on Vietnamization and on the nature of the Nixon administration itself. The way in which it was conducted broke rules of good policymaking, ignored vital intelligence, and disregarded political realities. Congress, to whom the Constitution assigns the power to declare war—in order, as Lincoln put it, that "no man should hold the power of bringing this oppression upon us"—was totally ignored. So was almost everyone else. Writing about the Cuban missile crisis, Richard Neustadt suggested that Congressional debate could no longer be a realistic constraint on modern Presidential crisis management and that more effective was argument within the Executive Branch. But even this unofficial, unrecognized restraint was missing in April 1970. Decision making was already so centralized in the White House that it was not true, in Neustadt's phrase, that the President stood "at the center of a watchful circle with whose members he cannot help but consult." There was little to prevent Cambodia from assuming an importance that was more symbolic than real.

Throughout the month Nixon was visibly angered by the Senate's rejections of the two men he had nominated for the Supreme Court seat left vacant by the resignation of Abe Fortas. After his first choice, Clement Haynsworth, was thrown out, Nixon publicly demanded that his second, G. Harrold Carswell, be approved automatically. The Senate, however, found that Carswell had no legal qualification for the task and was a segregationist; he too was rejected. In his book *Six Crises*, Nixon had described how he had always tried to control his impulsive rages. This time he wheeled into the White House press room, stuttered out a denunciation of the sixty-one "vicious," "hypocritical," "prejudiced" Senators who had thwarted the people's wishes as he had expressed them, and jerked out again leaving a slightly awkward press corps behind him.

His distress did not abate during the month, and it was apparent to members of the NSC staff that, whatever else he thought of Cambodia, Nixon also saw it as a chance of restoring his slighted authority. "Those Senators think they can push me around, but I'll show them who's tough," he warned Kissinger after one Congressional appeal for caution. "The liberals are waiting to see Nixon let Cambodia go down the drain just the way Eisenhower let Cuba go down the drain." His belligerence was increased by another irrelevant factor. Early in April he had a private viewing of the film *Patton,* in which George C. Scott gives a compelling performance as the gifted, demagogic, lonely and naïve World War II general who defied conventional restraints and risked everything to achieve a success in the Battle of the Bulge. The film appealed to Nixon's self-image, and he had a second showing as the Cambodian crisis deepened. William Rogers was dismayed to hear the President repeatedly citing *Patton* in this context, almost as he quoted his triumph over Alger Hiss during domestic troubles.

In response to the aggressive sounds from the White House, the Joint Chiefs in Washington and General Abrams in Saigon began to fire across the world proposals and counterproposals for escalation. Abrams asked first that he be allowed to send the Special Forces Salem House teams deeper into the country. "Lucrative targets would be engaged by tac-air, artillery and/or exploitation forces," he wrote. Then, while American attention was fixed on the precarious flight of the Apollo 13 astronauts, Abrams asked for a month of tactical air strikes into Cambodia. At this time, according to the White House's public claims, the North Vietnamese were moving westward and threatening Phnom Penh, but Abrams stated that he had increased sightings of their troops in the borders of northeastern Cambodia. He guaranteed that "to preclude compromise," the bombing could be kept totally secret.

General Wheeler, the Chairman of the Joint Chiefs, replied that approval would have to be given "at higher level," and he was not optimistic. But, a clear master of bureaucratic maneuver, he added, "In interim suggest you consider Menu (B-52) Operations for area described. Would contemplate earlier approval in view of ongoing program." Abrams did not take up this attractive offer; he replied, "At this time it is not believed that the targets described are of sufficient persistence to qualify as lucrative Menu targets." It was not long before his patience was rewarded; he was allowed to send fighter bombers up to eighteen miles into the country. By the end of May, 156 tactical airstrikes had been flown under the code name *Patio* and, like Menu, they were concealed under false reports until 1973. In testimony after the bombing was finally made public, Abrams was frank about the reasons for the falsification and concealment. It was necessary, "Because we did not have authority to use Tacair in Cambodia."

As Abrams was making his request, the Vietnam Moratorium Committee announced on April 19 that it would close its Washington office by the end of the month for lack of funds and support for the antiwar movement. It was a symbolic moment, and Nixon might well have considered it a major vindication of Vietnamization. But the President was still unsettled, and that day he flew 5,000 miles to Hawaii to associate himself with the astonishing escape of the Apollo 13 astronauts. He was briefed on Cambodia by Admiral John D. McCain Jr., Commander in Chief of the United States Forces in the Pacific, known as CINCPAC, who was based in Honolulu.

McCain, whose son was a POW in North Vietnam, was to play an important part in the story of Cambodia. He is a tiny, sprightly, man with a straightforward view of the world. His military briefings were legendary. He would talk very excitedly for forty-five minutes on a subject that might be dealt with in ten and illustrate a doom-laden message with lurid maps of Southeast Asia. Extended from the bright-red belly of China were gigantic red arrows or claws reaching all over that part of the free world for which McCain felt responsible. Sometimes his sermons on the "Chicom" threat were so energetic, his cries of woe so violent, his passionate pleas for aid so draining, that at the end of a briefing he would drop into his chair, ask for questions, and fall fast asleep.

In the Pentagon McCain was known, because of his maps, as the "Big Red Arrow Man," and both generals and journalists spoke with mingled awe and amusement of "McCain's claws." Nixon apparently was impressed when McCain unfurled for him a map of Cambodia with half the country already stained red and the dreaded claws reaching south and west beyond Phnom Penh and on toward Thailand. Cambodia must be saved, cried the Admiral, the President must act decisively. If he were still intent on announcing the withdrawal of another 150,000 men from Vietnam, then it was essential to protect Saigon's western flank. Lon Nol needed more than just a few thousand old rifles; what was required was an assault on the sanctuaries. Nixon flew McCain back to San Clemente to give the same message to Henry Kissinger. Kissinger's reaction is not recorded. The next day, April 20, Nixon addressed the nation on Vietnam. It was an optimistic speech; he promised that "pacification is succeeding," that "we finally have in sight the just peace we are seeking"; he hoped to withdraw another 150,000 troops within the next year. The President gave no hint of impending crisis, though he did refer to "the enemy's escalation in Laos and Cambodia" and warned that "I shall not hesitate to take strong and effective measures" to deal with any resulting threat to United States forces. After the speech, reporters with him observed that the President was very tense. To their dismay he decided to fly home to Washington that night; they arrived at the White House some time after 1 A.M. Six hours later Nixon was briefed by Richard Helms, the Director of the CIA.

Helms informed the President and Kissinger that the NVA were now threatening Phnom Penh itself; this, Kissinger later confided to reporters, made Lon Nol's appeal for arms very poignant. What Helms did not say, either then or at any stage during the next week, was that he had just received a National Intelligence Estimate on the Cambodian situation. Entitled "Stocktaking in Indochina: Longer Term Prospects" and drafted by the CIA's Indochina specialists, the paper dealt with the implications of Sihanouk's removal. It considered that if Hanoi could be denied Cambodian sanctuary its strategy would be endangered. But there was no way this could be enforced by Lon Nol. It "would require heavy and sustained bombing and large numbers of foot soldiers, who could be supplied only by the United States and South Vietnam. Such an expanded allied effort could seriously handicap the Communists and raise the cost to them of prosecuting the war, *but, however successful, it probably would not prevent them from continuing the struggle in some form*" (emphasis added).

Helms did not forward the memorandum to the White House. Instead, he sent it back to the Chairman of the CIA's National Estimates Board, Abbott Smith, with a handwritten note: "Let's take a look at this on June 1st and see if we would keep it or make certain revisions." Helms has since declined to explain his coyness; one member of the Board testified later that the Director would have considered it "most counterproductive" to send such a negative assessment to the White House, where he and the CIA had already encountered hostility. George Carver, Helms's Special Assistant for Vietnamization Affairs, objected to this explanation of Helms's action, but inadvertently confirmed it; he testified that Helms thought it would be fatuous to send the estimate forward for although Helms knew Nixon was already planning an invasion, his analysts did not.

Carver's view is hardly coherent. The CIA Indochinese experts' ignorance of Nixon's desire to send troops into the sanctuaries freed them of political pressures and would have tended to make their conclusions more, not less, relevant. But such was the fear of the White House within the CIA that Nixon was deprived of the considered opinion of the specialists that invasion was unwise. Whether it would have had any influence must remain a matter of speculation, but the incident is illustrative of the way in which inconvenient views were suppressed.

Sideshow

Helms's self-censorship was the prelude to ten days of somewhat negligent and emotional decision making. There was no consensus within the administration on North Vietnamese intentions. In Saigon, MACV offered captured documents that showed that Hanoi expected a United States invasion of the sanctuaries, and others that showed that the Communists expected the United States to provide only indirect aid to Lon Nol. Still others, produced later in Washington, purported to show that the North Vietnamese and the Viet Cong were massing in the sanctuaries for an attack on Saigon at the same time as they were supposed to be encircling Phnom Penh. A Senate Foreign Relations Committee investigation noted later, "There seem to be captured documents to prove almost any point or to support, retrospectively, almost any conclusion."

The Chiefs were surprised but not displeased by the depth of the President's anguish. On the evening of April 21, General Westmoreland cabled Abrams: "As you are certainly aware, there is highest-level concern here with respect to the situation in Cambodia." He saw it as a mood to be exploited: "The threat to Phnom Penh and the present concern of higher authority may be conducive to relaxation of some of the constraints under which we are operating. If this happens we should be prepared to take advantage of the opportunity." He asked Abrams how best the United States could involve itself more deeply in South Vietnamese attacks across the border. He needed a reply overnight so that he could advise "higher authority" next day.

Abrams needed little prodding. He had been keen on an invasion since he had arrived in Saigon. Moreover, as one of his deputies said later, "South Vietnam was relatively tranquil then. We were looking for something to do." Abrams responded that "our present degree of participation [in South Vietnamese invasion plans] is considered adequate," but he also supported the selective use of American troops "in most productive base areas, if U.S. policy permits." He suggested the dispatch of the Khmer Serei to Phnom Penh and the delivery of about 10,000 carbines to Lon Nol; "Problems are not foreseen for either covert or overt delivery."

Abrams proposed an elaborate scenario for widening the war. One section of his cable is worth quoting at length.

A pattern of progressive escalation in U.S. participation, coupled with continuing ARVN cross border operations, is suggested in the following counter measures which warrant consideration:
A. Maintenance of pressure of military force in Northern and Southern Laos.

138

B. Encourage programs of cooperation and coordination between the GVN and the Lon Nol Government.
C. Provisions of weapons, munitions and communications material support to the Lon Nol Government. This support is essential.
D. In support of RVNAF, use of U.S. gunship, artillery and tacair in Cambodia.
E. Selective combined US/RVNAF military operations against high payoff targets which might develop in Cambodia.
F. Exploit status of Mekong river as an international waterway.
G. Plan for quarantine of Sihanoukville prepared and imposed at an appropriate time.
H. Selective application of military force against selected military targets in North Vietnam.

That was very much how it happened. The next day Kissinger informed a National Security Council meeting that whether the North Vietnamese were intent on capturing Phnom Penh or merely setting up a provisional government, Vietnamization was now endangered. General Westmoreland, representing the Chairman of the Joint Chiefs, told him of Abrams' suggestions and said that he himself thought that an invasion by South Vietnamese troops alone would be adequate. That night, the twenty-second, Nixon authorized the final planning for a South Vietnamese attack on the Parrot's Beak, just northwest of Saigon. General Wheeler cabled Abrams to say that the South Vietnamese invasion was to begin on April 27. "Our objective is to make maximum use of ARVN assets so as to minimize U.S. involvement, and maintain lowest possible U.S. profile."

Laird and Rogers were anxious that nothing more than that should be done. Rogers told a House subcommittee—in phrases that were to haunt him—that the United States had "no incentive to escalate . . . We recognize that if we escalate and get involved in Cambodia our whole [Vietnamization] program is defeated." Rogers' opposition meant that the State Department was now even more excluded from the planning process. The White House suspected State officials of leaking the information that Nixon, not Thieu, had authorized the supply of arms to Lon Nol, and insisted on a new internal caption—"No-Dis Khmer"—designed to prevent distribution of top-secret cables about Cambodia to the Department's Cambodian experts. It remained in force until after the invasion. In the Pentagon the Vietnam Task Force, the group principally concerned with Vietnamization, was not consulted, perhaps because earlier in the month it—like the CIA—had decided that an invasion would make no long-term difference.

The main policy-making body now was WASSAG, but Secretary Laird's representative, Warren Nutter, was forbidden to attend some of its crucial meetings. "Only Kissinger and Nixon really knew what was going on," says one of Kissinger's staff. This is a little exaggerated; Nixon was also taking advice from Attorney General John Mitchell and from his friend Bebe Rebozo.

On the twenty-third, Nixon began to suggest that if the South Vietnamese were to be sent into some of the sanctuaries, it might be worth sending American troops into others. He called Kissinger, who was at the home of Senator J. William Fulbright, Chairman of the Senate Foreign Relations Committee, to ask for plans for such attacks by the following day. Kissinger told the Senator nothing of this. The next morning, he and Nixon met with Helms, Admiral Thomas Moorer, representing General Wheeler, the Chairman of the Joint Chiefs, and Helms's deputy, General Robert Cushman. The proposed target for an American attack was Base Area 352 and Area 353 in the Fish Hook section of the border, north of the Parrot's Beak. Area 353 was the Breakfast site, where Abrams had claimed to locate COSVN over a year earlier. Area 352 was Dinner. Since the bombing had begun, the two locations had been plastered with about 29,000 tons of bombs, but even so, Abrams claimed that COSVN was still in place, and some United States officers continued to conjure visions of a Communist Pentagon East, telling the gullible that COSVN was a reinforced-concrete bunker, 29 feet underground, that housed about 5,000 officials and technicians. *Newsweek*, among others, believed and reported it. So did Nixon.

Laird was not at this discussion on the twenty-fourth, and according to William Watts of Kissinger's staff, who was present, Admiral Moorer asked what he should relay back to the Secretary. He was informed that he was attending the meeting as the President's military adviser not as the representative of the Chairman of the Chiefs; he was to tell Laird nothing. Kissinger, however, phoned Laird to ask for plans of attack on the two bases. Laird's ignorance of the President's intentions is clear from the fact that his main concern at that time was to limit the number of American personnel that would accompany the South Vietnamese invasion of the Parrot's Beak. He had just sent General Wheeler a long list of questions to be put to Abrams; he said, "It is absolutely essential that we have *no* U.S. personnel involved in the initial phases or so called 'first wave' of the operation . . . It is likewise essential that *no* U.S. ground advisers be introduced into Cambodia at any time during the operation." Wheeler sent Laird's remarks to Abrams with suggestions as to how to deflect the Secretary's concern.

At the same time, however, Laird was beginning to believe that, by its requests, and by such questions as "How can you be absolutely certain that ARVN alone can do the job?" the White House was deliberately encouraging the Joint Chiefs and Abrams to argue that United States troops were essential. In an attempt to dampen White House enthusiasm, Laird suggested that Kissinger seek Congressional reaction to the idea of American forces invading a neutral nation. Instead, Kissinger and Nixon chatted informally with John C. Stennis, the Chairman of the Senate Armed Forces Committee, a Vietnam warrior who could be expected to endorse the plan but who had no constitutional authority alone to approve it.*

Laird's concern seems to have been warranted. Abrams now sent a proposal for an American attack on Base Area 352/353, to coincide with the South Vietnamese invasion of the Parrot's Beak. Wheeler replied that he was sympathetic, but "It is unlikely that we would be authorized to employ U.S. forces alone, except *in extremis*. An all-out attack on Phnom Penh would be an example. Therefore, recommend you not surface proposal at this time. Suggest you continue to march with planning for joint operations in 352/353 area but have in your hip pocket, on U.S. Eyes Only basis, suitable unilateral plans for extreme contingency. Warm regards."

On the evening of April 24, Henry Kissinger summoned his so-called "house doves"—William Watts, Roger Morris, Tony Lake, Larry Lynn and Winston Lord—to a staff meeting in his office. Its purpose was to discuss American options in Cambodia. Of these five, only Lord remained with Kissinger after the invasion.

Kissinger claimed that the encounter was "stormy and emotional"; but, in retrospect, Roger Morris felt that "not for the first or last time a policy in Indochina that warranted screaming was too gently opposed." If so, it was in part because Kissinger managed not to reveal exactly what was planned, still less what was being contemplated. With great skill he

---

* When Georges Bidault asked John Foster Dulles for United States air support around Dien Bien Phu in 1954, Dulles replied that the President could not authorize a single airstrike without Congressional approval. This was not mere diplomatic flimflam; Admiral Arthur Radford, the Chairman of the Joint Chiefs, had been pressing for just a strike and was even prepared to consider the use of nuclear weapons. But Eisenhower decided that there would be no United States commitment to Indochina without specific agreements with the French and the British and, more importantly, without complete Congressional support. The difference between the Eisenhower/Dulles approach and the Nixon/Kissinger attitude is instructive. The first pair could act as true conservatives or strict constructionists.

conveyed the impression that this was an entirely South Vietnamese show with, at most, a few American spotter planes helping out.

Nonetheless, Kissinger was made aware that at least four of his staff considered any attack on Cambodia disastrous. Lord said nothing, but Kissinger's Special Assistant, Tony Lake, told him it would represent an extension of the war that would cause real problems both in Cambodia and at home; William Watts saw it as part of the escalation discussed in September 1969, leading inexorably to an invasion of Laos and then to the bombing of Haiphong as well; Morris said that no one had any idea what North Vietnamese intentions were, and Lynn felt that the risks outweighed all possible gains and that salvation could be found, if at all, only on the fields of South Vietnam. He thought that resources should be concentrated on improving South Vietnamese provincial governments and local forces. Lynn's were the only arguments that seemed to impress Kissinger, because, Kissinger said later, he talked in terms of the military aspects of the invasion rather than emotion, law, morality or public opinion.

General Westmoreland, in his memoirs, asserts that Kissinger pressed for the invasion. Certainly he did not exercise the independence of his office; once it was clear that Nixon was interested more in the views of John Mitchell and Bebe Rebozo than in those of Rogers or Laird, he made little protest. As a result Kissinger's stakes in the invasion were high, and Nixon made this clear in a number of ways. One evening the President called to discuss the plans. As usual, Kissinger had one of his staff on the extension to take notes for history; this time it was William Watts. Nixon seemed drunk and said, "Wait a minute—Bebe has something to say to you." Rebozo came onto the line: "The President wants you to know if this doesn't work, Henry, it's your ass." "Ain't that right, Bebe?" slurred Nixon. There was some truth in this. By declining to try to argue the President out of invading Cambodia, Kissinger was pitting himself against both Rogers and Laird, and was committing his future influence to at least the appearance of success.

In Saigon, Abrams drew up a plan for a combined American-South Vietnamese assault on Base Areas 352-353—"Operation Shoemaker." Because of the hastiness of the request and the demands for secrecy, the General was not able to make very detailed preparations. The intelligence officers on the Cambodian Desk, ignorant of the proposal, could not be asked for an assessment. No one counted the number of bridges on the roads into Cambodia, and two days before the invasion the Operational Staff did not know the length of the frontier between Cambodia and South Vietnam. Aerial intelligence on North Vietnamese troop movements inside Cambodia was far from accurate. Neither Mike Rives nor Lon Nol was allowed to know of the plan, so no coordination with the Cambodians could be arranged.

As a result, Abrams' plan for the American invasion, cabled on April 26, one day before the South Vietnamese invasion was due to begin, was little more than a revision of previous JCS proposals, and it lacked a full account of Communist deployments since the end of March. When Kissinger asked Larry Lynn to review it, Lynn was horrified by its brevity and sloppiness. He realized that basic questions relating to the effect on South Vietnam and on Vietnamization, the disposition of air resources and so on, had hardly been posed, let alone answered. No one from the National Security Council had been dispatched to Phnom Penh to examine the situation on the ground. The few reports that did come in were from Mike Rives, who had very little idea of what was happening in the eastern provinces. To the fury of the White House, he reported a Cambodian claim that the Chinese People's Liberation Army was marching south from Yunan province through Laos. Nixon cursed Rives, but he sent no one he trusted to make an assessment.

In the past, Lynn had usually found Kissinger rather meticulous. On this operation astonishingly little analysis had been done. Lynn sat by himself in the Situation Room studying the plan, and listing questions on a yellow pad. When he had finished, Kissinger passed them on to the Joint Chiefs; but Lynn did not have the impression that Kissinger considered them urgent. It seemed, in fact, that the decision had already been taken.

Throughout this period, the White House was assuring reporters that the administration hoped that the rather ambiguous Soviet proposal for another convocation of the Geneva Conference would succeed. But since Premier Kosygin had rebuffed Sihanouk, and since the Prince was now in Peking, the extent of Soviet influence seems questionable. Peking was already dominating the growth of resistance to Lon Nol.

Over April 24–25, the Chinese sponsored a conference near Canton attended by Sihanouk; Prince Souphanouvong, leader of the Pathet Lao; Nguyen Huu Tho, President of the National Liberation Front; and North Vietnamese Prime Minister Pham Van Dong. The conference pledged all

four revolutionary movements to joint action against "the imperialists."
Chou En-lai attended the final session to give it his endorsement. Nonetheless, the Chinese had still not wholly committed themselves to Sihanouk, and in Phnom Penh Chinese officials were still trying to persuade
Lon Nol that he should accommodate the Viet Cong in the border areas.
As men and arms began to flow from Saigon, and as, in Nixon's words,
the border areas were "softened up" by even more B-52 attacks to "convey our concern," the possibility of accommodation in Indochina became
more and more remote. In Washington, Nixon saw *Patton* again. He
seemed to Rogers to be "a walking ad for that movie."

In the last few days before the launching of Operation Shoemaker a
series of tense meetings was held in the White House. On the morning of
the twenty-seventh, Nixon met with Laird and Rogers. Only then did it
become clear to them that he was on the verge of committing United
States troops to the Fish Hook, with the approval of General Abrams.
Rogers wondered if Abrams was simply telling the President what he
wanted to hear. Nixon then drafted a back-channels cable to ask Abrams
to repeat his views directly to the White House. Subsequently, this was
presented as an attempt to get at the "unvarnished truth." Its inevitable
effect was to encourage Abrams to ask for everything the President
seemed prepared to offer. Only a few days back neither he nor the Chiefs
had expected the use of United States troops to be part of "Presidential
policy"; they had been ready to invade the sanctuaries with the ARVN
alone. Now, given the choice, there was no reason for Abrams—or any
other commander—to ask for less rather than more. He confirmed that
United States troops would increase the chances of success.

Nixon made his final decision to send in American troops next morning,
the twenty-eighth. He subsequently explained to Nelson Rockefeller, "I
sat right here with two cabinet officers and my national security adviser,
and I asked what we needed to do. The recommendation of the Department of Defense was the most pusillanimous little nit-picker I ever saw.
'Just bite off the Parrot's Beak.' I said you are going to have a hell of an
uproar at home if you bite off the Beak. If you are going to take the heat,
go for all the marbles. . . . I have made some bad decisions, but a good
one was this: When you bite the bullet, bite it hard—go for the big play."

It was Kissinger, Presidential Assistant H. R. Haldeman and Attorney
General John Mitchell—not the Secretaries of State and Defense—whom
he informed first. Not one Congressional committee knew anything about
it. Indeed, the day before, at a closed hearing, Rogers had given the
Senate Foreign Relations Committee no hint that any such action was

contemplated. The Senators, however, had explicitly warned him that the Senate was opposed to substantial aid to Lon Nol.

When the White House told him the news, General Wheeler sent Abrams a cable which began, "Higher authority has authorized certain military actions to protect U.S. forces operating in South Vietnam. Authorization is granted for conduct of a combined U.S./GVN operation against Base Area 352/353." Attacks could be mounted up to 30 kilometers into Cambodia. Only now did Kissinger ask his staff to begin to consider all the implications of the use of American troops. William Watts was chosen to coordinate the NSC staff work on the invasion, but he went to Kissinger's office to tell him he objected to the policy and could not work on it. Kissinger replied, "Your views represent the cowardice of the Eastern Establishment." This, on top of the strain of recent weeks, was too much for Watts. He strode toward Kissinger, who retreated behind his desk. Watts stalked out to write a letter of resignation. In the White House Situation Room he was confronted by Alexander Haig, who, by contrast, was delighted by Nixon's decision. Haig barked at Watts that he could not resign: "You've just had an order from your commander in chief." "Fuck you, Al," Watts said, "I just did."

For Haig, to refuse any order was unthinkable, and he was disgusted when two more of the staff, Roger Morris and Tony Lake, wrote a joint letter of resignation. In it they put forward their objections to the invasion and added that "the reasons for our resignation, involving an increasing alienation from this Administration also predate and go beyond the Cambodian problem. We wished to inform you now, before the public reaction to our Cambodian policy, so that it will be clear that our decision was not made after the fact and as a result of those consequences." They handed the letter to Haig but, fearful of driving Kissinger into one of his rages at this difficult time, they suggested it be delivered only after the invasion had begun.

Even the ordinary White House staff was somewhat alarmed. Kissinger was asked at a meeting whether the invasion did not expand the war. "Look," he replied, "we're not interested in Cambodia. We're only interested in it not being used as a base." The wider justifications he cited dealt with superpower relations. "We're trying to shock the Soviets into calling a Conference," he said, "and we can't do this by appearing weak." William Safire asked if it did not breach the Nixon Doctrine, and Kissinger replied, "We wrote the goddam doctrine, we can change it." At the end of the meeting Haig stood up and shouted, "The basic substance of all this is that we have to be tough." That was indeed a point.

Another, as Kissinger instructed his staff, was that "We are all the President's men."

Nixon disregarded advice that Abrams simply make a routine announcement of the invasion from Saigon. He was apparently determined to make the most of the occasion and he worked on his speech himself until 4:15 A.M. on the morning of April 30, the day it was to be delivered. A few hours later he called Haldeman and Kissinger into his office and, slumped in his chair, he read it to them. They had only minor comments.

It was much later in the afternoon that the speech was taken over to Laird and Rogers. They were horrified. "This will cause an uproar," Rogers told his staff, and Laird called Kissinger to suggest fundamental changes. Under his prodding Kissinger did now suggest some; Nixon rejected almost all of them. The final speech was very much his own, and as delivered, it ranks with "Checkers," the 1962 "last" press conference, and the 1974 "farewell" to the White House staff, as among the key Nixon texts. As Jonathan Schell, of *The New Yorker*, pointed out, it reflected his attitudes toward himself, his place in America and America's place in the world, and it explains much about why he acted as he did. It had almost nothing to do with the realities of Cambodia.

Ignoring Menu, Nixon began with the lie that the United States had "scrupulously respected" Cambodia's neutrality for the last five years and had not "moved against" the sanctuaries. This falsehood was repeated by Kissinger in his background briefings to the press. That same evening he told reporters that the Communists had been using Cambodia for five years but, "As long as Sihanouk was in power in Cambodia we had to weigh the benefits in long-range historical terms of Cambodian neutrality as against any temporary military advantages and we made no efforts during the first fifteen months of this administration to move against the sanctuary." The next day he said of Sihanouk's rule, "We had no incentive to change it. We made no effort to change it. We were surprised by the development. One reason why we showed such great restraint against the base areas was in order not to change this situation."

In his announcement of the invasion, Nixon stated that his action was taken "not for the purpose of expanding the war into Cambodia, but for the purpose of ending the war in Vietnam"; he would give aid to Cambodia, but only to enable it "to defend its neutrality and not for the purpose of making it an active belligerent on one side or the other."

He promised that in the Fish Hook area American and South Vietnamese troops "will attack the headquarters for the entire Communist military operation in South Vietnam"; Laird had repeatedly told him that except in the wider reaches of military fantasy, no such "key control center," as Nixon put it, existed. He alleged that "the enemy . . . is concentrating his main forces in the sanctuaries, where they are building up to launch massive attacks on our forces and those of South Vietnam." Melvin Laird had, in fact, reluctantly approved the invasion only because he was sure that the movement of the Communists westward *out of* the sanctuaries would render United States casualties tolerably low. Nixon then "noted"—incorrectly—that "there has been a great deal of discussion with regard to this decision I have made."

More important than the specific falsehoods are the illusions upon which Nixon's speech was based. Underlying it was the notion that there is always some unknown but awaited threat, in anticipation of which current actions must be formed and judged. "Plaintive diplomatic protests" were no longer enough; alone, the President said, they would simply destroy American credibility in areas of the world, "where only the power of the United States deters aggression." The destruction of the sanctuaries would save American lives in Vietnam, but it was more important for the service it could render elsewhere.

The President's image that night, on television screens across America, was not comforting. His tone was strident, his words were slurred and he mopped the sweat from his upper lip. His emotion was understandable, for his vision of the world was truly a nightmare. "We live in an age of anarchy. We see mindless attacks on all the great institutions which have been created by free civilization in the last five hundred years. Even here in the United States, great universities are being systematically destroyed. Small nations all over the world find themselves under attack from within and from without." It was to these threats that the United States and he, the President, must respond. "If, when the chips are down, the world's most powerful nation, the United States of America, acts like a pitiful, helpless giant, the forces of totalitarianism and anarchy will threaten free nations and free institutions throughout the world."

Nixon introduced himself, as he so often did, into the discussion by promising that "I would rather be a one-term President and do what I believe is right than to be a two-term President at the cost of seeing America become a second-rate power and to see this nation accept the first defeat in its proud 190-year history." He compared his action with the "great decisions" made by Woodrow Wilson in the First World War, Franklin Roosevelt in the Second, Eisenhower in Korea, and Kennedy during the missile crisis. "It is not our power but our will and character that is being tested tonight," he intoned. Would America have the strength to stand up to "a group"—by which he presumably meant the entire North Vietnamese population and the Viet Cong together with their supporters in Moscow, in Peking and across the world—that flouted its President's will? "If we fail to meet this challenge, all other nations will be on notice that despite its overwhelming power the United States, when a real crisis comes, will be found wanting."

Despite the secrecy and the rhetoric, this was not, it seems, a *real crisis*. Cambodia was a test, a trial through which Nixon was putting the American people, let alone the Cambodians, so that if a real crisis did come one day, the world would beware. "This is not an invasion of Cambodia," Nixon insisted. (Officials were ordered to call it an "incursion" instead.) At one level this was just another lie, but at another it was true. Cambodia was a testing ground for United States resolve.

Arthur M. Schlesinger, Jr., has pointed out that Nixon's view of the world recalls that of the Romans, as Joseph Schumpeter described it. "There was no corner of the known world where some interest was not alleged to be in danger or under actual attack. If the interests were not Roman, they were those of Rome's allies; and if Rome had no allies, the allies would be invented." This was precisely what happened in Cambodia. United States troops were now committed to its forests, rubber plantations and villages to assure the world that the giant was in full training for the ultimate test.

The law was not relevant. Then, and subsequently, Nixon justified his action in terms of his responsibility as Commander in Chief to protect American troops, and he explained his refusal to consult Congress by citing Kennedy's secret moves at the time of the Cuban missile crisis. Afterward the White House asked the Justice Department to prepare a legal justification. The task fell to William Rehnquist, an assistant attorney general, whom Nixon later elevated to the Supreme Court. His arguments are not impressive. He asserted that the Commander in Chief clause of the Constitution was "a grant of substantive authority" that allowed all Presidents to send troops "into conflict with foreign powers on their own initiative." In fact; the clause only gave the President such powers as the commanding officer of the armed forces would have had if he were not President. Rehnquist suggested that the invasion was only a very mild assertion of Presidential prerogative.*

* During the Algerian war of independence the United States rejected France's claimed right to attack a Tunisian town inhabited by Algerian guerrillas, and in 1964 Adlai Stevenson, at the U.N., condemned Britain for assaulting a Yemeni town used as a base by insurgents attacking Aden. Even Israel had frequently been criticized by the United States

Mike Rives and the U.S. mission in Phnom Penh learned of the invasion by listening to Nixon's speech on Voice of America. Rives hurried around to tell Lon Nol what was happening in the eastern provinces of his country. Lon Nol was shocked. He declared publicly that the operation violated Cambodian territorial integrity. All that day United States and South Vietnamese troops, tanks and planes churned across the earth and the air into the provinces of Ratanakiri, Mondolkiri, Kompong Cham and Svay Rieng. Reporters flying westward by helicopter to cover the invasion noticed that the unmarked border was easily discerned. On the South Vietnamese side the buffalo grazed calmly, well used to the noise of the war above and around them. In Cambodia the animals ran into each other and scattered, terrified.

---

for attacks on enemy bases outside its territory. Now Rehnquist claimed that the United States Commander in Chief has powers under international law that French, Israeli and British political leaders did not have. Arthur Schlesinger noted that rather more relevant was Marshall's rule that "an army marching into the dominions of another sovereign may justly be considered as committing an act of hostility; and, if not opposed by force, acquires no privilege by its irregular and improper conduct." When Herndon advised Lincoln that the President could invade a neighbor if this were necessary to repel invasion, Lincoln had replied "Study to see if you can fix *any limit* to his power in this respect, after you have given him so much as you propose."

CHAPTER 10

The Outrage

COSVN WAS never discovered. The American troops plowed past its supposed site in the Fish Hook and through the plantations and villages beyond. Commanders were astonished by the lack of opposition as their tanks smashed jagged swathes through the trees and as landing zones for helicopters were blasted clear. Communist troops were hardly to be seen.

The small town of Snuol became the first of scores of Cambodian towns to be destroyed by the war. Until the second squadron of the 11th Armored Cavalry Regiment arrived at its outskirts on May 3, about two thousand people had lived quietly there, tapping rubber on the trees around. When the cavalry came under fire, their commander, Lieutenant Colonel Grail Brookshire, ordered his tank crews to fire their 90-mm. guns straight into the town and called in airstrikes to discourage further resistance. After twenty-four hours of bombardment, Brookshire judged Snuol safe for his men, and the tanks moved into the center. Only seven bodies could be seen, four of them Cambodian civilians. A small girl lay near the ruins of shops. When Brookshire was asked by reporters why the town had to be destroyed, he replied "We had no choice. We had to take it. This was a hub of North Vietnamese activity."

As they drove past shattered shops soldiers leaped off their tanks to kick down doors that still stood, and they looted the town. Grail Brookshire later recalled the event, laughingly describing himself as "The Butcher of Snuol." But he admonished a reporter, "You guys said my men systematically looted the town. My God, my men couldn't do anything that was systematic.''

The destruction of Snuol was repeated in Mimot, a much larger plantation town, the village of Sre Khtum, and dozens of villages and hamlets. The annual monsoon rains turned the red clay to clinging mud, but American and South Vietnamese troops advanced, fir. ug and burning whatever might be of use to a returning enemy, capturing caches of rice, ammunition and arms, driving the residents, Vietnamese and Cambodian, before them. The Americans found it almost impossible to separate friend from foe, and the South Vietnamese made no effort to do so. They plunged into Cambodia raping, looting, burning in retaliation for the murder of Vietnamese in Cambodia the month before. Their behavior persuaded many of those Vietnamese who still lived there that it would not be wise of them to stay, and during the first two weeks of the invasion about fifty thousand of them fled, to sit listlessly under tents in the overcrowded refugee camps of South Vietnam. ''We cannot possibly accommodate them,'' said South Vietnam's Minister for Refugees. Soon the numbers had doubled.

The pattern of the next five years in Cambodian history could be detected in the weeks that followed the invasion. Relationships and attitudes that if not destructive in themselves, were very destructive in combination, were formed almost at once.

On the ground the invasion pushed the battlefields farther westward into the heavily populated villages and rice fields around and beyond the Mekong river. The Lon Nol government proved itself unable to defend the country, and it entered into a dependence upon foreign aid that would eventually choke it. In Peking, Sihanouk was now encouraged by his new sponsors to form a government in exile containing a preponderance of his recent enemies from the Khmer Rouge. In Washington the manner of the invasion—its secrecy and Nixon's rhetoric—excited widespread protest, locked the White House into support of its aims, tended to exclude State and Pentagon more than ever, and pushed the Congress into unprecedented opposition. It was now that Nixon's misapprehensions about government were to have their most destructive impact, at home and abroad, both publicly and in secret.

The morning after the invasion, before its full impact on America was clear, Nixon drove with Kissinger across the Potomac for a briefing at the Pentagon. His remarks in the corridor about ''bums blowing up campuses," and "get rid of this war, there'll be another one," were published, and they fired the rage that was beginning to spread among students everywhere. His conduct inside the briefing was even more alarming. The Joint Chiefs were there, as was the Secretary of Defense; they had assembled to inform the Commander in Chief of the progress of the operation. To their consternation, Nixon did not seem interested. Agitated, he cut the briefing short and began an emotional harangue, using what one of those present calls "locker-room language." He repeated over and over again that he was, "going to clean up those sanctuaries," and he declared, "You have to electrify people with bold decisions. Bold decisions make history. Like Teddy Roosevelt charging up San Juan Hill—a small event but traumatic, and people took notice." General Westmoreland tried to warn him that the sanctuaries could not really be cleaned up; within a month the monsoon would make the area impassable. (Laird later thanked Westmoreland for trying to introduce a note of realism.) Nixon was unimpressed and threatened to withdraw resources from Europe if they were needed in Indochina. "Let's go blow the hell out of them," he shouted, while the Chiefs, Laird and Kissinger sat mute with embarrassment and concern.

From all over the country Senator George McGovern received about $100,000 in contributions to buy television time to reply to Nixon. And, in Vietnam, Major Hal Knight, who was still burning the true records of the continuing Menu missions, was appalled at the President's assertion that until now the United States had respected Cambodia's neutrality. The invasion and its aftermath increased his disillusionment with the Army and later led to his decision to resign and eventually to reveal the Menu story. For Robert Drinan, a Jesuit priest running for the House of Representatives in the Fourth District of Massachusetts, the invasion was an enormous boon: "It turned the district around," he said. He won the seat, and when Knight testified before Congress about Menu in July 1973, it was Drinan who, to the consternation of his more cautious colleagues, asserted that the President had been waging an illegal war and introduced an early motion to impeach.

After the invasion a third of American colleges and universities closed or were disrupted as the rejuvenated Vietnam Moratorium Committee called for "immediate massive protests." The President reacted belligerently in both public and private. He assured his staff that the fact that few enemy had been found was not important; it was the infrastructure of the sanctuaries that he was after. His language was crude: "It takes ten months to build up this complex and we're tearing the living bejeesus out

of it. Anything that walked is gone after that barrage and the B-52 raids."
He abused members of Congress who criticized the invasion, and he
declared, "Don't worry about divisiveness. Having drawn the sword,
don't take it out—stick it in hard . . . Hit 'em in the gut. No defensive-
ness."

On many campuses the Reserve Officers Training Corps buildings were
attacked or sacked. One, Kent State in Ohio, already had a connection
with Cambodia: Sihanouk had once been given a fine welcome there by
students who listened, raptly, to his denunciations of the American press.
Afterward the Prince wrote that "My short stay at Kent somewhat con-
soled me for all the disappointments we have had with America and the
Americans." Now Kent and Cambodia were to be forever linked. After
the ROTC building was burned, Governor James Rhodes, taking his cue
from Nixon and Agnew, declared that he would "eradicate" rioters and
demonstrators there—"They're worse than the Brown Shirts and the
Communist element and also the nightriders and the vigilantes. They're
the worst type of people we have in America." The next day the National
Guard that he had ordered onto the campus turned and, in a volley, shot
fifteen students, four of them dead.

The White House reaction to the killings was that they were predictable. So was the response. Over the next few days between 75,000 and
100,000 protestants converged on Washington. Buses were drawn up all
around the White House, and Alexander Haig told one journalist that
troops had been secretly brought into the basement in case they were
needed to repel invasion. It was a trying time. When Walter Hickel,
Secretary of the Interior, warned Nixon (in a letter that was leaked to the
press) that history showed that "youth in its protest must be heard," he
was fired. But Nixon did seem to realize, for a time, that concessions
must be made.

The most important—which made nonsense of any military rationale
for the invasion—was to declare that United States troops would penetrate only twenty-one miles into Cambodia and would be withdrawn by
June 30. Then on May 8 the President gave a rather low-key press conference at which he identified his goals with those of the students. During
that night he made over fifty telephone calls, including eight to Kissinger,
seven to Haldeman, and one each to Norman Vincent Peale and Billy
Graham. After one hour's sleep he started playing Rachmaninoff's First
Piano Concerto and then at 5 A.M. on May 9 took his Cuban valet, Manolo
Sanchez, to talk to students who were holding vigil at the Lincoln Memorial. It was a stilted encounter. Nixon tried to assure them that he and

they were really fired by the same purposes, talking to them about surfing, football and the way travel could broaden minds. Egil Krogh, an aide to Presidential assistant John Ehrlichman, followed Nixon to the Memorial and was deeply moved by the episode. This, he felt, was a President for whom he would do almost anything. Nixon himself had fewer illusions. When he finally got back to the White House after a detour to the House of Representatives, where he had his valet deliver a speech to the empty chamber, he said, "I doubt if that got over." Indeed, his soft approach soon wore thin. A few days later, as he leafed through photographs of two more students shot dead protesting the invasion at black Jackson State College in Mississippi, he asked its black president, "Look, what are we going to do to get more respect for the police from our young people?"

Kissinger later confided that Nixon was on the edge of a nervous breakdown in May 1970. According to Nixon, Kissinger also had doubts about the "incursion" after Kent State. Nixon says he reminded Kissinger of Lot's wife: "I said Henry, we've done it. Never look back." In public Kissinger took the advice. This was a trying moment, but it was one that required firmness. "They'd driven one President from office," he later remarked. "They'd broken Johnson's will. Were they trying to break another President?" Whether Kissinger thought this was the real problem, he realized, according to Nixon's speechwriter, William Safire, that the invasion offered him perhaps a unique opportunity, in Safire's words, for "winning on another front: the battle between his National Security Council and William Rogers' State Department."

As far as the White House was concerned, Rogers had not distinguished himself by his advice or attitude before the invasion; Melvin Laird had done little better. Laird issued public denials of the reported rift between him and the White House on the invasion. But within the circle of his own staff he expressed his dismay. At one of his daily Vietnamization meetings he complained that he had been led to understand that the invasion of the Fish Hook would be principally a South Vietnamese effort. In fact, there were now 12,000 American and only 6,000 Vietnamese troops there. He was concerned that Kissinger was running WASSAG without proper consultation with his office.

On May 2, the White House learned that William Beecher, of *The New York Times,* had still another story that the President did not wish to see published. He was about to reveal that just before the invasion Nixon had resumed the bombing of North Vietnam. Kissinger made several calls to *New York Times* editors to pressure them into dropping the story. He failed. Alexander Haig called Robert Haynes, the FBI agent who had brought over previous transcripts of taps for Kissinger and Nixon to read. According to an FBI memo, Haig said the new leak had been "nailed down to a couple of people," but he asked for four taps, on "the highest authority"—that is, the President himself. Among them, for the first time, was William Beecher. Haig also asked for a tap on William Sullivan, the Deputy Assistant Secretary of State for Asian Affairs, and that the tap on Laird's military assistant, Colonel Robert Pursley, which had first been placed in May 1969, then lifted, be replaced. And it was now that Richard Pedersen, Rogers' assistant, was tapped. For the first time, Haig asked that office as well as home telephones be tapped.

Pursley's tap, and Pedersen's, can have had little to do with plugging leaks. Pedersen had, on White House orders, been cut off from all information regarding Cambodia since mid-April. When he obtained his file from the FBI Pedersen says he was convinced that the White House's purpose was to catch him or his superior, William Rogers, in an indiscretion or criticism of the President's policy that could be used against them. It could apply to Pursley and Laird as well. William Safire has pointed out that the two taps "enabled Kissinger to preview the opinions of their bosses, Laird and Rogers. This gave Henry a bureaucratic advantage, to say the least." (On May 12 Haig again called the FBI and said Kissinger wanted two more taps—on Tony Lake, who had submitted his resignation to the National Security Council, and Winston Lord, Kissinger's loyal Special Assistant. The taps were installed, but from now on the FBI summaries were sent to Haldeman.)

Rogers' misgivings about the invasion were reflected in the ranks of the State Department, where virtually no one knew what was happening in Cambodia. Two hundred and fifty foreign-service officers signed a petition of protest, and sent it to Rogers. The story leaked to *The New York Times,* and Clark Mollenhoff, a reporter from the *Des Moines Register,* who had become, for a time, a diligent Nixon aide, called Pedersen to demand that the list of signatories be sent over to the White House. Although he was angered by the demonstration, Rogers refused; he knew the effect this would have on the careers of those involved.

Within a few days of the invasion, columnists and diplomatic correspondents were speculating on the division between the White House and Rogers. Kissinger complained to Safire that the foreign-service establishment was taking advantage of Rogers' vanity to circulate the story that his reasonableness toward Hanoi was being overruled. Kissinger himself saw clearly that his duty lay in giving the fullest support possible to the President in his hour of need. "We are all the President's men," he repeated, "and we must act accordingly." His loyalty and the fervor with which he tried to rally morale was, for his colleagues, very moving. "Henry was a fighter, a real inspiring leader," John Ehrlichman later recalled.

Inevitably, there was a price to be paid; total loyalty to the President on this issue was not compatible with the intimate relationship that Kissinger had hoped to maintain, and till now had largely succeeded at, with his liberal friends at Harvard. On May 8 a group of them, led by Thomas Schelling, descended upon him. (They discovered, to their embarrassment, that Kissinger had provided them all lunch at his expense; it was not a very convivial occasion.) Schelling began by saying he should explain who they were.

Kissinger interrupted, "I know who you are . . . you're all good friends from Harvard University."

"No," said Schelling, "we're a group of people who have completely lost confidence in the ability of the White House to conduct our foreign policy, and we have come to tell you so. We are no longer at your disposal as personal advisers."

Each of the men around the table—among them, Richard Neustadt, author of *Presidential Power;* Adam Yarmolinsky, Professor of Law and adviser to both Kennedy and Johnson; Francis Bator, who had worked on Johnson's National Security Staff—put his objections to Kissinger. They pointed out that the invasion could be used by anyone else in the world as a precedent for invading another country in order, for example, to clear out terrorists. Schelling told him, "As we see it there are two possibilities. Either, one, the President didn't understand when he went into Cambodia that he was invading another country; or, two, he did understand. We just don't know which one is scarier." Kissinger said he thought he could persuade them all was well if he could talk to them off the record. They refused to be drawn in; they shook hands and left.

Others of his friends suggested that Kissinger should resign, as his aides, Lake, Morris, Watts and Larry Lynn had done, but he brushed aside all such demands. "Suppose I went in and told the President I was resigning," he was reported as saying. "He could have a heart attack and you'd have Spiro Agnew as President. Do you want that? No? So don't keep telling me to resign."

In fact, though the public and the private denunciations of his former colleagues and the criticism of the "Eastern establishment," together with the defection of the "liberals" on his staff, may have been personally painful to Kissinger, professionally they were useful. If he had, as he sometimes claimed, been concerned to demonstrate to men like Mitchell, Rebozo, Haldeman and Ehrlichman that his loyalty, as well as his intellect, had been transferred with other baggage from Harvard to the White House, it was the invasion of Cambodia that enabled him to do so. This was, from the start, the President's battlefield and his chief foreign-policy adviser never discouraged him. To judge by the interest he subsequently showed in Cambodia, Kissinger did not share Nixon's enthusiasm for this new theater of war. But his unstinting support during the invasion and willing participation in decisions that were made from April 1970 on helped to ensure the final eclipse of William Rogers. As the war spread through Cambodia, Henry Kissinger's control over policy was underwritten.

Tom Charles Huston, a former Army Intelligence officer, was something of an intellectual in the Nixon White House, and his ambition, according to John Dean, was "to become the domestic equivalent of Henry Kissinger." Huston served on the White House's Internal Security Committee, which kept in touch with the police on demonstrations. He kept a scrambler telephone locked in his safe, and he studied Communism. Detente, however, was of little interest to Huston. Since the summer of 1969, at John Ehrlichman's request, he had been examining the role of foreign Communists in United States campus disorders.

To his disgust, neither the CIA nor the FBI had been able to discover such links. Huston was sure that this was because of the pusillanimity with which they approached the task—even J. Edgar Hoover was now reluctant to allow FBI "black bag jobs" and wiretaps without specific authorization from the Attorney General, and he refused absolutely to cooperate with the CIA. Huston was placed in charge of internal security affairs in the White House, and in April 1970 he persuaded Haldeman that the President must order the country's intelligence chiefs to draw up a coordinated plan for gathering intelligence on domestic dissidents. The meeting, fixed for early May, was postponed by the howls of anger that greeted the invasion.

His task, Huston later testified, became "even more important" after the invasion and Kent State. H. R. Haldeman later confirmed this, saying that "Kent State marked a turning point for Nixon, a beginning of his downhill slide toward Watergate." The protests over the invasion demonstrated as nothing else had ever done, Huston said, the need for controls upon, and information about, American protest. "We were sitting in the White House getting reports day in and day out of what was happening in the country in terms of the violence, the number of bombings, the assassination attempts, the sniping incidents—40,000 bombings, for example, in the month of May . . ." (*sic*).

The session Huston had suggested took place on June 5. Nixon met with Hoover, CIA Director Richard Helms, Vice-Admiral Noel Gaylor (Director of the National Security Agency), General Donald Bennett (Director of the Defense Intelligence Agency), and Haldeman, Ehrlichman and Huston. He showed no trace of the publicly conciliatory President who had tried to identify himself with the aims of the protestants. Speaking from a paper prepared by Huston, Nixon asserted that "hundreds, perhaps thousands, of Americans—mostly under thirty—are determined to destroy our society." They were "reaching out for the support—ideological and otherwise—of foreign powers." He complained about the quality of the intelligence that had so far been gathered, and appointed Hoover chairman of a new Inter Agency Committee on Intelligence. It was to have a staff working group, which would write a report on how better information could be gathered.

Hoover made his objections to the intrusion by Huston, "a hippie intellectual," very clear; but, goaded on by Huston, the working group did produce recommendations for the removal of almost all restraints on intelligence gathering. Many of its suggestions involved breaking the law. The other agency directors did not object, but when Hoover saw the more extreme options, he refused to sign the report unless his objections were typed onto each page as footnotes. This infuriated his colleagues, but eventually, to Huston's relief, they all signed the document and he carried it back to the White House.

Huston had a few good days. He informed Richard Helms that from now on everything to do with domestic intelligence and internal security was to be sent to his own "exclusive attention" in the White House, adding "Dr. Kissinger is aware of this new procedure." He then selected the most radical options in the ad-hoc committee's report and recommended their implementation to the President. "The Huston Plan," which Senator Sam Ervin of North Carolina, Chairman of the Select Committee on Presidential Campaign Activities, later described as evidence of a "Gestapo mentality," suggested that the intelligence community, with the authority of the President, should now be allowed to intercept and transcribe any international communication; read the mail; burgle homes; eavesdrop in any way on anyone considered a "threat to the internal security"; spy on student groups. Huston admitted to Nixon that "Covert [mail] coverage is illegal and there are serious risks involved" and that use of surreptitious entry "is clearly illegal; it amounts to burglary. It is also highly risky and could result in great embarrassment if exposed." But in both cases, he assured the President that the advantages outweighed the risks.

Nixon approved the plan, and though Hoover quickly managed to have it rescinded, the fact of the President's blessing was to be a key cause of his fall. The discovery of the plan in the summer of 1973 helped enormously to build such Congressional outrage that the legislature was finally able to force the White House to end the massive bombing of Cambodia, which was just beginning to spread as Huston formulated his proposals in summer 1970. It would become a crucial part of the impeachment proceedings. When, much later, Nixon was asked by David Frost to justify his action he blandly produced a new version of Presidential infallibility: "Well, when the President does it, that means that it is not illegal." *

Huston's rationalization resembled the reasons Henry Kissinger gave for the need to prolong the war as long as he thought it necessary to allow him to claim an "honorable" withdrawal. Huston thought of himself as a conservative but, as did Kissinger, he professed that the real threat to the United States was the rise of the reactionary right, and that the New Left would provoke every repressive demagogue in the United States. He argued that he and the intelligence community were protecting the country from its worst enemy, the far right, by "monitoring" its second-worst enemy, the New Left. As the Church committee put it, to Huston the plan was justified because it "would halt repression on the Right by stopping violence on the Left." †

After Huston's ambition "to become the domestic equivalent of Henry Kissinger" was thwarted, he came to realize that he had been wrong. He now believes that the sanctions of criminal law are a more appropriate

* After Nixon's resignation it emerged that the intelligence agencies had been undertaking most of these activities for years before 1970, without Presidential authorization.

† In similar vein Kissinger told a group of editors in Hartford, Connecticut, some months after the invasion, "It has been our conviction that if political decisions were to be made in the streets, the victors would not be upper-middle-class college kids, but some real tough guys. . . . The society which makes its decisions in this manner will sooner or later be driven towards some form of Caesarism in which the most brutal forces in the society take over. Therefore, we believe that what really was at stake here was not this President. What was at stake here was the problem of authority in this society altogether."

response to the threat of violence than unrestrained, illegal intelligence gathering, and he dismissed the right-wing backlash argument as specious. Henry Kissinger's attitude did not change. Long after the war ended he still called up the fear of the right not only to justify his decisions but also to refuse further discussion of Indochina. "The time has come to end the Vietnam War debate," he said on one occasion in 1977. "It could backfire, you know. If it continues, sooner or later the right wing will be heard from, too. And then we could have a very nasty controversy."

CHAPTER 11

The Doctrine

IN ITS first issue after the invasion *Time* magazine reported, "As he briefed White House staffers last week Henry Kissinger announced with a straight face that the Cambodians 'had sent in a request for enough stuff to equip an army of 200,000. We asked them to take it back and reconsider' Kissinger went on, 'and then they came back with a request for enough stuff to equip an army of 400,000.' " As so often, Kissinger's joke served to mask the truth. Within a year the Lon Nol army was being built, at Kissinger's insistence, into a force of 220,000 men.

At the time of the invasion Nixon declared, "The aid we will provide will be limited to the purpose of enabling Cambodia to defend its neutrality and not for the purpose of making it an active belligerent on one side or another." This was not the truth. The aid provided was designed almost entirely for the second purpose. As Kissinger told one WASSAG meeting that summer, "The President is determined to keep an anti-Communist government alive in Phnom Penh."

Alexander Haig was dispatched to Phnom Penh soon after the invasion. It was the first important solo mission that he had been entrusted with, a first opportunity to demonstrate his ability to act for the President in his own right rather than as Henry Kissinger's military assistant. (The State Department was not at first informed of the trip; when Marshall Green, the Assistant Secretary of State, heard of it he called Elliot Richardson and said, "We can't fight it but we can mitigate it . . . let's get one of our

161

best men on Cambodia to go along . . . Haig does not have the substance
. . . It would get the State Department into the action.") Haig would visit
Cambodia many times over the next three years. He was vital in defining
the relationship between the White House and Lon Nol, between the
White House and the United States embassy, between the White House
and reality.

United States military aid had already begun, secretly, in April, with
the supply of automatic rifles and several thousand Khmer Krom troops
from South Vietnam. Now Haig's mission was to decide not whether a
United States aid program should be extended, but how it could best be
implemented. The decision to support Lon Nol was, in one sense, implicit
in the decision to invade (or, rather, the invasion rendered aid almost
inevitable). The first of many reports on Cambodia by the Senate Foreign
Relations Committee pointed out that "Cambodia has now been linked
inextricably to the war in Vietnam and . . . the terms of reference of that
war have been permanently changed because its geographic area has been
expanded." Vietnamization was now on a wider stage.

After an inadequate briefing in Saigon (no one on Abrams' staff seemed
to have a complete idea of what was happening in Cambodia), Haig and
an official from State to whom Haig paid little attention, flew up to Phnom
Penh. John Court, from the NSC staff went to inspect the Cambodian
army in the field. Haig arrived at Pochentong airport in his battle fatigues,
to be met by the chargé, Mike Rives, who was dressed in his usual languid
style. Haig did not take to Rives, who has described himself as a "perfectly average" diplomat—not a popular species in the White House. He
is a rather mild, self-effacing type who, one of his colleagues says,
"would seem a stuffed shirt to a man like Haig, who is into *machismo*."
Like most foreigners in Phnom Penh, Rives and his staff were bewildered
by the speed with which the country disintegrated; communications, both
within Cambodia and to the outside world, were poor. His reporting of
the hectic events of March and April was often very good, but sometimes
he had been reduced to simply passing on Cambodian intelligence reports,
and these—as in the case of the advancing Chinese People's Liberation
Army—could be unreal.

Rives ran a low-key mission, suitable to the discreet presence that the
State Department had wished to maintain in Sihanouk's capital. He lived
in a small house near the Bassac river; the chancery was in the servants'
quarters in his garden. There was no air-conditioning, and the filing system consisted of cardboard boxes. A big metal container in the garden
was used as a safe. To Haig it was most unsuitable for an American

embassy and he made his distaste clear before he set off for his interview with Lon Nol.

It is normally considered courteous and efficient for the ambassador or head of mission to accompany any official visiting the rulers of the country to which he is accredited. Breaching this convention diminishes the status of the representative in the eyes of the host government. In the Nixon-Kissinger years, it was ignored whenever the State Department was to be excluded from policymaking. Haig had no intention of taking Rives to see Lon Nol, despite the fact that Rives spoke far better French than the major whom Haig had brought with him from Saigon as interpreter. Afterward Haig refused to tell Rives, State's representative or anyone else in the mission exactly what had passed between him and Lon Nol. Eventually, officials learned that the encounter was as critical as it was painful.

Lon Nol was clearly frightened by the forces unleashed by his move against Sihanouk. His original spontaneous reaction to the invasion had been to protest. He told an Asian diplomat, who told the U.S. Embassy, that he greatly regretted that the United States had not consulted Cambodia first. He wished that the Americans had blocked the Communists' westward escape route before attacking, instead of spreading them across Cambodia. (He did not seem to appreciate that Nixon was more interested in avoiding American casualties than in finding the North Vietnamese or that the invasion was actually *intended* to push the Communists away from South Vietnam's border.) The Cambodian leader told Haig that there was no way his small force could stop them. His country was in danger. Only the American army could help.

When he had finished talking, Haig began. He informed Lon Nol that President Nixon intended to limit the involvement of American forces in Cambodia. They would be withdrawn at the end of June. Then the President hoped to introduce a program of restricted economic and military aid.

As the implications of Haig's words for the future of Cambodia became clear to Lon Nol, he began to weep. Cambodia, he said, could never defend itself. Unable to control his emotions, he walked across to the window and stood there, his shoulders shaking, his face turned away from Haig. Haig then went across the room to try to comfort the General. He put his arm around his shoulder and promised him, through the interpreter, that President Nixon supported him and would give him what help he could, despite the political constraints in Washington.

By now, the attitude of the Congress was clear. The day after the

invasion the Senate Foreign Relations Committee, which reported telegrams running at eight to one against the adventure, demanded an audience with Nixon and approved a bill to repeal the Tonkin Gulf Resolution.* The Committee charged the President with usurping Congress'
war-making powers by neglecting to consult them before the invasion and
averred that he was "conducting a constitutionally unauthorized war in
Indochina." The White House declared that Nixon was acting on his
constitutional authority as Commander in Chief. On May 11 the Committee approved, over the administration's strenuous objections, an amendment proposed by Senator Frank Church and Senator Sherman Cooper
to the Foreign Military Sales Act, which restricted future operations in
Cambodia. In the modified form in which it was finally passed by the
Senate, "the Cooper-Church amendment" outlawed the introduction of
any troops into Cambodia after June 30, forbade the provision of American advisers to Cambodian forces and prohibited all air operations in
direct support of Cambodian forces. It also proclaimed that assistance
given by the United States did not constitute a commitment to the defense
of Cambodia.

It was an historic act, the first time in the history of the war that
Congress legislated to restrict the President. It had far-reaching implications. Politically, the important point is that it was not spontaneous; the
legislature had been provoked by the President into taking this step. Already the invasion was "dysfunctional."

When Haig first met Lon Nol the final language of the amendment was
unwritten, but the Senate's anger over the commitment to Cambodia was
clear. Still, the Colonel promised the General that everything possible
would be done, that he had a friend in the White House, and that he could
deal directly with the President.

It was not a commitment Haig made blindly. He and John Court understood some of the misgivings expressed by Mike Rives about the Cambodians' ability to defend themselves under their new leaders. There was
enthusiasm, but a visit to the battlefields along the Cambodian-Vietnam-
ese border showed how much it had to make up for. (Court met one
"Cambodian general" who was apparently a South Vietnamese deserter

---

* The Tonkin Gulf resolution was passed in August 1964, after President Johnson announced that two United States destroyers had been attacked in international waters off
Vietnam by North Vietnamese torpedo boats. The resolution supported the President in all
measures necessary to repel armed attack on American forces. As such it provided the
executive with basic legislative approval for its actions as the war developed. It later
emerged that Johnson had been less than candid in his description of the attack.

in disguise.) Evidence on the ground bore out the gloomy conclusions of the Pentagon's Systems Analysis Office, which had just studied the Cambodian army and discovered that it "suffers from lack of combat experience, equipment deficiencies, understrength military units, fragmented dispersal throughout the country and lack of mobility." Its "greatest shortcoming" was its incompetent and corrupt officer corps. Training was inadequate; equipment was "a considerable mix"; artillery was "limited"; "the aircraft are obsolete and maintenance of both the aircraft and airfields is poor." Only one airfield, Phnom Penh, had fuel pumps. Naval equipment was "also obsolete." The armed forces could quickly be raised to 90,000, but the experience of South Vietnam suggested they could not be properly trained and controlled for about four or five years.

These findings and many more were presented in May 1970. Haig, moreover, had personal reason to question Lon Nol's value as a leader. He looked at the maps showing the Chinese army's march south, he learned that Lon Nol had been involved in smuggling to the North Vietnamese, and it was clear after only a short visit that the General's mind tended to take flight. But he knew also that the White House had made the basic decision—Lon Nol was to be aided, the new war was to be underwritten.

Back in March and April the administration had had freedom of choice in reacting to events in Cambodia. If it had decided not to encourage, let alone to arm Lon Nol, it could have compelled either the return of Sihanouk or, at least, an attempt, by Lon Nol, to preserve the country's flawed neutrality. This would not have been an ideal solution for Washington, it would probably have meant a government dominated by Hanoi and at the very least it would have allowed the Communists continued use of Sihanoukville (which Lon Nol renamed Kompong Som) and the sanctuaries. But as the suppressed National Intelligence Estimate had pointed out, short of permanent occupation the sanctuaries would always pose a military problem for a South Vietnamese government; that was a fact of both geography and revolutionary warfare.

When Haig went to Cambodia, Washington's options were already limited by the White House's recent decisions. Without any knowledge of him, aid had been handed to Lon Nol and, without any consideration of the implications, the Communists had been driven deeper into his territory. The government's predicament was more serious than ever. The decision to expand aid to Lon Nol now was made on the basis of three factors: the idea of providing a new protective shield for American troops in Vietnam; the personal emotional investment that Nixon had already made in Cambodia; and the President's desire to experiment with the "Nixon Doctrine."

This was the doctrine that had been offered in a hastily assembled press briefing in Guam in July 1969. Nixon had said he could not be directly quoted, but a full account of his talk in indirect speech, reproduced in the *Congressional Record,* gives an authentic flavor.

He began by saying that his first trip to Asia had been in 1953 "with the usual four days in each country." This time he was spending only one day in each, but that was just as good, particularly if you believed, as he did, that the really important thing about a foreign country was its leader. What they all wanted to know was what America's role in Asia would be "after the end of the war in Vietnam." He understood that the reaction of many Americans was to withdraw, but he believed that the United States must stay if it was to avoid involvement in another war. America was a Pacific power; Guam was in the Pacific. World War II came from Asia, so did the Korean war. So did Vietnam. Today, "the major world power that adopts a very aggressive attitude in its foreign policy, Communist China, is of course in Asia," as were two minor but also very belligerent powers, North Korea and North Vietnam.

He described the achievements of South Korea, Taiwan, Thailand, Japan, the problems of the Philippines, the poverty of India and Pakistan, the growth of national and regional pride in Asia. For the future, he said, "The United States was going to encourage and had a right to expect that [defense] would be increasingly handled by, and the responsibility for it taken by, the Asian nations themselves." As for the difference between internal and external threats, Nixon dismissed that; internal threats—as in Thailand—would not exist but for the external support they received. If another "Vietnam-type problem" occurred America must avoid "that creeping involvement that eventually submerges you." If any Asian country faced internal subversion the American role should be "to help them fight the war but not fight the war for them." This was "a good general principle, one which we would hope would be our policy generally throughout the world." Military involvement and aid "would recede," but economic aid "would be adequate to meet the challenge as it develops." That was the lesson of Vietnam.

The implication of the "Doctrine" was that America's ends remained unchanged, but the means had altered. Specifically, Asian forces would be required to fill the gap between Washington's ambitions and the willingness of American citizens to die on behalf of those ambitions in foreign fields. The Doctrine was, in fact, Vietnamization internationalized, and all the risks implicit in Vietnamization attended it. Neither in his background talk nor later did Nixon ever seem to consider what effect the introduction of American assistance might have upon a client country or what might happen if, after Washington had committed its prestige, that client proved unable, in a Nixon phrase, "to hack it." Should or could Washington ever disengage from a government that it had encouraged if that government should prove incompetent, or were they bound to sink together? These and other questions remained unasked until Cambodia provided the test case.

On his return to Washington, Haig helped to develop the scheme by which the Doctrine should be implemented in Cambodia. His plan included an expanded United States mission with a large military attaché's office for intelligence gathering, and an extensive communications system both within the country and connecting Cambodia to the outside world. The United States should concentrate on equipping the Lon Nol army with light weapons; an integral part of the plan was the use of American air power in the border areas and, when necessary, deeper into the country to support Lon Nol's troops.

Haig's visit was the first of what became known to American diplomats as the White House's "stroking missions" to Lon Nol. Over the coming years Spiro Agnew, John Connally, Admiral McCain, the Commander in Chief Pacific Forces (CINCPAC), the Commander of the Seventh Air Force, and most frequently Haig himself would go out to comfort Lon Nol with assurances. Their visits were interspersed by spear carriers from the National Security Council, eager and aggressive young men with direct orders from Kissinger or Haig.

One of the commodities in which these men traded was the naïveté and credulousness of the Khmer leaders. Sihanouk had never allowed the emergence of an independent or self-confident ruling class; there was no one and nothing to replace him. Many Khmers found the vacuum more frightening than liberating and eagerly accepted the Americans' protection. They did so, for the most part, in good faith. Lon Nol himself had no understanding of international affairs—he knew little of the exigencies of Vietnamization, the balance of power, the attitudes of the United States Congress; six years after he came to power he said in an interview that he had never known that Kissinger supported detente. Insofar as he was trained in international politics at all, it had been by contact with United States officers in the fifties and early sixties and by watching the war in Vietnam. There, he considered and he said as much, that the United States had "lost face"; he believed that he offered Washington a chance to regain prestige. To him, American support was automatic in any war against demon Communism; he had never dreamed it might be qualified or curtailed.

Little was done to enlighten him. As if the "stroking missions" were not enough, Nixon began to write Lon Nol a series of warm and optimistic letters praising him for past achievements and exhorting future efforts. Delighted by the correspondence, Lon Nol seized any excuse—the Fourth of July or Buddha's birthday—to write the President. Some of his letters were in longhand, written, he said, in the middle of the night. They could be filled with vague and wandering mysticism, with praise for Nixon, with accounts of the shadows of the moon; they almost always requested aid.

His letters could have been merely acknowledged. Instead Nixon sent effusive replies. Lon Nol took the correspondence, which continued until Nixon's indictment, very seriously. He would keep the latest letter from Nixon in the breast pocket of his tunic and pull it out to show his friends the newest promises from *"mon ami, Monsieur le Président."*

Soon after Haig's return from Cambodia Jonathan "Fred" Ladd, who was on a trip to San Francisco, received an urgent call from Henry Kissinger. He asked if Ladd would be interested in a senior State Department position in the Far East. Ladd said he might be, and Kissinger persuaded him to take the night flight to Washington.

In 1969, Ladd had retired from his post as commander of U.S. Special Forces in Vietnam and set up a charter-boat business in Florida. In March 1970, at the time of the coup, he had had an unexpected call from the Pentagon asking whether he would like to return to "the area with which I was familiar." He said then that he would consider an offer, but it was only now, after the invasion, that the suggestion was followed up.

The next morning at the White House, Kissinger and Haig, whom Ladd had known in Korea, told him that Cambodia was the assignment, and that the President wished to open an aid program to be run by a civilian. Ladd was doubtful. As a Green Beret, he had been critical of the regular army's massive buildup in South Vietnam. He used to say that it made as much sense to send American troops to the Mekong Delta as it would for Chiang Kai-shek to dispatch the Kuomintang army to help out south of the Mason-Dixon line. This attitude had cost him his stars; he had known in 1969 that he would never make General. Still, he was interested in Cambodia, had known the Khmer Serei troops well and, when Haig and Kissinger assured him that this time it would be different—that the program would be limited, that few Americans would be involved, that the lessons of Vietnam had been learned, and that he could apply them— Ladd agreed to try. "Don't think of victory; just keep it alive," Kissinger said.

Ladd immediately became aware of bureaucratic tensions. Kissinger told him that he would deal directly with the Cambodian head of state, the Prime Minister, the United States ambassadors in Bangkok and Saigon, General Abrams, and Admiral McCain, who was already speaking of Cambodia as "my war." But the State Department, which had been ordered to give this retired soldier a foreign-service rank to do a military job for which it had little enthusiasm, tried to fob him off with a low grade. When Ladd complained, the White House overruled State; but it was a sign of conflict to come. In a brief visit to the Pentagon he sensed that the military was as wary of his unusual position as were the diplomats. When he stopped in Saigon en route to Phnom Penh he learned that Abrams, like Haig, was contemptuous of the way in which Mike Rives ran his mission. It also seemed clear that the military in Saigon had little idea what was happening beyond the twenty-one-mile zone of Cambodia that United States and South Vietnamese forces had invaded.

When Ladd arrived, the United States embassy was still housed in Mike Rives's shabby servants quarters. Ladd's office, shared with two military assistants, was an unconverted bathroom. There was still only one ordinary telephone line out of the building, and it was often out of order. Rives was still resisting expansionist pressure from Saigon, but as Larry Bonner, one of Ladd's military assistants, wrote to a friend, "a bemused smile from time to time revealed an inner conviction that he was just shoveling shit against the tide."

Like every official coming to Phnom Penh from Saigon or Washington, Ladd was warned that the White House was anxious to keep Cambodia out of the press. After the invasion by United States troops, correspondents had flocked to Cambodia. Arnaud de Borchgrave, *Newsweek*'s one-man world bureau, had set up his command post in a bungalow by the pool of the Hotel Royal. He spent most of his time with ambassadorial contacts and both briefed and debriefed other journalists as they returned each evening from the front. (Seventeen did not return; the front was a movable line in the first weeks of the war, and almost all the journalists who were captured were killed.) De Borchgrave wrote some exotic stories and confided one scoop to his friend, columnist Joseph Kraft; the Chinese, he said, really were coming. Kraft laughed.

One of Kraft's own columns was to have an astonishing influence. It mocked the Defense Attaché, Colonel William Pietsch, not a very effective diplomat. Kraft described "Colonel P" as "a creature of comedy and maybe pathos, chiefly distinguished by the wearing of a white bartender's jacket." He quoted him as saying "Now here's the line for you. What we're seeing here is a reverse domino theory. People are standing up to be counted. The Vietnamese, the Thais, the Cambodians. The enemy is on the run. He's running for his life. Let me speak not as a colonel, but as a man in the street, Mr. USA. I think that what President Nixon did was a brave decision. If there was anything wrong, it's that he waited as long as he did. Even so, the enemy is hurt. The enemy is taking a licking. I'll bet my professional reputation that we'll bring it off." The column caused consternation in the White House; Pietsch was immediately recalled. The incident made a lasting impression on the embassy, and few people ever dared to speak freely to reporters again. Ladd, who loved to gossip over a bottle of Scotch about the antics of the military, was an exception.

Like other visitors from Washington, Ladd was at first struck by the enthusiasm of the Cambodians he met and by the apparent popularity of the coup among the urban population. Many American officials, ignoring Lon Nol's mysticism, compared him with President Suharto of Indonesia. William Colby, who wanted the CIA to run Cambodia like Laos, was quite impressed; Lon Nol assured him that the war had "a spiritual basis" and derived from the glories of Angkor. Nixon's Foreign Intelligence Advisory Board was remarkably enthusiastic after meeting Lon Nol, but Mike Rives cabled Washington: "Lon Nol's optimism, as usual with visitors, was encouraging, though somewhat startling and is based perhaps on some naïveté and failure realize Cambodia probably embarked on long hard struggle. . . ."

At first, Ladd had the two bureaucratic essentials to success—access and information—both in Phnom Penh and Washington. He would visit Lon Nol at his home almost daily. They pored over maps on the floor and former colonel Fred Ladd, now Foreign Service Officer Grade Two, told the general what he should do with such men and matériel as he commanded. Ladd was Lon Nol's direct channel to the White House. Haig had told Ladd that he could communicate with the NSC through an American he would meet outside the embassy in Phnom Penh. This secret instruction started a proliferation of channels—which was, in the future, to cause great confusion in the embassy.

In his first weeks Ladd tried to discover just what the Cambodian army possessed in its Soviet, Czech, French, Chinese, American arsenals. His initial budget, till the end of June, was just $7.9 million, and much of this went to the purchase of ammunition for the varied weapons systems from a variety of sources. He set aside the rest for uniforms, medical supplies, radios, training of truck drivers and repairs to the small T-28 bomber planes that were the backbone of the Cambodian air force.

The fact that a budget existed at all and the manner in which it was obtained is more important than its small size. The money was not authorized nor appropriated by Congress. To avoid having to go before a hostile legislature for funds before the Congressional elections in November, Nixon diverted funds from other military-assistance programs by "presidential determination"—largely, in fact, from South Korea. In July he supplemented the first installment with $40 million for the fiscal year 1971. This was later raised again. When he eventually came to Congress at the end of 1970 for funds, he was daring the legislature, in effect, to discontinue it—which was much harder for Congress to do.

On June 30 Nixon marked the withdrawal of American troops from Cambodia with an enthusiastic television report on the brilliant success of the invasion. He cited the considerable quantities of arms, ammunition and rice captured and the 11,000 Vietnamese or Cambodian enemies killed. He praised the quality of the ARVN, of the U.S. Army, and of his own decisions. (He made no mention of COSVN, the supposed target when the invasion began.) His evaluation has been accepted and repeated uncritically by Kissinger, Ford and Theodore White, among others. (In his book on Watergate, *Breach of Faith*, White describes the invasion as one of the two major achievements of Nixon's rule, environmental policy being the other.) In fact, Nixon's assessment was very nearly irrelevant to what had really happened in the past two months.

Early in the operation Melvin Laird had sent a memo to the Chairman of the Joint Chiefs arguing that "the success of the military activities in Cambodia will be reflected in: Lower U.S. casualties. Increased Vietnamization. Continuing U.S. troop redeployment, in fulfillment and even in excess of the President's announced goals. Progress in negotiations." By these standards the invasion was not very successful. In the short term it certainly disrupted North Vietnamese logistics and attacks down "Rocket Alley" from the Parrot's Beak to Bien Hoa slackened for some months. But negotiations and Vietnamization were set back by the venture. Troop redeployment was not much affected and, despite Nixon's and Kissinger's subsequent claims to the contrary, it had only the most marginal impact on American deaths. Casualties did fall, but this was principally because American troops were withdrawn from the country while a South Vietnamese shield was placed between them and the enemy. This was, of course, the primary purpose of Vietnamization.*

Over the course of the war, the death rate for American forces averaged 1.8 percent per year. (This compares with annual losses of at least 2.5 percent for South Vietnamese troops, 5 percent for United States forces in Korea, and about 6.7 percent for the French Expeditionary Force in every year of the First Indochina War.) More than half of all combat deaths occurred in the north of South Vietnam, far from Cambodia, and about 70 percent of them were in United States maneuver battalions engaged in offensive action—such as the invasion itself, which increased combat deaths for May and June 1970 by 20 percent. From 1969 on, combat troops were withdrawn faster than support troops, and maneuver battalions fastest of all. These plans had been drawn up before the Cambodian invasion; they were not contingent upon it. By the spring 1972 Communist offensive, almost all American troops were safely in rear areas; nearly half of all United States deaths during that year occurred out of combat, many of them in helicopter accidents.

The success of Vietnamization in this regard is shown most starkly in a year-by-year comparison of American and South Vietnamese casualties. The South Vietnamese official figures are not very reliable, but they give a broad impression. In 1969, 9,414 Americans and 21,833 Vietnamese died in combat; in 1970, the figures were 4,221 and 23,346; in 1971, 1,380 and 22,738. The 1972 offensive made that year the worst for the South Vietnamese. Almost 40,000 of them died, along with 300 Americans. Vietnamese combat deaths in 1972 were about 5,000 fewer than American combat deaths in the entire war. Their attrition rate fell only slightly after the Paris Peace Agreement of 1973.

A June 1970 Rand study, "U.S. Casualties During Vietnamization," warned that one effect of the invasion might be a shift of the Communist focus of attack. This did begin to happen. A post-factum analysis, conducted soon after the invasion began by two systems analysts on Kissinger's staff, found that the Delta, the Central Highlands and Binh Dinh

---

* The White House impressed upon the entire administration how important it was that casualties should at least appear to fall after the invasion. At Laird's morning Vietnamization meeting on May 28, 1970 Admiral William Lemos stated that it was essential U.S. casualties be cut back sharply in July. "If necessary we must do it by edict."

province along the coast of central Vietnam had been left vulnerable and exposed when the American forces went into Cambodia. Their post-factum analysis of captured documents and supplies could not substantiate any of the premises on which the invasion had been based. The CIA drafted a Special National Intelligence Estimate (SNIE) that showed that United States interests in Indochina had been seriously compromised by the invasion. An account by the Assistant Secretary of Defense (Systems Analysis) was given to Laird in August 1970. He wrote, "Although U.S. and ARVN cross-border operations have disrupted NVA operations in Cambodia to some extent, these operations have not substantially reduced NVA capabilities in Cambodia. Approximately 25% of the Vietnamese Communists' reserve stocks have been lost. Captured supplies can be reconstituted in about 75 days with the opening of additional supply routes through Laos and continued high level supply operations into the rainy season."

In its bullishness the White House took no account of the political impact of the invasion abroad. In his speech of April 30, Nixon had stressed that one principal purpose of the invasion was to sustain America's credibility in the world; it had, in fact, the opposite effect. The United States Information Agency surveyed foreign opinion and concluded that the invasion had caused "a traumatic reaction in the world at large" and a blow to American prestige.

Nor did official assessments take into account the dangers that the invasion had raised in Cambodia and the way in which it drained Vietnamization. Now South Vietnamese troops and air power would fight in two countries. American planes would be spread thinner, the Saigon government would have to cope with at least another 100,000 refugees, and a limited supply of Congressional patience and American resources would be further strained.

By the end of May, State and Defense Department officials were admitting privately that they had never expected the fighting in Cambodia to spread so far so fast, and that it was clear that South Vietnamese troops would have to stay there indefinitely. Melvin Laird was exasperated. "The South Vietnamese are wandering all over Cambodia protecting the government while we, in turn, are in South Vietnam protecting the South Vietnamese," he complained at a morning meeting in the Pentagon.

The realities were spelled out not by Nixon, nor by those who spoke for him, but in a June 1970 cable from the Joint Chiefs to General Abrams: "Although scheduled reductions in United States troop strength in the Republic of Vietnam will soon place additional in-country responsibilities on RVNAF forces, operations should be conducted by these forces in Cambodia, particularly during the next few weeks . . . to prevent loss of major objectives to NVA/VC . . . It is considered that the preventation of total take-over of Cambodia by the NVA/VC is a prime objective and that RVNAF ground forces and United States air interdiction should be used to achieve this objective." There was now a new hostage.

The reference to "air interdiction" is vital. As the covert use of bombing had been integral to Vietnamization, so it became essential to the pursuit of the Nixon Doctrine in Cambodia. As we shall see, it was deployed with a disregard for controls and procedures that seems remarkable.

The "Patio" strikes by tactical aircraft, which Abrams had requested before the invasion, ended in May; they had been successfully concealed under falsified reports. Then, at the insistence of the White House, the bombing—by tactical aircraft and B-52s—was again extended farther and farther into Cambodia. Under the terms of the Cooper-Church amendment it was illegal for the United States to bomb Cambodia after June 30, except to intercept Communist men and supplies en route to Vietnam. By the end of the summer much of the country was a free-fire zone for United States aircraft and since their postoperational reports were almost all deliberately inaccurate, there was little follow-up to see what targets were actually being attacked. Pilots had far more liberty than in Vietnam to bomb any target they wanted.

At the same time Cambodia was open house for the South Vietnamese Air Force. They and the army were free, for the first time in decades, to give expression to their historical contempt for the Khmers. They behaved as if they were conquering a hostile nation, rather than helping a new ally; every Cambodian was a VC and a target. Perhaps the most chilling evidence of the pleasure that the pilots took in it all was contained in a cable sent by Abrams to the Pentagon. He reported that until now it had been virtually impossible to induce the South Vietnamese to fly on Sundays. Now they were paying bribes of 1,000 piasters each to be allowed to go out seven days a week—over Cambodia.

It was the same with the South Vietnamese ground troops. ARVN soldiers returned home with looted Hondas, bicycles and radios, and their commanders did not deter them. Throughout the later part of the summer, the 495th ARVN battalion rampaged through the villages around the town of Takeo. According to a CIA report from Phnom Penh, the ARVN commander, Captain Le Van Vien, frequently called in air strikes "to drive the people from the villages"; he and his men would seize the villagers'

animals and force them to buy them back. Rives reported to Washington
that ARVN troops frequently ambushed and killed Cambodian officers;
the governor of Svay Rieng made constant complaints about the way in
which the South Vietnamese stole cars, sandwiched them into military
convoys and barreled through border posts firing at the Cambodian sen-
tries. Rives informed his superiors that even Lon Nol was "getting increasingly fed up" and was considering how he might get rid of his
"ally." But he could not. Thieu began to demand that the Cambodians
pay for ARVN's presence. Kissinger's response was to suggest that Cambodia's other traditional enemy, Thailand, send troops.

Throughout the summer Kissinger and Nixon promoted this idea, in
the end without success, over the skepticism of the Defense Department.
The agony it aroused in Phnom Penh could have been understood in most
places. Cambodian Assistant Chief of Staff General Sak Sutsakhan told a
Filipino officer who was a CIA agent that the Lon Nol government feared
that South Vietnam and Thailand were trying to annex the territory each
had claimed for years. For their part, Thai ministers made their contempt
for Lon Nol quite clear to American officials; it was on this as much as
anything else that the proposal foundered. Even so, training in Thailand
and logistics of support from the Thais became part of the Nixon Doctrine
as applied to Cambodia.

The effects of the invasion were clear enough to some. While it was
still going on, three American journalists—Richard Dudman, Washington
Bureau Chief of the St. Louis *Post-Dispatch,* Elizabeth Pond of the *Christian Science Monitor,* and Michael Morrow of Dispatch News Service—
were captured in Cambodia by the Viet Cong and spent forty days in their
hands. In a book about the experience, Dudman wrote that the invasion
had simply spread the sanctuaries and that "the bombing and the shooting
was radicalizing the people of rural Cambodia and was turning the countryside into a massive, dedicated and effective rural base. American shells
and bombs are proving to the Cambodians beyond doubt that the United
States is waging unprovoked colonialist war against the Cambodian people." When Elizabeth Pond took the same message to Melvin Laird he
listened. But later he was assured by the military that even Pond's press
colleagues considered her pro-Viet Cong.

Mike Rives also understood a good deal. Throughout the summer he
reported cautiously and critically. It was evident that he had no great
enthusiasm for this venture, and he greatly irritated the White House,

175

where the blurred line between intelligence and policy was by now virtually erased. Rives's careful reporting had already earned him abuse from the NSC staff and Haig also thoroughly disliked him. The visit of Spiro Agnew to Phnom Penh in July 1970 almost ended his career.

When Vice-President Agnew flew in from Saigon, a group of Cambodian officials and children stood at the steps of the plane to greet him. The door opened and a squad of Secret Service men, Uzi machine guns at the ready, burst out. They rushed down the steps thrusting aside the welcoming party, and hustled Agnew toward a heavily armed helicopter, which had been sent from Saigon to take him the perfectly safe three-mile drive to the palace.

Agnew was greeted there by Acting President Cheng Heng. They had gifts to exchange. Agnew had brought a set of world maps, some silver cocktail glasses and a pair of leather-covered "In" and "Out" trays. He was given some finely worked traditional Cambodian silver. He left it behind when he departed from Phnom Penh.

Wherever Agnew was led in the palace by the diminutive Cheng Heng, the Secret Service went also, their machine guns over their arms. When the Acting President wanted to show Agnew one room that they had not cleared, the Secret Service men pulled Agnew away and refused to let him enter. During lunch they sat around the table, their guns still at the ready. It was all too much for the impeccably polite Mike Rives. When he saw one Secret Service man openly training his gun on the Acting President's back, he finally lost his temper and asked the agent to behave more graciously.

Rives did not have enough credit at the White House to insult such a sacred cow as the Secret Service. Agnew's guards complained to him, he complained to Nixon, the White House complained to State. Rives, the Department was told, must be sacked. His colleagues managed to protect him to the extent that he was just shunted into the backwater of African research before being quietly moved back onto the Laos-Cambodia desk. But his career never recovered, and his treatment reinforced the conviction of his colleagues that skepticism, especially about Cambodia, was an unprofitable business. It was a lesson that his successor in Phnom Penh, Ambassador Emory "Coby" Swank, would learn, and that he first applied and finally disregarded at a time when such nonchalance was possible only at high personal cost.

CHAPTER 12

The Strategy

THE NIXON DOCTRINE proposed that the United States could provide the material and counsel for an Asian country to withstand internal or external attack while remaining politically detached.

In this spirit, the White House professed the Cambodian government to be independent, a friendly power whom Washington was helping to help itself. But from the start the United States attempted to control events there. In the fall of 1970, the administration debated just what sort of war Cambodia should fight. This discussion helps to establish that the "limits" implicit in the declared Nixon Doctrine had little place in the real relationship.

The debate began over interim aid. By September 1970 there was a financial crisis. The military, despite Ladd's caution, had already spent almost all the forty million dollars that had been intended to last until July 1971. More money was required at once. Both the White House and the State Department had hoped to continue the surreptitious funding by Presidential determination, which evaded Congressional approval. Laird, however, refused to divert more funds from other Pentagon programs; he was concerned about arousing further Congressional ire and there was not very much left in other programs anyway. "State and the NSC staffs seem to think that Defense has all kinds of ways to finance the Cambodia operations," he complained to his staff one morning in early September. They agreed that Indochina policy was now a shambles; everyone had a hand in Vietnam, CIA and State ran Laos, and now the NSC was running Cambodia. Any coordination was quite impossible.

On September 11 Laird sent a memo to Kissinger: "We are involved in *a real crisis* in military aid programs." The resources currently available and now being requested from Congress were "inadequate to support ongoing implementation of the Nixon Doctrine and to assist in maintaining adequate balances of power throughout the world . . . *I strongly urge immediate action*" (emphasis in original). Congress must be asked "now" for an extra $260 million for military-assistance programs, $60 million of it for Cambodia. Another $130 million was needed in support-assistance. Otherwise Lon Nol might fall and then, Laird warned, "Our already significant investment in terms of military equipment and prestige could be lost." Just four months after the invasion the "credibility" scare was being invoked to obtain more support for Lon Nol. Eventually, Laird had his way. A supplemental aid request was put to Congress.

Laird was less successful in trying to influence Washington's decisions as to what kind of army Cambodia was to have, and what kind of war Cambodia was to fight. Part of the argument took place within the framework that Mort Halperin had devised back at the Pierre Hotel in December 1968; its vehicle was National Security Study Memorandum 99, "U.S. Strategy for Southeast Asia." One of the main questions it addressed was the correct mix of direct American military aid (and American air power) and South Vietnamese armed assistance. Should Lon Nol be given South Vietnamese men and American matériel, or just one or the other? What should be done in the case of a real Communist threat to Phnom Penh? On this last, three "strategies" were discussed.

Strategy One, supported by the Secretary of Defense's office, called for reliance principally on Cambodian troops to defend Phnom Penh, but would allow the South Vietnamese to intervene in a crisis.

Strategy Two represented the State Department's view, and it was more cautious. It proposed that Lon Nol should be given American aid, and argued that if Phnom Penh still were in danger of falling, this would show that conditions in Cambodia had deteriorated "beyond hope." State argued that involving the South Vietnamese with a regime that could not defend itself would only widen the scope of the defeat.

Strategy Three was more elaborate. It suggested that the defense of Phnom Penh was essential to United States policy, but it would be largely a matter of deterrence: the Communists were unlikely to attack so long as they were convinced that the South Vietnamese and United States air power would come to the city's defense. This sounded reasonable, but it demanded a much greater commitment of both American and South Vietnamese resources; the deterrent effect of the ARVN and the U.S. Air Force could be established only if they were both active in Cambodia before any Communist assault on Phnom Penh was mounted. Strategy Three, the most ambitious, was opposed by both Laird and Rogers. It was Dr. Kissinger's choice.

Strategy Three contained three subordinate possibilities, known as "Variants." These offered three answers to the concurrent question of how much of Cambodian territory should be defended. By now there was consensus in Washington that the old strip of border that had contained the Communist "sanctuaries" was a free-fire zone and that the South Vietnamese would continue to sweep it regardless of the fate of the Lon Nol government. The question was how far out of Phnom Penh Lon Nol's forces should try to extend their control.

The most modest proposal was Variant One. It called for the defense of a small southeast triangle of Cambodia between Phnom Penh, Kompong Som (Sihanoukville) and the Vietnamese border. Variant Two added to this triangle a corridor northwest from Phnom Penh through Battambang to Thailand. Variant Three spread that corridor much wider. Each of the Variants called for a progressively larger Cambodian army and the commitment of more Vietnamese forces and American air power.

Even before any decision was made, Laird's aides were concerned about the extent to which the South Vietnamese were involved in Cambodia. By early September 1970, there were twenty-one South Vietnamese battalions scouring the country and fully one quarter of all airstrikes and troop lifts flown by the Vietnamese Air Force were committed to them. Even so, the Cambodians had lost the northeast quarter of the country. A "Top Secret" talking paper prepared for Laird, dated September 14, warned that "at a time when U.S. units are redeploying, ARVN may not be able to support a strategy which requires successively more ARVN to offset a fixed number of enemy. . . ." The Secretary's Office was anxious. "It appears that the more ambitious Variants are counterproductive, tying down far more ARVN forces than justified by the enemy threat." Laird agreed; he considered that NSSM 99 should be rewritten to include a much cheaper, less ambitious plan. Once more he and the State Department were overruled.

On September 15 the Senior Review Group, chaired by Kissinger, met. Under his pressure, it recommended that the United States should adopt Strategy Three, Variant Three. Washington would build up a Cambodian army that, with South Vietnamese and Thai ground and air support and

179

American air power, must try to hold about half of Cambodia against the Communists.

To Laird's office it was evident that Kissinger had pushed through the policy without proper examination of its feasibility or expense. Although this was a two- or three-year program, no financial costs for the United States beyond July 1971 had been assessed, and neither the financial nor the opportunity costs of dispatching more South Vietnamese battalions into Cambodia had been considered. Philip Odeen, now Principal Deputy Assistant Secretary, Systems Analysis, told Laird it was a very disturbing decision: he was doubtful it would work at all and was sure it could not be paid for. Previous studies had shown that at least two years would be needed to build the Cambodian army up to the size now required, and in April the NSC itself had concluded that a crash expansion would be counterproductive, because the Cambodians "lacked the leaders and training necessary."

At least thirty-five South Vietnamese battalions would be needed for the new strategy, and if the Communists concentrated their forces against a limited number of targets, this could rise to 67, an enormous force. The Joint Chiefs themselves were unhappy with it, and even Admiral McCain, not a man to underplay his hand, warned that if more than twenty-five South Vietnamese battalions were sent to Cambodia "this would adversely affect Vietnamization." Systems Analysis agreed. To many of Laird's advisers it seemed horrifyingly clear that history was repeating itself. Kissinger was dragging the United States into another ill-advised and ill-considered conflict. One of Laird's civilian deputies complained in a memo to Colonel Pursley, "I have not seen a clear statement of the basic U.S. interest in Cambodia. Why should we be willing to pay to keep Cambodia afloat? Most disturbing to me is that an explicit decision on our Cambodia strategy will probably never be made. Events will make it for us."

In theory, Kissinger's decision of September 15 was provisional. A final binding decision was to be taken at another Senior Review Group meeting on October 16. In the interim Laird attempted to get a more modest strategy adopted. He failed totally—in part, as he discovered to his fury, because various agencies had already informed the field that the decision had been made and the Cambodians themselves had been given the news. Nothing now could be changed lest it appear that the United States was indecisive and unable to stand by its "commitments." On October 16 Strategy Three, Variant Three, was confirmed as United States policy.

On October 26, Kissinger dispatched into the bureaucracies National

Security Decision Memorandum 89, "Cambodian Strategy," a document that was to govern American policy for the foreseeable future. It informed the government that the President had reviewed the first phase of NSSM 99 and approved Strategy Three, Variant Three. "In implementing his decision, special attention is to be given to the development of capable Cambodian light-infantry forces with supporting weapons as appropriate and to the establishment of effective GKR [government] control in the countryside."

Kissinger understood what America's most valuable asset was. "In all cases," he wrote, "our policy will be to capitalize on Cambodian nationalism. . . ."

The United States would support Cambodian "neutrality" and promote the country's "self-sufficiency"; at the same time, cooperation with Bangkok and Saigon must be encouraged and international support must be aroused. The South Vietnamese army and air force would operate "mainly (but not exclusively)" in the eastern half of the country. Plans for the use of Thai troops would also be drawn up. Kissinger outlined a way of securing additional funds if Congress should fail to meet the administration's request for a Cambodian Supplemental on time. He wrote that the President had authorized the Defense Department to use Section 506 resources to cover the balance of the fiscal 1971 program and AID to divert Development Loan funds either to Cambodia directly or to third countries "so as to free supporting assistance for Cambodia." Both State and AID felt that such use of development loans for security assistance as Kissinger proposed, was "contrary to Congressional intent and the administration's new foreign-policy approach." Laird's office, moreover, had already warned that Kissinger's proposed use of the Section 506 funds would be seen as "a circumvention of Congressional intent" unless there was a Presidential determination that their use thus was "vital to the security of the U.S." Kissinger gave the orders nevertheless.

And so, only a few weeks after Fred Ladd was sent to Cambodia to administer a discreet aid program designed to emphasize Special Forces and guerrilla-type operations, Kissinger and Nixon began to impose the logic of a fully equipped main-force army upon the Cambodians, and to demand that the Lon Nol government pursue a strategy for which, most of their own advisers agreed, it was totally unequipped. This was almost exactly what their predecessors had done in Vietnam in the middle sixties, and the policy was designed not, as Kissinger claimed in NSDM 89, to support Cambodia's "neutrality," but, rather, to eliminate that concept once and for all.

This was all accomplished with little attention to the underlying problems. There was almost no consideration of the impact of "Strategy Three, Variant Three" on either Vietnam or the United States Congress, let alone upon Cambodia itself. One of Laird's senior officials wrote, "I don't want to appear overly pessimistic but I must admit some concern that the best interests of the nation are not being served by the NSSM 99 study." And in Cambodia, the application of this first phase destroyed the government it was supposed to help and nurtured its enemy.

After it all was over, administration officials maintained that the United States had had no alternative but to aid Lon Nol, because when the program began in 1970 he was immensely popular and there was no reason to doubt that he was the best man to carry the country. In fact, the disintegration of his government and his support occurred very early on and was related, as it took place, to Washington. By the fall of 1970 Kissinger knew exactly upon what manner of regime he was pressing "Strategy Three, Variant Three."

There had been Mike Rives's reports. These had shown that Lon Nol lived in a fantasy world in which the achievements of the Kings of Angkor had more importance than threats from Hanoi. Through the summer of 1970, Rives consistently warned Washington about the General's inflated hopes and "over-grandiose dreams," and in one cable he begged for help to bring him "out of the clouds of his planning." Rives's concern was echoed not only in Laird's office but also in the CIA. The Agency, as is now better known, had never been popular in the Nixon White House. Recent events in Cambodia had further damaged its credibility with the President. Documents captured during the invasion showed that it had consistently underestimated the use that the Communists had made of Sihanoukville for transporting supplies into South Vietnam. During the summer of 1970, senior CIA officials urged that the Agency be given control of Cambodia as it had been given control of Laos. William Colby explained later that the strategy he had suggested to Lon Nol was: "Arm the population. Like an oil spot gradually spreading out. Don't worry about killing the enemy. Get your own people involved. Build a political base in communities anxious to defend themselves." The White House had rejected this idea in favor of a conventional military approach. The Agency's role in Cambodia was restricted but its reporting was often very good.

In August 1970, the station chief reported on the political situation to Washington. He concluded that "there are several reasons for pessimism about the situation in Cambodia." Among them was the inability of the government to communicate at all with the people. Sihanouk had accustomed Cambodians to highly visible leadership, but Lon Nol "is a poor speaker and he lacks the oratorical talent to persuade, encourage and sustain the revolutionary spirit." (He noted that Lon Nol's colleagues were, if anything, worse.) Altogether he believed "the initial enthusiasm generated by the overthrow of Norodom Sihanouk has dissipated to a large extent." The blame, he was sure, lay with Lon Nol, who did not have any idea that such problems existed. At one meeting when subordinates attempted to point out the problems, he said, Lon Nol "did not seem to grasp the points being made, giving the impression that they were above his head." The only solution he could offer was appropriate enough —a propaganda campaign in which "the government should even resort to making promises it knows it cannot keep simply in order to raise the spirits of the people. Sihanouk got away with this for fifteen years."

But times had changed. By now Phnom Penh was clearly at war, and promises would arouse skepticism. When Sihanouk was overthrown it had been a comfortable residential city of around 600,000 Khmers, Chinese and Vietnamese. As the fighting and the bombing spread in April and May, refugees had begun to flee toward its shelter and that of the provincial capitals the government still held. By August hundreds of thousands had arrived; eventually, when the war ended, Phnom Penh was ragged and bursting and had a population of somewhere between two and three million; no one really knew how many.

By the fall of 1970 the traditional economy had almost vanished. Rubber production was at a standstill, rice production was slowing too. Other produce was still reaching the city, and the stalls in the huge covered central market were still stacked with fresh fruit and fish and vegetables. But as prices rose, more of the traders switched to a new line of business and began to sell surplus American equipment—C rations, huge boots that no Khmer could ever wear, enormous green uniforms—smuggled in by South Vietnamese troops.

Harsh plank barricades had been nailed in front of government buildings, sandbags (often filled with only husks) were stacked up against the walls of schools, ministries and banks. The anti-Sihanouk posters plastered onto walls in March and April were peeling and tattered now, fading under the monsoon rains, but new wooden bunkers, covered with fresh paint and plastic sheets, filled with earth, were placed at major crossroads.

Along the boulevards and in the parks and gardens the flame trees, the teak, the frangipani, the jasmine and the hibiscus were being hacked away by soldiers—sometimes for firewood, sometimes on the grounds that Viet Cong snipers might hide in the branches. (Later in the long war the trees would die as the starving population stripped their barks for food.)

The small square in front of the Post Office, where journalists, diplomats and Cambodian civil servants ate couscous and sipped Chablis at La Taverne, was no longer picturesque; it was decorated with barbed wire. Business there and at the best restaurants, the Café de Paris and La Cyrene, was changing. The old French trading firms were closing down; planters had fled their rubber groves in the eastern half of the country, driven off by air attack and ground assaults.

Filipino, Australian, Indonesian, American, Australian contractors, lured by the aroma of war and the influx of American aid, began a five-year descent into the city. They rented the best rooms at the Hotel Monorom or at the journalists' favorite hotel, the Royal (which had been renamed the Hotel Phnom) and they hired large cars and cruised around the capital hawking airlines, trucks, training programs, medicines, obsolete weapons, drugs. Diligently they paid their respects to Fred Ladd and those other American embassy officials they considered most important, and generously (but often crassly) they tried to entertain senior and underpaid Cambodian bureaucrats.

The civil service had degenerated since Sihanouk's removal. Most officials, denied responsibility for so many years, now refused to take it, and often there was no discipline or order at all. Ministries worked from 7:30 A.M. to 12:30 P.M., with an hour off for coffee in midmorning. Whole rows of desks were empty almost all the time, with many of their occupants moonlighting to earn enough to live on. The station chief reported a little later that the situation was leading to discontent among "youth and intellectual elements, who see the same old faces in the same old jobs performing at their usual level of inefficiency and continuing to pocket essentially the same payoffs that were previously customary." He saw no prospect for improvement.

New frictions between military and civilian officials were developing. He noted that the civilians felt that the military were generally incompetent, overconfident, and careless of civilian needs, while the civilians were often envious of the greater opportunities for corruption enjoyed by the soldier. These opportunities were a function of army expansion; no one had any idea how many troops there were. It seemed that government forces had tripled by the end of July and grown five times—to about 150,000—by the end of the year. But each battalion did its own recruiting, and records were informal. In the early, rather carefree months of the war groups of students would try out one battalion after another to see which suited them best. Battalion commanders quickly realized that submitting to the paymaster inflated figures on troop strength was an easy way of providing themselves with a large surplus of riels—an ideal material with which to line the pocket.

Training was not very extensive. Civil servants spent hours each day marching outside their ministries, a few in berets or khaki shirts, most not, some with old rifles, most not, a few in step, most not. Students were drilled up and down their campuses or schoolyards, and the city's golf course was now converted into a simulated battlefield. (Later it became an ammunition dump.) In order to circumvent Congressional restrictions on American training in Cambodia itself, the United States began to arrange for Khmer units to be sent to South Vietnam and to Thailand. Even so, few of the boys who were carried off to war in Coca-Cola trucks and buses had any idea of combat.

It was haphazard, and by fall the station chief was concerned. There was an alarming lassitude in Phnom Penh particularly among the rich, who till now had been largely cushioned against the worst effects of war. At the same time discontent was growing generally. The station reported that one could hear complaints around town that the generals ran the war "from their Mercedes cars and restaurants, while the young people, civilians and soldiers, are dying each day." It warned that the excesses of the South Vietnamese army had caused "grave physical and moral suffering" and that "it will be difficult to hold down the rising tide of hatred and rancor." An economic crisis was looming, and "the possibilities of an internal political explosion cannot be discounted."

Some of these problems were inevitable in any war, but Lon Nol exacerbated them and it was reported that he had absolutely no understanding of the real world. Sihanouk had always considered Lon Nol a fool, according to Charles Meyer, Sihanouk's long-established French counselor. But Lon Nol also had a certain guile. The combination did not make him very effective, but it rendered him rather more dangerous.

Lon Nol's greatest assets were the many loyalties he had bought over the years in the officer corps. To preserve them, he tolerated and indeed encouraged military corruption. But he did not always use associates in the most sensible manner. Convinced that, since he had replaced the God-King he must rule in a similar manner, he insisted on maintaining personal control over the war effort. He bypassed the army's general staff and called unit commanders whom he knew directly by field telephone.

He instructed them to conduct maneuvers that were often absurd in the face of enemy dispositions he knew little about. His tactical advice depended on his mood, which could be gauged at the daily military briefings he insisted on giving. If he was cheerful, he would launch into long monologues—sometimes lasting two or three hours—on ancient Khmer history. If the news from the field was bad, he would close down the briefing abruptly. A CIA station report noted that none of his generals ever questioned his interpretation of the past, because "no other participant has any interest in it."

General Abrams too was concerned. Early in 1971 Laird reported to Nixon himself that on his recent trip to Vietnam "Abrams confided that Lon Nol and the Cambodian leadership did not fully comprehend the military situation in their own country. . . . Of special concern is General Abrams' assessment that Lon Nol and his key leaders are strangely detached from the implications of the immediate military situation."

The quality of Lon Nol's leadership and the reality of the war were brought home to inhabitants of Phnom Penh on January 22, 1971. In the early hours of the morning Viet Cong sappers crept up to the perimeter of Phnom Penh's airport, Pochentong, and fired hundreds of rounds of mortar and 122-mm. rockets. The government was caught by surprise; although the attack lasted four hours, no attempt whatsoever was made to send reinforcements the two and a half miles from the city. The entire air force, an admittedly ramshackle affair, was destroyed.

The assault caused a panic in the capital and raised doubts as to whether the government could defend the city at all. Information was replaced, as it often was in Phnom Penh, by rumors; the most widespread was that the assault had been arranged by the South Vietnamese. The American Ambassador Emory Swank cabled home to say it was psychologically the most sobering event since his arrival in September; he asked for stand-by authority to evacuate embassy dependents.

Washington's response showed the extent to which the war was controlled from far away. The planes, Lon Nol was promised, would all be replaced. In the meantime Swank was instructed by the State Department to order Lon Nol to write to President Thieu and to the Thai prime minister to ask for a loan of T-28 fighter planes. Lon Nol was also to ask Thieu if he would increase the number of Vietnamese air force missions flown over Cambodia. Despite the justified hatred that almost all Cambodians now felt for Vietnamese pilots, Lon Nol did as he was told. His letter to Thieu asked him, "to amplify and intensify cover and support provided by your Air Force, within the framework of cooperation between our two countries for common defense against Communist invasion."

A few weeks later Lon Nol suffered a stroke. He was dispatched to Hawaii for treatment (the Pentagon and State Department later squabbled over the bill) and recuperated in Admiral McCain's guesthouse. When he returned to Phnom Penh he suffered from a serious limp, a slur in his speech and his grasp upon reality seemed more tenuous than ever. Swank informed the State Department that even Lon Nol's partner in the coup against Sihanouk, Sirik Matak, now felt that the general had to go. "He said that Lon Nol is obviously not in physical or emotional state to bear burdens of his office; his articulation is uncertain, and his emotional anxieties are acute, precluding his exposure to multiple decisions which would be demanded of him."

In April 1971 Lon Nol did resign, and the title of Marshal was conferred upon him. But he was not long deprived of power. Thanks to the machinations of his younger brother, Lon Non, no other government could be formed, and Lon Nol hobbled back to office. Well before his illness, senior army officers and officials had complained to the United States Embassy that his romantic visions and impetuous interventions were jeopardizing the war effort. Such tendencies were now far more pronounced. And yet Lon Nol would remain in power, sustained by Washington and in particular by the White House, for four more years, the symbol of the American policy that President Nixon called "the Nixon Doctrine in its purest form."

CHAPTER 13

The Embassy

EMBASSIES OFTEN have personalities that reflect not so much their transient staffs as the mission to which they are committed. An embassy is also a coalition. In an American embassy, the ambassador may be a member of the State Department, but he is appointed by the President, and his domain contains State Department officials and also men from the Pentagon, the CIA, the Agency for International Development and others. Inter- and even intra-departmental rivalries in Washington itself are rarely subsumed by the fact that all these persons are now representing their country out of one building in a distant land. But when they are all engaged on a single, agreed mission, the rivalries can be controlled.

No such harmony was possible in Cambodia. The embassy was a short-lived and frantic affair. Created in 1969, it grew like a military Topsy in 1970 and 1971, settled into a resigned torpor in 1972, and died in 1975. Its personality throughout the period was split by the fact that no consistent, well-considered policy toward Cambodia ever existed in Washington. Rivalries and disagreements were, if anything, intensified by the time they reached Phnom Penh.

By the end of 1970 Mike Rives's small house had been discarded, like Rives himself. "Coby" Swank, his successor, moved into a larger building.

Swank is a slim, stylish, mild-mannered man, a traditional and conscientious diplomat of the type that those who despise it would call "striped pants." He had served in Laos in the middle sixties, and Secretary of State Dean Rusk thought highly of him, but his main interest was Eastern Europe and the Soviet Union. When his appointment to Cambodia was announced his *New York Times* profile stated, "He has gradually emerged as the acknowledged leader of the group of Soviet specialists in the Foreign Service." This may have been an overstatement, but he was a competent officer.

Swank did not believe in "making waves" or "throwing off sparks"; he thought more could be done quietly. He liked his instructions to be precise, and he was painstaking in the way he carried them out. Conversely, he did not enjoy acting in either a policy vacuum or a policy morass. He was unsuited to be a proconsul in Indochina, and that was one reason for his being chosen. His low-key diplomatic manners would help reassure the Senate that Cambodia was not to be another Laos, where the ambassador, with the CIA, ran the war.

When he left Washington, Swank was told by Kissinger and Nixon that Lon Nol was to be given everything necessary for his survival. He was not told how far he should intervene in Cambodian politics, but he was warned that the American presence must be kept on a "low-profile." Swank understood from both that White House policy was, quite simply, to help Vietnamization. It was a policy that Swank was prepared to implement, but after he had been in Cambodia some time, and as the futility of the war became apparent to him, he began, as diplomats do, to question whether the country that he had been sent to might have interests very different from those of his own. More and more he considered that his country's policy was "essentially a very selfish business." Henry Kissinger destroyed him for his qualms.

Swank was confronted almost at once with disagreements as to how the cause of Vietnamization was to be furthered in Cambodia, and—every ambassador's nightmare—a multiplication of channels of communication. To his surprise he found the American effort had been run almost singlehandedly by Fred Ladd. Ladd spoke little French and rarely ventured outside Phnom Penh, but his instincts were good and his relationship with Lon Nol excellent. Every evening they discussed the current action and Ladd tried to persuade the General to rational conduct. Although Ladd had State Department rank, he was still a military man, and outside Cambodia he dealt directly with a small "Cambodian Support Office" on Abrams' staff in Saigon. He also had his direct channel to Haig. Swank knew nothing of that.

Ladd's methods and attitudes were compatible with the White House's desire for a "low profile." But they were not suited to Kissinger's "Strategy Three, Variant Three." When it was adopted, McCain, who was impatient with modest ideas, demanded a large and formal American military presence in Phnom Penh. He had the support of the White House and the Joint Chiefs, though not of Melvin Laird or State.

Although the Cooper-Church amendment outlawed a traditional military *advisory* group in Cambodia, once Congress formally appropriates funds for military aid to a country (as it did to Cambodia in December 1970, when it passed the Supplemental Appropriation that Laird had demanded) the Pentagon is by law required to monitor it. It has to establish that the recipient actually needs the equipment requested; has the trained personnel to use it; can deploy and maintain it; and does in fact do all of those things in pursuit of military goals that conform with United States policy. Inevitably such requirements plunge American personnel deep into the operational systems of recipient nations, regardless of profiles or any "Nixon Doctrine."

McCain continually exploited this requirement, complaining that no one ever told him what the Nixon Doctrine actually meant, and warning day after day that there was no way of knowing what was happening to the equipment Ladd was requesting and receiving. He disturbed Melvin Laird, who foresaw a Congressional uproar if the equipment was being mislaid, and on December 28, 1970, the Secretary's opposition to military expansion gave way. In the middle of his morning Vietnamization meeting he called Admiral Moorer to tell him to organize a "Military Equipment Delivery Team" for Cambodia. Kissinger concurred, and the State Department's resistance was overridden. On January 8, 1971, Swank received a joint State-Defense cable: "The purpose of this message is to inform alcon of the decision at the highest level to authorize the activation of a Military Equipment Delivery Team (MEDT) type group for Cambodia." This was "essential to meet the rapidly increasing demand of an expanding military-assistance program for Cambodia." But "the retention of as low a U.S. profile as possible" was still "equally important." Only sixteen of the new team's sixty officers were to live in Phnom Penh; the rest were to remain in Saigon.

Although Cambodia was considered an extension of Vietnam the program was to be controlled not by Abrams but by McCain in Hawaii; this confirmed the Admiral's proprietary feelings about the new theater. But the choice of the officer to run the team was left to Abrams; he was not anxious to lose one of his better men, and he chose Theodore Mataxis, a one-star general close to retirement.

Mataxis' service in Vietnam had been mainly with the Americal division, which had become notorious after the story of the My Lai massacre was published. He was a hearty fellow, who saw himself as a military intellectual. He admired Kissinger. He hated "peaceniks," "pansies" and "pinkos," and he liked to crush beer cans in his fist as he regaled junior officers with stories of how the Americal "neutralized longhair grunts" and other troublemakers. The Cambodians found him astonishing; he is powerfully built and had a huge round face dominated by a shining hairless scalp and heavy spectacles. One Phnom Penh magazine published his photograph with the caption, "The man seen here is not from Mars. He is only General Mataxis."

Mataxis and McCain worked well together. McCain's cables to Laird for more air power, more ammunition, more heavy equipment, more men were so constant and so predictable that Laird's staff quipped that he had boiler-plate texts ready for every occasion and merely had to insert the date. Mataxis was just as keen to build his own empire, and he understood what the White House wanted in Cambodia. It was, he said later, "a holding action. You know, one of those things like a rear guard you drop off. The troika's going down the road and the wolves are closing in, and so you throw them something off and let them chew it."

"That was Cambodia?" he was asked.

"Yeah," replied Mataxis, "of course it's an overstatement but still . . ."

It was, in fact, hardly any exaggeration, and throughout 1971 Mataxis and McCain forced increases in the size of their team and Americanized the Cambodian soldiers before they were to be thrown off the troika.

Soon after he won his battle for control in Cambodia, McCain sent several military survey groups from Hawaii to examine the Cambodian armed forces' supply methods, ammunition procedures, equipment distribution, and so on. Their recommendations were expensive and sophisticated. They wanted the entire logistics system computerized. Mataxis agreed; the Khmer system just did not "interface" well with American methods. And so, for example, the old requisition forms, printed in French and Khmer, were replaced by standard American forms. Few Cambodian quartermasters spoke English and in desperation the Cambodians devised a Khmer-English form. Mataxis' men refused to let the Cambodians use it, on the grounds that they "had no ability to interface carbon paper between the copies." Mataxis had an easy solution; Filipino bookkeepers who understood American logistical methods were imported to take over from Khmer quartermasters.

Mataxis also overrode Fred Ladd's decision to buy cheap, simple commercial trucks from Australia and ordered more complicated American military trucks with dual fuel systems. The Cambodians had no idea of how to maintain them. Mataxis hired Filipino mechanics and asked the Cambodians to reopen an old truck and repair depot at the town of Lovek, twenty-five miles north of Phnom Penh. This depot had been built with United States aid in the early sixties; when the new vehicles were now brought there they were surrounded by acres of American trucks imported ten years before and then junked. Most of the new machines were soon added to the pile.

As soon as his first group of officers was in Phnom Penh, Mataxis began to insist that he needed more men, and McCain bombarded Laird with cables warning that corrupt Cambodians would continue selling their new equipment to the Communists unless more Army officers could be provided to monitor its "end use." In April, McCain demanded another thirty places in Phnom Penh itself; Swank, mindful of Kissinger's low-profile notions, resisted and would agree only to fifteen. The Admiral was annoyed, and on April 17 he cabled Laird to complain: "Ambassador Phnom Penh apparently has instructions to maintain a low U.S. profile, which being vigorously observed, prevents stationing of sufficient MEDTC personnel in Cambodia to do the job." Under the requirements of the Military Assistance Manual, Mataxis' duties in monitoring "end use" could have been interpreted in a flexible manner. But neither McCain nor Mataxis had any interest in doing so, and McCain insisted that a decision be made "at the national level" as to whether "low visibility" or "end use" was more important. "Should that determination favor low visibility, the United States must accept that we have no way of knowing the equipment being furnished Cambodia is being used and maintained properly and that significant amounts are not going to the VC/NVA."

The increasing demands of the military coincided with a new debate over America's commitment to Cambodia. The first stage had been the NSC deliberations of April 1970; the second was Decision Memorandum 89. Now another bureaucratic dispute began over military aid for the next fiscal year, 1971–72. Once again Kissinger acceded to military demands.

This is not to suggest that "Stage Two" had ever ended. Kissinger had originally set September 30, 1970, as completion date for NSSM 99. In fact, NSSM 99 dragged on through 1971 as the National Security Council commissioned more and more studies from different agencies and offices, accepting some, sending others back for further review. Laird was convinced that the intention was to exclude State and Pentagon from real decisions by tying them up with irrelevant material. He and his staff agreed that the original purpose of NSSM 99 had long since been submerged in paperwork. Laird worried that he would never be able to influence final policy; nothing, he complained, was brought to him for review. How long was NSSM 99 going to last?

Some time yet. More meetings, more papers were arranged and commissioned; by the ninth of April there were six different papers under preparation. Most of them were already overtaken by events, but the White House was pushing the departments to complete them all and was planning to hold Senior Review Group meetings on each of them. Then Kissinger sent out another memo on the action to be taken on NSSM 99. It appalled Laird, who considered that Kissinger was simply ignoring key problems; he complained bitterly to his staff that Kissinger had made no mention of negotiations, redeployment rates, over-all strategy, or how far the original objectives of Vietnamization were being met. Above all Kissinger had completely disregarded the political context of the war and was trying to make policy without considering its impact on Congress, on the public, on the over-all defense effort or on the Administration's general position. These piecemeal studies were dangerous; they almost always resulted in bad decisions, Laird complained. It was essential to try to look at problems in perspective, he said, otherwise the wrong conclusions were inevitable. He found it disturbing that Kissinger presented issues to the President in this manner.

Laird attempted to arouse William Rogers, but, to his disappointment, the Secretary of State seemed unable to appreciate how he and his department were being manipulated by the NSSM process. He did not share Laird's concern about the number of pointless studies the NSC commissioned. "We should cooperate, because they keep Henry busy and they don't matter. In the real world they have no impact on policy," he told Laird. (In fact, of course, it was not Kissinger or his staff, but the specialists in the agencies who were kept busy on work that had "no impact.") Anyway, said Rogers, the final decisions were always political, so what did the studies matter? Laird's concerns were lost on Rogers.

On June 7, 1971, Kissinger raised the stakes in Cambodia once again. Decision Memorandum 89 had at least paid lip service to the notion of Cambodian neutrality. Now even the theory of it was abandoned. Kissinger informed a meeting of the Senior Review Group that the United States now had three objectives in Cambodia. First, to retain an anti-North Vietnamese government there. Second, to give the Cambodians enough material, "so that they can deny to the NVA most of the rural Khmer population." Third, to encourage the army to move onto the offensive

193

against the North Vietnamese. He then sent out a memo asking for a new military-assistance plan that would accomplish all this and more.

Laird and his staff considered Kissinger's request on June 10, three days before *The New York Times* began to publish the Pentagon Papers. The memorandum of their meeting shows that Laird's real concern was with the influence that the Joint Chiefs would be able to bring to bear on the aid decision. The Chiefs were already busily pushing the case of McCain and Mataxis for an expanded team in Phnom Penh. To Laird's horror, they had now gone so far as to demand that the Team be increased from 60 to 2,000 officers. To Laird it was obviously absurd, but he was anxious lest the White House give it a sympathetic hearing.

His staff had complained to Laird that the Chiefs' ambitions for Cambodia were identical with those they used to have for Vietnam. One memorandum to the Secretary said, "The question arises: what have we learned in the meantime?" More frightening still was that the White House appeared to accept so much of what the Chiefs had to say. The NSC, Laird grumbled, seemed to think that all the problems of Cambodia could be solved by pumping in more and more men and equipment. From now on, he insisted on June 10, all the studies prepared by the Chiefs must be submitted to him before they went on to the White House. "Let's keep ahead of the power curve and not let the NSC staff push us too fast," he said.

As Laird feared, the Chiefs responded to Kissinger's request with ambitious swiftness. They submitted a plan for the Cambodian army to be increased to 220,000 men, for a paramilitary force of 143,000, for a larger United States training program in South Vietnam, a pacification and counterinsurgency effort, and another increase in Mataxis' team, this time to 1,003. It would cost $350 million for the next year, and they claimed it would enable Lon Nol to move into northeast Cambodia against the enemy.

The plan ignored the fact that only 15,000 Communist troops had easily tied down 150,000 government soldiers. It also ignored the spirit if not the letter of the Cooper-Church amendment and the economic impact on Cambodia of such an increase in the army. (The Office of International Security Affairs in the Pentagon noted that altogether the plan was "a marked change in the character of the U.S. program," which "probably stretches the legal constraints that apply to Cambodia.") The State Department and AID calculated that Cambodian inflation would soar to at least 34 percent if the Chiefs had their way. Higher if, as the Chiefs also wished, economic aid was diverted into military hardware.

To meet these and other objections, the Chiefs produced a revised plan.

The 220,000 men army remained but, at a stroke, they had cut the cost from $350 million to $275 million. How had this 21 percent saving been achieved? Simply by cutting back the ammunition that the United States would provide to the new Cambodian troops. The Chiefs still ignored the impact of this plan on the Cambodian economy.

The discussions stretched out to Indochina and to General Mataxis, who was still based in Saigon. He took the opportunity to demand that he now be allowed to move with a still bigger staff into Phnom Penh itself. The State Department attempted to show that the position of Fred Ladd would be absurd if Mataxis did so and that Mataxis was incompetent anyway. Swank, however, did not argue strongly for Ladd—his inclination, he says now, was to let the military have the resources they thought they needed. The White House agreed. Just one year after Kissinger and Haig had pressed Ladd to take the post, he was dropped, and although he remained for some time in Phnom Penh, he lost almost all of his original influence. On July 1, 1971, Kissinger sent a memo to Laird and Rogers to say that Nixon had agreed that Mataxis' team in Phnom Penh should be raised to fifty, with another sixty-three back in Saigon. Mataxis, who had just been passed over for promotion to major general, was allowed to move to Phnom Penh himself. The State Department sent Swank a list of ready-made answers to give at a press conference, to show how delighted he was. Once again the expansionists were carrying the day. In Washington, members of the Senior Review Group then received a memo from Kissinger (signed by Haig) confirming that the National Security Council had agreed to the Joint Chiefs' main proposal. The Cambodian army was to be increased to 220,000 by January 1973. The troika gathered speed, but the wolves were never left behind.

By now the militarization of policy was well under way both at home and abroad. The National Security Council's relationship with the Chiefs was never closer (by the end of the year it was damaged to some degree by the revelation that the Chiefs had been spying on Kissinger), and somewhat to Kissinger's discomfiture, Haig was in the ascendant on the NSC itself, importing other officers to serve with him. In Phnom Penh a new prefabricated building was put up to house Mataxis' empire. Every other person on the embassy staff was now a military man. One of the embattled diplomats later complained that "Swank was just the doorkeeper to a Pentagon whorehouse."

Apart from Mataxis' men, there was also a large military attaché's office. Its role needs to be examined briefly, because it contributed to the internal entanglements of the embassy. Defense attachés are employed by the Defense Intelligence Agency, an organization with serious difficulties. It is supposed to provide intelligence and analysis for both the Chiefs and the Secretary; but, as we have seen, the two often disagreed. Furthermore, it has usually been staffed either by officers on short tours whose analyses tend to reflect the biases and budgetary requests of their own services, or by aging colonels who have been put out to pasture. When Lieutenant General Donald Bennett took it over in 1969, he immediately sacked thirty-eight attachés for incompetence; many marginal cases, like Colonel William Pietsch in Phnom Penh, remained. After his summary removal in 1970, he was replaced by Colonel Harry Amos.

A member of the class of '46 from West Point, Amos had served in Phnom Penh in the early sixties. He was a meticulous, rather taciturn soldier nearing the end of his career, and he liked the Cambodians. But from the beginning he advocated large-scale military aid to Cambodia. He disagreed with Ladd's proposals for minimum unconventional support and agreed with the Chiefs that the Cambodian army should be built into as large and fully equipped a fighting force as possible.

Amos took the secondary, diplomatic function of his office seriously and appointed one of his most gifted subordinates, Captain Peter Piazza, his "Protocol Officer." Piazza was a good intelligence officer, and his analyses of the Cambodian army's problems were excellent. But he found himself spending time arranging cocktail parties where the attachés indulged in low-grade spying on each other and he had to translate the Soviet attaché's bad jokes. To cheer himself up, Piazza adapted a Gilbert and Sullivan song to describe his predicament:

> I am the very model of an Officer of Protocol,
> I know the social graces, I drink anything that's potable.
> I smile at the Ambassador with unctuous insincerity,
> I sneer at lower ranks as if my presence were a charity.

> Although I'm just a captain, at my job I'm very serious.
> When making seat arrangements, I've authority imperious.
> In short, in matters sociable, promotable, and potable
> I am the very model of an Officer of Protocol.

The principal task of the attachés was to travel to the various fronts of the war and report daily on the state of the fighting. This they did diligently. But one of the serious problems they and Mataxis' men, who inspected "end-use" of equipment, faced was the Congressional prohibition on giving combat advice to the Cambodians. The line between reporting and advising was often impossible to draw. Certainly it was impossible for most Cambodian officers to comprehend. They tended not unreasonably to assume that the Americans were in Cambodia to help them. The arcane constraints of American politics and legislation were not persuasive to an ill-trained Khmer captain under enemy fire in a bunker along Route Five.

Amos' attachés were on the whole disciplined, and some, like Piazza and Major Alan Armstrong, who served two tours during the war, were gifted soldiers. They contrasted well with the Mataxis team. Members of the team tended to behave as a military "in" group; hardly any of them spoke French, their tours were very short, and few had any understanding of the country. Their conduct was often raucous, and they accepted girls from Cambodian officers. They offered advice; they tended to tolerate military corruption. By his own admission Mataxis was generous both in the way he interpreted Congressional restrictions and in the manner he treated commanders who padded their payrolls at United States expense. "I had been long enough in Asia to consider corruption part of life, unlike some of those pristine young guys from State," he said later. In very serious cases he used to intervene, telling the Cambodians, "We don't want to upset the embassy, do we?"

Swank did his best to restrain Mataxis and to limit the visits of his team members to the field. But the General, aware of his backing in Hawaii and Washington, was cavalier; he ignored Swank's instructions if he disagreed with them and, so that Swank should not see his cables, he flew them to Saigon for dispatch to Washington or Hawaii. Today Mataxis makes no secret of his contempt for Swank, whose main concern, he says, was to avoid getting a bad press.

In fact, very few stories about the extraordinary factionalism of the embassy surfaced in the press. Partly this was because everyone, from Swank down, was conscious of the intense displeasure with which the White House read revealing reports from Cambodia and so was cautious with journalists. But it was also because the media in general treated the war as the administration did—as a sideshow. Most journalists loved Phnom Penh, but few American or European papers had full-time correspondents there. Their Saigon correspondents paid occasional visits; for the rest of the time they relied on stringers. Many of these worked extremely hard (they wrote far more than their editors wanted to publish), but, as well as often being antiwar, they were usually also young, inexperienced and poorly paid. As a group they appealed little to American embassy officials, and there was scant contact, let alone socializing, between them. Many journalists spent their evenings in Madame Chantal's delightful opium parlor. French and other diplomats would join them: it was an excellent place to relax, to gossip, and to try to forget the sadness of this war, but American embassy staff were not allowed to go there.

It was hard to gather information from other sources. In Vietnam, reporters were recognized officially and given access and superb transport facilities. In Cambodia, the United States embassy claimed that there was nothing they could do, that everything was run by the Khmers. Privately, embassy officials urged that the Khmers not help reporters, and even deny them seats on helicopters or military planes. In at least one case, an embassy official asked the Cambodian government to expel an American reporter. To travel by taxi to the fighting was extremely dangerous, because the roads were always being cut, if only for short periods, by the Communists. Very few reporters who were captured ever returned; altogether, during the war twenty-one Western and Japanese journalists were lost. It was very inhibiting, and it helps to explain why so few of Amos' or Mataxis' men were ever discovered giving combat advice on the battlefield. Once, reporters out in the field did come across Amos himself with a group of Cambodian officers; they were poring over a map spread on the hood of a jeep. When Amos saw them he tried to disguise himself by speaking French. But Alabama accents are hard to conceal.

It was only after Mataxis won his battle with Ladd that any mention of the feud appeared in the press. The first story, in September 1971, was written by Craig Whitney, *The New York Times* Saigon correspondent. It was followed by a stronger and substantially accurate account in *Newsweek*, written by its stringer, Sylvana Foa, after talks with Ladd and others. Her story suggested that Swank was "knuckling under" to pressure to increase the military establishment, and that Ladd was being eclipsed by Mataxis.

She quoted one embassy official as saying that one reason for the buildup was that officers displaced from Saigon by Vietnamization were anxious for new work—"These men are worried about their careers and you don't become a general sitting behind a desk in Washington." She also suggested that some of Mataxis' men were directly advising Cambodian troops.

The only serious error in the article was the suggestion that the outcome of the battle was yet to be decided. Mataxis had, in fact, already won. But the White House was said to be furious, and Swank also reacted angrily, cabling Rogers to give him "the background on the reprehensible and indeed vicious story" that Foa had written. He charged that her editors had shown her Whitney's article and that "she was in effect given instructions to exploit this theme." She had talked to Fred Ladd and other officials socially and had attended two of Swank's "backgrounders," but "nothing in these contacts or backgrounders furnished a basis for the quotations attributed by *Newsweek* to embassy or U.S. officials."

Swank suggested that her material, "itself probably a composite of inaccuracies, was further edited and embellished in Washington or New York." He asked the State Department to deny that there were any rifts in the embassy and claimed that since July "We now have here what in old-fashioned language has been called a fine team spirit." This was not so, and Foa was correct to state that embassy officials gave advice to combat troops; it was often unavoidable. (Indeed a few days before her piece appeared, an indiscretion by Admiral McCain had caused a short flap in the Pentagon. He had cabled to suggest that more "U.S. advisors" should be sent to the country. When rebuked for using the term so openly, he offered to withdraw the cable formally. He was told by Laird's office that this would only draw attention to it and instead he should call the field and order all copies destroyed.)

The State Department declined to rebut Foa's story, but Swank wrote to her and to *Newsweek* to complain. The magazine published the Ambassador's rebuttal and noted that the magazine stood by her story. The affair lingered and reinforced the mutual distrust between embassy and the press corps, which had begun with Joseph Kraft's story about Colonel Pietsch in June 1970 and had gradually hardened. Reporting of the war continued to be a sporadic affair and, at least until 1973, the embassy was able to proceed sheltered, as the White House wished it to be, from fully informed criticism.

It was not only the press who were hampered in their work. When the House Foreign Affairs Committee or the Senate Foreign Relations Committee sent teams to report on the war, the embassy was encouraged by Washington to make their work as difficult as possible and to withhold all information they could possibly manage. The Joint Chiefs were able to suppress one 1971 House report that they considered, rightly, critical. It has still not been published.

CHAPTER 14

The Battle

THE WAR quickly took on a pattern that changed little during its five years. Communist offensives began with the dry season in January and ended as the monsoons spread the waters over the land in May and June. During the wet seasons the scale of the warfare depended in part on how badly either side had been mauled in the months before.

Within months of the 1970 invasion the Communists had isolated Phnom Penh, gained half the country and over 20 percent of the population. Each year they captured more. It became a war over the lines of communication. Despite the ambitions Kissinger expressed in "Strategy Three, Variant Three," the government controlled only a number of enclaves around Phnom Penh and provincial capitals—Kompong Thom, Kompong Cham, Svay Rieng, Takeo, Kampot, Kompong Som (the renamed port of Sihanoukville), a large area around Battambang in the northwest, and a strip of land between Battambang and Phnom Penh. Apart from Battambang, none was self-sufficient and all depended increasingly on Phnom Penh for rice and other essentials. Lon Nol's troops were engaged principally in trying to keep the roads to them open. As they failed, more and more goods had to be transported first by water and then by air.

For the North Vietnamese too, communications were the key. After the invasion they rebuilt their supply routes into South Vietnam. They came down from southern Laos along the Mekong by water, path and

The Battle

road and some then turned straight east into Vietnam, while others curled
westward and southward around Phnom Penh, eventually ending in the
Mekong Delta. In the northeast, where the North Vietnamese began training Khmer Rouge recruits, some Communist battalions defended these
new supply lines while other forces were used to push Lon Nol's troops
back toward Phnom Penh and keep them preoccupied with their own
survival. For Hanoi, as for Washington, Cambodia was a stalemated war.
The aim was not to capture Phnom Penh but to tie down as many South
Vietnamese and Cambodian troops as possible while Hanoi pursued its
unchanging ends in Vietnam.

Reporters who talked to government soldiers found an air of apathy
settling over them through 1971. By the middle of the year it was almost
impossible to hear such expressions of patriotic fervor as had been common in 1970; naïveté had been replaced by resignation. "There is too
much *bonjour* everywhere," people would claim, using the popular epi-
thet for corruption. Cambodians of all sorts found the Americans' attitudes depressing and confusing. They knew that aid to Vietnam was
unlimited, and that incomprehensible restrictions were placed on aid to
Cambodia although the enemy was the same. *"Pourquoi, Monsieur?"*

Younger and younger boys were being drafted to fill the ranks of the
army. When Australian officers in Vietnam refused to accept one Cambodian unit sent for training because they were only children, an American officer explained: "The little fellas were so anxious to fight that unit
commanders didn't have the heart to turn them down."

The government soldiers' habit of sticking to the roads was reinforced
as they were provided with more and more heavy American equipment.
In the early years the majority of actions were small unit skirmishes that
took place along or close to the highways. The most fiercely contested
points were those where government and Communist lines of communication crossed. There were, to begin with, few grand battles, few single
enormous losses, just a constant drain—twenty men killed here, forty
wounded there. The fighting was usually brutal and without mercy; neither side took prisoners. One of the lasting photographic images of the
war was of a grinning Cambodian soldier with a severed enemy head in
either hand. But, to the disappointment of American officials, the army's
"kill ratio" was poor; the number of Communists it killed for every loss
of its own was as low as that of the worst troops in South Vietnam. The
CIA station reported that the army's tactics "tend to be based on a desire
to permit enemy attack and to rely on air power and ARVN to inflict
casualties."

Individual soldiers often fought very bravely, but their officers were rarely worthy of them. At the same time, very little command or control was exercised over the sprawling new battalions. Poor communications were compounded by traditions of regional autonomy; many battalion commanders acted as if they were feudal chieftains fighting private battles rather than individual commanders in an integrated army engaged in a national war. Ties with Phnom Penh rested on whatever personal loyalty commanders felt for Lon Nol (and he managed to dissipate that fairly fast) rather than on any military traditions or institutions.

Often local commanders saw accommodation with their old neighbors and friends who had chosen Sihanouk—and therefore, at first, Hanoi—as the better part of valor. American arms and ammunition were constantly sold to the other side. The collaboration was especially common in the 3rd Military Region of the country, the section that stretched northwest from Phnom Penh up the Tonle Sap Lake to Thailand and included Battambang and Angkor Wat.

The limitations of the huge army the Nixon Doctrine was creating were never made clearer than at the end of 1971 in the battle of Chenla II.

This operation, named after the sixth-century kingdom, was an attempt to relieve the besieged town of Kompong Thom, which lies on Route 6, the road to Angkor Wat, northward out of Phnom Penh. The town had been under fairly constant siege since the beginning of the war; the only way in, for men or supplies, was by air. A halfhearted attempt to relieve it, Operation Chenla I, was made at the end of 1970. This second venture was entrusted to Colonel Um Savuth, Commander of the 5th Military Region. He was an astonishing personality, a thin, twisted man who walked with a long white cane, drove his jeep at terrifying speeds, and was nearly always drunk. Early in his military career he had, in a moment of high spirits, ordered a subordinate to place a cat on his head and then, from a considerable distance, shoot the animal off. The subordinate refused. Um Savuth insisted that it was a direct order. The man pulled the trigger and a part of Um Savuth's head was blown away. Ever since, half his body had been paralyzed, and he had to drink quantities of beer and Scotch to kill his constant pain.

The relief expedition was Lon Nol's idea, and as usual he retained daily control over it. When the force set out, the monsoon was full upon the country; low clouds hung over the sky and mists arose from the flooded fields on either side of the road. The water deterred any inclination that

Um Savuth might have had to move his men off the exposed, raised surface of the highway and into the comparative cover the paddy and the trees afforded.

Company by company, the troops drove and marched up the road, their women and children straggling along behind them as they always did. No one thought to secure the flanks by establishing outposts. No patrols were sent off the road to ascertain the exact dispositions of the North Vietnamese 5th and 7th Divisions, which were based in rubber plantations just to the east. One of the Communists' supply lines from the northeast down to the Cardamom mountains in the southwest of the country crossed Route 6 just south of Kompong Thom, but the Vietnamese did nothing to hinder the army's blithe advance. On October 11 the vanguard reached Kompong Thom and relieved the city with almost no fighting.

Great were the celebrations in Phnom Penh as the government began to rejoice in a famous victory. In Saigon, General Abrams was not so enthusiastic. "They've opened a front forty miles long and two feet wide," he complained. At the end of October, the North Vietnamese counterattacked. The thin line of soldiers along the road could do nothing to protect themselves; the men, desperate to protect their families, fled in panic.

Lon Nol paid a visit to the field and, back in Phnom Penh, continued his practice of issuing contradictory and irrelevant orders to Um Savuth. He sent one of his frequent personal letters to Admiral McCain in Honolulu requesting more helicopters and amphibious vehicles: "We have determined that our weakness is attributable to the lack of mobility of our reaction forces . . . I count on your kind understanding to help me resolve my difficulties and I am sure that you will not hesitate to use all your influence in coming to our aid . . . Admiral and great friend."

Despite especially intense B-52 attacks coordinated by the American embassy, the North Vietnamese broke the Khmer column between the towns of Baray and Tang Kuok. The troops defending Baray were the First Brigade Group under the command of Lieutenant Colonel Ith Suong, considered by many embassy officials to be one of the most incompetent officers in the country. His men had been without pay for three months; their morale was low. As the North Vietnamese approached, they fled through the paddies, abandoning their equipment, including their artillery pieces, which they neglected to spike.

The rout was complete and the losses enormous. No one knows how many men were killed. From the towns of Rumlong and Baray alone,

Sideshow

Lon Nol's troops, FANK (*Forces Armées Nationales Khmer*), lost four tanks, four armored vehicles, one scout car, twenty buses, twenty-one quarter-ton trucks, one 2½-ton truck, two 105-mm. howitzers and hundreds of machine guns. At Kompong Thom itself, they lost 300 men, two armored personnel carriers, eight 2½-ton trucks, four Land Rovers, twenty quarter-ton trucks, eight buses, one bulldozer, one 105-mm. howitzer. Um Savuth later remarked that he was impressed by the North Vietnamese and the extent of the American armaments they carried.

The debacle, which might have shown once and for all that Lon Nol was incapable of performing the ambitious tasks Kissinger had set him, caused panic and political crisis in Phnom Penh. For a time it seemed that the North Vietnamese might decide to roll all the way into the capital. (In fact, they had no wish to do so.) Rumors of coups abounded in cafés and in ministries. Almost everyone with an interest bent the ear of the United States embassy official he knew best. Son Ngoc Thanh, the leader of the Khmer Serei, who had returned to Phnom Penh, put out the word that it was finally time he became Prime Minister. He had the support of Khy Tang Lim, the Minister of Public Works, who told a member of the U.S. embassy that he himself was planning the coup that would bring Son Ngoc Thanh finally to power. The embassy reported this news to Washington under the rubric: "WARNING. This information must not be used in any way which risks disclosure of even a portion of the report to any foreign nationals, including officials of the Cambodian Government."

Sirik Matak, the acting prime minister and Cheng Heng, the head of state, tried to persuade Lon Nol to abdicate some of his power. Members of his general staff begged him to relinquish over-all command. He refused them all. The embassy, as usual, tried to pretend supreme unconcern or ignorance of the politics and the *démarches*. But Swank cabled Washington, "At issue are not only Lon Nol's highly personal and arbitrary methods of operation but very possibly the future of his government should Sirik Matak and others choose to resign. The dilemma which Sirik Matak and these contenders face, however, is that none of them would appear to be a politically viable substitute for Lon Nol, with all his faults."

Swank's cable found its way into the hands of the columnist Jack Anderson, who published it on December 17. (A second Swank cable, which Anderson published on January 11, 1972, criticized Lon Nol's "haphazard, out-of-channel and ill-coordinated conduct of military operations.") This sort of publicity was not what the White House had in mind when it demanded a "low profile" by the embassy in Cambodia. Swank was rebuked from Washington, and his relationship to Lon Nol, never close, was not improved. The incident led him to be even more cautious in committing any criticisms to paper, and he became still more circumspect with the press.

Nonetheless, his reprimand was less severe than it might have been. The White House was preoccupied with a more important leak, which eventually helped to reveal one effect Kissinger's conduct of foreign affairs had in Washington and the nature of his relationship with the Joint Chiefs.

Ever since Kissinger had refused Laird's January 1969 request to close the Liaison Office between the Chiefs and the NSC, it had been used, as Laird had feared. to strengthen their relationship at his expense. Kissinger later said that the officer in charge of it "would sometimes give us some advance information of what the Joint Chiefs were considering." In fact, according to J. Fred Buzhardt, the Pentagon's General Counsel, who investigated the matter for Laird, the Chairman would actually send Kissinger the drafts of memoranda he was writing to Laird so that Kissinger could revise them, if he wished, to his own advantage.

But although Kissinger flattered and used the Chiefs on some matters, he was less forthcoming on others, like SALT, where their views did not coincide. So the Chiefs began to use the Liaison Office not only to bypass Laird but also to spy on Kissinger. Navy Yeoman Charles Radford worked in the Liaison Office through 1970 and 1971. He later testified to the Senate Armed Services Committee that his superior, Admiral "Robbie" Robinson (who had since died) had told him to try to obtain any NSC documents that might interest the Chiefs and that Kissinger's staff might not provide.

One of Radford's most important tasks was to obtain the agenda of NSC meetings in advance. When Kissinger wanted the Chiefs to be well prepared, these documents and Kissinger's own talking papers were easily obtained. But if Kissinger wished the Chiefs to be at a disadvantage the papers had to be secured surreptitiously. Radford frequently rifled the "burn bags" in which the day's rubbish was accumulated for safe destruction. In December 1970, he accompanied Alexander Haig, as stenographer, to Saigon and Phnom Penh for one of Haig's "stroking missions" to Lon Nol. Radford testified that he was ordered to obtain anything of interest to the Chiefs—talk of troop cuts, agreements between the White House and Thieu, meetings with Swank, assurances to Lon Nol. By making himself extra photocopies of documents wherever possible and by rifling Haig's briefcase, Radford came back with an impressive haul. His boss seemed well pleased. The performance was repeated on another Haig trip to Vietnam and Cambodia in March 1971.

Radford's greatest haul came in July 1971, when he accompanied Kissinger on a trip to Asia. During his visit to Pakistan, Kissinger slipped away and made his historic secret flight to Peking. Then, when the whole party flew back from Islamabad to the United States, Radford rummaged through the burn bags in the plane and through Kissinger's briefcase. He read as much as he could of the transcript of Kissinger's meeting with Chou En-lai. Quite apart from that, he recalled, he obtained about 150 different documents on the trip.

All went well for Radford and his superiors until December 14, 1971, when Jack Anderson published an account of an NSC meeting on the Indo-Pakistan war in which Kissinger had stressed that United States policy was to pretend neutralism but actually to "tilt" toward Pakistan. The leak caused a furor in the White House, and John Ehrlichman assigned the White House Plumbers the task of tracing it. This investigative team had been set up following Daniel Ellsberg's release of the Pentagon Papers and their publication in *The New York Times* in June 1971. It was led jointly by Egil Krogh, from Ehrlichman's staff, and David Young, Kissinger's former appointments secretary; they employed Howard Hunt and G. Gordon Liddy. In September the Plumbers had burgled the office of Ellsberg's psychiatrist in an unsuccessful attempt to find material damaging to Ellsberg. Now they were ordered to place more wiretaps. Egil Krogh refused; he was removed from the team. David Young did as he was told. Four wiretaps were applied, and officials were polygraphed.

Admiral Robert Welander, who had replaced Robinson as Radford's superior, was convinced the leak must have come from Radford. He confessed to Haig what Radford had been doing. Radford himself denied the leak but admitted the spying. When Kissinger heard this, he was, he claimed later, "outraged" and "beside myself . . . precisely because the relationship with the Joint Chiefs had been so close." But J. Fred Buzhardt says, "Henry was very good at showing outrage when it was needed. He was really concerned because it had been a two-way street." In his sworn testimony Radford also maintained this.

Documents show that one of Kissinger's first reactions was to denounce Alexander Haig, whose links to the Army were strong and whose rise to a position of great influence on the NSC staff, in good part through his day-to-day handling of Cambodia, Kissinger now seemed to resent. Some of the internecine flavor of the affair appears through Ehrlichman's handwritten notes of a meeting with Haldeman and Nixon on December 23:

> Talk to HAK
> Not to be brot up w P
> E handling w A/G
> P knows bec of rel w/ JCS. . . .
> K tell Bob what to do re the channel
> Will prosec. Yeoman, Admiral.
> Dont let K blame Haig.

Ehrlichman tried to have Welander sign a prefabricated confession that he had spied on the National Security Council. The Admiral refused. Then, instead of being prosecuted, he and Radford were merely transferred in silence. Despite his "outrage" and despite the fact that the affair went to the heart of his conduct of foreign policy, Kissinger later claimed he knew nothing of the investigation, had "no personal knowledge of any wiretaps," did not know whether any act of treason had been committed, and had no idea why the two men were treated so leniently.

This insouciance may not be characteristic, but it is consistent with the general attitude Kissinger has always publicly taken toward the Plumbers; he claimed constantly that he knew absolutely nothing about them or about Young's work until the operation became public during the Watergate disclosures of 1973. However there are apparent problems in this statement of ignorance. Evidence exists to show that it was principally Kissinger's concern at the publication of the Pentagon Papers that led to the Plumbers' creation in the first place. Other documents show that David Young did remain in touch with Kissinger after he took up his new task.* And the then British ambassador recalls that when he commented unfavorably to Kissinger on the "leaks" of 1971, Kissinger replied, mystifyingly, "Don't worry, we have the Plumbers onto that." Kissinger also listened to a taped interview conducted by Young and read his report on the affair. In 1974, Kissinger admitted this in sworn testimony to the Senate Armed Services Committee.

Eventually the manner in which David Young investigated the affair

---

* Kissinger's concern is very evident in the handwritten notes John Ehrlichman took during meetings with the President to discuss the publication of the Papers. These notes appear in Book IV of the House Judiciary Committee's Statement of Information on the impeachment of President Nixon. In a July 30, 1971, memo to Ehrlichman, Krogh and Young, the Plumbers, wrote: "We have asked Mr. Smyser for an opinion (for Henry A Kissinger) on the relationship of timing between October South Vietnamese elections and the political exploitation of the Democrats' involvement in the 1963 coup against Diem. . . ."

became part of the evidence accumulated by the House Judiciary Committee for the impeachment of President Nixon for abuse of power. Once again the conduct of foreign affairs was responsible for domestic malpractice.

In December 1971 publicity and indictment were a long way off. At that time the only action Kissinger took was to close down the Liaison Office. He did not, he said later, allow the incident to affect his warm relationship with the Chiefs. They continued to collaborate well, particularly on Vietnam and on Cambodia.

The Chiefs agreed with the National Security Council staff that Swank's misgivings about Lon Nol's ability to lead the country—published by Anderson—had to be played down. This is not to say that Swank's analysis was considered incorrect. It was confirmed by an American government psychiatrist, a colonel in the U.S. Army, who was sent to examine Lon Nol's mental condition in December 1971. A few months later, one of the papers generated by National Security Study Memorandum 152 noted that the psychiatrist

> found no significant deviations in his [Lon Nol's] cognitive functions [but] observations by his close associates indicate his mental faculties have deteriorated markedly as a result of his February 1971 stroke . . . available medical data indicate that Lon Nol has extensive vascular disease involving one or more intracranial vessels. It should be noted that even before his stroke Lon Nol was reported to be a vague and unstructured individual. . . . Medical opinion is that it is reasonable to predict that within the next six to eighteen months there may be clinical manifestations either as a stroke which could be incapacitating or fatal, or a deterioration of his emotional stability, cognitive functioning and physical stamina.

This was the man into whose hands the United States was entrusting Cambodia. An explanation was offered by the President:

> [The] aid program for Cambodia is, in my opinion, probably the best investment in foreign assistance that the United States has made in my lifetime. The Cambodians, a people, seven million only, neutralists previously, untrained, are tying down 40,000 North Vietnamese regulars. If those North Vietnamese weren't in Cambodia they'd be over killing Americans. . . . The dollars we send to Cambodia saves [sic] American lives and help us to bring Americans home.

CHAPTER 15

The Bombardiers

EVER SINCE the First World War, air power has held political allure, seeming to offer the promise of almost painless victory. The promise has not always been fulfilled, but it is part of the nature of air power that its real effects are often difficult to separate from those claimed; it is often distant if not invisible, and a pattern of organizational misreporting has, from the start, accompanied it.*

Strategic bombing of the enemy's war-making capacity and attacks upon civilian areas to destroy his morale were first attempted during the Sino-Japanese war in the middle thirties. In the Second World War the British and American air forces pursued radically different approaches to the concepts; the British made much greater use of massive bombing of German cities than the Americans. Some of the reasons were technical: the Americans developed more effective bomb sights, which enabled them to hit critical industrial targets on daytime raids. Without such mechanical efficiency, the British had to rely on nighttime area bombing. But there were also philosophical differences. The Americans believed

---

* In 1919 the infant British Royal Air Force claimed credit for having destroyed the "Mad Mullah" of Somalia after all else had failed. In fact, the Mullah was not harmed by random bombing of the desert, but was chased across the border into Abyssinia by camel-mounted troops. Nevertheless, as Hastings Ismay, Commander of the Camel Constabulary, noted in his memoirs, "The field was open for the Air Ministry to peg out claims for the efficacy of independent air action, which no one in Whitehall had the desire or knowledge to question."

that civilian morale was unlikely to be destroyed by such attacks; indeed the Japanese bombardment of China could be shown to have the opposite effect. And the Americans tended to be more scrupulous. In January 1945, General Ira C. Eaker, an Air Force commander, wrote to his superior, General Carl Spaatz, Strategic Air Commander, Europe, to advise against bombing transportation and other targets in small German towns for fear of excessive civilian casualties. "You and Bob Lovett [Special Assistant Secretary of War for Air] are right and we should never allow the history of this war to convict us of throwing the strategic bomber at the man in the street." Hiroshima helped destroy such ideals.

After the war was over, jealous organizational imperatives began to assert themselves. The U.S. Air Force emphasized the importance of strategic bombing over tactical bombing (close air support for ground troops) in part to guarantee its independence from the army. The Air Force had no real strategic mission in Korea but it immediately saw possibilities in Vietnam. Although the Joint Chiefs could find only eight industrial targets worth striking in their first survey of North Vietnam, the Air Force officers insisted they had a vital role to play in the destruction of Hanoi's industrial infrastructure.

North Vietnamese industry was not destroyed by air strikes, and the CIA later noted: "Twenty-seven months of U.S. bombing of North Vietnam have had remarkably little effect on Hanoi's overall strategy in prosecuting the war, on its confident view of long term communist prospects and on its political tactics regarding negotiations." Other reports gathered in the Pentagon Papers showed that Hanoi's war-making capacity had hardly been affected, that its will had been strengthened by the bombing, its links with the USSR and China had been improved, and civilian morale had hardened.

Throughout the Vietnam buildup, 1965–69, the principal in-house critics of the air war were to be found in the Systems Analysis Office of the Secretary of Defense. Their *South East Asia Analysis Reports* contained many scathing evaluations of the recommendations and the data of the military (the twelve volumes have been obtained under the Freedom of Information Act). Their skepticism over the air war convinced Secretary of Defense Robert McNamara but infuriated the Joint Chiefs, who issued constant rebuttals and demanded that distribution of the papers within the Pentagon be restricted. The Chiefs also enlisted Congressional support against McNamara. Because the political appeal of bombing was so strong, this was easy to do.

The first report on the war Nixon and Kissinger commissioned in January 1969, National Security Study Memorandum One, offered little evidence of the military value of strategic bombing, particularly by B-52s. It showed that close air support of ground troops by tactical aircraft was far more effective—but this accounted for only 8 percent of the total of all missions flown in Indochina. There was no agreement between military and civilian officials as to how many Communists were killed in the "boxes" ground out by the B-52s, but the evidence demonstrated that the bombing of base camps was the least effective technique of all. Moreover, despite the enormous number of "interdiction" flights against the Ho Chi Minh Trail in Laos over the past three years the Communists were getting through adequate supplies. Evidence in NSSM 1 suggested that no amount of air power could prevent them. The American embassy in Saigon, going further, warned that neither the bombing of the North nor that of the Trail had affected Hanoi's ability to wage the war it wished in the South. The embassy concluded, "With this experience in mind there is little evidence to believe that new bombing will accomplish what previous bombings failed to do, unless it is conducted with much greater intensity and readiness to defy criticism and risk escalation."

The new administration considered that the criticism was indeed to be defied. Particularly in the use of air power, escalation was part of their strategy. Menu was launched in March 1969, and in 1970 Nixon expanded the free fire zone in Laos, sent B-52s over the Plain of Jars in Laos for the first time, and approved targets in North Vietnam that Lyndon Johnson had never allowed. One intention was to demonstrate to Hanoi the political point that bombing would not be constrained by domestic opposition.

In its "P.R. offensive" the White House always insisted that it was "winding down" the air war. It is true that the number of sorties by both tactical aircraft and B-52s was reduced during the first Nixon administration. But since many sorties had been judged ineffective, this was fairly easily done. And in 1971 a single B-52 squadron still dropped in one year half the tonnage dropped by U.S. planes in the entire Pacific Theater in World War Two. Furthermore, the White House failed to advertise that bomb loads per raid were increased enormously. In 1968, the average fighter bomb load was 1.8 tons. In 1969, it was 2.2 tons and by 1973, the planes were laden with 2.9 tons of bombs. Each year proportionately more use was made of the B-52, which was militarily the least effective plane, but politically and emotionally the most awe-inspiring. In 1968, B-52s accounted for 5.6 percent of all sorties; by 1972, their share had risen to 15 percent. To the Air Force it was altogether clear that Nixon was doing anything but wind down its role. Its official secret 1969 history was entitled, "The Administration Emphasizes Air Power," and that of 1970, "The Role of Air Power Grows."

The political use of bombing coincided with the Chiefs' desire to keep their planes and pilots flying. It aroused the concern of Melvin Laird. He understood the "firehose" use of air power and accepted the arguments of his civilian staff that many sorties were flown only for reasons of interservice rivalry and for organizational purposes. He never publicly criticized the Chiefs as McNamara had done, but within the Pentagon he persistently attempted to counter their and the White House's efforts to keep the level of bombing as high as possible. Inevitably, his views were unpopular within the Air Force, and its 1970 secret history disparages him as "the chief apostle of Vietnamization and budget cutting." Laird insisted that Congressional concern must be seen as a real constraint and argued that "escalatory acts on our part" would not help reach a negotiated settlement. This was the opposite of the White House perception. The Air Force history notes that in 1970 Nixon realized that the South Vietnamese Army was improving more slowly than troop withdrawals and so "bridged the gap . . . by applying air strikes for political purposes and by extending the geographic area of air interdiction—into Cambodia and back into North Vietnam. Thus the role of air power, though slated for reductions, continued to be emphasized."

Laird was unwilling to place either political or organizational need for bombing before its purely military use.* He and his civilian staff felt that the White House accepted uncritically every claim the Air Force or the Chiefs made for air power, and they frequently voiced their frustrations at the morning meetings on Vietnam that Laird held in the Pentagon. At one stage in early 1970 even the Joint Chiefs wished to withdraw from Southeast Asia B-52s that were not currently required there. The White House refused, demanding that they remain on station "for contingency purposes." A contingency did arise; it was the overthrow of Sihanouk and the invasion of Cambodia. Just before the invasion, Laird's representative, Warren Nutter, suggested at a meeting of the Senior Review Group

---

* There was a parallel and an intriguing dispute in the first half of 1971 between Laird and Kissinger on the maintenance of South Korean troops in South Vietnam. On this occasion, Laird and the Chiefs agreed. The popular image of the Koreans was that they were marvelous, but General Abrams found them atrocious mercenaries. He did not want them. Once when he tried to get them to move a few miles along Route 19 they insisted on $40 million worth of additional helicopters, tanks and armored personnel carriers before they would do so. When they were asked to move from the center of South Vietnam to the Demilitarized Zone in early 1971 they demanded between $200 and $300 million first. Abrams figured out that it cost the United States $730,000 for each Communist the Koreans killed. Nonetheless, the White House insisted that they remain.

that enemy activity did not justify the current sortie rates and that these could be made more flexible in future. Kissinger refused to hear of it and demanded that the number of tactical airstrikes and B-52 sorties that had already been approved for the next financial year be flown regardless of the military situation. Laird was furious. "Anyone that addresses the problem starting with a set number of sorties doesn't understand the problem and isn't qualified to discuss it," he said the next day.

Subsequently, Laird tried to introduce a banking system to mitigate the worst effects of interservice rivalry. He proposed that sorties be saved for future use if on any day no worthwhile target was available. Thus each service would eventually fly its full complement of sorties but at least the targets could be more sensibly chosen.

The Joint Chiefs resisted the innovations; so did Kissinger. Laird had to give way.

The invasion of Cambodia led to an extension of the use of bombing; it needs to be considered in some detail. The Air Force 1970 history notes that when the North Vietnamese recovered from the "temporary setback" of the invasion and began to mount new operations, "the JCS insistence on countering these moves, as well as possible later ones, intensified, and Presidential agreement with the JCS turned the tide in favor of a greatly expanded air interdiction effort."

For a short time in May 1970, Laird attempted to limit the bombing in Cambodia. The White House kept trying to extend it. Kissinger told one meeting of the Washington Special Action Group that the United States would even give close air support to Thai troops in Cambodia if necessary. By early June Laird had stopped resisting. "We're taking so much heat in Cambodia that we might as well bomb as much as possible," he told his Vietnamization group on June 5. But he and his aides were still concerned that Kissinger and Nixon had no idea of what air power could and could not do. He asked Philip Odeen to produce a briefing "to begin educating Dr. Kissinger." "It's a very big job," commented Colonel Pursley, Laird's military assistant. "The President and Dr. Kissinger both believe everything the Seventh Air Force has told them."

The language of the Cooper-Church amendment (limiting U.S. involvement in Cambodia), which was being debated at this time, forbade the use of American air power in close support of Lon Nol's troops. After June 30, 1970, it was to be used only to interdict men and supplies en route to Vietnam. Publicly the administration accepted this restriction, but in fact it was ignored from the start. On the fifteenth of June, Nixon interrupted a WASSAG meeting to insist on more bombing in Cambodia. Its primary purpose might be interdiction, he said, but "I want this purpose interpreted very broadly." The President ordered Laird's deputy, David Packard, to see how more air power could be made available to Lon Nol. Packard suggested that bombing might not be the most effective aid but, he told his colleagues later, "This didn't seem to get through." It was clear to Packard that Nixon was determined to have almost limitless bombing in Cambodia. And so, on June 17, a "Top Secret, Exclusive" cable was sent to Abrams by the Joint Chiefs to authorize more United States and Vietnamese bombing "in any situation which involves a serious threat to major Cambodian positions, such as a provincial capital whose loss would constitute serious military or psychological blow to the country." The Chiefs ordered Abrams, in accordance with Nixon's instructions, to "conduct the most aggressive U.S. and R.V.N.A.F. [South Vietnamese] air campaign in Cambodia which is feasible. . . ." Laird, realizing that the White House was obdurate, secretly recommended that poststrike reports no longer be divided between close support and interdiction; this allowed the support role to be concealed much more easily.

The White House was concerned not to provoke the Congress into banning all air power, as well as advisers, in Cambodia. While the debate over the Cooper-Church amendment was taking place, the extent and purpose of the bombing were publicly played down. But when, at the end of 1970, the amendment finally became law, without any bar on bombing in Cambodia to interdict men and supplies en route to Vietnam, some pretenses were dropped. The Pentagon admitted openly that it would now use the full range of its air power in Cambodia, since any enemy there might "ultimately" threaten United States forces in Vietnam. Laird publicly dismissed the distinction between "interdiction" and "close air support" as "semantics." Rogers declared, "We are going to continue to use that air power, because it protects American lives. It's the least costly way to protect our men—and why we should have any restrictions on the use of that air power to protect American lives, I don't know." Unnamed officials told *The New York Times* that Cambodia was being used as a laboratory to test "public acceptance of the general process of gradually substituting helicopters and attack planes for foot soldiers, as American combat units are withdrawn from the Vietnam war."

There were fewer controls and restraints on targeting in Cambodia than in Vietnam. The South Vietnamese Air Force, as we have seen, considered Cambodia an open field, and although most American pilots were, as a rule, more careful, several have testified that almost anything in Cambodia constituted a legitimate target. The original Menu strikes on the border sanctuaries ended, still a secret, in May. By now, Menu was a recognized procedure, not merely a geographic area. "I would like to retain the Menu cover," Laird wrote to the Chiefs. One of his aides subsequently explained that the Menu procedures required the Chiefs to ask Laird's approval for specific attacks and thus placed some control on the bombing. At the same time, however, it meant that the falsification of Cambodian bombing reports was now accepted as normal.

The main area of the new, extended bombing was known as Freedom Deal. Originally a box of Northeastern Cambodia between the border and the Mekong, it was gradually pushed southward and westward into more heavily populated areas, as the fighting spread. Bombing outside Freedom Deal was reported as being inside, and bombing in populated areas inside as being in wild, uninhabited places. The misreporting meant that there was very little follow-up, or "bomb damage assessment," after missions. In Saigon, little or nothing was known about the location and shifts of Cambodian villages, particularly in Khmer Rouge areas. At the same time, the battle zones of Cambodia were even more inaccessible to the press than those of Vietnam. Carelessness and callousness were easier to practice and tolerate.*

There were different procedures for bombing inside and outside Freedom Deal. In the eastern half of the country, B-52 missions were controlled (and targets were selected) by the Seventh Air Force in Saigon. West of Freedom Deal—west of the Mekong river, in effect—B-52 strikes could be requested by the Cambodians.

Much of the tactical bombing of the country was controlled by American spotter planes known as FACs (Forward Air Control planes). Their job was to call the "strike birds" or bombers into targets. Because American ground advisers were forbidden, the United States trained Cambodian soldiers to liaise with the pilots from the ground. They were known

* Accidents were sometimes pursued. In February 1971 a B-52 mission over Cambodia missed its target. Investigation showed, according to an Air Force memorandum of the event, that the radar site guiding the strike was manned "by a newly formed crew with varied levels of experience. There were several instrument indications during the bomb run that singularly did not indicate a withhold but, when considered collectively, a withhold was imperative. . . . The potential serious political impact of bombing friendly non-combatants led to an immediate generation of reconnaissance of the suspected impact area." No casualties were seen but it was noted that "a repeat of this error could have serious political implications affecting the outcome of the Southeast Asia conflict. Therefore it is imperative that action be taken to preclude recurrence of this nature."

as FAGs (Forward Air Guides), and they spoke either a little French or a little English and were equipped by the United States with FM radios on which they could speak either to the "strike birds" or to the spotter planes above. They developed a close rapport with their American counterparts in the sky, and together the FAGs and the FACs actually controlled many battles. The American pilot was often able to see just what a situation was, and he frequently gave encouragement and instructions, through his FAG, to the ground-unit commander, to whom the Cooper-Church amendment denied such help. (Problems arose after the Communists captured or bought the radio sets and started to ask pilots to bomb FANK positions, and jammed the wave bands by shouting or playing Radio Peking down them.)

The story of the river convoys illustrates how the use of American air power expanded in Cambodia. As the Mekong narrowed with the recession of the flood waters, toward the end of 1970, the convoys to Phnom Penh became more vulnerable to attack from the banks. In early January, Swank cabled Rogers to warn that supplies of petroleum in the city were dangerously low. In Saigon, the military worked out an emergency plan to provide Vietnamese naval support and United States air power to push the convoys through.

The task of guarding the convoys was given to the U.S. Air Force, and to Army helicopter gunships. This drew instant protests from the U.S. Navy, which wanted its own planes involved as well. In Saigon, the Air Force categorically claimed that, "Sufficient air assets were available," and refused to allow the Navy in. But the Air Force had also assumed prime responsibility for keeping Cambodia's roads open. As the 1971 dry season progressed, North Vietnamese attacks on the roads grew so heavy that the Air Force was compelled to divert planes from the river convoys. The Navy was called upon.

Once the Navy, the Air Force and the Army were involved, they all made sure they stayed. Although the convoy protection was meant to be short-term, it expanded along with every other American effort in Cambodia. Even after the river widened with the summer flooding, and became safer for the convoys, air attacks over it were extended again and again. They remained an integral part of United States air activity in Cambodia until 1973.

Throughout 1971, the White House hoped to conclude a settlement and withdraw all but an advisory mission of United States troops from Saigon before the 1972 election. This meant, if anything, more bombardment. President Nixon made frequent public threats to step up the bombing, asserting, for example, that he had "laid down" a new "understanding" with Hanoi on the use of air power. And he warned, "I am not going to place any limitations on the use of air power in Indochina—except to exclude nuclear weapons." The reliance on bombing increased after the catastrophic defeat of ARVN soldiers invading Laos on Operation Lam Son 719 in February 1971.

Laird had recently returned from Saigon. He wrote a bullish report for Nixon in which he praised Vietnamization, and endorsed General Abrams' suggestions for such an invasion. But the ARVN was weaker than he believed, and the enduring image of the operation was of wretched South Vietnamese soldiers desperately clinging to the skids of American helicopters, often falling from great heights as they attempted to flee the disaster.

The Laotian debacle must have given comfort to Hanoi; in the White House its effect was to underscore Nixon and Kissinger's conviction that the Chiefs, and not Laird, were right about the limits of Vietnamization and the need for expanded bombing. The Air Force history of 1970 records that his " 'positive' optimistic positions were eroded more and more by increasingly strong enemy initiatives . . . and by Presidential agreement with the JCS." The 1971 Air Force history records, "Past critics of air interdiction had often suggested that ground forces could achieve more effective results, but now they were less optimistic." In his memoirs Nixon later described his general mistrust of Laird's opinion—"I once jokingly remarked that Laird . . . would answer questions and state his views whether he was informed or not."

It is important to remember that Vietnamization never envisaged the withdrawal of American airplanes from Indochina. Laird publicly acknowledged that, after American troops were removed, American planes would "remain on duty in South East Asia" to form part of the "realistic deterrent which we will maintain." He failed to mention that the White House intended to keep the planes not only "on duty" but at work. In private he expressed his concern. "The roof would come flying off the Capitol if they knew we were seriously considering flying large numbers of sorties in 1973 and 1974," he told his staff in early 1971. "We must keep some considerations very quiet," he warned.

Whatever the tactical relevance of American air power in Cambodia (it helped Lon Nol's troops in the short term and made them dependent in the long run), it was employed both to keep the planes flying and as a strategic symbol. Menu had taken up some of the slack after Johnson halted the bombing of North Vietnam and it was supposed to demonstrate Nixon's "toughness." After the 1970 invasion, the growing South Vietnamese Air Force was diverted to Cambodia; Pentagon studies show that this was deliberately done to prevent the South Vietnamese from displacing the U.S. Air Force in Vietnam. Throughout 1970 and 1971 Kissinger was anxious, for political reasons, to keep the sortie rates high; it was the expanding battlefield in Cambodia that enabled him to do so.

The statistics show the way in which the country was used. In 1970, 8 percent of American combat sorties were flown in Cambodia; the figure rose to 14 percent in 1971. In the first quarter of 1972, Cambodia accounted for 10.5 percent of all USAF sorties and 14 percent of the B-52 missions. But suddenly in April 1972 the planes were withdrawn. At the end of March, Hanoi launched its massive spring offensive into South Vietnam. Soviet-made tanks and North Vietnamese divisions poured over the Demilitarized Zone and across the Cambodian border, demonstrating how short-lived the "brilliant success" of the 1970 invasion of the sanctuaries had been. The war seeped across Vietnam, and for a few weeks in April it seemed that the South Vietnamese might be routed and Nixon confronted with a defeat a few months before the Presidential election.

Air power was called upon to avert the awful possibility. Nixon launched hundreds more planes against the North. Haiphong was bombed and mined. In the South immense numbers of strategic and tactical bombers were thrown into close air support of Thieu's beleaguered troops.

Some of this new armada was flown from bases far from Indochina, but the rest were diverted from Laos and Cambodia. The skies around Phnom Penh were unusually quiet that summer. In 1971, 61,000 American and Vietnamese sorties had been flown there; in 1972 only 25,000. Over these two years Cambodia's share of the bombing fell from 10.5 to 4 percent. But then in 1973, when the Paris Peace Agreement prevented American bombing of first Vietnam and then Laos, the entire Seventh Air Force was switched back to Cambodia. All of this had more to do with political and organizational requirements in Washington and South Vietnam than with the military needs of the Lon Nol government.* Until August 1973,

* Nixon had a furious dispute with the Pentagon over the number of extra B-52s to be sent to Indochina at this time. Dr. Robert Seamans, the Secretary of the Air Force, described the argument in the "Secret" Oral History interview he gave after he left office: "The President wanted to send a hundred more B-52s. This was appalling. You couldn't even figure out where you were going to put them all, you know. How were you going to

when Congress brought the bombing to an end, hundreds of thousands of bombs dropped by the American, South Vietnamese and Cambodian air forces onto Cambodia fell unreported and uncontrolled on areas occupied first by the North Vietnamese and then by the Khmer Rouge.

It could be argued that this use of air power constitutes a prima-facie case of breach of international law. Article 6 (b) of the Charter of the International Military Tribunal following World War II defined "war crimes" as "violations of the laws or customs of war. Such violations shall include, but not be limited to, murder, ill treatment or deportation to slave labor for any other purpose of civilian population of or in occupied territory, murder or ill treatment of prisoners of war or persons on the seas, killing of hostages, plunder of public or private property, wanton destruction of cities, towns or villages, or devastation not justified by military necessity."

---

base them? And you had to base them in a place like the International Airport at Bangkok. And the Thais were pretty supportive, but they didn't want a whole bunch of B-52s right there. They finally agreed to adding some tankers there but not very many. . . . Mr. Rush and Admiral Moorer went over to brief Kissinger on the reason why we shouldn't increase the number more than a certain amount and got a negative response to that. I think it was at the same time the President was going over to Moscow . . . so, anyway, a message was sent to the airplane—this was that timely—as to why we couldn't send those B-52s over there. As I understand it, the response when he touched down really burned the wires, and he said he wanted them over there. . . . The total never did quite reach one hundred, but it was a pretty large number. . . ."

CHAPTER 16

The Decay

As the bombing transformed the countryside, American aid transformed the cities. It was clear, from 1970 on, that Lon Nol needed economic support to continue the war and that his political stability had to be subsidized. The aid program was applied more broadly than military assistance; its failure demonstrates the contradictions of the Nixon Doctrine more starkly.

From the beginning of 1971 until April 1975 (and in some ways, beyond), United States aid was the dominant factor in almost every aspect of political, economic and military affairs in Cambodia. Since the Doctrine demanded a pretense that the United States was not involving itself in the affairs of this small country, economic aid, like military, was handed over with few strings attached. Embassy officials with "low profiles" watched as the money they provided destroyed the will of the recipients.

The initial grants were to help Cambodia import commodities that had previously been financed by its exports. Despite the stagnation of the economy under Sihanouk, in 1969 exports of rice, rubber and corn had brought in $90 million; a sizable portion of the Gross National Product of $450 million. By the end of 1970, the government was spending five times its revenue and earning nothing abroad. The rubber plantations in the east of the country were burned down, bombed or occupied by the Communists;* thousands of hectares of paddy field had been abandoned, and those still being harvested, around the city of Battambang, were required for domestic consumption. Within a few months the country's economic independence was destroyed.

As well as financing a Commodity Import Program, the United States began to sell the Cambodians surplus American agricultural products—wheat, flour, vegetable oil, tobacco, cotton fiber and cotton yarn under the "Food for Peace" program, the standard vehicle for distribution of food to the Third World. The agricultural goods (like other commodities imported) were purchased with Cambodian riels, which—until the U.S. Congress legislated against such practices—were placed in a blocked account in Phnom Penh and used to pay the salaries of the expanding army. The "sales" of American agricultural produce financed a new military machine.

As more economic aid was invested in Cambodia every year, the economy deteriorated. One can glance at the consumer price index for food; the figures are the government's and are perhaps slightly exaggerated, but not greatly. From the base of 100 representing 1949 prices, the index had risen to 348 in March 1970, the last month of Sihanouk's rule. By the end of 1970 the index was 523; by the end of 1971, 828; by the end of 1972, 1,095; by the end of 1973, 3,907; and by the end of 1974, 11,052.

By mid-1971, it was clear that economic management required more refined tools. The United States encouraged the International Monetary Fund to set up an Exchange Support Fund that could create a flexible exchange rate. (It was the American experience from Vietnam that a fixed exchange rate was unrealistic in time of war and inflation, distorted economic performance and encouraged corruption.) The Fund was supposed to sell foreign exchange to commercial importers twice a week on a modified auction basis. These auctions would determine the rate of the riel. The United States pledged a 50 percent share of the Fund, and after Washington applied varying amounts of pressure the rest was provided by the governments of Japan, Britain, Australia, Thailand, New Zealand and Malaysia.

The Fund proved useful for generals and merchants to continue importing luxury goods that were not eligible under the Commodity Import Program. In the early years of the war new Mercedes, Peugeots, Audis blocked the streets; and throughout, Courvoisier and Dom Perignon

* Subsequently officials in Phnom Penh devised methods of buying Communist-produced rubber to sell abroad for hard currency.

flowed into the country. By itself, however, the Fund was not as financially influential as AID officials had hoped. Cambodian government bankers tended to be conservative in monetary policies and, influenced by powerful private importers, often resisted American advice to devalue the riel. Embassy officials found they had to threaten to withhold or to cut the Commodity Import Program in order to secure reforms they thought desirable. Only then would the haggling reach a compromise barely acceptable to both sides.

Almost every month of the war the government's enclaves shrank, the numbers of refugees in them grew, and the country's per capita agricultural and industrial production declined, even with AID-financed imports taken into account. The Commodity Import Program changed constantly, and less-essential goods were dropped in favor of rice, petroleum and medicines. From mid-1972 onward, there was rarely enough food in Phnom Penh and from 1973 until the end of the war, AID officials raced from one rice crisis to another. But official reports show that Washington kept the imports of rice as low as was consistent with avoiding food riots. This was ostensibly to encourage greater domestic rice production on the declining areas of paddy left to the government. But it was also to disguise the serious nature of the problem.

The U.S. AID mission's draft termination report notes, "The record shows that mission requests from 1973 forward stayed on the low side of requirements and that PL 480 rice requested was never more than the basic amount needed to avert serious food-supply shortages among the deficit population." The amount of rice available per head fell annually, and gradually malnutrition increased, particularly among refugees.

Like many Cambodian statistics, the number of refugees who fled their homes during the war is still disputed. Several hundred thousand were uprooted by the end of 1970; the CIA reported that Phnom Penh's population doubled to 1,200,000 within the first months of the war. By the end of 1971, the Cambodian Ministry of Health estimated that more than two million of Cambodia's seven million people had been displaced, and the government reckoned that over 20 percent of property in the country was destroyed.

The first refugees—some plantation workers and fishermen, but mostly farmers—said they were fleeing the bombing, the fighting, the combatants, most especially the South Vietnamese. (Later the rigors of Khmer Communist control were increasingly cited.) Despite American and Cambodian complaints, the South Vietnamese continued to regard Cambodia as a free fire zone, pillaging, burning, raping. At the town of Kep in Kampot province they ate the animals in the zoo. (A Joint Cambodian-South Vietnamese Committee appointed to examine the outrages had, by September 1971, examined three hundred cases and paid compensation on only two—$90 for a rape and $180 for a murder.)

Many refugees initially made their way to provincial capitals. The town of Svay Rieng, one of the government's few enclaves in the east, became saturated, and its camps filled to overflowing. On every spare patch of street, makeshift thatched huts were erected. Work was almost impossible to find. All through 1971 and 1972 some three hundred refugees streamed in each month, many of them without money or belongings. As conditions in this and other provincial towns worsened, refugees pushed on to Phnom Penh in hope of improvement. They were disappointed. Some at first managed to find sanctuary with relatives or friends and after a few months of war it was not uncommon to find three or four families in one small home. As the economy deteriorated, it became almost impossible for the head of the original household to support all his dependents even though some of them found casual work as day laborers, *cyclo* drivers, street vendors, prostitutes. Shanties began to appear on the roads leading into Phnom Penh and other towns. Refugees built shelters out of bamboo, thatch, cardboard or, if they were lucky, corrugated iron. These huts gave little protection against the rain, and sanitation was scarce. In Phnom Penh, the largest encampment of this kind was just south of the city in the Southern Dike area, and month by month it grew into an intractable slum half drowned in stagnant water.

Refugees housed in government camps were little better off. The Chak Angre camp was built in the middle of Phnom Penh in December 1970. Within a year almost all of its small houses leaked, the drainage and the latrines had broken down, and morale was poor. Many of the families had lost their men to the war, and the women and children rarely earned enough money to survive. By the end of 1971 malnutrition and stomach disorders were widespread in the camp.

Under a policy laid down in Washington and faithfully implemented by the embassy in Phnom Penh, American officials were actually discouraged from admitting that a refugee problem existed. Refugee work was considered incompatible with a "low profile," and it was feared that recognizing the problem might encourage further Congressional hostility toward the Nixon Doctrine. Two of the staff of Senator Edward M. Kennedy's Refugee Subcommittee visited Cambodia in September 1970 and reported that "although U.S. officials were obviously aware of the widespread displacement of people, there was little evidence to suggest they were much concerned about the situation, its tragic potential if the war in Cambodia continued, or the impact of United States military activities on the civilian population." Nobody in the embassy was given full-time responsibility for the problem.

In Washington, William Sullivan, then Deputy Assistant Secretary of State for East Asian and Pacific Affairs, claimed that "people who are displaced have been taken care of, except the small group of people who are encamped on the outskirts of Phnom Penh itself." In Phnom Penh, embassy officials, from Ambassador Swank down, insisted that the Khmer family system was coping, that the government was proud of its independence. In fact, the Lon Nol regime was incapable of managing the flow of indigents. It never developed any coordinated refugee program and its agencies differed by a factor of one thousand percent on how many refugees there were.

If journalists, officials from charities like Catholic Relief Services or Congressional investigators asked why no humanitarian aid was being given, Swank and his superiors replied that the Cambodians had never officially asked for it. It is true that the Cambodians did not make many requests of the United States; the embassy had made it clear that they would not be granted.

Health services throughout the country began to collapse very fast under the impact of war. In 1971, a team from the Congress' General Accounting Office found that there was a critical shortage of medicine and that conditions in many hospitals were deplorable. As casualty lists lengthened and the need for medical treatment grew more acute, the facilities were further strained. Extra cots or mats were pushed into hospitals, but there was a shortage of doctors and nurses. The Ministry of Health's share of the national budget was slashed; in the first year of the war, fiscal 1971, it fell to 2.6 percent—the lowest percentage for years. In the Khmer-Soviet Friendship Hospital, which was built during Sihanouk's time, patients lined the wards and the corridors wall-to-wall, sleeping on cots, rush mats, wooden benches, the floor. Staff offices were converted into an emergency unit, but it had almost no equipment. The latrines were usually underwater. In the maternity ward mothers and newborn babies lay together on cots without any cover.

In 1969, before the war began, Cambodia had imported $7.8 million worth of drugs, paid for by exports of rice and rubber. (Some of this medicine went to the Vietnamese Communists.) In 1970, the demand for drugs soared, but only $4.1 million worth was imported. The next year, with demand still higher, the figure was almost exactly the same. By the summer of 1971, the shortage was critical; hundreds of people were dying for want of proper treatment. In one Phnom Penh hospital, a serious gastric disorder was killing off 15 percent of all infants. It would have been easily controlled with appropriate drugs. The doctor in charge complained that none was available.

Cambodian health officials asked the U.S. embassy that drugs be included under the Commodity Import Program. The request was refused. The official explanation was that the Cambodians did not control drugs carefully and much of it would be sold to the Viet Cong. This was also true of arms; hundreds of weapons were ending up on the other side, but that was never used as a reason for denying military aid.

On June 1, 1971, Dr. Pheng Kanthel, the Ministry of Health representative on the Khmer Red Cross, came to see Robert Blackburn, a second secretary in the embassy, to ask for help in obtaining medical equipment and supplies from the American Red Cross. Blackburn agreed to contact the organization. According to his own memo of the conversation, he also told the doctor that there was little possibility of such supplies or equipment being financed by United States aid. Then, Blackburn continued, "I strongly recommended that he seek assistance through other embassies, including those of the socialist countries, as it was clear that he was seeking humanitarian assistance for civilian casualties." Blackburn wrote on the bottom of his memo: "Comment: I have the impression that he has been launched by the Minister, that he hopes the Red Cross will provide everything he needs—even though he has no idea what he needs. I will inform the American Red Cross that there is this interest but I do not recommend that we take any further action." His advice was accepted.

Two and a half months later, after hearing nothing, Dr. Kanthel wrote to Samuel Krakow, the Director of International Services of the American Red Cross. He began by thanking Krakow for aid offered by the American Red Cross in 1968 and reminded him that they had met at a conference in Vienna, "an encounter which will always remain vivid in my memory." Now, wrote the doctor, Cambodia was in difficulties. Since March 1970,

Communists aggression against Cambodia generated medico-sanitary problems. Hospitals of Phnom Penh both civilian and military are over-crowded with the sick and wounded. People have fled from insecure rural areas, taken refuge in the capital whose population has increased from 600,000 to 2 millions. In the provinces, also, people have flocked in urban areas whose medical facilities are destroyed by the aggressors either kill or wound the medical staff and the civilians population. . . . The war is going on, casualties are increasing steadily resulting in an alarming rapid decline of our medical, clothing and food stockpiles although we did receive a large number of aids from friendly countries.

He was "taking the liberty" to ask the American Red Cross

to send us in the shortest possible time such drugs as antibiotics, vitamins, antimalaria, etc. . . . and such medical articles as dressing materials, surgery equipment, clothing and food. . . . We sincerely hope your friendly and urgent intervention with American Red Cross will help us assume our responsibilities. We did approach the U.S. Embassy in Phnom Penh but no response has yet been obtained.

Dr. Kanthel waited for over six months for a reply. On February 17, 1972, Krakow wrote to offer the Cambodians 6,433 bottles containing 385,900 vitamin tablets. "Before these can be shipped to Khmer, we must have your Society's acceptance of the shipment, with a statement regarding duty-free entry."

The Blackburn memorandum was leaked to Senator Kennedy's Refugee Subcommittee; and some months later, at a hearing on Cambodia, Kennedy asked how Washington had followed up Dr. Kanthel's request. Thomas Corcoran, State's Cambodian desk officer replied, "We received this request in order to pass it on to the American Red Cross, and we did pass it on to the Red Cross."

"Continue," said Kennedy.

"We have heard no more about it," said Corcoran.

"Do you follow it up at all? Do you just pass the buck? Is there any humanitarian aid in the budget?" Kennedy demanded. There was a silence in the hearing room.

Finally, an AID official, Roderic O'Connor, tried to explain why the United States did not send medicines to Cambodia.

Kennedy interrupted. "I simply can't understand how a request of this sort—for needed medical supplies for refugees and victims of a war which we help fuel—how you can allow such a request to be handled in this fashion. . . . If that request had been for military aid—for guns or air support—how many hours do you think it would take for us to respond?"

It was not until second half of 1972, after increasing pressure from

Kennedy and other members of Congress, and after the embassy could no longer pretend that the plight of the refugees did not exist, that the administration was prepared to admit a serious problem. A modest relief program was begun. Largely because Congress had by now imposed a ceiling of 200 personnel on the American embassy, funds were given to charities like Catholic Relief Services and World Vision to expand their own relief efforts in the country. Of the total $244.1 million given in American aid between July 1972 and July 1973, $1.2 million was for refugee assistance.

. Graft had been one of the issues that encouraged urban support for Sihanouk's removal; it was nothing new. But before 1970 it had been controlled, in part by the Prince's authority, in part because Cambodia's economy was small and self-sufficient. As the economy became dependent on American aid and as Cambodians exercised less and less control over their own economic and political life, a sense of responsibility and caution diminished.

Three ministries took most of the wartime budget—Defense, Education and Finance. The most corrupt was Defense. Given the speed with which the Army was expanded from about 37,000 to over 200,000 in two years this was perhaps understandable. The biggest source of "bonjour" lay in the pay packets of "phantom soldiers." Individual commanders, recruiting whom they could, submitted their own units' pay claims and were supposed to distribute salaries when (and if) the money was produced. Throughout the war dishonest commanders inflated the rolls and pocketed the salaries of nonexistent men. Many colonels would not pay the troops who really did exist, and hungry soldiers often resorted to pillaging villages, alienating the peasants. When men and their families were on the point of riot the Ministry of Defense would demand more funds from the Ministry of Finance. Then Lon Nol endorsed the demands, and the money had to be found or printed.

No one will ever know just how much was stolen and dissipated in this way. But the sums were not inconsiderable, and they grew every year as the Joint Chiefs, Kissinger and Haig insisted on expansion of Lon Nol's forces. One FANK census of July 1971 showed there were already at least 22,000 "phantom soldiers," with another 46,000 real troops actually untraceable. At the end of 1971, Laird's office sent out auditors, who concluded that between 6 and 8 percent of all salaries were being paid to "ghosts" and that in one month alone $280,000 was padded onto the payroll. This was nothing to what was to come. In the second half of 1972, Lon Nol decided he needed to buy more loyalty from his officer corps and told regional commanders that they could raise their recruiting levels. As a result, by the end of the year payrolls leaped by another 50,000, to over 300,000. In Washington the General Accounting Office determined that in 1973 between $750,000 and $1.1 million was being paid to "phantoms"—that is to their officers—every month. In its Termination Report, the Agency for International Development concluded that 20 to 40 percent of all military salaries were lost in this way.

In the face of this corruption the United States embassy, acting on orders from the White House, did almost nothing. General Mataxis scoffed at those who complained. His successor General John Cleland· did attempt some reforms, but he was, if anything, even more easily angered by criticisms from individual diplomats within the embassy. Both men could and did insist that the logic of the Nixon Doctrine supported their inaction.

One of those who were most indignant about their attitude was William Harben, who came to the embassy in January 1972 as Chief of the Political Section. Harben's first assignment in the Foreign Service had been in Bonn in the early fifties; he had served directly under John Paton Davies—who was soon to fall victim to the McCarthy purge of the State Department because he had reported from China (over twenty-two years before it was accepted) that Mao Tse-tung was an effective leader with whom the United States should deal. Davies taught Harben the value of skepticism about official attitudes, and by the time he reached Cambodia, at fifty, Harben, who had never taken easily to the niceties of diplomatic life, found it hard to tolerate lies: his reporting style was as pungent as Khmer political life.* Today Harben argues that "American toleration of military corruption led directly to defeat. Every imported motorcycle cost the Army a squad, every car a platoon." He spent most of 1972 writing

---

* One of Harben's reports recounted a fight in the Assembly between two deputies, Hoeur Lay Inn and Ung Mung. Hoeur Lay Inn, he wrote, "is fond of the meat of the Cambodian wild ox, which acquires a special piquancy due to its habit, in the dry season, of urinating into a hole it stamps in the ground and quaffing the contents." Harben related how Hoeur Lay Inn retained the friendship of both the Russians and the Americans, serving the Americans baksheesh vodka and caviar given him by a man from TASS. He was "built like a Cambodian wild ox and has a temper to match", he had survived a succession of beautiful wives. Ung Mung, on the other hand, was "unpopular, sharp-tongued, opportunistic." During a recent angry debate in the Assembly, "Ung Mung unwisely advanced to the podium to escalate the vituperation still further, but collided with Hoeur Lay Inn, who kicked him painfully in the groin and chased him through the hall, pounding him with his fists and overturning tables."

long memos to Swank and to the Deputy Chief of Mission, Thomas Enders, about embezzlement of funds; nothing ever happened. One memo to Enders complained about the huge villas that unit commanders were building all over Phnom Penh with their "phantom money." Harben pointed out that there was an extreme shortage of military accommodation and suggested the villas should be seized by the government and used to house military families or refugees instead of the mistresses of the officer corps. Enders ignored his suggestion. When Harben complained to a visiting Washington official, the man replied, "Oh well, it's better they spend the money here than take it to Switzerland." (Some did that as well.) Another of Harben's papers was attacked by General Cleland as "anti-Lon Nol propaganda."

To his fury Harben found that Ambassador Swank would not take his side against the United States military on the issue of corruption. Admitting this, Swank argues that "this was their society. We were not there to reform it." Even talk of corruption was discouraged for fear of the press and for fear of increasing Congressional reluctance to continue funding the war.

Harben was also appalled by Lon Nol. He wrote a long paper entitled "The Anthropological Lon Nol" in which he detailed the Marshal's bizarre idiosyncrasies. Swank allowed the paper to be sent to Washington, and members of the NSC staff were furious, accusing the embassy of "racism." (The State Department has refused to declassify the paper under the Freedom of Information Act.) Harben was right. Month by month the Marshal's behavior became more autocratic. The debacle of Chenla II only temporarily restrained his meddling in the conduct of battles. His political interference was at least as damaging. In October 1971, he suspended the Assembly and assumed emergency rule, saying that he would no longer "play the game of democracy and freedom." At the same time Sirik Matak, the Prime Minister-designate, imposed new restrictions on the press. These moves, together with Chenla II, infuriated Phnom Penh students, who by now realized that Lon Nol was far more corrupt and dictatorial than Sihanouk had ever been. In March 1972 students began to demonstrate against the government and especially to demand the dismissal of Sirik Matak, who had himself dismissed a critic of government, Keo An, the Dean of the Law Faculty.

Lon Nol chose the moment of this crisis to overthrow Cheng Heng, the Chief of State. He declared that he was now Chief of State himself (as well as Prime Minister and Supreme Commander of the Armed Forces) and dissolved the Assembly. Even Sirik Matak refused to serve in his new regime, and so Lon Nol appointed Son Ngoc Thanh "First Minister." After twenty-five years of fighting with American help, the leader of the Khmer Serei had achieved a powerful position in his country.

The students retreated, then attacked again. At the end of April, government forces fired on a group of them, hitting at least twenty. Lon Nol proclaimed a new constitution that gave the executive branch overwhelming powers. It was approved by a referendum after the populace was warned that a vote against it was a vote for Communism. Under the provisions of the new constitution, Lon Nol then put himself forward for election as President.

In the midst of this turmoil Kissinger launched another of his National Security Study Memoranda—No. 152, "Cambodia Assessment"—into the bureaucracy. "The President has directed," he wrote on March 27, 1972, "the preparation of an assessment of the current situation in Cambodia, prospects for the next eighteen months and actions we might take to advance our objectives in Cambodia." He wanted to know how stable Lon Nol was, how Cambodian-South Vietnamese relations could be improved, how the Cambodian Air Force could be developed, how the army could be made more effective and "the importance in military terms to Vietnamization of various Cambodian contributions including denial of supply through a Cambodian port, allied air operations against supply routes in Eastern Cambodia, cooperation with ARVN in cross-border operations against logistics and training areas, and diversion of NVA and VC combat forces away from Vietnam."

Kissinger asked for two studies, one military, to be chaired by the Pentagon and one political, by State. As usual, they stretched beyond the nominal deadline he set. For months dozens of offices and scores of officials throughout Washington were occupied with seeking, acquiring, ordering and analyzing information for the White House, and being told to take it back for modification and review. The papers demonstrate how clearly Washington understood the nature of the regime it had already supported for two years and would sustain for almost three years more.

The memoranda were dominated by Lon Nol and by the effect of his incompetence upon the country. The U.S. Army psychiatrist's report was cited, and there was general agreement that "his own erratic actions" had eroded a great deal of his original support. His meddling in battlefield tactics had alienated the army; "his authoritarian actions" had lost him the support of the Buddhists, students and many politicians. The coalition that had overthrown Sihanouk had fallen apart. Ambassador Swank reported that Lon Nol, "gives the impression of a rider astride a somewhat rebellious horse whose actions he cannot fully control."

A military paper, written by Brigadier General A.P. Hanket, the Chairman of the Military Study Group, noted five deficiencies in the Cambodian army: leadership and discipline; strategy and force utilization; the personnel system; the logistics; training. Behind all of these lurked the problem of Lon Nol:

> He is a political figure and uses the FANK for political as well as military ends. He insures that promotion and good assignments go to the loyal officers, not all of whom are capable. He ignores normal staff procedures, in many instances, going to officers whom he knows and trusts. . . . This proclivity of the Marshal to ignore the established command/staff system makes the development of an effective chain of command and a functioning staff at FANK HQ difficult if not impossible. Field commanders bypass the HQ or ignore HQ directives to the extent they believe their political affiliations will allow.

This, the paper stated, undermined almost every aspect of the war effort. It harmed personnel actions, encouraged late or inaccurate reports from unit commanders, hurt the intelligence system, since commanders relied on personal networks, not FANK, and disrupted logistics.

> As a consequence the staff is frustrated and cautious, and the commanders in the field castigate the staff in Phnom Penh for inactivity and lack of support.

The report noted that

> it isn't enough to produce trained units complete with qualified officer and non-commissioned officer personnel; these leaders must operate within a system that gives them direction and insists on results. If malaise, nepotism or weakness is allowed to exist at the top it will pervade the entire organization.

From Phnom Penh, Swank agreed that Lon Nol was almost exclusively to blame for the spirit of "drift and futility" that now slouched through Phnom Penh's streets and the ranks of the army.

The political section of NSSM 152 identified possible successors to Lon

Nol. There was First Minister Son Ngoc Thanh, whom one of the NSSM documents called "Cambodia's George Washington." But, it noted, if he became President, "This would represent a propaganda windfall for the enemy, since it has been charged and is apparently believed in some U.S. circles and even in the Congress that Thanh's Khmer Serei was supported by the CIA and was instrumental in bringing about Sihanouk's overthrow at the behest of the U.S."

An alternative was Sirik Matak. The papers stated that he had, for many years, maintained extremely close relations with the United States. He was a competent politician and an adequate administrator. But, NSSM 152 noted, his conspicuous wealth and dictatorial methods denied him support among students and intellectuals. Next was Major General Sak Sutsakhan, the Defense Minister and Deputy Chief of Staff, who had managed the singular feat of staying honest and close to Lon Nol. NSSM 152 believed that he was highly regarded by the military, who would probably support him in a crisis, and that his frustrations over the malaise of the war might induce him to make a bid for political power.

The most plausible candidate appeared to be In Tam, former Brevet General, Governor of Kompong Som, First Deputy Prime Minister, Assemblyman, leader of the Democratic Party. One NSSM paper noted that he is "among the most politically experienced of possible pretenders to the leadership position." Unlike many of his peers, he lived simply and unpretentiously and had preserved a reputation for honesty. He had the support of youth, intellectuals, civil servants and some military officers. However, the regular army did not like him, and he was criticized for his "mandarin" attitude and for refusing to listen to subordinates' advice. In Tam had little experience in foreign affairs and had "a tendency to become emotional when frustrated." Nevertheless, he "has a popular following, an integrity and personal courage rare in Khmer leaders . . . He displayed a very good sense of military organization and tactical ability in Kompong Cham in 1970."

As these conclusions were being made in Washington, In Tam proposed himself for election as an alternative to President Lon Nol in the summer 1972 election. Keo An, the ousted Dean of the Law Faculty, also entered the electoral lists. In Tam's platform promised that the military was to be reformed, and the direction of battlefield tactics would be left with the general staff, where they belonged. Keo An capitalized on the growing pro-Sihanouk sentiment by promising to allow the Prince to return home "as a private citizen." Each man's program was popular.

The contest presented Washington a unique opportunity. Although al-

232

most no one was now prepared to defend Lon Nol's mental or military competence, United States policy had always been to give absolutely no support to his political opponents. Asked why, Swank would cite the murder of Vietnamese President Ngo Dinh Diem in the 1963 coup, which was backed by the CIA. That was certainly an unhappy precedent; the United States embassy wished, with good reason, to avoid a repetition. But the election offered the prospect of Lon Nol's removal with no such risks. All that Washington need do was to insist that it be conducted fairly.

The result could not have been predicted with confidence, but in May 1972 there was consensus in the American and Western embassies that the most popular candidate was In Tam. Many diplomats believed that he might be able to rally and rejuvenate the weary country. He might also attract back from the Khmer Rouge, whose growth was beginning to concern the United States embassy, those who had defected out of horror at Lon Nol's government rather than revolutionary zeal. If the embassy insisted on visibly fair electoral procedures, In Tam's victory would be possible, and then Lon Nol could be gently retired.

No such pressure was applied. Despite the evidence produced, the papers of NSSM 152 concluded that Lon Nol was "the key to stability" and "to the extent that political instability develops the war effort will suffer, an eventuality contrary to U.S. interests and the prospects for the success of Vietnamization." They went further and argued against an attempt to persuade Lon Nol to attack corruption or reform the staff structure. The results of such pressure "would be difficult to predict but would be highly dangerous and could well eliminate or seriously reduce our existing influence and the effectiveness of our assistance program." Exactly the same arguments had been applied in Vietnam years before.*

From Phnom Penh, Swank urged that the United States should let the Khmer politicians "play out their hand without outside interference." In Washington, participants on NSSM 152 agreed that "we should refrain from overt or covert acts designed to manipulate the outcome of the evolving political situation in Cambodia."

At the same time, the Joint Chiefs were pressing, at General Cleland's request, for more military aid to Lon Nol. They wanted more assistance to the Khmer military personnel system; money for a separate finance

---

* The Pentagon Papers noted that after the big U.S. buildup in South Vietnam in 1965, neither Washington nor the embassy would find a "compelling reason to be tough with Saigon; it would only prematurely rock the boat. To press for efficiency would be likely, it was reasoned, to generate instability."

directorate of the army; more military advisers, perhaps from Korea; more military training, perhaps in Indonesia; more Filipino logisticians; more help from New Zealand and Australia; and more bombing by the Thai Air Force. The tasks that Congress had forbidden Americans to perform were to be farmed out to allies and clients. Most important, they wanted direct United States involvement in Lon Nol's vague plans for a "General Mobilization" of the countryside.

It was a crucial feature of the Nixon Doctrine that the United States give military support to Lon Nol, tolerate his corruption, and also assert that it was not intervening in Cambodian politics. One American official reflected his own despair over the charade when later, in an official report, he likened America's intervention in Cambodia to the arrival of a 25-foot shark in a backyard swimming pool filled with children who cannot escape. Even if the shark assumes a "low profile" and lies motionless, he displaces a great deal of water and interest over his intentions begins to affect everyone's behavior.

If, in addition, he also brings some toys for a few of the children and casts a baleful eye at anyone who appears to want-to interfere with the enjoyment of the few, behavior will become almost ritualistic in its predictability. Even if those receiving toys ruin life in the pool for everyone else, there will be no interference with their activities. The shark's awesome potential will assure that.

During the election campaign Lon Nol announced that if he were not reelected all United States aid would immediately be suspended. Washington did not deny it. His brother, Lon Non, returned from Paris with the avowed purpose of seeing that Lon Nol won under any circumstances. The vote took place on June 4. Army units voted in serried ranks with their officers—those same officers whom Lon Nol allowed to pad their payrolls—counting the ballots. According to the official figures Lon Nol won 55 percent of the votes cast, In Tam had 24 percent and Keo An 21 percent.

Harben, together with other American and Western diplomats, was convinced that the count, especially in the provinces where there was little foreign observation, was fraudulent. Lon Non boasted that he had raised his brother's share of the vote from 35 percent. Harben prepared a paper in which he detailed the electoral malpractices; the ambassador refused to send it to Washington. Swank now says, "There were too many unsubstantiated allegations in it."

Harben's comment was typically angry. "Washington collaborated in delivering total control of its military aid into the hands of a man who had been appointed *because of* his incompetence," he wrote later. "Far out on a limb in an election year with its 'Nixon Doctrine,' the administration did not want anyone to see the albatross around its neck." He was right. It is clear from almost all the papers in NSSM 152, which rolled on and on through the summer of 1972, that Lon Nol's incompetence was not only irrelevant, it was actually valuable. The crucial point was that neither Washington nor Hanoi wanted a cease-fire in Cambodia before Vietnam. At least until 1973 each wished its associate to continue a limited war. So long as Lon Nol remained to conduct his holy struggle against the demon Communists no cease-fire was likely. A more realistic leader might have tried a path of accommodation. One NSSM 152 paper pointed out what would happen if a separate peace were arranged in Cambodia. For now the Thais and the South Vietnamese were ostensibly Cambodia's allies, but a unilateral settlement by the Khmers "would likely bring South Vietnamese and possibly Thai incursions, which would subject the Khmer countryside to continued damage and destruction and possible foreign domination of another stripe." The threat was clear; the Cambodians could not win, but if they tried to retire, war would be waged against them as aggressively as now—by their current friends.

CHAPTER 17

The Others

ALL THROUGH the war diplomats and journalists at Phnom Penh dinners and cocktail parties spoke of *"les autres"* only in the vaguest terms. They were thought of as shadowy, insubstantial, inconsequential, wraiths almost, inhabiting that unknown, fearsome world "out there," where the bombs that rattled the windows and shook the glasses actually fell. It was not until well into the war that the idea that the Khmer Rouge could in any way differ from, actually be independent of, the North Vietnamese and Viet Cong was entertained.

Such ignorance was fostered and exploited by Washington and by the American embassy. The intention was at first to establish that it was a wholly North Vietnamese army that Lon Nol's gallant men were fighting and later to explain why a settlement was impossible. The Khmer Rouge leadership was said to be unknown and divided, and three of its supposed leaders were pronounced dead—"ghosts"—in Washington; there was no one with whom Kissinger could talk.

It is true that there are fewer written sources on the origins of Cambodian Communism than on Vietnamese or Lao, that its beginnings are confused, and that since there had been no American embassy in Phnom Penh between 1965 and 1969, American knowledge of opposition in the countryside was sketchy. Moreover after May 1970, the CIA found it harder to place agents among the Khmer Rouge than among the Viet Cong. Nonetheless, for those who cared to inquire, there was evidence enough. The cable traffic between the embassy and Washington shows that from the start of the war there was no justification for Nixon and Kissinger to claim, as they did, that the Cambodians were North Vietnamese puppets with invisible leadership and unknowable aims.

All Indochinese Communism originates from Vietnam. The Indochinese Communist Party, formed in 1930, originally consisted entirely of Vietnamese cadres. They followed Comintern policy of the period and envisaged the replacement of French Indochina by a socialist federation of the three countries. One Communist document of 1934, for example, stated: "there is no place for considering a Cambodian revolution on its own. There can only be an Indochina revolution."

In 1941 the Indochinese Communist Party went underground. The struggle against the French and Japanese was led by a new united front, the Viet Minh, which was dominated by the Party. The Viet Minh was active in all three countries of Indochina recruiting Laotians and Khmers. It was not very successful in Cambodia; many of those Khmers who did join came from the anti-French Khmer Issarak ("Free Khmer") guerrillas. By the end of the decade the Viet Minh was still the only important anticolonial force in Indochina, and it was overwhelmingly Vietnamese.

In 1951 the Vietnamese dissolved the Indochinese Communist Party into national components. In Hanoi the Lao Dong (Workers') Party was constituted, and in Cambodia the Revolutionary Cambodian People's Party was formed under a Central Committee of figures tied to the Viet Minh. This party later encouraged the formation of a legal political party, the Pracheachon group, under the terms of reconciliation imposed by the 1954 Geneva Accords. The Khmer Communist Party itself remained a clandestine ally of the Lao Dong Party and the People's Revolutionary Party in Laos. It was much weaker than either of them.

Today the Vietnamese leadership claims that 1951 marked the end of all ideas of an Indochina Federation; the Cambodian Communists maintain that the Vietnamese never abandoned the dream. Evidence can be found to support either position, but at the very least it is clear that the Vietnamese, then and subsequently, saw the revolutionary struggle in Indochina first in terms of Vietnamese national interests and only secondly in terms of proletarian internationalism.

In 1954 the North Vietnamese accepted the terms of the Geneva Agreement, which required the Cambodian Communists to integrate with Sihanouk's political structure. They endorsed Cambodian neutrality, and the Viet Minh were withdrawn to Hanoi. The bulk of those Cambodians who had already chosen Communism went with them—estimates of just how many this involved vary between two thousand and four thousand, the lower number probably being closer to the truth.

Geneva marked a historic split among Khmer Communists. Those who were taken to Hanoi remained there, growing older, more pro-Vietnamese and more remote from their country. But a few hundred Khmer Communist guerrillas disobeyed Hanoi and stayed in the *maquis* after 1954. They saw Geneva as an outright betrayal of the Cambodian revolution. Twenty-three years later, the Communist Prime Minister of Cambodia complained that "this revolutionary struggle of our people and the war booty that was subsequently captured, dissolved into thin air through the Geneva Agreements." The trouble in those days, he said, was that Cambodians did not know which direction to follow and "which forces to rely on." Evidently Hanoi was not a reliable force and, in order to distance the Khmer Rouge from their Vietnamese origins, the Party's history was rewritten and its founding dated in 1960, not 1951.

The Party did not prosper in the fifties and sixties; the *maquis* scratched out a thankless existence in the jungles and hills of the northeast and the Cardamom mountains of the southwest. Hanoi's policy throughout the period was to cooperate with Sihanouk, and the Vietnamese Communists gave very little aid to their Cambodian comrades. At the same time the Prince's success in winning independence and maintaining reasonable standards of living deprived the Party of both a national and an international base.

Before its history was rewritten, Party leaders defined 1954–67 as the "period of political struggle" that preceded their taking up arms. The rigors of that struggle depended very much on the unpredictable nature of Sihanouk's current political activities. In 1955 and 1958 the Pracheachon group fought in the elections though it was severely harassed. The revised version of the Party's history drastically shortens the political-struggle period and declares that in 1960 "we then took up the task of mobilizing the masses to fight against imperialism . . . to achieve true independence." The countryside was given the leading place in the revolution.

From then on, certainly, more left-wingers trickled out of Phnom Penh, Battambang and other towns into the traditional refuge of opposition that the hills and forests have afforded throughout Cambodian history. After Sihanouk forced the Pracheachon group underground, the number of exiles grew faster—even when he also moved leftward and renounced American aid. It was now that the real core of the Khmer Rouge began to form in the countryside, and it was from these recruits that the movement took, and retains, its leaders. They were, from the start, an extraordinarily close-knit community, bound by class, by intellectual training, by the ordeal of opposition, even by marriage.

For almost all of them, socialist commitment had begun in Paris in the 1950s, when study at a French university or technical college was considered *de rigueur* for middle-class Cambodians, and young people of all backgrounds and political views avidly sought scholarships.

The Khmer Students' Association in Paris was dominated by the left. It made good use of the freedom France afforded to form students' views in ways that were unacceptable at home. There were limits to development, however, and these were set by the French Communist Party, an organization difficult to rival for dogmatic orthodoxy, which taught hatred of the bourgeoisie and uncritical admiration of Stalinism, including the collectivization of agriculture.

The intellectual and political voyages of the future Khmer Rouge leaders were so similar that only a few need be charted here. Saloth Sar (who would emerge after the war as Prime Minister and Party Secretary with the pseudonym Pol Pot) was born in Kompong Thom in 1928. By his own account he was a peasant child, worked the fields himself, and spent six years in a Buddhist pagoda. After attending the Collège Technique in Phnom Penh he went to Paris in 1949 to study radio electronics. He failed his examinations three times; this, he has said, was because of his greater interest in revolutionary work. After his return to Phnom Penh he taught history and geography in a private school, joined the Pracheachon and became well known as a left-wing journalist. By 1962 he had apparently risen in the underground Communist Party to the post of Deputy General Secretary. He fled to the hills in 1963 when, like others, he interpreted an invitation from Sihanouk to thirty-four left-wingers and "subversives" to enter the government as a feint, a prelude to repression.

With him went Ieng Sary, who was born in South Vietnam in 1930 and was educated in Cambodia and Paris, where he studied first commerce and then politics. In France, he too was active in student politics, traveled widely, and then became President of the Khmer Students' Association. He returned to Phnom Penh in 1957 and worked as a schoolteacher until 1963. His wife, Khieu Thirith, was also a left-wing student in France, and after 1963 she followed her husband into the *maquis*—undoubtedly becoming the only Cambodian revolutionary to have a diploma in Shakespearean studies. Her sister, Khieu Ponnary, another activist, was the wife of Saloth Sar.

Son Sen, born in 1930, went to France to train as a teacher in 1950.

Five years later, he lost his Cambodian government scholarship for sponsoring a meeting of left-wing Khmer students but was nonetheless able to return to Phnom Penh and teach. In 1958 he joined Sihanouk's party, the Sangkum, and became a director of curriculum at Phnom Penh's National Pedagogical Institute, but by 1962 Sihanouk was accusing him of stirring up left-wing demonstrations, and he too fled the capital in 1963.

Some leftists remained in Phnom Penh after 1963. Among them was Hu Nim, who had returned from France in 1957 to work as a customs and treasury official. He too joined Sihanouk's Sangkum and held a number of government posts, becoming Secretary of State for Commerce in 1962. His dissertation, "Les Services Economique au Cambodge," is one of the texts that help to explain the evolution of Cambodian revolutionary doctrine. It is a detailed Maoist analysis of the peasantry and attempts to show that although land ownership was broken up, it was becoming concentrated in fewer peasant hands. At the same time, he argued, the gradual "feeble development" of capitalism in Cambodia prevented technological advance and encouraged the exploitation of the poorest peasants, who were burdened with debt.

Hu Nim's work holds some interest today, but more extraordinary—in view of what happened after the Khmer Rouge victory in 1975—is the thesis of Khieu Samphan, the Khmer Rouge commander in chief during the war and the head of state afterward. He was the son of a minor civil servant from Svay Rieng; Khieu Samphan's widowed mother made a meager living selling vegetables. He won a scholarship to France in 1954. He became Secretary General of the Students' Association, but he is remembered by his contemporaries as an immensely studious, serious young man who devoted all his time to his work and to his politics, none to socializing.

His thesis, "Cambodia's Economy and Industrial Development," was completed at the University of Paris in 1959. It argues that the strength of Cambodia lay in the villages, where 90 percent of the people lived, that the cities were parasitical, and that integration into the world economy retarded the country's development. It was essential that Cambodian industry be developed. But this could be done only if agriculture were developed first and this, in turn, depended on very different terms of trade from those that were now in effect, and a transfer of the population out of the towns into productive work, first in the fields and then in industry.

Industry in the late fifties provided only 10 percent of GNP and it was, he argued, geared much more closely to the needs of the international

240

market than to those of Cambodia; it was an extension of Western capitalism. At the same time, agriculture was atrophying in a precapitalist phase. In the last sixty years the state of feudalism had hardly been affected, the merchant economy barely altered; indeed, "integration" with capitalist economies encouraged landlordism. Public investment—such as the railway—financed by France had only helped in the penetration of French industrial products, not the development of Khmer industry.

It was true that most Khmer peasants, unlike the Vietnamese, owned between two and seven hectares of land, their own equipment and animals. But, he claimed, since they often had no working capital and had to rely on moneylenders, who charged rates of up to 300 percent, the independence conferred by land ownership alone was illusory. Moreover, the situation was actually deteriorating, because landlords were spending more of their income on imported goods and were demanding rent in cash, not in kind. Peasants, therefore, had to sell their produce, the mercantile class increased, and the rent was dissipated into the foreign-exchange markets instead of remaining at least in the area, if not in the hands, of the producer. The multiplier effect was thus lost. He argued that "without this considerable leakage, development of the country might well proceed at least as rapidly as that of European countries."

That rural debt existed in Cambodia and constituted, in some areas at least, a serious burden on the peasantry, is not a matter of dispute. But other studies of the countryside do not demonstrate that landlordism was the overriding problem that Khieu Samphan asserted. It was, however, true that as family land passed through generations plots became smaller and smaller, especially along the fertile banks of the rivers and the Great Lake. In one crowded village along the Mekong, 83 percent of the farming land was divided into six thousand holdings that averaged only one quarter of a hectare each.

Now in the fifties, Khieu Samphan asserted, precapitalist stagnation was being deepened by the flow of American aid. The import of cars, refrigerators, radios, created a wasteful service or commercial class in the cities. Very few people in Phnom Penh were even registered to work, and of those who were registered 85.43 percent were engaged in unproductive labor—as waiters, maids, *cyclo* drivers, civil servants. The bureaucracy was too large, in part because the slow growth of industry meant that the civil service provided the only work the middle classes considered suitable.

At the same time, he argued, in terms similar to those used by Sihanouk himself in the middle sixties, the nature of American aid and the presence of the large American mission helped nourish "the desire of a particular part of Khmer society to imitate the American way of life." The country's economy was becoming increasingly geared to satisfy the needs of foreigners and of those rich Khmers who sought to mimic them. Luxury goods (candies, perfumes, cognac, silk, raincoats, porcelain) were bought by only 10 percent of the population but made up 49 percent of the value of all imports. Products consumed by the masses (cotton, tools, fireworks, household goods) constituted only 4 percent of all imports.

Khieu Samphan argued that the provincial towns were even more parasitical than Phnom Penh and concluded that if Cambodian society were to be reorganized (and corruption checked), then people must be transferred into productive work. The only way was to alter the country's present links with the outside world. But he did not recommend severing all ties and developing a siege economy; he agreed that isolation would cause national bankruptcy. He believed that foreign trade must be not abandoned, but exploited, in order to accelerate domestic transformation. "We would hope to profit from a century's accumulation of technical innovation in developed countries," he wrote. American aid, designed to shore up traditional relationships, would be forsworn, but French aid, which was less conservative, could continue. At the same time, the government should nationalize trade in such basic commodities as rice, corn and rubber. This would enable it to control most of the country's foreign exchange, limit illegal and wasteful imports and use export earnings to bolster the industrial sector. Banking should also be controlled by the state (though foreign banks would not be expelled), interest rates should be lowered to make capital accessible to peasants, artisans and small industrialists; credit for nonessentials like alcohol and soft drinks would be limited. The government should give priority to developing the country's electrical system, and must encourage the production of chemicals, bricks, bicycles, textiles, soap, food and pharmaceuticals. Everything must be done to divert resources into investment, and the state must set the example in fighting waste. All prestige projects must be cut out of the budget—no "magnificent exteriors and sumptuous decorations" were needed. Surplus bureaucrats and others rendered unemployed by the proposed changes would be transferred into productive work.

Once the economy was protected against the worst of external influences, the structural reform of the countryside, which was essential to the creation of a strong industrial base, could begin. Rents should be reduced, moneylending suppressed. Peasants must be encouraged to form cooperatives. This should not be too difficult, for it is "not unusual to see our peasants organizing themselves into teams of several families to help each other with transplanting and harvesting, all the while singing well-known songs. The task at hand is to generalize this practice in a systematic way. With cooperatives, new lands could be opened up. . . . Agricultural development will stimulate industrial expansion and is at the same time dependent upon it." He understood that not all peasants would immediately realize the value of such doctrines and that intensive political education was necessary. But, Khieu Samphan wrote—in terms which were forsworn when the experiment was eventually begun in the seventies—"Peasants must be treated with patience and understanding." None of his proposed structural changes would be imposed by force. They could occur only if the government could persuade the people to adopt them and could "ally itself with a broad democracy and enjoy general support from the masses of the population." The methods this twenty-eight-year-old Marxist prescribed in 1959 for the transformation of his country were essentially moderate.

After Paris, Khieu Samphan returned to Phnom Penh and founded a biweekly paper, *L'Observateur*, a well-produced journal in which he rehearsed his ideas for economic change and rural development, wrote sympathetically of all the socialist countries and frequently attacked (in Sihanouk's own words wherever possible) the corruption of civil servants and their lack of interest in the problems of the people. He felt that there should be far more contact between administrators in Phnom Penh and the peasantry. "To learn from the people," he wrote, "is to perfect one's knowledge, to verify the theory learned at school by the experience of life. It is to learn to really love the people."

It was a philosophy that he himself practiced, but that immediately brought him to the attention of Sihanouk's aggressive Ministry of Security. In 1960 he was called in for interrogation, and one day in August that year plain-clothes police thugs set upon him in the street, stripped him naked, photographed him and pushed him, unclothed, on his way. That is not the sort of humiliation that men forgive or forget, but despite the assault upon him, Khieu Samphan and other leftists, like Hou Yuon, Hu Nim and Chau Seng, still look a moderate line toward Sihanouk. In 1962, when Sihanouk was trying to preempt left-wing opposition by his own move left, Khieu Samphan joined the Sangkum and won a seat in Parliament. Sihanouk made him Secretary of State for Commerce. He was immensely popular among the poor in Phnom Penh, for even as a minister he lived unpretentiously, shunning the "cognac and concubine circuit." His mother continued selling vegetables. He had no large car and drove around on a motorcycle. He lost his job when he refused to accept the bribe of a Mercedes in exchange for issuing a trading license.

During the same time, Communists like Ieng Sary, Saloth Sar, and Son Sen were taking a much harder line, denouncing Sihanouk (privately) as the principal enemy of the Cambodian people and the revolution. These were the men who fled the city in 1963, while Khieu Samphan, Hou Yuon and Hu Nim stayed.

The divergence of views was subsequently rationalized by the Khmer Rouge in the long official history published in 1977. Since Sihanouk had made membership in their front, the Pracheachon group, extremely hazardous, the Party "assigned us to act separately. Some were asked to work in the open in the guise of representatives of Parliament or functionaries in the administration. . . . Some were asked to operate openly in various other mass organizations or to be journalists. All this was aimed at inciting the masses." The Party was working in the cities and in the countryside with the rural areas as the main base. "The cities could not be used as a base area. . . . The enemy was everywhere; the Parliament, the Court, the jails, the police and the military were there. The enemy networks were too close, and the class composition in the cities was too complex, too varied." The basic role of the Party was to educate the peasantry, "to feel class indignation. This was the key, the basic question determining our victory."

Despite this explanation, a split between the two groups became evident after the Communist victory in 1975. Most of those who emerged in the important leadership positions were men and women who had taken the hard anti-Sihanouk position early and had joined the *maquis* in 1963.

In 1966, Sihanouk for the first time allowed an open slate of candidates from his party for election to the Assembly. A right-wing legislature was returned, and it chose Lon Nol as the new Prime Minister, whereupon Sihanouk formed a "counter government" of the left—it included Hou Yuon, Hu Nim and Khieu Samphan. They did not long remain members of the loyal opposition. The next year peasants revolted in Battambang province, an event that has since been seen as a turning point of the Cambodian revolution.

Sihanouk put the blame for the insurrection on Chinese agents acting in the flush of Chairman Mao's Cultural Revolution. The clandestine Party was aligned with Peking—Saloth Sar and other leaders of the *ma-*

quis had secretly visited China in 1965—but the revolt seems to have been spontaneous. Its causes included long-standing resentment against usurious Chinese middlemen and a crude attempt by local authorities to drive peasants off their land to make way for a sugar refinery. The outbreak took the Party by surprise, and Pol Pot (Saloth Sar) later said that it could not be backed, because such isolated, premature revolts would be crushed by the government.

That is what did happen. Sihanouk's reaction was inhumane as well as tactically foolish. He ordered Lon Nol to liquidate the rioters. The deed was done bloodily: villages were razed and peasants were clubbed to death. Hundreds fled to the *maquis*, forever embittered. In Phnom Penh, Sihanouk suppressed the Chinese-Cambodian Friendship Association and publicly accused Khieu Samphan, Hu Nim, Hou Yuon and other leftists of having inspired the uprising. Fearful of his revenge, they separately joined their comrades who had fled in 1963.

It says something of the nature of political debate in the kingdom at the time of their disappearance that it was believed by many—including United States intelligence officials—that Sihanouk had had the three men put to death. It was these three the American embassy called the "Three Ghosts" when their names appeared in the ranks of the government in exile that Sihanouk formed in 1970 after his overthrow.

The Khmer Rouge later described the period between the Battambang revolt and the 1970 coup as "the civil war." It was now, according to the Party, that the Revolutionary Army of Kampuchea was formed. The Party afterward made much of its victories in those years; in fact although the Communists exploited peasant grievances—such as the low price of paddy—those victories were not impressive. The Communists executed several village chiefs. Sihanouk pursued them relentlessly. He broadcast continuous tirades against "les Khmers Rouges" (it was he who had so christened them), and his army and police attacked them ferociously. Khmer Rouge prisoners often had their stomachs slit and were then hung in trees to die slowly; others were flung into ravines. One authority notes, "Enemy villages were razed and the villagers were beaten to death by peasants conscripted by the army specifically for the task."

But it was not only, not even principally, repression that explains the failure of Cambodian Communism before 1970. Apart from Battambang and the northeast, where the government tried to bring the self-assertive Khmer Loeu hill people under control, discontent was not sufficient to thrust large numbers of peasants into the rigors of rebellion. Living standards in much of the country were certainly low, malaria was prevalent in many areas, infant mortality was high, but 90 percent of the peasants owned some land and the burdens of rural debt of which Khieu Samphan, Hu Nim and others complained were not insupportable. By 1970, Marxist teachers had been scarcely more successful in proselytizing than the Christian missionaries had been in the late nineteenth and early twentieth centuries. At the time of the coup the Khmer Rouge was still tiny. By its own account it had 4,000 regular troops and 50,000 guerrillas, but those figures are almost certainly exaggerated. Captured documents show that the regulars were grouped into companies. Such small-scale organization suggests that they were scattered and not nearly as numerous as 4,000. One Vietnamese leader later claimed that the Khmer Rouge numbered only a few hundred in 1970. Their impact had been minimal. The pagoda remained the center of cultural and political life in almost every Cambodian village; the seasons of the year were celebrated with the rituals of church and monarchy. The class anger that the Khmer Rouge sought to arouse was softened by the personality of the Prince.

Sihanouk's first impulse after his overthrow was to retire to his house at Mougins in the South of France. Under pressure from Chou En-lai, whom he considered an old friend, and of North Vietnam's Premier Pham Van Dong, and from whatever motives—petulant revenge, injured vanity, nationalist zeal—within days he sacrificed the independence and the chance for unilateral action that a waiting period in France might have afforded him. He agreed to an alliance with his enemies. His broadcast of March 23—an appeal for the country to rise against Lon Nol under the banner of his own new National United Front of Kampuchea—was immediately welcomed in a statement from Hanoi signed by Khieu Samphan, Hou Yuon and Hu Nim.

The Communists' instant approach to the man who had for years been abusing, threatening, killing them, was not surprising. Their relations with him were understandably strained and continually deteriorated, but for the moment they used Sihanouk in two ways. His task in Peking was to lead a diplomatic offensive designed to isolate the Lon Nol government and attract international support to his own Royal Government of National Union (which was announced after the United States invasion had made reconciliation impossible). At home his persona was employed to win precisely that mass support which the rhetoric of revolution had failed to engender. In Sihanouk the Khmer Rouge at last had a national and international identity and appeal.

It was not only they who turned to him. In Cambodia, feudal chiefs, village leaders and their people, and in Paris, leftists and neutralists all flocked to the Prince. In appearance both the Front and his new government were genuine coalitions. The government was based in Peking, and the Prime Minister was Penn Nouth, an old left-of-center politician who had served Sihanouk devotedly as Premier in the past. Increasingly, however, power came to lie not in Peking but in the "liberated" area of Cambodia itself, first with the North Vietnamese and then with the Front. And as the Front expanded so the Party secretly increased its control over it. Sihanouk's request to be allowed to leave Peking for Cambodia was denied by the Khmer Rouge. His popularity in the countryside was valuable, but it was also threatening, an asset to be diminished even while it was exploited.

Their past history had taught the Khmer Rouge that their new comrades in arms, the North Vietnamese, were hardly more reliable than their new leader. (Hanoi's principal supporter, Moscow, recognized Lon Nol and maintained a mission in Phnom Penh until late 1973 leaving some diplomats there until the very end of the war.) The North Vietnamese might have finally embraced the cause of Khmer Communism, but there was no reason to expect that they intended it to serve any interests save their own. Hanoi had now two principal concerns. The first was to rebuild its lines of communication, and the second was, for the first time, actually to encourage the growth of a Khmer resistance movement, which could later relieve Vietnamese divisions from the defense of these lines and the sanctuaries against attack by Lon Nol forces.

The first aim was fairly easily achieved. One new route was by water. Arms, ammunition and food were floated by raft and sampan down the Mekong from southern Laos to the Khong Falls, carried round the torrent by porter and then taken by truck and cart to the town of Kratie, which the North Vietnamese had emptied of its population after they captured it on May 5, 1970. The town now served as an administrative headquarters. From there some equipment was moved by night along hunting trails and cycle tracks east toward Vietnam and whichever of the new shifting base areas required it. The rest, destined for the southern Delta of South Vietnam, was circled by sampan, bicycle, truck, porter, in a counterclockwise direction around Phnom Penh through the foothills of the Cardamom mountains and finally into the fertile lands of rice and river of the Mekong Delta.

These and other lines of communication became important targets of the B-52s, the American and Vietnamese tactical aircraft, the helicopter

247

gunships, the South Vietnamese ground troops and many of the Cambodian battalions. They were harassed and cut, but they were never broken. The principal effect of the American invasion on North Vietnamese logistics had been to extend the lines of communication, not to destroy them.

The construction of an effective Khmer Rouge took longer and undoubtedly presented the North Vietnamese with a dilemma. Although for the first time they needed a Khmer Communist movement, they had every reason to fear that the stronger the force became the more independent of Hanoi it might be. Nonetheless, the process began right away, and although there was no agreement in Washington on the nature of the Khmer Rouge there was never any basis for the pretense that its emergence could be neither foreseen nor monitored. Many of the incidents cited below are from Embassy reports of the time. They show how much more was known about the new movement and, in particular, about its relations with the Vietnamese than Kissinger and other officials claimed.

There appear to have been three stages to the Khmer Rouge wartime progress. Until mid-1971 they were allied with the Sihanoukists (known as Khmer Rumdoh, or "Khmer Liberators") and, under North Vietnamese supervision, simply took over those areas of the countryside abandoned by the Lon Nol government. They did not at that time implement political programs. During the second stage, between summer 1971 and early 1973, the growing Khmer Rouge started to break away from Hanoi's control and to discard the totem of Sihanouk and his supporters; collectivist measures were begun. Then, from the time of the Paris Peace Agreement in January 1973 onward, the Khmer Rouge were largely on their own; they depended on North Vietnamese logistics but had no guaranteed aid from any foreign power and were free to launch their own military initiatives. It was in this third period that they embarked on the radical transformation of the country, which climaxed in their victory and the evacuation of Phnom Penh in April 1975.

CIA reports suggest that in the early months of the war both the North Vietnamese and the Khmer Rouge were concerned to behave in an exemplary fashion toward the local people. For their part, the North Vietnamese were anxious to dispel traditional peasant dislike and the fear that fighting for them meant fighting for the hegemony of Hanoi in Indochina. They were, they told villagers, the personal emissaries of the Prince, and they carried recordings of his speeches from Peking to prove it. A 1971 Agency report stressed that in Takeo province the Khmer Rouge

> take great care not to antagonize the peasantry. They help them with
> the harvesting, offer to pay a reasonable sum for the supplies they

need, treat the women with respect and refrain from abusive language or behavior. . . . They have gained considerable sympathy from the local peasantry, who support them . . . and warn them of the arrival of [Lon Nol] troops. The only people in this area who do not actively support the VC/NVA and Khmer Communists are the wealthy merchants, local functionaries and professors.

In Kompong Speu province, the station in Phnom Penh reported, "By maintaining tight discipline and carefully avoiding actions which might antagonize the local population the VC/NVA have been able to convey the impression that they have the true interests of the peasants in mind." Such claims were especially persuasive in areas the South Vietnamese had already crossed. For example, the village of Chebal Monn [sic], outside the town of Kompong Speu, had been pillaged by the ARVN in June and July 1970. When the North Vietnamese won control of it in September, they reminded the villagers that they had never had to worry about South Vietnamese looting before Sihanouk's removal and promised to help them defend themselves in the future. The Agency reported that they were careful to use the village chief to recruit and persuade. He "was not and probably is not now a communist [but] like many peasants in the area was merely dissatisfied with the inability of the Cambodian Government to protect them." Communist efforts, according to the station, had already won at least a hundred recruits in this one village alone.

Not all Washington agencies were oblivious of the fact that the new war was creating an enemy where none had previously existed. On January 9, 1971, the Defense Intelligence Agency noted in the Far East summary of its secret Intelligence Bulletin, "Unless the Government is able to reassert its influence and maintain some semblance of control over the rural sector, the communist infrastructure will probably continue to grow." In a detailed ten-page Intelligence Appraisal entitled "Communist Infrastructure in Cambodia," the Agency commented a few months later: "The Vietnamese communists have been successful in establishing an indigenous infrastructure to support their military and logistic efforts and in creating a rudimentary, functioning political apparatus staffed by Khmer in more than half of Cambodia's 19 provinces." They now controlled 65 percent of the land and 35 percent of the people and they numbered between 35,000 and 50,000—with up to 10,000 soldiers.

The troops were organized, as in Vietnam, in three tiers—a main force, a local force and a guerrilla militia with units at the national, regional, provincial, district, village and hamlet levels. From company level up, the commander of each unit was flanked by a political commissar who exercised undisputed authority over the combatants. By summer 1971 the village and hamlet guerrillas were already almost totally Khmer. The Vietnamese still provided the logistics and almost all of the military muscle, but local leaders were being developed. So were tensions between the two allies.

After the coup Hanoi dispatched down the Trail the two thousand or more Cambodian Communists it had been preparing since 1954 for just such a moment as this. Their task was to take control of the fledgling movement. They were at first given command of new battalions and entrusted with the training of recruits. But unlike Eastern Europe after the Second World War—when those Communists who had spent the war comfortably in Moscow virtually eliminated those who had fought at home—the "Hanoi-Khmers" never achieved important leadership positions in Cambodia. Indeed it appears that the indigenous *maquis,* led by men like Saloth Sar and Son Sen, regarded them from the start as Vietnamese agents intent on suppressing Cambodian independence.

As early as June 1970, the CIA station chief was reporting that relations between the North Vietnamese and Khmer Rouge were not always easy. Apparently there were, for example, clashes in Kratie province over whether Ho's or Sihanouk's portrait should be more prominently displayed. During an assault on the town of Kompong Thom in September 1970, Khmer Rouge soldiers were said by the CIA to have fired on North Vietnamese troops from behind.

Reports from the province of Takeo described how the Khmer Rouge were organizing a new civil administration in which the Viet Cong were allowed only an advisory role. The Khmers were also forbidding the Vietnamese to form their own political infrastructure among those few Vietnamese who had chosen to remain in Takeo. Nor would they allow them to collect taxes. William Colby, the former CIA Director, recalls that reports of actual fighting between the Khmer Rouge and Vietnamese Communists in Takeo began to come through in 1971.

In summer 1972 an Agency report described an anti-Vietnamese demonstration organized by the Khmer Rouge in Kompong Cham. Villagers marched around, brandishing machetes and shouting, "We do not fear to die from bombs dropped from airplanes," and "We all agree to die together in order to get the VC/NVA out of Cambodia." A few months later another report asserted that villagers and Khmer Rouge alike had been complaining of the way in which the Vietnamese Communists based themselves in villages in an effort to evade airstrikes. Such attempts were not always successful. The report noted that 75 percent of the houses in one village had been destroyed; the surviving villagers had expelled the North Vietnamese. Racial hatred was obvious and clashes between the two Communist armies were increasing. "In some instances VC/NVA food and ammunition supplies were confiscated by the K.C. [Khmer Communists] and the VC/NVA managers of the supply sites were arrested . . . the expropriation of weapons and supplies continued at an alarming rate and had become a major problem for COSVN. As a protective measure, COSVN units were advised to travel in large groups. When challenged at K.C. checkpoints they were not to react against the K.C. but were to await the liaison teams who would then take the necessary actions to effect their release."

The CIA also reported from the start how Lon Nol's troops collaborated with the enemy. (They were encouraged by the fact that Lon Nol's main source of foreign exchange—after Washington—was rubber bought from the Communists and resold abroad.) One agency report of September 22, 1970, noted that in one district of Kampot the major in charge of government troops realized he was no match for the Communists and agreed to keep his men in their quarters. The Communists were allowed free run of the countryside and, in return, no attacks were made on the barracks themselves.

The Khmer Rouge later claimed that 80 percent of their arms and ammunition was either captured from or bought from the Lon Nol side. This is a very great exaggeration; what is certainly true is that the North Vietnamese very carefully rationed the amount of material they entrusted to the army they were creating—this became one of the principal sources of contention between the allies. And it is also true that a considerable proportion of the cornucopia that poured through the hands of United States Generals Mataxis and Cleland ended up on the other side.

The fullest account of wartime life under the Khmer Rouge comes to us from Ith Sarin, a left-wing primary-school inspector, who left Phnom Penh to spend nine months in the bush as a candidate for Party membership in 1972. This was during the second stage of the Khmer Rouge development when the Front was purging the Sihanoukists. They were maturing as a fighting force, asserting independence of the North Vietnamese and beginning to embark on the radical transformation of the areas they controlled.

Ith Sarin left Phnom Penh disillusioned by the failure of the March 1970 "revolution" and the corruption and the incompetence of the Lon Nol government. But his experiences of the Khmer Rouge were such that he never became a full Party member; he returned to the capital to write a book, *Regrets for the Khmer Soul*. It was intended to convince the population of the dangers of the Khmer Rouge and encourage the replacement of Lon Nol's government by one that could accept and defeat the Communists' challenge. After a few days the police apparently decided his book was pro-Communist, and it was banned for a time. With this history in mind, the book provides a useful, indeed unique account. At the time almost no foreign journalists paid any attention to it; the only long piece written about it was by Elizabeth Becker, a stringer for the *Washington Post*. The U.S. Embassy, however, did realize its importance; a political officer, Timothy Carney, filed several long reports to Washington on its significance.

Ith Sarin noted that the Party was not referred to in the "liberated areas." In order to preserve the idea of a National Front, the Party's very existence was still secret; government of the liberated areas was ascribed to the *Angka*, or "Organization." The country was divided into five geographical regions with another for the capital, Phnom Penh. The Chairman, or Secretary of each region was a long-standing member of the Khmer Rouge. Each region was divided into functional sector, district, township (*khum*) and village or hamlet (*phum*) committees, whose ultimate orders came from the Party's Central Committee. In 1970, the committees had been filled with Sihanoukists; by 1972 there were some committee members who "still believed they were making the revolution simply in order to hand authority back to Sihanouk," but most of them were being replaced. Each committee was now run by a political commissar, who had to ensure that party instructions on production, recruitment and population control were carried out.

The concept of what Khieu Samphan had called, in his thesis, "mutual aid groups" was being implemented; the lowest level of government was an interfamily group of about twelve to fifteen members headed by a chairman chosen by the hamlet chief. These groups were responsible for organizing agricultural production; as in China and in North Vietnam, this revolution began in agriculture. But in Cambodia there was scarcely any reform stage; collectivization began as early as 1971.

Ith Sarin found ample evidence of tensions between the Khmer Rouge and the North Vietnamese. He quoted Hou Yuon as saying that the Party "has foreseen all in preparing for danger from the VC/NVA." He thought the Khmer Rouge "seems to have control over all activities in its zones. The VC/NVA are far from being the masters."

He described how the war had already hardened as well as strengthened the movement. There were still very few experienced cadres and rigorous political education was emphasized. "They educated and trained youth and their cadre to become socialists and to become communists by means of a series of increasingly tougher standards." Liquor, gambling, adultery and feudal terms of address were eliminated, personal characteristics were to be replaced by a collective spirit. A cadre who became irritated easily was accused of having "thick individual traits." Everyone was required to observe his comrades and criticize them in order to help them become socialists. Ith Sarin considered this was "a step in 'taming' a man to become a 'machine' contrary to natural evolution." Everyone had to hand himself over to the *Angka* to be built. "One must trust completely in the *Angka*, because the Organization has as many eyes as a 'pineapple' and cannot make mistakes."

Ith Sarin warned that it would be almost impossible to come to terms with these new cadres. One of the other lessons they were taught was "mortal hate for the Republican government of Phnom Penh." The party accused the government of being "the valet of American imperialists, of being puppets, of being reactionary, of corruption." Administrators were taught to "have burning rage toward the enemy." They were enjoined to "awaken in order to make the revolution by oneself; do not depend on others or foreigners or let anyone replace one."

At the same time, Ith Sarin understood some of the reasons for the appeal of the Khmer Rouge. Cadres were taught to respect "the ways of the people," to be modest and forswear authoritarianism. (These were ideas that Khieu Samphan had expressed in his newspaper *L'Observateur* in the early sixties.) Now, according to Ith Sarin, the Khmer Rouge advised "study from the people in order to be like the people." He recorded that "if a peasant is sick the Khmer Rouge will often go to the house to give an injection or leave medicine even at night or during a storm." The cadre had to help bring in the harvest and, as a result, "the farming people of the base areas quickly began to love and support the Angka because of its sentiments of openness and friendliness."

But he noted also that peasants, like cadres, had to monitor each other's activities "in order to educate each other in the way which communists call 'construction.'" Political sessions were held to exhort greater production, and dramas were enacted to whip up rage against the Lon Nol "puppets" and their American "masters." By the end of 1972 he considered that the movement had become genuinely totalitarian, but he believed the peasants "remain passive, very attached to their habits

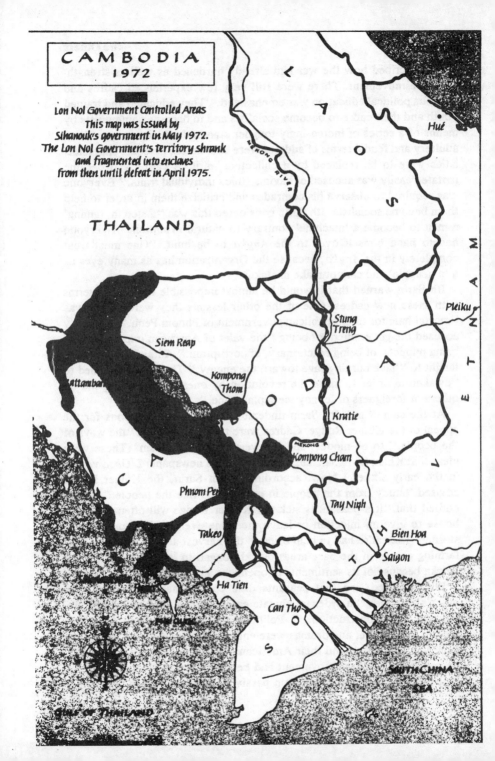

CAMBODIA
1972

Lon Nol Government Controlled Areas
This map was issued by
Sihanouk's government in May 1972.
The Lon Nol Government's territory shrank
and fragmented into enclaves
from then until defeat in April 1975.

THAILAND

Hué

MEKONG RIVER

L A O S

V I E T N A M

Pleiku

Stung
Treng

Siem Reap

Kompong
Thom

C A M B O D I A

Battambang

Kratie

MEKONG R

Kompong Cham

Phnom Penh

Tay Ninh

Bien Hoa

Takeo

Saigon

Ha Tien

T H I

Can Tho

L A O S

GULF OF THAILAND

SOUTH CHINA
SEA

and customs. The new collective life being imposed upon them frightens them. Most keep secret their attachment to Sihanouk and his regime."

It was clear to Ith Sarin that although they had removed the Prince's followers from positions of influence, the Khmer Rouge considered conservative, superstitious monarchism the greatest threat to them. By the end of 1972, cadres started to attack the Prince personally. Ith Sarin heard some maintain that even though Sihanouk was now leading the liberation movement from Peking, he was still the symbol of comprador feudalism. Ith Sarin wrote that the Prince's popularity at home and abroad was being siphoned through the Front and into the Khmer Communist Party. "The Central Committee of the Khmer Communist Party pulled Sihanouk into their trap by means of Peking. Having got him in hand, the Khmer Rouge got ready to squeeze him dry."

Sihanouk lived well in Peking. He was given a large old embassy as a residence, and the Chinese built him a heated swimming pool. He retained some of his *bon vivant* habits and enjoyed entertaining, particularly journalists he had liked in Phnom Penh. His table was one of the best in town, often laden with gooseberries and guinea fowl "from my good friend Kim Il Sung," the leader of North Korea. He had nine chefs "because I am a gourmet. They prepare me Cambodian food, French food, Chinese food, anything you want."

The display had some purpose. Sihanouk was anxious to convince the world that he really did dominate the Front, and that the Khmer Rouge recognized his authority as Head of State. Any journalist who cabled him to solicit his views on a particular subject would get an instant and characteristically expressive reply. Every day his aides hurried around to the Agence France Presse office with the latest *"plis urgents,"* and *"dépêches immédiates"* from the Prince.

In fact, his relationship with the Khmer Rouge was strained from the start, and he did nothing to improve it by his treatment of their representatives in Peking. In mid-1971 Ieng Sary, the Party's principal liaison with the Vietnamese, was transferred from Hanoi to Peking as the "Special Representative of the Interior," with the mission of controlling the Prince. Sihanouk made no attempt to conceal his dislike of him. He considered Ieng Sary, wrongly, an agent of North Vietnam. "We all know that for you the *maquis* means central Hanoi," he would say. "Why don't you allow people to speak English? After all, your own wife is an English teacher." One of his favorite jokes was to borrow whatever mildly pornographic or risqué films the French embassy might have and invite Ieng Sary to attend a soirée. Ieng Sary could not refuse his Prince's summons, and he would sit stiffly, smiling when Sihanouk smiled, applauding when the Prince applauded, and obviously hating the experience. When he had gone, Sihanouk would roar with laughter with his intimate aides—"Ieng Sary will have to go through terrible self-criticism tomorrow," he would say.

For his part Ieng Sary tried to split Sihanouk's entourage. He played upon the tensions between his wife, Monique, and other members of the royal family, who still resented the way she had broken up the relationship between Sihanouk and his first wife, Princess Norleak—who also came to Peking. Ieng Sary constantly told Monique that the Khmer Rouge had enormous regard for her, giving her to understand that this was because she was a commoner, not a member of the royal family. He also tried to persuade Penn Nouth, Sihanouk's nominal Prime Minister, that the men in the field valued his experience and views very highly.

Although Sihanouk continued to use the foreign press, as he had done in Phnom Penh, to convey his views and moods, his principal contact with the outside world was more discreet—it was through his friend, Etienne Manac'h, the French ambassador to Peking. Manac'h is one of those who emerge with credit from the story of the destruction of Cambodia. The longer the war dragged on, the harder he tried to find a solution to it.

An able career diplomat, Manac'h was also an uncompromising figure. In the early fifties the Communists had expelled him from Czechoslovakia when he made plain his dislike of their brutality. For the rest of his career he was involved exclusively in Asian affairs. He helped negotiate Cambodia's independence in 1953 and subsequently came to know Sihanouk quite well. In 1966, he drafted the famous speech which de Gaulle delivered in Phnom Penh in praise of Indochinese neutrality. The speech infuriated the Johnson administration; Manac'h, however, believed that for Indochina, and particularly for Cambodia, there was no reasonable alternative.

As a result of his views Manac'h was always regarded with some suspicion in Washington even after he became head of the Quai d'Orsay's Asia Department. Nonetheless, in 1968 he played a vital part in setting up the first secret round of talks between the Americans and the North Vietnamese. After he was appointed ambassador to Peking in 1969, his blunt integrity, his knowledge of Asia, above all, perhaps, his understanding of the Indochina war, soon won him the respect not only of the entire diplomatic corps but also of Chou En-lai himself. His views were widely sought.

Manac'h was not only a highly intelligent expert—he cared. He regretted the destruction of Cambodia's neutrality. And he believed that Sihanouk, for all his faults, was still the best ruler Cambodia had had or was likely to have.

Sihanouk's own hopes for the future varied enormously according to his mood and to political developments. At times he was certain that the Khmer Rouge would discard, if not kill, him when he had served their purposes. When he was feeling more cheerful he would tell those few aides whom he trusted—and Manac'h—that although the Khmer Rouge might be exploiting him, he was using them as well. His alliance with them was tactical. Cambodia could never be the same again, but he felt that he could better secure its future than the Khmer Rouge. He wanted to return in his own right, not under their control. All he needed was the support of China and of Washington.

In the early years of the war China's support—and particularly that of Chou En-lai—was very obvious. Ever since 1954 it had been the Chinese policy to support a Cambodia independent of Vietnam, under Sihanouk. After his overthrow the Prince became the first exiled head of state the Chinese allowed to establish himself in Peking. Given their feelings about the other "Chinese government" in Taipei, this was a singular concession. He was accorded the full honors due a national leader, and Chou's personal commitment was generous. There was the fine residence and the pool, and Chou's wife accompanied him on trips to seaside resorts. Chou gave him constant audiences, even though Sihanouk could rarely resist bragging about them. Chinese priorities were sharply expressed when Ieng Sary arrived in Peking. The Chinese supported the indigenous *maquis* against the "Hanoi-Khmers." Nevertheless, Ieng Sary and his entourage were billeted in the Friendship Hotel, several miles from the center of the city, and, unlike Sihanouk, they had to depend on public transport. Both Sihanouk and Manac'h were convinced from their separate conversations with Chou that the Chinese did wish to see Sihanouk return to lead a neutral Cambodia. Manac'h believed that despite Sihanouk's mercurial nature and his attacks on Peking during the Cultural Revolution, the Chinese considered him more useful than the Khmer Rouge who might (at least in theory) eventually emerge as pro-Soviet.

Washington was unresponsive. And Manac'h's cables to the Quai d'Orsay—concerning both Sihanouk's desire to talk directly with Kissinger and Chou En-lai's support of the Prince—were never well received when their substance was relayed to the relevant American officials. In the Oval Office as well as in the White House basement, Sihanouk was treated with contempt. Kissinger distrusted Sihanouk just as he did Archbishop Makarios, the independent-minded ruler of Cyprus. He argued that the Prince was yesterday's man, he represented no one but himself, there was no evidence that the Chinese took him seriously. Contempt is self-fulfilling. In the early years of the war the Chinese did make their commitment to Sihanouk clear. Though it is true that real power lay increasingly with the Khmer Rouge on the ground, Sihanouk was nonetheless the leader of the resistance and came to be recognized as such by forty nations. His international stature could have been exploited, at least acknowledged, by the United States. Instead, he was ignored. The result was that eventually, and with apparent reluctance, the Chinese began to transfer their support to the Khmer Rouge. In this way, American policy sustained the growth of Cambodian Communism.

CHAPTER 18

The Peace

IN PARIS on January 27, 1973, one week after Nixon's second inauguration, the United States, the Republic of Vietnam, the Democratic Republic of Vietnam, and the Provisional Revolutionary Government of South Vietnam signed an "Agreement on ending the war and restoring peace in Vietnam." Soon after dawn on the morning of January 29, 1973, the crump of mortars, the whistle of bullets and the whine of artillery shells began to die all over South Vietnam. In the wreckage of the provincial capital of Quang Tri, men on both sides tentatively lifted weary heads from foxholes and gazed silently upon one another.

It was a moving moment, and a short one. *Time* Magazine named Nixon and Kissinger its Men of the Year, and *Newsweek* proclaimed "PEACE" on its cover.* But while the agreement was certainly an achievement, it was not designed or destined to bestow peace. In Laos a sort of peaceful transfer of power was arranged. In Vietnam casualties remained almost as high as ever over the next two years. During 1972, according to the Pentagon, over 39,000 South Vietnamese soldiers had died in combat; in 1973, the figure would be almost 28,000, and in 1974 over 31,000. In Cambodia the war continued even more dreadfully than before.

Given the role that the Cambodians were expressly supposed to play in

---

* H. R. Haldeman later recalled that Nixon "was close to white-lipped in anger when Henry squeezed him aside as *Time* magazine's Man of the Year. Nixon ended up as part of an unprecedented dual selection, both appropriately carved in stony images."

saving American lives, it would have been unreasonable to have expected the administration to try to find an end to their war before the United States withdrawal from Vietnam was completed. It is less easy to demonstrate why no solution to the war in Cambodia was found after the Paris Agreement. Kissinger's explanation of why the fighting was continued and even intensified over the next two years needs examination.

The principal purpose of the peace agreement was to extract American uniforms from South and North Vietnam while sustaining President Thieu in office for Kissinger's "decent interval." The accord had been made possible by fundamental concessions on each side. Hanoi agreed to allow Thieu to remain in place while elections were arranged. The Americans acknowledged the presence of North Vietnamese troops within S uth Vietnam. By the middle of 1972 this was a huge concession; altogether, Hanoi had now moved about 145,000 men into the South. It was the legitimation of Hanoi's presence that most enraged Thieu, and it was his understandable resistance that had snatched "peace" from Kissinger's hand in October 1972.

After Nixon's reelection, United States policy was directed toward inducing the South Vietnamese president to accept the basic terms negotiated. Under the code name "Operation Enhance" the administration shipped an astonishing new armory to Saigon; this made the South Vietnamese air force the fourth largest in the world. Then the White House demonstrated its resolve by the Christmas bombing of Hanoi and Haiphong. Designed partly, in General Haig's words, to "brutalize" the North, the bombing was also intended to assure Thieu that Nixon was prepared to go to considerable lengths to impose and preserve "peace with honor" and to demonstrate the fearsomeness of Presidential "irrationality." One might have thought that Nixon's own "Madman Theory of War" had proved rather ineffective by now, but at the height of this unprecedented bombing campaign the President assured a journalist, Richard Wilson, that he "did not care if the whole world thought he was crazy. If it did, so much the better. The Russians and the Chinese might think they were dealing with a madman."

At the same time Thieu was warned in a series of secret letters from Nixon that there could now be no further argument about his signature; but Nixon promised "to take swift and severe retaliatory action" and to "respond with full force" to any Communist violation of the agreement. This secret commitment was to have an important effect upon Cambodia.

The language of the Paris Agreement placed no real formal obligations on Hanoi or Washington with regard to Cambodia or Laos. Article 20 called on all foreign countries to "put an end to all military activities in Cambodia and Laos, totally withdraw from and refrain from reintroducing into these two countries troops, military advisers and military personnel, armaments, munitions and war material." The internal affairs of each country "shall be settled by the people of each of these countries without foreign interference." But no deadline was given and a secret State Department analysis, entitled "Interpretation of the Agreement on Ending the War and Restoring Peace in Vietnam," asserted that the commitment to withdraw was only one of principle; Article 20 "was carefully drafted . . . to avoid stating a time or period of time for the implementation of these obligations. . . ."

During the course of his talks with Le Duc Tho, Kissinger had attempted to obtain an assurance that cease-fires could be arranged in Cambodia and Laos as well as in Vietnam. The North Vietnamese were able to give satisfactory assurances on Laos; Hanoi had always dominated the Pathet Lao. In Cambodia, however, no such guarantees could be given, because of the growing tensions between the North Vietnamese and the Khmer Rouge. During 1972, when almost all North Vietnamese combat divisions were withdrawn from Cambodia for the offensive in South Vietnam, reports of fairly constant fighting between the allies reached Phnom Penh and Washington. By the end of the year the Khmer Rouge were fielding an army of around 50,000 men, organized in regiments, and were strong enough to hold their own against Lon Nol, with only logistical support from the North Vietnamese. They could now act independently of Hanoi.

Kissinger, however, apparently persisted in the belief that Hanoi could and would deliver the Khmer Rouge, and during the final round of talks with Le Duc Tho he tried to link a Cambodian cease-fire to the provision of postwar American aid to North Vietnam. Although Kissinger subsequently assured Congress there were no secret clauses to the Paris Agreement, Nixon had, at North Vietnamese insistence, written a secret letter to the North Vietnamese Prime Minister, Pham Van Dong, promising such aid.

On January 23, during the final session of the talks, Kissinger read a unilateral statement on Cambodia into the record. He said that after the agreement took effect on January 29, Lon Nol would suspend all offensive operations, and the United States would halt its bombing of Cambodia. If the other side reciprocated, a *de facto* cease-fire would come about; if not, "Government forces and the United States Air Force would have to take necessary counter measures." He warned that the bombing of the country would then resume until a cease-fire was achieved.

The next day, at a press conference called to explain the accords, Kissinger declared. "We can say about Cambodia that it is our expectation that a *de facto* cease-fire will come into being within a period of time relevant to the execution of the agreement."

It is not clear what role Kissinger himself was prepared to take in any Cambodian negotiations at this precise moment. Before and after January 1973, he usually insisted that any Cambodian peace talks—unlike those concerning Vietnam—must take place between "the two parties," and that the United States could not be directly involved. Since each Cambodian side had always explicitly denied that there was any possibility of its negotiating with the other "traitors" (each, indeed, had condemned the leaders of the other side to death) the prospects for such talks were dim. At the same time both Kissinger and Nixon maintained that one of the serious difficulties in negotiation lay in the fact that the other side was divided and had no clear leadership. Kissinger spoke of the "innumerable Cambodian factions."

From Washington's point of view, there was a more fundamental problem. Any cease-fire and negotiated settlement in Cambodia would have necessarily involved the replacement of the Lon Nol government by a coalition that at the very least included members of the other side. It could not, therefore, be an ally of President Thieu. Yet Thieu himself and many American officials insisted that the existence of an anti-Communist allied government in Phnom Penh was essential to the survival of South Vietnam. The evidence suggests that while Kissinger was talking publicly of the need for a cease-fire in Cambodia, the administration was doing what it could to shore up Lon Nol.

A few days before the Paris Agreement was signed, Alexander Haig—whose service on the NSC had now won him promotion to full general—flew into Phnom Penh on another of his "stroking missions" and to inform Lon Nol of the terms. (In October 1972 Kissinger had made his only visit ever to Phnom Penh. He stayed two hours. Lon Nol later said he had revealed very little of Washington's plans for Cambodia's future.) Haig promised him more military supplies and, according to a cable from Swank to Rogers, he assured him "of our continuing support, for which the Marshal expressed appreciation." Lon Nol was evidently disturbed by the notion of a cease-fire; Swank soothed him by guaranteeing that "enemy actions of any scope against Cambodia involving a cease-fire in Vietnam would be regarded as a violation of any agreement reached with

Hanoi, and I stressed that air power based in Thailand would be deployed on his behalf in case of need." Swank also promised Lon Nol "that he can count on our continued support for equipment and training through our military-assistance program and that its size would depend less on the administration's volition, which is to provide all the assistance the FANK can absorb, than on Congressional attitudes. . . . I referred to the accelerated deliveries of MAP equipment over the last three months and promised him to do whatever we can to continue such deliveries."

Haig was followed by Spiro Agnew, who also assured Lon Nol that Washington was constant and that military aid would continue. Swank cabled Washington that "in and of itself the visit constituted a striking gesture of our continuing interest in sustaining a friendly government in Phnom Penh, and this was doubtless its principal accomplishment." The visits and Swank's promises demonstrate both how little pressure was put on Lon Nol to achieve, let alone observe, a cease-fire and the American attitude to a change in government in Phnom Penh.

However, on January 28, the day before the Paris Agreement took effect, Lon Nol made what passed for the cease-fire offer Kissinger had promised Le Duc Tho. His statement makes clear his refusal to appreciate that a Khmer Communist organization existed and shows how qualified his gesture was:

> By virtue of the Geneva Agreements of 1954 we have the right to repossess the parts of our country which have been illegally occupied by the North Vietnamese and Vietcong forces. To enable them to leave our territory in the shortest possible time, we will order our troops . . . to suspend their offensive operations and to establish contacts with the people to ascertain their welfare and to assure their protection. Incidents which might impede their passage or jeopardize their installations will be regarded as actions by intruders who will bear full responsibility for any misfortunes which ensue. We will continue to exercise our right of legitimate self-defense through defensive military operations throughout our territory.

Given that Lon Nol's troops had been on the defensive almost everywhere since the rout of Chenla II in 1971, an offer to cease offensive operations was meaningless. Nonetheless in the next few days the tempo of the fighting did slacken, and Washington ordered the B-52s and tactical aircraft confined to their bases in Guam and Thailand. The respite was brief.

The sequence of diplomatic and military moves that led to a full-scale resumption of the war is still unclear. One crucial point is that despite the partial nature of Lon Nol's offer, the North Vietnamese did now encourage their Khmer allies to enter into negotiation. At the end of January, Sihanouk publicly declared that the Front was reevaluating its policy. "If the United States is prepared to act in a friendly manner with an independent and nonaligned Cambodia, we are prepared for a rapid reconciliation with Washington," he said. "We are not warmongers. We don't want a bloodbath. We don't want to throw oil on the fire that is now dying out in Indochina."

The Prince ascribed this change to pressure from "our friends," who claimed that the Front's adversaries were "accusing us of bellicosity while peace was being built." He said he hoped he could meet now with Kissinger. Hanoi issued a strong statement endorsing Sihanouk's position. The response from Washington was negative. The White House announced that Kissinger had "no plans" to see Sihanouk during his forthcoming trip to Hanoi and Peking.

The Khmer Rouge were no more cooperative. In Cambodia they launched an attack on Kompong Thom; in Hanoi their representatives apparently insisted to the North Vietnamese and to Sihanouk—who was there for the Tet celebrations—that the struggle would continue. Years later the Khmer Communists explained their refusal to compromise in terms of their historic fear of Vietnam's intention to incorporate Cambodia into an Indochina Federation dominated by Hanoi; the 1954 Geneva Conference did not provide them a reassuring precedent. Publicly, at least, Hanoi now acceded to its ally's demands: on February 7, 1973, a joint communiqué from the North Vietnamese government and Sihanouk's government insisted that in Cambodia the fight would continue. On February 9 the American bombing began in greater intensity than ever before. Within a few months an enormous new aerial campaign had destroyed the old Cambodia forever.

There was a straightforward military explanation for part of the armada—the defense of government enclaves against Communist attack—but at the same time the bombing provided an important piece of theatrical business in the sideshow.

Once again Thieu's position has to be considered. Nixon's secret promises of military support undercut any incentive the South Vietnamese might have had to implement the political sections of the Paris Agreement. They provided Thieu with the insurance necessary to continue prosecuting the war. But for clear political reasons there was only one way the Nixon administration could now meet such commitments—by the use of air power.

Bombing had always been integral to "peace with honor"; the planes were to be kept in Indochina after the men had been withdrawn. Now the Paris Agreement proscribed further bombing of North or South Vietnam and, if a cease-fire was reached in Laos or Cambodia, there as well. Once a total cease-fire had been installed over all of Indochina it would be hard to muster in Washington the arguments necessary for the maintenance of Thieu's secret defense on station in Southeast Asia. If the war lingered in the sideshow, however, then "the firehose" could be given play.

This is not the whole explanation for the extended 1973 bombing of Cambodia. Lon Nol's forces were dependent on air power. Thieu's insurance was, however, an important strategic consideration, and when William Colby was asked to explain why the country was bombarded so ferociously, he replied that after the Peace Agreement "Cambodia was then the only game in town."

New rules were drawn up by General John Vogt, now Commander of the Seventh Air Force, which moved its headquarters to Thailand after the Paris Agreement. On February 8, Kissinger flew to Bangkok summoning the ambassadors from South Vietnam, Laos and Cambodia to explain to them the current situation and his intentions for the future. Emory Swank was told that his embassy was to become the command post for the new aerial war in Cambodia.

Until now the embassy had been a conduit, passing Cambodian requests for bombing strikes on to the Seventh Air Force. From now on, it was to be actively involved in the entire bombing process, selecting, examining, approving and controlling the bombing, passing judgment on all potential targets. This certainly violated the spirit, perhaps the letter, of the Cooper-Church amendment, which specifically forbade American officials in Phnom Penh from giving combat advice. Swank was told that complete secrecy was essential; no one was to know of the embassy's new duties. Although the general instructions were laid out in a cable from the State Department, William Rogers (who, as Secretary of State, was responsible for everything done by any United States embassy) was not told how fully his subordinates in Phnom Penh were now involved in the bombing.

Swank delegated the day-to-day responsibility to his Deputy Chief of Mission, Thomas Enders. As so often in this war, accidents of personality had a marked effect on the conduct of the war itself.

Thomas Ostrom Enders is six feet eight inches tall, too tall for the U.S. Army, and the most common description given of him is "absolutely

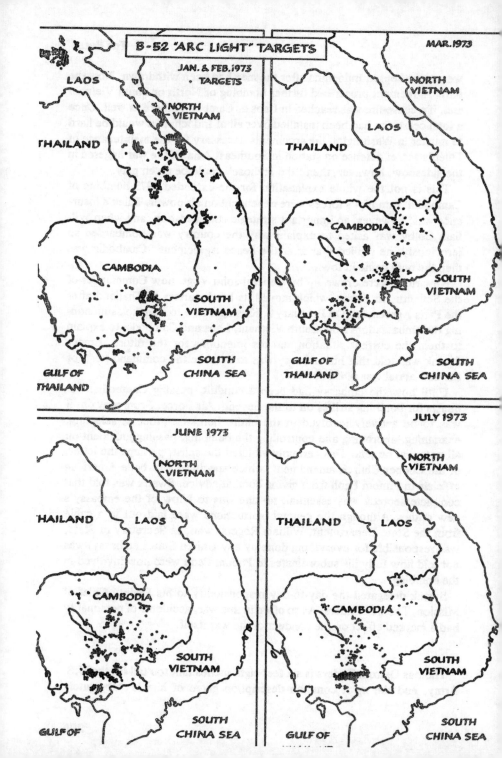

B-52 'ARC LIGHT' TARGETS

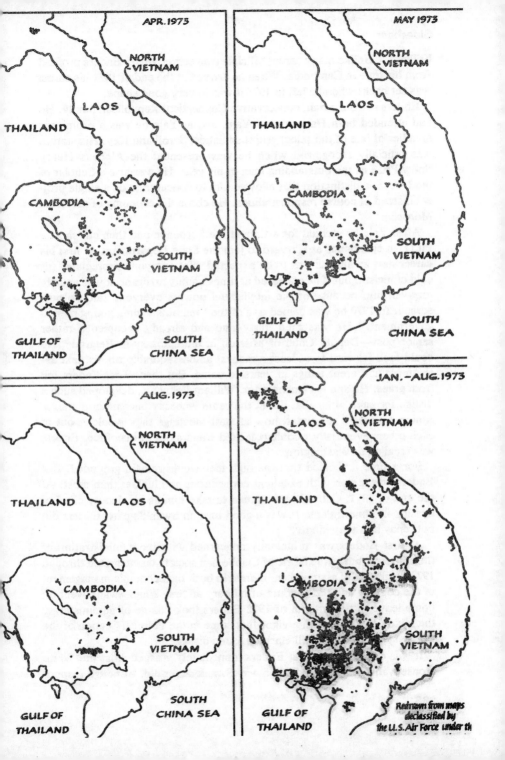

APR. 1973

NORTH VIETNAM

LAOS

THAILAND

CAMBODIA

SOUTH VIETNAM

GULF OF THAILAND

SOUTH CHINA SEA

MAY 1973

NORTH VIETNAM

LAOS

THAILAND

CAMBODIA

SOUTH VIETNAM

GULF OF THAILAND

SOUTH CHINA SEA

AUG. 1973

NORTH VIETNAM

THAILAND

LAOS

CAMBODIA

SOUTH VIETNAM

GULF OF THAILAND

SOUTH CHINA SEA

JAN.–AUG. 1973

LAOS

NORTH VIETNAM

THAILAND

CAMBODIA

SOUTH VIETNAM

GULF OF THAILAND

Redrawn from maps declassified by the U.S. Air Force under th brilliant." Unlike many career officials who served there, Enders profited from his time in Cambodia. When he arrived at the end of 1971 his career was set back; when he left in 1974 it was in very good shape.

Enders is from a rich, conservative Connecticut Republican family. He had attended both Harvard and Yale, and at Yale he was a prominent member of one of the select secret societies, Scroll and Key. His stature was officially recognized when he was presented the Alpheus Henry Snow Prize as the outstanding man of his year. He was also a Scholar of the House, a distinction that allowed him to concentrate on a single project instead of course responsibilities. He chose the economy of medieval Morocco.

After Yale he studied for a time at the Sorbonne and then cut short a Ph.D. in economics at Harvard to join the State Department. At first his career flew as high as was to be expected. Not everyone appreciated his cold clinicism, but if he appeared at times unduly arrogant, it was usually forgiven him because of the intellectual powers everyone said he possessed. In 1970 he was named one of the "ten outstanding young men in government." He was then thirty-nine and already occupied a rather senior post—Deputy Chief of Mission in the embassy in Belgrade. He could look forward to at least a modest ambassadorship on his next assignment and great things in years to come. But then, Tom Enders fell from grace. He and his ambassador, William Leonhart, developed such a dislike for each other that life in the same embassy became intolerable. Junior diplomats recounted how at staff meetings they would shout at each other; eventually Leonhart locked Enders out of his office. Enders was recalled to Washington.

For a time it seemed that the high flier would remain grounded. But Enders was a man with excellent connections and luckier than most. At the end of 1971, Coby Swank agreed to take him as his deputy chief of mission in Phnom Penh. It was a good turn on Swank's part; Enders did not repay him very kindly.

At first Enders was principally concerned with the administration of the embassy, but as the fabric of Cambodian society disintegrated through 1972 he gradually assumed an interest in both the economic management of the country and the conduct of military affairs. When Swank went on home leave in the autumn of 1972 Enders took charge of administering the Nixon Doctrine with a vigor that some in the Political Section of the Embassy, particularly Bill Harben, found distasteful.

It was clear to them that Enders immediately grasped what the White House wanted of Cambodia in a way Swank never did. Although responsible for running a war, Swank refused to act like a proconsul (unlike his counterpart, George McMurtrie Godley, in Laos). He had a genuine concern for the Cambodians.

Swank had supported White House policy in Cambodia so long as it seemed to him necessary for the withdrawal of American troops from Vietnam. Once that was accomplished, in early 1973, he became increasingly disillusioned with the failure to secure an end to the war. What he failed to understand was how little the White House was interested in Cambodia for itself. John Negroponte, who, as one of Kissinger's Indochina specialists, was actively involved with the war and the peace talk, says, "I never knew very much about Cambodia. I don't think anyone did. I am a Vietnam expert, and I always thought of Cambodia as just an adjunct to the whole damn thing. I knew what I had to know, but I didn't get involved in the gory details."

Swank's anxiety for Cambodia did not favorably impress Haig or any of the other NSC aides who came out to Phnom Penh. John Bushnell, another of those who defined White House policy, says, "Swank didn't seem to comprehend the White House view that Cambodia was secondary to Vietnam. For him Cambodia was primary. He would ask 'What do you want me to do? What solution are we going to find for Cambodia?' Kissinger is not very patient and didn't like it." Kissinger wanted an ambassador who would act on his own responsibility without precise instructions. Brent Scowcroft, Kissinger's deputy and later his successor as National Security Adviser, says, "We felt Swank's attitudes were not healthy. He was pessimistic and therefore a bad influence on the Lon Nol government. He had a negative attitude towards what we were doing; didn't put his heart into it." Swank's problem, says John Bushnell, was that "he was not an operator, not a can-do sort of guy. We didn't have much confidence in him."

Tom Enders was a "can-do sort of guy," and to his colleagues in the embassy it seemed that he was not burdened by much interest in the Cambodians. Scowcroft says, "We were delighted with him. He was strong, aggressive, exuded confidence." Bushnell thinks that he "had a much broader perspective than Swank; he understood that Cambodia was secondary to the main problem." He was obviously prepared to fight the war as the White House wished it to be fought, and he was prepared to support Lon Nol whatever his inadequacies. (In June 1972, he wrote a telegram to Washington in which he described Lon Nol's rigged election victory as "a step forward for Cambodian democracy.") Within the embassy he gave no support to political officers like Bill Harben, who questioned policy. Harben's conviction that only radical political change, including the promotion of In Tam to power and a concerted attempt to rally deserters from the insurgents, could save the Republic, was dismissed with contempt.

When investigators from Congressional committees or Congress' General Accounting Office appeared, Enders did what he could to block their inquiries. He was openly hostile to and contemptuous of the press (the feeling was reciprocated), and he made a considerable effort to have the Cambodians expel one of the most dogged of the American journalists in Phnom Penh, Sylvana Foa of UPI and *Newsweek*. He soon became Haig's favorite diplomat in the embassy, and Kissinger was equally impressed. "That sort of man appeals to Dr. Kissinger," said Swank later.

Enders had a natural ally in General Cleland, Mataxis' successor as the Chief of the Military Equipment Delivery Team. Unlike Mataxis, Cleland was a combat soldier; he had commanded a battalion in Vietnam and he possessed both ideas and powers of analysis. Like Enders he was "a can-do sort of guy" and he too abhorred criticism of the war effort, inside or outside the embassy.

After he arrived in Cambodia in early 1972 Cleland had decided that the 1970 plan to create a light-infantry force had been ill conceived. As he pointed out later in his end-of-tour report, such a force had been intended "to combat the 'Khmer insurgents.' That such 'insurgents' might one day evolve into main-force units in their own right, thus requiring a rethinking of the 'light-infantry concept' was a possibility never fully addressed. . . ."

That was correct, but the way in which Cleland chose now to address the problem was controversial. He decided that the army must be reorganized from battalions into divisions. Given the poor quality of most of the officer corps, starting with the Chief of Staff, Sosthene Fernandez, and the way in which Lon Nol abused the entire command and staff structure, this was extraordinarily ambitious. Cleland himself wrote later that Lon Nol's conduct made it "difficult if not impossible" for the army to be administered effectively. He realized also that the army's base was "a non-technical society that is seriously deficient in technical expertise." And yet he insisted that an even more complicated command structure be imposed upon it.

By the time of the Paris Agreement, Cleland's reorganization plans were under way and, with Enders, he had began to dominate both the political and the military side of the embassy in a way in which no other military man had yet managed.

Cleland and Enders agreed that the extensive use of American air power in Cambodia was vital. (Cleland described it in his end-of-tour report as "the one sacrosanct absolute" in all American planning.) When control of the bombing was secretly shifted into the embassy in February 1973, an embassy panel, chaired by Enders and containing Cleland, became responsible for bombing strikes in all parts of the country except the eastern Freedom Deal area, which was still a virtual free fire zone. Most requests for strikes came direct from Cambodian army headquarters, but targets could be proposed by the embassy or by the pilots of the American spotter planes. Such targets had to have clearance from the Cambodians but they were rarely, if ever, rejected. As one air attaché, Mark Berent, recalls, "They never plotted anything. We could have given them the coordinates of the palace and they would have said yes."

By now most Cambodian officers considered air power an essential part of any action, however insignificant. Often they refused to move without it. The Cambodian Psychological Warfare Directorate referred to it as "The Garuda of the Legends" and "Magic Arrow," an omen of divine support. Lon Nol seemed to invest it with supernatural powers, and air attachés at the United States embassy spoke with awe of his habit of simply erasing from the map any enemy unit he had ordered bombed.

Cambodian generals took a casual view of the risks to civilians. The attitude was summed up by Sosthene Fernandez, who, despite his ineffectiveness, was about to be promoted to commander in chief. If a village was suspected of harboring "VC," he said, the government first appealed to the villagers to leave. Then Cambodian Air Force planes strafed around the village to frighten the villagers away from their homes. "Once they have left the village they come to ask us to bomb it. They themselves come to ask us to destroy everything, because they hate the VC. Of course, the villagers are very sad about their belongings, their houses, their lands, but they want us to bomb everything to drive out the VC. We do all we can to avoid civilian casualties, but one cannot always be certain that all civilians have fled."

Given such statements, the embassy might have been expected to consider Cambodian requests for American strikes carefully. But the maps used by the bombing panel were only 1:50,000 in scale and several years out of date; the embassy had no recent photography to show the location of new settlements in the massive forced migrations that the Khmer Rouge were now imposing on the areas they controlled. Maps of the same scale were being used by United States fighter pilots. According to their own official history (April 1 to June 30, 1973) the pilots of the 8th Tactical Fighter Wing actually complained that these maps "lacked sufficient detail and currency to pinpoint suspected enemy locations with some degree of confidence." They asked for up-to-date maps with a scale of 1:5,000—ten times as large. They did not get them.

Inside the embassy, Harben was appalled and now did what others might have done. He cut out, to scale, the "box" made by a B-52 strike and placed it on his own map. He found that virtually nowhere in central Cambodia could it be placed without "boxing" a village. "I began to get reports of wholesale carnage," he says. "One night a mass of peasants from a village near Saang went out on a funeral procession. They walked straight into a 'box.' Hundreds were slaughtered."

Throughout this period, Congress and the American press appeared to be paralyzed by the scale of Nixon's reelection victory and by the withdrawal of the last American soldiers and POWs from Vietnam. Over and over again, White House janissaries repeated that "the President has a mandate." Members of the cabinet made little attempt to conceal their contempt for the Congressional committees that questioned them.* Nothing demonstrated the attitude of the administration as well as the renewed bombing of Cambodia.

In all of 1972 the B-52s had dropped just under 37,000 tons of bombs onto Cambodia. In March 1973 they dropped over 24,000, in April about 35,000 and in May almost 36,000 tons. So with the fighter bombers. In 1972 they had loosed 16,513 tons of bombs at their targets. In April 1973 alone, they dropped almost 15,000 tons, and the figure rose monthly to over 19,000 tons in July. In Washington, some questions were asked, but few answers were given. The Pentagon brushed aside reporters, referring them to CINCPAC headquarters in Hawaii "because it's nearer the action." One explanation frequently offered was that the strikes were being flown against North Vietnamese lines of communication into South Vietnam. This was not entirely true. Maps from one official secret history of the B-52 campaign that year show that many of the bombs were falling on the most heavily populated areas of Cambodia. Another Air Force history states that in March the Joint Chiefs of Staff "increased the scope of air

---

* The White House revealed its intentions by asserting vastly exaggerated Presidential rights to impound funds already appropriated by Congress and to withhold the testimony of any member of the Executive Branch on grounds of "executive privilege." On April 10, 1973, the Attorney General, Richard Kleindienst, told a joint hearing by two Senate Subcommittees that the President could extend this privilege to cover every single federal bureaucrat in the nation; if Congress did not like it then Congress should impeach him.

operations throughout the Khmer Republic to permit strikes against targets posing a potential threat to friendly forces and population centers."

Such studies were not available outside the administration at the time, and at the end of March 1973 the Deputy Assistant Secretary of State for East Asian and Pacific Affairs, William Sullivan, was asked, at a briefing for Senate aides, to justify what had been happening. He laughed and said, "It is interesting you should ask that. I have got a couple of lawyers working on it. I guess what I would say is the reelection of the President." "By that theory," the *Washington Post* pointed out, "he could level Boston."

By March 1973, the Lon Nol government had reached its nadir. Within Phnom Penh and provincial capitals still held by the government, there was acute disappointment at the failure of the Paris Agreement to have brought more than a four-day lull in the fighting and a one-week halt to the bombing. In Tam, who had been given the task of rallying defectors from the Khmer Rouge, resigned after sixteen days because of the restrictions the government, to Bill Harben's fury, placed upon him. A general strike that closed sixteen industries in Phnom Penh was followed by strikes of teachers and students demanding an end to corruption and inflation. In Phnom Penh food ran short after the Khmer Rouge cut the road to Battambang. Oil ran shorter still, and the United States had to airlift supplies. Faced with another collapse of morale and a high rate of desertion from the army, the government introduced conscription.

The bombing was doing little to improve the government's performance. The secret history of one B-52 unit—the 43rd Strategic Wing—acknowledges that in spite of the raids, "the enemy remained steadfast, while Lon Nol's troops continued to decline in effectiveness." As the bombing spread, more and more villagers, pushing carts and carrying bundles or babies on their hips, straggled into the government's enclaves and into Phnom Penh. In the U.S. embassy there was still no adequate refugee program, and only one man with any responsibility for refugees. Tom Enders' Italian wife, Gaetana, set up a home for war widows, "The House of Butterflies," unaware that in Khmer "butterfly" means whore. But those who mocked her had to admit her work was better than nothing —and until well into 1973, not much else was being done.*

The students and the teachers stayed out on strike, and one of their

* The United States government made its first grant of funds to an international relief agency on December 1, 1972. It was to $50,000 to the International Committee of the Red Cross. And on May 2, 1973, grants of $500,000 each were made to Catholic Relief Services and Cooperative for American Relief Everywhere.

meetings, supposedly guarded by the *Gendarmerie*, was disrupted by secret-police agents, who flung grenades into their midst. Two students were killed and eight wounded while the *Gendarmerie* stood idly by. The students accused Lon Nol's younger brother, Lon Non, of setting up the incident. That same day the lover of one of Sihanouk's daughters, a former pilot, hijacked an Air Force T-28 fighter-bomber, roared off the runway at Pochentong airport and swooped down onto the Presidential Palace. He missed Lon Nol, but killed forty-three members of the palace entourage and their families and flew off to the "liberated" areas of the Khmer Rouge.

Lon Nol declared a state of siege, suspended all but the most progovernment newspapers and arrested all the princes and princesses left in town. Prince Sirik Matak, his collaborator in the coup of three years ago and his former prime minister, was placed under house arrest for criticizing the regime. In an interview with *The New York Times*, Sirik Matak then warned that the regime could not survive, and he said that Sihanouk would win easily in a free election. He appreciated Washington's reluctance to interfere in Cambodian affairs, but if the White House insisted on continuing to sustain such an unpopular regime, "We will fall to the Communists."

It was an accurate prediction of inevitable defeat and an unexceptional assessment of the revival of Sihanouk's popularity. Desire for the Prince's return was barely concealed now; almost nothing of the urban contempt in 1970 remained. Rumors of coups were to be heard in every café and every camp in the capital. There were few American diplomats or military men who were not approached by their Cambodian contacts and asked discreetly about Washington's attitude to a change in government. One group called "The Free Patriotic Khmers" petitioned the embassy to protest the "neo-Hitlerism" of Lon Nol and to beg President Nixon to act quickly to change the government. But Lon Nol was still the White House choice, and after the bombing incident Nixon sent him a telegram "to renew our expression of admiration for the Khmer people's courage and steadfastness under your leadership."

A few days later William Porter, the Under Secretary of State for Political Affairs, spoke of the "large degree of political stability in Cambodia under the leadership of Lon Nol." The embassy received instructions from Washington; any journalist who asked about the political situation was to be informed that Lon Nol represented the majority of the Cambodian people. The notion was greeted with derision by correspondents, and relations between the press and the embassy deteriorated further. "We were torn apart by the press," says Harben, "because our line was so ridiculous."

Kissinger was more sanguine. In a background briefing to Richard Valeriani of NBC news he remarked, "We can't go around bashing our allies . . . If you replace a government then you're responsible for its successor and we've just been through that in Vietnam. We didn't go through the agony of getting out of Vietnam in order to get reinvolved in South East Asia." Alexander Haig left on another mission to Phnom Penh. His over-all task was to sustain policy. Lon Nol was offered a trip to the United States for medical treatment, but he was to be bolstered, not replaced. Haig had some success. He persuaded the Marshal that his younger brother Lon Non ought to go on an extended tour of the United States. William Harben, who had just been reassigned to Washington, accompanied him. Harben's Political Section was merged with the Political Military Section so that political reporting from the embassy was further restricted.

Haig also induced Lon Nol to form a more "representative" government by effecting a rapprochement with Sirik Matak, and reuniting the men of the 1970 coup into a four-man ruling council. For a few weeks brave new promises of responsible, collegial government were made, but they soon lapsed. Neither Lon Nol nor the White House was seriously interested in change. Lon Nol refused to relinquish any control of the army. Gradually the other members of the Council—Sirik Matak, In Tam, Cheng Heng—fell away. As Harben later put it, "As soon as Washington was distracted elsewhere, Lon Nol, with the usual [United States] army backing, resumed his dictatorship, and the Americans acquiesced again."

The Senate Foreign Relations Committee sent its seasoned Indochina investigators, James Lowenstein and Richard Moose, to Phnom Penh once again. They were appalled: "We found it generally agreed among all observers that the political, military and economic performance of the Lon Nol government had reached an all-time low. Furthermore, it was our impression that the feeling of apathy and futility on the part of government officials was so profound that it obscured any sense of crisis, which, by any Western standards, they should have felt, given the facts of the situation."

The way the embassy, and in particular Enders, dealt with them is instructive. Moose and Lowenstein were anxious to discover the nature and the extent of the bombing. They found neither Swank nor Enders helpful. What they could not have known was that while their visit was being arranged, Enders had proposed to State that if they asked about the bombing they simply be told that the Defense Attaché's office screened requests from FANK and transmitted them to the Seventh Air Force in Thailand. If they were to ask whether the embassy recommended targets he should reply that it shared certain intelligence that sometimes entered into the Cambodian decision to request strikes. Enders' cable proposed that any questions about numbers of targets or bomb-damage assessment be referred to Washington or CINCPAC. These parameters, described as the "essential elements," were approved by State. Both Swank and Enders subsequently referred to their "special instructions" on how to deal with the investigators, though those "instructions" had originated in the embassy.

Even the "instructions" were at first ignored. To begin with, Moose and Lowenstein reported, "We were told that the embassy possessed only limited information regarding tactical air operations and the locations of B-52 strikes." However, an air attaché told them that he had much more information, which he was forbidden to divulge to them. Then, on a cheap transistor radio belonging to the UPI and *Newsweek* correspondent Sylvana Foa, the two men heard embassy personnel giving bombing instructions directly to United States warplanes.* When they confronted Swank, he referred to Washington's "instructions"; this was the first that Moose and Lowenstein knew of any restrictions on what they could know. They cabled Senator Stuart Symington to complain. Symington spoke to William Rogers, who said that he knew nothing about it. Then Moose and Lowenstein were told a little more—that American spotter planes were radioing ground requests for airstrikes direct to the embassy and that the embassy "validated" every strike request in order to "minimize unnecessary collateral civilian damage." This was still a good deal less than the truth.

Enders' attitude was summarized in another cable warning the State Department that Moose and Lowenstein could be expected to assert a new degree of United States involvement in Cambodia "backed up by detail to the extent we make it available." Rogers ignored this caution and sent two aides over to the Pentagon to try to discover just what was happening in the Phnom Penh embassy. Only then did Rogers learn the full extent to which Enders had been controlling the bombing. He sent an angry cable to Swank, ordering him to brief Moose and Lowenstein fully

---

* Following this incident Sylvana Foa was expelled by the Cambodian government. Cambodian officials said that the initiative came from Enders. Enders later admitted to the Foreign Relations Committee that he considered her stories "tendentious," and had told Cambodian officials that her presence was not what their government or his government needed.

and pointing out that he had been unaware of any "special procedures" used by the embassy to coordinate air strikes until informed by the Pentagon "a few minutes ago."

Enders later argued that State knew the details and that he made no attempt to conceal the embassy role. Swank acknowledges the deception, and he regrets it. "I think it can be explained only on the basis of the extreme sensitivity of our mission, and Washington itself, to Congressional criticism. The whole history of the U.S. in Cambodia is of conflict between the legislature and executive. It was one of the tragedies of the situation. We were always trying to work between them."

The Moose-Lowenstein report was released by a subcommittee of the Foreign Relations Committee at the end of April. Senator Symington, concluding that the embassy's activities were "illegal," called for hearings. The State Department was compelled to fashion a defense of the bombing-control operation, and it was Rogers who had to present it. But attention was diverted. As he drove up Capitol Hill on the morning of April 30, an aide said to him, "This will be hot."

"No," replied Rogers. "The President is about to make a statement which will far overshadow this."

That evening Nixon announced that H. R. Haldeman, John Ehrlichman and Attorney General Richard Kleindienst had resigned after the first revelations about Watergate.

The legal arguments were important. The justification for bombing Cambodia had been to protect Americans in Vietnam. Since October 1970 the Congress had included in every military appropriation bill a proviso expressly forbidding bombing in Cambodia except for that purpose. By the end of March 1973 there were no American troops left in Indochina. Still the bombing of Cambodia increased. The administration now based its case on Article 20 of the Paris Agreement. Rogers now claimed that American withdrawal from Vietnam did not affect the situation in Cambodia, and that Article 20 legalized the bombing "until such time as a cease-fire could be brought into effect."

Such an argument was unpersuasive. Article 20 did not call for a cease-fire, and it did not give any of the signatories unilateral authority to enforce any settlement in Cambodia. As we know, a secret State Department analysis of the Article stressed that it was carefully worded to be only in agreement in principle. No public mention was made of that now. Furthermore, Article 20 applied only to those parties that had signed the Paris Agreement; no Cambodians were among them. Since the obligation on "foreign countries" to withdraw troops and end all military activities in Cambodia was not conditioned on a cease-fire, the absence of a cease-fire could not properly be cited as authority for continued United States involvement.

The memorandum also asserted that the bombing was justified because the continued presence of North Vietnamese troops in Cambodia threatened the right of self-determination in Vietnam. This argument was weakened by the fact that the Paris Agreement had countenanced the continued presence of "approximately 145,000" North Vietnamese soldiers in South Vietnam. The memorandum also ignored the fact that on March 2 Rogers had signed the Declaration of the International Conference on Vietnam which pledged the signatories, if the Agreement were violated, to consult "either individually or jointly . . . with the other parties to this Act with a view to determining necessary remedial measures."

The logic of the administration's position was that the President could involve the country in war whenever he determined that an executive agreement had been violated; it ignored the fact that, even if the United States did have the authority under international law to retaliate against any North Vietnamese breach of the accord, this did not supply the President with a constitutional right to do so. In effect the administration was justifying the bombing as an extension of the Vietnam war; it was to help prevent the imposition of a Communist government on South Vietnam. Rogers claimed that to stop it now would imply "a Constitution that contains an automatic self-destruct mechanism designed to destroy what has been so painfully achieved." In fact, all that the Constitution required was that the President ask for Congressional authority to bomb Cambodia in order to prevent the Communist takeover of Vietnam, if that were indeed its purpose. Instead, the White House merely insisted on its right to continue the campaign.

Secretary of Defense Elliot Richardson asserted that despite the fact that over the years Congress had stated that aid to Cambodia "shall not be construed as a commitment by the United States to its defense," the Lon Nol government was now an American "ally." This assertion provoked Senator George McGovern to comment that it was "a fascinating question of law how a country which has refused protection under a treaty (SEATO), a country whose defense by the United States is prohibited by law, nonetheless qualifies as an 'ally.' " He pointed out that Cambodia was obviously "a super ally," since Lon Nol's "request" for bombing was taken by the White House as conferring the authority for it, whatever the attitude of Congress.

This was the situation at the end of April 1973, and there is no reason

Prince Norodom Sihanouk, an immensely popular ruler, preserved the fragile neutrality of his kingdom throughout the 1950s and '60s. President Richard Nixon and his National Security Adviser, Henry Kissinger, extended Vietnam's war into Cambodia. Its neutrality was effectively destroyed; the "sideshow" began.

Nixon made his only visit to Cambodia in 1953, when he was Vice-President. He considered Sihanouk "vain and flighty . . . totally unrealistic." Sihanouk believed that friendly relations with China were essential for Cambodia: here he is with Chou En-lai in 1956 and with Mao Tse-tung in 1965.

The leaders of the March 1970 coup against Sihanouk: Prime Minister Lon Nol and Prince Sirik Matak. Sihanouk was told the news by Soviet Premier Alexei Kosygin just before he flew to Peking with his wife, Monique, to be greeted by Chou En-lai.

ម៉ែនជាក្បួនសិទ្ធិរបស់ងកជនណរាម្ម

The Lon Nol government immediately published scurrilous posters of Sihanouk and forced unarmed Vietnamese residents of Cambodia to march on Communist troops in the town of Sa'ang. In Peking, Sihanouk abandoned neutrality and made an alliance with the Cambodian Communists and with Hanoi's Premier Pham Van Dong against Lon Nol, South Vietnam and the United States.

On April 30, 1970, President Nixon announced on television that American and South Vietnamese troops had crossed into Cambodia. He showed where the "incursion" had taken place. His Secretary of State, William Rogers [below], and his Secretary of Defense, Melvin Laird [above, with General John Vogt], were opposed to the scale of the operation.

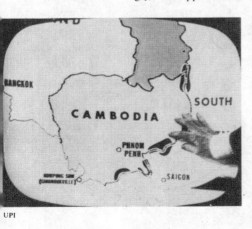

From 1970 onward, Kissinger's aide Alexander Haig made frequent visits, known to U.S. officials as his "stroking missions," to Lon Nol. When Vice-President Agnew met the new Chief of State, Cheng Heng, in August 1970, his Secret Service men openly toted machine guns. Emory Swank, the new U.S. ambassador, was ordered to assume a "low profile" in Cambodia.

In October 1970, Lon Nol abolished the monarchy and proclaimed a republic. Already the country was engulfed in war.

Cambodians fought each other brutally, and rarely took prisoners. Younger and younger boys were drafted into Lon Nol's army. The Communists grew stronger; in April 1973 Sihanouk, their nominal leader, visited them and embraced their commander, Khieu Samphan. In Phnom Penh, the U.S. deputy ambassador, Thomas Enders, coordinated a fierce bombing campaign on White House orders. Kissinger and North Vietnam's Le Duc Tho were unable to negotiate a cease-fire in Cambodia.

Lon Nol, who suffered a stroke in 1971, never seemed able to appreciate the destruction that was being wrought. In one Communist bombardment of Phnom Penh in February 1974, some 10,000 homes were destroyed.

In April 1974 Mao Tse-tung endorsed Khieu Samphan's drive for a military victory in Cambodia. The French ambassador in Peking, Etienne Manac'h, made a last attempt to have Sihanouk returned to power; the effort failed after President Ford and Dr. Kissinger met French President Giscard d'Estaing at Martinique.

During the final Communist offensive in early 1975, thousands were killed, thousands more made homeless. On April 1, Lon Nol fled; he was followed on April 12 by U.S. Ambassador John Gunther Dean and his staff.

UPI

On April 17, 1975, the victorious Khmer Rouge entered Phnom Penh and immediately began to empty the city by force. Three years later Phnom Penh and all other towns were still deserted; the entire population was laboring in the countryside.

By 1978 the two most important men in Cambodia were Pol Pot and Ieng Sary, the leaders of the tiny Communist elite. Sihanouk had been stripped of power. This picture of him and his wife, Monique, with Khieu Samphan, the new head of state, at a Khmer Rouge banquet in Phnom Penh was a rare emergence from house arrest. Hanoi now called Cambodia "a land of blood and tears, hell on earth."

to suppose that the administration intended to shift its attitude or that Congress could, without unusual pressures, have affected it. But then, as the White House abuses of power were revealed, as officials from Nixon and Kissinger on down became more obviously involved, Congress found the will to reassert itself. As an attempt was being made in the courts to have the bombing declared illegal, the legislature finally managed to restrain the President and to accomplish what Nixon and Kissinger had failed to achieve—an end to direct American military involvement in Indochina.

The Bombing

CHAPTER **19**

The Bombing

HENRY KISSINGER blames the Congress for the failure to secure a cease-fire in Cambodia. He has consistently maintained that "delicate negotiations" were underway in the summer of 1973 and were undercut by the Congressional vote to stop the bombing. When Kissinger later asserts what might have been, it is often hard to establish the validity of his claims. His style of diplomacy frequently prevented others having full access to the facts. Among those who did have such access there are not many who are willing to contradict him. It is important to try to examine the record.

In February and March 1973, Sihanouk was finally allowed to make a trip to the liberated areas of Cambodia by his Khmer Rouge allies. In the greatest secrecy, his Peking entourage confined to a hotel outside Canton, he was driven in a jeep, down the Ho Chi Minh Trail into eastern Cambodia. He and his wife, Monique, were taken to a political rally. Wearing the black pajamas and checkered scarves of the Khmer Rouge, they were photographed with Khieu Samphan, Hou Yuon and Hu Nim, Washington's "three ghosts." To his distress the Prince was not allowed to meet or mix with any peasants; he was confined within a close circle of cadres. He returned to Peking with mixed feelings. He told his friends that he was depressed by what he saw as the rigors of collective life under the

Khmer Rouge, but he spoke fiercely about what seemed to be Hanoi's betrayal of the Cambodian cause.

After the Khmer Rouge refusal to negotiate with Lon Nol in February, the North Vietnamese began to restrict their supplies of arms, apparently to stop them from fighting. When the quarrel between Communist Vietnam and Cambodia became public in 1978, Phnom Penh broadcast the confession of a Vietnamese soldier who stated that in 1973 Vietnamese cadres were told that Cambodia must be forced to accept the Paris Agreement, and "whether Cambodia agrees with us or not is not the problem, because Cambodia has a small population." He maintained that cadres were taught that "after finishing the war in Indochina, we would become the big brother in Indochina. . . . As the big brother we had to govern the younger brothers and not allow them to do anything at will. . . . We should, as a common duty, force Cambodia to accept the Paris Agreement . . . a great success achieved by Vietnam in the international arena." In the same vein a Cambodian Communist diplomat later complained that in 1973, after the Khmer Rouge refused to talk with Lon Nol, "The Vietnamese signed their own agreement with the Americans and the B-52s which bombed Vietnam were all sent to pulverize Cambodia. . . ."

Such historical analyses were made after the event, for their propaganda value. But they coincide exactly with what was said at the time. When Sihanouk returned from his trip to Cambodia he told Ambassador Etienne Manac'h that Khieu Samphan, the Khmer Rouge commander in chief, had said to him, "Hanoi has dropped us." Sihanouk asserted that Khmer Rouge independence of North Vietnam was increasing, that nationalism, not just Communism drove the movement now.

The Prince was welcomed back to Peking in triumph, and on April 12 the Chinese gave him a banquet at which Chou En-lai praised him warmly. For his part, Sihanouk gave vent to his feelings in a diplomatic manner. He criticized "peace-loving" countries that sought to impose a cease-fire on Cambodia. He said American claims that North Vietnam was still fueling the war were untrue—the resistance was no longer receiving aid. He denounced American peace plans which involved the partition of the country.

During the toasts at the end of the dinner, Chou walked across the great room to the table at which Etienne Manac'h was sitting. He took Manac'h aside and told him that the longer the war in Cambodia continued, the more extreme and harsh would be the final victory. Would the French please try to persuade Kissinger of this? France, he said, was better placed than anyone else to explain the reality of the situation to Washington. They must do so.

Manac'h understood the seriousness of Chou's appeal. But, say French officials, when the French ambassador to Washington passed Chou's words and Sihanouk's assessment on to William Sullivan at the State Department, he was visibly unimpressed. In both Washington and Phnom Penh, American officials openly scoffed at the reports of Sihanouk's trip. The photographs had been faked, they said; Sihanouk had never left China and, whatever any superficial resemblances in the pictures, the "three ghosts" were certainly dead. Eventually Chou En-lai gave the head of the new American Liaison Office in China, David Bruce, a copy of the film of the trip, "in case you don't believe it happened."

All American troops and POWs had left Vietnam by the end of March. In April the administration began to warn that a breakdown of the ceasefire was possible because of Communist breaches in both Vietnam and Cambodia. In Washington officials claimed that the North Vietnamese were shipping new men and matériel into South Vietnam and publicly alleged that there were still five thousand North Vietnamese troops "operating against Cambodian forces." As threatening gestures, the United States resumed bombing of Laos, suspended mine-clearing operations in Haiphong and restored reconnaissance flights, banned by the Paris Agreement, over North Vietnam. Kissinger requested a new round of meetings in Paris, first between William Sullivan and Hanoi's Vice Foreign Minister, Nguyen Co Thach, later between Le Duc Tho and himself.

The intention apparently was to wave the stick of renewed bombing of the North and to offer again the carrot of postwar reconstruction aid. But then, as Senator Ervin's investigation of Watergate gathered steam, as accounts of the wiretaps caused by the secret bombing, of the illegal Huston plan that had followed the invasion, and of the activities of the Plumbers were headlined across the papers and the television news, the White House's plans for increasing force in Indochina had to be shelved. Both houses of Congress, provoked by Watergate and by the continued bombing of Cambodia, began to debate a War Powers Bill designed to limit the President's right to commit troops abroad without Congressional agreement. (It was eventually approved in the fall, and Nixon's veto was overridden.) Of more immediate concern, both houses began legislation to end the bombing.

On May 10, 1973, the House of Representatives took an unprecedented step: it blocked any use of funds from the Supplemental Appropriations Bill for the bombing of Cambodia. This was the first time in the war that the House voted to undercut a military action on which the President was insisting. The conservatives summoned traditional arguments: the President's hands should not be tied; this was not the time; the United States was bombing for peace. Representative George Mahon of Texas rose to entreat, "Give him a little more time. Join not the multitude to do evil." When the votes were counted, the majority (219–188) was against the President.

Immediately the White House asserted that peace in Cambodia, now close at hand, would recede if the House persisted in such folly. A loud campaign was begun to assure Congressmen, Senators and journalists that all would be well in Cambodia if only Kissinger were given a little more time. Nonetheless, the Senate broadened the amendment to block the use of any funds, from no matter what source, to bomb Cambodia.

Cambodia was certainly a major subject of discussion in the new round of Paris talks. The Americans tried again to tie reconstruction aid to North Vietnam to a Cambodian cease-fire. Le Duc Tho, according to American participants in talks, protested once more that Hanoi was in no position to deliver the Khmer Rouge. In fact, as he knew, the Khmer Rouge had responded to Hanoi's restriction on arms supplies not by caution but by pressing an all-out assault toward Phnom Penh.

In the meantime, Sihanouk had left Peking for his first foreign tour since 1970. He visited eleven countries in North Africa and Eastern Europe, using the freedom the trip gave him to try again to establish his own contact with Washington. From Mauritania and from Guinea he sent messages asking for direct talks with Kissinger. A few days later he said publicly that he had been refused. This was confirmed by the State Department.

Within a fortnight after his last meeting with Le Duc Tho, Kissinger appears finally to have realized that Hanoi could not deliver the Khmer Rouge. He announced that the future of Cambodia "depends not only on decisions taken by Hanoi and Washington but also on decisions taken by other sovereign parties." (Le Duc Tho pointedly denied rumors that he and Kissinger had reached any secret agreement on Cambodia.) To selected journalists, Kissinger began to offer a revised opinion of Sihanouk.

Bernard Gwertzman of *The New York Times*, who had previously noted that the administration dismissed Sihanouk's role, now reported that the Prince "seems to represent the insurgent forces." Kissinger let it be known that he would be delighted to meet Sihanouk on a trip he was planning to Peking in July. Gwertzman called this "a major shift," but its importance remains a matter of speculation. William Steerman, one of

Kissinger's NSC aides dealing with Cambodia, and whose attitude toward the Khmers is described by some of those in the embassy as unconcerned, claims now that Kissinger never really thought Sihanouk could offer anything at all. David Bruce said later that Kissinger's instructions to him in Peking were to "talk to anyone except Sihanouk" about Cambodia. (Among others, Bruce talked to Manac'h; he found his views on Cambodia persuasive.)

One year earlier, veiled promises of peace from Kissinger would have been enough to turn the Congress around. Now his hints were submerged by the intensity of the bombing and by the flood of "White House horrors" that poured daily from Senator Ervin's hearings. Despite Kissinger's entreaties, both houses enacted an amendment to stop the bombing at the end of June. It was sent to Nixon on June 26. The President vetoed it, claiming that it would "cripple or destroy" any chance of a negotiated settlement in Cambodia, would jeopardize the future of the Lon Nol government, and would call into question America's international credibility. The House attempted to override the veto by mustering a two-thirds majority. It failed, and the measure died.

But the President's demands were no longer accepted so obediently as in the spring. Mike Mansfield, the Senate Majority Leader, warned that the amendment would be attached to other bills "again and again and again, until the will of the people prevails." Both houses added the language to financial bills whose enactment by the end of June was essential to keep the federal government funded. The prospect of the government actually being halted was real enough for talk of compromise to begin. Melvin Laird, who had resigned as Secretary of Defense at the end of Nixon's first term, and who was now back in the White House to offer Nixon advice (which Nixon did not take) on how to handle Watergate, announced that the President would veto every bill that contained an immediate ban on the bombing, whatever happened to the government. But he suggested that Nixon might accept a fixed date in the future by which the bombing should end.

The unacknowledged implication was that the President had assumed the power to wage war, not only without Congressional approval, but in the face of express disapproval of the majority. Since it was clear to the Democrats that the votes to override another veto did not exist, such a compromise was made. When the President publicly agreed to respect a deadline of August 15, and not to increase the intensity of the bombing in the interim, the Congress gave him another month and a half to bomb Cambodia and to produce the cease-fire that he and Kissinger claimed was within grasp.

The paradox was clear. Senator J. William Fulbright remarked, "I don't think it is legal or constitutional. But whether it is right or not, he has done it. He has the power to do it because under our system there is not an easy way to stop him." That was an accurate political assessment but it did not satisfy all of his colleagues. Senator Thomas Eagleton of Missouri complained that bombing was "not an issue that yields to compromise. Congress cannot sanction an unconstitutional and illegal endeavor for 'just a little while.' There is no way of just being a little bit unconstitutional or just a little bit illegal." Senator Edward Kennedy called it an "infamous" agreement, totally careless of Cambodian lives. Another view was expressed by House Majority Leader Thomas P. "Tip" O'Neill. He said the bombing should stop because "Cambodia is not worth one American life."

Kissinger and Nixon have ever since claimed that the bombing halt immediately killed all possibility of peace talks, because the United States was no longer negotiating from strength. In his memoirs, Nixon asserts that after the vote "I had only words with which to threaten," and he relates that when Kissinger discussed "Communist violations of the cease-fire in Cambodia" with Anatoly Dobrynin, the Soviet ambassador, the latter "scornfully asked what we had expected, now that we had no negotiating leverage because of the bombing cut-off imposed by Congress. Kissinger tried to be as menacing as he could, even though he knew that Dobrynin was right."

Nixon evidently believed in 1973 (and still in 1978) that the Khmer Rouge were controlled by Hanoi and were amenable to Moscow. Neither was true.* At the same time, neither he nor Kissinger appears to have considered the possibility that it was the continuation of the bombing through the summer, not its eventual ending, that hindered negotiations by placing Sihanouk in an impossible position and rendering the Khmer Rouge more intransigent.

Kissinger was still assuring the diplomatic press corps that he was anxious to see Sihanouk in Peking in July. But early in the month Sihanouk himself told Etienne Manac'h that he could not possibly talk to Kissinger now that the bombing had been turned into such a clear form of duress. On July 5 he announced publicly that he had made three attempts to see Kissinger and had been rebuffed. This time, he would not be in Peking when Kissinger arrived.

* In his memoirs Nixon recounts that in one conversation with Brezhnev in June 1973, "I turned the conversation to Cambodia, a subject I had already raised several times during our meetings. I pointed out that the renewed North Vietnamese activity there was a major threat to world peace."

The Chinese clearly supported his position. The next day Chou En-lai complained about the bombing to a group of American Congressmen. When their leader, Senator Warren G. Magnuson of Washington, suggested that the Cambodians "be patient," Chou asked with obvious anger, "How can a man be patient when bombs are falling on his head?" He warned that although Sihanouk was a "peace-loving Buddhist," Washington was "forcing him to put himself into the battle." China's own patience, he said, "is not unlimited." A few days later David Bruce was informed by the Chinese Foreign Ministry that a visit by Kissinger would not be "convenient" just now. Then, in Cambodia itself, the first Congress of the United National Front of Kampuchea met and announced that it would never negotiate but would fight on until total victory.

It is almost impossible to assess now the extent to which Cambodian and Chinese policies were influenced by the U.S. Congress. The fact that the Khmer Rouge pressed an almost suicidal attack upon Phnom Penh throughout July, despite the promise of an imminent end to the bombing, suggests that other factors were more important in determining their strategy.

Kissinger has never revealed details of the "delicate negotiations" that the Congress had undercut. They must have been very closely held. Dennis Doolin, then Assistant Secretary of Defense for East Asian and Pacific Affairs, says "I never saw any negotiations"; Tom Enders says he was unaware of any. Brent Scowcroft says there was "nothing more than a generalized hope that China would do something—no specific negotiations." David Bruce said later that in Peking he saw no sign of any talks. In Washington Um Sim, the new Cambodian ambassador, was unable even to get an appointment with Kissinger before the bombing ended— "What could he say to me? They were pretending to help us and in fact they were using us," he says. Emory Swank comments that "the only possibility of peace then would have been if we had taken the dramatic step of drastically reducing our support for the Phnom Penh government. It was one of the possibilities I suggested. The Chinese and North Vietnamese might have taken it as a step toward a negotiated settlement. But to Kissinger it would have been leading from weakness."

The reality of the administration's position was probably best expressed publicly by Doolin, testifying to Congress in June. "Cambodia became an integral part of the battlefield in the continuing conflict for South Vietnam. It remains so today." Many American officials, including Nixon, believed that the survival of Lon Nol was essential to that of Thieu, and the thrust of Doolin's message was repeated many times to

Congress. Thieu himself constantly agreed. This priority clearly restricted the administration's quest for peace in Cambodia. By the middle of July Kissinger began to modify his assertion that "delicate negotiations" were under way.

It was now, as Senator Sam Ervin delved further and further into the White House, and as the countryside around Phnom Penh was punished as never before, that the origins of Watergate emerged. In December 1972, Major Hal Knight, the radar operator who had had to burn the records of the Menu bombing and substitute false poststrike reports, had written to complain to Senator William Proxmire of Wisconsin. Knight was no longer in the Air Force. His misgivings about the falsifications had soured his relations with his commanding officer, Colonel David Patterson, who had given him bad efficiency ratings. Knight had one bad rating overturned on appeal, but his career was jeopardized. In October 1972, he was told that he would be discharged, and two months later he wrote Proxmire to say that he felt the American people "have the right to know how the war has been conducted."

Proxmire forwarded the letter to Senator Harold Hughes of Iowa, who had taken a more aggressively skeptical attitude toward the conduct of the war than any other member of the Senate Armed Services Committee. For various reasons, including the mugging of the Committee's chairman, Senator John Stennis, Hughes did not immediately act upon it. But on March 28, 1973, he asked Elliot Richardson, the Secretary of Defense, to provide a complete record of all United States bombing in Indochina since the war began in 1965. Though Richardson was aware of Menu, the classified print-out that he sent the committee showed that no bombing had taken place in Cambodia until May 1970. A declassified version was then requested of the Pentagon. It too was false.

On July 12, General George Brown came before the committee for confirmation as Air Force Chief of Staff. Brown had been Commander of the Seventh Air Force and General Abrams' Deputy for Air Operations from August 1968 to August 1970. Hughes asked him, "Did the United States in fact conduct air strikes in Cambodia prior to May 1970, utilizing B-52s or tactical aircraft or both?" The question was to lead to hearings and a public response of excuses and lies that were perhaps more alarming than anything that was coming from the Ervin Committee. They raised fundamental questions of military discipline and honesty, of civilian control over the military and of Congressional effectiveness. Many of the questions still remain unanswered, many of the conflicts of testimony are still unresolved, and many of the crucial documents are still classified.

In some confusion, Brown asked the committee to go into secret session. There he admitted that B-52 bombing had taken place in Cambodia before the invasion. In this spontaneous testimony the General agreed that reports had been falsified. But after he returned to the Pentagon he withdrew this admission in a letter that argued that, "so long as the reports met in every detail the requirements imposed, they were not intended to deceive those with a security 'need to know.' "

The committee immediately scheduled public hearings. Knight appeared to explain the complicated way in which he had burned the records. Randolph Harrison, the Special Forces lieutenant, came to tell of the secret Salem House and Daniel Boone missions, and of the first, disastrous B-52 strike in Cambodia. Gerald Greven, the pilot who had been told "with a smile" that his maps were in error when he had reported seeing bomb craters in Cambodia in 1969, came to confess that he had been involved in bombing an enemy hospital there. Other junior officers came to say that that was commonplace and described how they had tortured enemy suspects.

But the senior military and civilian officials who were called to testify were not so forthcoming, and the hearings were disappointing for the two Senators—Hughes and Symington—who took them most seriously. These two considered that the fundamental questions were: who exactly had ordered that the Constitution be ignored and the Congress not be informed of an act of war against a neutral country; and who had instructed that military reports and procedures be corrupted. They were continually frustrated in their attempts to find the answers. Both inside and outside the hearing room, the administration mounted a successful campaign to divert attention from those issues by insisting that the bombing had been essential to protect American lives and that the secrecy had been crucial to protect Sihanouk.

The Sihanouk factor dominated all the justifications, even though little or no documentary evidence of his complicity in the bombing was produced. As has been noted, Chester Bowles's visit in January 1968 was cited, and so was Senator Mansfield's in August 1969. Admiral Moorer, Chairman of the Joint Chiefs, said that Kissinger had told him Sihanouk would tolerate secret bombing. Later Kissinger referred the Senate Foreign Relations Committee to a May 1969 press conference in which Sihanouk had said he had no control over what the Americans did in those parts of his country occupied by the North Vietnamese. He also secretly sent the Senate Foreign Relations Committee copies of the letters and cables between Nixon and Sihanouk in 1969, to prove that the Prince had not objected.

Even if diplomatic concerns were, in 1969, the most vital, no one explained why Sihanouk had still to be protected, and the Congress deceived, into the summer of 1973. When the Pentagon's press spokesman, Jerry Friedheim, was asked why the Pentagon had so recently submitted false statistics to Congress, he at first replied, "Obviously it was a blunder of some magnitude. . . . We weren't smart enough to foresee" the testimony of Hal Knight. He said he knew at the time it was wrong and now regretted it. But this was not the answer required of him, and five hours later he issued a "clarification," stating that on further recall he had not known that the B-52 statistics were incomplete until after they were sent to the Committee in June. He claimed that the Pentagon had then been in a "state of flux," with Elliot Richardson moving to the Justice Department and James Schlesinger not yet confirmed as Secretary of Defense.

Friedheim first blamed the Strategic Air Command for the falsification of reports, but the Pentagon then stated, in his name, that the dual reporting procedures "were fully authorized and directed by senior military and civilian officials here in Washington." Laird and General Wheeler then denied that they knew anything about it, and Kissinger claimed he thought the practice "deplorable." Wheeler, however, pointed out that it was the President who insisted continually on the need for total secrecy. Later in sworn testimony to the Foreign Relations Committee, Kissinger initially claimed that "we" in the White House had no knowledge of the double bookkeeping system. But then he inserted into the written record a statement that suggested that either he or members of his staff certainly did. Kissinger said "The President did not know of the dual reporting channels. The President and the NSC unanimously did agree on the need for secrecy, however, for the reasons that have been explained. It was in carrying out this requirement that special double accounting procedures were developed within the Department of Defense."

The administration refused to declassify the crucial documents on the bombing (none of the cables quoted in Chapter One of this book was released), but the Pentagon did provide the November 1969 memorandum from Wheeler to Laird in which the Chairman asked the Secretary to authorize more Menu strikes. The memorandum explained the cover procedure: simultaneous strikes in South Vietnam "will provide a resemblance to normal operations thereby providing a credible story for replies to press inquiries." And, "All sorties against targets in Cambodia will be programmed against preplanned alternate targets in [South Vietnam] and strike request messages will so indicate.''

Harold Hughes was delighted to have the memo. ''This is a direct order to enter targets in the record that are not the targets bombed?'' he asked William Clements, the Deputy Secretary of Defense.

''Yes, sir, it is part of the cover. That is what we said a while ago,'' replied Clements.

''There is an order?''

''That is exactly right.''

''It is signed by Secretary Laird, isn't it?''

''That is exactly right,'' repeated Clements.

Hughes was satisfied. It was, he said, the first solid written evidence of instructions to misrepresent the actual bombing positions, to enter false coordinates.

Laird was displeased by Clements' admission. At a press conference the next day he refused to have parts of the memo read out to him, and claimed that although he had approved a separate reporting procedure he had not sanctioned any falsification of records. Asked whether Kissinger or Nixon had seen the Wheeler memo, Laird replied, ''I can assure you that I did not approve the strikes without total and complete discussion at the highest level of government.''

In an interview for this book, Laird repeated that in 1969 he had wanted to bomb the sanctuaries publicly, that it was Nixon, Kissinger and Rogers who insisted that it be done in secret. In 1977, Nixon told David Frost that Sihanouk's position was

> the reason that Secretary Laird, Laird, took the positions he did, that this should be kept secret for diplomatic reasons. . . . The charge that the Pentagon, Secretary Laird gave two sets of orders, ah to the plane crews in when the, when the bombings were to take place. Ah, but, he did that in order to protect the security of the operation. And, ah, in, in war there are times when you have to, in dealing with the enemy, in order to mislead them, you may not be able to level with your friends, or even with your own people.

Nixon then cited in defense of the procedure the way in which the Allies attempted to mislead the Germans about the site of the Normandy landings.*

---

* Nixon appears to have confused Laird with Kissinger. It has never been suggested elsewhere that it was Laird who was concerned to "protect" Sihanouk. This statement, recorded by Frost, was edited out of the broadcast interviews. It is reproduced direct from the transcript.

The Congress never was able to discover precisely who had initiated the false-reporting procedures, nor who had approved them, nor which White House officials actually knew about them. The characteristic response was that all the Menu procedures "were devised by the highest military authorities on the basis of requirements imposed by the senior civilian authorities."

Donald Dawson was a young Air Force captain, a Christian Scientist, serving as a B-52 copilot at Utapao, Thailand. He had been flying B-52s since the end of 1971, but throughout 1972 he found it impossible to ignore the consequences of his work. When he returned home at the end of his first tour he found himself obsessed with the deaths he had inflicted. Watching *West Side Story* on television one night, he could see nothing but falling bombs and screaming people. In the spring of 1973 he was sent on a second tour to bomb Cambodia; he found each of the twenty-five missions he flew more difficult to reconcile with his conscience. He became particularly upset by a report that a Cambodian wedding party had been "boxed" by B-52s. This made him think constantly of the "reverence" in which he held his own wedding—he considered it the most important event in his life, and "having the actual ceremony devastated by a B-52 attack is beyond comprehension." It forced him, he said, to realize that the Cambodians were human beings and to recognize that nonmilitary targets were being hit.

Then he read Solzhenitsyn's *1914* and appreciated more fully the impact that iron missiles have upon human flesh. On June 19, 1973, he refused to fly. He talked to the chaplain and the flight surgeon about the chances of applying for conscientious-objector status. The doctor advised that he be taken off flying duties, but his commanding officer Colonel Bill V. Brown gave him a direct order to fly. Dawson disobeyed it and court-martial proceedings were begun.

With the help of a competent young military counsel, he then joined three other B-52 officers and a first-term member of Congress from New York, Elizabeth Holtzman, in a lawsuit the American Civil Liberties Union was conducting to have the United States courts declare the bombing of Cambodia illegal. Since the courts have traditionally refused to become involved in the conduct of foreign affairs, the case was of some judicial importance. Throughout the summer of 1973, its legal journey paralleled Congress' attempt to end the bombing.

The first judgment was given on July 25; a Republican judge, Orin Judd, of the Federal District Court in New York, found in favor of the plaintiffs.

He decided it was evident that, since 1970, the Congress had made clear that aid to Cambodia was approved only for the protection of American lives in Vietnam. Since there were no Americans left to protect, the continued bombing had no basis in law. Congress' acceptance of the August 15 compromise reflected only an admission of the President's power to bomb, not approval of his doing so. The judge stressed that "it cannot be the rule that the President needs a vote of only one third plus one of either House in order to conduct a war, but this would be the consequence of holding that Congress must override a Presidential veto in order to terminate hostilities which it has not authorized." He issued an injunction to stop the bombing within forty-eight hours.

The administration appealed, and a stay was granted by the Second Circuit Court. The plaintiffs then appealed to the Supreme Court to have the stay lifted. The Court was in recess, and so Mr. Justice Thurgood Marshall, who had supervisory jurisdiction over New York, heard the case alone. He was sympathetic and said that he "might well conclude on the merits that continued American operations in Cambodia are unconstitutional." But since the Supreme Court as a whole had not considered the issue, he did not feel that he could alone reinstate the injunction.

The rules of the Supreme Court allow plaintiffs in such a situation to appeal to another Justice, and so the ACLU sent one of its lawyers, Burt Neuborn, across the country to find William O. Douglas, then the oldest and most liberal member of the Court, in his home in the mountains of Washington State.

Neuborn flew to Seattle, drove five hours to the town of Goose Prairie, and walked for an hour up through the woods to deliver the appeal to Douglas' cabin. Douglas agreed to hear the arguments, and on August 3 the post office in the river-valley town of Yakima opened as a hearing room. Several hundred local people crowded in, and Douglas came down from the hills in an ill-fitting suit, listened, and then retired to his cabin to write a judgment that was moving if not entirely convincing in terms of law.

Douglas argued that the appeal "involves the grim consequences of a capital case" and would decide "whether Mr. X (an unknown person or persons) should die. No one knows who they are. They may be Cambodian farmers whose only 'sin' is a desire for socialized medicine to alleviate the sufferings of their families and neighbors. Mr. X may be the American pilot or navigator who drops a ton of bombs on a Cambodian village. The upshot is that we know that someone is about to die." That, he considered, was far more important than any possible harm that might be done to foreign policy by ending the bombing.

Recalling the Court's decision that President Truman had no power to seize the steel mills during the Korean war he observed

> property is important, but if Truman could not seize it in violation of the Constitution I do not see how any President can take "life" in violation of the Constitution . . .
> When a stay in a capital case is before us, we do not rule on guilt or innocence. A decision on the merits follows and does not precede the stay. If there is any doubt whether due process has been followed in the procedures, the stay is granted because death is irrevocable. . . . Denial of the application before me would catapult our airmen as well as Cambodian peasants into the death zone. I do what I think any judge would do in a capital case—vacate the stay entered by the Court of Appeals.

It was now only eleven days before the bombing had to end anyway. The White House was no longer pretending that it was necessary to help the United States "negotiate from strength," and the Khmer Rouge offensive had slackened. But to Nixon the bombing of Cambodia had evidently become an important symbol of his embattled presidency. Under the procedures of the Supreme Court only the Court in a proper meeting could now overturn the stay imposed by Douglas. So, the Justice Department argued that he had not, in fact, issued a stay at all, but had simply vacated the order of the Second Circuit Court, and that the government therefore had the right to seek its own stay on the original ruling. The Department went back to Thurgood Marshall. He accepted the argument and telephoned his colleagues across the country to find a consensus. All but Douglas—who protested that such a telephone poll was alien to the court's procedures—agreed that he should reimpose a stay on the first injunction. The bombing continued.

By the time the original stay—rather than the appeals—reached the Supreme Court early in 1974, the lower courts had decided that the only plaintiff who had arguable standing was Donald Dawson, since he was the only one of the five whose interests were directly affected by the bombing. The ACLU lawyers were confident that they would win the case in the Supreme Court and that the bombing of Cambodia would be declared, retrospectively at least, unconstitutional. That would have been a historic judgment, but it was not one that Nixon, more decayed than ever, could risk. A few weeks before the Court was due to hear the arguments, the government suddenly dropped the court-martial proceedings against Dawson, and conscientious-objector status was granted to him. His standing now gone, the High Court never heard the case. There was to be no final judgment on the bombing.

Neak Luong was a strategic ferry town on the Mekong between Phnom Penh and the Vietnam border, vital to the Lon Nol government's control of the river. In the middle of the town was one of the radar beacons essential to the B-52 bombing of Cambodia. Unlike in Vietnam, there were no ground radar sites to help planes to their targets in the country. Some missions came under the control of a guide plane flying out of Thailand; this program was known as "Pave Phantom Lead." On other missions the navigator himself plotted the plane's final bomb run, calculating the coordinates from fixes taken off the nearest radar beacon on the ground. That done, the navigator had to flip an offset switch on his radar scope, otherwise the plane would home in on the coordinates of the beacon instead of those of the target. Early in 1973 one beacon was placed on top of the American embassy in Phnom Penh. Despite the fact that embassy officials constantly praised the accuracy of bombing, it caused a certain nervousness among them, and in April it was removed. At the same time more and more beacons were installed in Cambodian towns to cope with the expansion of the bombing. On August 7 one navigator who was using the Neak Luong beacon forgot to flip his switch. Six miles above the town the plane's belly opened and the long thirty-ton string of bombs "boxed" without warning onto the people below.

Rumors of the accident quickly reached Phnom Penh, where dozens of journalists had gathered to await what everyone expected to be the Khmer Rouge "kill" after the bombing ended on August 15. Colonel David Opfer, the United States embassy's air attaché, told them the accident was "no great disaster. The destruction was minimal." Nonetheless, he and other embassy officials did everything they could to prevent reporters from traveling to Neak Luong. Sydney S. Schanberg of *The New York Times* managed to do so. He found that one string of bombs had marched right down the main street, the hospital was destroyed, 137 people had been killed and 268 wounded.

The accident inevitably raised the question of how often such errors occurred in parts of the country where reporters could never penetrate.*

---

* The bombing of Cambodia was now so intense that the Seventh Air Force was faced with serious logistical problems. At one stage B-52 sortie rates were as high as eighty-one per day. In Vietnam the maximum had been sixty per day. The Seventh Air Force history

Commiserating with the townspeople, Ambassador Swank pointed out that "in war one learns to suffer, but it is especially disheartening to receive death and destruction from your friends." The United States government promised funds to rebuild the hospital and pay compensation of about $100 per casualty. A survivor thanked Swank for his generosity. The navigator was later fined $700 for his carelessness.

In 1973 the war did not slacken when the onset of the monsoon in May turned the red earth to mud and brought the waters of the Mekong tumbling over the land. Despite the ferocious and ever-increasing bombardment to which they were subjected, the Khmer Rouge fought throughout the summer more fiercely than ever before—even through July, when the bombing was in its final spasm. The North Vietnamese, like the Americans, had sought a stalemate war in Cambodia. But the Khmer Rouge were seeking victory. After attempting to cut the government's supply lines they now closed in on Phnom Penh. The airplanes moved above them.

Their principal motive, it is apparent, was fear that the North Vietnamese might betray them completely. In Cambodian terms that betrayal had already begun. Sihanouk complained to *The New York Times* in July that the North Vietnamese were now far more interested in American aid than in helping Cambodia. "Suddenly you see Dr. Kissinger smile and Mr. Le Duc Tho smile at Dr. Kissinger. They shake hands, and they go arm in arm and leave us alone." He later told another journalist, T.D. Allman:

> We do not have enough ammunition. I look back to the Treaty we signed with the Pathet Lao, with the North Vietnamese and with the (Viet Cong) at the South China Conference in 1970. We promised to fight to the end. Now the North Vietnamese sign agreements with Kissinger. No matter, we will fight on alone. . . . The North Vietnamese want American aid so they do not help as much as they

---

for the period notes that, with the Cambodian sky so crowded, the problems of air-traffic congestion were considerable; sorties were so frequent that it was impossible to give adequate "Air Strike Warnings" to other aircraft. Errors were made. In late May a mistake was made in transcribing the coordinates of a proposed B-52 strike which needed the approval of FANK. (After the Moose and Lowenstein investigation in April, control of the bombing was shifted from the United States embassy to FANK headquarters.) "The incorrect target card was then used as the reference for drafting the validation request message which was submitted for FANK validation. The requested area was cleared for Arclight strike although it was, unknown to the FANK, sixty miles from the desired strike area . . ." The strike took place, but the history does not record its results.

could. The Chinese play the big power game with America. Brezhnev and Nixon are friends. But we will not play the big power game. We will fight for the unity of our country. . . . Nixon continues to pour arms into Phnom Penh. We get very little from our Communist allies. Still we will fight for Cambodia.

On several occasions he said that he feared that Washington and Hanoi might agree to the partition of Cambodia. Certainly that idea had occurred to some American officials—indeed it was the basis of what passed for one peace proposal. In these matters Sihanouk expressed ageless Cambodian fears, and there was no reason to suppose that he did not represent the feelings of the Khmer Rouge as well. Later the Khmer Communists claimed that the North Vietnamese "entered into negotiations in 1973 in an attempt to swallow us, but they did not succeed." Pol Pot, the Party leader and Prime Minister after the war, commented: "If we had agreed to have a cease-fire in 1973 in accordance with the maneuvers of the U.S. and Vietnamese enemies, we should have suffered a heavy loss. First of all, we should have lost to U.S. imperialism and its lackeys; and secondly, we should have become slaves of the Vietnamese, and the Cambodian race would have entirely lost its identity." The Khmer Communists also asserted, "During the U.S. imperialists' air war in 1973, during which Cambodia was the only country to hold high the offensive banner of attacking the U.S. imperialists, the U.S. imperialists mobilized all types of aircraft from Southeast Asia and the Pacific to bomb Cambodia in a most barbaric and cruel manner. . . ."

The Khmer Rouge numbered now some 60,000 men organized into about 175 battalions. They were well disciplined and excelled at infantry assaults and at quickly digging in and holding ground against superior fire power. Through June and July they rolled up vital government outposts on the roads leading to Kompong Cham and to Phnom Penh, but they failed to take the capital. This was in part because they had not yet developed an effective command and control structure, full strategic mobility or communications security. As a result they tended to commit units in an uncoordinated, piecemeal fashion. These shortcomings, together with a scarcity of munitions, helped Lon Nol's troops to resist their assaults around the capital during July. So did the final, frenzied use of American air power.

The White House ignored its agreement with Congress that the intensity of the bombing during the last forty-five days not be increased. In

June, 5,064 tactical sorties were flown over Cambodia; in July this was raised to 5,818; and in the first half of August, 3,072 raids were flown. In those forty-five days, the tactical bombing increased by 21 percent. The B-52 bombing also increased, though those planes were already almost fully committed. By August 15, when the last American planes dropped their cargoes, the total tonnage dropped since Operation Breakfast was 539,129. Almost half of these bombs, 257,465 tons, had fallen in the last six months. (During the Second World War 160,000 tons were dropped on Japan.) On Air Force maps of Cambodia thousands of square miles of densely populated, fertile areas are marked black from the inundation.

The immediate and the lasting effects of that massive, concentrated bombardment will probably never accurately be known. At the time, Tom Enders defended the policy vigorously as essential to Lon Nol's survival. Now, he claims that it took hardly any lives and that its purpose was essentially diplomatic, based on Kissinger's belief that Hanoi controlled the Khmer Rouge.

The Air Force does not undervalue its contribution thus. The history of the activity of B-52s in the 43rd Strategic Wing, based in Guam, summarizes those months:

> FANK units failed to contain the insurgents in many areas of the country. The enemy succeeded in partially isolating the Cambodian capital from the main lines of communications. . . . Some foreign observers were virtually convinced that the fall of Phnom Penh was expected to occur within a matter of days.
>
> Steady pounding by ARC LIGHT crews perhaps saved the day for Cambodia. . . . ferocious B-52 bombing rained upon the enemy and kept the insurgents from amassing reinforcements and staging resupply activities. . . . [Then] the insurgents after achieving sizeable gains near the Cambodian capital, were beginning to disperse in mass numbers as ARC LIGHT strikes continually flushed them out.

The Chief of the Targets Division, based in Thailand, described the situation in his end-of-tour report:

> For the first time since the defense of An Loc in South Vietnam during the 1972 Communist offensive, B-52s were used close in with ARC LIGHT boxes within [deleted] of besieged friendly positions. With its greater accuracy, the F111 was targeted even closer, to [deleted]. This tactic countered the enemy tendency to move close to the friendlies when under bombing attack on the presumption we will not risk bombs on friendly forces. . . . By saturating the banks

[of the Mekong] at vulnerable points with pre-planned airstrikes in advance of river convoys and maintaining F4s and A7s overhead during the ships passage, the command effectively reopened the Mekong to Phnom Penh. . . . The enemy shifted to a direct assault upon Phnom Penh. . . . Although he drove the FANK back, the assault exposed his concentrated troops to air attack. As a second tactical error, he began a "scorched earth" policy, burning villages as he overran them, possibly with a view toward increasing Phnom Penh's refugee problem. Initially it was very difficult to target the enemy's forces with B-52s and F111s close enough to the fighting to be effective: the area is almost suburban in character with close-spaced villages throughout. However, by driving the inhabitants out and destroying the villages, the enemy developed areas that the command could legitimately target without hazard to noncombatants. In defiance of the "conventional wisdom that air cannot take ground or hold it," we have done it. . . . The Cambodian army is as hapless and helpless as could be imagined. The application of sound principles in the use of U.S. air by a determined Commander, skillful staff, and well trained and disciplined air crews took and held ground by making it untenable for the enemy. The FANK did not fight its way to the positions it held at the end of the air campaign. It walked to them standing up.

General John Vogt, the Seventh Air Force Commander, also speaks with pride today of 1973. The bombing, he says, saved Phnom Penh by killing about 16,000 of the enemy. It is important to consider the implications of this figure, even if, as is probable, it is exaggerated. About 75 of the Khmer Rouge's 175 battalions were put into the battle for Phnom Penh, and each battalion numbered some 340 men. This meant a force of about 25,500 attacking the capital. If most of Vogt's casualties were where the bombing was heaviest, on the city's approaches, then the Khmer Rouge would have lost well over half of its assault force. Even if one spreads the loss across the entire army, this means 25 percent killed. There is a military rule of thumb, generally accepted by battle commanders, that units cannot sustain losses of more than 10 percent without suffering often irreversible psychological damage.

That summer's war provides a lasting image of peasant boys and girls, clad in black, moving slowly through the mud, half-crazed with terror, as fighter bombers tore down at them by day, and night after night whole seas of 750-pound bombs smashed all around. Week after week they edged forward, forever digging in, forever clambering slippery road banks to assault government outposts, forever losing comrades and going on in thinner ranks through a landscape that would have seemed lunar had it not been under water. They pushed toward the enemy's capital, urged on by their commanders, a small group of hardened zealous men who had lived up to ten years in the isolation of the jungles, whose only experience of alliance was betrayal, whose only knowledge of war was massive retaliation.

For those men, 1973 confirmed a historic conviction that survival, let alone victory, could be guaranteed only by absolute independence and an astonishing fixity of purpose. They faced an enemy who at least appeared to have enormous support from his sponsor, while they themselves could not trust even their own leader, let alone their friends. Their attack upon Phnom Penh was a madness born of desperate isolation, which bred a dreadful hatred of their enemy and a contempt for the attitudes of the outside world. But for the bombing and their shortages of munitions, they might have won the war that summer. As it was, the indifference of their allies and the assault upon them by the supporters of their enemy stamped out thousands upon thousands of them, and the survivors had neither the men nor the firepower for a final assault upon the capital when, after August 15, 1973, the rains reinherited the skies.

CHAPTER 20

The Secretary

SEVEN DAYS after the bombing ended, Richard Nixon nominated Henry Kissinger to be his second Secretary of State. The announcement delighted many people, including members of the diplomatic press corps. When one of them asked, "Do you prefer to be called Mr. Secretary or Dr. Secretary?" Kissinger replied in the style they enjoyed: "I don't stand on protocol," he said. "If you just call me Excellency it will be O.K."

Kissinger's elevation was sensible enough. For years he had controlled the levers of foreign-policy power, and William Rogers had often been used for little more than ceremonial purposes or for testifying to Congress on subjects about which Kissinger did not keep him properly informed. Morale in the State Department, an organization whose deficiencies do not justify its exclusion from decision making, had rarely been lower.

The nature of Rogers' role was revealed in a conversation between Nixon and H. R. Haldeman, his chief of staff, on June 23, 1972. (The tape of this conversation was the "smoking pistol" which finally caused Nixon to resign. After discussing Kissinger and Rogers, Nixon and Haldeman went on to plot how to limit the FBI's investigation of the Watergate burglary.) Kissinger was expected back from another trip to China at 4:30 that afternoon:

> PRESIDENT: I told Haig that I'll see Rogers at 4:30.
> HALDEMAN: Oh, good. O.K. . . .

PRESIDENT: Well, I have to, I'm supposed to go to Camp David. Rogers doesn't need a lot of time, does he?

HALDEMAN: No sir.

PRESIDENT: Just a picture?

HALDEMAN: That's all. He called me about it yesterday afternoon and said "I don't want to be in the meeting with Henry, I understand that, but there may be a couple of points Henry wants me to be aware of."

PRESIDENT: Sure.

PRESIDENT: [Unintelligible] call him and tell him we'll call him as soon as Henry gets here, between 4:30 and 5:00 [unintelligible] good.

HALDEMAN: O.K., that's fine.

HALDEMAN: Now, on the investigation, you know, the democratic break-in thing, we're back in the problem areas because the FBI is not under control. . . .

Given the humiliation to which he had been subjected, Rogers behaved with dignity. Kissinger, however, found the situation intolerable. In his memoirs Nixon recounts, "The problem became increasingly serious as the years passed. Kissinger suggested repeatedly that he might have to resign unless Rogers was restrained or replaced." After the 1972 election, according to Haldeman, Nixon decided to replace Rogers with Ambassador Kenneth Rush, but Rogers refused to leave before summer 1973, and Nixon gave in. Kissinger, Haldeman recounts, was furious. "You promised me, Haldeman. You gave me your *word!* And now he's hanging on just like I said he would. Piece by piece, bit by bit. He stays on and on and on." By the time Rogers finally did go, Watergate had already weakened Nixon, and he needed the luster that Kissinger's appointment might lend his administration.

Kissinger had succeeded in creating a wide constituency outside the White House, even while he strengthened his relations with the President. At the same time Nixon apparently now believed that his adviser was not always to be depended on. In his memoirs, the former President claimed that he had installed his secret taping system in part to provide a record, because "any President feels vulnerable to revisionist histories—whether from within or without his administration—and particularly so when the issues are as controversial and the personalities as volatile as they were in my first term." Haldeman was more explicit in his own book about the reasons for the taping system.

One of the prime focal points of Nixon's concern was the unpredictable Henry Kissinger. Nixon realized rather early in the relationship that he badly needed a complete account of all that they discussed in their many long and wide-ranging sessions. He knew that Henry was keeping a log of these talks, a luxury which the President didn't have time to indulge. And he knew that Henry's view on a given subject was sometimes subject to change without notice. He was frequently given to second thoughts on vital matters that the President assumed had been settled.

Nixon quoted in his memoirs a letter Kissinger had sent him on Election Day 1972, thanking him for the privilege of serving the last four years and praising his "historic achievement—to take a divided nation, mired in war, losing its confidence, wracked by intellectuals without conviction, and give it a new purpose and overcome its hesitations." Yet only a few weeks later, after Kissinger had encouraged Nixon to embark on the Christmas bombing of Hanoi, he carefully suggested to James Reston of *The New York Times* that he was opposed to the decision. Reston reported this. According to Haldeman, Kissinger then denied he had given Reston an interview. It transpired that he had talked to the columnist on the telephone. Nixon was not pleased.

When the taping system was revealed in 1973 Kissinger was, by all accounts, dismayed. Haldeman maintained that it was Kissinger who had most to lose if the conversations between him and Nixon were ever published and that he had urged Nixon to destroy them. They would presumably show Kissinger as much more aggressively hawkish than he cared to suggest to the public and would be filled with unflattering comments on those who considered themselves to be his friends. Ray Price, a Presidential speechwriter who remained consistently loyal to Nixon, wrote that one of Kissinger's traits, "which he seemed to carry to compulsive extremes, always particularly irritated me and contributed to my feeling of distrust: his incessant backbiting of anyone who in any way might be perceived as his rival for power or influence. While cordial enough to their faces, he was ruthless behind their backs." Price said that whenever he met Kissinger to discuss papers for the President "the entire meeting would be punctuated with Henry's put-downs of those in State or Defense or one of the other agencies, who had anything to do with the project. The constant theme of these animadversions was that unless checked (implicitly by Henry himself) these others would undermine all that the President was trying to do. I had to assume that as soon as my own back was turned I was subject to the same treatment." Nixon's tapes would reveal similar performances in the Oval Office. They might also show conclusively the extent of Kissinger's involvement in two of what John Mitchell called "the White House Horrors"—the Cambodia wiretaps and the Plumbers.

Kissinger has always denied any knowledge of the Plumbers' activities until these became public in 1973. As we have noted in Chapter Fourteen there are apparent problems in his statement of ignorance. Kissinger has given many varied and conflicting accounts of the wiretaps. One of the first journalists to question him on the subject, when the taps were revealed in May 1973, was Bob Woodward of the *Washington Post*. Woodward's attitude was not what dealing with the diplomatic press corps had taught Kissinger to expect from journalists. He asked Kissinger if it were true that he had authorized taps on two aides.

"It could be Mr. Haldeman who authorized the taps."

"How about Kissinger?" Woodward asked.

"I don't believe it was true."

"Is that a denial?"

"I frankly don't remember," Kissinger replied. He thought he might have provided the FBI with names and they might have taken this as an authorization.

When Kissinger told him he had "almost never" authorized any taps himself, Woodward asked if that meant "sometimes." Kissinger shouted, "I don't have to submit to police interrogation about this," and then tried to insist that the whole conversation be put, retroactively, on "background." Woodward refused, Kissinger hung up and then complained angrily to Woodward's superiors.

Asked at that time at a press conference whether he had known that the home telephone of one of his staff (Halperin) was being tapped (a truthful answer would have been "Yes") he replied:

The CIA and the FBI submit reports through my office when they concern national security. In the overwhelming majority of these cases these reports are always at the direction of the Director of the Agency . . . and follow duly constituted processes. My office has not handled or been aware of any activities that were conducted by other processes. The overwhelming majority of reports that come through my office from both of these agencies concern matters of foreign intelligence. In a very few cases where it concerns allegations of the mishandling of classified information that was within the purview of the NSC, I would receive summaries of reports from agency heads concerning these activities.

On May 29, 1973, after further questioning, he conceded, "My office supplied the names of some of the individuals who had access to the information that was being investigated."

His confirmation hearings did not provide a full review of the facts. Many of the Senators trod warily, and Kissinger managed to direct the discussion to the semantic, and essentially irrelevant, question of whether he had actually "initiated" the taps or merely acquiesced in them. Serious questions as to their morality or legality were easily deflected. They nonetheless remained and would continue, occasionally, to haunt him.

Kissinger's confirmation hearings—the first public testimony he had ever given before Congress—did provide an opportunity to examine the foreign policy of the last four and a half years, but many of the Senators were restricted either by their regard for Kissinger, by their wish to identify with, rather than criticize, the statesman before them, or by their imperfect knowledge of the facts. In some cases this was not important; there were considerable achievements for which Kissinger deserved praise and which might alone justify his elevation to the Secretaryship. Poor young Americans were, at last, no longer dying in Indochina, Nixon had visited Peking and ended more than twenty years of destructive hostility toward China. He had visited Moscow as well, and although both he and Kissinger had oversold the process they called "détente," American-Soviet relations were certainly now conducted more rationally than ever before. It was hard to quarrel with Kissinger's basic premise that the peace of the world and the lives of hundreds of millions of people depended on the stability of that relationship. The first SALT treaty that he had negotiated with considerable skill undoubtedly helped secure those lives.

Some of the changes were more cosmetic than real, and others—indeed, the visit to China—had been overdue, principally because of long years of opposition by men like Nixon. Nonetheless, the new civility between Washington and Moscow and Peking did seem a stunning success, one which tended, not unnaturally, to overshadow other aspects of the past four and a half years of stewardship.

First, of course, there was the continuing, extended war in Indochina, where no real peace had ever been sought, and where détente had failed to produce real benefits. There was the fundamentally careless acquiescence in General Yahya Khan's attrition of East Pakistan and the "tilt" away from India in the Indo-Pakistan war of 1971. There was the deliberate attempt to "destabilize" the government of Salvador Allende in Chile. "I don't see why a country should be allowed to go Communist through the irresponsibility of its own people," Kissinger had remarked at the time of Allende's election in 1970. Most of the American attempts to disrupt the Chilean economy and arm, not merely encourage, Allende's opponents were still undiscovered. But they helped—ironically, as Kissinger's nomination was being considered by the Senate—to secure Allende's death and his replacement by a brutal right-wing junta. When Kissinger was asked about CIA involvement in the coup, he denied that there was any such thing; this was a fundamentally misleading answer.

There had been the refusal to apply United Nations sanctions against Rhodesian chrome. With it had gone a tolerance for the white minority regimes of southern Africa, based on accepting the option in National Security Study Memorandum 39 that argued that "the whites are here to stay, and the only way that constructive change can come about is through them." This judgment led to years of neglect, which were to have extremely serious consequences when it was inevitably proven wrong. Coinciding with it was Kissinger's proclaimed ignorance of economic affairs and his early lack of interest in the "Third World" in general. As so often, his attitudes were to change, but not before considerable damage had been done.

Then there was the Middle East, the area of the world where Kissinger was later to win so much credit. In the first Nixon administration United States policy had failed there. It had been the one topic for which William Rogers was allowed some responsibility, but he was never given proper support. In 1970 Kissinger and Nixon had given no backing to the Rogers' Plan for a comprehensive settlement; it had been dismissed by the Israelis even before the Jordanian crisis destroyed it. After that, Nixon and Kissinger insisted that United States policy must be a full alliance with Israel against the Soviet Union. Three times in 1971 and 1972 Sadat's overtures to the United States and his declared readiness to accept a peace agreement were rejected. Kissinger saw Sadat's expulsion of his Soviet advisers not as an opportunity for settlement but as a vindication of American support for Israel. He considered Israel had no need of a settlement then. Such errors of judgment helped lead to the Yom Kippur war.

There were other mistakes, and underlying many of them was a state of mind that was itself perhaps more troubling than any specific decision. Kissinger had a fundamentally pessimistic vision of Western society. He seemed inspired by the notion that the Soviet Union was ultimately invincible and that his task was to negotiate the best possible deal for the West in the meantime. While the West was filled with "intellectuals without conviction," the USSR was run by men of iron will. He was therefore impatient with Western democracies and tended to undervalue their achievements. On one occasion he would claim that scarcely any of them had been legitimate since 1914. Not surprisingly, his "Year of Europe" in 1973 was a fiasco.

Kissinger has often been described (and, rightly or wrongly, his experience of the chaos of Weimar has been cited as an explanation) as placing order before justice. Years before, in his book on Castlereagh, Metternich and the Congress of Vienna, he wrote that a stable international order required a sense of legitimacy that had less to do with justice than with "an international agreement about the nature of workable arrangements and about the permissible aims and methods of foreign policy." The record of the first Nixon administration demonstrates that even when the existing order was manifestly unjust, he felt an impatience with demands for change, especially when the consequences of change could only partly be predicted. Inevitably this led to a confusion of status quo and stability: Greece, Iran, and South Africa are just three examples. When the Shah of Iran asked in 1972 for secret American military aid to be given to the Kurdish rebels in Iraq, Kissinger agreed over the opposition of the CIA station in Teheran. When the Shah later embarked on a policy of conciliation with Iraq the Kurds were abruptly cut off; at least 35,000 were killed and more than 200,000 refugees were created. On another occasion the White House ignored CIA protests and channeled funds to a neo-fascist group in Italy in the hope that this would harm the Italian Communist Party. These policies were unkind; they were also foolish.

In one sense his very successes contributed to his failures. His overriding interest in détente prevented him from considering the characters, priorities, incentives, imperatives of countries in their own rights. Nations could not be seen as untidy groups of disparate people with complicated lives and inconvenient histories. Instead they had to be regarded as subordinate parts of a seamless strategic design. This notion, which Kissinger called linkage, was not original. But he did seem to apply it more rigorously than his predecessors. Thus, Allende had to be "destabilized" much less for the threat he posed to United States' commercial interests than for the fact that the emergence of a Marxist state in the hemisphere would itself "destabilize" United States-Soviet relations. Each side recognized spheres of influence, and those spheres had to be preserved, however painful that might be for those within them.

A few months before the Soviet invasion of Czechoslovakia in 1968, Kissinger (still a private citizen then) talked with Alexander Dubcek's foreign minister, Jiri Hajek. According to Hajek, Kissinger "confirmed that the existing division of the world was regarded by both sides as an element of stability based on peaceful coexistence. And that every disruption of the equilibrium would have to lead to unfathomable consequences." Four and a half years in office had strengthened this view. Once again, it was not exceptional, but his critics argued that he took the practice of *real politik* to an unacceptable extreme, and that in his schemes the concept of individual rights had no place.

This may be unfair. It seems likely, for example, that the record will show that Kissinger argued with the Soviet leaders on behalf of individual dissidents and others persecuted in the USSR more frequently than has yet been revealed. But, as he himself frequently maintained, the appearance of American attitudes is often as important as any hidden reality. He extended approval to regimes like the Portuguese, Spanish, Greek and post-Allende Chilean, which were most obviously intent on denying the ideals on which European civilization and American government are based. Such support had obvious strategic purpose, but it meant that the United States appeared to care little for human suffering and democratic rights. This policy comforted dictators and discouraged democrats everywhere. It was shortsighted.

Equally disturbing could be the lengths to which he was prepared to go to effect his plans. He never really concealed his irritation with conventional procedures and restraints of the law. "The illegal we do immediately, the unconstitutional takes a little longer," he once said. It was a joke, but Kissinger often attempted to mask his real attitudes in humor. (When asked about the exacting way he treated State Department officials, he once replied, "Why, Thomas Jefferson was a fine Secretary of State, and he had slaves." At his last meeting with the press as Secretary of State in January 1977 he asked "What makes you think this is going to be my last press conference?" Speaking at the historic first meeting of the Washington ambassadors of Egypt and Israel, he said "I have not addressed such a distinguished audience since dining alone in the hall of mirrors.") He seemed convinced that there should be few restraints on espionage, counter-intelligence paramilitary operations, wiretapping or any other covert activity that he thought might serve higher purposes. When William Colby, the Director of the CIA, began to tell Congress the truth about some of the CIA's abuses of power in 1975, Kissinger attempted to stop him. He complained that Colby, a Catholic, was simply "going to confession" on Capitol Hill. He himself did all he could to frustrate Congress' inquiries.

Kissinger argued that the new triangular relationship between Moscow,

Washington and Peking which he and Nixon helped create would itself promote a new international order or legitimacy. He believed, in particular, that the Soviet bear could be enmeshed in such a thick net of agreements that its own self-interest would force it to behave more cautiously abroad. Stanley Hoffmann has described the notion "The bear would be treated like one of B.F. Skinner's pigeons: there would be incentives for good behavior, rewards if such behavior occurred, and punishments if not. It may have been a bit pedantic, or a bit arrogant; it certainly was rather theoretical."

Events showed the limits of the theory. The Russians had, it could be argued, applied some pressure on North Vietnam in 1972, but only for a tactical change. The conduct of the war through 1973, 1974 and 1975 showed that they scarcely altered their support for Hanoi's unchanging strategic aims. In July 1973 Kissinger proclaimed after Leonid Brezhnev's visit to Washington that "it is safe to say that the Soviet Union and the USA agree on the evolution of the Middle East and how it should be resolved." The outbreak, just 103 days later, of the Yom Kippur war and Soviet threats to introduce their own troops into the conflict, showed just how unrealistic that belief actually was. After the collapse of the Caetano regime in Portugal, Moscow lent considerable support to the wild demands of Alvaro Cunhal's Communist Party there. Later still, the Angolan adventure showed again that for both parties the net of détente was, in fact, rather loose. What had not been appreciated adequately was that linkage works both ways. The agreements that the USSR signed—on SALT, European security, sales of American grain and technology— were binding on the U.S. government (and American corporations) as well. They could not easily be reneged on if Moscow subsequently refused to play by rules that Washington laid down. Indeed, in one sense the very structure of détente and its concessions to Soviet needs and Soviet power actually liberated the USSR and gave it more freedom for an adventurist foreign policy.

Kissinger's confirmation hearings did not fully reflect it, but by summer 1973 his attitudes, personality and priorities had excited some criticism. They would excite more. William Colby later complained that Kissinger's obsession with secrecy and his refusal to disclose his actions to his colleagues made proper intelligence gathering, and hence sensible policy formation, very difficult. Charges of insincerity abounded. Daniel Moynihan later claimed that Helmut Sonnenfeldt, one of Kissinger's principal aides, once told him, "Henry does not lie because it is in his interest. He lies because it is in his nature." Sonnenfeldt denies having made this remark. To Kissinger many of the critics must often have seemed superficial or naïve. In a study of Bismarck he had once written: "Sincerity has meaning only in reference to a standard of truth or conduct. The root fact of Bismarck's personality, however, was his incapacity to comprehend any such standard outside his will. . . . It accounts for his mastery in adapting to the requirements of the moment. It was not that Bismarck lied . . . this is much too self-conscious an act—but that he was finely attuned to the subtlest currents of any environment and produced measures precisely adjusted to the need to prevail. The key to Bismarck's success was that he was always sincere." Similarly, Kissinger had said of himself, "Conviction. I am always convinced of the necessity of whatever I'm doing. And people that feel that, believe in it."

Whether or not it would prove true in the long run, most people certainly wished to believe in Kissinger when he was confirmed. As Nixon sank, Kissinger not only became indispensable to his employer, he seemed to become invaluable to the Republic. Now that he was Secretary of State as well as the President's Assistant for National Security Affairs, almost all the reins of the nation's foreign policy were in his hands. The years to come would reflect his priorities even more than the years gone by.

The Secretary

CHAPTER 21
The Proconsuls

As THE Senate confirmed Kissinger, Emory Coblentz Swank left Cambodia. When he had arrived in 1970 the glow of enthusiasm at least among the townspeople for Sihanouk's removal and for the chance of fighting the North Vietnamese was dimming, but it was still perceptible. By the fall of 1973 it had long disappeared. When Swank presented his letters of credence, the embassy numbered only 60, and the tiny military assistance program was quietly administered by Fred Ladd. Since then the embassy was held to two hundred Americans only by specific act of Congress. Fred Ladd himself, who by the end of his time there was a mournful spinner of yarns over large glasses of Scotch, was long gone home, his modest ideas with him.

Since the Paris Accords, Swank had made little attempt to conceal from his staff his distaste for the continuing carnage in Cambodia. As he left the country he gave an emotional and candid farewell press conference at which he spoke publicly of the frustrations of recent months. He asserted that the war "is losing more and more of its point and has less and less meaning for any of the parties concerned." He could see no prospects for peace. To questions about Kissinger's "delicate negotiations" earlier in the summer, Swank replied, "I would not describe them as negotiations. There are diplomatic contacts from time to time. I don't mean to overestimate or underestimate them."

As to whether the United States had achieved its objectives in Cambodia, Swank replied that through the deaths of Cambodians "time was bought for the success of the program in Vietnam . . . to this extent I think some measure of gratitude is owed to the Khmers." It was not a valedictory that would heighten the regard in which Swank's superiors, particularly Kissinger, would hold him. One former CIA official suggests that he was, by the end, "about as popular as a polecat at a cocktail party" among the NSC staff. Swank's next appointment had already been announced, and it reflected Kissinger's opinion of him. Swank was to become Political Adviser to the North Atlantic Fleet, based in Norfolk, Virginia. He accepted the order without complaint, but in 1975, after two years in this wilderness, he asked what posting he could now expect. He was informed that there was no work for him in Kissinger's State Department.

Swank's was by no means the only career that Kissinger brought to an early end. The list of casualties among those who displeased the Secretary is probably longer in Kissinger's case than in that of any other recent incumbent. But some of Swank's colleagues did consider it a waste that, at fifty-three, the man whom *The New York Times* had described as "the acknowledged leader" of the State Department's Soviet experts and "a leading contender for the Moscow post" should instead be forced into retirement.

Kissinger did not replace Swank in Cambodia; the embassy was left in the hands of the Deputy Chief of Mission, Tom Enders. This arrangement was not widely welcomed in Phnom Penh. Enders' manner had alienated many Cambodian officials, and within the political section of the embassy there was concern that he would cut back political reporting even further than it had already been since Bill Harben was removed and his job abolished.

This was apparently what Enders was meant to do. Now that Kissinger's time was stretched even further than before, and now that the end of the bombing meant that he could, in his own perception, no longer "negotiate from strength," Cambodia appears to have been pushed even further into the recesses of his mind. When Enders returned from a meeting with Kissinger in Tokyo during November 1973, he seemed to his colleagues to be in no doubt as to what was required of him. He was to worry about neither the future nor peace. He was to keep the show on the road and out of the press.

The period of the war that followed is, in some senses, the most depressing of all. The military and social decay of the country has already been described. It continued now, without optimism in Phnom Penh, without concern in Washington.

Some feel for the period can be derived from the end-of-tour reports of General Cleland, Chief of the Military Equipment Delivery Team, and his successor, General William Palmer, who was in Phnom Penh from February 1974 until its fall in April 1975. These reports must be read with caution, since each man was anxious to promote his own career in the Army despite the Cambodian débâcle. Each, therefore, was concerned to attach all blame to the Cambodians and refused to analyze carefully the effect of his own work in Phnom Penh. Nonetheless, the reports do provide an extraordinary picture of the problems of the Cambodian army at this stage of the war—and of the difficulties inherent in the Pentagon's attempt to impose its models upon the country. It is clear from Palmer's report that he disagreed with many of Cleland's actions; he pointed out that the short length of American officers' tours, together with the fact that arriving and departing officers rarely overlapped, meant that it was "impossible to follow the rationale on which program decisions had been made, particularly when a rapidly changing tactical situation may have rendered that rationale invalid in the meantime."

In August 1973, the fall of Phnom Penh had been widely expected. Journalists flocked to be there when the American bombing ended. Given the fact that United States air power had indeed been, as Cleland wrote, "the one sacrosanct absolute" in all American planning for Cambodia, this was reasonable. In fact, however, now that they could no longer shelter behind the curtain of falling iron, Lon Nol's troops fought, for a time, more bravely and aggressively.

They were helped also by the Khmer Rouge's continued shortage of ammunition. The day after the bombing ended, the Communists launched an assault on the provincial capital of Kompong Cham, a vital road-and-river junction northeast of Phnom Penh. Through the summer they had easily rolled up the garrisons defending the approaches to the town along Routes 6 and 7. Now they captured a large part of the city, led 15,000 people away into the countryside, and came within one hundred meters of the governor's mansion. But the government troops did not break as they had done a few weeks earlier in the town of Skoun. (The commander there had seized the first available helicopter for himself and fled the city.) After a long and bloody street battle the Communists finally withdrew. Sihanouk later complained bitterly that, but for the treachery of Hanoi in withholding supplies, the town would have been captured.

Ammunition, at least in the narrow military sense, decided the outcome of the war. While Communist advances were, to some extent, dependent on provisions from Hanoi, Lon Nol's army became hostage to American matériel. Under the code names "Nimble Thrust" and "Nimble Voyage," shiploads of new equipment were rushed to Phnom Penh to replace American air power. There were 105-mm. and 155-mm. artillery pieces, over one hundred more armored personnel carriers, more heavy river craft, hundreds of 81-mm. mortars, grenade launchers and recoilless rifles, 45,000 more M-16 rifles—altogether a vast new store of treasure. With them came the equipment for the headquarters and the combat support elements of four divisions that Cleland was creating.

To the extent that he was anxious to protect FANK blood and bone, Cleland's demand for such massive supplies was commendable enough. But the effect of the new bounty was predictable: the troops simply began to fire off more and more ammunition. In July 1973, 200 short tons were issued a day; by January 1974 this had tripled to 600 tons. Cleland explained the rationale—and, unconsciously, its serious implications—in his end-of-tour report: "The FANK depend on firepower to win. Seldom has FANK outmaneuvered the enemy—he has outgunned him." But his own actions made this inevitable; instead of improving the intrinsic fighting quality of Lon Nol's troops, Cleland created a fatal new dependency in them. By mid-1974 fully 87 percent of all American military aid was being spent on ammunition. If the Congress began to cut back aid or if the Khmer Rouge closed all lines of communication, then the government's troops would be deprived of "the quickfix" (to use another Cleland expression) which the Americans had thrust upon them. Both these things did happen and each contributed toward making the fall of the regime inevitable.

The fundamental military problems of incompetence and corruption were, if anything, exacerbated by the actions Cleland took. FANK was unable to absorb the sophisticated accouterments of divisional reorganization he pressed upon it. Congressional restrictions on advice meant that the Khmers were denied the over-all training, management skills, and technical know-how essential to the sort of army that Cleland was creating. At the most basic level, the Cambodians could not maintain equipment. Army engineers earned so much more in the city that they would spend only a 30-hour week in the field. Servicing was rare; guns, trucks and armored personnel carriers would simply be used until they stopped. When it proved impossible to shift spare parts through Khmer Rouge roadblocks, equipment was abandoned or cannibalized. Parts were sold to whoever was in the market, friend or foe.

Like his predecessor Mataxis, Cleland failed to move adequately against corruption. It was, for example, only when Elizabeth Becker stringing for the *Washington Post*, began to investigate how officers were selling brass artillery shell cases abroad, that real action was taken by the embassy. However, some restrictions were placed on "phantom" soldiers. The embassy now had personnel and financial experts working in FANK's pay units, Lon Nol had been forbidden to increase the over-all payroll beyond 253,000 men, and individual unit commanders had been deprived of their previous total control over their men's wages. As Cleland delicately noted, "there was considerable resistance" to this last change and "there were some incidents, including overt acts of force and intimidation on the part of some commanders." The embassy had to order Lon Nol to send letters to unit commanders instructing them to obey the new procedures. But still no one knew how strong individual units really were, and neither Cleland nor Enders was determined to insist on effective change. Enders would argue within the embassy that the United States actually had no authority over individual commanders. In the end, as General Palmer later noted, the fact that so many "phantoms" were defending Phnom Penh helped ensure its collapse.

The command structure had not been reformed. Lon Nol, whose title was now "Supreme Commander," still bypassed his general staff, forbade any proper coordination between army, navy and air force, and guarded the right to make all important strategic and even tactical decisions personally. The untrained prewar officer corps, which had been elevated en masse with the expansion of the army in 1970–71, still occupied most of the key positions. Group loyalties still prevailed over national consciousness; in 1974 one brigade was entrusted to an officer who was actually a deserter. Many battalion and brigade commanders were more often to be found in Phnom Penh villas they had built or bought on phantom salaries than with their men. All this had serious effects upon the morale of effective officers. One CIA Information Report noted that "junior and field-grade officers blame the FANK high command" for the country's predicament. "Officers openly state that Cambodian President Lon Nol is incompetent because of mental illness."

Ammunition disappeared faster and faster, in many different directions. The troops expended it as generously as they could, and hundreds of thousands of rounds were sold every month to the Khmer Rouge. One of the worst offenders was the military commander of Battambang province, who supplied the Communists with weapons on the understanding that they be used against any government positions save his own.

After the Yom Kippur war and the oil price rise, the black market in petrol was uncontrolled. By the end of 1973, $100,000 worth of gasoline was vanishing every month. Boys and young soldiers stood on street corners all over Phnom Penh with bottles for sale. Corrupt officers always found ways of evading such restrictions as the embassy did attempt to impose. Units equipped by the Military Equipment Delivery Team would be dissolved overnight, their matériel shifted elsewhere or sold. Despite the objections of the embassy, Lon Nol created the 9th Infantry Division as his Palace Guard. He placed it under one of the most ineffective and corrupt commanders in the entire country, who, in General Palmer's words, "then used his strong political position to circumvent organizational restraints and diverted unauthorized personnel and equipment into a large unauthorized divison base . . . the result was three under-equipped, poorly trained brigades that successively collapsed under minimal combat pressure."

There were by now few volunteers to the falling flag. The government had passed a Conscription Act, and in summer 1973 the army rounded up 16,000 boys and young men in Phnom Penh. Cinema queues were a favorite hunting ground; army trucks would rush up in the evening and drag young customers away at gunpoint. Army life began as it ended—in squalor. The boys were packed off for inadequate training. General Cleland's account of the system and how the problems were met is of some interest. "The new troops faced primitive living conditions, lackadaisical cadre at some training centers, and lack of command interest." As more and more recruits deserted, the government, he says, "finally realized . . . that something had to be done." What was it? "Money previously allocated for training-center construction was released, security forces at some training centers were increased, barrier material was provided (not to keep the enemy out but to assist in keeping the recruits in). . . ."

Military pay was, as Palmer said, an insult: a soldier received $13 a month—if he was lucky. Rice was usually sold by unit commanders to their men on pay day. If, as frequently happened, monthly pay was late or was stolen, then the men and their families went without. Inevitably soldiers were often far busier fishing, farming, gathering firewood, stealing chickens, than in manning their defensive positions. Moonlighting of some sort was essential for almost everyone.

Battlefield tactics reflected both the incompetence of the officers and the poor training of their men. The army had built small mud huts around the government's remaining enclaves. These could have been effective only with cleared fields of fire, active day and night patrolling to disrupt infiltration and accurate indirect fire by both mortars and artillery to prevent the enemy concentrating his forces. None of this was achieved.

Enemy targets were not usually well observed, and machine guns were rarely positioned properly. Artillery officers worked only to a very strict schedule: from 0630 to 1300 or 1400 hours five days a week. On Saturdays and Sundays they invariably rested. Lon Nol's command and control structure prevented coordination of artillery with infantry assaults.

The army's infrequent offensives were no better. General Palmer noted that "the normal attack pattern of the Khmer Republic's army was characterized by a dull plodding, belated advance, devoid of surprise, coordination or innovation. When the enemy chose to resist, friendly casualties were high and objectives rarely attained." (Once again, Palmer failed to question how far this reflected his own and his predecessor's impact on the army.) If by midafternoon on the day of an operation they had not gained terrain to their liking, the troops would simply retreat to their original positions for the night. Day after day this would happen, and casualties were such that, after seventy-two hours, units often had to be withdrawn altogether. The Khmer Rouge now mounted superb nighttime operations, but Lon Nol's troops rarely ventured out of their foxholes after dark.

The air force had grown considerably since Sihanouk's day, but it was still the least efficient of the three services. Cleland called it "undisciplined"; Palmer pointed out that it had a "totally inadequate motivation, incentive and salary system" and that "the necessity to survive" led to the sale of equipment, falsified reports, evasions of responsibility and cynicism.

Despite the almost total lack of maintenance, planes remained airborne, even if not strictly airworthy. However, many of the missions the pilots flew were useless. There was almost no cooperation on either strategy or tactics between the services, and often the only link between operational headquarters and the air base was by ordinary commercial telephone; radio contact with combat units in the field was erratic, communications security nonexistent. Pilots were keener to fly for contraband than for combat, and then often demanded bribes from ground units before providing air support. The T-28 fighter-bomber pilots would not descend below 3,000 feet; bombs and napalm dropped at sharp angles from that height were usually inaccurate. They undoubtedly killed a lot of people but not necessarily those who were targeted.

By this time the economy was in ruin. Inflation ran at about 250 percent a year, industrial and agricultural production was permanently declining, exports were almost nonexistent. The government and the population it controlled were now on American welfare—about 95 percent of all income came from the United States—and the welfare officer was Tom Enders. It was he, together with the U.S. AID officials in the embassy, who determined what the exchange rate should be, how far electricity prices should be raised, how slumps in production might be slowed. The government was often reluctant to accept his orders; frequent harrowing meetings with ministers were necessary, and Enders would tower over Khmer officials bellowing, *"Vous comprenez, Monsieur le Ministre, que c'est absolument nécessaire, n'est-ce pas?"* *"Ah, oui, oui, Monsieur Enders, bien sur"* would be the reply, and eventually a halfhearted compromise would be effected. One American economist stationed in the Phnom Penh embassy later complained in an official report that the economic policies that Enders implemented were like "picking fleas off a dog that has cancer. . . . It will make him more comfortable, more faithful and save energy by keeping him from scratching and thus prolong his life. But the ultimate result will be the same unless the cancer is cured."

Those who could count themselves a part of the government's establishment continued to live well. Lon Non, Lon Nol's younger brother, was reported to have raised $90 million by arms trafficking and extortion. Lesser men had built lesser but still substantial fortunes, and for them conditions were tolerable. During 1974 there were frequent power cuts in Phnom Penh under the government's austerity program. But they almost all occurred in the poor parts of the city. In the villas the air conditioners and refrigerators usually had power, and at the Cercle Sportif, the city's smartest club, the floodlights were normally working for evening tennis. One journalist noted that "for the few privileged elite the good life of tennis, nightclubs, expensive French meals, and opulent, brandy-drenched dinner parties went on almost to the very end, while the vast majority of the city's swollen population sank into deeper and deeper misery."

For ordinary people the more urgent problem now was always food. Eighty percent of the country's prewar paddy fields had been abandoned, and the government's own figures showed that in 1974 rice production was only 655,000 metric tons—as opposed to 3.8 million tons in the last year before the war. The shortfall was not nearly met by imports. To deflect growing Congressional criticism of the amount of rice being shipped to Indochina, the embassy still requested only the minimum necessary to avert a repetition of the food riots that had already flickered through Phnom Penh. Even at the very reduced rations allocated per head, there was never now more than a two- or three-week supply on hand, and at one stage in 1974 there was only three days' rice left in the capital. None of the rice from the United States was provided free, and food prices were rising catastrophically high—from a base of 100 in May 1971, they were 1,604 in 1973 and 4,454 in 1974. A bowl of soup which had cost 4 riels in 1970 now cost 300, a bread roll had risen from 2 to 100 riels. Real wages had dropped, and U.S. AID's draft termination report acknowledges that the vast majority of the population of Phnom Penh could afford to buy little more than one day's subsistence of rice in any week. Through the last eighteen months of the war most people in the cities were slowly starving.

Because the Communists were now concentrating on closing the government's lines of communication, hectic and chaotic profiteering developed in 1974. In 1973 it had cost 8,000 riels to shift one ton of cargo from Battambang to Phnom Penh by road; the price leaped to 30,000 riels now that the road was cut and part of the journey had to be made by water. (At the official rate of exchange this was an increase from almost $18 to $66.) It was simply explained: merchants had to pay protection money to the Cambodian navy to ensure safe passing along the river. The fees were demanded by the Association of River Carriers; its President was the brother of Sosthene Fernandez, the army commander in chief.

The skies were even more chaotic. Military pilots constantly overloaded their planes with food—sugar, salt, rice and fish in the engine casings made flying more hazardous and maintenance more difficult than ever. At the beginning of 1974 there were six registered airline companies; by the end of the year there were 23, flying a total of 57 planes, many of them battered old DC-3s, around the country. Food could be sold in Phnom Penh for up to four times the price paid in the provinces. Planes swooped into an enclave where, for some reason, there was a temporary food supply. Wounded soldiers waiting for transport to a hospital were ignored.

Refugees continued to press into the capital. By the end of 1973 they had swollen the population of Phnom Penh to over two million and, according to U.S. AID's Termination Report, their plight then "was desperate, serious health problems became evident, and thousands . . . were without housing, without work and completely dependent upon outside assistance for their very survival."

This was almost all being provided by charities like Catholic Relief Services (the most effective) and World Vision. The embassy itself was still only indirectly associated with the refugee crisis. The U.S. AID final report noted that Washington "assumed no responsibility for the generation of refugees in Cambodia."

By early 1974 the United States government had provided humanitarian aid of $2.5 million for Cambodia. It can be compared with $3.4 million provided by other countries, and by the voluntary relief agencies in the period January 1972–May 1973, alone—and with the $516.5 million in military aid and $216.6 million in economic aid that had flowed from Washington since the war began.

For the most part, the voluntary agencies coped well, though interdenominational arguments were sometimes squalid, and on occasion food was offered in exchange for religious conversion. But they had neither the manpower nor the money really to relieve the suffering of the refugees, and throughout 1974 conditions in and out of the camps grew ever more inadequate. By now lean-tos and shacks were propped against walls all over Phnom Penh, and thousands of people slept in the doorways of houses. Thousands and thousands of orphan children roamed the streets in rags. One twelve-year-old boy, Chum Pal, whose father was killed in battle and whose mother had been driven mad by the war, lived by begging. "Sometimes I go into shops. Some people give me five or ten riels. Some give me nothing, but they do not say bad things to me. They just say they have no small change." Chuon Yan, a thirteen-year-old village girl whose father had been badly burned in a shelling attack, also begged in order to supplement the 50 cents a day her mother made picking through garbage for plastic bags to sell.

Until August 1973 the refugees tended to cite American bombing as the main reason for flight. Through 1974 they spoke of the increasing violence of the Khmer Rouge. In March 1974, a government offensive into the province of Kompong Thom opened an escape route for the people living there. Around 35,000 stumbled with their bundles and their oxcarts over to the Lon Nol side. Altogether that year at least another 100,000 people pressed desperately into the government's shrinking, decaying enclaves. Many brought with them tales of alarming harshness.

"Out there" the Khmer Rouge were reorganizing. At the end of 1973 the Party finally asserted full control of the Front's military command structure. Political commissars were now assigned to assist and instruct officers down to company level throughout most of the country. Main forces were reorganized, like Lon Nol's, into divisions. But unlike in Lon Nol's army, Khmer Rouge officers were promoted for their performance.

When they launched their annual dry-season offensive against Phnom Penh in January 1974, they used dispersed patrols and stand-off attacks by fire, and they seeded areas with mines as they left. At night they pinned Lon Nol's troops down by fire and then mounted ground assaults through the darkness. By dawn they had often consolidated their positions and dug themselves into well-camouflaged protective emplacements that would withstand both 105-millimeter artillery fire and T-28 bombing attacks.

Once within range they demonstrated their attitude toward the people of Phnom Penh by showering rockets and artillery shells over the heads of the defenders into the city. Day after day, night after night the missiles fell haphazardly into the streets, smashing a group of children here, a family there, a rickshaw driver pedaling home after work, houses and schools. The principal line of fire was directly into an area in which thousands of refugees squatted, and so it was the most wretched of the city who suffered worst from this, as from every other, desolation of the war. On one day in February 1974 alone, Khmer Rouge gunners killed 139 people and blew to smithereens the houses and shacks that gave meager shelter to some ten thousand people. More than one thousand people died in this one series of attacks before Lon Nol's troops were finally able to push the guns and rocket launchers out of range of the town.

That 1974 dry-season assault failed because the Khmer Rouge command and control machinery was still inadequate; because the attackers committed units in an uncoordinated piecemeal fashion; because they were unable to replace casualties fast enough; and because they were still short of ammunition. Through the course of the year, as they maintained pressure on the government by cutting the roads, these deficiencies were largely repaired.

At the same time they were developing into an increasingly formidable political organization. As their relationship with Hanoi became more and more bitter and as their growing strength allowed them more and more independence, they started to eradicate among the people they controlled the three traditional elements of Cambodian life: respect for the monarchy, attachment to the village, and devotion to Buddha. Throughout 1974, reports reached Saigon, Phnom Penh and Washington that in areas where their military situation was relatively secure—such as the southeast—the Communists were accelerating their transformation of society. As well as the Sihanoukists, cadres who were known to be pro-Vietnamese were purged and replaced by militant officials who had never been seen before. According to one contemporary State Department study, the Communists embarked on intense programs of "psychological reorientation, mass relocation, total collectivization of agriculture, the elimination of religion and restructuring social customs."

The destruction of Sihanouk's authority was always inevitable if the war continued long enough; it began in earnest after his one visit to the liberated areas in spring of 1973, when the affection in which the peasantry still held him must have been evident, even though he was confined by cadres. The fiction of a united national front began to be dismissed; the word "Royal" (*Reach*) was removed from documents and proclamations of the Royal Government of National Union of Kampuchea. The Khmer Rouge started to destroy schools built in the Sihanouk period. The Prince was more frequently accused of living too long in the comfort of Peking and of supporting the hated Vietnamese. Such attacks were not always well received by peasants, and refugees to South Vietnam brought stories of fighting between the Khmer Rouge and those members of the Front who were still loyal to Sihanouk. But in Peking the Prince understood the drift of events. In a memorable phrase he told the Italian journalist Oriana Fallacci that he and the Khmer Rouge hated one another and that they would "spit me out like a cherry stone" when they had sucked him dry.

All Khmer Rouge policies, and in particular the relocation of villages, were obviously intended to effect a total and dramatic break with the past. When peasants were moved they were ordered to leave behind any private property; in the new villages, refugees reported, about two hundred people lived in a single shelter, all land was owned and worked communally, all day was spent in the fields, long indoctrination sessions followed at night, no religion could be practiced, monks were defrocked, all old songs were banned, traditional sexual and marital habits forsworn.

Younger and younger cadres began to appear; the Party used its Youth Organization as the cutting edge of social change. One party document of the time declared that the Party "educated, watched, nourished and built youth as the central force in the revolutionary movement of each area and as the central force for future national construction." The education seems to have had dramatic effects. In the southeast, teen-agers were removed from their families for two or three weeks of intensive indoctrination; according to refugees, this was enough to engender in them a passionately fierce commitment to the destruction of the old society and a total rejection of religion and all family ties. Throughout 1974 Cambodians who fled from the southeast of their country into Vietnam, and from other areas into the government's enclaves, spoke with awe of the fanaticism of these youths, who would allow no dissent nor any questioning of their directives.

It was now that the gruesome accounts of rule by terror, which after 1975 became commonplace, began to filter out of the "liberated" zones. Refugees repeated that those who questioned the orders of the young cadres were led away never to reappear. According to the State Department study, "some refugees said that the climate of fear was so great that even within the confines of their own home a husband and wife did not dare discuss Khmer Rouge policies for fear of being overheard." Its author, Kenneth Quinn, concluded that the exploitation of terror was the main way in which the Khmer Rouge enforced their will.

This analysis, based on reports of refugees in the Mekong Delta area of South Vietnam, was supplemented by newspaper reports of Khmer Rouge conduct elsewhere in Cambodia. In March 1974, for example, the *Baltimore Sun* correspondent remarked on the "incomprehensible brutality of the Khmer Communists." He recalled that the conventional wisdom had always been that Khmer did not wish to fight Khmer and that once the North Vietnamese withdrew from Cambodia good sense would prevail; in fact, however, the Khmer Rouge seemed to have indulged in "sheer brutality for brutality's sake." The *Washington Post* reported that the Khmer Rouge were "reconstructing" the people and often punished infringements of their regulations by death. The *New York Times* correspondent, Sydney S. Schanberg, described the joy with which the refugees from Kompong Thom escaped Khmer Rouge control. All of this information—and much more—was available to the State Department and the National Security Council. It does not appear to have created any sense of urgency.

In April 1974 Tom Enders returned to Washington. When he and Gaetana had arrived in Phnom Penh in 1971 she had told colleagues that the best Tom had expected after his Belgrade problem was a consular appointment; now Kissinger rewarded his unquestioning obedience in Cambodia by nominating him to be Assistant Secretary for Economic Affairs. The promotion infuriated those members of the Senate Foreign Relations Committee who recalled the attempts to frustrate their investigation of the bombing in 1973. The Committee delayed six weeks before it reported his nomination favorably. When it eventually did so, it issued an unusual rebuke in which it called Enders' original description of the embassy's role "grossly misleading" and concluded that the embassy had made "a conscious effort" to conceal its role in the bombing. In 1976, at the age of forty-five, Enders became Ambassador to Canada.

Enders' successor, John Gunther Dean, was the last American ambassador to Phnom Penh. He had a frustrating tour. Like Kissinger, Dean is a refugee from Hitler's Germany. He had been involved in Indochinese affairs since the middle fifties and, in the Paris embassy in 1968, he had taken part in the first, abortive round of peace talks with Hanoi. Dean had come to know and like Etienne Manac'h, who was then the head of the Quai d'Orsay's Asian Department. When Manac'h heard of Dean's appointment he wrote him from the French Embassy in Peking to wish him luck, calling him the "*chevalier de la retraite.*"

Dean arrived from Vientiane, where he had distinguished himself by forestalling a right-wing *coup d'état* that had threatened to wreck the fragile coalition peace that had been imposed upon Laos since the Paris Accords. His arrival and Enders' departure were widely welcomed in Phnom Penh. Many Cambodians hoped he could work the same sort of miracle there. For weeks people ran up to his car to pass notes through his window requesting help or advice.

Dean was a more canny bureaucratic warrior than Swank and less aloof than Enders. From his experience in Laos he was used to dealing directly with Kissinger, bypassing State Department officials. He accepted this, arguing that the man in the field has no alternative but to deal with real power, wherever it lies, whatever his personal or professional loyalties. The precise nature of Kissinger's instructions to him as he left for Cambodia is not certain. One senior State Department official says that, "Henry shot the dove off his shoulder," telling Dean, "Your job is to improve the military situation to enable us to negotiate from strength. I don't want to hear about Laos-type compromises." Certainly Dean saw one of his tasks as trying to improve the quality of the Lon Nol army and its image in the American press and the Congress.

Most journalists who were based in, or who visited, Cambodia felt a troubling ambiguity about the country. Phnom Penh still had enormous, poignant charm; it was an easy place to love—with sadness. The corruption of the regime was depressing, but the people, including officials, were invariably friendly, even warm. In the countryside small boys smiled as they walked toward the war, and incompetent officers would patiently explain their tactics to reporters. But most journalists were sickened by the killing, and their dispatches tended to reflect the war-weariness of the country. Sydney Schanberg filled *The New York Times* with powerful accounts of the effect of Washington's policies; H. D. S. Greenway, who had covered the whole length of the war, wrote moving descriptions of the people's suffering for the *Washington Post*.

Such accounts of the futility of war in the sideshow had an impact in Washington. As the House Judiciary Committee moved closer to impeaching Nixon, Congress began to question more critically the rationale of the "decent interval" in South Vietnam and the policy of supporting Lon Nol. In Vietnam, neither side had launched an all-out offensive since the Paris Agreement, but each had tried continually to increase its holdings of land and people at the cost of many thousands. The Senate Refugee Subcommittee claimed that the fighting in the first year of "peace with honor" had created 818,700 new refugees in Vietnam, far more than in any year since 1968, save 1972. An average of 141 people were being killed each day. "The Vietnamese have, in short, suffered more in one year of peace with honor than America experienced in a decade of war," the subcommittee reported.

Despite the fact that the August 1973 bombing cut-off meant that Washington could no longer respond, as Nixon had promised, "with full force" to North Vietnamese violations of the cease-fire, United States policy had not altered since Nixon declared, four days before the cease-fire, that Thieu's regime was "the sole legitimate government of South Vietnam." The United States continued to support Thieu in his attempts to ignore the political obligations of the agreement. Graham Martin, an unashamed hawk, who was ambassador to Saigon, fulfilled those instructions to the letter. When Senator Kennedy sent Kissinger a series of questions about United States policy in Indochina, Martin cabled the Secretary: "It would be the heart of folly to permit Kennedy, whose staff will spearhead this effort, the tactical advantage of an honest and detailed answer. . . ."

Kissinger's replies to Kennedy were certainly unusual. The crucial feature of the Paris Agreement (which had enraged Thieu) was that it tolerated North Vietnamese troops in large parts of South Vietnam. Now, however, Kissinger declared, "The presence of large numbers of North Vietnamese troops in the South demonstrates that the military threat from Hanoi is still very much in existence." This quicksilver shift, Kennedy pointed out, was "a new rationalization for our continued heavy involvement in Indochina."

Kissinger claimed that "a secure peace" in Vietnam was an important part of Nixon's search for "a worldwide structure of peace" and throughout the spring of 1974 the White House pressed for more military aid to Saigon. But Watergate was pushing even conservatives away from the commitment. Republican Senator Barry Goldwater of Arizona declared, "We can scratch Vietnam." The Senate approved an amendment to bar further military aid to Vietnam after July 1974.

Congressional impatience with Cambodia had always been greater, and Dean appreciated that restrictions on aid to Lon Nol would inevitably be imposed. After he arrived in Phnom Penh he saw that some sort of negotiation must be started if the war was not to end in the collapse of the government and the ignominious flight of the Americans.

But as impeachment approached, Nixon became more committed to his foreign-policy record. The trips to China and the USSR, the Paris Accords and the disengagement in the Middle East were the achievements he cited most frequently as proof of the extent to which he had built a "generation of peace." It was also clear to the NSC staff that Cambodia, the "Nixon Doctrine in its purest form," remained an emotional commitment of the President's. *The New York Times* reported that he was "taking a personal interest in Cambodia" and had pledged his support to Lon Nol despite the warnings of the intelligence community. Early in 1974 Nixon wrote to Lon Nol:

> I am convinced that under your vigorous leadership and that of your government, the republic will succeed . . . The United States remains determined to provide maximum possible assistance to your heroic self defense and will continue to stand side by side with the republic in the future as in the past. . . . The continuing warfare in Cambodia results solely, I believe, from the unreasoning intransigence of the North Vietnamese and their Khmer communist supporters.

To Dean, Kissinger seemed equally inflexible. Soon after he arrived Dean cabled Kissinger to suggest that the United States try to contact the Khmer Rouge commander in chief, Khieu Samphan, who was on a long tour of North Africa, the Middle East and Eastern Europe. Kissinger rejected the idea. Dean persisted, asking Kissinger to consider the proposal very carefully and arguing, in terms that he thought Kissinger would respect, that Washington had nothing to lose by the initiative. He suggested that whatever happened, it would make the administration look good in Congress and in the eyes of the world. Kissinger again refused to entertain the idea; the United States and the Lon Nol side would be "negotiating from weakness." That was true. But the evidence of the last four years was that the insurgents grew stronger month by month.

Dean, nonetheless, did what he could to muster the government side; "If you don't hang together you'll hang separately," he warned. In these early months, he was more optimistic that he could repeat his Lao success than circumstances warranted, and many journalists found his manner brash and arrogant. But some recognized that he showed more concern for the country than Enders.

In one cable to Kissinger soon after his arrival Dean commented on a rout of FANK:

> Although leadership failures from the platoon up lie behind the Kompong Luong defeat, shifting and unclear command responsibilities of the field commanders were a deficiency FANK need not have incurred. These came in part from the familiar personal intervention of the Marshal himself, from some unavoidable if unfortunately timed reassignments . . . giving the Kompong Luong and Lovek commands to unemployed and discredited generals. . . . We are making certain that these lessons are brought home to the Khmer. . . . We are requesting an appointment with Marshal Lon Nol for April 23 to . . . engage in a frank talk on the need to avoid future setbacks of this nature.

Dean forced the government to restrict the import of the more extravagant luxuries—Mercedes cars, televisions, canned asparagus—but his attempts to have the most corrupt officials and officers retired were not very successful. With General Palmer, he flew from enclave to enclave, haranguing ineffective commanders and praising the brave. He introduced the novel procedure of making personal wagers with individual commanders. He would issue precise instructions as to what he wished to see done; if the commitments were fulfilled he would hand out bottles of cognac or champagne as a prize.

Sek Sam Iet, the governor of Battambang province, was widely considered to be among the most corrupt of Lon Nol's commanders, selling rice to the Thais and ammunition to the Khmer Rouge. On a visit to Battambang, Dean upbraided him for his recent defeats; he gave him precise orders to reduce the size of his command, regroup his forces into large entities, improve his use of artillery and air support, and run more food convoys. "You must be mean and tough," he said, and he insisted that the siege of the town of Koh Kralor must be broken. "Would you like to bet as to how long it will take you to relieve Koh Kralor?" he asked. "I'll bet you a bottle of cognac you can't do it before Monday. Will you bet me you can do it sooner?"

Sek Sam Iet was interested in bigger wagers. His leadership remained execrable, rice and ammunition continued to disappear. Dean insisted on his removal, but Lon Nol was by now so used to the unconditional support of the White House that, after a brief transfer, he restored him to office.

Dean's behavior was a novelty—neither Swank nor Enders had involved himself so minutely in military or government affairs. A report by the House Foreign Affairs Committee noted that he was "energetic" in carrying out what he saw as his task. "By his own admission, he does not hesitate to give strategic military advice to Lon Nol or tactical advice to subordinate military commanders." This was against the law, but Dean rather airily asserted that when Congress passed the Cooper-Church amendment it did not mean to preclude advising at the level at which he performed.

In his early months in Cambodia the government did have some successes. In May 1974, as the monsoon rains began, the Khmer Rouge lifted their siege of the coastal town of Kampot, and then government troops relieved the towns of Oudong, the old imperial capital, and Lovek, which is north of Phnom Penh. After these victories Dean persuaded Lon Nol to offer, in a speech on July 4, "unconditional negotiations" with the Communists. The new proposals dropped Lon Nol's previous insistence on a prior cease-fire and the withdrawal of foreign troops. Dean thought Lon Nol's speech (of which he was the chief author) was "nicely Rooseveltian," but in Peking Sihanouk denounced it, reiterating that his government would never negotiate with the "puppets," particularly not with the "seven traitors," who had been marked for execution. From the interior, the Khmer Rouge dismissed Lon Nol's offer as a "fallacious maneuver."

Lon Nol's offer had been approved by Kissinger, but it was about the only concession Dean managed to extract from the Secretary that summer. Dean understood that any improvements he could effect in the government's position could only be marginal. The republic was fighting for survival alone, and nothing would change that. He sent a series of cables back to the State Department warning that "time is against us," arguing that "the ship must be found a port; we cannot abandon it on the high seas." He began to talk of the need for a "controlled solution," which he later defined as "a nonmilitary solution which would take account of the realities" while allowing the Cambodians to stop fighting and the Americans to withdraw with dignity. When one of his gloomy predictions was realized, Dean could not always resist the temptation of saying "As I pointed out in my cable . . ." or "As I warned some weeks ago . . ." Once, in frustration over his apparent inability to move Kissinger toward a settlement he asserted that but for his self-discipline he would have resigned by now.

Such cables infuriated Kissinger. He sent increasingly astringent messages to Phnom Penh informing Dean that the duties of an ambassador did not include giving strategic counsel to the Secretary of State. To Dean's demands that "we must do something," Kissinger would reply that he was indeed acting but it was no concern of Dean's: an ambassador had no right to know everything. When presented with his morning cable traffic Kissinger would ask his staff sarcastically, "What lectures has Professor Dean got for us today?" and he reacted with anger (understandable, perhaps) when *The New York Times* revealed that he had rejected Dean's proposal for a meeting with Khieu Samphan. He blamed Dean for the leak. Later, Dean diplomatically told a Congressional committee that he felt the number of cables he received from Kissinger was "amazing." Of their disagreements, he said he considered that "It is the role of an ambassador to be honest and not always say what is popular." This was never Kissinger's view.

Kissinger did face certain distractions at this time. Throughout the year he had been preoccupied with his Middle East shuttle and with the collapse of Nixon's Watergate defense. While Dean was proposing contact with Khieu Samphan, the White House was reeling under public reaction to Nixon's edited version of his taped White House conversations.

The row over the Judiciary Committee's demands for more tapes continued through May and June, and involved Kissinger once again in wiretap scandal. On June 6 Laurence Stern of the *Washington Post* revealed that the February 28, 1973, tape in the hands of the committee showed that Nixon had told John Dean that it was Kissinger who "had asked that it [the wiretapping] be done." That afternoon, at a State Department press conference, where he had expected to be questioned about his Middle East triumphs, Kissinger was instead asked "whether or not you have consulted or retained counsel for a defense against a possible perjury indictment." He flinched, said he was not conducting his office like a conspiracy, and tried to avoid the question. Clark Mollenhoff of the *Des*

Moines Register began to bellow about his "evasion and failure to recollect," and he demanded an answer to "the direct question—if you had any·role in initiating the wiretaps of your subordinates." Kissinger sidestepped; Mollenhoff shouted. Shaking with rage, the Secretary said, "I did not make a direct recommendation." *

More evidence to show that he had neglected to tell all the truth about the wiretaps appeared in other papers, and by the time Nixon departed on a diversionary "journey for peace" to the Middle East, Kissinger was upset. On June 11 in Salzburg he called an impromptu news conference. His eyes watering, he complained bitterly about the way in which his secret papers were being leaked and his motive impugned. Warning that "I do not believe it is possible to conduct the foreign policy of the United States under these circumstances when the character and credibility of the Secretary of State is at issue," he threatened to resign unless the Senate Foreign Relations Committee publicly cleared him of lying about the wiretaps.

Kissinger's outburst had the effect he desired. The idea that the nation might be deprived of its brilliant Secretary of State as well as its President was too alarming for the Senate; fifty-two Senators quickly signed a statement declaring that the Nobel Prize winner's "integrity and veracity are beyond reproach," and the Foreign Relations Committee promised to hold more hearings.† When it did so it was clear that it had no wish to probe. Senator Fulbright advised his colleagues, "It is not our responsibility to say whether it was legal or not, but whether Mr. Kissinger misrepresented his role." The Committee found that he had not.

In the course of his outburst in Salzburg, Kissinger explained his behavior in a revealing way. "I would like to think that when the record is written some may remember that perhaps some lives were saved and that

---

* Such confrontations were rare. Kissinger had by now more critics in the press but many of those who covered him most constantly still felt very close to him. The first major account of his period of office, by Marvin and Bernard Kalb, was published in the fall of 1974. It was useful as a log of his events and very admiring; the words "Chile" and "Allende" do not appear in its index. Soon after it was published Kissinger embarked with his press corps on another arduous Mid-East shuttle, and at the end of the trip, Marvin Kalb suggested to his press colleagues that they give presents to the crew of the plane. The journalists were delighted with the idea. What the crew wanted, Kalb said, were signed copies of his book. The journalists paid $5 each.

† Kissinger and Le Duc Tho had been awarded the 1973 Nobel Peace Prize jointly, in recognition of their achievement in negotiating the Paris Peace Agreement. In his book, *The Ends of Power*, H. R. Haldeman recalled that the award aroused Nixon's jealousy of Kissinger. Kissinger accepted the prize; Le Duc Tho refused to take his share, on the grounds that peace had not yet come to Vietnam.

perhaps some mothers can rest more at ease. . . . But I leave that to history. What I will not leave to history is a discussion of my personal honor.''

The corollary of the wiretaps was the concealment of the Menu bombing of Cambodia from Congress and the falsification of the Pentagon's computerized records. When this was revealed in 1973, Congressman Robert Drinan, the Jesuit priest from Massachusetts, introduced the first motion to impeach Nixon. His motion was later taken up by John Conyers, Jr., one of the senior Democrats on the House Judiciary Committee. A tiny staff was assembled for the committee to investigate the charge that Nixon had flouted the Constitution by waging a secret war in a neutral country.

It was an immensely important commission. The Committee possessed full authority to discover how the foreign policy processes of the United States had been corrupted.

But the Committee staff soon realized that the Democratic leadership had little wish to see the inquiry proceed. One reason was its breadth. Unlike the articles concerned with specific domestic crimes, Article IV, on the bombing of Cambodia, threatened to indict an entire system of policymaking. Furthermore, the introduction of the war into the Committee's proceedings would inevitably be emotional and would threaten the ''fragile coalition'' that Judiciary Chairman Peter Rodino was trying to build with moderate Republicans. Finally, a full inquiry would have demonstrated that Senator Mike Mansfield, the Senate Majority leader and other Democrats had known about the secret bombing at the time it was taking place.

Without real political support, the staff was able to obtain only a limited amount of material from either the Pentagon or the Senate Armed Services Committee. It did, however, receive all the cables to and from General Abrams that precipitated the bombing and are quoted at the beginning of this book. The papers showed that Nixon himself had ordered the concealment, and that the Senate had been lied to by men like Elliot Richardson. At the same time the texts of closed Armed Services Committee hearings revealed the extent of Democratic complicity in the deception. The White House refused categorically to allow Executive Branch documents to be declassified and the Committee leadership made almost no attempt to question this judgment. Rodino limited as strictly as possible his members' access to the papers.

Article IV survived through the summer only because of the obstinacy of Conyers. And it was eventually adopted by the Democratic caucus because the members knew it would be defeated in the full committee.

The Democrats met together in closed executive session on the morning of July 30, 1974. The Committee had already approved the first two articles of impeachment—on the Watergate cover-up and on the abuse of power (including the Cambodia wiretaps and the Huston plan.) The discussion of Cambodia in this private session (reproduced from the notes of a staff member who was present) provides a revealing demonstration of the caution with which Congress, by contrast, approached matters of foreign affairs.

Rodino soon made it clear that he wished Conyers to drop the Article. He agreed with Representative Walter Flowers, Democrat of Alabama, who said, "It's going to damage the credibility of the Committee to the extent of jeopardizing our efforts. If I was a prosecutor and a guy was up for five murders and I could prove only three, I would bring him up on only three. The primary charge is abuse of office and we have already proved that."

To this William Hungate, Democrat of Missouri, responded, "It's kind of hard to live with yourself when you impeach a guy for tapping telephones and not for making war without authorization." But Rodino warned that if the Article was introduced the Republicans would say, "Nixon's the guy who saved the world, brought peace and all that crap." "One of the hardest things in politics is being right and keeping quiet," sighed Hungate. The caucus ended with Conyers agonizing over what he should do.

Later that day the full Committee met before national television to debate Article III, which charged Nixon with contempt of Congress for refusing to provide papers and tapes duly requested by the Committee. In the middle of the debate Conyers passed around a note saying he intended still to offer Article IV. At this, Representative Harold Froehlich, a Wisconsin Republican, approached Rodino and whispered, "I seriously hope you will consider putting this off till tomorrow so it does not happen on prime time TV. That will cost us all our support with the American people."

Article III was approved, and the Democrats again caucused to decide how debate on Conyers' troublesome motion could be limited. Rodino asked Conyers if he would withdraw the Article if the Republicans attached an amendment attacking Lyndon Johnson as well. Conyers refused. "This is not frivolous, Mr. Chairman. This is not merely to make a record. I feel very strongly on this."

After the caucus Charles Wiggins, a conservative Republican from California, approached Conyers. "I hear you are offering your article. Well I might just have another article too. I understand the President has been having all these prayer breakfasts at the White House. I might just impeach him for not separating church and state."

Eventually the debate opened at 4:15 that afternoon—not prime time—and the members agreed to limit it to one and a half hours. Rodino left the chair, almost for the first time in the entire impeachment process.

Article IV charged that Nixon had violated his constitutional oath of office in that he, "on and subsequent to March 17, 1969, authorized, ordered, and ratified the concealment from the Congress of the facts and the submission to the Congress of false and misleading statements concerning the existence, scope and nature of American bombing operations in Cambodia in derogation of the power of the Congress to declare war, to make appropriations, and to raise and support armies, and by such conduct warrants impeachment and trial and removal from office."

The charge, said Conyers, was simple: "The President unilaterally undertook major military actions against another sovereign nation and then consistently denied that he had done so to both the Congress and the American people." Representative Elizabeth Holtzman, who had tried the year before to stop the bombing of Cambodia, pointed out that at issue was "whether or not the Congress can participate in decisions which it is given power over under the constitution." Robert Kastenmeier of Wisconsin acknowledged that the Article had no hope of approval but said he would vote for it nonetheless, for "the essence of the article is as fundamental as the three we have already adopted if not more so."

The opponents of the motion argued that this had been wartime, that the President was fulfilling his obligation to protect American lives, that Sihanouk had acquiesced, that some members of Congress had been told, and that previous Presidents, particularly Johnson, had been as deceitful. Perhaps the most interesting speech against the motion was made by John Seiberling, whose Ohio district includes Kent State University. He agreed with its spirit but had to vote against it, he said. With a flourish he held up in his hand the sheaf of cables to and from Abrams in which the Menu procedures were organized in 1969. The administration, he said, had refused to declassify them. "They are top secret. And yet there is no justification for the secrecy. The war is over. But they also, by doing that, prevent us from using as evidence in this case before the public some of the documents which tie the President into this very act of concealment. So the concealment is continuing and prevents us from effectively presenting the facts." Twelve members voted for the motion, twenty-six against. After the result was announced, ten of those who had voted in favor filed a dissenting view in which they remarked that the article was

> one of the most serious the Committee on the Judiciary considered during the course of its inquiry. It is difficult to imagine Presidential misconduct more dangerously in violation of our constitutional form of government than Mr. Nixon's decision secretly and unilaterally to order the use of American military power against another nation, and to deceive and mislead the Congress about this action. . . . The Constitution does not permit the President to nullify the war-making powers given to the Congress. Secrecy and deception which deny to the Congress its lawful role are destructive of the basic right of the American People to participate in their government's life-and-death decisions. . . . By failing to recommend the impeachment of President Nixon for the deception of Congress and the American public as to an issue as grave as the systematic bombing of a neutral country, we implicitly accept the argument that any ends—even those a President believes are legitimate—justify unconstitutional means.*

Perhaps Drinan was exaggerating only a little when he said, "Those who vote against this article will be saying, in effect, that the President, our next President, any President, can deceive the Congress, can have secrecy in the executive branch, can try to justify it by saying we didn't want to embarrass some foreign prince. . . ."

Richard Nixon's resignation was hailed by Sihanouk in Peking. President Gerald Ford, he remarked, was not bound by the errors and the obligations of his predecessor. He could break with the past and perhaps finally a solution to the war in Cambodia could be found. Then Ford made it clear, by retaining Henry Kissinger as his Secretary of State and National Security Adviser, that he intended to continue the foreign policies of the past five years.

When John Gunther Dean visited Washington at the end of August it was obvious to him that little had changed. He found it almost impossible even to talk to Kissinger. Once again the Secretary was preoccupied—this time with the failures of his policy during the Cyprus crisis. After writing Kissinger another long paper on the situation, Dean spent a good deal of time with influential members of the Senate and the House. In an obvious, and understandable, attempt to protect his future should there

---

* The dissenting view was signed by Representatives Holtzman, Kastenmeier, Edwards, Hungate, Conyers, Waldie, Drinan, Rangel, Owens, Mezvinsky.

be a rout in Cambodia, he made it clear, discreetly, that he was rather more in favor of negotiations than was Kissinger. He also hinted at the difficulty he was having in getting to see the Secretary.

The investment paid off. After several calls from Capitol Hill to the State Department Kissinger did see Dean briefly and extended what Dean took to be grudging approval of the idea of a "controlled solution." Several months later Congressman Donald Fraser, to whom Dean had talked, pointed out at a public hearing on Cambodia, "It is reasonably common knowledge that when the Ambassador from Cambodia was back in Washington a while back he had great difficulties getting the attention of the Secretary." Choosing his words carefully, Fraser observed, "the impression one gets is that we are prepared to continue financing this war to the last Cambodian."

CHAPTER 22

The Negotiators

FOR FOURTEEN months after the bombing ended in August 1973, Kissinger made no effort to end the war in Cambodia. A State Department summary of negotiating efforts, produced in March 1975 in an effort to persuade Congress to increase military aid, stated that "a number of major efforts toward negotiation were made in 1973, efforts which were thwarted by the forced bombing halt in August of that year. In October, 1974, we broached the idea of an international conference on Cambodia. . . . We received no substantive answer to these overtures. . . ."

The summary suggested that after Nixon's resignation Cambodia did once more become a concern. It listed six attempts made between October 1974 and February 1975 to try to find a solution to the war. To show the exact nature of these efforts it is useful to consider in some detail one of the more significant attempts that were made. This is how the summary described it: "In December, 1974, and early January, 1975, we concurred in an initiative to open a dialogue with Sihanouk in Peking. Sihanouk at first agreed to see an emissary, but later refused." The initiative was taken by the French.

In September 1974 a summit meeting was arranged between Giscard d'Estaing, who had succeeded Georges Pompidou to the French presidency in May, and Gerald Ford, who had just replaced Richard Nixon. It was to take place in December on the French Caribbean island of Martinique, and its principal purpose was for the two leaders to become acquainted and to discuss oil, energy and gold prices. Giscard, anxious to act the statesman, also began to consider what other topics he could raise.

After Giscard's elevation to the presidency, the Secretary of the Elysée, Claude Pierre-Brossolette, had shown him the file of messages from Etienne Manac'h in Peking, messages that dealt with Chinese hopes for a settlement in Cambodia. Now Giscard cabled his ambassador to ask if there was still, at this late stage, any chance of France playing a useful role. Manac'h's optimism was guarded. He still believed that Chou En-lai wished to see Sihanouk leading Cambodia again. But it was clear to him, as it was to other diplomats, that Chinese policy had changed in the spring of 1974. Manac'h was convinced that this was because of Kissinger's apparent lack of interest in either Sihanouk or negotiations.

In early April 1974 Khieu Samphan, vice-president of Sihanouk's Government of National Union and commander in chief of the Cambodian People's National Liberation Army, had come to Peking. To Sihanouk's intense discomfiture he was welcomed almost with the honors due to a head of state. At a formal banquet given in his honor he attacked all "such vicious maneuvers as sham cease-fire, sham talks and sham peace," and he ruled out all compromise. He presented Chou En-lai with a grenade launcher; the Chinese Premier aimed it at the ceiling. It was a critical moment which symbolized an important shift in Chinese policy away from a political solution toward a military end to the Cambodian crisis. In talks with the Chinese government the Khmer Rouge commander requested a major commitment of military supplies from Peking; that request was granted. It was with the help of these new weapons that the Khmer Rouge were able to keep the fighting through the 1974 wet season at a higher level than ever before and then to launch the offensive that won them the war.

From Peking Khieu Samphan embarked on a long tour of African, Middle Eastern and East European countries sympathetic to the insurgent government. (It was now that Dean suggested to Kissinger that the United States contact him.) His message everywhere was the same: there could be no negotiations with Lon Nol. President Ceaucescu of Rumania attempted to act as mediator but Khieu Samphan was adamant: the GRUNK would fight on till total victory.

Manac'h knew that stated American policy—that the two sides should negotiate together—was quite impossible. As Sihanouk had recently told

The New York Times, "It is like putting a tiger and a dog in the same cage. Things will be settled only when one animal eats the other. And that is how it will be in Cambodia. We are the tiger, and Lon Nol and his people are the running dogs." At the same time, Manac'h was certain that unless a peace was negotiated an eventual Khmer Rouge victory on the battlefield was inevitable. He was aware of the rigor with which it enforced its policies and believed, from the perspective of a Western social democrat, that the prospect of its power was unattractive. He was convinced that, for all his failings, Sihanouk remained the best hope of the Cambodian people, and he realized that if the Khmer Rouge arrived first in Phnom Penh they would not agree to share power with him. It was essential to try to arrange Sihanouk's arrival in the city before the Communists. That, thought Manac'h, could be achieved only in one way. The United States must accept and arrange the departure of Lon Nol and his clique from the capital and then massive demonstrations must be organized there for Sihanouk's return. (That part of the plan would have been simple.) The Prince would fly home from Peking to assume control of a broad center-left coalition which integrated into his GRUNK all prominent Phnom Penh politicians not completely beholden to the other side. That was plausible; dozens of political figures in Phnom Penh, including Lon Nol's commander in chief and Prince Sirik Matak, had already sent him word that they would welcome his return. Even Lon Nol's ambassador to Washington, Um Sim, had been asking Senator Mansfield to try to find out from the Prince on what conditions he would come home.

Manac'h's proposal was, essentially, that the leader of the Royal Government of National Union should exercise his authority to extend its base. The Khmer Rouge would remain in the government, but they would be somewhat balanced by other figures. Instead of being a powerless figurehead in exile, he would be at home in control of the capital, half the population, the bonzes, the bureaucracy and an army whose morale would have soared. The successor of the kings of Angkor, at the head of a popular front in the real sense of that term, could then unilaterally declare a cease-fire. Manac'h recognized that the Khmer Rouge leaders would be outraged, but he believed they would have to accept the *fait accompli.* Thousands of their troops would undoubtedly defect, were they ordered to continue to fight, their indoctrination against Sihanouk notwithstanding.

It was an attractive scheme, but Manac'h realized that enormous difficulties were implicit in it. It demanded that the United States reverse a policy of four and a half years, and it required the cooperation of the

Chinese. Peking had already made a public commitment to Khieu Samphan; and Sihanouk's principal champion, Chou En-lai, was now in the hospital much of the time, suffering from the cancer that would soon kill him. Nonetheless, on the basis of his conversations with such officials as Foreign Minister Chiao Kuan-hua, Manac'h understood that Peking was still prepared to consider such an "initiative."

(The scheme was further complicated by the nature of French relations with Cambodia. The French had attempted to have the best of both worlds since 1970. In order to protect substantial commercial interests in Cambodia they recognized Lon Nol—but reduced their mission in Phnom Penh below ambassadorial level—and at the same time attempted to remain on friendly terms with Sihanouk. Any move toward the exiled government now reflected not only Manac'h's personal desire to end the war but also the French government's wish to be associated with the winning side.)

On October 31 Giscard made his first approach—a telegram of greetings to Sihanouk, who was then in Algiers. The French ambassador, Jean Marie Soutou, told the Prince that Giscard was anxious to help end the war. Sihanouk adamantly attacked the American demand that he negotiate with Lon Nol. French officials later confided that he had said, "The Americans lack realism. I had a white handkerchief. The Americans have soaked it in blue ink. Absurd! The handkerchief turned red. Now they want to dye it white again. Well it's not possible." But, he said, the *integration* of Lon Nol's Phnom Penh opponents into GRUNK which Manac'h proposed, might work.

On November 20 Manac'h saw Foreign Minister Chiao Kuan-hua once more and asked if Chinese policy remained as Chou En-lai had outlined it to Pompidou. He was told that it did, but that it might not do so for much longer. The Chinese attitude at this stage was equivocal. So long as Hanoi's blockade of arms supplies denied the Khmer Rouge their full military potential, Peking appeared willing to connive at a settlement that would result in a government of which it could be certain, a government controlled by Sihanouk. But if and when a Khmer Rouge battlefield victory became imminent, the Sihanouk card could no longer be played, and Peking would have to accept a Khmer Communist government, with all the risks of alignment toward Moscow that that, in theory, posed.

(The ambiguity of Chinese policy was displayed in a long article published by Hsinhua, the Chinese news agency, on November 24. It was an analysis of the Phnom Penh economy and made no attack on political personalities in the city except to refer to the "phantom government of

[Prime Minister] Long Boret." As for negotiations it said simply, "The Cambodian people have rejected completely the proposal of negotiations concocted by the Lon Nol clique with the support of the U.S. It is determined to pursue the struggle till final victory." Significantly, the article did not denounce the kind of negotiations the French had proposed. Similar equivocation was demonstrated in the treatment now accorded to Ieng Sary, the Khmer Rouge's main representative in Peking. On November 24, Ieng Sary visited Chou En-lai in the hospital. He was then given a banquet at which he denounced all talk of negotiations. But his host Li Hsien-yen made no mention of negotiations.)

Still more uncertainty was added by the fact that the United Nations was holding its annual debate on whether Lon Nol's government should be replaced in the General Assembly by Sihanouk's. Since 1970 more and more countries had recognized the Prince's government, and even the Russians had closed their embassy in Phnom Penh and were now making approaches to the Prince. In 1973 the move to unseat Lon Nol had only just been defeated, by postponing the decision for a year, after vigorous American lobbying. This year American pressure was even more intense, and John Gunther Dean sent Long Boret, one of the most effective Prime Ministers Lon Nol had ever had, on a trip to the Middle East to win Arab support. The efforts were successful, Lon Nol retained the seat by a margin of two votes. The French abstained: Giscard said publicly that this "should not be interpreted as indicating indifference to the sufferings of the Khmer nation."

On November 25 Manac'h saw Sihanouk. The Prince realized that the French were offering him a last chance to return home in his own right, and with some influence over the country's future. He was clearly anxious about any commitments that Chou En-lai might have made to Ieng Sary, whom he loathed. He agreed that if the United States removed Lon Nol and "his clique" he would be prepared to return to Phnom Penh and allow various politicians there to join a broadened GRUNK. He would establish a government of national unity in which the Khmer Rouge would, of course, be dominant but which would, he hoped, be less radical than an administration in which they had complete control and he had no part. He knew that the Khmer Rouge would resist any such compromise bitterly. He insisted to Manac'h that the proposal must be kept secret.

Manac'h then flew to Paris to brief Giscard. Over a four-hour lunch on November 29 he outlined his proposal, stressing the need for speed and secrecy. Giscard accepted his logic, and on December 2 the Quai d'Orsay informed Washington that the French President wished to discuss Cambodia at Martinique. There was no objection. Manac'h returned to Peking.

Kissinger had just completed his seventh trip to the Chinese capital; just what he proposed on Cambodia is still disputed. Some American officials claim that he had by now drastically altered his position and was prepared to remove Lon Nol. But Chou En-lai later told Sihanouk—according to the Prince—that Kissinger remained adamant that any negotiation must be between Sihanouk and Lon Nol. On December 6, Chiao Kuan-hua told Manac'h that Kissinger was elated by Lon Nol's success at the U.N.; the Chinese foreign minister thought it barely relevant to the situation in the field. Manac'h was led to understand that Chiao Kuan-hua still supported the French proposals to be made at Martinique.

Manac'h's impressions of Kissinger's attitude coincided with those of John Gunther Dean, who flew to Hawaii for a briefing of American ambassadors in Asia after Kissinger's Peking trip. Dean knew of Manac'h's hopes and had recently written him an encouraging letter about his attempts to start a dialogue with Sihanouk. He believed now more than ever that time was against Lon Nol, particularly since Congress was beginning to impose unprecedented restrictions on aid to Cambodia.

On December 4 the Senate had accepted a foreign-aid bill that placed an absolute ceiling of $377 million in economic and military aid to Cambodia for the year July 1974–July 1975. (In the previous year the United States had provided the country with over $708 million in aid.) The same measure was passed by the House and even though a House-Senate conference subsequently added another $75 million military aid it was a historic and, for the Lon Nol government, fatal vote. The Pentagon's current plans called for military spending of $362.5 million for the year. About half of this had already been spent, and now the Congress had reduced the military budget to $275 million. With such restrictions, it was inevitable that the government would run out of ammunition.

In pushing for a "controlled solution" Dean even had the support of Graham Martin, the United States ambassador to Saigon, who believed, correctly, that Cambodia was draining resources and Congressional patience from Vietnam and wished to see Sihanouk return to Phnom Penh. Nevertheless, Dean still did not detect any sense of urgency on Kissinger's part. Kissinger, says Brent Scowcroft, considered any attempt to remove Lon Nol too risky. Dean returned to Phnom Penh depressed.

The New York Times correspondent Sydney Schanberg, with whom Dean was on good terms, now quoted "an embassy official" as saying he hoped that Washington would put as much effort into peace negotiation as it had put into the U.N. vote. Schanberg wrote that there was little sign of movement in Washington and that the impression in the embassy was that it was Kissinger who had to be persuaded to talk—"He has never seemed to place any obvious urgency or high priority on this little country."

Still, as far as Manac'h could see, the conditions for his Cambodian proposal seemed good when Giscard flew to Martinique on December 13. The day before, the ambassador had seen Sihanouk again and the Prince had told him that the Khmer Rouge were still short of arms. In his optimism Sihanouk even speculated that the North Vietnamese might themselves now be playing "the Sihanouk card" against the Khmer Communists. He said he knew the Khmer Rouge would kill him one day if they had the chance and told Manac'h he was grateful for his efforts, but begged above all for secrecy.

It was secrecy that was denied.

The history of American-French cooperation on Indochina has not been altogether happy. Officials of each country have tended to despise the performances and the opinions of the other. During the seventies many of France's notions seemed to the Americans to be hopelessly out of touch. The French persisted in the belief that the Viet Cong were genuinely independent of Hanoi and that the South would never be governed from the North. In the final weeks of the war, it was the French who insisted the loudest that the North Vietnamese would negotiate if only President Thieu was removed.

At Martinique, Giscard introduced Manac'h's proposal cautiously after he and his foreign minister, Jean Sauvarnagues, had had an informal lunch with Ford and Kissinger on the second day of the talks. He suggested that it would offer the United States a dignified solution to the dilemma it faced in Cambodia and at the same time assure China (and France) a solid, friendly regime in Phnom Penh. In the easy ambience of the occasion the proposal seemed to the Frenchmen to be surprisingly well received. Kissinger made no objections; he simply asked that the French send someone from the Quai d'Orsay to Washington to work out the details. But the next day the official communiqué on the talks was issued.

Ideally the communiqué should have made no mention of Cambodia at all. In fact it stated: "Regarding Cambodia they [the two presidents] expressed the hope that the contending parties would enter into negotiations in the near future rather than continuing the military struggle." This represented a reversal of French policy on Cambodia; it was just what Sihanouk, the Khmer Rouge and the Chinese had always rejected. It was Kissinger's peace proposal. It virtually destroyed Manac'h's idea before its inception.

In Peking, officials at once demanded that Manac'h tell them why France had abandoned its policy; what did this "betrayal" mean? Sihanouk told Manac'h that the Khmer Rouge leadership now realized what was afoot and that the communiqué had dealt a "truncheon blow" to the initiative. The Quai hurriedly instructed all French ambassadors to state "without hesitation" that France's policy had not in fact changed and Giscard even made a humiliating retraction on television. "Quite frankly," he said, "the communiqué imperfectly reflects what I had in mind . . . negotiations between the parties . . . does not seem suited to the situation at present. Other forms of political evolution of a different type and that we ourselves consider desirable should be sought. I told President Ford of our concern in this field and at the same time of our ideas regarding a type of political solution that does not exactly consist of negotiations between parties."

It was too late. To protect himself Sihanouk issued a public statement denouncing France's "inadmissible interference" in Cambodia's affairs, and Manac'h was left with the unenviable task of persuading the meticulous and skeptical Chinese that a genuine mistake had been made. On the French side this was undoubtedly true. The communiqué had been produced in a hurry. That particular sentence had been drafted by Kissinger's staff and presented by him to Giscard and Sauvarnagues. Although Manac'h had proposed that they do so, the French had brought no Asian specialist to Martinique, and neither Giscard nor Sauvarnagues knew enough of Cambodian politics to understand the implication of the words.

Despite the fiasco, two French officials, Henri Froment-Meurice and Hubert Argod, flew to Washington to discuss Manac'h's plan just before Christmas. Here the politics of the Quai intrude slightly upon the story. Froment-Meurice had succeeded Manac'h as head of the Asia Department. He and Manac'h are not similar in either politics or personality. Froment-Meurice has the reputation of being pro-American, but even American officials have expressed wariness of his character. It is said in the Quai that he envied Manac'h's position and reputation. In any case, the two men had never liked each other. Froment-Meurice had little enthusiasm for Manac'h's current idea, since he thought Vietnam far more important, and he did not press it with vigor at the State Department. Indeed, he scarcely concealed his skepticism.

Kissinger, for his part, did show some interest, but he insisted that Washington could have nothing to do with the idea unless specific conditions were fulfilled and absolute guarantees were obtained from the Chinese. This was understandable enough, particularly in light of China's apparent public endorsement of a military victory. But, somewhat to the surprise of the French, Kissinger was not prepared to solicit help from the U.S. Liaison Office in Peking or to ask for a more detailed report from Manac'h. On the contrary, he insisted that American officials in Peking not even be informed of the discussions, and he refused to accept Manac'h as a reliable witness or negotiator, apparently thinking him too close to Sihanouk. (This was arguable, but had Manac'h not had the Prince's confidence he would never have been able to make his "integration" proposal in the first place, let alone have Sihanouk accept it.) Instead, Kissinger insisted that either Argod or Froment-Meurice fly to Peking to take over the negotiation from Manac'h. Froment-Meurice did not demur.

When Manac'h was told that the Quai was asking the Chinese for a visa he was appalled. Inevitably it would increase both publicity and suspicions, and he doubted that Peking would wish to be seen to cooperate in a venture that could only have been designed to circumvent the Khmer Rouge. He was right. The Chinese simply did not respond to the request.

Soon after Christmas Manac'h cabled the Quai to say that the venture had now been so compromised that it had better be abandoned. A few days later, the Khmer Rouge launched what was to be their final offensive against Phnom Penh. When Manac'h next saw Sihanouk, the Prince was very depressed. He believed that the Khmer Rouge were more suspicious, that his relations with them were, as a result, worse than ever, and that his hopes of a moderate socialism akin to Yugoslavia's must now be dismissed totally. Now only force would prevail. Stalinist Albania, he said, would be the model.

CHAPTER 23

The End

THE FINAL battle for Phnom Penh began as government officials and division commanders, at a party given by John Dean, raised their glasses to the new year, the fifth year of the war. At 1 A.M. on the first of January, Communist artillery and rockets were unloosed on government positions north, east and west of the city and in the enclaves across the country. North of Phnom Penh government positions crumbled at once and artillery pieces were abandoned. The 1975 dry-season offensive was underway.

Lon Nol's troops were not well placed to meet it. The level of fighting during the previous rainy season had been much higher than in earlier years. At General Palmer's urging, the army had attempted to drive the Communists out of the "rocket belt"—their launching area in the swampy lands southeast of Phnom Penh between the Bassac and Mekong rivers. Casualties in the 1st Division there were so high that other units had to be rotated in to absorb the losses. Several military attachés in the embassy urged that the offensive be broken off. Palmer refused. Instead, he says, he urged the army leadership to "whipsaw" the Khmer Rouge by exploiting FANK's superior mobility and shifting the attack quickly against the Communists' main east-west supply line north of the city once they were heavily committed in the Bassac area. This was not done. Palmer blames the army. Some American military attachés criticize him. In any case, as Palmer complained in his end-of-tour report, the failure represented "a major tactical turning point of the war." By January 1 dozens of Lon Nol's units had been badly mauled, very few had been able to rest and refit, and no effective gains had been made.

Now, in these final three months, each side fought with extraordinary bravery and each suffered losses that would have been intolerable for most armies. In the end, differences in training, morale, discipline and, perhaps most important of all, supplies, were crucial.

It was clear within days of the start of the offensive that Hanoi was no longer withholding arms—the Khmer Rouge had far more weapons and ammunition than ever before. It was also obvious that they had improved their communications security, that they now exercised efficient command and control over their forces, that they were able to replace the killed and wounded, and that they had devised an effective plan for pinning down government troops around Phnom Penh. On the government side, not only had nothing changed, but it was now that what Palmer called "the past sins of Lon Nol's officers" took their final, critical toll. Once more he was unable to acknowledge the extent to which he and his predecessors had tolerated, even encouraged these sins.

There was still no sense of urgency at the command level, and in the field officers still demanded money before cooperating with other units. Lon Nol still insisted on personal control, and the old pattern of late-morning attacks, heavy afternoon losses and dusk retreats continued as ever. In the past, fire power had been used to shore up incompetence. Now that Congress was cutting back aid, Palmer noted, "the only remaining option appeared to be manpower." Often the manpower did not exist. In Siem Reap, near Angkor, one battalion commander paled when told to redeploy his full unit strength to Phnom Penh; for years he had carried four hundred phantoms on his payroll and in fact had only forty soldiers ready for combat. The defense of Battambang, where Dean's foe Sek Sam Iet had ruled, soon proved impossible for the same reason. Losses mounted. The phantom soldiers marched their comrades to defeat.

Within weeks the foxhole strengths of many units had fallen to only 30 percent of their authorized strength. The American embassy made frantic efforts to overcome the shortages. Lon Nol was encouraged to introduce general mobilization. He was even urged to end deferments of middle-class students, but that was politically impossible. All day long, army press gangs roared up and down poorer streets seizing boys. General Palmer urged FANK to transfer around 10,000 men from its headquarters staff into combat units; he later acknowledged that only a small portion of these men were reassigned to the field and that many of them, particularly officers, deserted.

And yet, those of Lon Nol's soldiers who did fight, fought on and on and on, often displaying such tenacity that Palmer was astonished. "Despite the flagrant absence of their officers during critical actions, the failure of their top leadership to even visit them or recognize their heroic deeds, the long periods that they and their families were without pay or enough food because of their officers' incompetence or dishonesty, and the unimaginative tactics that they were ordered to execute, Khmer foot soldiers continued to fight for their country until defeat was inevitable."

It was not really their country that Lon Nol's troops were fighting for. Like soldiers anywhere they frequently fought for their own lives and those of their families. Many of them fought out of fear of the Khmer Rouge. They fought against atheism. They fought for their comrades, for their squads and for their platoons. They fought because they had nowhere else to go.

After the war was over, the new government of Cambodia declared over Radio Phnom Penh that "the Mekong was the key to our great victory. It was also the enemy's weakest point. Blocking the Mekong meant completely defeating the enemy and winning total victory."

Before January 1975, all roads into Phnom Penh had been decisively cut. Ninety-two percent of all the rice, fuel and ammunition on which the government depended for survival was brought by barge sixty miles up the winding river from South Vietnam. Through December, as the rains ended and the waters receded, the banks closed in and the convoys became more and more vulnerable. One convoy managed to pass up river just after Christmas, but as soon as the New Year offensive began, the Khmer Rouge committed over 5,000 troops to the banks of the lower Mekong between the Vietnamese border and the ferry town of Neak Luong.

The government had failed to appreciate that the defense of the Mekong was far more vital to its survival than, say, that of the enclave of Takeo. Inadequate forces were committed to keep the river open. For almost all of January no convoys came through, and the capital's stocks of rice, fuel and ammunition were diminished. Finally, at the end of the month, one small convoy did manage to reach Phnom Penh.

For the Vietnamese, Taiwanese and Korean crews, the voyage on the rusty barges and tugs was perilous. In the past they had usually had to brave an hour of heavy fire at a few well-known choke points along the river. This year the fire was extraordinarily heavy and almost continuous. Hour after hour, thousands of machine-gun rounds and hundreds of B-40, B-41 and 107-mm. rockets, grenades and mortars crashed into the sand-bagged bridges of the boats and against the steel cages with which the ammunition barges were protected. For much of the trip many of the crew members were in panic, screaming "Back up, VC. Back up, VC." The wheelhouse of one tug took a direct hit and collapsed on the Cambodian pilot. Even as the convoy finally straggled into Phnom Penh's little dock, a rocket sizzled across the water, smashed into a harbor tug and killed a man.

The convoy brought just two weeks of supplies. It was the last ever to reach Phnom Penh. By the time the crews had recovered from their ordeal and set off back to Saigon, the Khmer Rouge had introduced a fatal new weapon. They stretched nylon line and wire rope, salvaged from tugs sunk in earlier operations, across the river. The lines were supported by bamboo floats and attached to them were small mines, supplied by China, which were detonated from the shore as ships passed over them. Several vessels in the empty convoy were sunk.

With American advice, the FANK leadership developed plans for co-ordinated army, navy and air-force sweeps of the river. The navy was to cut the barricades, while artillery was unleashed on Khmer Rouge positions, helicopters were to leapfrog troops up the riverbanks just before convoys passed, and the ships were to run the most dangerous of the choke points at night. The scheme was, as General Palmer pointed out, "an excellent piece of staff work from a U.S. Staff College viewpoint," but it was never implemented. There were not enough men and "for the Khmer it was simply a grandiose 'joint plan' beyond their level of sophistication." Instead, the navy alone made haphazard attempts to clear the river. They were not successful, and by the end of March the navy had lost about a quarter of its ships and had 70 percent of its crewmen killed or wounded. The river was never reopened, and the city began to starve.

With the Mekong closed, Washington revived old contingency plans for a massive airlift of food and fuel to Phnom Penh. For 48 days through February, March and early April a shuttle of DC-8s flew rice up from Saigon. At the same time the Pentagon began to fly in fuel and ammunition from Thailand. To abide by at least some of the spirit of the Cooper-Church amendment, the U.S. Air Force did not do this job directly.

Instead, the contract was given to a firm named Bird Air. The planes were lent by the Pentagon, their official markings were painted over, and about half the pilots were U.S. Air Force reservists.

The airlift of food prevented famine, but it did not stop starvation spreading through the city. In 1973 the government's estimate of the daily rice needed in Phnom Penh was 770 metric tons. During 1974, as tens of thousands more refugees arrived, the daily distribution fell to about 694 metric tons. Still more refugees streamed in during the new offensive, but after the Mekong was closed the amount of rice distributed fell further almost every day. Its average for that period was 543 metric tons a day. Throughout February and March the airlift managed to bring in only about 440 metric tons a day. Dean made continual complaints. By now, according to AID, about a thousand tons a day would have been necessary to provide adequate nutrition. By the middle of February the maximum amount of rice that anyone could buy at the subsidized price (which was still far too high for most families) was 270 grams a day; the World Health Organization considers 450 grams a day to be the minimum nutritional requirement.

Reports by the various charitable relief organizations and investigations by the World Health Organization and by the Senate Refugee Subcommittee had already showed that malnutrition was a serious problem in 1974. In February 1975, the office of Inspector General of Foreign Assistance at the State Department asserted that "children are starving to death" in Cambodia. That conclusion was hard to avoid. In the camps and in the streets, in the cardboard shelters, in the Cambodiana Hotel refugee center, one could see sick children everywhere. Those who suffered from kwashiorkor, extreme protein deficiency, had distended bellies and swollen hands, feet and ankles. Their hair was falling out or turning light brown, and so was their skin; they behaved as listlessly as one might expect.

Other children had simply far too little to eat to be able to grow properly and were suffering from marasmus. Their matchlike limbs hung over the empty skin folds of their bodies, they had almost no muscular control, and eight-year-olds looked like shriveled babies. For most of them there was no hope. The World Vision child nutrition center had to turn away 1,758 severely malnourished children between December 1974 and February 1975; they had beds for only 235 of the worst new cases. The Inspector-General's report noted: "It requires little imagination to picture these wretchedly frail and sickly little bodies, borne away in their weak mother's arms, carried to an alley somewhere, to die; certain to suffer, untreated, unhospitalized, unfed."

The End

Sydney Schanberg of *The New York Times* wrote from the besieged ferry town of Neak Luong,

> The children gathered by the dozens around a Western newsman. . . . Some have swollen bellies. Some are shrunken. A 10-year-old girl has dehydrated to the size of a 4-year-old. Harsh bronchial coughs come from their throats, marking the beginnings of pneumonia and tuberculosis. All have dysentery. Their noses run continuously. Their skins have turned scaly. Every scratch on their legs and arms becomes an ulcer.

It was only now, under extreme pressure from Congress and the relief agencies, that the White House finally agreed to ship free rice to Cambodia under Title II of the Public Law 480 program. Previously only Title I rice had been used—which had to be bought by the Cambodian government and resold to those who could afford to buy. Supplies were now increased to 700 metric tons a day. Administration policy was still limited; Lieutenant General H. M. Fish, Director of the Pentagon's Defense Security Assistance Agency, told Congress, "We seek only to keep them alive and fighting through the remainder of this fiscal year."

No one knows how many thousands of children died in Cambodia in those final months before the end of the war. Their suffering was perhaps the most poignant demonstration of the government's inability to sustain its population, but in these final weeks the majority of the population collapsed into the sort of half life that the refugees had always endured. The U.S. AID Termination Report commented later that although more and more people were still pushing desperately into the enclaves and thus exacerbating the refugee crisis, "paradoxically, as the refugee situation became more and more critical, it was at the same time less and less readily identifiable as a distinct problem . . . [and] became inseparable from the larger social economic collapse of the country." By now, "There was little or no food to be had by anybody—refugee, civilian or soldier. Malnutrition became rampant, especially in Phnom Penh, and spread to all classes of the Khmer society."

At the beginning of February Etienne Manac'h left Peking, his tour completed, to retire to his house in Brittany. Before he departed, he saw Sihanouk one last time; the Prince was extremely dispirited. At the beginning of January the Khmer Rouge had told him that they did not expect to take Phnom Penh this year. But in the last month they had moved so

349

far so fast that an imminent victory seemed likely. He said he would have to reject any further attempts the Americans made to reach him; it was too late. He knew now that he could never expect any authority in the new Cambodia; the Khmer Rouge would rule the country harshly.

Publicly, however, Sihanouk was still not prepared to break with the Khmer Rouge. Throughout February and March he issued a stream of statements discounting fears of a blood bath, insisting that only Lon Nol and certain "traitors" in his "clique" need fear execution. In one telegram to Congressional Democrats, he claimed that the new government would have "no intention of making Cambodia a socialist or popular republic, but a Swedish type of kingdom." It was nonsense and he knew it, but many of his admirers in the West were deceived.

The U.S. Congress had, in a sense, been radicalized (temporarily) by the lies it had been fed—not least about Cambodia—during the long Watergate investigations. Until now, American military and economic aid to Lon Nol had totaled $1.85 billion. (On top of that, the cost of bombing Cambodia had been around $7 billion.) In December 1974 strict restrictions had been placed on aid to Cambodia, and now a large number of new and assertive members, elected in the fall of 1974, were moving into both Houses. Several conservative committee chairmen, in particular Edward Hebert, leader of the House Armed Services Committee, were removed, and it was evident that requests for vast new aid for Indochina would have slight chance of success. Nonetheless, the White House sent Congress a request for an additional $300 million emergency military aid for Vietnam and $222 million for Cambodia. At the same time it began expending considerable energy abusing Congress and warning that the "loss" of Cambodia would be a "foreign policy disaster" for the United States.

That Congress bore a measure of responsibility for the last five years of Cambodian history is beyond dispute; the legislature had constantly intervened to alter the relationship but, until December 1974, had always provided the funds adequate for White House ends. It was true, as Assistant Secretary of State Philip Habib now put it, that "year by year we built up a historical relationship and a historical dependency."

But Kissinger once again saw the Cambodian problem only in a wider context. He said that unless Congress acted "within the next few weeks, it is certain that Cambodia must fall, because it will run out of ammunition. I know that it is fashionable to sneer at the words 'domino theory,'" but unless the Congress provided the aid that the administration demanded, there would be "the most serious consequences" for American credibility. The validity of American commitments around the world would be called into question. "I don't believe we can escape the problem by condemning those who have dealt with us to a certain destruction," Kissinger said.

Kissinger's warnings were repeated by President Ford, who posed the "moral question" of whether the United States would "deliberately abandon a small country in the midst of its life-and-death struggle." He declared that it was American policy to aid "allies" so long as they were "willing and able to carry the burden of their own self-defense." Cambodia, he asserted, "has been such an ally."

The administration now maintained that it sought merely to give Phnom Penh enough ammunition to survive until the May rains checked the Khmer Rouge offensive. Then perhaps the Communists would finally negotiate. But neither Kissinger's own previous attempts at negotiation, nor the Khmer Rouge's declared policies gave any reason for such optimism. Anthony Lewis of *The New York Times* commented that just as the "Kissinger Doctrine" demanded that the United States conspire against another country's legal government if it feared that country might slip out of its orbit (he had Chile in mind), so it also required that if any regime take its country into the United States sphere of interest, Washington would do everything to sustain it, no matter how little support it had from its own people or how terrible the cost to them.

What Kissinger was, in fact, trying to do was to pin the blame for the failure of the "Nixon Doctrine in its purest form" on that branch of government that had always been most skeptical of the venture. When Cambodia fell, as the administration knew it would, the "catastrophe" could be laid entirely on Congress, and in the resultant furor, the legislature might then accede to the executive's demands over Vietnam. Even at this late stage, there were performances to be given in the sideshow. One problem, however, was that by insisting on linking American "credibility" to a cause that was already lost, Kissinger actually helped to manufacture the very crisis of confidence that he ostensibly sought to avoid.

With some difficulty the administration persuaded a group of members of Congress to visit Saigon and Phnom Penh. In Phnom Penh they were greeted by hostile newspaper editorials. One urged, "Congressmen, don't misunderstand. Cambodia helps America, not America helps Cambodia." They spent eight hours in Phnom Penh and were visibly shocked by what they saw of the suffering on the government side and, in most cases, by what they heard of the brutality of the Khmer Rouge. From both Lon Nol and Dean they gathered that Lon Nol was finally prepared to step aside if that were a precondition of aid or peace talks. Dean told them that 2,400 government soldiers had been killed in January and 1,857 in the first twenty days of February. These figures, he pointed out, were "staggering." The army, he felt, was fighting with great courage but could not continue without further aid. Should it collapse,

> all indications are that an uncontrolled solution will lead to an effort by the communists to impose their will rapidly, with brutality, in order to establish a new system in Cambodia. . . . This is the way they have been operating in the zones which they presently control. . . . It will be the first time since 1948 in China that an uncontrolled solution will occur, except that in this case, unlike China, there is not even a Formosa to which those who have been fighting the communists can escape.

Many of the legislators were genuinely unable to decide how best American moral responsibilities for the human disaster that Cambodia now constituted should be exercised. The dilemma was best summed up by Representative Pete McCloskey, a liberal Republican from California, who had consistently opposed both the war and Nixon, and who went to Phnom Penh determined to vote against emergency aid. After the trip he changed his mind and offered a compromise: the government should be helped through the rest of the dry season in the hope that this would force the Khmer Rouge to negotiate. "But then," McCloskey said, "after June 1, I don't believe the United States ought to have one man, one dollar, or one ambassador in Cambodia."

The compromise had considerable support, but in the end the Congress took no definite action either way on the administration's request. It was allowed to lapse, despite administration demands. McCloskey summarized his feelings with some bitterness: "I can only tell you my emotional reaction, getting into that country," he said. "If I could have found the military or State Department leader who has been the architect of this policy, my instinct would be to string him up. Why they are there and what they have done to the country is greater evil than we have done to any country in the world, and wholly without reason, except for our own benefit to fight against the Vietnamese."

By now the appalling casualties and the lack of food and pay were reducing the spirit of Lon Nol's forces. There is no doubt that Congress' long deliberations also had a debilitating effect. By juggling with supplies,

Palmer and the Pentagon managed to keep some ammunition flying into Phnom Penh but the stocks were diminishing.

Lon Nol's troops had always expended ammunition at an extravagant rate, firing off twenty 105-mm. artillery shells when one stray mortar crumped nearby. Had FANK units been properly led, a cut in the flow of ammunition could have been sustained at no very serious military cost. But because ammunition had always been provided in lieu of leadership it was the only form of protection on which many units could draw. To have supplies cut by almost 40 percent at the height of the most serious attack they had ever faced was a shock many found impossible to bear.

The 36th Brigade, the 72nd Brigade, the 38th Brigade, the 12th Brigade, the 4th Brigade, the 20th Brigade fell away one by one from the defense of Phnom Penh's perimeter. When troops on the 13th Brigade, 3rd Division, defending Route 4, finally received some of the pay they had been owed for months, about fifty of the men took their families and walked away from the war. The brigade was unable to withstand the next enemy assault and ran away. By early March every company commander in the division had been either killed or wounded. From almost every unit more and more men followed the ghosts into the mists.

There was no consensus, either in the embassy or among United States government agencies, as to how the Khmer Rouge would behave after victory. Dean was a pessimist. He warned visitors that he now feared an "uncontrolled and uncontrollable solution" in which "the entire infrastructure . . . the army, navy, air force, government and Buddhist monks were killed." He would retell the story of Sarsar Sdam, a village near Siem Reap which had been captured by the Khmer Rouge in August 1974. The whole village had been burned down and, according to Catholic Relief Services workers, over sixty peasants had been brutally killed: old women had been nailed to the walls of their houses before they were burned alive, children had been torn apart by hand. In another incident in January, about forty civilians were reported to have been massacred and mutilated at Ang Snuol on Route 4. As he told the Congressional delegation, he believed that the Communists would impose a brutal revolution if they won.

But the blood-bath theory had been invoked so often, and over so many years, that it did not now arouse much interest. Even members of the embassy were divided on what the Khmer Rouge would do; some shared Dean's gloom, others considered that he was exaggerating in order to obtain more aid. The Cambodians themselves seemed uncertain of the future. Many refugees were terrified of the Khmer Rouge. Other people appeared confident that, once the fighting ended, old friendships would be restored, enmities forgotten. Officers began to reminisce about days spent in cold Paris flats with boys now on the other side. Everyone quoted Sihanouk's constant, soothing assurances that only a handful of "traitors" would die, and some noted that in a recent radio broadcast Khieu Samphan himself had declared, "Every Cambodian has his role in national society regardless of his past." Many foreign journalists in the city, disgusted by the present horror, hoped that all would be well; the embassy Cassandras were hawks who wished to prolong the war, they decided. Drinking whiskey in their rooms in the Hotel Phnom they sang a little ditty to the tune of "She was poor but she was honest":

> Oh will there be a dreadful bloodbath
> When the Khmer Rouge come to town?
> Aye, there'll be a dreadful bloodbath
> When the Khmer Rouge come to town.

"Out there" the same problems were being discussed. It was now evident to the Khmer Rouge leadership that total military victory was almost within their grasp. If Lon Nol's troops continued to fall away as they were now doing, Phnom Penh would be in their hands within weeks. According to Sihanouk's *chef du cabinet,* they had not expected this. At the end of February, delegates were summoned to the Second National Congress of the Front, under the auspices of the Communist Party of Kampuchea. They considered the implications of imminent success and, in particular, the problems of feeding and governing the three and a half million people crowded into the enclaves on the losing side. In total secrecy, they decided that as soon as victory was theirs, the cities would immediately be emptied of their populations.

The people of Phnom Penh had little way of judging the effects of the bombs, shells and rockets the FANK had rained on Communist positions and ordinary villages, but one criterion was their own fear and the destruction caused by the Communists' random shellings of Phnom Penh. These had taken place throughout the war, whenever the Khmer Rouge had managed to push within range. Now the fire was much more frequent, and the principal target was the airport. Over these first three months of 1975, more than 2,500 rockets and shells were fired at Pochentong in an attempt to halt the airlift. Hardly a day went by when a plane or a runway was not damaged. All civilian airlines except Air Cambodge suspended their flights. (On the Air Cambodge's Caravelle from Bangkok glasses had to be gripped and seat belts fastened well as the plane dived at an extraordinary angle or corkscrewed tightly down to avoid the rocket launchers in the normal approaches and then jolted across the pocked runway to the sandbagged terminal, where ground crews in flak jackets tended the flight.)

The city itself suffered rather worse from the bombardment. One day in early February, a rocket landed just outside Le Collège de Phnom Watt and shot shrapnel and flying glass into a classroom. Eight children were killed and thirty-five wounded, many terribly, by that one missile. By the middle of February, over 700 rockets had skewered across the river into the city, killing over one hundred people. On March 10 a single 107-mm. rocket struck just outside the door of the Monorom Hotel in the international section of the city. Eleven people were killed and twenty wounded. The security guard on duty at the door died in the arms of an American television correspondent.

The army's paper strength was 230,000. By the middle of March there were about 60,000 men in the foxholes. Over 8,000 soldiers had deserted since the offensive began and around 15,000 had been killed or wounded. The seriously wounded rarely returned to fight, for the hospitals were unable to help them. There were only 1,394 beds in the city, and soldiers wounded in the 1974 Bassac campaign were already lying two or three on a bed when the New Year offensive began. Now the wounded were being carried into town like bunches of broken flowers—600 or so a week. Their families straggled after them, camping where they could, and within weeks the hospitals had degenerated into stagnant slums, where boys with open, untreated wounds lay with only their extraordinary patience to sustain them. In the entire army there were only 66 doctors and of these only 18 were qualified surgeons. Almost all were in Phnom Penh. There, the blood bank began to run dry and although drugs were plentiful on the black market or in ordinary pharmacies, government supplies were soon exhausted. Conditions were worse in the enclaves. In their request for the additional $222 million aid, Ford and Kissinger had made no mention of such needs.

Khmer Rouge casualties throughout these final weeks were even higher than FANK's. A squad leader of the Communists' 1st Division, captured on March 21, said that his regiment had lost 800 of its original 1,200 men in the fighting. Three wounded soldiers from the Khmer Rouge 3rd Division fighting southwest of the city claimed that their battalion strength had fallen from 700 to around 200. They said that morale was low, desertions were increasing, malaria was widespread, and medical supplies were insufficient. Dean, who had now adopted the White House's policy of attempting to keep the government alive until the rainy season, cabled Kissinger: "This is not intended as a light at the end of the tunnel message." However, he thought it "possible, perhaps even probable" that the Khmer Rouge were already fully committed. "In short, making allowances for the well-known and widely publicized deficiencies and problem areas of FANK, one arrives at the picture of the proverbial two punch-drunk fighters staggering around the ring, neither of which appears to have enough power left to push the other over on his face."

Major Alan Armstrong, an able soldier known to his friends as "Red Dog," was the military attaché to the 7th Division, which was defending the northwest sector of Phnom Penh. Already by the end of January, the division was fielding only about 130 men per battalion, the logistics and engineer battalions were no longer functioning, nearly all officers and NCOs had been killed or wounded, the squadron commander had typhoid, and one of the finest officers in the division was taking a training course in Taiwan. There had not been a single staff meeting during the month, and the command structure was falling apart. The divisional commander had devoted much of his energy to giving frequent parties for which the division had to pay, he rarely left the security of his bunker, giving all his orders by radio. Armstrong recommended to Palmer and Dean that the man be replaced. He was not.

This was Armstrong's second tour in Cambodia. He found the contrast between now and 1971 depressing. Early in March, as Kissinger and Ford were demanding more military aid, Armstrong gave vent to his frustrations in a report on the army for Palmer and Dean. "FANK is tired and uneasy," he wrote. A general mood of resignation was interrupted by outbreaks of naïve confidence that Washington would find a solution. No one talked of victory, only of peace. The soldiers were now so badly fed that they could no longer fight properly; their families lived worse than refugees. There were reports of cannibalism in the besieged town of Kompong Seila. These were documented. If soldiers were posted where they could not fish, morale collapsed. Many units looked like pirate bands with men fighting in rubber shower clogs, blue jeans, sarongs, nothing but a sweatband around their heads. Commanders rarely now inspired any loyalty in their men, and soldiers simply wandered away from the field. At the same time "a silent but desperate *sauve-qui-peut* sentiment is spreading among the officers."

Armstrong complained to his superiors that the corruption of the Republic had produced "a constant pus of disaffection and disillusion." Decent officers could not understand why the United States had not purged the thieves. The American position that the government must clean its own house was "absurd." United States aid to Cambodia was like a heart or lung machine. "Once the patient has reached that stage, it is folly to expect him to operate on himself."

Armstrong then asked what the United States was really doing now in Cambodia. "Is the U.S. Government here as a result of using [Cambodia] to disengage from Vietnam or is [it] here to help Cambodia? If the former, the mission is terminated. If the latter, the U.S. Government has been 90 percent unsuccessful." His own view was that "the Khmer Republic is unworthy of the supreme sacrifice by any of its citizens." The only hope of improving the situation was for more aid to be provided conditional on a real clean-up of corruption. "The Cambodians have just about given up on Americans as a redresser of wrongs. . . . To survive at the negotiating table with options, the Khmer needs a new revolutionary spirit within the Republic; one that matches the quixotic, touching and deeply emotional spirit which existed here in 1970." Armstrong knew that that was gone forever.

In the middle of March Lon Nol's commander in chief, Sosthene Fernandez, was finally removed in an attempt to regenerate the morale and the tactics of the army. Next it was Lon Nol's turn. While Dean hovered by encouragingly, the Japanese and other Asian ambassadors in Phnom Penh began to try to persuade him and other senior politicians that if only he left the country the U.S. Congress might finally authorize the additional aid that would allow the republic to survive until the rainy season.

On March 23, a group that included Long Boret, the Prime Minister, General Sak Sutsakhan, Sosthene Fernandez's successor, Saukham Khoy, the President of the Senate and Lon Nol's brother, Lon Non, wrote Lon Nol a memorandum in which they advised a "tactical" visit to Hawaii while peace talks were explored. Faced with this ultimatum, Lon Nol demanded written assurances that a Communist government would not be accepted in his absence and that he would be allowed to return if his absence did not result in more aid to Cambodia. On March 28, Long Boret sent him a memorandum that stated:

> 1. Our American friends are not working for our surrender;
> 2. Our friends need the provisional departure of the Marshal to obtain (a) aid from Congress, (b) a margin of maneuverability for negotiations for peace between Khmers. . . .

As a further incentive, Lon Nol was given half a million dollars and his Socio-Republican Party "baptize(d) [him] a national hero who has made a brilliant contribution to the nation and to all of us." On April 1, 1975, the Marshal finally left the ruins. His departure and calls by Prime Minister Long Boret (one of the seven "traitors") and by the new acting President, Saukham Khoy, for peace talks were dismissed with contempt by both Sihanouk and the Khmer Rouge.

That afternoon the Khmer Rouge finally broke through the government's last defenses on the Mekong, the strategic ferry town of Neak Luong. After a three-month siege, in which the population of 70,000 suffered terribly, the town fell that evening in bloody hand-to-hand street fighting. Six thousand more Communist troops and their artillery were freed for the final assault on the southern perimeter of Phnom Penh.

In its final assessment of the war the defense attaché's office in the embassy was straightforward about the campaign along the Mekong river. "Suffice it to say that FANK was outthought, outmaneuvered, outfought and outdesired [*sic*]—in a word, outclassed—every step of the way." The fall of Neak Luong was fatal, psychologically and strategically. The Communists now had control of the lower Mekong and could now redeploy two divisions and a separate brigade. But, in the words of the military attaché's office, "The most terrifying aspect of the situation lay in the realization of what these forces were bringing with them in terms of FANK munitions captured . . . 10–14 operational howitzers with thousands of unexpended rounds and literally hundreds of crew served weapons with associated ammo. . . ." Soldiers in FANK's 1st and 2nd divisions guarding the southern approaches of the city threw away their weapons and uniforms, and gathered their families for a last flight to the capital.

The government's ammunition stocks were constantly diminishing.

Ambassador Dean began to agitate to leave Phnom Penh. Plans for evacuation of the embassy had been brought up to date by his deputy, Robert Keeley. The first of the staff were flown out through the rocket fire at Pochentong on April 3. Dean wanted to evacuate the rest on April 5, but Kissinger refused. Dean warned that, given the speed with which the Khmer Rouge were now closing on the airport from the north and the town from the south, the final exodus would almost certainly have to be made by helicopter from near the embassy in the center of Phnom Penh.

As government positions tumbled, the mood in the embassy became distraught. Military and diplomatic officers were forced by the circumstances to review their experience in Phnom Penh and the ends they were pursuing. Some blamed Congress for its restrictions, others blamed the administration for its tolerance of the corruption that drained the Republic. Many were somewhat disgusted by the spectacle of General Mataxis, the first head of the Military Equipment Delivery Team. He was now working for an arms dealer in Singapore, and had suddenly reappeared in Phnom Penh. He was offering to buy from Cambodian officers, matériel that had previously been handed to them under the American military aid program.

For almost all embassy officials the strain of attempting to implement Kissinger's policy was immense. In recent weeks the head of the AID program, Thomas Olmsted, had died at his post, Robert Keeley had had to be given emergency treatment for bleeding ulcers, and another official had a heart attack; one military attaché was drinking heavily. Dean himself was suffering from high blood pressure and the effects of extreme fatigue. When a British journlist asked him rather roughly just what he thought he was doing in Cambodia, Dean burst out, "You guys think you know everything, but I've got orders to fight to the last Cambodian."

In those days, indeed, Dean was not always very diplomatic, and sometimes he made his contempt for Kissinger and his policies obvious. It was clear to his colleagues that after it all was over, Dean would not go quietly as Swank had done. Everyone knew that he had kept a complete file of all his cables to and from Kissinger, and that he would use them as he saw best. Some of his colleagues believed that unless he was treated carefully he would resign from the State Department and write a book.

On April 6, Dean gave a dinner for the American journalists who were still in Phnom Penh. One of his purposes was to persuade the press to leave with him when the time came. He served a good wine and told his guests that they were so lucky only because he did not want to abandon it to the Communists. When one reporter asked him what he expected to do after Cambodia, Dean looked at him and said slowly, "We would hope our efforts to negotiate a sensible solution would be rewarded with a suitable European embassy." In reply to a question of whether things might have been better had Kissinger accepted his advice about a "controlled solution" Dean replied, "You said it, I didn't."

At the other end of the table, Robert Keeley was openly even more morose and explicit. Keeley, never a man to accept policies and orders without question, had jeopardized his career while in Greece by criticizing the Nixon administration's close support for the Colonels. He had become even angrier in Cambodia. "One day," he said slowly, "Henry Kissinger will write his memoirs. And we will all go out and buy them. And there will be a chapter on Cambodia. And I will write a footnote on every page."

Dean's departure was further delayed by an extraordinary last-minute ploy by Kissinger. Throughout March and early April Sihanouk had conducted a daily public propaganda war, promising reconciliation with the United States if only his government were recognized and the "lackeys," "puppets," "bandits" and "traitors" left Phnom Penh. But at the end of March he had also, in despair, reestablished a secret link with the United States through the French embassy in Peking. On his request his *chef du cabinet*, Pung Peng Cheng, met with John Holdridge, the deputy to George Bush, the man who had replaced David Bruce in the U.S. Liaison Office, at the French embassy. Pung said that Sihanouk had a favor to ask of President Ford: in his old home in Phnom Penh were copies of the films of Cambodia he had made in the sixties when he had been an enthusiastic *cinéaste*. They constituted a unique cultural record of a Cambodia that was gone forever: would the Americans please rescue them? Kissinger ordered Dean to find the films and also instructed Bush to seek a meeting with Sihanouk. The Prince refused, and during the first ten days of April, as the noose around Phnom Penh tightened, he continued his public tirades.

By April 11, the Khmer Rouge had moved all their forces up from Neak Luong and were about to launch a full-scale attack on the capital's southeast sector. FANK troops on the east bank of the Mekong had now been forced into little pockets dependent on tenuous water-borne supplies and with no land route of escape. To the northwest the Khmer Rouge had moved through FANK's 7th Division defenses—FANK did not have enough ammunition to drive them back, and the Communists were about to cut the division off from the rear as they swept on to Pochentong airport. Only in the southwest was FANK holding. President Ford's declaration that day that any aid voted for Cambodia now would be "too late" was very discouraging in Phnom Penh, but it was accurate enough.

It was now, on April 11, 1975, as Dean was telling government leaders he might soon be leaving, that Kissinger decided that Sihanouk should be brought back to Cambodia. In Peking, George Bush was ordered to seek another meeting; that afternoon John Holdridge met once more with Pung Peng Cheng at the French embassy. The American diplomat explained that Dr. Kissinger and President Ford were now convinced that only the Prince could end the crisis. Would he please ask the Chinese for an aircraft to fly him straight back to Phnom Penh? The United States would guarantee to remain there until he arrived. Dr. Kissinger wished to impose no conditions. Monsieur Pung smiled behind his dark glasses, shook Holdridge's hand and said he would talk to the Prince.

As Holdridge was meeting with Pung, the Khmer Rouge had moved to within a mile of the airport. It was now under constant fire, and a chartered DC-3 had gone up in flames. The airlift of rice and ammunition had been suspended. Dean was anxious to evacuate his remaining staff by helicopter to a carrier that was waiting in the Gulf of Thailand. On April 12 at 5 A.M. Peking time, Holdridge met again with Pung. He told him that the Phnom Penh perimeter was degenerating so fast that the Americans were pulling out at once. Sihanouk had already issued a statement rejecting and denouncing Kissinger's invitation.

At 6 A.M. on April 12, Dean sent letters to members of the government and to other politicians offering them places on his helicopters in two and a half hours' time. To his astonishment the only senior official to arrive at the embassy was Saukham Khoy, the acting President. The day before, Saukham Khoy had sat, weeping for Cambodia, and told some journalists, "The United States led Cambodia into this war. But when the war became difficult the United States pulled out." Dabbing his eyes, he had speculated on the future: "There are some Cambodians who say that if the United States stops aiding Cambodia then we should turn to some other great power. Who? Russia. We could change our policies and become socialist. Then they would help us." When Saukham Khoy arrived at the embassy gate the next morning, the guards ordered him out of his official car. He was bundled into a jeep and driven to the helicopter landing zone just like any embassy employee. The Prime Minister, Long

Boret, who was on the Khmer Rouge's public "death list," declined Dean's invitation along with all but one of his cabinet. So did Lon Nol's brother Lon Non. So did Prince Sirik Matak, another "traitor" and the only leader of the 1970 coup still in Phnom Penh. He sent Dean a letter:

> Dear Excellency and friend. I thank you very sincerely for your letter and for your offer to transport me towards freedom. I cannot, alas, leave in such a cowardly fashion.
>
> As for you and in particular for your great country, I never believed for a moment that you would have this sentiment of abandoning a people which has chosen liberty. You have refused us your protection and we can do nothing about it. You leave and it is my wish that you and your country will find happiness under the sky.
>
> But mark it well that, if I shall die here on the spot and in my country that I love, it is too bad because we all are born and must die one day. I have only committed this mistake of believing in you, the Americans.
>
> Please accept, Excellency, my dear friend, my faithful and friendly sentiments. Sirik Matak.

At about 9 A.M. that morning the first of the huge transport helicopters swooped down onto "Landing Zone Hotel," a football ground several hundred yards from the embassy. Three hundred and sixty heavily armed Marines, equipped with M-16 rifles and grenade launchers, leaped out to secure the area in a dramatic show of force. Some American officials had feared there would be riots in the city and a rush for the landing zone—as there had been in Danang in South Vietnam—when the people finally realized the Americans were abandoning them. There was nothing of the sort. The gap between Khmer and American perception remained as large as ever.

About one hundred Cambodians gathered outside the embassy and the landing zone, watching curiously this final spasm of American effort. Some of them actually seemed to believe that the helicopters were bringing in reinforcements and they offered to help control the traffic. When Major Alan Armstrong arrived at the landing zone he saw in the crowd his personal driver, a young soldier who was immensely proud to be working for the Americans, and who had for months driven Armstrong with courage and skill through countless rocket barrages along the scarred roads to the war. He and Armstrong liked each other very much, and he smiled at the major now. Armstrong could not smile; he realized that the boy had no idea what was happening.

By just after 10 A.M. the full complement—82 Americans, 159 Cambodians and 35 "third-country nationals"—had been loaded without incident into the relays of helicopters. They were given leaflets that read "Welcome Aboard, Marine Helicopter Inc. (Flight 462) Non-Stop to the Gulf of Thailand. . . . The Pilots and Crew of this aircraft are the most professional and highly trained known to man. We hope you enjoy your flight." Dean sent a last message to Washington. "A.m. Embassy Phnom Penh is closing down its communication facilities. . . ." and, dressed in a dark suit with a striped tie and matching striped handkerchief in his breast pocket, the last American representative was driven to the landing zone. He carried under his arm the Stars and Stripes. When he strode toward his helicopter, Cambodian children behind the Marines waved and called out "O.K., bye-bye. O.K., bye-bye." As the last machine lifted out the last load of Marines, the Khmer Rouge began to fire on the landing zone from across the river. A mortar round killed one of the bystanders who had stood patiently watching the caravan disappear.

The blow that was dealt to morale by the flight of the Americans can be imagined. Nonetheless, with remarkable courage, the army continued to fight, and Prime Minister Long Boret tried to devise an orderly surrender. He received no response to his overtures. The Communists moved steadily in on Phnom Penh. In Washington, Lon Nol's ambassador, Um Sim, expressed his emotions: "Let's face it," he said, "you took advantage of us, of our inexperience. As you are much cleverer than we are, you could induce us into this fighting. . . . If the United States had respected our neutrality then the fighting, the killing and things might not have happened." Kissinger, asked to comment on this accusation, replied:

What has happened in Cambodia is heartbreaking. Our political opponents speak of our intervention in Cambodia as if we had not had enough war on our hands and involved a neutral country for the fun of it. In fact, we went into Cambodia because there were 60,000 North Vietnamese soldiers in the sanctuaries all along the frontier. We captured 15,000 of them and we seized 20,000 tons of material. After that our losses in Vietnam fell from 100 to 50 a week and finally to 10. Our operations in Cambodia prevented the North Vietnamese from launching planned offensives in regions 3 and 4, against Saigon and in the Delta. We did it to protect the evacuation of our troops from Vietnam and, from this point of view, Cambodia was a success.

Moreover, from the beginning, from 1970, we abstained from all activities in Cambodia apart from those helping the withdrawal of our troops. We fixed a limit of 21 miles for our penetration and we avoided operations which could have been interpreted as support for the government in Phnom Penh. I must say that I have great admiration for the Cambodian government, which stayed in place after our departure, and I am sad that, in these final days, we were not able to provide it with ammunition. I am not proud of that.

CHAPTER 24

The Beginning

WHEN THE first strange soldiers walked along Monivong Boulevard early on the morning of April 17, they waved as the townspeople cheered, embraced them and wept. Small children danced around, the government ordered all troops to cease fire. At last, it seemed to those who saw the scene, the fratricide was over, guns would be laid aside, the "gentle, smiling Khmers" would reunite.

It was a cruel deception, and a short one. This first contingent was a tiny group, mostly students from Phnom Penh acting, some say, under the influence of Lon Nol's brother Lon Non, who still apparently imagined that victory could be denied the Communists if only a new government seized power from Long Boret. In less than two hours, the Khmer Rouge themselves arrived.

They marched in from all sides of the city, those from the south arriving first. All in black, wearing checked scarves and Ho Chi Minh sandals, their most obvious qualities were their youth and their exhaustion. Hung around with bandoliers and shouldering their AK-47s, they strode through the town.

Within a few hours they had stationed themselves at strategic crossroads all over the city. They did not smile much, and the relief with which most people had begun the day began to dissipate; joy was replaced by concern, concern by trepidation, trepidation by fear.

Toward the end of the morning a platoon of the young victors marched into the grounds of the Preah Ket Melea hospital. Many of the doctors had already fled, and here, as in most other hospitals, patients lay untended in filth and agony. A mother had been sitting motionless with her children; she waved the flies off the bloated, patchy body of one dying baby. Wrapped in brown paper beside her, its feeding bottle by its head, lay the dead body of her other child. A soldier with a gaping, untreated stomach wound gasped for water he could not have swallowed. The corridors, on which bodies, alive and dead, were piled, were awash with blood and excrement.

The soldiers marched through the wards, and then they ordered all those patients who could walk to get off their beds and push out through the doors those who could not move. And so, in the heat of the day, a most dreadful parade began.

From hospitals all over the city crawled and hobbled the casualties of the war, the first victims of the "peace." Men with no legs bumped down stairs, and levered themselves on skinny arms along the street; blind boys laid their hands on the shoulders of crippled guides, soldiers with one foot and no crutches dragged themselves away, parents carried their wounded children in plastic bags that oozed blood. Beds were pushed slowly, jolting along, the blood and plasma bottles breaking. One father stumbled through the heat with his daughter tied in a sheet around his neck. A man with a foot hanging only by skin to the end of his leg begged Father François Ponchaud, a Jesuit priest, for refuge as he passed his house. The priest refused him, feeling as he did so that he had lost the last shred of human dignity. With thousands of others the man stumbled along toward the countryside.

This was only one stage in the purification of the city. At the same time soldiers ordered everyone out of the grounds of the Hotel Phnom, where the Red Cross had hoped to establish a neutral zone. Many Cambodians and almost all the foreigners who remained in Phnom Penh now made their way to the French embassy, which, despite Sihanouk's order to close, was still manned by the vice-consul. All together, about 800 foreigners and 600 or more Cambodians, among them Sirik Matak, now facing the consequences of his brave refusal of John Dean's escape offer, crowded into the compound.

It afforded no refuge. Within forty-eight hours, the vice-consul was informed by the Khmer Rouge that Cambodia was owned by its people and that the new government recognized no such concepts as territoriality or diplomatic privilege; if he did not expel all the Cambodians then the lives of the foreigners would also be forfeit. Cambodian women married

to foreigners could remain; Cambodian men in the same situation could
not. A few marriages were hastily arranged so that some women could
acquire French citizenship. No resistance was offered. The foreigners
stood and wept as their husbands, friends, lovers, servants, colleagues
were hustled through the embassy gates.

Within a fortnight the foreigners were taken out of the country in
trucks. Almost none of those Cambodians has ever reappeared. The new
authorities later announced that Sirik Matak had been executed. So was
Prime Minister Long Boret, who had surrendered to the victors with great
dignity. So was Lon Nol's brother Lon Non.

When the hospitals had been emptied, it was the turn of the ordinary
townspeople and the refugees. They were ordered to abandon their
houses, their apartments, their shacks, their camps. They were told to
take with them only the food they could carry. Those who were separated
from their families were not allowed to seek them. No demurral was
allowed. As the sun began to sink that afternoon, men, women and children all over Phnom Penh straggled bemused out of the side streets and
onto the highways. The roads became clogged; people could shuffle forward only a few yards at a time. In the crush, hundreds of families were
split, and as they moved on more and more people fell under the strain.
The old and the very young were the first to go; within a few miles of the
city center more and more bodies were to be seen lying where their
relatives had been forced to leave them.

Out on the roads the evacuees found that the Communists had accumulated stocks of food in places. But these and supplies of water were
not adequate for more than two and a half million people. When the
townspeople asked how they were to eat, where they could find drugs,
where they were to go, the response was one with which they were soon
to become familiar. *"Angka"* or *"Angka Loeu"*—"The Organization"
or "Supreme Organization"—would provide. *Angka* would instruct
them. The nature of *Angka* was not clear to the evacuees at first, but
within hours millions of Cambodians had realized that its orders, transmitted through the fierce young soldiers who supervised their trek, were
to be obeyed instantly, and that complaints were often met by immediate
execution. As they walked into that first night of April 17, 1975, they were
told that from now on only *Angka* ruled and that Cambodia was beginning
again. This was "Year Zero."

It is not the purpose of this book to describe conditions in Cambodia,
or Democratic Kampuchea, as the country was renamed, in Year Zero

and the years that followed it, in minute detail.* Information on conditions there has been difficult to obtain and often impossible to verify. In April 1975, Cambodia was almost completely cut off from the outside world, and for three years it hardly opened its frontiers, except to Chinese technicians and advisers. Throughout that time it was in a state of siege; the new regime was engaged in wars against the country's past and against its external enemies.

The principal sources of news were refugees who fled to Thailand, and Radio Phnom Penh, the official voice of Democratic Kampuchea, and then refugees in Vietnam and the Vietnamese media. When the refugees first arrived in Thailand in the summer of 1975, they brought such terrible tales that there was a tendency among Western journalists and experts to dismiss them; they seemed to fit too neatly with the predictions of blood bath that American officials had been making for years in Vietnam and that had not, in the event, proved accurate there. Refugees, it was argued, inevitably decry the land they have fled. But refugees' descriptions have often proved accurate enough; those from Stalin's Russia and Hitler's Germany in the 1930s provide two contemporary examples. Moreover, people who fled from different parts of Cambodia over a three-year period to either Thailand or Vietnam spoke of Khmer Rouge conduct in similar terms. Their accounts were indirectly underwritten by Radio Phnom Penh's explanations of government policies and then, in 1978, by the commmentaries that the Vietnamese media made on Democratic Kampuchea. When the bias of all these sources was discounted they tended to complement rather than contradict one another and provided a consistent, if not necessarily complete, account of life in Democratic Kampuchea.

It seemed a vast and somber work camp where toil was unending, where respite and rewards were nonexistent, where families were abolished and where murder was used as a tool of social discipline. The refugees claimed that after that terrible march out of Phnom Penh and other towns the "new people" had to write biographies of themselves. Anyone, they claimed, associated with the Lon Nol government—officers in the army, civil servants, teachers, policemen—risked death. So, they said, did those who were educated, those who questioned the *Angka* or complained, those who made love outside of marriage, and those who

---

* Readers who wish to obtain a full account of the nature of Khmer Rouge rule should read *Cambodia: Year Zero*, by François Ponchaud. The French Jesuit lived ten years in Cambodia until May 1975 and has devoted most of his time since to trying to understand Khmer Communism.

could in any way be associated with Vietnam. The wives and families of these "traitors" faced execution too. The manner of execution was often brutal. Babies were torn apart limb from limb, pregnant women were disemboweled. Men and women were buried up to their necks in sand and left to die slowly. A common form of execution was by axe handles to the back of the neck. That saved ammunition.

During 1977 and 1978 the purges extended into the *Angka* itself, and so an increasing number of Khmer Rouge officials themselves began to flee to Thailand. They confirmed the stories that earlier refugees, their victims, related.

In 1978, under pressure of a new war with Vietnam, the country began to open slightly. Relations with other Southeast Asia nations were strengthened, and trade was increased. A group of Yugoslav journalists were invited to visit. They produced articles and a film in which they made only a thin attempt to disguise their dislike of the regime. Scandinavian ambassadors on a visit from Peking were dismayed by what they saw.

Three years after its fall, Phnom Penh was still an almost empty city. Some quarters were carefully tended. In others, wrecked cars lay where they had been abandoned in April 1975, and grass grew through the cobblestones. Some parks and gardens were now vegetable gardens; shops, hotels and kiosks were all closed. None of the apparatus of modern government existed; almost every office in the various ministries was deserted. About ten thousand workers were trucked in daily to run the few services essential to the *Angka*'s leadership. There was no postal system, no currency, no telephone. The main link to the outside world was one fortnightly flight to Peking. The few foreign diplomats stationed in Phnom Penh were confined to their houses in a single street, refused permission to communicate with each other, and denied such normal diplomatic privileges as secure mail or radio contact with their capitals.

Both the Scandinavians and the Yugoslavs noted that young people were far more in evidence than the old. In factories, lathes were worked by children so small they had to stand on boxes to reach them; at the Port of Kompong Som, small boys manned the docks and crewed fishing boats. Children were servicing Phnom Penh, and the Scandinavians said they saw only young people in the fields they passed. The diplomats refused to speculate on what had happened to the adults, but one of them said of the country, "It was like an absurd film. It was like a nightmare. It is difficult to believe that it is true." But it was even more difficult to deny, and it demanded an attempt at explanation.

369

The first act of Khmer Rouge rule—the instant evacuation of Phnom Penh and other towns in April 1975—symbolized its absolute nature. Such an action was unprecedented in recent revolutionary history. The Chinese did not empty Shanghai, the Algerians left Algiers, Castro was prepared to face up to the corruption of Havana. After the event several explanations were offered by Cambodian Communist officials. The first of them was the problem of feeding the urban population. By April 1975, Cambodia was destitute. Vast areas of the countryside were desolated by bombardment and neglect, and about three and a half million people in the cities were totally dependent upon the inadequate American airlift. U.S. government documents show that after this was ended by the rocketing of Pochentong airport on April 11, the government possessed stocks that would have fed the population for at most ten days.* Private hoarding may have been considerable—François Ponchaud estimates that there may have been about one month's supply of food in the city—but when the Khmer Rouge entered Phnom Penh on April 17 they faced an acute food crisis.

The Communists lacked the transport necessary to move supplies into the cities, particularly Phnom Penh. As the American government itself formally acknowledged, there was no way in which the urban population could be fed in place without outside help and, specifically, without an airlift. By its nature such help could be provided only by the United States, or by the United Nations, or perhaps by the independent relief organizations. Each of these presented the Khmer Communists with obvious political problems. American aid was out of the question. The United Nations had twice denied the GRUNK a seat in the General Assembly and to retain Lon Nol there, while the relief organizations had been working, in effect, for the Khmer Rouge's enemy, sustaining those who had fled their control. If the victims wished to seek help from none

---

* The U.S. embassy's weekly summary of events for the State Department, "The Khmer Report," of April 1, 1975, noted that "Opening rice stocks March 31 amounted to 6,122 metric tons representing a nine-day supply based on daily distribution of 545 metric tons to the population at large and 100 metric tons under P.L. 480 Title II program. The rice airlift increased in the last two days to 20 and 23 sorties which compensated for interruptions on March 23 and March 28. The daily average since the inception of the airlift on February 27 now stands at 12.5 sorties/505 metric tons." The draft U.S. AID Termination Report sub-. sequently noted that "As of mid-April GKR [Government of the Khmer Republic] owned rice stocks to feed the estimated two to three million people who lived in Phnom Penh and the enclaves or served in the FANK (otherwise termed the 'rice-deficit population') were about 6,500 metric tons." There were, of course, other foods besides rice. A U.N. official, W. G. Sampson, later wrote that he saw abundant supplies of fish and vegetables around Phnom Penh in March 1975.

of these three, the only alternative was to take the people to where at least the possibility of food existed.

But the food imperative cannot fully explain the evacuation. Other government-held towns, like Battambang, did not present the same logistical problems—yet they too were summarily emptied. Moreover, supplies in the countryside were limited. Over the past three years and in particular since the end of the American bombing in 1973, the Khmer Rouge had repaired some of the worst damage in the areas they controlled, had rigorously collectivized agriculture, and had accumulated some rice stocks. Exactly how large these were is not known, but there is no evidence that they were adequate to feed the population of the entire country for long. The starvation the people experienced through the summer of 1975 was, according to refugees, far worse than anything during the war.

Furthermore, even if abundant stocks in the countryside had existed, they might have explained the principle of the evacuation, but not its absolute, brutal nature, its failure to make provision for the sick, the very young and the old. Such behavior was dictated by political priorities. To understand these one has to consider such factors as the comparative sizes of the forces involved and the expectations the Cambodian Communists held of their enemies.

The reactions of the world outside to a Khmer Rouge victory must have been nearly impossible for the men in the jungle to predict. But the historical fear of Khmer leaders that their country would be swallowed up can scarcely have been more acute than in April 1975. To the west were 44 million Thais with a strong army and economy, and the backing of the United States. To the east was Vietnam, which was about to be reunited after thirty years into a nation of 48 million with all the captured military hardware that the United States had poured in over the past decade. In the middle there were somewhere between seven and eight million Khmers, almost all of them exhausted, about half of them crammed into the towns. Huge areas of the countryside, particularly the eastern borders with Vietnam, were uninhabited and undefended.

Although the North Vietnamese had, at Chinese insistence, allowed more supplies of arms down the Trail, relations between them and the Khmer Rouge leadership had continued to deteriorate through 1974 and early 1975. Almost the whole length of the frontier, including the offshore islands, where oil deposits were thought to lie, was in dispute. We know

now that the indigenous Cambodian Communists feared that Hanoi intended to incorporate a socialist Cambodia into a Vietnamese-dominated Indochinese Federation. Radio Phnom Penh has declared that "they wanted to swallow us in 1970, but they could not. They entered into negotiations in 1973 in an attempt to swallow us, but they could not succeed. They tried again in 1975." According to the Cambodians, Hanoi's plan in 1975 was to capture Saigon and then immediately march upon Phnom Penh "in order to impose their control over us. This time again, they were a step behind Cambodia. Cambodia won victory before them." Saigon fell thirteen days after Phnom Penh.

There was also the fear of aggressive American reaction to the defeat of Lon Nol. The CIA had had agents in the last enclaves held by the government. Communist leaders later said they feared that these networks would have remained behind in radio contact with controllers in Thailand, under orders to exploit discontent, sabotage Communist policies, provoke insurrections and incite food riots. The fear was justified. In his book, *Decent Interval,* the former CIA agent Frank Snepp describes how the Khmer Rouge decision to evacuate the towns broke all the agency's spy rings. One CIA agent has separately recounted how he listened in Bangkok in April 1975 as one of his operatives in Kompong Speu screamed over her radio: "They are breaking down the door. What should I do with the radio?" He did not reply. "What should I do?" she cried again. He still said nothing. Her last words were, "You people are worse than the French."

As the Khmer Rouge herded the population out of Phnom Penh some cadres explained to the people that the United States was about to bomb Cambodia again—this time the cities, not the countryside. Such a prediction might now sound absurd; it may not have seemed so there and then. There was the Christmas 1972 bombing of Hanoi as precedent, and throughout the final stages of the war Kissinger and Ford had warned that the United States could not afford such a blow to its credibility as defeat in Indochina. Had not Kissinger himself espoused the need for irrational and unpredictable behavior in international politics? Was he not the artisan, if not the architect, of the "Madman Theory" of war? We know, from their own accounts, that the North Vietnamese leaders—who had considerable worldliness and understanding of American politics—feared almost until the end that their 1975 drive on Saigon would provoke armed American intervention. To men who had lived for up to twelve years in the dark mountains and jungles of Cambodia, with almost no direct contact with the world outside, and who had felt the impact of the American bombardment, the laws passed by the U.S. Congress almost three years before must have seemed slight protection. The way in which the United States reacted to the Cambodian seizure of an American container ship, the S.S. *Mayaguez*, on May 12, 1975, and immediately bombed Cambodia again (with Kissinger demanding B-52 strikes against the country) to reassert American "toughness," showed that these laws were indeed inadequate and American intentions unpredictable.*

The uncertainties of external threat can only have been compounded by enormous problems of internal social and political control. The army had been rebuilt since that devastating summer of 1973, when American air power had ravaged it. But the slaughter had only abated since then, it had not ended. By the best accounts the army numbered around 70,000 regulars at the start of the year, many of them politically inexperienced boys and girls. How many died in the final three months is not known, but Communist casualties were, as always, terrible. As on the Lon Nol side, children were thrust continually into the war with almost no military training and no ideological commitment. The Party's cadres were hardened now, but they were still not numerous. (Pung Peng Cheng, Sihanouk's *chef du cabinet*, estimated that by the end of the war they numbered around one thousand.) Many of them were fully occupied in administering the four million or so people who already lived (often unwillingly, to judge by the refugee movements in 1974) in the "liberated" areas. They were too few to be able to supervise the raw army once the discipline that war imposes had gone.

The Communists, according to Pung Peng Cheng, did not expect the 1975 dry season to bring them victory when it began on January 1. By the middle of February, however, it was clear to Khmer Rouge leaders that what John Gunther Dean called "an uncontrolled solution"—their total victory—was imminent. They took the decision to empty the cities at the Second National Congress of the Front, which met at the end of that month. How they would have behaved had their assumption of power been more orderly, gradual or controlled, is impossible to assess. The Prime Minister of Democratic Kampuchea, Pol Pot (previously known as Saloth Sar) subsequently admitted that the evacuation had been an unplanned reaction to the unfolding of events. But the towns, of course, were incompatible with the new society that they intended to construct

* The *Mayaguez* incident provided in microcosm an illustration of the way in which U.S. policy toward Cambodia had been conducted since 1969. A synopsis of the affair, based principally on Pentagon documents declassified under the Freedom of Information Act, is included in the Notes.

on the ruins of Sihanouk's and Lon Nol's Cambodia. Khieu Samphan had denounced them in his 1959 thesis. They were the Sodoms that men like Saloth Sar, Ieng Sary, Hou Youn, Hu Nim and Khieu Samphan himself had rejected. They had also become the fortresses from which they had been pursued in the sixties and from which outright war had been launched against them in the seventies. Khmer Rouge leaders later explained that they greatly feared the corrupting effects the towns would have upon their unformed troops. Pol Pot declared that the evacuation was "one of the important factors" in safeguarding "the fruits of the revolution. . . . [It] was decided before victory was won, that is, in February, 1975, because we knew that before the smashing of all sorts of enemy spy organizations, our strength was not enough to defend the revolutionary regime." Implicitly confirming refugee accounts of the ferocity with which perceived "enemies" had since been pursued, Pol Pot continued, "Judging from the struggles waged from 1976 to 1977, the enemy's secret-agent network lying low in our country was very massive and complicated. But when we crushed them, it was difficult for them to stage a comeback. Their forces were scattered in various cooperatives that are in our grip. Thus we have the initiative in our hands."

Refugees have constantly spoken of the starvation as well as the terror they have endured since April 1975. The government's determination to carry the Maoist principle of self-reliance to lengths of which Mao himself had never dreamed, made this inevitable. But any government would have been confronted with almost insurmountable problems of food and agriculture in April 1975. Their scale was well described in the draft Termination Report prepared by the U.S. AID team. It was written just after John Gunther Dean and his staff fled Phnom Penh, and it reflects to some extent the anguish of junior officials forced to implement policies they felt were destructive.

The report noted that "Cambodia slipped in less than five years from a significant exporter of rice to large-scale imports, and when these ended in April 1975, to the brink of starvation." The country faced famine. "To avert a major food disaster Cambodia needs from 175,000 to 250,000 metric tons of milled rice to cover the period July 7 to mid-February 1976." Yet the vast bulk of Cambodia's rice would not be harvested until December. "Even with completely favorable natural conditions, the prospects for a harvest this year good enough to move Cambodia very far back toward rice self-sufficiency are not good. . . ." Too much damage had been done. The report noted that the land would be seriously over-grown, seed and fuel would be short, and that up to 75 percent of draft animals had been destroyed by the war. Moreover, most of the planting would have to be done "by the hard labor of seriously malnourished people. . . . Without substantial foreign aid the task will be brutally diffi-cult and the food-supply crisis can be expected to extend over the next two or three years. . . ."

Given how the Khmer Rouge actually behaved, U.S. AID's conclusion was significant:

> If ever a country needed to beat its swords into plowshares in a race to save itself from hunger, it is Cambodia. The prospects that it can or will do so are poor. . . . Therefore, without large-scale exter-nal food and equipment assistance there will be widespread starva-tion between now and next February. . . . Slave labor and starvation rations for half the nation's people (probably heaviest among those who supported the republic) will be a cruel necessity for this year, and general deprivation and suffering will stretch over the next two or three years before Cambodia can get back to rice self-sufficiency.

That is very nearly how refugees and, by implication, the Phnom Penh Radio described what has happened in Cambodia since April 1975.

Throughout 1975 the population (particularly the "new people" from the towns) suffered terribly from lack of food; hundreds of thousands may well have died of starvation and of disease. Western medicine was dis-carded, and there were almost no drugs in the country; at one stage the Prime Minister himself admitted that traditional herbal remedies had been ineffective and that 80 percent of the people were suffering from malaria. In 1976 slightly more food was available and Chinese quinine was im-ported. The 1977 harvest was poor, but by the summer of 1978 Radio Phnom Penh was claiming that every Cambodian received 900 grams of rice a day. Refugees asserted that daily rations were usually much less, but certainly rice supplies should by then have been adequate. Immense efforts had been made to rebuild the country's agricultural system, and the eleventh century rather than the 1960s was the model.

The civilization of Angkor was founded upon the control of water in an area where the monsoon is too heavy and too short. The enormous res-ervoirs, intricate canals and careful dams prevented flooding, created hydraulic power, allowed the building of the wats, increased rice produc-tion, and provided year-long labor for the slave population. It was the dams and the canals—not the wats—that the Siamese invaders destroyed. Between 1969 and 1975 the agricultural system had been destroyed again, and in April 1975 the entire population was mobilized to construct a new one.

Phnom Penh Radio emphasized the importance of irrigation, and the population was directed to build new dams and canals. "The key question in agriculture is the water supply. Solidarity groups are building dams, digging ditches, constructing checkerboards of new field embankments. In the fertile northwest . . . they are building ditches several kilometers long. These are also used as communications lines. Seedlings are transported along them in boats sailing to distant fields."

During the Angkor period agriculture supported the city. This time—as Khieu Samphan's 1959 thesis had proposed—it was eventually intended to sustain industrialization. "Grow, grow everything," the radio exhorted. "Particular attention must be paid to rice, for rice means everything. Rice means steel, factories, energy, fuel and tractors." Only a strong agricultural base could provide the people of Democratic Kampuchea with the independence or "sovereignty" they required and deserved. The people must "master" everything—the elements, production, territory; they must "rely on our own strength," "defend and construct the country," and "take our destiny in our hands."

The nature of those hands was drastically changed; the creation of a new Cambodian man was even more important than the construction of a new Cambodian economy. The old individualism, which had contributed to the corruption of former regimes, was replaced by collectivism; the old villages, where life revolved around the seasons, the pagoda and respect for the monarchy, gave way to work camps or cooperatives controlled by the *Angka*.

Family life was subordinate to that of the cooperative. Men and women often lived apart. Food was gathered and cooked centrally; from January 1977, meals were eaten communally. The chairman of the cooperative, usually a Khmer Rouge veteran, was responsible for production. In most areas work began before dawn at around 5 A.M. and continued until dark with a break for lighter work in the shade of the trees in the heat of the day. In some areas floodlighting or a full moon meant that an extra shift was added. As the radio said, "Democratic Kampuchea is one huge work site; wherever one may be, something is being built."

All forms of address that betokened social or family relationships were abolished, and names were simplified. Father, mother, doctor were all replaced by "comrade." Theravada Buddhism, which had been so closely integrated into every aspect of Cambodian life since the thirteenth century, was abolished as the state religion. Article 20 of the new 1976 constitution declared, "Every Cambodian has the right to worship according to any religion and the right not to worship according to any religion. Reactionary religion, which is detrimental to Democratic Cambodia and the Cambodian people, is absolutely forbidden." The bonzes were driven from their wats, derobed of their saffron and sent into the fields; they were dismissed by the radio and by cadres as parasites. The wats became rice stores.

Refugees who came to Thailand during the first year after April 1975 said that political instruction was then minimal—partly perhaps because fifteen-year-olds with AK-47s do not necessarily have much to say, and partly because communications with the central government developed slowly. Subsequently, the training of new cadres allowed the spread of political education. Evenings not spent at work were devoted to group sessions in which workers "reflect on their lives" and "learn from their experience at work." Every ten days, larger educative sessions were called.

At first the *Angka* was everything—the source of all power, of all influence, of all decisions. As François Ponchaud has pointed out, the radio spoke of it in terms of almost religious respect. The *Angka* was "believed in," it was "loved," its "blessings" were "remembered," it was the source of all happiness and inspiration. This "happiness" of the Cambodian people, now that the inequalities and the exploitations of the past were renounced, was constantly acclaimed by the radio. For the first time, the people were told, they were free of all corrupt and thieving outsiders. Until now they had been oppressed and wretched, in particular under the yoke of the fascist Lon Nol and his imperialist supporters. Now, at last, Kampucheans had mastered their soil and were free to live joyously and independently. "The imperialists, the capitalists and the feudalists utterly destroyed our national soul for hundreds of years. Now our soul has risen again, thanks to our revolutionary *Angka*." "For thousands of years the colonialists, imperialists and reactionary feudalists have dragged us through the mud. Now we have regained our honor, our dignity; now we smell good again."

The radio constantly declared that Kampucheans reflected the revolutionary spirit, the spirit of *Angka*, "a spirit of combative struggle, economy, inventiveness and a very high level of renunciation." "Renunciation," said the refugees, had three components: "renunciation of personal attitudes," "renunciation of material goods," and "renunciation

377

of personal behavior." The individual must find complete joy in working for the *Angka*, must forswear personal property, family relationships and such attitudes as pride, contempt, envy.

As during the war, special attention was paid to the development of children. They were often brought up communally; if they still lived with their parents, they were taught to have no regard for the concept of family and to treat their relations simply as anyone else in the group. Parents, on the other hand, were taught to honor their "comrade children," whose spirits are uncorrupted by the past. Children were often used as spies within villages; the radio has said that many of them "have held aloft their spirit of vigilance and creativity [and] . . . have become engaged in patrolling their villages and communes with the highest revolutionary spirit."

From the moment of victory in April 1975 it was clear that the new rulers had no place for Sihanouk in Democratic Kampuchea. He was not officially informed of the capture of Phnom Penh; a wire-service message was given him at an embassy reception in Peking. He refused to believe the first reports of the evacuation of the cities, denouncing them as Western lies. After that he received no word at all from his country, and to avoid the persistence of reporters he went into "voluntary exile" in North Korea to be spared "indiscreet questions." It is said that in his conviction that he would never again go home he wrote a song called "Farewell Cambodia."

It seemed that the revolutionary leadership did not seek his return; his popularity could only have been destabilizing. However, Chou En-lai apparently insisted on it, and Sihanouk agreed, with some trepidation, after Khieu Samphan came to Pyong Yang and promised that he could remain head of state for life. Chou congratulated the Prince on his courage and patriotism, and on September 9 Sihanouk flew home with his wife, Monique, but without the entourage that had supported him in Peking. He was quoted by the Associated Press as saying to friends, "My return to Cambodia does not mean that I approve the cruel policy of the Khmer Rouge, but I must sacrifice my own views out of consideration for China and His Excellency Chou En-lai, who have done so much for Cambodia and myself."

At Pochentong airport he was greeted with honors and driven through the town to one of his homes. He later told friends that he was appalled by the echoing emptiness of the city he had built, with just a few pedestrians, a few bicycles, very few cars and scores of soldiers silhouetted on balconies and roof tops. One of the rare sorties he was allowed was to a textile factory that had resumed production near Pochentong. Women workers fell at his feet crying. After that he was kept pretty much to his quarters.

The Prince was allowed to preside over one meeting of the government but not to take any real part in it. However, the new leadership did still have one task for him—to journey abroad and add some luster to the regime. He flew back to Peking and told his cabinet and family about life in the new Cambodia. Without exception these men and women, who had worked with him throughout the war, bade him farewell and set off on the Trans Siberian railway, bound mostly for an uncertain, penurious future in Paris.

Sihanouk himself flew to New York to denounce the United States at the U.N. General Assembly. Then in Paris he gave a talk to a small group of correspondents. Sitting under a photograph of himself being handed an AK-47 rifle by Khieu Samphan, flanked by Khmer Rouge associates, he gave an unconvincing account of the glories of the new regime. Everything the Khmer Rouge had done was *"très raisonnable,"* and he was looking forward to returning. There would be 300,000 people in the capital eventually; this was ideal. (In 1978, there appear to have been only between ten and twenty thousand.) The evacuation was a good decision—starvation made it essential. Socialism in Cambodia was also fine; after all, Buddha was "a real socialist." Asked about reports of massacres he laughed his high laugh and said, "I was not there, but I do not think so. Our government has succeeded perfectly in establishing authority and order. Fighting exists only in the minds of some ugly Cambodians in Thailand and Paris. They fight from their nightclubs there."

He claimed that 600,000 people had been killed in the war, and over a million seriously wounded. Asked if Cambodia, like North Vietnam, would demand United States aid as reparations, he shouted, "We will never do so. Our blood is not to be commercialized. The United States will have to pay for its crimes in the pages of history."

As for himself, he lived alone with Monique. "Food is brought to me every morning by the food service of the army. I have three little revolutionary cooks working for me and my aunt is teaching them cuisine. I sleep in the bed I once had made for my hero, General de Gaulle. As I am very small, I am very comfortable. I just tell you this little detail for the lady readers." He claimed that Phnom Penh was fine now; it was not Sodom or Gomorrah but "Spartan with no nightclubs, no taxi girls." In the future he would be like the Queen of England inspecting schools and receiving ambassadors. "That keeps me quite busy, you know. And the revolutionaries who took arms and fought the United States—they deserve the government."

One month later he was in Peking's Friendship store for foreigners. Surrounded as usual by a small group of men and women, he was buying wooden animals for a trip he was about to make to sympathetic African countries. He said he was looking forward to it, but had no time to talk— he was so very busy. In January 1976, he returned with his wife and two children to Phnom Penh just in time to declare the new constitution, which abolished the monarchy of the last thousand years—"excellent."

In February 1976, Chou En-lai, Sihanouk's great friend and supporter, died. Sihanouk's protection was gone, the "Gang of Four" was in the ascendant in Peking, and Khieu Samphan's promise of life tenure of the presidency was forgotten. The Prince was immediately removed from office, and Khieu Samphan replaced him. In an emotional address over Radio Phnom Penh on April 4, 1976, Sihanouk declared, "It has been my great pride and honor from March 1970, to this day to accompany the most beloved Cambodian people in the great and prestigious historical march which is now leading Cambodia to a new era in which the people are the only true masters of their destiny and of the nation and fatherland. . . . All my wishes have been resolved without exception." The Council of Ministers expressed "regret" at his decision to retire "so as to have more time for the private life of his family," but they accepted it and proposed to build him a monument; he was awarded a pension of $8,000 a year—in a country where there is no currency.

Then the Prince disappeared. For over a year nothing was heard of him and some of his friends in the West began to fear for his life. Etienne Manac'h tried to discover his whereabouts; so did Senator Mansfield. Then, it seems, President Tito, an old comrade from the early days of the Nonaligned movement, insisted that his ambassador to Phnom Penh be allowed to confirm that the Prince was still alive. The Yugoslav diplomat was taken from his embassy and driven past Sihanouk's house, where the Prince could be seen in his garden. In 1978, as the war with Vietnam worsened and the men of Phnom Penh came under increasing pressure, they began to exploit Sihanouk's old appeal among the population; his name was attached to several denunciations of Hanoi.

The precise makeup of the government that succeeded Sihanouk was at first unclear. Refugees spoke much more of *Angka* than of individual leaders. Names like Khieu Samphan, Ieng Sary and Pol Pot did not readily come from their lips, nor did the Radio at first make much mention of them. Despite the obvious emphasis on collective measures, it was not until 1977 that the leading role of the Communist Party was acknowledged.

What happened among those few men and women who came out of the fields and the forests into the capital they had emptied in April 1975 is not yet known. But it is certain that the struggle among them was intense. Their disputes were influenced, above all, by the fighting that broke out immediately with their former Vietnamese allies and, to a lesser extent, by the upheavals in Chinese politics that followed the death of Chou En-lai and then that of Mao Tse-tung. It was not until the second half of 1977, by which time the struggle with the Vietnamese had intensified to the point of war, that the composition of the government began to become clear.

In some ways the new rulers of Phnom Penh conformed to Cambodian tradition; they were drawn from a tiny, inbred and self-perpetuating oligarchy. Lon Nol had replaced Sihanouk's scheming court with an equally scheming and much more corrupt military-bourgeois clique. The new elite was equally unrepresentative of Cambodian society. By 1978 the government appears to have been in the hands of about ten people related not only by intellectual training and shared revolutionary experience but also by marriage. The government was led by Pol Pot, the Secretary of the Cambodian Communist Party since 1963. Now he was Prime Minister as well. In charge of foreign affairs was Ieng Sary; defense was in the hands of Son Sen. The important post of Minister of Education, Culture and Information was held by Yun Yat, Son Sen's wife. The Minister of Social Action was Khieu Thirith, the wife of Ieng Sary. Her sister, Khieu Ponnary, was married to Pol Pot and ran the Association of Democratic Women of Kampuchea. The Vietnamese referred to them as either "the Pol Pot-Ieng Sary clique" or as "The Gang of Six." "All power is in the hands of Pol Pot and Ieng Sary and their wives who, to crown it, are sisters," commented *Nhan Dan*, the Vietnamese party paper in September 1978. "This kind of regime is cynically termed a 'democratic' regime."

The Vietnamese army paper published a profile of Pol Pot, noting accurately that "those who watched the Yugoslav television film on Democratic Cambodia could see that Pol Pot was the only smiling Cambodian in the film. 'When did you first come to know about Pol Pot?' I asked a Cambodian. He said, 'When I came home from the rice field one day I saw my two-year-old child lying dead in a heap of ashes with a half-finished piece of pumpkin soaked in blood in his mouth and my wife dying of a head wound. She was panting and whispering to me—"Try to find the murderer of our son and revenge me and our son." Then, I found out about Pol Pot.'

"Pol Pot," the paper continued, "became famous following the bloody purges involving not only hundreds of thousands of civilians killed and dealt with like rubbish and the disappearance in a way that is hard to understand of basic and middle-level cadres in the ruling machinery, but also of some of the well-known Cambodian leaders. . . . It seems that the Cultural Revolution has been copied by Phnom Penh in a hasty, but no less horrible manner.

"Pol Pot is a quiet man. We know of only a small number of talks he has delivered over the radio and some guiding documents he has written. . . . In commending a new group of cadres who assumed their duties in August 1977, Pol Pot told them about the Party-building task: 'Although a million lives have been wasted, our Party does not feel sorry. Our party needs to be strong.' "

Apart from blood and marital ties, the principal characteristics shared by these and many other leaders of the Cambodian government was their French education in the fifties and their graduation into the *maquis* in the year 1963. Those who, like Khieu Samphan, Hou Yuon and Hu Nim, fled Phnom Penh only in 1967, had played important roles during the war, but by 1977 they had all been eclipsed by the men of 1963. Khieu Samphan's duties as Chief of State were largely ceremonial, Hu Nim and Hou Yuon had disappeared altogether. According to Hanoi they had been executed.

Such exclusivity and other features of the Khmer Communist party remained mysterious. But some of its philosophy was elucidated by Pol Pot when he emerged as the country's undisputed leader—after he had disappeared for months—in September 1977. His five-hour speech over Radio Phnom Penh and his subsequent press conference in Peking provided the first detailed account of how the Khmer Rouge saw its own history.

He acknowledged for the first time that Democratic Kampuchea was run not just by the *Angka* but by a Marxist government, and that the Communist Party of Kampuchea was a Leninist organization in the vanguard of the revolution. Some of his rhetoric came straight from Mao, and the speech openly aligned Cambodia with China. As well as stressing self-reliance and collectivism, he spoke in strong terms of the persecution that the Khmer Communists had faced and overcome. The rift with Vietnam was not yet publicly proclaimed, but Pol Pot made obvious attempts to disassociate Cambodian Communism from that of its neighbor. It was now that he complained of the way in which the 1954 Geneva Conference had forced Khmer Communists to retire to Hanoi.

Pol Pot also described with bitterness the ruthlessness with which Sihanouk's police and army ("the enemy") had pursued the *maquis* in the sixties, and he emphasized the theme that the war and the revolution had unleashed a vast anger accumulated during long years of persecution. He acknowledged the undoubted truth that it was only the war that had made the Khmer Rouge, and Cambodia, what it was today. In 1970, he said, "Our force was still relatively isolated and inadequate. The situation underwent a tremendous change after the Lon Nol clique staged the reactionary coup of March 18, 1970. The whole nation quickly swung over to the side of the revolution . . . a broad national united front was thus formed . . . changes also took place in the world attitude toward us . . . this situation enabled our nationwide struggle to develop apace."

In talking of the new national anthem * he said, "Its essence is in the blood of our entire people, of those who fell for centuries past. The blood call has been incorporated into the national anthem . . . the blood has been turned into class and national indignation." It still had an outlet. The evacuation of the cities had scattered the enemies of the revolution but still, he declared, "In our new Cambodian society there also exist life-and-death contradictions, as enemies . . . are still planted among us to carry out subversive activities against our revolution."

By 1977, it seemed, the regime's zeal was directed more against those suspected of sympathy with Vietnam than against those suspected of harboring a reactionary past. The poor relations between the two Communist parties deteriorated further with their captures of Phnom Penh and Saigon. The exact course of events cannot yet be determined, but the public claims of the two sides, after their disputes became public in 1978, can help chart its direction.

In April 1975 the Vietnamese were still in the sanctuaries just inside

---

* The official translation of the national anthem of Democratic Kampuchea reads:

Bright red Blood which covers towns and plains
Of Kampuchea, our motherland,
Sublime Blood of Workers and peasants,
Sublime Blood of revolutionary men and women fighters!

The Blood changing into unrelenting hatred
And resolute struggle,
On April 17th, under the Flag of the Revolution,
Free from slavery!

Cambodia's eastern border that Sihanouk had given them in 1965 when, in Radio Phnom Penh's sarcastic words, "they had nowhere to stay in South Vietnam." Their refusal to depart "shows how ungrateful they are." Quarrels over the offshore islands and their promised oil deposits proved even more intractable. The Cambodians demanded that the Brevie line, which the French had drawn through the sea in 1939 for administrative purposes, be accepted as the border. The Vietnamese refused. The Cambodians laid claim to the large Vietnamese island of Phu Quoc and the Vietnamese occupied several islands of the Wai group, which Cambodia had controlled. In June 1975 Pol Pot flew to Hanoi and Peking in a vain attempt to find a solution. Talks continued sporadically, and the Vietnamese returned the Wai islands. But in May 1976, discussions over the frontier broke down completely, because, according to Phnom Penh, the Vietnamese presented a new draft map "which took away a vast part of Cambodia's territorial sea."

Skirmishing increased through 1976 and early 1977, and Radio Phnom Penh broadcast oblique references to the need for self-defense along the eastern border. The Cambodians have since claimed that the Vietnamese attempted several *coup d'états,* using cadres trained in Vietnam in the fifties and sixties, against the Phnom Penh government. There is good reason to believe that this is so. After one serious attempt in April 1977, the fortnightly flight from Peking was stopped for a time, and later the North Korean leader Kim Il Sung congratulated Phnom Penh's rulers on eradicating traitors in their midst. It was now that rigorous purges within the *Angka* itself began, and thousands more people died, accused of being agents of Vietnam.

The fighting along the border worsened through 1977, and in September that year General Giap flew from Hanoi to inspect the area. Cambodia claimed that Vietnam then began to attack in force. This is how Vietnam, for its part, described a Khmer Rouge attack on a Vietnamese village in October 1977:

All the houses were surrounded by Cambodian soldiers, who immediately opened fire and used machetes, axes, sabers and sharpened sticks to slay the villagers . . . A fleeing child was caught by a soldier who cut off his leg and threw him into the flames. All seven members of Mrs. Truong Thi Rot's family were beheaded. Rot was disemboweled and had a seven-month fetus placed on her chest. All eight members of Nguyen Van Tam's family were beheaded and the heads were put on a table for amusement. All eight persons in Nguyen Thi

Nganh's house were disemboweled, the intestines piled in one shocking heap. Mr. Quang's wife was also disemboweled. The killers took out her five-month fetus, then cut off her breast and chopped her body in three parts. Her two-year-old boy was torn in two and dumped into a well.

Such accounts are fairly characteristic of the way in which totalitarian governments speak of their enemies in wartime, but in this case they gain credibility both from refugee stories of life inside Cambodia and from the way in which the Khmer Rouge are known to have behaved in disputed villages along the Thai border. After a similar incident there, the foreign ministry in Phnom Penh merely asserted that the village was Cambodian anyway, and so of no concern to anyone else.

At the end of 1977 Phnom Penh denounced Hanoi publicly, broke diplomatic relations and treated the world to the unprecedented spectacle of two fraternal socialist nations at war. The Vietnamese immediately launched a massive invasion in January 1978. They attacked in main-force units, using tanks and artillery left behind by the Americans. The Cambodians relied upon the guerrilla methods with which they had repelled the Vietnamese a century before and with which the Viet Cong had, in the past, so successfully resisted American attacks. Tactical and logistical mistakes by Vietnamese commanders, together with fierce resistance by the Cambodians, halted the drive.

There was no way of knowing exactly how the fighting ebbed and flowed across the frontier through the 1978 dry season. Journalists were taken to the Vietnamese side of the border. Ha Thien, a pretty little harbor on the South China Sea, was deserted; its 30,000 people had fled from the Khmers. Tinh Binh, further east, was a ghost town, the wind banging the shutters, dogs roaming the streets. In Moc Hoa, the district capital of Kien Tuong province, the bulk of the population was evacuated. Village after village on either side of the border was empty, their rice fields left untended. Refugees huddled under tents; everywhere there were freshly dug graves. To the correspondents this Third Indochina War looked very like the First and Second. To the people themselves it may have felt even worse.

As the fighting continued, so did the purges within the *Angka*. Hanoi claimed that by early 1978 all the "Hanoi-Khmers" who had been sent back down the Trail after March 1970, and whose politics clearly clashed with those of the indigenous *maquis*, had been murdered. There is no reason to believe that this is false. "It is most enraging," said Hanoi

Radio, "to see that on the bodies of those murdered there are inscriptions reading 'Convicted for (sympathy) with Vietnam.' "

The Vietnamese army paper's profile of Pol Pot stated that

> In 1970 when Lon Nol staged a coup to overthrow Sihanouk . . . Pol Pot himself went over to our base asking us to help. . . . When the time came to liberate Phnom Penh, Pol Pot had six divisions in hand. Clad in black pajamas and wearing a striped scarf around his neck, Pol Pot once said with half-closed eyes and with a smile on his face: "How close our two fraternal countries are! What you comrades have done will be recorded in our country's history. . . ." Although we did not see his eyes clearly, we felt the tone of his words to be [honest] . . . But [after liberation] Pol Pot . . . ordered the arrest of all leading cadres of the divisions and units that had been trained by Vietnam . . . All Khmer cadres who returned from Vietnam to participate in the fight against the U.S. aggressors and their puppets to save the country have been murdered . . . Anyone who happens to speak a single word of Vietnamese is considered as committing a crime.

In another broadcast Hanoi said,

> What grieves us most is the case of 250 children of Khmer cadres who were sent to study in Hanoi during the war. They were called home by their parents after Cambodia was liberated. . . . They were all killed by Cambodian troops only some 300 meters inside the border. They screamed, cried and yelled to Vietnamese cadres on the other side of the border, "Please, come and help us, uncles." But the Vietnamese uncles stood powerless. . . .

Such accusations were not denied by the Cambodians. Indeed, Radio Phnom Penh exulted that "the Party has flushed out the Khmer-Vietnamese running dogs of the aggressor, expansionist and annexationist Vietnamese enemy who have sneaked their way into the ranks of our party . . . our youths have basically smashed and wiped out these agents."

By the middle of 1978 Hanoi was openly inciting the Cambodian people to rise and overthrow "the clique . . . the most disgusting murderers in the latter half of this century." The Vietnamese organized a resistance movement in the eastern provinces, said to be under the control of So Phim, who was formerly in the Khmer Communist leadership.

Each side asserted that the border disputes were only a minor part of the struggle. Hanoi declared that the rulers of Phnom Penh wished to distract their own and other people's attention from the suffering they [of Phnom Penh] had imposed upon Cambodia. Phnom Penh continued to claim that the war was caused by the Vietnamese Communists' old ambition of imposing a federation dominated by Hanoi on all Indochina. Hanoi's intention was "to annex Cambodian territory within a fixed period of time and eliminate the Cambodian race by Vietnamizing it." Radio Phnom Penh described how this threat could best be met: every Cambodian should kill thirty Vietnamese. This would eliminate the disparity in the sizes of the two nations.

The war between the two countries was slowed by unusually severe flooding during the 1978 rainy season, but at the end of the year, when the waters receded, the Vietnamese embarked on a new invasion of Cambodia's northeast. Pol Pot admitted in an interview that "some of our places may fall into their hands but since they will meet many difficulties, the longer they fight the more they will be worn down." Hanoi certainly appeared to hope that international distaste for the Khmer Rouge government would mute criticism of its offensive. But it must have been daunted not only by the courage with which the Cambodians had fought even for this government against Vietnam and by the prospects of administering a hostile conquered country, but also by the attitude of the Khmer Rouge's only sponsor, Peking.

A Cambodia independent of Vietnam had been a principle of Chinese foreign policy at least since the Geneva Conference of 1954. China had been the Cambodian Communists' only reasonably consistent supporter throughout the 1970–75 war, and when it ended only China was allowed real access to the country. Conversely, China's relations with Vietnam had deteriorated after Nixon's 1972 visit to Peking and after Hanoi's victory in 1975. Peking, evidently fearing the power of a united Vietnam, cut off all military aid to its southern neighbor. The Vietnamese then turned increasingly to the Soviet Union, and at the same time the Chinese began to build up the Cambodian army. The Vietnamese claimed that China encouraged Khmer Rouge harassment along the border and that Peking's purpose was "to provoke a disease that is not fatal to us, but would keep us always sick." Vietnam's fears of encirclement by China and Cambodia matched Chinese fears of encirclement by the USSR and a pro-Soviet Vietnam.

Throughout the first half of 1978, relations between Peking and Hanoi deteriorated rapidly. After Hanoi imposed severe restrictions on private business in Vietnam, about 150,000 Chinese fled to China. The Vietnamese blamed the exodus on groundless fears aroused by Chinese propaganda; Peking asserted that the Chinese were being persecuted. China cut off economic aid; Vietnam's three consulates in China were closed. Talks broke down, and by the end of the summer there was skirmishing along the Chinese-Vietnamese border. Vietnam asked its people to prepare for "a large-scale war of aggression."

It was in this context that the future of the Pol Pot regime had to be considered. One Vietnamese commentary claimed that "the reactionary Pol Pot–Ieng Sary clique is a bloodthirsty lackey clique, badly needed by the Chinese authorities to carry out their expansionist policy in Southeast Asia. The Chinese authorities are using the barbarous social system in Cambodia as a tool to oppose Vietnam and undermine its activities and then to proceed toward conquering all Southeast Asia."

By the middle of 1978 it was unclear how far the Chinese were still prepared to underwrite the Phnom Penh regime. Relations cannot have been improved by the fact that Phnom Penh had hailed the rise of "the Gang of Four" and the fall of Teng Hsiao-peng in 1976, nor by the Khmer Rouge's wholesale murder of Chinese residents of Cambodia. The Khmer Rouge's image abroad did not accord well with the broadly based foreign policy of entente that China pursued. Western leaders, including President Carter's Adviser for National Security Affairs, Zbigniew Brzezinski, complained to Peking and asked that the Chinese moderate Cambodian conduct. The British, American, Canadian and Norwegian governments submitted detailed dossiers on human-rights abuses in Cambodia to the United Nations Human Rights Commission in Geneva. Amnesty International also asked the Commission for an investigation. As a result of pressure of this sort, Western diplomats in Peking believed that the Chinese began to try, in the summer of 1978, to persuade Pol Pot to abandon his sectarian policies and create a broad-based front that would involve even Sihanouk once again.

As a result, the Prince's name was attached to more ritualistic denunciations of the Vietnamese and at the end of September Phnom Penh announced that he had attended a "banquet" with Pol Pot. In other concessions to world opinion, Ieng Sary invited Kurt Waldheim, the United Nations Secretary General, to Cambodia and the first American journalists were then allowed in. When the Vietnamese attacked in December, Cambodia was more vulnerable to being swallowed by its old enemy than at any time since the French imposed their protectorate in 1864. At the end of 1978 it seemed just possible that this weakness, together with the displeasure of China, might finally force the regime to eschew some of its more draconian policies. Sihanouk was the only man who had ever given Cambodia the semblance of peace, and the Chinese had always recognized his worth. If they could now compel his successors at least to pay lip service to their old enemy, perhaps power would one day be restored to him. It was only a glimmer of hope, but in Democratic Kampuchea hope was a scarce commodity by 1978.

By then the war in Cambodia had lasted eight and a half years. No one knew how many Khmers had died.* Casualties during 1970–75 were not counted; one figure that has often been cited is 500,000, but this could be an exaggeration. By the beginning of 1975, about five hundred people were thought to be dying on each side every week. It is even harder to assess the number of deaths over the natural rate since April 1975. Estimates have ranged from several hundred thousand to two million. Father Ponchaud, who had by then interviewed over a thousand refugees, himself believed that the higher figure was more accurate by spring 1978, and that, as a result of starvation, disease and execution, around a quarter of the population had died. This was what the Vietnamese claimed. Comparable figures for the United States would be fifty million deaths; for Britain, fourteen million. Such a massacre is hard to imagine, and the figure could not be verified. But, in a sense, this was not critical. What was important was to establish whether an atrocity had taken place. Given the burden of evidence, it was impossible not to agree with Hanoi's assertions that "In Cambodia, a former island of peace . . . no one smiles today. Now the land is soaked with blood and tears . . . Cambodia is hell on earth."

All wars are designed to arouse anger, and almost all soldiers are taught to hate and to dehumanize their enemy. Veterans of the combat zone are often possessed of a mad rage to destroy, and to avenge their fallen comrades. It does not always happen, however, that victorious armies have endured such punishment as was inflicted upon the Khmer Rouge. Nor does it always happen that such an immature and tiny force comes to power after its country's social order has been obliterated, and the nation faces the danger of takeover by a former ally, its ancient enemy. In Cambodia that did take place. In the last eight years, degree, law, moderation had been forsworn. The war and the causes for which it was fought had brought desolation while nurturing and then giving power to a little group of zealots sustained by Manichean fear.

---

* Population figures for the country have always been inadequate. In 1970 the generally accepted estimate was about seven million. In 1974 a report by the U.N. Economic and Social Commission put the population in 1974 at 7.9 million.

Sideshow

On Christmas Day 1978 their fears were realized. Under the transparent banner of a new "Kampuchean National United Front for National Salvation," the Vietnamese launched a dry season blitzkrieg toward Phnom Penh. Cambodian positions fell with extraordinary speed and the Khmer Rouge finally realized that they could not do without Sihanouk. He was dispatched to plead Kampuchea's case to the world. But, like Kissinger before them, the Communists had turned to the Prince too late. On January 7, 1979, hours after he arrived in Peking, Phnom Penh was captured and the Vietnamese installed a new "People's Revolutionary Council" to govern Cambodia on Hanoi's terms. The Khmer Rouge leaders fled to the jungles whence they had emerged less than four years before, vowing that they would mount a new guerrilla war against the enemy in Phnom Penh.

The Chinese leadership promised to support the Khmer Rouge in their struggle against "hegemonism" and accorded Sihanouk the same respect they had always shown him. Both in China and then at the United Nations, the Prince demonstrated that his consistency still lay in his concern for Cambodia. He wept when he was asked about Khmer Rouge abuses of power; the regime, he said, had denied his people "the basic rights of humanity: the right to be loved, to choose your wife and to be with your wife all the time; to have classical justice with lawyers; to be judged publicly." At the same time, however, he praised the Communists for their resistance to Vietnam and promised he would support their fight from abroad.

In an interview with the author in New York, Sihanouk reflected on the events of the last ten years. "In the sixties Cambodia survived because Lyndon Johnson rejected all the requests of his military that the United States invade Cambodia and remove Sihanouk. He thought the consequences would be very dangerous. But Nixon accepted those ideas. I did not know about the B-52 bombing in 1969. In 1968, I had told Chester Bowles, *en passant*, that the United States could bomb Vietnamese sanctuaries, but the question of a big B-52 campaign was never raised. I was not happy when the Vietnamese came further and further into Cambodia in 1969. Nor was Lon Nol. But what separated me and Lon Nol in 1970 was that he wanted to make war against the Communists and invite the United States into Cambodia. I knew that if we did so we would be completely involved in the Vietnamese war, we would lose our peace, and everything in Cambodia would be destroyed.

"If the United States had refused to help Lon Nol after the coup, he would have collapsed. Sihanouk would have returned and stopped the war. It didn't happen because Nixon and Kissinger did not want Sihanouk back. Nixon called Cambodia his "best investment." Kissinger hated me. For most of the war he refused to see me—until the Khmer Rouge were so strong it was too late. In 1970 the Khmer Rouge were only a few hundreds. In 1973 the Vietnamese tried to make them negotiate but it was too dangerous for them. They would then have had to share power and they wanted it all alone. They got it in 1975."

During his three years of house arrest since then, said Sihanouk, "I did not really know what was happening in my country. The BBC and Voice of America said it was terrible; every day I had to think about the possibility of being executed." Asked to explain the brutality, he spread his hands in a gesture of incomprehension and said, "Well, many of the soldiers I saw were only twelve or thirteen years old. Then their leaders were very ambitious. They wanted their names in history. They wanted to establish the most advanced and purest form of communism in the world. They told me that was their plan."

For the future he was uncertain. He now had to speak out in defense of the Pol Pot regime "because, despite its abuses of human rights, it is the genuine and the only government of Cambodia. It sprang from popular resistance to the United States and Lon Nol. If I fought against it, I would be a traitor. I feel capable of negotiating a settlement with Hanoi; I know the Vietnamese well. But Pol Pot will not now allow it. In future, we shall see. If we don't find a solution soon the Vietnamese will be in Cambodia forever."

Asked about the lessons of recent history, Sihanouk said that there was no one country to be blamed for the state of his nation. "There are only two men responsible for the tragedy in Cambodia today, Mr. Nixon and Dr. Kissinger. Lon Nol was nothing without them and the Khmer Rouge were nothing without Lon Nol. Mr. Nixon and Dr. Kissinger gave the Khmer Rouge involuntary aid because the people had to support the Communist patriots against Lon Nol. By expanding the war into Cambodia, Nixon and Kissinger killed a lot of Americans and many other people, they spent enormous sums of money—$4 billion—and the results were the opposite of what they wanted. They demoralized America, they lost all of Indochina to the Communists, and they created the Khmer Rouge."

One hundred and twenty years ago, in 1859, Henri Mouhot, the French naturalist, noted: "The present state of Cambodia is deplorable and its future menacing. . . . The population is excessively reduced by the incessant wars carried on against neighboring states." By 1979 incessant wars had once again reduced the population; once again the state of Cambodia was deplorable, its future menacing. "The humble people of Cambodia are the most wonderful in the world," said Sihanouk in New York. "Their great misfortune is that they always have terrible leaders who make them suffer. I am not sure that I was much better myself, but perhaps I was the least bad."

Afterword

AFTER THE collapse of the American effort in Indochina in April 1975, Secretary of State Henry Kissinger and President Gerald Ford asked that there be "no recriminations." Perhaps because the war had drained from the United States so much energy, their plea was acceded to. A "great debate" about America's role in Indochina did not take place.

For a time there was a reaction in the press and in Congress against the Presidential uses of power and against Kissinger's style of conducting foreign policy. Congress turned down his attempt to thrust the United States into Angola. During the 1976 election campaign, Kissinger's record became an issue. Right-wing Republicans criticized him for his greatest success—the achievement of more rational relations with the USSR—and some Democrats for his expediency and disregard for human rights. Candidate Jimmy Carter promised that if he were elected there would be no more Cambodias.

This backlash was brief. By the middle of President Carter's first term, the facts were hard to recall in Washington, and Carter's approach to foreign policy was unfavorably compared with Nixon's and Kissinger's techniques. Many of Carter's difficulties, including the way in which Congress was then beginning to assert itself, stemmed from the manner in which his predecessors had used their power. But Vietnam and Watergate were frequently referred to as "traumas" or "tragedies" rather than as specific acts and decisions by officials. Kissinger established himself in a

Washington exile, receiving statesmen and offering criticisms of his successors. His relationship with the press was even closer than when he had been in office. In Washington and in London, journalists wrote that if it had not been for Kissinger's brilliance, Carter's ineptitude would have resulted in chaos, and even urged Carter to invite Kissinger into his administration.

Neither Nixon nor Kissinger addressed the dimensions of the disaster in Cambodia. Nixon's memoirs, which were published in 1978, lacked understanding of the country at any time in recent years. He referred to the "highly organized" Khmer Rouge in March 1970 and to a close alliance between them and Hanoi throughout the war. David Frost, in his television interview, suggested to Nixon that American policy had brought Cambodia "into the holocaust which created the Khmer Rouge and destroyed a country which might otherwise have survived." He asked the former President, "Do you have, in a Quaker sense, on your conscience the destruction of this rather pitiful country?"

"If I could, if I could accept your assumption, yes," replied Nixon. "But I don't accept your assumption, I don't accept it because I know the facts. I think I know the facts, at least. I do know that without United States assistance, that instead of having a situation in which Cambodia is not neutral, in which Cambodia is one of the most ruthless, cruel, vicious communist dictatorships in the world—500,000 dead, a million and a half off to relocation centers—the country is in pitiful shape. But, for five years, from 1970 till 1975, Cambodia enjoyed, for whatever we may call it, at least had, 'enjoyed' is not the best word, it had what you called a flawed neutrality. But as far as that neutrality was concerned, yes, during that five-year period, lives were lost, but on the other hand, they, as far as this savage, cruel, a vicious extermination of a people that has taken place, of a class of people since the Communists took over. They avoided that and that was something."

Kissinger was equally unresponsive. His fullest statement on Cambodia was given to Theo Sommer, the editor of the respected West German paper *Die Zeit*, in the summer of 1976. Tales of Khmer Rouge atrocities were already widespread. The interview was conducted in English, and it bears careful reading.

Sommer asked Kissinger whether he had pangs of conscience at night about Vietnam or Cambodia. "What is there to have pangs of conscience at night about with Vietnam?" Kissinger replied. "We found 550,000 American troops in Vietnam and we ended the war without betraying those who in reliance on us had fought the Communists. And to remove 550,000 troops under combat conditions is not an easy matter."

"You don't think it took too long?" asked Sommer.

"It was important," Kissinger said, "that the war not be ended with the United States simply abandoning people whom we had encouraged to resist the Communists. No one could possibly foresee that Watergate would so weaken the executive authority that we could not maintain the settlement that was in itself maintainable. And if you look at what our opposition was saying during that time, their proposals were usually only about six months ahead of where we were going anyway. Some said we should end the war by the end of '71. Well, we ended it by the end of '72. After all, it took de Gaulle five years to end the Algerian war. And it was a very difficult process.

"Now, with respect to Cambodia, it is another curious bit of mythology. People usually refer to the bombing of Cambodia as if it had been unprovoked, secretive U.S. action. The fact is that we were bombing North Vietnamese troops that had invaded Cambodia, that were killing many Americans from these sanctuaries, and we were doing it with the acquiescence of the Cambodian government, which never once protested against it, and which, indeed, encouraged us to do it. I may have a lack of imagination, but I fail to see the moral issue involved and why Cambodian neutrality should apply to only one country. Why is it moral for the North Vietnamese to have 50,000 to 100,000 troops in Cambodia, why should we let them kill Americans from that territory, and why, when the government concerned never once protested, and indeed told us that if we bombed unpopulated areas that they would not notice, why in all these conditions is there a moral issue? And, finally, I think it is fair to say that in the six years of the war, not ten percent of the people had been killed in Cambodia than had been killed in one year of Communist rule."

Kissinger's argument, in its best light, is that his decisions were justified because the North Vietnamese were in Cambodia first; their presence there was causing American casualties; Sihanouk did not publicly object to their enclaves being secretly bombed; and more Cambodians had been killed since American policy collapsed than while it was being sustained.

Any American administration would have faced dreadful decisions in Vietnam from 1969 onward. It has not been the purpose of this investigation to suggest that there were any easy answers. But given what happened, the discussion cannot be confined as narrowly as Kissinger would seem to wish. At every stage of the war, choices—although difficult ones—did exist. The record shows that those choices that Nixon and Kissinger actually made were made wrongly.

Kissinger's defense ignores crucial issues. Sihanouk was in an impossible position. He was no more able to prevent the American bombing in

1969 than he was able to prevent the North Vietnamese from usurping his country in the first place. His collaboration with both powers, such as it was, was intended to save his people by confining the conflict to the border regions. It was American policy that engulfed the nation in war. That war did not end when helicopters lifted Americans out. It took another form.

Kissinger has said that he will deal fully with Cambodia in his memoirs. If the questions raised by the history of the last decade are to be answered, then more details on Sihanouk's attitude, on the unhelpfulness of the U.S. Congress, or on Kissinger's contacts with foreign governments will not alone suffice. The legality of the 1969 bombing; the way in which Menu and then the invasion spread the fighting; the deliberate extension of the war and the sustenance of Lon Nol; the indiscriminate bombing of 1973; the inadequate attempts to reach a peace settlement; finally, perhaps, the way in which the Khmer Rouge were born out of the inferno that American policy did much to create—these are just some of the issues which have to be addressed. Statesmen must be judged by the consequences of their actions. Whatever Nixon and Kissinger intended for Cambodia, their efforts created catastrophe.

No one could have foreseen the consequences at home and abroad of their decision to override the American Constitution and wage war in a neutral country. But constitutions are devised and laws are written to protect and guard against human frailty. For the highest officers in the land to abuse them is tyranny and encourages tyranny. There were achievements during the Nixon-Kissinger years. But just as their relations with each other and with their associates were often scarred by falsehoods, so were many of their relations with the rest of the world. Together they pursued ends that frequently had a tenuous link with reality, using means that were not merely disproportionate but counterproductive and untrue to those values they were meant to defend. In fact neither man demonstrated much faith in those values.

In Cambodia, the imperatives of a small and vulnerable people were consciously sacrificed to the interests of strategic design. For this reason alone the design was flawed—sacrifice the parts and what becomes of the whole? The country was used to practice ill-conceived theories and to fortify a notion of American credibility that could in fact only be harmed by such actions. Neither the United States nor its friends nor those who are caught helplessly in its embrace are well served when its leaders act, as Nixon and Kissinger acted, without care. Cambodia was not a mistake; it was a crime. The world is diminished by the experience.

A Short Chronology

1864   Franc imposes a protectorate over the kingdom of Cambodia.

1941   Prince Norodom Sihanouk is crowned King of Cambodia.

1953   Sihanouk gains Cambodia's independence from France.

1954   The Geneva Conference on Indochina recognizes Cambodia's neutrality and orders the withdrawal of the Communist Viet Minh and Khmer Rouge to Hanoi.

1955   Sihanouk abdicates the throne in favor of his father. As Prince he becomes the country's principal political leader.

1963   Leaders of the left-wing opposition to Sihanouk leave Phnom Penh for the jungle and mountains.
Sihanouk renounces American aid.

1965

February 28. The United States announces "continuous limited airstrikes" against North Vietnam.

March 8. The first U.S. Marine Infantry (3rd Battalion, 9th Marines) lands in South Vietnam.

May 3. Cambodia breaks relations with the United States.

1966–67   Sihanouk allows the Vietnamese Communists to use the border areas of his country adjoining South Vietnam and to land supplies at the port of Sihanoukville. The United States protests. South Vietnamese and American forces mount frequent small raids across the border. The Cambodian government protests many of these raids.

Sideshow

1967   Sihanouk's armed forces crush a left-wing peasant revolt in Battambang
province. More left-wingers flee from Phnom Penh to the *maquis*, which
Sihanouk calls "les Khmers Rouges."

1968
January 8–12. U.S. Ambassador to New Delhi Chester Bowles visits Cambodia
to explore restoration of relations between Cambodia and the United States
and ways to limit Communist use of the border areas.
January 30. The Vietnamese Communists launch their Tet offensive in South
Vietnam.
November 5. Richard Nixon is elected President of the United States.

1969
February 9. General Creighton Abrams, Commander of U.S. forces, Vietnam,
requests B-52 bombing attack on a Communist base camp inside Cambodia.
March 17. Abrams' request is approved by President Nixon.
March 18. Operation Breakfast, a B-52 strike against Base Area 353, takes
place.
May 9. The New York Times reports that base camps inside Cambodia are being
bombed for the first time.
May 10. The White House demands the first of seventeen wiretaps on govern-
ment officials and journalists.
June 11. Prince Sihanouk announces that Cambodian–U. S. relations will be
restored.
July 25. President Nixon announces the "Guam" or "Nixon" Doctrine on
future American commitments in Asia.

1970
March 11. An estimated 20,000 Cambodians demonstrate against Vietnamese
Communist presence in the country and sack the North Vietnamese and Viet
Cong embassies in Phnom Penh.
March 18. Prince Sihanouk is deposed as Cambodia's head of state while on a
trip to Moscow and Peking. Power is seized by the Prime Minister, General
Lon Nol, with Prince Sirik Matak and Cheng Heng.
March 19. The U. S. government states that Sihanouk has been legally deposed;
the question of recognition of the new government "does not arise."
March 23. In Peking, Prince Sihanouk announces that he has formed a National
United Front of Kampuchea with his former enemies, the Khmer Rouge, to
struggle against the Lon Nol government.
April 14. Prime Minister Lon Nol makes an international appeal for aid.
April 20. President Nixon announces the withdrawal of 150,000 troops from
Vietnam.
April 30. President Nixon announces that American and South Vietnamese
troops have crossed into Cambodia to attack Communist bases.
May 1. Prime Minister Lon Nol states that the U.S.–South Vietnamese assault
has been mounted without his knowledge or approval.

May 4. Four students are fatally shot by the National Guard at Kent State University.

May 5. In Peking, Prince Sihanouk announces the formation of a government in exile, the Royal National Union Government of Kampuchea. His government is immediately recognized by China and North Vietnam.

May 6. China, North Vietnam and North Korea break diplomatic relations with Cambodia.

May 11. The Senate takes the first step to approve an amendment introduced by Senator Sherman Cooper and Senator Frank Church to prevent any future U.S. military operations in Cambodia.

June 29. U.S. ground troops withdraw from Cambodia.

June 30. In a report to the nation, President Nixon praises the "successful" completion of the Cambodian "incursion," citing the amount of enemy supplies captured.

July 5. A Cambodian court condemns Prince Sihanouk to death on grounds of treason and corruption.

July 14. President Nixon approves the "Huston plan" for illegal intelligence gathering in the United States.

September 12. Emory Swank, the first U.S. ambassador since 1965, arrives in Phnom Penh.

October 26. National Security Decision Memorandum 89 defines the administration's "Cambodia Strategy" as to "capitalize on Cambodian nationalism."

December 22. The Cooper-Church amendment becomes law and prohibits the use of authorized funds for sending American troops into Cambodia or for attaching American advisers to Cambodian forces. It proclaims that any assistance given by the United States does not constitute a commitment by the United States to the defense of Cambodia.

1971

January 10. The American Military Equipment Delivery Team Cambodia is formed.

February 13. Lon Nol leaves for Hawaii for treatment of a stroke.

April 12. Lon Nol returns.

April 21. Lon Nol is proclaimed Marshal.

October 20. Lon Nol declares a state of emergency, saying he will no longer "play the game of democracy and freedom," because it stands in the way of victory.

October 27. Lon Nol's Chenla II expeditionary force is attacked by the North Vietnamese.

December 1. The Chenla II forces abandon all their major positions and fall back in disorder with heavy losses.

1972

February 5. The U.S. Senate Refugee Subcommittee of the Judiciary Committee reports that two million Cambodians have been made homeless by the war.

March 10. Chief of State Cheng Heng resigns, transferring his powers to Prime Minister Lon Nol. Lon Nol accepts, dissolves the National Assembly, and declares himself President of Cambodia, Commander in Chief of the Armed Forces and President of the Council of Ministers.

June 4. Lon Nol wins the Khmer Republic's first presidential election.

June 17. Watergate break-in.

September 7–9. Rice shortages and rising prices lead to food riots in Phnom Penh.

October 22. Henry Kissinger makes his only visit to Cambodia, remains four hours and tells Marshal Lon Nol of the progress made in his talks with the North Vietnamese.

November 7. Richard Nixon is elected President for a second term.

December 18. President Nixon orders bombing of Hanoi and Haiphong.

1973

January 27. The Paris Agreement on ending the war in Vietnam is signed. Article 20 deals with the withdrawal of foreign troops from Cambodia.

February 8. Massive B-52 and F-111 bombing of Cambodia resumes after a halt since the January 27 cease-fire.

April 11. Prince Sihanouk returns to Peking after a six-week tour of the Communist-controlled areas of Cambodia.

May 10. The U.S. House of Representatives blocks the use of funds for the continued bombing of Cambodia. This is the first time in the war that the House has voted to undercut a military action on which the President insists.

June 3–4. European news agencies report that Sihanouk has attempted to make contact with President Nixon through third countries, but that his overtures have been rejected. The State Department confirms these accounts.

June 14. Le Duc Tho, Hanoi's negotiator, tells the press that "no tacit agreement" exists between him and Henry Kissinger on Cambodia.

June 30. The Congress and the administration reach agreement on a compromise over the Cambodia bombing; it will continue till August 15.

July 19–21. A "National Congress" of the Cambodian resistance movement, held in the "liberated zone," decides that there will be no peace until all U.S. military activities in Cambodia are ended and Lon Nol is replaced by leaders from Sihanouk's government.

August 7. An off-target B-52 plane bombs the government-held town of Neak Luong, killing over 125 people and injuring more than 250.

August 15. The American bombing of Cambodia, and thus all direct American military intervention in Indochina, ends.

September 4. In a farewell press conference, Ambassador Swank calls Cambodia Indochina's most useless war. No new ambassador is appointed.

September 21. Henry Kissinger is confirmed as Secretary of State.

1974

January 6. Khmer Rouge open 1974 dry-season offensive with attack on the northwest perimeter of Phnom Penh. A bombardment of the city by 105-mm.

artillery culminates in a shelling on February 11, killing 139 people and leaving 10,000 homeless.

March 28. Khieu Samphan, the Deputy Prime Minister in the insurgent government, and commander in chief of its army, leads a delegation from the interior of Cambodia to Hanoi, Peking, and nonaligned countries.

April 3. John Gunther Dean presents his letters of credence as American ambassador to Cambodia.

July 27. The House of Representatives' Judiciary Committee approves Article I—on the Watergate cover-up—in the impeachment of Richard Nixon.

July 29. The Judiciary Committee approves Article II—on abuses of power, including the wiretaps.

July 30. The Judiciary Committee approves Article III, which charges the President with contempt of Congress; it votes down Article IV, which accuses the President of waging secret illegal war in Cambodia.

August 9. Richard Nixon resigns the Presidency and is succeeded by Gerald Ford. Ford announces that Henry Kissinger will remain his Secretary of State.

December 16. President Ford meets with French President Giscard d'Estaing in Martinique; the final communiqué states that "regarding Cambodia, they expressed the hope that the contending parties would enter into negotiations in the near future rather than continuing the military struggle."

1975

January 1. The Khmer Rouge launch annual dry-season offensive against Lon Nol forces.

February 5. The Communists close the Mekong river, preventing any convoys of food, fuel or ammunition reaching besieged Phnom Penh.

April 1. President Lon Nol and his entourage leave Cambodia for Hawaii, via Indonesia. The ferry town of Neak Luong falls to the Communists.

April 12. The U.S. embassy is evacuated from Cambodia by Marine Corps helicopter. Acting President Saukham Khoy leaves with the Americans; most other Cambodian Cabinet officers remain. The army continues to fight.

April 17. The Khmer Rouge enter Phnom Penh and begin to empty the city. All other towns held by the government are also emptied.

April 30. Saigon falls to North Vietnamese assault.

May 3. Fighting begins between the new governments of Cambodia and South Vietnam, in the border area and among the offshore islands.

May 12–15. Cambodian naval forces capture the U.S. container ship *Mayaguez*. President Ford and Secretary Kissinger order the Cambodian mainland bombed in retaliation.

September 9. Prince Sihanouk returns to Phnom Penh after a five-year absence.

1976

April 4. Sihanouk resigns his position as head of state.

1977

December 31. Radio Phnom Penh suspends diplomatic relations with Hanoi and announces that the two countries are engaged in heavy fighting along the border.

1978   Throughout 1978 the Socialist Republic of Vietnam and the Republic of Democratic Kampuchea confront each other in increasingly fierce polemics and in bloody fighting. Relations between Vietnam and China deteriorate. The Cambodian government accuses Vietnam of wishing to "swallow up" Cambodia and impose an Indochina Federation, dominated by Hanoi. The Vietnamese call upon the Cambodian people to overthrow their regime. Vietnam describes Cambodia as "a land of blood and tears, hell on earth." Hanoi announces the formation of a new "Front" to "liberate" Cambodia. In December the Vietnamese launch a large scale invasion of Democratic Kampuchea.

Additions to the new edition

Afterword from Cambodia

AT THE END OF 1979, roughly ten years after the destruction of Cambodia began, the world finally awoke to the scale of that destruction. The suffering of the Khmers briefly fanned the flame of international conscience; Cambodia, or "Kampuchea," became synonymous with horror, with evil in our time. At last the Cambodians, who had been denied so much in the last decade, were extended assistance.

In the fall of 1980 I visited Cambodia. I stayed a month and traveled widely in the north, east and south of the country to places where no foreigner, save Vietnamese, had been since the war began in 1970. Eleven years after Operation Menu was launched I went to the border provinces in which the secret bombing had taken place. Ten years after Sihanouk's overthrow and the United States invasion, I wandered through his palace (which was strangely well preserved) on the banks of the Mekong in Phnom Penh. Nine years after the bloody battle of Chenla II, I drove up the road on which the North Vietnamese had routed Lon Nol's army—all along it were the rusting remains of tanks and armored personnel carriers and the wreckage of towns and villages bombed and never rebuilt. It was more than five years since the Khmer Rouge defeated Lon Nol and emptied the towns. Now, almost two years since the Vietnamese invaded to impose their own regime, the towns were beginning to refill, a semblance of normal life was resuming; I talked to people about the horror of the last decade and particularly the rule of the Khmer Rouge. It was very moving.

To travel through Cambodia was to travel through a land that had been cast into the outer reaches of hell and only barely retrieved. Those who had survived lived now in a broken society that had little chance of regaining the calm and prosperity it had enjoyed before 1970. It was a land that local and international politics seemed likely to condemn to a long twilight existence of decay rather than development. The 1970s were the decade in which Cambodia died; it did not seem at the beginning of the 1980s that there was very much chance of its fully reviving.

For almost all Cambodians the Vietnamese invasion of January 1979 was a liberation. The Khmer Rouge had become more not less brutal, more not less paranoid, as their rule continued. By the end of 1978 the killing had become almost frenetic in many areas. I was taken, immediately after my arrival, to a mass grave outside Phnom Penh. Here about six pits had been excavated; they were filled with the remains of hundreds of people. Skulls were blindfolded, wrists tied as they had been when the victims were killed—at the very end of 1978, it was said. The terrible sweet-sour smell of decaying flesh hung like a pall over the whole place.

Such graves are to be found all over Cambodia. Just how many people were murdered by the Khmer Rouge and how many died of starvation, disease or exhaustion under their rule is not clear. The Vietnamese claim that three million died seemed to be an exaggeration, but the number was probably between one and two million. In any case, the terrible nature of the crime was evident.

The Vietnamese invaded in January 1979 in response to Khmer Rouge attacks into Vietnam, not the Khmer Rouge massacres inside Cambodia. The Khmer Rouge leadership fled Phnom Penh and found refuge principally in the jungles and mountains of Southwest Cambodia, close to the Thai border. They took with them as many civilians as they could seize, probably several hundred thousand people. Those who escaped that fate were allowed, even encouraged, by the Vietnamese to leave the work camps into which they had been corralled by the Khmer Rouge and to return to their original villages.

The invasion, scattered resistance by the Khmer Rouge and mass migration of people in early 1979 seriously disrupted the harvesting of the country's main annual rice crop due at the beginning of the year. Both armies destroyed rice stocks or unharvested fields if there was any risk of these falling into their enemy's hands. Such food stocks as were not requisitioned or burned were consumed by peasants making their way across the country.

For similar reasons very little planting of a 1979 rice crop was carried out in the summer of 1979. Neither seed nor tools nor fertilizer nor even labor were available when needed. Rumors of impending famine reached the west by May and June. But officially, the new regime that the Vietnamese had installed under a former Khmer Rouge officer named Heng Samrin, stalled on offers of help from relief organizations until July. They then issued an appeal for assistance, warning that 2.5 million Cambodians faced death from starvation. Only four million Cambodians, out of a 1970 population of over seven million, remained alive, they said.

The first two international relief officials to visit Cambodia in four years arrived in Phnom Penh at the end of July 1979. They were appalled by what they saw: a still empty city, an orphanage in which children were dying of starvation, a high school that the Khmer Rouge had made into a prison and in which over 16,000 people had been tortured to death. Together with officials from voluntary agencies and a few journalists who were also allowed into Phnom Penh, they returned to the West to describe in graphic, emotional terms the immense and urgent needs that the country faced.

The films and photographs of the mass graves and of the ruined, deserted towns came at almost the same time as thousands of dying Cambodians stumbled out of the Khmer Rouge areas in the southwest into Thailand. They were walking skeletons, suffering from malaria, TB, starvation. Many died where they fell. To those interested in the West it seemed as if all Cambodia must be a charnel house, where the dying picked their way through the dead. At last an outcry occurred; governments responded to public horror.

Negotiation over the delivery of aid took weeks. The Phnom Penh authorities were prepared to allow only very few foreign aid personnel into Cambodia. The Thai government, for its part, insisted that any organization shipping food from Bangkok (the only logical base) must also put food across the border to the Khmer Rouge. Underlying this demand was the fact that Thailand, in common with other non-Communist Southeast Asian countries and, indeed, most of the world, refused to endorse the Vietnamese invasion of Cambodia and still recognized the Khmer Rouge as its legitimate government.

Large quantities of international food aid finally began to arrive in October 1979. But the country's infrastructure was in such wretched shape—no trucks, no cranes, almost no rolling stock, an exhausted labor force—that it was not until early 1980 that significant amounts were widely distributed. Even then large rations went almost exclusively to government workers.

Several hundred thousand Cambodians flocked to the Thai border and settled in makeshift camps, where they were fed by the international agencies—Unicef, World Food Program—and given medical care by the International Committee of the Red Cross. Others came to pick up food supplies handed out at the border and returned into the interior. A massive black market developed at the border, in which Thai traders made fortunes selling to Cambodians everything of which they had been deprived since at least the Khmer Rouge takeover—cloth, needles, soap, nails, fishhooks, matches, candles, yeast, sugar, salt, watches, hats, bicycles, sandals and so on. The Cambodians paid principally in gold, which they had miraculously hidden from the Khmer Rouge. Vast quantities of gold flooded across the border through the first half of 1980, but by the end of the year the trade had diminished. It seemed hard to believe that there was then any more gold left in private hands in the country.

At the same time as the border traffic helped feed and reequip ordinary Cambodians, it also greatly benefited the Khmer Rouge. The Thai government demanded that Unicef and the International Red Cross feed and care for them at the same time as the Thais were arming them, mostly with weapons supplied by the Khmer Rouge's principal ally, China. By the end of 1980 the Khmer Rouge had been rebuilt into a guerrilla force said to number some 40,000 and capable of tying down and harassing the 200,000 troops that the Vietnamese had deployed in Cambodia. The awful irony of humanitarian organizations being used to shore up one of the most inhumane regimes in recent history is clear enough.

At the same time the Khmer Rouge embarked, with the blessing of their

Chinese sponsors, upon a macabre public-relations campaign around the world. Pol Pot was officially removed from the party leadership, and Khieu Samphan, who had been a figurehead chief of state in Phnom Penh after Sihanouk's removal, was pushed to the fore. In interviews with journalists who were brought to a camp near the Thai border he claimed that the Khmer Rouge were no longer Communists but Social Democrats; that a few mistakes were made but these were being greatly exaggerated by the Vietnamese; that now all would be well if only they were given another chance. All they asked for were free elections.

Ieng Sary, the foreign minister, continually traveled the world, as did other spokesmen, delivering this same message. I met one of their representatives, Thiounn Moumm, in Geneva during 1980. He was one of those Khmer Rouge intellectuals who had been educated in Paris in the fifties; indeed, he had been one of the most brilliant scholars of his generation and he spoke fluently and calmly, gently trying to persuade me that the mass graves and the gruesome prison in Phnom Penh were all creations of Vietnamese propaganda. I told him that I did not believe him and that despite the distasteful strategic game whereby the Khmer Rouge retained Cambodia's seat at the United Nations there was not one Western or Third World government that wished to see their return to power in Phnom Penh. I found his eloquent intelligence in service of such a regime literally terrifying.

Most depressing of all was the inability of the world through 1979 and 1980 to find any compromise political solution for the continued crisis in Cambodia. The Vietnamese insisted that their occupation was "irreversible," the Chinese that it was "intolerable." The Vietnamese position was the more realistic, in that with the help of international aid they had built up a regime in Phnom Penh that, though not necessarily popular, controlled and administered the vast part of the countryside without great difficulty. But it cost the Chinese almost nothing to arm the Khmer Rouge and thus to tie down Vietnamese troops. Chinese policy was to bleed Vietnam; it was a policy supported by Thailand and, at least tacitly, by most Western and other Southeast Asian countries, who still argued that to recognize the Heng Samrin regime would be to legitimize invasion. The dilemma was real enough for many countries, like Yugoslavia, whose governments have good reason to fear anything that seems to lessen the world's resistance to the notion of invasion. And the Vietnamese seemed unprepared to offer even token concessions to their concerns.

It was clear through 1980 that the Vietnamese people were enduring with pain the economic costs of the Cambodian occupation, but the government in Hanoi remained unwilling to compromise at all. Any suggestion of even minor changes in the Heng Samrin government to broaden its base, and thus make it easier for Western and Southeast Asian countries to accept without losing face, was dismissed in Phnom Penh and Hanoi.

Throughout the period Prince Sihanouk was mentioned fairly frequently as another possible way to end the crisis. The Chinese endeavored to persuade him to rejoin the Khmer Rouge. But he, until early 1981, refused and continued to denounce their atrocious record. Toward the Vietnamese he was more ambiguous. He made a trip to the West at the end of 1979, ostensibly seeking support for armed resistance to the Vietnamese. When this failed to generate much support he returned to his places of exile, China and North Korea, and threw out occasional hints that he might be willing to make some sort of deal with the Vietnamese. They, however, gave no sign of being interested at all, and by mid-1980 Sihanouk was saying that he had given up politics forever, and that if he ever did return to Cambodia it would only be to die there as a private citizen. By early 1981, however, he was beginning to accede to Chinese pressure and even met with Khieu Samphan to discuss an alliance with the Khmer Rouge.

In the refugee camps along the border in Thailand, Sihanouk's name still commanded respect. But I found when traveling around Cambodia itself in the fall of 1980 that the Heng Samrin regime had done everything it could to discredit him at home. In each part of the country I visited, people told me, when asked, that Sihanouk had encouraged them to support the Khmer Rouge before 1975 and that after Vietnamese "liberation" he had gone to the United Nations to criticize the Vietnamese. It seemed that the Vietnamese felt that they had no need of Sihanouk to gain public acceptance of the government they had installed; fear of the return of the Khmer Rouge was enough to do that. His flirtation with the Khmer Rouge in 1981 further damaged his reputation in Cambodia.

At the same time, however, it was hard to detect widespread enthusiasm for the Heng Samrin regime in its own right. That regime was an uneasy mixture of a few "Hanoi-Khmers"—those Cambodian Communists educated in Hanoi who had survived the Khmer Rouge purges of almost all those associated with the Vietnamese, defectors from the Khmer Rouge, like Heng Samrin himself, and a few "bourgeois" educated people who had survived the Khmer Rouge years. Through 1980, as the Heng Samrin regime consolidated its hold on the country and became more autocratic—imposing restrictions on movement, on meetings with foreign aid officials, and on the private economy that had developed during 1979 and early 1980. Those who were the most uncomfortable were not the defectors from the Khmer Rouge but the "bourgeois." Through 1980 there was a steady trickle of doctors, engineers and nurses to the Thai border, and sometimes beyond into the diaspora.

At the end of 1980 Cambodians began to harvest the annual rice crop. It was much larger than that of 1979, thanks to the import of large quantities of rice seed by the international relief effort. The country would not be self-sufficient in rice in 1981, but it seemed that this might be possible by 1982. Over-all the food situation seemed so remarkably much better than it had been reported by the first aid officials and journalists who had visited the country in the summer of 1979, that it was difficult to believe that two and a half million people had ever really risked dying of starvation. Recovery from famine can be fast, but by the end of 1980 many aid officials considered that the threat of the "extinction of a nation" in 1979 had been exaggerated.

This is not to say that Cambodia had not needed and did not still need massive international assistance. Perhaps the food that had been brought into the country during 1979–80 had been of more direct help to government officials than to peasants. But Cambodia had desperately required a stable and relatively benevolent regime after the Khmer Rouge. One of the most touching sights I saw, in the town of Kompong Thom, was lines of children walking through the morning mist to school. In their hands they had slates provided by Unicef. Under the

Khmer Rouge there had been no schools. Now they existed because the Heng Samrin government had been able to pay teachers, like other government workers, in international food aid.

By the beginning of 1981, as the prospect of famine receded, so Western nations became more reluctant to send aid to the Heng Samrin regime. The international organizations were experiencing considerable difficulty in raising funds for what was termed "development" rather than "emergency" aid. But after the destruction of the last ten years Cambodia evidently needed such "development" aid—if only to repair the crumpled roads, to build and equip hospitals and schools adequately, to rebuild irrigation systems and a thousand other things besides.

But once again politics intruded. So long as the Heng Samrin regime was unrecognized by the United Nations, the UN's development agencies were not allowed to work in the country. Unicef alone is allowed to aid countries outside the UN system, but its principal donors (the United States, the European Economic Community, Japan, Australia and Canada) were not willing to fund the organization to carry out "development" work in what was seen as a Vietnamese —if not, by extension, Soviet—satellite. As of this writing it seemed, therefore, as if aid to Cambodia would be sharply cut back in 1981 and that the people's struggle to rebuild the ruins in which they lived would be long and painful. Once again the country had become peripheral.

WILLIAM SHAWCROSS

London
January 1981

BY 1986, very little had changed for the better. The Vietnamese still occupied Cambodia and most decisions in its government were still taken by Vietnamese officials. Vietnamese troops had conducted several dry season offensives against the Khmer Rouge and non-Communist resistance camps along the border. Civilian casualties had been heavy.

The Khmer Rouge were still by far and away the strongest of the resistance groups. Indeed, the others had virtually collapsed through internecine squabbles and an inability to marshal adequate forces in the field. The Khmer Rouge reach, by contrast, had lengthened, and they were able to attack Vietnamese targets over wide areas of Cambodia. This greatly increased the insecurity of the country.

There was still no prospect of a political settlement; Vietnam and the ASEAN countries remained as far apart as ever on the issue. Cambodia remained out of the United Nations and therefore ineligible for U.N. Development Aid which it so badly needed. All emergency relief had long since ended. The deadlock continued, and no one seemed to have any wish to end it and to begin repairing the fabric and the soul of the country, whose destruction had begun so many years before.

WILLIAM SHAWCROSS

London
April 1986

Kissinger and *Sideshow*

WHEN *Sideshow* was published in April 1979 Kissinger was en route to China, to join his wife, who was there modeling clothes for *Vogue*. In Peking, Kissinger made a point of meeting, for the first time, Prince Norodom Sihanouk. The Prince, who is willing to make friends of the bitterest enemies, invited him to lunch. Later in the year, in Paris, Sihanouk gave me his account of the encounter. He seemed to find it funny.

"Before lunch Kissinger said he wanted a special conversation with me. He began by saying he wanted to get things absolutely straight. That is to say, he had never been anti-Sihanouk, he had always been a Sihanouk supporter. . . . He insisted that the Americans had had nothing to do with the Lon Nol coup.

"I answered, 'But why, immediately after the coup, did you extend *de jure* recognition to Lon Nol? The United States government was the first in the world to do so. And after that President Nixon asked the U.S. Congress to give Lon Nol tremendous amounts of dollars to help his regime survive.'

"And Kissinger said, 'Yes, but we wanted you to return to power very quickly in Cambodia.'

"I answered, 'Why did you refrain from telling me about it? Not only that, but you wanted Lon Nol to resist to the end my return.'

"He said, 'No. No. No. You *must believe* that we were favorable to your returning to power and we did not like Lon Nol. We liked *you*.' [Sihanouk's emphasis]

"I said, 'Thank you very much.'

"And Kissinger said, 'I want you to *believe* it.'

"I said, 'Excellency, let bygones be bygones.'

"He said, 'No. No. No. I want you to *say* that you believe me.'

"I said, 'I apologize. I cannot say I believe you.' "

This exchange with Sihanouk does not appear in Kissinger's memoirs, *White House Years*, which were in galleys when the conversation took place. But Kissinger did insert other extracts from the conversation—which, presumably, he deemed more useful to his case. At the same time, he made significant alterations to the Cambodia section of his book in response to the charges made in *Sideshow*.

Through the summer of 1979, Kissinger avoided any substantive public comment on *Sideshow* or on Cambodia, merely remarking, "I am amazed that a book

409

so inaccurate and distorted should have been accepted as gospel truth." He declined to list the inaccuracies and distortions for the record; he made it a precondition of several interviews he gave when his book was published in October 1979 that *Sideshow* not be mentioned. In England his publishers, Weidenfeld and Nicolson, tried to demand that journalists attending a Kissinger press conference submit their questions to be vetted. This process broke down when the editor of *Punch*, a humorous weekly, sent in the question, "Does Dr. Kissinger expect Prince Charles to be married next year?"

For months Kissinger denied that he had made any real changes to his memoirs as a result of *Sideshow*. To *People* magazine he said, "I added one or two footnotes to my manuscript, but I really did not change it in any significant way." To André Fontaine of *Le Monde* he said, *"J'ai ajouté deux notes au texte, et deux references à la fin du livre. Autrement je n'ai rien changé."* When David Frost asserted, in a celebrated encounter on NBC, "It's common knowledge that the Book-of-the-Month Club went berserk, that you had to rewrite the Cambodian sections," Kissinger replied, "That just isn't true . . . I added to the book itself one paragraph and I added one or two footnotes."

On October 31, 1979, *The New York Times* published a long article based on Kissinger's galleys and entitled "Kissinger revised his book more than he reported." It was evident that some of the changes Kissinger had made in the Cambodia section shifted what he himself would call the "nuance" of his argument; others involved changes of fact.

David Frost tried to examine Kissinger closely on the whole Cambodian story. Under his pressure Kissinger gave inadequate answers and he then attempted to have NBC—with whom he had a contract as an adviser—give him the opportunity to answer some of Frost's questions a second time. Frost resigned from the project and publicly criticized it. NBC released the entire transcript of the Cambodia discussions.

Privately Dr. Kissinger demanded, under the Freedom of Information Act, those United States government documents that I had thus obtained. His aide Peter Rodman then prepared and distributed to sympathetic journalists a 17-page memorandum entitled "Shawcross's Documents." This claimed to be an "independent" analysis, and was unsigned. Those to whom it was given were asked not to hand it on to me. When, eventually, I did obtain a copy I decided to give Kissinger's anonymous memorandum plus my signed rebuttal, a wider circulation. I sent both memoranda to journalists and academics interested in Cambodia. I also sent my response to Kissinger. He did not reply, but finally, in March 1981, he authorized Rodman to publish a revised version of this memorandum in *The American Spectator*. I responded, and the editor, who sympathized with Kissinger, gave the final word to Rodman. I have included this exchange in this edition.

But what of *White House Years*? Kissinger's book was received by many critics as an "exhaustive" study of foreign policy in the first Nixon administration. They were deceived by its length; the book is a partial and incomplete account. Kissinger devotes only 8 of 1,500 pages to Iran and discusses Cambodian affairs in only 1969 and 1970.

He writes at length about the secret 1969–70 B-52 bombing of the Vietnamese Communist sanctuaries in eastern Cambodia, Operation Menu. He also covers the March 1970 overthrow of Sihanouk by General Lon Nol and the subsequent American invasion. After that Cambodia disappears from the book for more than nine hundred pages covering two and a half years. The most destructive period of modern Cambodian history began in the summer of 1970. Kissinger does not describe this period, nor the White House's essential role in it.

Bearing in mind that what Kissinger omits about Cambodia is more important than what he includes, his Cambodia sections on the Menu bombing and the events of 1970 (together with the last-minute changes to them) need to be examined in somewhat laborious detail if the inadequacies of his arguments are to be clear.

MENU:

Kissinger's case includes the following points: He claims that the bombing had to be done secretly because, if it were public, Sihanouk would have to demand an end to it. He says that the sanctuaries were uninhabited or only lightly populated by Cambodians. He asserts that the effect was, if anything, to push the Vietnamese Communists back into South Vietnam rather than further into Cambodia. He claims that the decision to bomb the sanctuaries was in response to an "unprovoked" Communist offensive launched in South Vietnam in February 1969. He states categorically that the North Vietnamese had violated the agreement under which the bombing of the North had been stopped in 1968 by Lyndon Johnson. (On this last point Kissinger does not acknowledge that there was debate within the top levels of the Nixon Administration as to whether the offensive did constitute such a violation. At the last minute he excised a sentence that would have appeared on page 244 noting that Melvin Laird, Secretary of Defense, "was not even sure whether the violation of the bombing halt understandings had been unambiguous.")

Kissinger insists that protection of American lives was the principal reason for the bombing. This would be reasonable if it were true. It is not. The "unprovoked" Communist offensive began in February, and fighting was fierce until the monsoon dampened it in May. This happened every year. Yet during that time the Menu campaign was, according to Kissinger (and according to Nixon in his own memoirs) intermittent. There was one strike in March, one in April and a few more in May. The strikes did not become regular until the fall of 1969. But by then the "unprovoked offensive" had long since ended. If the bombing had been principally intended to save American lives, it would have been most intense from March to May. In fact, United States casualties rose proportionally during the first half of 1969 in the Vietnamese province of Tay Ninh, which was closest to many of the sanctuaries bombed. In 1968, 4 percent of United States deaths were in Tay Ninh; between January and August 1969 the figure was 9 percent. Kissinger does not mention this fact.

On the question of how many Cambodians lived in the bombed areas, Kissinger at the last minute added to his galleys claims that the relevant sanctuaries were "all unpopulated" (p. 247) and "affected no Cambodians" (p. 250). On page 251, he added the sentence, "No one doubted the legality of attacking the base areas being used to kill American and friendly forces, from which all Cambodian authority had been expelled and in which, according to Sihanouk himself, not even a Cambodian buffalo had been killed."

This quotation comes from a press conference given by Sihanouk on May 13, 1969. Kissinger asserts that this was "nearly two months after the bombing had begun." But by his account the bombing was still only occasional then. Moreover, he ignores a press conference on March 28, 1969, which Sihanouk called specifically to deny a UPI report from Saigon that he would not oppose B-52 attacks on the sanctuaries. In an emotional and prescient speech Sihanouk had said, *inter alia*, "I do not want to run the risk because of their bombing of the Communists, of seeing an escalation of the war extend to Cambodia—that is, I will in all cases oppose all bombings on Cambodian territory under whatever pretext." (When David Frost quoted this press conference to Kissinger, the former Secretary claimed he had never heard of it.)

Kissinger's claims that the sanctuaries were unpopulated are untrue, as the Defense Department memoranda quoted in chapters one and six of *Sideshow* demonstrate. Those memoranda also show that it is untrue that no Cambodians were killed in the raids. The point is not that thousands of peasants died in the Menu campaign; no one knows how many were killed. The point is that Kissinger simply does not tell the truth.

At the bottom of page 253 and into page 254 of his book, Kissinger added at the last moment a long section attempting to refute the notion, advanced in *Sideshow* and elsewhere, that the Menu bombing forced the Communists further into Cambodia. His addition begins: "Nor is it true that the bombing drove the North Vietnamese out of the sanctuaries and thus spread the war deep into Cambodia. To the extent that North Vietnamese forces left the sanctuaries it was to move back into Vietnam, not deeper into Cambodia—until after Sihanouk was unexpectedly overthrown a year later."

The idea of a "sanctuary" is not that it be moved closer to the front line when attacked. There is ample evidence that the Communists moved further into Cambodia through 1969 and early 1970—Sihanouk himself complained publicly about it. There is no evidence that the sanctuaries were moved into Tay Ninh or other Vietnamese provinces that year. Nor does Kissinger cite any.

When David Frost taxed Kissinger with this claim that the Communists leaped from the fire into the frying pan, Kissinger was visibly discomforted and admitted, "I have no evidence that [the bombings] moved them in either direction and I'm not saying that they moved them one way or the other."

White House Years is also internally inconsistent on the effects of the bombing on Communist disposition. Kissinger's assertion above conflicts with his own, largely correct analysis of the causes of the coup against Sihanouk in March 1970: "Cambodia's tragedy was that its internal stresses finally upset the delicate equilibrium that Sihanouk had struggled to maintain. . . . The precipitating issue was the communist sanctuaries from which the North Vietnamese had tormented our forces. These increasingly aroused the nationalist outrage of Cambodians. . . ." (p. 459)

That is true. The sanctuaries had been just about tolerable to most Cambodians through the late sixties. In 1969 and 1970 they became intolerable to some because they became larger. The North Vietnamese and Viet Cong usurped much of eastern Cambodia. Kissinger quotes statements from Sihanouk and from other Cambodian leaders to this effect. To maintain as he does in *White House Years,* that this movement out of the sanctuaries had nothing to do with the bombing of those sanctuaries (an operation that Kissinger says was extremely successful from the United States military view) is surely ridiculous. Menu did not push the Communists hundreds of miles across Cambodia. But a few miles deeper into the country was enough to help upset what Kissinger calls its "delicate equilibrium."

Kissinger claims that on June 11, 1969, he and President Nixon "fully briefed" Senators Stennis and Russell on Menu. This is untrue. By his own account, the bombing had not yet become regular and intense—there was no way the Senators could have been "fully" briefed. Stennis himself later said, "I couldn't recreate any distinct recollection of having been especially briefed on that matter. . . . I was told about it, yes . . . but the vastness, I didn't? that point . . . not the volume of it. I just wasn't told—I wasn't, about the extent of it, and all about the false records and everything."

Kissinger acknowledges that, "We were wrong, I now believe, not to be more frank with Congressional leaders." But he claims that the minimal, informal briefings that took place were "at that time the accepted practice for briefing the Congress of classified military operations" (p. 253). Again, this is not true. Under Lyndon Johnson far less expensive cross-border operations into Laos and Cambodia had been reported to the Appropriations Committees as "classified projects." No breach of security was ever said to have resulted from such briefings. Admiral Thomas Moorer, later Chairman of the Joint Chiefs, subsequently said that the method by which the bombing was kept secret "was completely unique. It was occasioned by one thing and that was President Nixon's insistence on the utmost secrecy."

When Nixon announced the invasion of Cambodia on April 20, 1970, he lied when he claimed that hitherto the United States had "scrupulously respected" Cambodian neutrality and had not "moved against" the sanctuaries. Kissinger inserted a last-minute acknowledgment of this on his galleys: "And he added a sentence that was as irrelevant to his central thesis as it was untrue, that we had heretofore not moved against the sanctuaries—overlooking the secret bombing." (p. 505) Kissinger does not add that he too told the same lie in a background briefing to the press that day.

David Frost asked Kissinger about Nixon's lie. Kissinger replied: "That statement should not have been made."

> FROST. Why did he make it?
> KISSINGER. Because he was given to hyperbole.
> FROST. Why did you make the same statement in your background briefing to the press on the same day?
> KISSINGER *(looking angry).* Because I suppose to us this bombing of the sanctuaries had become so much part of the landscape that we did not really focus on that. But that was not a correct statement.

After the interview was taped, Kissinger moved heaven and earth to have NBC executives delete this exchange from the broadcast show. He called dozens of times from Europe. But NBC was working under great public pressure because of Frost's resignation from and criticism of the project. The exchange was not erased.

Kissinger fails to note in his book that the lie was made not just once but over and over again. Nixon repeated it in his report to the nation on the invasion of June 30, 1970; this report was written by Kissinger. It was repeated again in the President's Foreign Policy Report to Congress on February 25, 1971; that report too was written by Kissinger. Countless other reports, briefings, computer print-outs sent to Congress through 1970, 1971, 1972 and early 1973 reiterated it. The story came out in summer 1973, not because Kissinger or anyone else in the administration revealed it, but because Major Hal Knight, a radar operator, wrote to Senator William Proxmire about it. But for Knight, there is no reason to suppose that Kissinger or any other administration official would have told any of the truth.

In summary: There were Cambodians in the areas bombed; Kissinger does not tell the truth when he says there were not. The principal intention of the bombing was not to protect American lives; Kissinger does not tell the truth when he says it was. There were Cambodian casualties; Kissinger does not tell the truth when he says there were not. The bombing pushed the Communists further into Cambodia; Kissinger does not tell the truth when he says they moved the other way.

The 1970 Coup and Invasion

Among Kissinger's contentions are that:

1. The U.S. had no prior knowledge of, let alone involvement in the coup, was in fact disappointed by it, and would have liked Sihanouk back.
2. That it was a new North Vietnamese invasion of Cambodia, right after the coup, which made the U.S. "incursion" inevitable.
3. That the planning for the "incursion" was careful and rational.
4. That the "incursion" was very helpful to Vietnamization, cut U.S. casualties, and protected Cambodia from the fury of the Khmer Rouge for five whole years.

Kissinger's arguments are incomplete, distorted and dishonest. This was true of the original account in the galleys. It is even more true of the revised version he produced after the publication of Sideshow.

On the question of responsibility for the coup, much has been alleged and little has been proved. I did not demonstrate in Sideshow that Washington organized or arranged the coup. It was, however, clear that American officials in Vietnam were aware of its planning and were indirectly in touch with the plotters. In some circumstances there is only a fine line to be drawn between foreknowledge and complicity.

Kissinger asserts that within days of the coup the situation was out of control. Sihanouk, he claims, was "unreachable" in Peking. This assertion appears in Chapter Seven and it is remarkable above all because of the way it contrasts with claims he makes in Chapter Six. That chapter, "First Steps to China," describes lovingly and at length the succession of discreet moves that the White House made toward Peking in 1969. (The fact that the initiative had come from the Chinese is mentioned only fleetingly. Peking's eagerness in the face of the Soviet threat is less important than Kissinger's subtlety.) By the beginning of 1970 relations had progressed as far as a meeting between the United States Ambassador and the Chinese chargé in Warsaw. This, according to Kissinger, "went extraordinarily well . . . both sides avoided polemics . . . procedural issues were amicably settled. . . . Thus one year to the day after Nixon's inauguration the People's Republic of China and the United States were to engage in substantive discussion for the first time in over twenty years. But these were to be different from any of the 134 meetings that had preceded them. They had been painstakingly prepared over months, by messages, first indirect but growing increasingly explicit, of a willingness to bring about a fundamental change in our relationship. . . . It was a moment of extraordinary hope. . . ." (p. 193)

Ten weeks and three hundred pages later, close contacts in Warsaw and moments of extraordinary hope are completely forgotten. Kissinger needs to devise an excuse for not contacting Sihanouk in Peking immediately after the coup; China's revolutionary remoteness is blamed. Peking became "the most revolutionary capital in the world and with which, moreover, we had no means of communication whatever" (p. 485).

Kissinger attempts to show also that within a very few days of the coup Sihanouk had thrown in his lot with his former enemies, the North Vietnamese and Khmer Rouge Communists and that the "Sihanouk card" was therefore quite lost. When he made his corrections on his galleys he went to some lengths to strengthen this assertion. Thus, on page 468 the original language that Sihanouk had "identified himself with the communists" became "irrevocably joined forces with" them. In fact, as I tried to show in Chapters Eight and Nine of *Sideshow*, both the Chinese and the North Vietnamese greeted the coup ambiguously; they did not embrace Sihanouk at once.

There is no doubt that the fighting in eastern Cambodia spread during March and April. Nor is there any doubt that the North Vietnamese moved westward. Did they move freely, bent on immediate conquest, as Kissinger alleges, or were they pushed?

Kissinger goes to considerable lengths to conceal the fact that since February —before the coup—the South Vietnamese had been authorized by Washington to launch limited ground attacks upon the sanctuaries in an attempt to push the Communists further away from the border (and deeper into Cambodia) than Menu had already done.

On page 588 there is some serious rewriting to hide these operations. Originally Kissinger had acknowledged "Since February the South Vietnamese had undertaken occasional shallow crossborder operations." On galleys he changed this to "Since February the South Vietnamese had considered" such operations.

Originally Kissinger wrote that after a visit to Vietnam in January, Alexander Haig had "recommended limited hit-and-run raids by the South Vietnamese" at certain base camps. In the final version he deleted that recommendation altogether. (It would have been on page 488, in the paragraph beginning "Since February . . .")

Originally he wrote, "Laird had encouraged General Abrams and President Thieu to begin these when he visited Vietnam in February." In the revised version, Laird's "encouragement" is modified. It becomes instead "Laird had authorized General Abrams to give logistical support to South Vietnamese forces for shallow penetrations when he visited Vietnam in February."

The extent to which these attacks began to drive the Vietnamese into Cambodia even before Sihanouk's overthrow is unknown. But when Lon Nol seized power the Communists tried to reach an accommodation with him. Some of these efforts are detailed in Chapter Eight of *Sideshow*. Kissinger mentions none of them in his book. It is his purpose to show that from the moment of the coup the North Vietnamese were intent on capturing Cambodia forthwith. Attempts at compromise do not fit into that design.

Kissinger makes no mention of the contracts between Son Ngoc Thanh, the leader of the Khmer Serei in South Vietnam and the organizers of the coup. He makes very little of the South Vietnamese attacks into Cambodia through the last ten days of March.

Instead, Kissinger says (p. 467) that "in early April the North Vietnamese and Viet Cong forces began making good their pledge of 'support' (for Sihanouk in Peking). Communist forces left their base areas and started penetrating deep into Cambodia to overthrow the new government." (To Kissinger, Communist attacks are always "deep," United States–South Vietnamese attacks always "shallow," though in fact at this time they were often similar in extent.)

Kissinger mentions that on April 3 the Communists attacked government positions in Svay Rieng province. He does not mention that on April 4 General Abrams asked to send Special Forces teams into the country, nor that on April 5 two South Vietnamese battalions thrust ten miles deep into Cambodia. He says that on April 10 Cambodian troops were forced to evacuate positions in the Parrot's Beak. He does not acknowledge another South Vietnamese operation that began on the same day. Nor that joint South Vietnamese–Cambodian military planning also began then.

Kissinger produces long lists of specific Communist attacks to show Hanoi's aggressive intent. What is interesting is that many of these incidents have never been mentioned before—neither in Nixon's announcement of the invasion, nor anywhere else. This is not to say that they did not happen. But it does suggest that they were not considered very significant at the time. Kissinger has searched the files for the slightest incident that he can use to support his current assertion that the Communists were intent in April 1970 on capturing all of Cambodia and would have done so but for the United States invasion. He has also exaggerated many such incidents.

This process went on right until the book went to press. On page 472, for example, Kissinger had written that "On April 13 and 14 several Cambodian outposts in Takeo province south of Phnom Penh and near the South Vietnamese border were captured." This apparently did not sound serious enough; on galleys the "outposts" were rewritten as "military positions" and the fact that they were near the border was deleted.

Similarly, on page 485 Kissinger changed, "April saw a wave of communist attacks to ensure the free use of Cambodia for military purposes against South

Vietnam and us" to "April saw a wave of communist attacks to overthrow the existing governmental structure in Cambodia." On page 487, "Helms' briefing showed that the North Vietnamese had broken out of the sanctuaries and were attacking all over the country" becomes "showed that the North Vietnamese were attacking all over the country and that Phnom Penh could not long withstand this assault."

These retrospective claims of imminent North Vietnamese hegemony over Cambodia are vital to Kissinger's case that the United States had no alternative to the actions it took there. But there is no evidence whatsoever to support that case. His own analysts on the NSC—John Court, Larry Lynn and Robert Sansone—were ordered in the summer of 1970 to try to prove it on the basis of captured documents, radio intercepts and all other available material. They were unable to do so.

The most detailed and authoritative survey of contemporary Communist intentions was published by the United States Embassy in Saigon in January 1971. This was a long paper in the Embassy's series "Vietnam—Documents and Research Notes"; it was entitled "The Viet Cong's March–April 1970 plans for expanding control in Cambodia." It did not mention any plan by Hanoi to take over the government of Phnom Penh in 1970. Nor did a similar, less sophisticated paper published by the Ministry of Information in Phnom Penh in 1971 entitled, "Documents of Viet Cong and North Vietnamese Aggression Against Cambodia." Had any such evidence existed, it is certain that both of these documents would have included it. To be fair to Kissinger, he does not produce any evidence himself. He merely asserts.

What the Vietnamese Communists were trying to do in March–April 1970—after their attempt to work out a modus vivendi with Lon Nol had failed—was to control large enough areas of eastern Cambodia to guarantee the security of their sanctuaries and supply routes. In the long term, certainly, they planned to build up an indigenous Communist army to battle Lon Nol. And in the long term, certainly, they wanted Cambodia to be part of an Indochina Federation dominated by Hanoi. But that is not relevant to decisions made in 1970; then their principal concern was Vietnam, and any attempt to "conquer" and control Cambodia would have been a wasteful diversion of resources.

Kissinger is equally disingenuous in his description of the atmosphere and manner in which the invasion was planned in Washington, and particularly in the White House. He disregards the fact that at the beginning of 1970 Nixon was anxiously seeking a way to demonstrate American "credibility" and that Cambodia provided such an opportunity. He tries to downplay the chaotic, emotional way in which the decision to invade was reached. In this he is not very successful, because so much is already on the public record about Nixon's disturbed, drunken state at the time. He also has difficulty in dismissing the charge made in *Sideshow* and many other places that the Secretaries of State and Defense were cut out of the planning of the invasion because they were opposed to it. Here he has had the rewrite gremlins extra busy on the galleys.

On page 597 Kissinger is describing events on April 24. A decision to send the South Vietnamese into the sanctuaries had already been made; discussion over the use of American troops was continuing. Originally he had written, "All plan-

Sideshow

ning so far had been conducted without the participation of the Secretaries of State and Defense, who in fact devoted much of their energy to cutting back on even the South Vietnamese operation into the Parrot's Beak." In his revised version this admission has gone; instead he writes only, "Since the NSC meeting two days earlier the Secretaries of State and Defense had not been heard from."

The most severe of Kissinger's last-minute alterations is designed to show that the invasion was a last-minute decision, forced upon a reluctant Administration by Hanoi's lack of restraint, rather than an operation long planned.

On page 487, there is a short paragraph that begins, "There had been no consideration of attacking the sanctuaries before April 21. The final decision was taken on April 28." This paragraph was added at the last minute; it bears reading twice.

At the same time Kissinger deleted from the galleys a memorandum that he wrote to Nixon in preparation for an April 26 meeting with Laird, Rogers, Helms and Wheeler. This memo, which would have appeared on page 499, read: "The purpose of today's meeting should be to consider the ramifications of authorizing the combined US-ARVN operation into Base Area 352–353. . . . Conceptually this operation would constitute a second punch when combined with the already approved ARVN operation into the Parrot's Beak scheduled for the early morning hours of April 28 Saigon time. The combined US-ARVN into Base Area 352–353 operation has been under preparation by MACV for several weeks but up until now Secretary Laird has not been aware of the likelihood of its being approved and opposition can be anticipated from him as well as from the Secretary of State. The Joint Staff and MACV, however, have been proceeding with the view towards early implementation of the plan in the event you decided in favor of it."

This is an extraordinary document and one can see why Kissinger had to delete it. Not only does it flatly refute his last-minute claim that no invasion had been considered before April 21 and that it was only decided on April 28. It also demonstrates more clearly than anything else that the White House was making vast military plans without the knowledge of the Secretary of Defense. It is in direct contradiction to the assertion that Kissinger added at the last moment on page 502, that "The decision was not made behind the backs of his senior advisers, as has been alleged—though later on others were. Nixon overruled his Cabinet members; he did not keep them in the dark."

So much for the causes and the planning of the invasion; what of the effects? Kissinger acknowledges that its successes were restricted by the fact that the domestic uproar (which Laird, unlike Kissinger, had predicted) forced Nixon to limit the adventure to two months and thirty kilometers. But he claims that "the main goals" were won. The invasion "made our withdrawal from Vietnam easier; it saved lives; even after the sanctuaries were partly reoccupied by the Communists they had been deprived of stockpiles for a sustained offensive." (P. 507)

The first two of these claims are without foundation. As I tried to demonstrate in *Sideshow*, the Communists quickly rebuilt their stockpiles in the sanctuaries and the damage that the invasion inflicted at home was incalculable.

But what of casualties? Kissinger says, understandably enough, that for Americans "the key criterion was our casualties." He claims that after the invasion

418

"the number of men killed in action dropped to below one hundred a week for the first time in four years. They continued to drop with every month thereafter. For each month beginning with June 1970 the casualty figure averaged less than half of that of the corresponding month of the previous year. By May 1971, a year later, it had fallen to 35 a week; in May 1972 ten a week. To be sure the withdrawal of American forces was a factor; but we had several hundred thousand Americans in Vietnam through 1971, and had Hanoi possessed the capability it could have inflicted substantially higher casualties than it did. That it did not do so was importantly due to the breathing space provided by the Cambodian operation." (p. 508)

This is, for Kissinger, rather a modest claim. And well it might be. For the invasion had little effect on United States casualties, beyond raising them for the period it lasted. Casualties dropped afterward, but for other reasons.

These points must be made:

a. Casualties were cyclical. Every year they were highest during the annual campaigning season, January–May, and fell through the summer and fall. June 1970 was no different.

b. Every year from 1968 onward this over-all pattern was repeated with lower peaks every year.

c. Over 50 percent of all American casualties occurred right up in the north of South Vietnam, near the DMZ, far from Cambodia and largely unaffected therefore by the bombing or invasion of the sanctuaries.

d. Over 76 percent of American deaths were incurred in combat, specifically in the United States maneuver battalions engaged in offensive action. American deaths fell in direct relation to the withdrawal of maneuver battalions; from 1969 —long before the invasion—these battalions were withdrawn faster than any other United States troops in Vietnam. By 1972 United States deaths had dropped significantly—only 300—because by then almost all Americans were ensconced in rear areas, protected by South Vietnamese troops.

No one would argue that Nixon and Kissinger did not have a primary responsibility to protect their own troops. But what responsibility should they accept for the lives of their allies? In discussing casualties Kissinger does not mention those of the Cambodians or Vietnamese. In 1971, for instance, U.S. deaths were certainly down. But South Vietnamese deaths were the same, and Cambodian deaths had grown enormously. Over-all, the number of young men dying in Indochina was almost identical with the year before. Obviously Kissinger could not be expected to weight Southeast Asian deaths as heavily as American. But some consideration of them was due.

In a section entitled "The Balance Sheet," Kissinger attempts to show that United States action actually saved Cambodia for five whole years from the horrors of the Khmer Rouge. "Without our incursion the Communists would have taken over Cambodia years earlier. That the rule of these fanatical ideologies would have been more benign under those conditions is not very likely; when tyrants are so remote from their people, so committed to frightful experiments of social transformation, so doctrinaire, no normal criteria apply."

Sideshow

This is a skillful but contemptible elision. By using the phrase "the Communists" Kissinger disregards the distinction between the Khmer Rouge and the Vietnamese. He ignores the fact that the indigenous Khmer Rouge could not have taken power in 1970; they were only about 4,000 strong and had no political base. By 1975 they had waxed on the war, exploiting nationalism, and numbered some 70,000 soldiers, capable (just about, and by using terror) of taking over the country. It may be that "no normal criteria" can be applied to the Khmer Rouge leaders. But Kissinger will not face the fact that in 1970 they could not have had power; in 1975 they won it after a five-year war that destroyed Cambodian society.

Kissinger ignores also his own principal argument—that in April 1970 it was Hanoi's quest for hegemony that forced the United States invasion. If so, Hanoi would never have allowed leaders from the Cambodian Communist maquis to take control in 1970. Had they sought and won control of Cambodia at that time, they would have installed their own leadership, as they did after they invaded in 1979; they had Cambodian Communists in Hanoi groomed since 1954 for just such an eventuality. (By 1979 the Khmer Rouge had killed most of these "Hanoi-Khmer"; defectors from the Khmer Rouge had to be installed.)

In a section added (p. 517) at the last minute Kissinger obliquely refers to *Sideshow*, saying, "The bizarre argument has been made, with glaring lack of substantiation, that the cruelty of the Khmer Rouge in history was the product of five years of American and Cambodian efforts to resist them. No one can accept this as an adequate explanation except apologists for the murderous Khmer Rouge rule. Sihanouk does not believe this; they were men he had kicked out of Cambodia in 1967 because they were a menace to his country. He told me in April 1979 that the Khmer Rouge leaders were 'always killers from the beginning.' "

The argument is not as "bizarre" as Kissinger misrepresents it. Whether or not the Khmer Rouge were "always killers"—and the evidence is that they became much more brutal as the war progressed—the point is that it was only after the five-year war that they were put into the position of being able to kill so many, so indiscriminately. The five-year war did not "resist" them; it created the conditions, the *only* conditions, in which they could grow. Just as the Bolsheviks could come to power in Russia only after the destruction wrought by World War I, so the Khmer Rouge were brought to control Cambodia only by the 1970–75 war.

Menu and the invasion—that's almost all there is of Cambodia in Kissinger's book. At the end of his section on the invasion he added at the last minute two pages (518–520) of ritualistic regret: "Poor Cambodia gradually turned into the butt of our national frustrations. . . ." But this new section does not address the issues raised by United States policy in Cambodia after the invasion; it is merely a favorable review of a Senate Foreign Relations Committee report by staff who were touched by Cambodia's plight at the end of 1970.

White House Years covers 1969–73 but there is no mention at all of Cambodia between pages 520 and 1,414, between June 1970 and a hastily rewritten paragraph concerning November 1972. The most destructive period of all, after the

420

invasion, is evidently of no interest to Kissinger. He does not mention that he and Nixon sent Alexander Haig to Phnom Penh to decide how to run this new war in summer 1970. He does not acknowledge that the original, rather modest and sensible proposals for military assistance were overridden by the Pentagon with White House support, in favor of a constantly expanding military presence in Phnom Penh.

He does not discuss National Security Study Memorandum 99, in which tactics for the defense of Cambodia against the Communists were discussed in Washington in the fall of 1970. He ignores the fact that it was he who insisted that the United States implement the most ambitious and impractical of the proposals for the militarization of Cambodia, while Melvin Laird and William Rogers advised against that implementation. There is no reference here to National Security Decision Memorandum 89, "Cambodian Strategy," in which he gave this instruction.

Kissinger does not reveal his reasons for increasing the size of the United States military team in Phnom Penh again in summer 1971. He does not say anything about the terrible battle of Chenla II in November 1971, when Lon Nol's pathetic, overextended new army was decisively routed by the Vietnamese. He never mentions the problems of leadership and corruption that the military expansion imposed by the United States caused in Cambodia. He does not deal with the fact that State and CIA officials in the United States Embassy became more and more despairing as the war progressed, that they constantly warned Washington of Lon Nol's incompetence and corruption, and that these warnings were ignored.

For Kissinger the spread of the fighting and of United States bombing are not matters to be discussed. The flood of peasants off the land, fleeing the warfare and then the growing cruelty of the growing Khmer Rouge is not relevant. He has no interest in the collapse of Cambodian society through 1970, 1971, 1972 and 1973. None of these things, none of these terrible stages in the calvary of the Cambodian people is mentioned once by Kissinger. Indeed, *White House Years* demonstrates more forcefully and more conclusively than any of his critics could do that for Kissinger Cambodia was a sideshow, its people expendable in the great game of large nations.

Sideshow

Kissinger's authorized response to *Sideshow*, written by his aide, Peter W. Rodman, for *The American Spectator*, March 1981, and published under the title: SIDESWIPE: KISSINGER, SHAWCROSS AND THE RESPONSIBILITY FOR CAMBODIA

In April 1975, the Communist Khmer Rouge took power in Cambodia, emptied Phnom Penh of its entire population and embarked on a nationwide campaign of terror and destruction that claimed the lives of somewhere between one million and three million Cambodians—out of a total population of seven million.

Four years later, British journalist William Shawcross produced a book entitled *Sideshow: Kissinger, Nixon and the Destruction of Cambodia*. As its subtitle suggests, it attempts to prove *American* responsibility for the horrors wrought by the Khmer Rouge. Shawcross argues in essence that American bombing in 1969 "destabilized" the neutral government of Prince Norodom Sihanouk; that the U.S.-South Vietnamese incursion of 1970 triggered the bloody war in Cambodia that engulfed the country; and that America's prolongation of the conflict for five years paved the way for the victory of the Khmer Rouge and accounted for their genocidal brutality after they took power.

The Shawcross book was widely praised for its impressive documentation, even by some who did not entirely swallow its conclusions. The book advertises itself as based on "thousands of pages of classified U.S. Government documents" obtained under the Freedom of Information Act (FOIA). Without the time or inclination to verify his evidence, reviewers seemed mesmerized by invocation of the Freedom of Information Act, as if it were a voodoo incantation that paralyzed all critical faculties. I have had the opportunity to examine a duplicate set of the government files that Shawcross obtained under the FOIA. It was an experience full of surprises. Close scrutiny of the materials shows that the evidentiary basis of the book is so seriously flawed as to discredit his whole enterprise. He had no White House documents, since they are exempt from the FOIA, yet he presumes to pass judgment above all on White House decisions. His vaunted research turns out to be slipshod, distorted by bias, and in some cases bordering on the fraudulent. It is a compendium of errors, sleight of hand, and egregious selectivity; he has suppressed entirely a mountain of evidence in his possession that contradicted his principal points.

The chronicle of Shawcross' errors is in itself a brief history of Cambodia's tragedy.

Beginning in about 1965, North Vietnam established a string of military bases on the territory of neutral Cambodia, along the border, just opposite South Vietnam. From these sanctuaries North Vietnamese forces launched forays into South Vietnam, attacking South Vietnamese and American troops and escaping back across the border into Cambodia where self-imposed restraints prevented our pursuit or retaliation.

The Nixon administration in early 1969 lifted some of these restraints. At a time when major American troop withdrawals were being planned, the North Vietnamese shelled a number of cities in South Vietnam in flagrant breach of the pledge that had been the *quid pro quo* for President Johnson's halt to the bombing of

North Vietnam. No one in the Nixon administration was eager to resume the bombing of the North; a less explosive form of retaliation seemed warranted. President Nixon undertook the bombing of the Cambodian sanctuaries in the knowledge that 1) Prince Norodom Sihanouk, Cambodia's neutralist leader, did not object to American military action against the North Vietnamese bases, and that 2) the risk of harm to Cambodian civilians was minimal.

Shawcross struggles without success to prove that both these propositions were false.

CHESTER BOWLES: THE MISSING QUOTATION

Sihanouk was powerless to prevent North Vietnam's expropriation of Cambodian territory for prosecution of the Vietnam war. The Prince went considerably beyond acquiescence, however; he allowed the Communists to ship war material to the port of Sihanoukville and then to transport it by a leisurely truck route to the sanctuaries along the border. Even Shawcross describes this (p. 64), and anyone wanting an authoritative account of the active help Sihanouk gave to the North Vietnamese will find it in Sihanouk's recent memoirs.* This would seem to say something about how "neutral" Cambodia was under Sihanouk.

In fairness to the agile Prince, however, in the late 1960s he began to feel put-upon by the heavy-handed North Vietnamese and tried to square accounts by telling American officials that he would not object at all if the United States attacked the Vietnamese Communist bases and drove them out of Cambodia. He said this to various visitors, one of the most important being Ambassador Chester Bowles, who on January 10, 1968, met with the Prince in Phnom Penh on a mission for President Johnson.

Sihanouk's conversation with Bowles has become controversial. The Nixon administration cited it when the Cambodian bombing became a *cause célèbre* in 1973. Shawcross devotes a great deal of effort to the Bowles mission, attempting to discredit, evade, deny, or dismiss the administration's contention. The reason for this exertion is obvious. If Sihanouk invited us to attack the North Vietnamese bases, then we were defending Cambodia's neutrality, not violating it, and the bombing of Cambodia appears in an entirely different light.

Shawcross pronounces the claim "questionable" (p. 28). For three and a half lengthy pages he walks us through the Bowles mission (pp. 66–71), citing Bowles' State Department briefing papers, Bowles' escort officer's summary report, and Bowles' cables to Washington. Never does Shawcross quote a word of what Sihanouk said to Bowles on the subject. He apologizes that his documentation is incomplete and therefore not "conclusive evidence"; "whether Sihanouk actually told Bowles that the United States was free to bomb the sanctuaries cannot be definitely determined from the sanitized State Department papers," he writes. Nevertheless, Shawcross is confident enough to inform his readers that his documents "suggest that it is not so."

A look at the documents is illuminating. While Shawcross may not have had a verbatim transcript, he had an explicit summary of what Sihanouk said. The State Department escort officer's report of the Bowles mission, which Shawcross received

War and Hope: The Case for Cambodia, London and New York: Pantheon Books, 1980.

under the Freedom of Information Act, contained evidence that could not be more conclusive, which Shawcross chose to conceal from his readers:

> Then, in one of his amazing reversals [the report read], the Prince said he would not object if the U.S. engaged in "hot pursuit" in unpopulated areas. He could not say this publicly or officially, but if the U.S. followed this course it would help him solve his own problem. Of course, if the U.S. engaged VC/NVA [Vietcong/North Vietnamese Army] forces on Cambodian territory, both sides would be guilty of violating Cambodian soil, but the VC/NVA would be "more guilty" (sic). If we pursued VC forces into remote areas where the population would be unaffected he would "shut his eyes."

The same thing could have been found in Chester Bowles' memoir *Promises to Keep*, published in 1971:

> Later, in a quiet private visit, Sihanouk volunteered that he would not object to the United States' engaging in "hot pursuit" in unpopulated areas of Cambodia. He pointed out that while he could not say this publicly or officially, if the United States followed this course, it might even help him to solve his problem.

Bowles was skeptical, but Sihanouk's position never deviated from this. After the B-52 bombing started in 1969 and was reported in the American press, Sihanouk responded in similar terms publicly: he complained if Cambodians were hurt but did not object if we attacked Vietnamese Communists who were illegally occupying a portion of his country. Sihanouk drew closer to the United States. In July 1969, four months after the bombing started, he invited President Nixon to pay a visit to Phnom Penh and promised a warm reception. He began to write and speak more openly against the North Vietnamese. This avid observer and barometer of the balance of power now saw the United States as a potent counterweight to the hated North Vietnamese, restoring his country's freedom of action and enhancing—yes, enhancing—its neutrality.

Shawcross' treatment of the Bowles mission is a sham. Kissinger has published part of Sihanouk's verbatim remarks in his memoirs but it adds little to what was already available. In a lecture at Harvard in March 1980, Sihanouk admitted what he said to Bowles. Stephen Young, Assistant Dean of Harvard Law School, heard Sihanouk's lecture and called it "an incredibly significant admission." For "that means that, in the debate that has riven our country for 10 years, Henry Kissinger is right and William Shawcross is all wrong."

WHAT THE CHIEFS' MEMORANDUM REALLY SAID

Nixon ordered the B-52 bombing of certain North Vietnamese sanctuaries on the Pentagon's assurance, secondly, that attacking them posed minimal danger of Cambodian civilian casualties. The Joint Chiefs of Staff examined 15 North Vietnamese base areas in Cambodia with the explicit mandate, *inter alia*, to consider the risk of harm to civilians. General Earle Wheeler forwarded the results to Secretary of Defense Melvin Laird on April 9, 1969, in a lengthy memorandum with numerous appendices and maps. Only the base areas in which the danger to civilians was found to be "minimal" were recommended for targeting.

This exercise might suggest to an impartial observer that the United States took extraordinary pains to avoid civilian casualties. But not to Shawcross. He quotes from the memorandum in the most selective fashion (*Sideshow*, pp. 28–29) to imply a callous disregard for human life—exactly the opposite of the memorandum's obvious meaning. Shawcross accomplishes this by quoting at length only from the caveats that the memorandum's draftsmen included for the sake of honesty: that all estimates of likely civilian casualties were "tenuous at best," that "some Cambodian casualties" would likely be sustained in certain kinds of military operations, and that the "surprise effect" of attacks could tend to increase the danger, "as could the probable lack of protective shelters around Cambodian homes to the extent that exists in South Vietnam."

On reading the Chiefs' memorandum carefully one finds, first of all, that these acknowledged risks to civilians applied to combined air and ground operations against the sanctuaries, not to aerial attacks on specific military targets as ordered by Nixon. What is more, Shawcross acknowledges only in passing what the memorandum emphasized over and over again: that civilian casualties would be "minimal," for the simple and obvious reason that the North Vietnamese did not allow any Cambodians anywhere near their military dispositions. The point was made repeatedly, in passages that Shawcross found inconvenient to call to the reader's attention. For example:

> a. There is very little mixing of the VC/NVA Forces with the Cambodian populace. Conversely, Cambodians rarely go into areas under de facto control of the VC/NVA.
>
> b. Cambodian villages and populated areas are readily identifiable and can be essentially avoided in conducting preplanned operations into the base areas.
>
> c. Very few permanent structures exist in the base areas outside the Cambodian villages. Virtually all those that do exist are enemy-occupied. (JCSM-207-69, April 9, 1969, Appendix E, p. 27)

> [T]he enemy's military forces in Cambodia habitually occupy areas close to the SVN [South Vietnam] border and away from significant Cambodian presence. (Cover memorandum p. 2)

> Extreme care would be taken to attack only known enemy bases in Cambodia, thus minimizing the risk of engagement with Cambodian forces or of causing Cambodian casualties. (Appendix B, p. 8)

The canard that we callously assumed the risk of massive harm to civilians should finally be laid to rest by Prince Sihanouk's recent memoirs. Before the March 1970 coup that overthrew him, Sihanouk writes, the North Vietnamese sanctuaries were "limited to a few outlying and uninhabited sectors along the Cambodia–Vietnam borderline."

There is more to this April 9, 1969 memorandum. It sets out in detail the strategic importance of the enemy sanctuaries and the danger that they presented. Indeed, it is one of the most impressive statements ever made of the case *for* attacking them. For example:

> An appropriate time to undertake operations to destroy an enemy force is subsequent to a contact in which the enemy has been defeated and is withdrawing. It is at this point that the enemy force is most disorganized and vulnerable. The option of conducting pursuit operations has essentially been withheld from COMUSMACV [the U.S. Command] because the best place to conduct such operations is against his rallying and collection points in Cambodia.
>
> Authority to conduct pursuit operations to limited depths in Cambodia could result in destruction of enemy units involved as effective fighting forces, and could require the enemy not only to provide filler replacements to regenerate such units but also to provide new cadre leadership. Pursuit operations also could result in capture or destruction of munitions and supplies in the sanctuaries to which enemy forces are withdrawing. Possibly most important of all, however, is the fact that once US/RVNAF [U.S./South Vietnamese] pursuit operations have been undertaken, the enemy would be forced to adjust to the possibility of future pursuit operations, and would not be able to operate in border areas with confidence that sanctuary was available nearby. Reestablishment of bases deeper in Cambodia would be very difficult for the enemy, due to increased visibility and the likelihood of confrontation with the Cambodian populace and forces, the International Control Commission, and the foreign press. . . . It is estimated that, as the enemy reaches his full deployment for the current offensive, and his operations begin to run their course, an opportunity will be presented in the III Corps area to strike a strategic blow of major proportions. If successfully exploited, this blow could change the whole balance of forces in Vietnam, severely curtail enemy capability in the vital III Corps area, and shorten the war. (Appendix C, pp. 23–24)

Shawcross preferred not to call this strategic analysis to his readers' attention.

BASE AREA 704: THE WRONG BOX

From the Joint Chiefs' memorandum of April 9, 1969, the White House selected as targets only six base areas minimally populated by civilians. The target areas were given the codenames BREAKFAST, LUNCH, DINNER, SUPPER, SNACK and DESSERT; the overall program was given the name MENU.

With only six base areas, one might have thought that Shawcross would get it right. But he did not. To his embarrassment, a glaring error was discovered during the taping of David Frost's interview with Henry Kissinger in October 1979. Frost hurled at Kissinger the accusation that the White House ordered hundreds of B-52 attacks against a North Vietnamese base area in Cambodia that the Joint Chiefs of Staff had specifically recommended *against* attacking because it was heavily populated by Cambodians. Frost based the accusation on the following passage in *Sideshow*:

> Three of the fifteen sanctuaries—base areas 704, 354 and 707, which had

"sizeable concentrations of Cambodian civilian or military population" in or around them—were not recommended for attack at all. . . . The Chiefs' warning seems to have made no difference. Base Area 704 appeared on the White House's Menu as Supper. In the course of events, 247 B-52 missions were flown against it. (p. 29)

The only problem with this is that Base Area 704, because of its sizeable number of civilian inhabitants, was *never* a target of the B-52 bombing. The target area code-named SUPPER, against which 247 B-52 missions were flown, was Base Area *740* in eastern Cambodia—minimally populated by civilians and about 200 miles away from Base Area 704 which is in southern Cambodia along the Mekong River. Shawcross' assertion that Base Area 704 was attacked by B-52s is totally wrong. The map on page 27 of his book labeling Base Area 704 as target area SUPPER is also wrong.

Shawcross has admitted the error. The map and the relevant pages in his book were redone in subsequent editions. David Frost, informed of the error by Kissinger, was sufficiently embarrassed to request that the taped segment be deleted from the NBC program broadcast on October 11, 1979. It was deleted. But Shawcross was unapologetic. In a letter to Nigel Ryan of NBC News on October 10, 1979, Shawcross acknowledged that his book was wrong—and then offered an explanation as false as the original error. Shawcross excused his mistake on the ground that he had relied on a Defense Department White Paper submitted to the Senate Armed Services Committee in September 1973. This Defense Department statement indeed listed Base Area 704 as one of the six base areas targeted in the MENU program, apparently by a typographical error. What Shawcross failed to mention to NBC News is that he had two documents in his possession making clear that Base Area 740, not 704, was one of the six targets of the B-52 bombing program. A memorandum for Secretary Laird from General Wheeler dated November 20, 1969, recommended "additional" B-52 strikes against Base Area 740 in the MENU series. A similar memorandum of November 25, 1969, again listed Base Area 740 as a MENU target. The first memorandum was published in the Senate Armed Services Committee hearings of 1973 (pp. 151–153), to which *Sideshow* refers frequently; the second memorandum was released to Shawcross in 1977 under the Freedom of Information Act.

A meticulous scholar would have noticed the discrepancy between the 1973 White Paper with the typographical error and the contemporaneous 1969 documents listing Base Area 740 as a MENU target. Had Shawcross noticed the discrepancy he might have guessed that the contemporaneous documents were more authoritative than the after-the-fact summary of 1973. Or he could have checked with the Defense Department, as he did in October 1979, six months after the publication of his book and only after Kissinger pointed out the error. Shawcross did neither. The erroneous figure "proving" American barbarity was too tempting to admit of noticing discrepancies.

It is interesting to read what else the 1969 documents contain. According to the JCS memorandum of November 25, 1969, Base Area 740 contained enemy troop concentrations; anti-aircraft, field artillery, rocket, and mortar positions; eleven North Vietnamese base camps and bivouac areas; two storage areas; road and trail networks including six bridges; as well as numerous bunkers, trenches, and defensive positions—none closer than one and one-half kilometers to any civilian habitation. None of this is mentioned in *Sideshow*.

"DESTABILIZING" SIHANOUK: THE ELUSIVE EVIDENCE

Sihanouk was deposed as Cambodian Chief of State on March 18, 1970, by his own government and National Assembly. This set off a chain of events that ultimately engulfed Cambodia in ten years of bloody conflict.

It is an article of faith in anti-American demonology that the United States had a hand in the coup. (In fact, the United States was taken by surprise.) Shawcross naturally pursues this line of enquiry, only to admit in the end that he can find "no direct link" between the U.S. government and the coup plotters (*Sideshow*, p. 112). He would earn credit for his honesty were it not for two paragraphs of thick insinuation that the United States had plenty of motive and its denials must always be suspect, as if only bad luck can account for his failure to unearth the "direct link."

Shawcross then resorts to a more complicated line of argument to establish American responsibility. Most observers ascribe the coup to Cambodian popular resentment at the continuing North Vietnamese occupation of Cambodian territory tolerated by Sihanouk. Shawcross' thesis is that American B-52 bombings of remote sanctuary areas in 1969–1970 forced the North Vietnamese and Viet Cong troops to push their supply bases "deeper into the country" and "spread the fighting out from the border areas," thereby disrupting Cambodian politics and "destabilizing" Sihanouk's rule. (*Sideshow*, pp. 35, 95, 113–114)

It is difficult for anyone at this point to reconstruct North Vietnamese movements under the American bombings. Undoubtedly they moved to evade the precisely targeted attacks. The crucial questions are where, and to what extent, and with what traceable consequences. Shawcross's documentary evidence is so weak and so tendentiously handled that it casts serious doubt on whether his thesis holds any water at all.

The first document cited by Shawcross is General Wheeler's memorandum of November 20, 1969, to Secretary Laird, which we saw earlier. Shawcross cites it as evidence for the following:

> . . . in Cambodia, as the Chiefs reported, it [the bombing] forced them to 'disperse over a greater area than before.' The raids spread the fighting out from the border areas. . . . (*Sideshow*, p. 95)

General Wheeler's memorandum, however, turns out not to refer to "spreading the fighting" at all. It refers rather to the enemy's dispersal of *supplies* "over a greater area than before." And far from endorsing Shawcross's claim that they moved "deeper into Cambodia" into conflicts with Cambodian authorities, the passage describes the North Vietnamese as dispersing supplies, and secondarily personnel, into more *isolated* areas on the immediate periphery of the main base areas, or in between the various base areas, which were strung out along the Vietnamese border. The passage cited by Shawcross actually reads:

> Supplies have been dispersed over a greater area than before; and supplies have

been moved into densely covered, unstruck areas. This tends to be confirmed by the increased activity noted since mid-October approximately mid-way between Base Areas 350 and 351. . . . However, even with his increased dispersal of personnel and supplies, the enemy continues to use portions of his old areas. (Wheeler memorandum, 20 November 1969, quoted in the 1973 Senate hearings, p. 152)

Thus the source cited by Shawcross is not only irrelevant to his main point but in direct contradiction to it. His use of the document is either deceptive or notably inept.

But there is more. Shawcross then invents a phony quotation from General Creighton Abrams:

To escape the bombardment [Shawcross writes], the Vietnamese Communists had begun to move deeper into Cambodia—"thus," as Abrams later acknowledged to the Senate, "bringing them into increasing conflict with the Cambodian authorities.". . . The effect was inevitable. . . . Sihanouk's balance of right against left became more precarious. The bombing was destabilizing him. (*Sideshow*, p. 113)

It turns out that the quoted words attributed to General Abrams in testimony to the Senate Armed Services Committee were spoken in reality by Senator Stuart Symington. In a book so fawned over for its scholarship, this is remarkable sleight of hand. Senator Symington put forward the proposition that U.S. bombings and ground probes from South Vietnam must have induced the North Vietnamese "to expand their areas of control or operations, thus bringing them into increasing conflict with the Cambodian authorities." Abrams indeed "acknowledged" this in the vaguest terms ("Yes, I think that is a fair statement"). Unfortunately we do not have General Abrams's own analysis because Senator Symington moved to a different subject. Nor is it likely that the Army Chief of Staff would tell a powerful senator on the Armed Services Committee that he was full of baloney. And neither General Abrams nor Senator Symington even touched upon the two central steps in Shawcross' argument: that the bombing drove the Vietnamese and the war "deeper into Cambodia" and was responsible for undermining Sihanouk's government. The Abrams/Symington exchange, even if quoted honestly, does not establish the crucial points.

The claim of North Vietnamese "spreading in Cambodia" is repeated in another passage shortly thereafter. This time Shawcross invokes an article published in Sihanouk's monthly journal *Le Sangkum* in October 1969 written by Sihanouk's Prime Minister and Defense Minister, Marshal Lon Nol:

. . . their spread [Shawcross writes] was due [in Lon Nol's words] to flooding and to "the operational pressure exerted by their adversary," that is, to clearing operations by American and South Vietnamese troops. (*Sideshow*, p. 114)

Lon Nol was writing of incidents of conflict between the North Vietnamese and Cambodian troops, thus confirming what General Abrams "acknowledged" to

Senator Symington. But rather remarkable in this article, seven months after the beginning of the MENU bombing, is the absence of any reference to North Vietnamese "spreading" and, indeed, the complete absence of any mention of the U.S. bombing. Lon Nol is describing a totally different cause and a totally different effect. He writes of the increase in numbers (*accroissement*) of Vietnamese Communist forces *in* their base areas—not the spreading *out* of these bases. And he blames not the enemy's flight from American bombing in Cambodia but the enemy's withdrawal (*repli*) from South Vietnam, made necessary (as Shawcross notes) by American and South Vietnamese clearing operations *in South Vietnam*. Seven months after the bombing began, if Shawcross is to be believed, the Cambodian government should have complained of the American bombing as the cause of disruption and "destabilization" that Shawcross is so eager to prove. Yet Sihanouk and Lon Nol saw the menace elsewhere; they placed the condemnation precisely where it belonged. The article was entitled: "The Implantations of Viet Cong and North Vietnamese Along Our Frontier."

Shawcross has been backtracking lately, writing in a recent *Harper's* that the movement of North Vietnamese "deeper into the country" may not have been very extensive but that "a few miles deeper" was enough to disrupt Cambodia's political equilibrium. Considering how much of the weight of Shawcross' entire argument rests on this complicated syllogism, it is striking how weak is the evidentiary basis for it. (Even the map on page 27 of *Sideshow* showing the Communist base areas in the 1969–70 period offers no indication of any change in their location or extent over those two years.) Prince Sihanouk is rather more honest, telling the Cambodia Affairs Institute in Washington ten years after his overthrow: "If I lost my *Fauteuil presidentiel* and my Chamcar Mon Palace in Phnom Penh to Marshal Lon Nol who occupied them for five years, it was because I tremendously helped the Vietcong and the North Vietnamese."

NORTH VIETNAMESE ASSAULT ON CAMBODIA: THE MISSING MONTH OF APRIL

Like Sherlock Holmes' dog that didn't bark, the most striking distortion in *Sideshow* is an epic event in Cambodian history that is simply omitted from the book.

The new Cambodian government, even before it stripped Sihanouk of his powers, formally asked the North Vietnamese and Viet Cong in mid-March 1970 to vacate their Cambodian sanctuaries. The North Vietnamese responded with the humanitarianism for which they are renowned: they invaded the rest of Cambodia. Sweeping out of their bases along the border, they attacked and overran Cambodian military outposts, Cambodian towns, Cambodian roads, and Cambodian river communications all over the eastern half of the country, linking their scattered sanctuaries into one massive continuous base area aimed at South Vietnam and advancing westward on Phnom Penh, surrounding and menacing the capital with the evident intention of intimidating the new government into passivity, surrender, or collapse.

It was this wholesale North Vietnamese assault on eastern Cambodia, beginning late March 1970, that plunged Cambodia into the Indochina war for the first time. To be sure, the remote sanctuaries along the border had been the subject of North

Vietnamese occupation and American counter-attacks; there had been occasional local incidents between North Vietnamese and Cambodian authorities. But Cambodia had never been at war; the Cambodian armed forces had never before been belligerent; in full-scale hostilities. The North Vietnamese changed all that. It was after a month of these assaults that the United States and South Vietnam launched the so-called Cambodian incursion on April 30 to block the North Vietnamese and to protect American and South Vietnamese lives against the vast new North Vietnamese military base ballooning over all of eastern Cambodia.

The reader turns eagerly to *Sideshow* to see what this brilliantly comprehensive investigative reporter has to say on the subject of this North Vietnamese invasion. Nothing. Absolutely nothing. There is but one disingenuous descriptive sentence, ascribing only defensive motives to the North Vietnamese:

> [T]he North Vietnamese moved westward into Cambodia with the apparent intention of securing their lines of communication. (*Sideshow*, p. 130)

There are one or two oblique references elsewhere in *Sideshow* that would indeed require Sherlock Holmes to piece them together and deduce that something was going on. It is not that Shawcross lacked information. Under the Freedom of Information Act, he had, for example, an important cable of April 21, 1970, in which Acting Chairman of the Joint Chiefs General William Westmoreland informed General Abrams in Saigon of the fact that Phnom Penh was surrounded and threatened:

> As you are certainly aware, there is highest level concern here with respect to the situation in Cambodia. This concern has been heightened by the following:
> a. It appears that the success of NVA and VC troops to date have encouraged them to expand what may have been limited objectives initially to a current drive to isolate Phnom Penh.
> b. Most lines of communication leading into Phnom Penh from the north, east, and south have been interdicted by enemy forces and the security of Phnom Penh and the Cambodian Government appears to be seriously threatened. (JCS 05495, 21 April 1970)

The North Vietnamese were systematically interdicting all the major roads and waterways that led into Phnom Penh, cutting off the highways particularly to the north, east, and south of the city and blocking traffic on the Mekong River that was the city's lifeline. This North Vietnamese assault would seem to have little to do with "securing their lines of communication," as *Sideshow* fatuously claims, but a great deal to do with strangling the lines of communication of the Cambodian capital.

None of this is to be found in *Sideshow*. Shawcross prefers to regard the U.S.-South Vietnamese incursion as gratuitous and unprovoked, explained by the psychic aberrations of the Nixon administration: "the White House's truculence," Nixon's eagerness for "restoring his slighted authority" after domestic setbacks, "negligent and emotional decision making," and other *ad hominem* imputations of pathological aggression (pp. 130ff). The whole month of April is practically missing from the book—except for minor *American* actions after mid-April, without reference to the North Vietnamese attacks to which they were a response.

When Kissinger described these North Vietnamese attacks in his book and the David Frost interview, Shawcross took evasive action. His first response was to claim that Kissinger's account of the North Vietnamese assault was an afterthought: "[A]t the time of the [U.S.–South Vietnamese] invasion, neither Nixon nor Kissinger mentioned these moves or used them to justify American actions," *Newsweek* reported him as claiming. Yet no one could possibly read the Nixon administration's public statements of the time—April 30, June 3, June 30, 1970; February 25, 1971—and not find that the North Vietnamese invasion of eastern Cambodia was *the* reason for the allied military operations of April 30, 1970. Shawcross later retreated to the narrower assertion that "many" of the individual clashes listed in Kissinger's book "have never been mentioned before, neither in Nixon's announcement of the invasion, nor anywhere else." This is ridiculous. *The New York Times* reported the rapid advance of the North Vietnamese invasion of Cambodia throughout the period and published a map on April 18, 1970, showing them already in control of a third of the country. If Kissinger's is indeed the most detailed and comprehensive description of the events of 1970—which it is—how this is a criticism of the Kissinger book is not obvious.

Shawcross' other tack has been to claim that Hanoi's *intention* in devouring eastern Cambodia in March–April 1970 "has never been proven" and has always been in dispute. The assertions that Hanoi really sought to topple the Cambodian regime, Shawcross now says, "have no basis in reality." This is first of all false and second of all a curious line of argument. Presumably it is possible to invade a country, occupy a third of it, lay siege to its capital, and yet claim sufficient ambiguity about one's motives to render any counter-measures not only unwarranted but immoral. The only account in *Sideshow*, remember, is that the North Vietnamese moved westward to "secur[e] their lines of communication."

What is the evidence? Shawcross certainly had enough documentation to show that the American government at the highest levels had good reason to believe the worst about North Vietnamese intentions. Witness Westmoreland's message of April 21, 1970, that Phnom Penh was surrounded, quoted above, not to mention all of Sihanouk's public statements including his March 23, 1970, five-point declaration calling for the overthrow of the Lon Nol government, and the declarations of solidarity from the North Vietnamese, Viet Cong, and Pathet Lao. On the ground, the North Vietnamese efforts to establish (and dominate) the insurgency aroused the resentment of, among others, the Khmer Rouge (the Cambodian Communists, who came to power in their own right five years later). The "Black Book" issued by the Khmer Rouge (Pol Pot) regime in September 1978 recounts:

> After the coup d'etat, of March 18th 1970, the [North] Vietnamese organized their nationals living in Kampuchea, they armed them and used them as particularly ferocious instruments of oppression against the people of Kampuchea. . . . [The North Vietnamese] secretly organized a shadow national administration in Kampuchea, particularly in the north-east zone. . . [They] organized a secret shadow army in Kampuchea. . . .

This was published seven months before *Sideshow* appeared but Shawcross does not refer to it.

Among North Vietnamese documents captured by the allies in the post-April 30 sweep through the sanctuaries were guidebooks for the organizing (by the North Vietnamese) of the Sihanouk-proclaimed "National United Front of Cambodia" (FUNK) at the hamlet and village level to take power after the overthrow of the Lon Nol government; directives pledging support by North Vietnamese cadre and armed forces for the FUNK; soldiers' notebooks detailing North Vietnamese activity in forming and training guerrilla units; military staff notebooks on the formation of Cambodian units led by North Vietnamese cadre and of signal battalions, and so on. This is public knowledge.

Even *Sideshow* contains a damaging admission by Shawcross that "a government dominated by Hanoi" was the probable outcome if the United States did nothing (p. 165). Nor have any of Shawcross' emotional rebuttals to the Kissinger book even addressed one of its most important revelations: that in secret talks with North Vietnamese negotiator Le Duc Tho on April 4, 1970, Kissinger proposed joint diplomatic steps to guarantee the neutralization of Cambodia. Le Duc Tho contemptuously dismissed the offer and insisted on the overthrow of the new Cambodian government.

It was the North Vietnamese assault of March–April 1970 that plunged Cambodia into war, whatever *Sideshow*'s evasions. In 1979, four years after the Khmer Rouge victory, the North Vietnamese invaded Cambodia again, demonstrating that the heirs of Ho Chi Minh never had the slightest intention of tolerating a truly independent Cambodia, even an independent *Communist* Cambodia.

THE STRANGULATION OF THE CAMBODIAN ARMY

The Cambodian Army resisted the assault of the North Vietnamese and Khmer Rouge for five years, succumbing finally in April 1975. Their struggle was prey to a host of difficulties: poor organization and logistics; lack of training and the technical know-how to maintain and use equipment; petty corruption and the progressive, Congressionally mandated withdrawal of American military support—from the 1970 ban on U.S. advisers, to the 1973 halt of U.S. air operations, to the 1975 strangulation of military supplies. Pentagon accounts document this well, and Shawcross under the FOIA had access to two of the best: the end-of-tour reports of two American officers who headed the Military Equipment Delivery Team in Cambodia (MEDTC), Major General John Cleland and his successor, Brigadier General William W. Palmer.

These accounts are quite moving, but Shawcross suppresses their principal points and turns the documents totally on their head. By quoting selectively he develops a tendentious thesis of his own to explain Cambodia's failure. He dismisses the generals' own analysis (without informing his readers of its contents) in a crude *ad hominem* attack:

> These reports must be read with caution, since each man was anxious to promote his own career in the Army despite the Cambodian debacle. Each, therefore, was concerned to attach all the blame to the Cambodians and refused

to analyze carefully the effect of his own work in Phnom Penh. (*Sideshow*, p. 312)

Shawcross second-guesses the American strategy and blames Generals Cleland and Palmer for the disaster that befell the Khmer National Armed Forces (FANK):

> Cleland explained the rationale—and, unconsciously, its serious implications—in his end-of-tour report: "The FANK depend on firepower to win. Seldom has FANK outmaneuvered the enemy—he has outgunned him." But his own actions made this inevitable; instead of improving the intrinsic fighting quality of Lon Nol's troops, Cleland created a fatal new dependency in them. By mid-1974 fully 87 percent of all American military aid was being spent on ammunition. If the Congress began to cut back aid or if the Khmer Rouge closed all lines of communication, then the government's troops would be deprived of "the quickfix" (to use another Cleland expression) which the Americans had thrust upon them. Both these things did happened and each contributed toward making the fall of the regime inevitable. (*Sideshow*, p. 313)

Shawcross' military critique is utterly disingenuous. Generals Palmer and Cleland stress an obvious and totally different point: that Congressional restrictions made any other strategy impossible. The ban on U.S. advisers meant that there was no possibility of "improving the intrinsic fighting quality of Lon Nol's troops," as Shawcross professes to recommend; escalating legislative prohibitions deprived the Cambodians of what assets they had. Shawcross is not really recommending an alternative approach to assistance; his argument is that no assistance should have been given the Cambodians in the first place. He faults the Congress, indeed, but only for the degree to which it acceded to administration requests at all. (*Sideshow*, p. 350)

General Palmer's end-of-tour report, for example, makes poignantly clear how even the minimum objective of achieving a military stalemate (for purposes of negotiation) was rendered impossible because the Cambodian Army's few advantages over the enemy were eroded by the progressive reduction of American aid. It is a powerful account that Shawcross understandably did not want his readers to see:

(1) *Congressional Restrictions*

In January 1971, the Cooper–Church Amendment specifically prohibited "advisors" in Cambodia. The Symington–Case Amendment of February 1972 prescribed that the total number of U.S. personnel in Cambodia should not exceed 200. In view of the U.S. Vietnam experience, the intent of these restrictions is understandable. However, their cumulative effect was to severely limit any MEDTC ability to ensure that millions of dollars in MAP [Military Assistance Program] funds were being well spent. FANK was provided modern equipment but was denied the overall training, technical know-how, and military professionalism desperately needed to modernize it in the areas of tactical leadership, staff planning and coordination, personnel and financial management or logistics operations. Proper management and effective use of the equipment provided was apparently to be learned by a trial and error, do-it-yourself process which time would not permit.

Lacking any authority to provide in-country advice on U.S. training, any improvement in FANK leadership was predicated on almost non-existent Khmer initiatives since American officers were too restricted to assist. (Palmer Report, April 30, 1975, Part One, IV/B(1))

(2) *Reliance on Firepower*

FANK was originally conceived as a "light infantry force" designed to fight "Khmer Insurgents." When it became apparent that the "insurgents" were rapidly evolving into main force units in their own right, the U.S. objective of keeping FANK alive and the GKR [Government of the Khmer Republic] viable was assured through the quick-fix of massive U.S. airpower. With the U.S. bombing halt in August 1973, the Khmer Army artillery and tactical air inventories were augmented because this solution provided less expensive and politically more palatable sources of firepower to offset the leadership and manpower deficiencies in the Khmer Armed Forces. As that firepower was increasingly denied to them because of escalating munitions costs and reduced funding, the only remaining option appeared to be manpower.

However the Army's inability even to maintain the strength of its intervention brigades, let alone achieve significant growth, soon became self-evident. Moreover, serious leadership and training deficiencies, combined with the absence of any U.S. advisory or training effort, obviated major changes in the Khmer force structure, battle tactics or doctrinal reliance on firepower, even if sufficient time had been available.

In sum, the U.S. taught the Khmer Armed Forces to survive through firepower. FANK was equipped with the means to employ it in large amounts. Outside sources of firepower were withdrawn so that they relied solely on their own firepower assets. Firepower and the logistics to support it became the two most important advantages FANK had over the KC [Khmer Communists], and by 1974 it was too late to change that orientation to any extent in the short term. Therefore, as escalating prices drove munitions costs progressively higher, increasing rather than decreasing levels of MAP funding were necessary to promote successful achievement of U.S. objectives in Cambodia. (Part One, IV/B (2))

FEELING SORRY FOR THE KHMER ROUGE

Shawcross at least acknowledges the genocidal brutality of the Khmer Rouge after they took power, in contrast to the other prophets of the Left who still consider the charges to be imperialist propaganda. But Shawcross nevertheless excuses the atrocities by another line of argument: that they were all America's fault. Apologetics nonetheless. His book is not subtitled "The Khmer Rouge and the Destruction of Cambodia," but "Kissinger, Nixon and the Destruction of Cambodia."

The viciousness of the Khmer Rouge he attributes to a paroxysm of vengeance, a seizure of "Manichean fear" induced by the severe "punishment" inflicted upon them in the years of their struggle—that is to say, by American and Cambodian efforts to resist them. This is one of the central theses of his book, and for it he offers no documentation whatsoever:

> All wars are designed to arouse anger, and almost all soldiers are taught to hate and to dehumanize their enemy. Veterans of the combat zone are often possessed of a mad rage to destroy, and to avenge their fallen comrades. It does not always happen, however, that victorious armies have endured such punishment as was inflicted upon the Khmer Rouge. Nor does it always happen that such an immature and tiny force comes to power after its country's social order has been obliterated, and the nation faces the danger of takeover by a former ally, its ancient enemy. In Cambodia that did take place. In the last years, degree, law, moderation had been forsworn. The war and the causes for which it was fought had brought desolation while nurturing and then giving power to a little group of zealots sustained by Manichean fear. (*Sideshow*, p. 389)

It is enough to make one feel sorry for the poor Khmer Rouge. How perfectly natural that they would up and murder three million of their own people! This is, of course, ridiculous. Most soldiers in combat have "endured . . . punishment" but none before have murdered a third of the population of their country after the war was over.

American bombing had ended twenty months before they came to power. The evacuation of Phnom Penh was planned months before. The savagery was systematic—forced dispersal of whole populations; destruction of traditional social structures, organized religion, and even the family; forced collectivization of agriculture; liquidation of the middle class and civil service; police terror—and it was all standard Khmer Rouge practice in all the areas they controlled in Cambodia from as early as *1971*. The genocide was premeditated, motivated by ideology, and the work of political fanatics. And the definitive evidence for this is found in Shawcross' own sources.

One of the best is *Cambodia: Year Zero* by Francois Ponchaud, a French Jesuit who lived through the early horrific phases of the Khmer Rouge victory. Ponchaud is a friend of Shawcross and no defender of American policy; nevertheless his book shows a clarity about Khmer Rouge motivations that Shawcross seems to have deliberately avoided. Shawcross cites Ponchaud extensively but never the passages stressing the ideological premeditation of Khmer Rouge policies dating back at least to 1972. Ponchaud writes, for example (emphases added):

> [A]ccusing foreigners cannot acquit the present leaders of Kampuchea: *their inflexible ideology had led them to invent a radically new kind of man in a radically new society*. A fascinating revolution for all who aspire to a new social order. A terrifying one for all who have any respect for human beings. (p. xvi)

So we must look elsewhere for an explanation of the deportation from Phnom Penh. The official reasons certainly had something to do with the decision to clear the city, but they do not seem sufficient. *The deeper reason was an ideological one*, as we later saw clearly when we learned that the provincial towns, villages, and even isolated farms in the countryside had also been emptied of their inhabitants.

The evacuation of Phnom Penh follows traditional Khmer revolutionary practice: ever since 1972 the guerrilla fighters had been sending all the inhabitants of the villages and towns they occupied into the forest to live, often burning their homes so they would have nothing to come back for. A massive, total operation such as this reflects a new concept of society, in which there is no place even for the idea of a city. The towns of Cambodia had grown up around marketplaces; Phnom Penh itself owed its expansion to French colonialism, Chinese commerce, and the bureaucracy of the monarchy, followed by that of the republic. All this had to be swept away and an egalitarian rural society put in its place. (p. 21)

On April 17, 1975, a society collapsed; another is now being born from the fierce drive of a revolution which is incontestably the most radical ever to take place in so short a time. *It is a perfect example of the application of an ideology pushed to the furthest limit of its internal logic.* (p. 192)

Shawcross had another important source as well: a U.S. government study by Foreign Service Officer Kenneth M. Quinn. From interviews with refugees fleeing Cambodia in 1973 and 1974, Quinn pieced together a detailed description of Khmer Rouge totalitarian practices and shows that they began in some areas in late 1971. Shawcross cites some of Quinn's account (pp. 321–322) but leaves the impression that it all dates from 1974. Another source, a Cambodian intellectual, is quoted at length in reference to the 1972–73 period, but all the quotes describe Khmer Rouge organizational structure and political indoctrination, including their "respect for the 'ways of the people.'" (pp. 251–255)

The distortion is calculated. American bombing reached its peak in the spring of 1973. The evidence of Father Ponchaud and Kenneth Quinn that the Khmer Rouge were totalitarian thugs in 1971 and 1972 contradicts the thesis that Shawcross struggles mightily but in vain to prove: that it was American bombing that turned the Khmer Rouge into butchers.

Sideshow is filled with countless other errors and distortions. On one page he asserts that "no Communist offensive had been launched" when the secret bombing began in 1969; yet the preceding page had quoted from a North Vietnamese document hailing the Communist spring offensive of 1969 because it killed more Americans than the Tet offensive of 1968 (pp. 109–111). His tendentious account of the role of the U.S. Embassy in the bombing procedures of 1973 (pp. 272–277) relies on a Senate Foreign Relations Committee staff report that is itself wildly erroneous. His chapters on alleged "missed opportunities" to negotiate a settlement are undercut by the mountain of evidence that the North Vietnamese and later the Khmer Rouge rejected all American and Cambodian overtures to compromise.*

* The "Black Book" published by the Pol Pot regime in September 1978 reveals the reason: The Khmer Rouge resisted all pressures for a cease-fire in 1972–73 because "if the Kampuchean

Sideshow

As a work of history the book is worthless. It is an elegant polemic in which scrupulous regard for evidence has been swept aside by political bias and emotional compulsion. Its elaborate documentation is impressive only if one has not seen the original documents. To understand it, one must leave historiography and explore the realms of psychiatry.

The antiwar movement's temptation to gloat at the long-predicted collapse of the "corrupt" anti-Communist regimes of Indochina was quickly stilled by the tales of holocaust that emerged from Cambodia. (The "boat-people" of Vietnam and the poison-gas campaign to exterminate the Hmong in Laos came a bit later.) For anti-war critics had assured us beforehand that the collapse of the Lon Nol government would end the killing and be a blessing for the Cambodian people. "What future possibility could be more terrible than the reality of what is happening to Cambodia now?" asked Anthony Lewis on March 17, 1975, urging a cutoff of American aid. Abandoning the Cambodian government was "for the good of the suffering Cambodians themselves," the *Los Angeles Times* assured us on April 11. "Indochina Without Americans: For Most, a Better Life," was the headline of a piece in *The New York Times* on April 13, datelined Phnom Penh. Its author, Sydney Schanberg, had comforted us a month before with a report that the Khmer Rouge would be more moderate after victory and that fears of a bloodbath were unfounded. These predictions turned out to be horribly wrong. The people of Cambodia paid the price. But there were no recriminations in America. The administration was stuck with a failed policy, and its opponents were understandably sheepish at the results of an outcome they had long urged.

Then along came Shawcross. Vietnam critics could now "resist all attempts to make them feel guilty for the stand they took against the war," as Stanley Hoffmann urged them in an enthusiastic review. Shawcross was a godsend. How psychologically comforting to have in hand a convoluted theory and purported evidence that *American* government decisions were the propelling force behind the horrible events after all. How politically convenient to be able to focus responsibility on a Republican administration for the most gruesome outcome of a failed military commitment begun under two liberal Democratic Presidents.

But it was too convenient to be true. The book's evidentiary basis is shoddy and deceitful. By no stretch of moral logic can the crimes of mass murder be ascribed to those who struggled to prevent their coming into power. One hopes that no craven sophistry will ever induce free peoples to accept the doctrine that Shawcross embodies: that resistance to totalitarianism is immoral. So whatever the book's value as psychotherapy, as a history of Cambodia it is a joke. And as political apologetics it is obscene.

revolution had accepted a cease-fire it would have collapsed." Later they rejected a compromise because they smelled victory. This will not be found in *Sideshow*.

William Shawcross' reply to Rodman, written in the form of a letter to the Editor of *The American Spectator*, April 27, 1981, and published in July of that year under the title: **SHAWCROSS SWIPES AGAIN**

Sir,

I have been away for some time in South-east Asia and I have only just seen the article by Dr. Kissinger's aide, Peter Rodman, in your March 1981 issue ("Sideswipe: Kissinger, Shawcross and the Responsibility for Cambodia"), attacking my book, *Sideshow: Kissinger, Nixon and the Destruction of Cambodia* (Simon and Schuster, 1979).

It is good that Cambodia should be the subject of interest and debate. And I suppose it is flattering that almost two years after the publication of my book, Kissinger should instruct his aide to attack it. But Mr. Rodman has misled your readers. What he should have acknowledged is that he had a great deal of help from me in preparing his article. Here is how:

This article is a rehash of a long memorandum prepared by Mr. Rodman on Dr. Kissinger's instructions in the second half of 1979. That memorandum, entitled "Shawcross's Documents," was anonymous and its authors saw fit to claim (anonymously) in its introduction that it was "an independent examination" of documents I had obtained under the Freedom of Information Act. It was distributed quite widely by Mr. Rodman and Dr. Kissinger—to journalists and others—with the strict instruction that I was not to be allowed to see it. Its inaccuracies, distortions, and omissions were deliberately misleading; they may even have misled you in the article which you published about my book at the end of 1979 in which you said that "rumors now circulate" that I had misused the documents.

In the summer of 1980, I obtained a copy of the Rodman–Kissinger anonymous memorandum. I immediately wrote a detailed response to it. I sent copies of both memos to a number of journalists, editors and academics interested in Cambodia. (A short article about the two memos appeared in *New York* magazine.) I also sent a copy of my response to Dr. Kissinger for his information; he did not reply. Later last year, my publishers decided to bring out a new edition of *Sideshow*; I decided that Rodman's memorandum and my repudiation of it should both be published in this new edition. The book will be out (Touchstone) in a few weeks time.

Perhaps it was because I had already given his covert attack such publicity that Kissinger decided to have Rodman go public himself—almost two years after *Sideshow* was first published. In any case, the article in *The American Spectator* is Rodman's memo rewritten with the help of my own memo. It would have been honest for Rodman to have noted this. As for you, Sir, either you knew the tale of the two memos, in which case you were hardly straightforward in telling your readers, "Now I have asked Peter Rodman . . . to illuminate the Shawcross method of cooking up history," or you did not, in which case Mr. Rodman was hardly straightforward with you.

So much for the history of Rodman's concoction. What of its substance? The best one can say is that in the light of my own repudiation, some of the most ludicrous charges have been removed, others tempered. But, even with my help, Rodman's work is unimpressive—long on abuse, short on honest argument. He also fails, like Kissinger himself, to address the real issues raised by the history of Cambodia. I apologize to your readers for the fact that this can be shown only at considerable length.

"CHESTER BOWLES: THE MISSING QUOTATION"

Chester Bowles visited Sihanouk in 1968. Kissinger and other Nixon administration officials subsequently claimed that Sihanouk, in effect, then gave the green light for the secret U.S. B-52 campaign which began in March 1969 against Vietnamese Communist sanctuaries in Cambodia. Rodman labors to show the same thing and that I concealed it. Sihanouk did not. I did not. Bowles talked with Sihanouk and his officials about "hot pursuit," not about B-52 bombing at all. Even if Sihanouk had authorized U.S. "hot pursuit" of Vietnamese Communists into Cambodia this could in no way be taken as authorizing a massive B-52 campaign against the sanctuaries. The record of what happened in the conversation is anyway ambiguous and I am scrupulous at showing this.

Rodman has shifted from the position he took in the memorandum. There he accused me of not quoting a direct statement from Sihanouk to Bowles which Kissinger quotes in his memoirs. The implication was that I had concealed it. In fact, as I pointed out in my reply, that statement had not before been published and was not in the documents released to me. Kissinger does not source it in his memoirs. Rodman has now dropped that attack.

But his new attack is just as fraudulent. He claims that the State Department's report, which I received in a sanitized form and which I quoted, "contained evidence that could not be more conclusive, which Shawcross chose to conceal from his readers . . ." He then quotes the report as saying that "in one of his amazing reversals Sihanouk said he would not object to 'hot pursuit' . . ." I did not conceal this passage. As Rodman must know perfectly well, it was not in the report as I received it. Perhaps it was in one of the sections excised for reasons of national security. In any case, I did not receive it.

Even if I had received it, I would not have found it conclusive of anything. There is enormous difference between "hot pursuit" and a B-52 bombing campaign sustained over more than a year. Moreover, Bowles' own talking paper stated, "we do not regard so-called hot pursuit as a desirable remedy," and the State Department report concludes at the end of the mission that the Bowles party believed that "there seemed little doubt that on the Cambodian side fears of hot pursuit had been allayed." Rodman does not mention that.

Rodman quotes Chester Bowles' autobiography, in which Bowles says Sihanouk took him aside and said he would not object to U.S. "hot pursuit" into unpopulated areas of Cambodia. Bowles, says Rodman, "was skeptical." Indeed he was. He wrote, "I doubted that he meant it." And what else did Bowles say of that visit? Quite a lot, all of which Rodman "conceals from his readers." He was sent there by Lyndon Johnson to discuss the Communists in the border areas. "The Pentagon had been pressing for the right of 'hot pursuit' across the Cambodian border, and my visit was obviously part of an effort to relieve this pressure." At the end of the trip, Bowles writes:

There seemed little doubt that on the Cambodian side fears of "hot pursuit" by U.S. and South Vietnamese troops, which had been strongly rumored in the American press had now been allayed; it never occurred to any of us that less than two years later we would actually invade Cambodia. . . Later events in Cambodia, the overthrow of Sihanouk and the subsequent introduction of U.S. troops there with the result of widening the scope of the war in Vietnam have served to emphasize for all to see what became evident to me during my visit. Sihanouk's policies, though often irritating to the United States, were an effective means of guarding the neutrality of Cambodia. (pp. 576–580)

But Rodman then says, "Sihanouk's position never deviated from this"—i.e., his aside on "hot pursuit"—"After the B-52 bombing started in 1969 and was reported in the American press, Sihanouk responded in similar terms publicly . . ." And in one press conference, which Rodman cites, he did indeed say that he would not object to the U.S. bombing the Vietnamese. But another was called *specifically to deny* a UPI report from Saigon that he would tolerate B-52 bombing. In that press conference, March 31, 1969, Sihanouk said, "Nobody, no chief of state in the world placed in the same situation as I am, would agree to let foreign aircraft bomb his own country . . . I do not want to run the risk, because of their bombing of the communists, of seeing an escalation of the war extend to Cambodia—that is, I will in all cases oppose all bombing on Cambodian territory under whatever pretext." Rodman and Kissinger have always concealed this press conference from their readers.

It was my view, expressed in *Sideshow*, that Sihanouk was a cunning fellow, whose statements did not always fully reflect his real views. The point is that it is untrue for Rodman to claim that "Sihanouk's position never deviated." In this as in many other matters, Sihanouk was a most accomplished deviator.

To make clear all the ambiguities and uncertainties, I actually agree (p. 94) that "It is possible that Prince Sihanouk was indeed a party to the conspiracy"—that he would tolerate bombing so long as it was kept secret. Rodman conceals this from his readers. And in an interview with Sihanouk after the rest of the book went to press, I quote him (p. 390) as telling me, "I did not know about the B-52 bombing in 1969. In 1968, I had told Chester Bowles, *en passant*, that the United States could bomb Vietnamese sanctuaries, but the question of a big B-52 campaign was never raised."

Rodman's treatment of my account of the Bowles mission is a sham. First, because he dissembles and second, because he ignores the vital point, which I stressed, that whatever Sihanouk told Bowles was quite irrelevant in terms of the U.S. Constitution. The administration had no right to conceal the bombing from Congress simply because that may have been convenient for Sihanouk. "The whims of and the constraints upon a foreign prince . . . are not grounds for the President to wage war . . . By informing only a few sympathetic legislators in a general way of the bombing, the White House was deliberately usurping the Congress' constitutional rights and responsibilities." That was the principal argument I was making, as Rodman knows. He does not dare address it.

"WHAT THE CHIEF'S MEMORANDUM REALLY SAID"

Rodman's complaint seems to be that I claim the United States "callously assumed the risk of massive harm to civilians" in the secret B-52 bombing of the sanctuaries 1969–70. I do nothing of the sort. I simply show from contemporary U.S. Government documents, of which this memo was only one, that it was a lie for Kissinger and other officials to claim later (and as Kissinger continued to claim in his memoirs) that the sanctuaries were "all unpopulated" by Cambodians. I did not, as Rodman seeks to show, exaggerate the danger to these Cambodians, as expressed in the Chiefs' memo; indeed, I said (p. 28) of the Chiefs' assertion that there were Cambodian "towns" in the sanctuary areas that "villages would be a more accurate description."

Rodman does not share with your readers the Chiefs' actual estimates of the numbers of Cambodians living in the areas which became MENU sites. They were:

Area 609,	LUNCH,	198
Area 351,	SNACK,	383
Area 352,	DINNER,	770
Area 350,	DESSERT,	120
Area 740,	SUPPER,	1,136

To Cambodians (as perhaps to many other people) these are communities, some of them sizeable.

"BASE AREA 704: THE WRONG BOX"

I repeated a mistake made by the Pentagon and as soon as it was discovered at the Pentagon—from enquiries made simultaneously by me and by Kissinger—I acknowledged it. Neither David Frost nor I was "embarrassed" by the error, as Rodman claims; when we learned of it there was no question but that the Frost–Kissinger exchange in which it was involved be deleted from the interview or that the three sentences in my book which referred to it be deleted also.

The error was first made not by me but in the Defense Department White Paper that Rodman mentions. This stated clearly that area 704 was SUPPER, when in fact SUPPER was area 740. It is true that I had other documents referring to the bombing of Area 740, though neither of them identified it as SUPPER. I did not notice the discrepancy. I should have. All I can say is that I am used to White Papers being accurate.

But how important was the mistake, in fact? Almost irrelevant. Rodman claims that Area 740, the *real* SUPPER was "minimally populated by civilians." But, according to the Chiefs' memo cited above, Area 740 contained 1,136 civilians. This was the second largest concentration of civilians in the sanctuaries bombed after BREAKFAST which was said to have 1,640. If communities of 1,640 and 1,136 are "minimal" to Rodman, I rest my case.

"'DESTABILIZING' SIHANOUK: THE ELUSIVE EVIDENCE"

Kissinger and Rodman are in the unhappy position of asserting (1) that the MENU bombing campaign successfully dispersed the Vietnamese Communists from their Cambodian sanctuaries, (2) that a principal reason for the overthrow of Sihanouk was that these same Vietnamese moved further into Cambodia in 1969–70, and (3) that there is no direct relation between (1) and (2). But at least Rodman has retreated from Kissinger's claim—scotched by David Frost—that the bombing actually encouraged the Vietnamese to move into South Vietnam rather than deeper into Cambodia.

Certainly I say that the bombing, together with the other U.S. and South Vietnamese operations, pushed the North Vietnamese further into Cambodia. It is nonsense for Kissinger and Rodman to attempt to deny it. This movement increased right-wing and military dissatisfaction at home with Sihanouk. U.S. officials in South Vietnam and Washington were well aware of this.

As Rodman says, I write that I found "no direct link" between the U.S. Government and the coup plotters (p. 112). But certainly I think there was American motive for replacing Sihanouk and that I established this without, as Rodman claims, "thick insinuation." The principal motive was a desire, by one means or another, to clean out the sanctuaries. I never deny, despite Rodman's claims in various parts of his article, that those sanctuaries were large and were seen by the U.S. commanders as serious military threats.

On p. 122 I write, "this account of the coup is neither complete nor conclusive; the extent of American complicity (if any) could probably only be uncovered by Congressional investigation." What I do is produce a good deal of evidence that at the very least American officials in Vietnam had prior knowledge of the plot, through their contacts with anti-Sihanouk exiles led by Son Ngoc Thanh. I quote William Colby, among others, on this. Colby said of the coup's leader, Lon Nol, at this time, "Lon Nol may well have been encouraged by the fact that the U.S. was working with Son Ngoc Thanh. I don't know of any specific assurances he was given, but the obvious conclusion for him, given the political situation in South Vietnam and Laos, was that he would be given United States support" if he overthrew Sihanouk. He was.

Rodman then claims that I "invent[ed] a phony quotation from General Abrams." I did not. This was the full exchange between Senator Symington and General Abrams:

Symington: During 1969 and early 1970 the North Vietnamese in Cambodia were under increasing pressure from U.S. ground probes, B-52 strikes and ARVN cross border operations. As an experienced military man, would you not think this pressure made it almost inevitable that they would have to expand their area of control or operations, thus bringing them into increasing conflict with the Cambodian authorities.
Abrams: Yes, I think that is a fair statement.

I included a paraphrase of this exchange in *Sideshow*, in a section which Rodman quotes selectively:

To escape the bombardment, the Vietnamese communists had begun to move deeper into Cambodia–"thus"—as Abrams later acknowledged to the Senate, "bringing them into increasing conflict with the Cambodian authorities." More and more reports of serious clashes between the communists and Cambodian villagers and troops reached Phnom Penh. The effect was inevitable (especially when it coincided with a deepening economic crisis); Sihanouk's balance of right against left became more precarious. The bombing was destabilizing him. (p. 113)

It is clear that I "invented" nothing; there was no "sleight of hand" as Rodman claims. Indeed, if anything, the original exchange makes the case more strongly than I made it in *Sideshow*. Moreover, despite Rodman, Abrams could perfectly well have said to Symington, "No, Senator, our intelligence showed that the bombing moved them back into South Vietnam" (as Kissinger claimed in his memoirs), or, "Well, Senator, I am afraid there's simply no evidence either way." Rodman gives the impression that the General was a complete patsy to "a powerful senator"; in fact the hearing shows he often disagreed with the questions or suppositions put to him. By saying that Symington had made a "fair statement," Abrams, as I wrote, "acknowledged" its validity. To "acknowledge" means "to admit to be true."

"THE NORTH VIETNAMESE ASSAULT ON CAMBODIA: THE MISSING MONTH OF APRIL"

Rodman claims that at this time, just after Sihanouk's overthrow, the North Vietnamese advance into Cambodia was made "with the evident intention of intimidating the new government into passivity, surrender, or collapse." This is a retreat—a welcome one—from Kissinger's own line, repeated *ad nauseam* in his memoirs, that the North Vietnamese were intent on capturing all Cambodia in April 1970. That is an assertion for which not a shred of evidence has been produced.

That the North Vietnamese spread further into Cambodia in April 1970 is evident; Rodman attempts to show that I deny it. I do nothing of the sort, as any reasonable reader of Chapter 9 of *Sideshow* can see. Rodman quotes a cable from General Westmoreland to General Abrams of April 21, 1970. The suggestion is that I ignored it. I did not. I quoted the first sentence Rodman quotes and then another section:

"As you are certainly aware, there is highest level concern here with respect to the situation in Cambodia." [Westmoreland] saw it as a mood to be exploited: "The threat to Phnom Penh and the present concern of higher authority may be conducive to relaxation of some of the constraints under which we are operating. If this happens we should be prepared to take advantage of the opportunity." He asked Abrams how best the United States could involve itself more deeply in South Vietnamese attacks across the border. . . (p. 138)

My account of April 1970 makes it abundantly clear that the North Vietnamese moved westwards. But I also raise the question of how far they were pushed—by

South Vietnamese and American attacks into the sanctuaries which had begun even before Sihanouk's overthrow and increased after it. Since then, I have indeed said that many North Vietnamese attacks mentioned by Kissinger in his memoirs had never been thought important enough to be mentioned before. And I have shown (*Harper's*, Nov. 1980) that in the alterations he made to the Cambodia section of his memoirs after *Sideshow* was published, Kissinger tried to exaggerate and magnify these incidents. I also record that although members of the NSC staff were specifically asked by Kissinger to prove, after the invasion and on the basis of captured documents and other evidence, that the North Vietnamese had been about to capture Phnom Penh in April 1970, they were able to do no such thing. Yet Kissinger constantly asserts in his memoirs that the North Vietnamese were about to establish their hegemony over all Cambodia at that time and that only the U.S. invasion stopped them. Rodman and Kissinger have never admitted to the existence of two rather important documents about that period. The first was published by the U.S. Embassy in Saigon in January 1971, as part of a regularly published research series. It was called "The Viet Cong's March–April 1970 plans for expanding control in Cambodia." The second, called, "Documents of Viet Cong and North Vietnamese Aggression against Cambodia" was published by Lon Nol's Ministry of Information in 1971. Neither document claimed that in April 1970 Hanoi had been bent on the conquest of Cambodia, as Kissinger claimed in his memoirs. Had any such evidence existed it is certain it would have been included.

Certainly I also maintain that Nixon was in a highly emotional state at the time of the invasion and looking for an opportunity to demonstrate "toughness." Nixon's mood was confirmed in Kissinger's own account, with its sly innuendoes that Nixon was so drunk on the *Sequoia* a few nights before the invasion that he could hardly stand.

Here, as elsewhere in his article, Rodman quotes Khmer Rouge assertions as evidence in his case against the North Vietnamese. (Kissinger does the same in his memoirs.) Yet Rodman also describes the Khmer Rouge as "political fanatics" and "totalitarian thugs." When are such people to be believed? It seems to me that it is legitimate to quote Khmer Rouge statements by way of illustrating their positions, their beliefs, their paranoias, as I do in *Sideshow*. It is quite illegitimate to quote them as giving irrefutable evidence. Does Rodman believe, for example, the Khmer Rouge assertion that it was the Vietnamese who murdered all those found in mass graves throughout the country? Apparently not, because Rodman also says that the Khmer Rouge murdered three million Cambodians. His use of the Khmer Rouge statements is not scholarly; it is utterly disgraceful.

Rodman complains that I have not addressed "one of the most important revelations" in Kissinger's book—that on April 4, 1970 he proposed the neutralization of Cambodia to Le Duc Tho. If this is indeed a startling revelation then that fact has escaped almost every other critic also. And Richard Nixon himself did not seem to think it very important. He made no mention of it whatsoever in his account in his own memoirs of that meeting between Kissinger and Le Duc Tho. I have found that on most matters Nixon's book is a more reliable account than Kissinger's.

"THE STRANGULATION OF THE CAMBODIAN ARMY"

Rodman complains about my use, or lack of use, of the end-of-tour reports of Generals Cleland and Palmer, the heads of the Military Equipment Delivery team in Cambodia. Actually I use them extensively; in the notes to Chapter 21 I acknowledge "the military information and descriptions in the following pages are from these reports unless otherwise noted." In the notes to Chapter 23 I say that my account of the final battle of Phnom Penh "is derived principally from General Palmer's end of tour report, reports of the military attaché's office in the U.S. Embassy, Phnom Penh, other declassified documents, interviews with American and Cambodian officials and soldiers, and contemporary press reports."

Rodman criticizes the reservation I express about the reports (p. 312). That paragraph continues by saying, "Nonetheless, the reports do provide an extraordinary picture of the problems of the Cambodian army at this stage of the war (1973 onwards)—and of the difficulties inherent in the Pentagon's attempt to impose its models upon the country. It is clear from Palmer's report that he disagreed with many of Cleland's actions . . ." Rodman ignores these complicating subtleties.

After quoting a passage in which I criticize the way in which Cleland encouraged the Cambodian army's dependence on firepower (p. 313), Rodman claims that I am "utterly disingenuous . . . Congressional restrictions made any other strategy impossible." He suggests that I pay scant and inadequate attention to those restrictions. Not true; in the very next paragraph I go on to argue that it was precisely those restrictions of which Cleland should have taken account.

> The fundamental military problems of incompetence and corruption were, if anything, exacerbated by the actions Cleland took. FANK (the Cambodian army) was unable to absorb the sophisticated accoutrements of divisional reorganization he pressed upon it. Congressional restrictions on advice meant that the Khmers were denied the overall training, management skills and technical know-how essential to the sort of army that Cleland was creating. . .

Rodman claims that I "blame Generals Cleland and Palmer for the disaster that befell" the Cambodian army. He knows this is not so. I am critical of Cleland (much less of Palmer), but if I attach any *blame* it is to Henry Kissinger. The point I made repeatedly through the second half of the book is that over and over again Kissinger disregarded advice from the ground and imposed upon Cambodia strategies that were so hopelessly ambitious, in military terms, as to be counterproductive. In fall 1970 the White House overrode the rather moderate, sensible proposals put forward by its first military emissary to Cambodia, Colonel Fred Ladd, that small guerrilla units be built up, in favor of creating at once a huge main force army. It was at Kissinger's insistence that the Cambodian army was expanded from about 37,000 to over 200,000 (at least on paper); the country's command structure could not possibly absorb such an increase.

Throughout the period there were constant pleas for restraint from State, CIA (which reported the war particularly well from the Phnom Penh station), from the military attaché's office, and from Melvin Laird himself. Almost all such appeals were overridden in favour of maximization—by Kissinger.

Rodman claims that I had no access to White House documents. This is untrue. He should note especially Chapter 12 where I discuss at length National Security Study Memorandum 99 and National Security Decision Memorandum (NSDM) 89. In NSDM 89 Kissinger dismissed all caution and authorized the most ambitious and most impractical of all the military options which had been discussed for Cambodia. That decision, made in fall 1970, was one of the single most disastrous of the war. One result was not, as Rodman airily claims, "petty corruption" but mammoth corruption which was seriously, perhaps fatally, debilitating to the Cambodian army. Here, as so often elsewhere, Kissinger indulged in overkill; and, as so often, it was quite counterproductive.

Not a single mention is made in Kissinger's memoirs (nor, of course, in Rodman's efforts) of NSDM 89.

"FEELING SORRY FOR THE KHMER ROUGE"

Given what has happened in Cambodia in recent years this is the most important section in Rodman's concoction. It is also the most shocking.

Rodman begins "Shawcross at least acknowledges the genocidal brutality of the Khmer Rouge after they took power, in contrast to other prophets of the Left. . ." I have never considered myself a "prophet" of the Left or any other cause, and as for "acknowledging" Khmer Rouge brutality, that was one of the principal reasons I embarked on my research in the first place. I went to talk to Cambodian refugees in Thailand in 1975, a few months after the Khmer Rouge victory. Their stories were being dismissed by some people, as Rodman says, as "imperialist propaganda" or CIA fabrications. It was quite clear to me, however, that they were telling the truth. I immediately began to write about the horrors of which they spoke. And I began to research into who the Khmer Rouge were and why they behaved in this appalling way. That research was embodied in numerous articles, in *Sideshow*, and will be part of the next book I am writing.*

Rodman goes on to claim that I "excuse the atrocities [of the Khmer Rouge] by another line of argument: that they were all America's fault. Apologetics nonetheless." This is a most childish smear. Nothing I have ever written has sought to "excuse" or "apologize" for the Khmer Rouge. But what I *have* done is to try and find explanations for their conduct. Some of those explanations are, of course, deeply uncomfortable to Mr. Rodman and Dr. Kissinger. But that does not make them excuses.

Rodman claims, falsely, that it is my thesis "that it was American bombing that turned the Khmer Rouge into butchers" and that in pursuit of this notion I ignored important sources—Ponchaud and Quinn. My claim is in fact that the Khmer Rouge became more and more vicious as the war progressed—both Ponchaud and Quinn bear that out.

Quinn writes in the summary of his study (*Naval War College Review*, Spring 1976, p. 6) of changes in Khmer Rouge conduct:

Mid 1971 to early 1973 . . . they took the first steps to change radically the nature

* *The Quality of Mercy: Cambodia, Holocaust and Modern Conscience*, London and New York, 1984.

of Khmer society. Distracted by the necessity to battle the Phnom Penh government's forces, this revolutionary program was, of necessity, limited. Cultural and social structures remained essentially intact but came under stiff attack through attempts to modify them . . . Early 1973 to February 1974. . . . During this final period [it is final only because Quinn ended his work then] the Khmer communists drastically accelerated and intensified their program to radically alter society. Included in this effort were mass relocations of the population, purges of lenient cadres, the use of terror and extensive remodelling of the economic system.

Nor do I ignore Ponchaud; apart from anything else, I recommend his book *Year Zero* as the best account of Khmer Rouge rule. In his original memo Rodman claimed that I cited Ponchaud only "occasionally"; in my response I pointed out this was false. So in *The American Spectator* Rodman says I quote him "extensively." (I wonder what Rodman actually *believes*?) Despite Rodman's efforts there is nothing in Ponchaud's book which contradicts my work. Indeed, we have long collaborated and we each believe that the other's work complements his own.

Rodman takes offense at a passage in my book, which he quotes: "All wars are designed to arouse anger. . ." This paragraph appears to be at the center of his assertion that I am an apologist for the Khmer Rouge. The passage (as Rodman knows from my response to his memo) was in part inspired by some of the observations made by J. Glenn Gray, the American soldier and writer, in his classic study, *The Warriors: Reflections on Men in Battle*. In this book, which Hannah Arendt describes in her introduction as "this singularly earnest and beautiful book," Gray tries to come to terms with the nature of evil in warfare:

Anyone who has watched men on the battlefield at work with artillery or looked into the eyes of veteran killers fresh from the slaughter, or studied the description of bombardiers' feelings while smashing their targets, finds it hard to escape the conclusion that there is a delight in destruction. A walk across any battlefield shortly after the guns have fallen silent is convincing enough. A sensitive person is sure to be oppressed by a spirit of evil there, a radical evil which suddenly makes the medieval images of hell and the thousand devils of the imagination believable. This evil appears to surpass mere human malice and to demand explanation in cosmological and religious terms. Men who have lived in the zone of combat long enough to be veterans are sometimes possessed by a fury that makes them capable of anything. Blinded by the rage to destroy and supremely careless of the consequences, they storm against the enemy until they are either victorious, dead or utterly exhausted. It is as if they are seized by a demon and are no longer in control of themselves. From the Homeric account of the sacking of Troy to the conquest of Dienbienphu, Western literature is filled with descriptions of soldiers as berserkers and mad destroyers.

I tried to relate that general observation to the specific circumstances of the Khmer Rouge—in particular their small numbers, the isolation of their leaders in the jungle for up to thirteen years, their ideological commitments, the surprisingly sudden nature of their victory, *and* the punishment they had endured at the hands of their enemies. I do indeed believe that the massive U.S. bombing, particularly in 1973, must have affected their conduct. But by enemies I meant not just the United States and Lon Nol, but also North Vietnam. Rodman is thoroughly dishonest when he says that my reference to their "Manichean fear" is to "American and Cambodian efforts to resist them." In fact the very next paragraph after the one he quotes relates to their "Manichean fear" of the Vietnamese:

> On Christmas Day 1978, their fears were realized. Under the transparent banner of a new "Kampuchean United Front for National Salvation," the Vietnamese launched a dry season blitzkrieg toward Phnom Penh. Phnom Penh was captured . . . the Khmer Rouge leaders fled to the jungles whence they had emerged less than four years before, vowing that they would mount a new guerrilla war against the enemy in Phnom Penh . . .

Rodman concludes by declaring: "By no stretch of moral logic can the crimes of mass murderers be ascribed to those who struggled to prevent their coming to power." Only by ignoring "moral logic" can Rodman, like Kissinger, invent such a formulation. Has he forgotten that it was the North Vietnamese America was fighting in 1970? The 1970–75 war did not *prevent* the Khmer Rouge coming to power; it *created* them and created the opportunity for them to come to power. Even Rodman seems to understand that, though he does not acknowledge it: his section on April 1970 is all about the North Vietnamese—the Khmer Rouge are not mentioned. Rightly, because they numbered only a few thousand then and had no hope of political power. By 1975 they were about 75,000 and Cambodian society had been overturned. Just as the Bolsheviks could come to power in Russia only after the destruction of World War I, so the Khmer Rouge were enabled to control Cambodia only by the 1970–75 war. This is one of the main points I made, and which Rodman, like Kissinger, fails to address.

To sum up: Rodman's article, like his memorandum, like Kissinger's memoirs, does not even dent the argument of my book. It was clear to me, when I first read the memo, that the feebleness of its criticisms, and its low intellectual quality, far from devaluing *Sideshow*, vindicated it. I was pleased to be able to distribute the memo widely and to publish it in the next edition of my book. Rodman's article is no more impressive, no more damaging. Even as a hatchet job it seems to me to fail completely.

In writing *Sideshow* I did not just have access to U.S. Government and other documents. I also used masses of material already on the public record and I was given a great deal of information by many of the people I interviewed—over 300 in all. What was significant was the consistency of all the sources I used, the way in which together they made a forceful history, the integrity of which no one, least of all Rodman, has been able to undermine.

Most of those I interviewed were American officials—from Cabinet ministers, ambassadors, on down to low level soldiers, diplomats, and secretaries who had had to do with Cambodia. One of the most striking things about those who knew the country well was their almost unanimous contempt for Henry Kissinger. They

Sideshow

blamed him for carelessness and callousness in his policies towards Cambodia and for sacrificing the country to a strategic design which was itself necessarily flawed. Reflecting this, I wrote at the end of *Sideshow* (p. 396), "Statesmen have to be judged by the consequences of their actions. Whatever Kissinger and Nixon intended for Cambodia, their efforts created catastrophe."

What is "obscene," to use Mr. Rodman's word, is not the attempt of a writer like myself to explore and explain what happened. It is the refusal of Dr. Kissinger to accept any responsibility for the results of a policy which Nixon himself called "the Nixon Doctrine in its purest form." Nothing that Kissinger has produced since the publication of *Sideshow* has shown that the grave charges I made against him were ill-founded. Rodman is no more successful. But how could he be? He is merely the sorcerer's apprentice.

> Yours,
> *William Shawcross*

Kissinger's further reply through Rodman, published in *The American Spectator* July 1981, under the title: **Rodman Responds**

With great abandon Mr. Shawcross flings accusations of war crimes and responsibility for three million deaths, yet he howls "smear" when someone challenges his scholarship!

I am saddened that Mr. Shawcross has reduced the debate to the level of personal abuse. My article in *The American Spectator* was a careful examination of his use of documentary sources. I found voluminous discrepancies between what the documents said and what *Sideshow* claimed they said. His "research" turned out to be filled with glaring errors, sleight of hand, and calculated omissions that amounted to suppression of inconvenient evidence that contradicted his arguments. I did commit the appalling crime of circulating an earlier draft of my findings, which obviously embarrassed him a great deal. I atoned for my sin by going public, which has upset him even more.*

Mr. Shawcross' real problem is not that he is being persecuted by the Thought Police but that he is unable to rebut any of my points. His attempt at rebuttal is as deceptive as his book. Amid all the overwrought and at times incoherent bluster, Mr. Shawcross is now in essence conceding that key arguments of the Nixon administration were true, that he has no answer to the new information revealed in the Kissinger memoirs and elsewhere, and that he has no new evidence to fill in the gaping holes that I found in his documentation.

Let me take my original points in order.

* My earlier version was hardly anonymous. My authorship was always known and indeed announced in the press. (See, e.g., Edwin M. Yoder, Jr., "Who Destroyed Cambodia? A Season for Scapegoats," *Washington Star*, Nov. 8, 1979; Leopold Labedz, "Of Myths and Horrors," *Encounter*, Feb. 1980, p. 47.) Mr. Shawcross' reprinting it without my knowledge raises some interesting legal questions, which I am looking into. My *American Spectator* article, of course, was far more complete, detailed, and damaging. I can see why he would not dare reprint that.

CHESTER BOWLES: THE MISSING QUOTATION:

Sihanouk's conversation with Chester Bowles in January 1968 was the earliest of many utterances in which the Cambodian chief of state invited American attacks on the illegal North Vietnamese military bases in Cambodia. In *Sideshow*, eager to show that the bombing was in defiance of Cambodia's wishes, Mr. Shawcross disputed this as "questionable."

It is interesting to watch Mr. Shawcross now in disorderly retreat, as the accuracy of the Nixon administration's account of what Sihanouk actually said has been established beyond doubt. The Kissinger memoirs quote from the verbatim transcript; my article quotes from the State Department summary. Mr. Shawcross' only excuse is that he did not have the information when he wrote his book; the truth is that Bowles published the same account ten years ago in his memoirs. The facts are now clearly in the public domain, and they destroy *Sideshow*'s argument.*

I am delighted to see Mr. Shawcross quote from his 1979 interview with Sihanouk, in which the Prince confirms yet again that he invited American bombing of the North Vietnamese sanctuaries.

That B-52s instead of fighter-bombers were used is a red herring. It made no difference to Sihanouk at the time. In his March 28, 1969 news conference, of which Shawcross makes so much, the Prince accused the *Communists* of "bring[ing] the war to our country." On the B-52 bombing which had begun ten days earlier, he took exactly the position he had told Bowles he would take: he could not endorse it publicly, even though he *really wanted us to do it*. In subsequent public remarks throughout 1969 he dropped even the pro forma criticism and virtually endorsed the bombing. In a May 13 news conference (and in August 22 conversation with Mike Mansfield), Sihanouk professed indifference to the B-52 attacks against the North Vietnamese bases and objected only if we injured Cambodians. He became much friendlier to the United States and warmly invited Nixon to visit Phnom Penh. In a November article in his journal *Le Sangkum* he continued to complain only of *Communist* "subversion, aggression, infiltration, and occupation" of his country. In December in the same magazine he praised the Nixon Doctrine and welcomed American military power as the only hope for Cambodia's survival.

There can no longer be any doubt that American bombing of the North Vietnamese bases had the explicit and continued support of Sihanouk.

WHAT THE CHIEFS' MEMORANDUM REALLY SAID:

One of Mr. Shawcross' principal charges in *Sideshow* was that American bombing of North Vietnamese bases wantonly risked the lives of Cambodian civilians. Since I have demonstrated that this was not true, he now assures us heatedly that he did not mean to exaggerate the danger to civilians. I take this as a welcome retraction of the clear and repeated insinuation in his book. In *Sideshow* he quoted selectively and

---

* The State Department summary as released to my office under the Freedom of Information Act purported to be identical to what was released to Mr. Shawcross. It included the paragraph in question. If Mr. Shawcross' copy omitted it, I grant him that much—except that a conscientious job of research would have found it in Bowles' memoirs. And the issue, of course, is what Sihanouk said—not whether Bowles agreed with it!

deceptively from a 1969 memorandum of the Chairman of the Joint Chiefs of Staff to make precisely that accusation.

The minimal population figures he lists in fact prove my point. Mr. Shawcross, alas, still seems not to understand his own documents. The base areas he lists ranged over dozens of square miles or more; the targets of aerial attack were specific military facilities *within* those base areas. All the JCS memoranda proposing B-52 missions specified that the designated targets were kilometers away from civilian habitation. And the 1973 Senate hearings provided repetitive evidence that the North Vietnamese *did not allow* Cambodians anywhere near their military complexes.

BASE AREA 704: THE WRONG BOX:

Mr. Shawcross has already admitted this blunder, and it is probably cruel of me to keep rubbing it in. In *Sideshow* he falsely accused the White House of ordering B-52 attacks against a particular base area that the Joint Chiefs had recommended against attacking because it was heavily populated by Cambodian civilians. He later admitted that the base area was *not* attacked—but he changed nothing in the book except one sentence and the label on a map. The insinuation of American barbarity was too important to the book; it remains, even though the "evidence" supporting it has been removed!

"DESTABILIZING" SIHANOUK: THE ELUSIVE EVIDENCE:

If I can understand his somewhat incoherent explanation under this heading, Mr. Shawcross is essentially admitting that he has no new evidence to salvage what I demonstrated to be yet another series of unsubstantiated claims.

He is still unable to show, first of all, any American involvement in the decision of Sihanouk's own parliament and government to depose him as chief of state on March 18, 1970. He has no evidence, only surmise and insinuation. (Kissinger's memoirs present considerable documentary evidence that the United States regarded the *status quo ante* as the best attainable situation and was caught by surprise by the coup. William Colby, by the way, remains convinced that the Cambodians acted completely on their own *without* American involvement, and tells me that he told this to Mr. Shawcross.) And as I have shown in my article, none of the documents that Mr. Shawcross invoked in *Sideshow* supports his alternative accusation: that the U.S. bombing drove the North Vietnamese so much deeper into Cambodia in 1969–70 that it "destabilized" Sihanouk's neutralist regime. Indeed, more of his documents contradict it than support it. (For example, he foolishly cited a JCS memo that really deals with Hanoi's dispersal of *supplies* in areas *between* the base areas, not the spread of the fighting to the interior, and an article by Lon Nol complaining of increases in numbers of Viet Cong *in* the base areas, not their being driven out of them into the country. The Abrams–Symington exchange, even if quoted honestly—as I stated in my article—does not establish Mr. Shawcross' conclusion either. It says nothing about forcing the North Vietnamese to spread deeper into the country, or about undermining Sihanouk.)

The theory that our bombing brought down Sihanouk is one of the most crucial points of Mr. Shawcross' argument. The fact remains that he cannot substantiate it.

On the contrary, Sihanouk's recent memoirs would seem to confirm that the Vietnamese sanctuaries remained quite limited in size until after Sihanouk was overthrown.* The map in *Sideshow* (p. 27) shows no change in their extent or location over the period of the bombing. The truth is that the illegal North Vietnamese sanctuaries were an affront to Cambodian dignity and a disruptive element in Cambodian politics *from the beginning* (1965)—which is why Sihanouk invited the American bombing in the first place. It was the North Vietnamese, not the Americans, who wrecked the equilibrium of neutral Cambodia.

THE NORTH VIETNAMESE ASSAULT ON CAMBODIA: THE MISSING MONTH OF APRIL:

How pleasing it is to see that Mr. Shawcross now acknowledges ("admits to be true"?) that the North Vietnamese launched major military operations throughout eastern Cambodia after Sihanouk's ouster, weeks before the U.S.–South Vietnamese incursion of April 30, 1970. This is one of the most important events in Cambodia's history. *Sideshow* somehow neglected to mention it.

Mr. Shawcross' book dealt with this whole episode dishonestly and he should not pretend otherwise. *Sideshow* fiddled with the evidence so that North Vietnamese actions appeared as minor movements for defensive purposes and as nothing more than a pretext for opportunitistic American aggression. The book's excerpt from General Westmoreland's cable of April 21, 1970, for example, conveniently *omitted* the passage (quoted in my article) in which the magnitude of the North Vietnamese threat to Phnom Penh is described. Nor were the North Vietnamese "pushed" into Cambodia, as Mr. Shawcross would have us believe. The first significant South Vietnamese cross-border operation took place only at the end of March, and with Cambodian permission, as reported in *The New York Times* of March 28, 1970—roughly "simultaneously" with the beginning of the North Vietnamese march westward (as *Sideshow*, p. 130, indeed admits). In fact the North Vietnamese invasion was "provoked" only by the new Cambodian government's demand that they leave Cambodian soil.

And what is the evidence of Communist intentions in that period? Prince Sihanouk, immediately after his first ouster, threw in his lot with the Communists and publicly demanded the overthrow of the new Cambodian government; on March 23, in Peking, he announced the formation of a liberation army and a government-in-exile. China, North Vietnam, the Viet Cong, the Khmer Rouge, and the Pathet Lao all immediately joined in the call for the overthrow of the Cambodian government and promised assistance. Hanoi's negotiator, Le Duc Tho, in his meeting with Kissinger on April 4, rejected the American proposal for neutralization of Cambodia and demanded the overthrow of the Cambodian government. At the end of March and beginning of April, North Vietnamese troops broke out of their sanctuaries and invaded the interior of Cambodia, overrunning Cambodian towns, military posts, and lines of communication, surrounding and laying siege to Phnom Penh, the country's capital, all the while recruiting guerrillas and building up a shadow army and shadow administration to take over the country. The North Vietnamese thus *announced* their intention to overthrow the Cambodian govern-

* Sihanouk, above, p. 33

ment, and they were on the way to doing so. If Mr. Shawcross regards all this as "ambiguous," he is beyond the reach of rational argument.

The evidence of what the North Vietnamese were doing is overwhelming, unambiguous, and irrefutable. Mr. Shawcross' evasions are feeble. The Pol Pot document of 1978 is accurate on Hanoi's organization of a guerrilla army and shadow government, however "disgraceful" Mr. Shawcross finds it; it is corroborated by all other evidence including contemporary news accounts.* The North Vietnamese attacks enumerated in the Kissinger book are taken from contemporary internal reporting; many were mentioned in Nixon's speeches and even reported in *The New York Times*. There is simply no way for Mr. Shawcross to deny that they happened! Likewise the meeting between Le Duc Tho and Kissinger on April 4, 1970, was indeed a pivotal event. (It was the first of a dozen occasions when the United States proposed the neutralization of Cambodia, and Hanoi flatly rejected it.) The Kissinger book quotes extensively from the official transcript. Is Mr. Shawcross claiming that the conversation did not take place? He will have to come up with something better than complaining that he never heard of this evidence before, for that only confirms that he wrote his book in woeful ignorance of much of what really went on.

If some of the systems analysts on Kissinger's staff were skeptical of a North Vietnamese intention to overrun the country in April, the Asian and military experts on the staff were not. (The systems analysts were wrong on this as they were wrong on the logistical importance of Sihanoukville, a similar example of intelligence analysis influenced by dovish preferences.) Mr. Shawcross never explains what he thinks the North Vietnamese *were* up to. Perhaps he thinks a "liberation army" is formed for the purpose of tourism.

I can understand his discomfiture. He has written a book on the Cambodian war that deliberately omits the most crucial event: the North Vietnamese invasion that began it!

THE STRANGULATION OF THE CAMBODIAN ARMY:

My point here was a very simple one and is unrebutted. Mr. Shawcross misleadingly and selectively used Generals Cleland's and Palmer's military reports to support a thesis very different from what the reports contained. Cleland and Palmer pointed out that congressional restriction on U.S. aid and advisers are what made it impossible to remedy the Cambodian army's weaknesses and unavoidable to rely on firepower. Shawcross suppresses their analysis, attacks their reliance on firepower, but has no alternative strategy to offer—because his real argument (*Sideshow*, p. 350) is that Congress should not have allowed any help to the Cambodians at all!

This is the same issue that was involved in the NSDM 89 directive. The real difference between Shawcross and Kissinger is that Kissinger thought the free Cambodians had a right to survive, and Shawcross did not. Mr. Shawcross got his wish.

---

* See, e.g., James P. Sterba, "North Vietnamese Reported Recruiting Guerrillas in Cambodia," *New York Times*, May 29, 1970.

FEELING SORRY FOR THE KHMER ROUGE:

Mr. Shawcross is quite proud of having written articles critical of the Khmer Rouge after April 1975. How nice. The debate, then, would seem to be between those who opposed the Khmer Rouge after 1975 and those who opposed the Khmer Rouge *before* 1975, when it could have made a difference.

Unfortunately, even that gives too much credit to Mr. Shawcross for his always guarded, qualified, half-hearted criticism of the Khmer Rouge. I have accused him of making excuses for Khmer Rouge genocide, and I maintain my view.

First, *Sideshow* is nothing if not an exercise in shifting the blame for Khmer Rouge atrocities onto others. It is not subtitled "The Khmer Rouge and the Destruction of Cambodia" (or even "The North Vietnamese and the Destruction of Cambodia") but "Kissinger, Nixon and the Destruction of Cambodia." Mr. Shawcross' "explanation" of Khmer Rouge behavior is always in terms of their response to dirty deeds done to them by others. In his famous paragraph on page 389 of *Sideshow*, the brutality of the Khmer Rouge in April 1975 is explained as the inevitable result of their "fear," their "rage to avenge their fallen comrades," and the "punishment" they had "endured" at the hands of the Americans. In fact, American bombing had ended twenty months before the Khmer Rouge carried out their systematic murder and destruction after victory in April 1975. As for the North Vietnamese, how their 1978 invasion of Cambodia could have prompted the Khmer Rouge to murder three million of their own people in 1975 is beyond me.

If Mr. Shawcross considers this a "singularly earnest and beautiful" analysis, I consider it an obvious evasion. The explanation he ignores—or rather suppresses—is the one explanation stressed clearly by two of his principal documentary sources: that the Khmer Rouge's motivation was ideological; that they *intended all along* to destroy Cambodian society in order to reconstruct it according to their fanatical theories. Kenneth Quinn showed that they carried out the same totalitarian practices systematically, as a deliberate act of policy, in all areas they controlled as early as 1971. Their early efforts were limited only by their limited means—as Shawcross' quotation from Quinn confirms! Khmer Rouge brutality increased as time passed because their power and territorial control increased as time passed. Father François Ponchaud was exactly on the mark when he described Khmer Rouge atrocities as "a perfect example of the application of an ideology pushed to the furthest limit of its internal logic."

These authors understood the Khmer Rouge with a clarity that Mr. Shawcross deliberately avoids. *Sideshow* did tell us, for example, about Khieu Samphan's doctoral thesis, written in Paris in 1959, which called for the wholesale uprooting and reshaping of Cambodian society. But Mr. Shawcross hastened to assure us that "the methods . . . prescribed . . . were essentially moderate" (*Sideshow*, p. 243)—the implication being that there could not possibly be a connection between this totalitarian doctrine of 1959 and the very same policy implemented with savagery in 1975!

Of course the Khmer Rouge grew from nothing. But it was the North Vietnamese who built them up as a military power and contributed decisively to their victory. Sihanouk makes this point at excruciating length in his memoirs, describing the logistical, materiel, training, artillery, and tank support provided to the Khmer

Rouge by Hanoi.* Had we turned Cambodia over to the North Vietnamese in 1970, as Mr. Shawcross urges, not only would South Vietnam and the 400,000 American troops there have been put in serious jeopardy, but the North Vietnamese would have had to resort to the Khmer Rouge to help govern Cambodia just as they resorted to the Khmer Rouge to help prosecute the war. The consequences for Cambodia would have been the same. The Vietnamese never objected to the Khmer Rouge's internal policies, only to their independence of Hanoi.

I can only guess at Mr. Shawcross' motives for trying to cover up the premeditated, ideological origins of the Khmer Rouge genocide. That his key sources had "almost unanimous contempt for Henry Kissinger" is a good clue to the personal bias that animated his whole enterprise. He is free to write a hatchet job on Henry Kissinger any time he wants. He should not pretend, however, that it is a serious history of Cambodia.

One final point, on the alleged unconstitutionality of the President's conduct of the Indochina war. Mr. Shawcross simply asserted this in various places in *Sideshow*, without analysis. It is interesting how he seems to wheel it out as a *deus ex machina* when other arguments fail, as in his reply here on the Chester Bowles conversation. Indeed he seems to rely on it more and more in his recent writings—as if conscious that his thesis about Cambodia is crumbling under the counter-evidence. (*Whatever* Nixon really did in Cambodia, it was wrong!)

American constitutional law is a subject Mr. Shawcross obviously knows nothing about. The Supreme Court of the United States, which usually decides such questions, never declared any aspect of the war unconstitutional; it stayed far away from an issue so clearly political. Nor did the U.S. Congress ever legislate such a view (only an antiwar minority espoused it). Key legislative leaders were consulted on the bombing of Cambodia under informal procedures for covert military operations that had been customary since the Lewis and Clark expedition: the House Judiciary Committee in 1974 *rejected* an article of impeachment on this issue by more than two-to-one. And, of course, four Presidents over fifteen years regarded their actions as a proper exercise of the commander-in-chief's power. Mr. Shawcross can set himself up as a Lawgiver over and above the three branches of government in this country, but his claim has no legal authority whatsoever. It is a fringe theory of the antiwar Left. Indeed, it is plain wrong. The balance of strength between the Executive and Congress in foreign affairs has been tested and shaped in political struggles over 200 years. Presidential powers exist whether Mr. Shawcross approves or not. If Franklin Roosevelt had followed such a constricted theory of executive authority before Pearl Harbor, Mr. Shawcross would have grown up speaking German.

Sideshow, in short, is a fraud.

* Sihanouk, above, pp. 14–15, 20–21, 25–27, 71–72.

Postscript

Rodman declares in this response that I "would not dare to reprint" his attack on *Sideshow* from *The American Spectator*. I am delighted to do so.

W.S., London 1986

Notes

Chapter 1

p. 19   Abrams' cable. This and the following cables cited were obtained under the Freedom of Information Act, as amended over President Ford's veto in 1974 [Title 5, U.S. Code, Section 552 (b)]. Abrams' request (MAC 1782) was followed by an interim response from General McConnell, Acting Chairman of the Joint Chiefs of Staff, on February 11 (JCS 01836), permission from the Joint Chiefs to begin planning the strike on March, 1, 1969 (JCS 03287), and the order for its execution on March 17, 1969 (JCS 03298). These and other highly classified documents were delivered to the House Judiciary Committee in 1974 when it was considering whether to impeach President Nixon for the secret bombing of Cambodia. The administration did not allow them to be declassified.

p. 20   Troop withdrawals. In an "Eyes Only" cable of January 28, 1969 (JCS 04184), General Wheeler informed Abrams that Secretary of Defense Melvin Laird had given the following guidance: "Continuation of US-GVN discussions currently underway in Saigon involving possible selected U.S. troop reductions in conjunction with increasing GVN capabilities is approved. However, these discussions must be on a strictly close-hold, need-to-know basis. At the present time, public discussion of withdrawals or troop reduction in Vietnam should be limited to mutual withdrawal within the context of the Paris negotiations. I myself propose to keep silent. . . ."

p. 21   Laird's skepticism. Laird has reiterated his position on several occasions since the secret bombing was revealed in 1973, including an interview with the author on June 30, 1977. Laird's account of his attitude has been confirmed by a number of his former associates, including his military assistant, General Robert E. Pursley, in interviews with the author, January 16 and 29, 1977.

Sideshow

p. 21 Wheeler's statement. Wheeler, in sworn testimony to the Senate Armed Services Committee on July 30, 1973. See Committee's Hearings—*Bombing in Cambodia*—July 16, 23, 25, 26, 30; August 7, 8, 9, 1973, pp. 131–89.

p. 23 For a full account of the diversion procedure, see Wheeler's testimony, *loc. cit.*

p. 24 Special Forces. For security reasons the code name of the missions varied from Daniel Boone to Salem House and finally to Thot Not (when the South Vietnamese took them over).

p. 24 This account of the Daniel Boone missions and of the first B–52 strike in Cambodia is based on Harrison's sworn testimony (*Bombing in Cambodia*, pp. 231–55), together with the diary Harrison kept at the time, and several telephone interviews with him during 1977–78.

p. 26 Halperin and Kissinger. David Wise, *The American Police State*, (New York: Random House, 1976) p. 33 and author's interview with Halperin.

p. 28 Sihanouk's motives and attitude are discussed later in this book; see pp. 93–94.

p. 28 Kissinger's assertions. Senate Foreign Relations Committee, *Hearings on Nomination of Henry A. Kissinger to Be Secretary of State*, September 1973, Part I, pp. 30, 244. Statement of 1976. *Die Zeit* (Hamburg), No. 28, July 2, 1976.

p. 28 Chief's description of bases. Contained in JCSM–207–69. This memorandum did not refer to Menu as such, but recommended combined ground-air attacks on the sanctuaries.

p. 29 Wheeler on lying. See *Bombing in Cambodia*, p. 148. When Dr. Robert J. Seamans eventually discovered he had been deceived he was angered, especially since he had in the meantime given false testimony to Congress, assuring a Senate committee that no bombing had taken place in Cambodia in 1969. In an interview for the Pentagon's Oral History Program, declassified under the Freedom of Information Act, he said later: "That to me is not the 'right way to run a railroad.' I think if you're going to have service secretaries, they have got to be entrusted with *all* significant operational information. . . . To use an old phrase, 'You cannot be halfway pregnant.' If you're going to be involved in it, they can't leave you in the awkward position of knowing some things but not something of the importance of bombing those sanctuaries."

p. 30 This account of Knight's activities and the preceding description of B–52 bombing procedures is based largely on his sworn testimony to the Senate Armed Services Committee, *Bombing in Cambodia*, pp. 2–70.

p. 32 ". . . bombing China." *The New York Times*, July 15, 1973.

p. 32 Gerald Greven's account comes from his testimony to the Senate Armed Services Committee, *Bombing in Cambodia*, pp. 275–333.

p. 33 Beecher's method. Author's interview with William Beecher, July 8, 1977.

p. 33 *U.S. News & World Report*, April 7, 1969; *The New York Times*, April 6, 1969.

p. 34 There are many published accounts of Nixon and Kissinger's initial reaction to the Beecher story. See *Dr. Kissinger's Role in Wiretapping*, from the report on hearings held by the Senate Foreign Relations Committee in 1974, for much of the primary material; also depositions in the civil case *Halperin et al. v.*

Notes

Henry A. Kissinger et al. (No. 1187-73) in the District Court of the District of Columbia and Halperin's appeal (No. 77-2014); also David Wise, *The American Police State*, pp. 31-107. These sources were supplemented by interviews with Morton Halperin and others who had been wiretapped.

Chapter 2

p. 38 Early history of Cambodia. D. G. E. Hall, *A History of Southeast Asia*, 2nd Edition (London: Macmillan, 1964); G. Coedes, *The Making of Southeast Asia* (London: Routledge & Kegan Paul, 1966); Bernard-Philippe Groslier, *Angkor et le Cambodge au XVI siècle d'après les documents portugais et espagnols* (Paris: Presses universitaires de France, 1948).

p. 38 Chinese texts. Coedes, *op. cit.*, p. 58.

p. 40 Chou Ta-kuan's account. Published in *Bulletin de l'Ecole Française d'Extrême Orient* (Hanoi: n.p., 1902), pp. 123-77.

p. 41 "One scholar . . . " David Chandler, "Cambodia before the French: Politics in a Tributary Kingdom 1794-1848," dissertation, University of Michigan, 1973.

p. 41 Minh Mang quote. Chandler, *op. cit.*

p. 42 Henri Mouhot, *Travels in the Central Part of Indochina*, 2 vols. (London: John Murray, 1864), Vol. 2, p. 21; Vol. 1, pp. 281-82, 272-75.

p. 43 King's attitude. D. G. E. Hall, *op. cit.*, p. 614.

p. 43 1907 Treaty. "The First American Advisers in Thai History," *Journal of the Siam Society*, Vo. 62, Part 2 (July 1974).

p. 44 French resident. See *Etudes Cambodgiennes*, No. 12, p. 23; quoted in Malcolm Caldwell and Lek Tan, *Cambodia in the Southeast Asian War*, (New York and London: Monthly Review Press, 1973), p. 21.

Chapter 3

p. 52 Penn Nouth. *The New York Times*, September 12, 1953.

p. 52 The Cambodian government requested United States military aid on May 20, 1954; it was approved in August.

p. 52 NSC study. No. 5612, approved September 5, 1956.

p. 52 NSC paper. May 12, 1957. See Pentagon Papers, Vol. 10, p. 1100.

p. 53 McClintock. In his book *My War with the CIA*, written with Wilfred Burchett (London: Penguin 1973), Sihanouk gives full rein to his feelings for McClintock. State Department officials who served under McClintock in Phnom Penh underwrite the Prince's complaints.

p. 54 Presidential study. Made by the Operations Coordinating Board, *Report on Southeast Asia*, January 7, 1959. Pentagon Papers, Vol. 10, p. 1156.

p. 54 NSC papers. See, for example, NSC 5809.

p. 54 Colby quote. Interview with the author, July 6, 1977.

p. 54 *Time* magazine, March 16, 1959

p. 54 *Psychological Operations: Cambodia*, was prepared under the direction

461

of Dr. Egerton L. Ballachey with Howard D. Kramer and F. Loyal Greer, by the Special Operations Research Office of the American University, Washington, D.C., under contract for the Department of the Army, April 1969.

p. 58 The tensions between French and United States military men are reflected in NSC documents from 1954 onward (see the Pentagon Papers, Volume 10, pp. 756, 859) in Sihanouk's *My War with the CIA*, and in the after-action report, "Discontinuance of the MAAG; Cambodia," by Brigadier General Robert Taber, January 9, 1964. They were confirmed and elaborated by interviews with U.S., French and Cambodian officials, including General William Yarborough, formerly Deputy Chief of the Military Assistance Group, Cambodia, on June 30, 1977; Charles Meyer, formerly adviser to Prince Sihanouk, on May 30, 1977; and General Nhiek Thioulong, formerly Sihanouk's Chief of Staff, on April 20, 1977.

p. 60 Description of Air Force. Taber, after-action report, January 9, 1964, p. B2.

Chapter 4

p. 64 Chou En-lai's request. Sihanouk interview, *The New York Times*, July 8, 1973.

p. 64 Sihanouk's unhappiness. *Ibid.*

p. 65 Ladd statement. Interviews with the author, May 17–18, 1977.

p. 65 Colby statement. Interview with the author, July 6, 1977.

p. 66 Joint Chiefs' admission on Cambodian villages. JCSM 207–69.

p. 66 LBJ on Sihanouk. Related to the author by James C. Thomson, Jr., in interview February 1, 1977.

p. 68 Nhiek Thioulong statement. Interview in Paris with the author, April 20, 1977.

p. 70 Meyer assertion. Interview with the author, May 30, 1977.

p. 71 Footnote. Kissinger statement. Senate Foreign Relations Committee *Hearings on Nomination of Henry Kissinger*, September 1973, Part I, p. 244.

p. 71 Sihanouk's affirmation. *Etudes Cambodgiennes*, No. 13 (January–March 1967), p. 11.

p. 72 Bowles' analysis. March 18 cable, New Delhi 128989.

p. 72 Debate over Sihanouk. Bunker argued that any move toward Sihanouk would be bad for South Vietnamese morale. He cabled Rusk on March 23, 1968, saying, "I believe that the disadvantages inherent in any early move toward resumption of relations with Cambodia outweigh the advantages. . . . Our immediate objective should be to put pressure on Sihanouk to do something about the existing situation." Rusk's decision to go ahead with exploratory talks was contained in a cable of March 26, 1968, State 135669. Bunker continued through June 1968 to demand that even exploratory moves be deferred.

p. 72 Eugene Black's visit. *Etudes Cambodgiennes*, No. 15 (July–September 1968). A copy of Black's report to the State Department was made available to the author.

Chapter 5

p. 74   Kissinger's telephone calls. *Wall Street Journal,* May 20, 1977.

p. 76   Nixon on nuclear weapons. *The New York Times,* March 18, 1954.

p. 76   Kissinger on "graduated amounts of destruction." Kissinger, *Nuclear Weapons and Foreign Policy,* p. 130–131.

p. 76   Kissinger on "credible irrationality." Quoted by Kalb, Marvin, and Kalb, Bernard, *Kissinger,* p. 47 (from Kissinger, *A World Restored*).

p. 76   Kissinger on "ban the bomb." Kissinger, *Nuclear Weapons,* p. 82.

p. 77   Kissinger on "molding reality." Quoted by Stephen Graubard, *Kissinger: Portrait of a Mind* (New York: Norton, 1974), p. 45 (from Kissinger, "The White Revolutionary: Reflections on Bismarck," in *Daedalus,* 1968).

p. 77   Kissinger on Soviets. Kissinger, *Nuclear Weapons,* pp. 59, 239, 241–42, 248–51. A succinct and cogent analysis of Kissinger's writing, containing some of the quotations used here, is by Sheldon Wolin, "Consistent Kissinger," *The New York Review of Books,* December 9, 1976.

p. 77   Kissinger on intellectuals. Kissinger, *Necessity for Choice,* pp. 348–54.

p. 79   Nixon on Kissinger during 1968 Presidential election campaign. *RN: The Memoirs of Richard Nixon,* pp. 323–30.

p. 79   Henry Brandon's articles. *The Sunday Times* of London, December 8, 1968 and December 5, 1976.

p. 80   Reston. *The New York Times,* December 4 and 18, 1968.

p. 80   Halperin remark. Interviews with the author, January 1977.

p. 82   Eagleburger's reaction. Roger Morris, "Uncertain Greatness," *Quartet,* London, 1977, p. 83.

p. 82   Kissinger's views on Goodpaster. Roger Morris, *op. cit.,* p. 84, and author's interview with Halperin, January 1977.

p. 83   Nixon on Rogers. Roger Morris, *op. cit.,* p. 85.

p. 84   Kissinger on secrecy and exclusion. *Washington Post,* November 14, 1976.

p. 84   Kissinger on spinning bureaucratic wheels. Kalb and Kalb, *op. cit.,* p. 90.

Chapter 6

p. 85   Nixon, "step up the buildup." Speech of February 15, 1962.

p. 85   Nixon 1964 advice. Statement of April 18, 1964.

p. 86   Nixon to Southern delegates. Quoted by Lewis Chester, Godfrey Hodgson, Bruce Page, *An American Melodrama* (London: André Deutsch, 1969), p. 464.

p. 87   Kissinger on America in Vietnam. Kissinger, "What Should We Do Now?" *Look* magazine, August 9, 1966.

p. 87   McNaughton memorandum. "Some Paragraphs on Vietnam," January 19, 1966. Pentagon Papers, *New York Times* edition, pp. 491–92.

p. 87   *Foreign Affairs,* January 1969.

p. 88   Kissinger on Vietnam war as "disaster." Television interview by William F. Buckley, Public Broadcasting System, September 13, 1975.

p. 89   NSSM 1 was reproduced in the *Congressional Record*, May 10, 1972, E 4975–5066. See *Rolling Stone* interview with Daniel Ellsberg, Parts I and II, reprint September 1973.

p. 89   Nixon's view of Vietnam as "short-term problem." Quoted by Kalb and Kalb, *op. cit.*, p. 120.

p. 90   Nixon's "Madman Theory." H. R. Haldeman with Joseph Di Mona, *The Ends of Power*, p. 83.

p. 91   Rogers' cable. State 024758 on diplomatic relationships. February 15, 1969.

p. 91   Joint Chiefs Quarantine study. JCSM 114–69, February 27, 1969.

p. 92   Pentagon on Johnson's refusal. Written response by General Wheeler to a question from Senator Harold Hughes, *Bombing in Cambodia*. p. 141.

p. 92   Nixon on Breakfast. *RN: Memoirs*, pp. 380–85.

p. 92   Firehose. Thomas C. Thayer, Office of the Assistant Secretary of Defense, "How to Analyze a War Without Fronts, Vietnam 1965–72," (P.A. and E) *Journal of Defense Research*, Series B: Tactical Warfare Volume 7B, Number 3 (Fall 1975), pp. 825–26. See also U.S. Senate, the Subcommittee on United States Security Agreement and Commitments Abroad, *Hearings*, October 20–22, 28, 1969. Senator Stuart Symington commented, "In fact, as the General just said—which I knew—orders were that if you do not need the planes against Vietnam, use said planes against Laos," (p. 713).

p. 93   Laird's view. Interview with the author, June 30, 1977.

p. 93   Laird memo to JCS on bombing sanctuaries. November 13, 1969.

p. 93   Target boxes and Cambodian habitation. "Authority for B-52 strikes Against Targets in Cambodia," CM-4739-69, November 20, 1969.

p. 93   B-52s and U.S. troops. General Creighton Abrams told the Senate Armed Services Committee that "we did not bomb with B-52s closer than 3,000 meters to our own troops. At Khe Sanh we reduced that to 1,500. In some emergency situations we reduced it to 1,000. In doing that, the battalion commander on the ground, who was going to get the support, is the one who had to agree to it. . . . He is responsible for his men. He is trusting in the faith and the discipline of whoever is running these things and whoever is flying them and whoever is pushing the button." *Bombing in Cambodia*, p. 350.

p. 93   "Lucrative targets." Memorandum for the Secretary of Defense, "Authority for B-52 strikes against Cambodia," CM-4739-69, November 20, 1969.

p. 93   The Chiefs' admission that casualties could not be assessed. On July 25, 1973, Congressman Michael Harrington asked the Pentagon for "documents giving the best available estimate of civilian and military casualties incurred by Cambodia and Laos during the period January 20, 1969, through April 30, 1970, including the targets of bombing in Cambodia and Laos." In its response the Pentagon said:

We have no documents with which to provide useful information on the totals of either civilian or military casualties in Cambodia or Laos during this time frame. Several factors prevented the maintenance of such records: A. Heavy jungle canopy precluded effective aerial photography. B. Heavy anti-aircraft fire frequently prevented low flying observation craft from making post strike reconnaissance. C. There were usually no on-scene ground observers to report casualties. D. Bomb damage reporting that does exist is fragmentary, occasionally inconsistent and inadequate to support any estimate of casualties. E. it is important to realise that many casualties in both Laos and Cambodia have been caused by enemy forces.

p. 93   The texts of the letters Kissinger supplied the Foreign Relations Committee follow. The translation of Sihanouk's messages, written in French, is by the State Department.

4th April, 1969

Mr. President:

I have just received, through His Excellency the Ambassador of Australia to Cambodia, the text of the declaration by which the United States recognizes and respects the present frontiers of the Kingdom of Cambodia. In the name of the Khmer people and in my own name, I must express to you, Mr. President, as well as to your government and to the great American people, our sincere gratitude for this act of justice and equity by the United States of America toward Cambodia. The resumption of normal relations between our two countries—a resumption which will follow in the near future the decision of the United States to recognize our frontiers—will open the way, I hope, to mutual understanding and good future relations between Cambodia and the United States of America.

I know, moreover, that this is also your desire, and I must thank you especially for the decision that you have just made which will permit this normalization hoped for by both sides. I beg you, Mr. President, to accept the assurances of my very high consideration.

Norodom Sihanouk

Mr. President:

I was pleased to receive your letter of July 28 and thank you warmly for it. I would wish that it were possible for you, at the time of your next travels in Asia, to visit Cambodia where the warmest reception will be reserved for you by the Cambodian people and the Royal Government.

Norodom Sihanouk

8th August, 1969

Your Royal Highness:

I was most appreciative of your note of July 31 with its invitation to visit Cambodia. I would indeed like to visit your lovely country again, and I hope that the occasion to do so will arise in the not too distant future.

I am taking advantage of the departure of Mr. Rives, our newly-designated Chargé in Phnom Penh, to transmit this note to you. I hope that his arrival and the re-establishment of functioning Embassies in our two capitals will mark the start of a new and auspicious chapter in the relations between our countries.

Sincerely,
Richard Nixon

465

Mr. President:

I thank you for your kind message of August 8, 1969, and for the hope that you will give us the opportunity to welcome you to Cambodia in the not too distant future.

I think, as you do, that the arrival of your distinguished Chargé d'Affaires in Phnom Penh and the installation of our Chargé d'Affaires in Washington will mark a new chapter in the history of our relations.

We welcome with honor at this moment Senator Mansfield, an old and faithful friend of Cambodia. He will tell you of our profound desire to put on a firm foundation the friendship which we all hope to see reborn between our two countries and our two peoples.

Sincerely,
Norodom Sihanouk

p. 94   Lack of Cambodian protest. In an airgram to the State Department on January 13, 1970, Rives relayed recent protest notes the embassy had received from the Cambodian Ministry of Foreign Affairs about attacks across the border. There had been seven such notes covering December 1969. They referred to specific attacks on Cambodian territory by American tactical aircraft, artillery boats, helicopters. No mention was made of B-52 strikes. That month 401 B-52 sorties were flown against Cambodia; 11,565 tons of munitions were dropped.

p. 94   Reply to possible Cambodian protest. See, for example, JCS 01762 from General Wheeler to General Abrams—"Operation Menu," February 5, 1970.

p. 94   Congressmen informed. In 1978 Nixon claimed that only Richard Russell and John Stennis, the chairman and the ranking member of the Senate Armed Services Committee, were told of Menu (RN: Memoirs, p. 382). John Stennis later claimed that he had been given only a very vague description of what was happening. "I just wasn't told—I wasn't—about the extent of it, and all about the false records and everything." (CBS TV interview, September 16, 1973.)

p. 94   Among the specific acts of deception were the following: Melvin Laird describing the 1970 invasion, to the House Subcommittee on Defense Appropriations, May 4, 1970, as the "first opportunity we have had to go into the sanctuary areas." Melvin Laird to Senate Armed Services Committee in hearings on Military Procurement, May 12, 1970, "Previously the Government (of Cambodia) had always objected to any activity on the part of U.S. or G.V.N. forces in the NVN sanctuary area of Cambodia." General Wheeler also said then the U.S. had "responded to attacks from Cambodia with artillery fire and with air strikes. . . . We have always made an announcement of it." Richard Nixon, Foreign Policy report to Congress, February 25, 1971, "In Cambodia we pursued the policy of the previous administration until North Vietnamese actions after Prince Sihanouk was deposed made this impossible." The Air Force presented false statistics to the Senate Armed Services Committee on March 31, 1970. On May 30, 1970, Acting Secretary of State Elliot Richardson wrote to William Fulbright, Chairman of the Senate Foreign Relations Committee, "For five years, neither the United States nor South Vietnam has moved against these North Vietnamese/Viet Cong sanctuaries because we did not wish to put ourselves at odds with the Sihanouk government." The same false statistics, showing no bombing in Cambodia before May 1, 1970, were again presented in May 1973. Admiral Thomas Moorer, Chairman of the Joint Chiefs, testifying to the Senate Armed Services Committee in hearings on military procurement, fiscal year 1974, on April 2, 1973, pp. 390–91, provided false information and confirmed Senator Symington's statement that Cambodia bombing began in the spring of 1970.

p. 95 Scowcroft statement. Interview with the author, February 16, 1978.

p. 95 Nixon on reasons for secrecy. *RN: Memoirs*, p. 382.

p. 95 Kissinger on Menu. Kalb and Kalb, *op. cit.*, p. 132.

p. 95 Chiefs on Communists' "dispersal." Memorandum for the Secretary of Defense, "Authority for B-52 strikes against Cambodia," CM-4739-69, November 20, 1969.

Chapter 7

p. 96 The section on Kissinger and the press is based in part on interviews with former members of Kissinger's staff and many Washington journalists. Other sources are Roger Morris, "Henry Kissinger and the Media: A Separate Peace," *Columbia Journalism Review*, May/June 1974, pp. 14–25 and *Uncertain Greatness*.

p. 97 Kraft statement. Interview with Stanley Karnow, "Kissinger in Retrospect," Public Broadcasting System, January 11, 1977.

p. 97 Brandon statement. Quoted in Lewis Chester et al., *Watergate: The Full Inside Story* (New York: Ballantine Books, 1973), p. 27.

p. 97 The section on the Nixon-Kissinger relationship and on life on the National Security Council staff is based partly on interviews with former members of the staffs of the two men. See also William Safire, *Before the Fall;* H. R. Haldeman and Joseph DiMona, *The Ends of Power;* Roger Morris, *Uncertain Greatness;* Bob Woodward and Carl Bernstein, *The Final Days* (New York: Simon and Schuster, 1977).

p. 99 Safire, *op. cit.*, p. 157.

p. 101 "Stalin/Lenin." Roger Morris in interview with the author and in *Uncertain Greatness*, p. 142.

p. 102 Safire on Kissinger's telephone transcripts. Safire, *op. cit.*, p. 169.

p. 103 Nixon on Kissinger and Rogers. Safire, *op. cit.*, p. 406; Nixon, *RN: Memoirs*, pp. 433–34.

p. 103 Statement of a subcommittee of Senate Armed Services Committee. Quoted in the Pentagon Papers, 4:204.

p. 104 Kissinger and ISA. Mort Halperin interview with the author, January 1977.

p. 104 For a full exposition of the bombing argument between Laird and Kissinger, see Chapter 15.

p. 104 Kissinger's moratorium proposal. Kalb and Kalb *op. cit.* p. 145.

p. 105 Laird recollection. Interview with the author, June 30, 1977.

p. 106 Laird and Pursley's views. Laird interview with the author, June 30, 1977, and Pursley interview with the author, January 16 and 29, 1977.

p. 106 Kissinger on Haig's trustworthiness. Senate Foreign Relations Committee, Hearings, *Dr. Kissinger's Role in Wiretapping*, p. 24 (1974).

p. 107   Nixon on wiretaps. Nixon, *RN: Memoirs,* p. 389.

p. 107   Kissinger on treatment of Halperin. *Wall Street Journal* May 20, 1977.

p. 107   Footnote. For a summary of the law on wiretaps, see David Wise, *The American Police State,* pp. 96–106. Also *Warrantless Wiretapping and Electronic Surveillance,* report by subcommittees of the Senate Judiciary and Senate Foreign Relations Committees, February 1975. The arguments in the Halperin case are contained in "Brief for the Plantiffs-Appellants" filed in the Court of Appeals, No. 77–2014, February 2, 1978.

p. 109   Systems Analysis report, May 1969, "Enemy emphasis on causing U.S. casualties: a Follow-Up."

p. 109   Kissinger's warnings to Russians. Nixon, *RN: Memoirs,* p. 396 and p. 399.

p. 109   "Savage, punishing blow." This account of the "September Group" derives in part from interviews with former members of Kissinger's staff. See also Roger Morris, *Uncertain Greatness,* pp. 163–68, and Tad Szulc, *The Illusion of Peace,* pp. 152–56.

Chapter 8

p. 113   Abrams' remark. *Bombing in Cambodia,* p. 358.

p. 113   Lon Nol's statement. *Le Sangkum,* Phnom Penh, October 1969.

p. 114   Sihanouk's complaints against Hanoi. Confirmed by his long-time French aide, Charles Meyer, in an interview with the author, May 30, 1977.

p. 115   Snepp. Interviews with the author, January 9 and February 8, 1977.

p. 115   Sawin. Telephone interviews with the author, July 1977 and November 10, 1978.

p. 116   Layton. Interview with the author, July 4, 1977.

p. 117   Laird's views. Interview with the author, June 30, 1977, and "Memorandum for the President, Trip report to Vietnam and CINCPAC, 10th–15th February, 1970," February 17, 1970.

p. 117   Abrams' view. Background interview with *The New York Times,* August 2, 1970.

p. 117   Richardson's statement. Letter from Representative Hamilton Fish to his constituents, May 13, 1970.

p. 117   Sihanouk's Paris dinner. The dinner, at the Cambodian Embassy in Paris on March 10, was attended by Jean de Broglie, the head of the French National Assembly's Foreign Affairs Committee. Sihanouk apparently complained bitterly about North Vietnamese behavior in Cambodia. He also said that he had opposed American policies in the sixties because he thought them counterproductive. He was right—they had forced the Chinese to arm Hanoi, and now American withdrawal would mean that Cambodia, Thailand and Malaysia would all fall to the Communists.

p. 118   Rives cable. No. 110235Z, March 70.

p. 119   Lon Nol explanation. Fred Emery, *The Times,* March 22, 1970.

p. 119   Queen's message. Her French doctor, General Riche, told Mike Rives of the Queen's fatal message to her son. Rives reported this to Washington, Phnom Penh 289, 200450Z March 70.

p. 120 Rosson's statement. Rosson interviews with the author, May 24 and November 23, 1977.

p. 121 Rives's cable on no "new ballgame." This message was relayed by State to the embassies in Bangkok, Saigon and Vientiane, 182248Z March 70 7-FF4.

p. 122 Kissinger's lunch was on January 9, 1977. This account comes from two of the journalists present.

p. 122 Prom Thos statement. Interview with the author, May 31, 1977.

p. 122 William Colby statement. Interview with the author, July 6, 1977.

p. 122 Melvin Laird statement. Interview with the author, June 30, 1977.

p. 123 Rogers' cable. State 040069, March 19, 1970.

p. 123 Thieu's response. At noon on March 18, before news of the coup filtered out of Phnom Penh, Thieu canceled a speech he was to make at an Asian press-seminar dinner that evening. Later in the day he said, "This is the Cambodians' last hope. I think South Vietnam and Cambodia could become very good friends in the future. . . ." *The New York Times,* March 18, 1970.

p. 123 Sihanouk, *My War with the CIA,* p. 28.

p. 124 Air France story. Interview with Etienne Manac'h, February 18, 1977.

p. 127 Bernard-Philippe Groslier and Jacques Arthaud, *Angkor, Hommes et Pierres,* Paris, 1965.

p. 127 Sword story cable. Phnom Penh cable 362.

Chapter 9

p. 128 "Stream-of-consciousness excursions." Roger Morris, *Uncertain Greatness,* p. 173.

p. 129 Marshall Green. Interviews with the author, May 19 and 26, 1970.

p. 129 Rives's warning. Phnom Penh 322, 240530Z March 70.

p. 130 Vietnamese Communist intentions. "The Viet Cong's March–April 1970 Plans for Expanding Control in Cambodia," Document No. 88, U.S. Embassy, Saigon, January 1971.

p. 130 Lon Nol government protest. Government statement April 2, 1970, "Cambodia will not in fact accept the right of pursuit carried out on its territory."

p. 130 Pursley reaction to Haig. Pursley interviews with the author, January 16 and 29, 1977.

p. 131 Press conference. *The Times,* London, April 3, 1970; *The New York Times,* April 4, 1970.

p. 131 "Men armed with sticks." *The Times,* London, April 13, 1970.

p. 131 Abrams remark. *Newsweek,* May 4, 1970.

p. 131 Westmoreland cable. JCS 05495, April 21, 1970.

p. 131 Abrams on Khmer Serei, MAC 5364, April 22, 1970.

p. 132 Lon Nol's aid demands. *The Times,* London, April 30, 1970.

p. 132 Takeo abattoir. Published reports and interview with Kevin Buckley, January 21, 1977.

p. 133 Capture of Saang. *Newsweek,* May 4, 1970.

p. 134 Neustadt. Afterword by Richard Neustadt and Graham Allison in Norton paperback edition of Robert F. Kennedy's *Thirteen Days*, 1971, pp. 118-19, quoted by Arthur Schesinger, Jr., *The Imperial Presidency*, p. 189.

p. 134   Nixon on toughness. Roger Morris, *Uncertain Greatness*, p. 174.

p. 135   Patton. Kalb and Kalb, *op. cit.*, p. 154.

p. 135   Abrams' request for Special Forces attacks. MACSOG 4432, April 4, 1970.

p. 135   Abrams' request for tactical air strikes, MAC 5163, April 18, 1970; Wheeler's response, JCS 05362, April 18, 1970; Abrams' refusal, MAC 5194. April 19, 1970.

p. 135   Abrams' frankness. *Bombing in Cambodia*, p. 343.

p. 137   Kissinger on "poignancy." Kalb and Kalb, *op. cit.*, p. 156.

p. 137   Story of suppressed National Intelligence Estimate. "Stocktaking in Indochina," Senate Select Committee on Intelligence Activities, Volume I, pp. 79-81. The estimate was obtained under the Freedom of Information Act.

p. 138   Senate report, "Cambodia May 1970." U.S. Senate Foreign Relations Committee, June 7, 1970.

p. 138   Westmoreland cable. JCS 05495, April 21, 1970; Abrams' response, MAC 5364, April 22, 1970.

p. 139   Westmoreland on Vietnamese adequacy. William Westmoreland, *A Soldier Reports*, (New York: Doubleday, 1976). p. 388.

p. 139   Abrams' deputy. Rosson, interviews with the author, May 24 and November 23, 1977.

p. 139   Wheeler on invasion by Vietnamese. JCS 05623.

p. 139   Rogers' statement. To House Appropriations Subcommittee, in *The New York Times*, May 5, 1975.

p. 139   "No-Dis Khmer." Interviews with State Department officials, and *The New York Times*, May 5, 1970.

p. 140   Nutter. Philip Odeen, memorandum for the record, morning meeting of the Vietnamization group in Melvin Laird's office, May 8, 1970. Extracts of these daily "Mem-Cons" were made available to the author, not by Mr. Odeen. When quoted hereafter they are referred to as "Odeen."

p. 140   Kissinger meeting with Fulbright. Kalb and Kalb, *op. cit.*, p. 157.

p. 140   Abrams on COSVN, MAC 4432, April 4, 1970.

p. 140   *Newsweek* on COSVN, May 11, 1970.

p. 140   Moorer and Laird. Watts interview with the author, June 4, 1976.

p. 140   Wheeler cable with Laird's questions. JCS 05660, April 24, 1970.

p. 141   Laird on effect of White House questions. Interview with the author, June 30, 1977.

p. 141   Footnote. Townsend Hoopes, *The Devil and John Foster Dulles*, pp. 211-12.

p. 141   Abrams' proposal for attack on 352/353. MAC 5504, April 25, 1970, Wheeler's reply, JCS 05715, April 25, 1970.

p. 141   "Stormy meeting." Kalb and Kalb, *op. cit.*, p. 158. Morris, *Uncertain Greatness*, p. 174.

p. 142   Westmoreland's assessment. *Op. cit.*, p. 388.

p. 142   Rebozo story. David Wise, *op. cit.*, p. 92.

p. 143   Lynn's review. Lynn interview with the author, February 1, 1977.

p. 144   B-52s "softening-up." *Washington Star*, May 6, 1970.

p. 144   Patton. Kalb and Kalb, *op. cit.*, p. 154.

p. 144   Nixon backchannels cable to Abrams. Nixon, *RN: Memoirs*, p. 450.

p. 144   Rockefeller statement. Safire, *op. cit.*, p. 102–3.

p. 144   Rogers and Senate Foreign Relations Committee. "Background Information Relating to Southeast Asia and Vietnam," Senate Foreign Relations Committee, December 1974, p. 101.

p. 145   Wheeler cable. JCS 05812, April 28, 1970.

p. 145   Staff-implications. *Look* magazine, August 11, 1970.

p. 145   Haig and Watts. Kalb and Kalb, *op. cit.*, pp. 161–2, and Watts interview with the author, June 4, 1976.

p. 145   Kissinger with White House Staff. Safire, *op. cit.*, pp. 186–87.

p. 146   "We are all the President's men." Kalb and Kalb, *op. cit.*, p. 169.

p. 146   Laird's view of speech. Interview with Melvin Laird, June 30, 1977.

p. 146   The best analysis of Nixon's speech has been made by Jonathan Schell, in *The Time of Illusion* (New York: Knopf, 1976).

p. 148   Schumpeter, *Imperialism and Social Classes* (New York: n.p., 1955), p. 51. Quoted by Arthur M. Schlesinger, Jr., in *The Imperial Presidency*, p. 184.

p. 148   Rehnquist. The memorandum even falsified the legal evidence. It invoked the recent case of *Mitchell v. Laird* and went on to say: "In the words of Judge Wyzanski, the President properly acted 'with a profound concern for the durable interests of the nation—its defense, its honor, its morality.'" What Judge Wyzanski actually said was: "President Nixon's duty did not go beyond trying to bring the war to an end as promptly as was consistent with the safety of those fighting and with a profound concern for the durable interests of the nation—its defense, its honor, its morality. Whether President Nixon did so proceed is a question which at this stage in history a court is incompetent to answer." In other words, the judge was referring to the President's obligation, not his actual performance. In a letter to *The New York Times*, Arthur Schlesinger, Jr., commented: "This is simply one more example of the instinct for duplicity and mendacity that, as recent events have made more clear than ever, is the hallmark of the Nixon style of government. I am sorry to see that the State Department has now been infected." *The New York Times*, May 9, 1973.

p. 148   Footnote. Schlesinger, *op. cit.*, pp. 187–93.

p. 149   Lon Nol's reaction to invasion. Senate Foreign Relations Committee Report, Background Information Relating to Southeast Asia and Vietnam, December 1974, p. 102.

Chapter 10

p. 150   Destruction of Snuol. *Washington Post*, May 7, 1970, quoting a UPI dispatch.

p. 150   Brookshire as "butcher of Snuol." Said to Kevin Buckley of *Newsweek* at Naval War College Seminar, May 1972. Buckley interview with the author, January 21, 1977.

p. 151   Vietnamese Minister of Refugees. *Christian Science Monitor*, June 12, 1970.

p. 151   Nixon's behavior at Pentagon. Westmoreland, *op. cit.*, p. 388, and interviews with two of those present.

p. 152   Knight disillusion. *Bombing in Cambodia*, pp. 2–70.

p. 152   Drinan. Interview with the author, January 18, 1977.

p. 152   Nixon on "the living bejeesus." Safire, *op. cit*, pp. 189–90.

p. 153   Sihanouk-Kent State. Michael Field, *The Prevailing Wind*, (London: Methuen, 1965), pp. 244–45.

p. 153   Nixon's telephone log. Reproduced in William Safire, *op. cit.*, p. 204.

p. 154   Krogh. Safire, *op. cit.*, pp. 205–22.

p. 154   Jackson State. Evans and Novak, *Nixon in the White House*, (New York: Vintage Books, 1972), p. 291.

p. 154   Lot's wife. Nixon television interview with David Frost, May 13, 1977.

p. 154   Laird on invasion and WASSAG. Odeen, May 7, 1975.

p. 155   Kissinger's battle with Rogers. Safire, *op. cit.*, p. 196.

p. 155   Pedersen's opinion. Pedersen interview with the author, June 23, 1976.

p. 155   Safire on taps, *op. cit.*, p. 167.

p. 155   State protest. Pedersen interview with the author, June 23, 1976.

p. 156   Ehrlichman on Kissinger. Kalb and Kalb, *op. cit.*, p. 168.

p. 156   Kissinger, heart-attack rationale. Kalb and Kalb, *op. cit.*, p. 165.

p. 157   Haldeman on Kent State. Haldeman and DiMona, *op. cit.*, p. 107.

p. 158   Huston testimony. Senate Select Committee on Intelligence Activities, 1976, Volume 2, p. 32.

p. 158   Huston memo. Senate Select Committee on Intelligence Activities, Volume 2, p. 246.

p. 159   Nixon on Presidential immunity. Television interview with David Frost, May 13, 1977.

p. 159   Footnote. Kissinger on Presidential activity. Kalb and Kalb, *op. cit.*, pp. 169–70.

p. 160   Kissinger's arguments. Interview with Kenneth Harris, *The Observer*, London, June 12, 1977.

Chapter 11

p. 161   Kissinger to WASSAG. Odeen, May 28, 1970.

p. 162   Senate report. *Cambodia May 1970*.

p. 162   Haig's mission. This account is based on several interviews with NSC and State Department officials.

p. 162   Rives's self-description. *The New York Times*, August 11, 1969.

p. 163   Treatment of ambassadors. The most famous "incident" that this practice provoked took place in Saudi Arabia in 1974. As Kissinger set off for a meeting with King Faisal, he told the ambassador, James E. Akins, that he was not expected to come. "In that case," said Akins, "you will find my resignation on the desk when you return." Kissinger allowed him along; but, despite the fact that Akins was one of the best Arabists in the Department, his career was ruined. He resigned.

p. 165   Cambodian army. *A Systems Analysis View of the Vietnam War 1965–1972*, Volume I, *Cambodian Armed Forces*, April–May 1970.

p. 166   Nixon Doctrine. *Congressional Record*, July 28, 1969, pp. S 8637–40, reproduced in Senate Foreign Relations Committee Report, "Background Information Relating to Southeast Asia and Vietnam," December 1974, pp. 356–67.

p. 167   Lon Nol on detente. *Los Angeles Times*, May 26, 1976.

p. 168   Ladd's role. Interviews with the author, May 17 and 18, 1976, January 8, 1977; February 11, 1977.

p. 170   Kraft column. *Washington Post*, June 11, 1970.

p. 170   Colby and Lon Nol. Rives reported to State that Lon Nol was very excited by Colby's visit. Colby lectured him on the "People's War" of North Vietnam.

p. 170   Rives's cable, Phnom Penh 1507, July 7, 1970.

p. 171   Laird memorandum to Joint Chiefs. May 15, 1970.

p. 172   Footnote. Odeen, May 28, 1970. For the comparative casualties, see Thayer, *War Without Fronts*, pp. 850–51.

p. 172   Rand Study. *U.S. Fatalities During Vietnamization*, Parts I and II, by F. J. West, Jr., RM 6376–ARPA, June 1970.

p. 172   Kissinger's analysts. Larry Lynn and Robert Sansone, interviews February 1, 1977, and February 11, 1977. John Court of the NSC staff also maintains that the NSC staff tried to prove with captured documents that the North Vietnamese had been about to capture Phnom Penh and that no such conclusion could be sustained. Telephone interviews February 3 and 12, 1977.

p. 173.   Invasion assessment. Memo to Laird, 1-35633-70, August 21, 1970.

p. 173   USIA survey. Described by Frank Shakespeare, USIA Director, on "Issues and Answers," December 20, 1970.

p. 173   Laird complaint. Odeen, May 19, 1970.

p. 173   Cable from JCS to Abrams, Limdis, Ivy Tree, 2835, June 17, 1970.

p. 174   Abrams on ARVN pleasure in Cambodia. Odeen, June 5, 1970.

p. 175   Rives's cable on South Vietnamese conduct. August 23, 1970.

p. 175   Thai troops. Published reports. Also interview with Jonathan Moore, February 1, 1977.

p. 175   Dudman analysis. Richard Dudman, *Forty Days with the Enemy* (New York: Liveright, 1971).

p. 175   Elizabeth Pond. Odeen, July 23, 1970.

p. 175   Rives and Agnew. Interviews with State Department officials.

Chapter 12

p. 177   Laird complaints. Odeen, September 3 and 10, 1970.

p. 178   NSSM 99. The study was launched on August 17, 1970. It stated that "As an initial interim step in the overall study alternative short range military strategies for Cambodia should be developed."

p. 180   Odeen on "disturbing decision." Odeen, September 18, 1970.

p. 180   CINCPAC's concern. Talking paper prepared for Laird's use at October 16, 1970, Senior Review Group meeting, and Odeen, October 22, 1970.

p. 180   The Cambodia Supplemental was to include: the transfer of $49 million in Supporting Assistance to the Military Assistance Program, for use in Cambodia; the institution of a $20-million PL 480 program for Cambodia; the commitment of $11 million in AID contingency funds to Cambodia, either through a MAP transfer or as grant assistance, after the Administration's request had gone forward; the authorization of DOD offshore procurement to the extent practicable.

p. 181   Laird's office's objections. Outlined in the talking paper prepared for Laird's use at the Senior Review Group meeting on October 16, 1970.

p. 181   Logic of main-force army. Already by September 1970, $8 million of the original $40 million transferred to Cambodia for the purchase of small arms and ammunition was being reprogrammed for helicopters.

p. 182   Rives's cable. Phnom Penh 1264, June 16, 1970.

p. 182   Colby explanation. Interview with the author, July 5, 1977.

p. 185   Charles Meyer statement. Interview with the author, May 30, 1971.

p. 186   Laird's memorandum for the President. "Trip to Paris, Bangkok, South Vietnam, and CINCPAC, January 5–15, 1971," January 16, 1971. In his communications with Nixon, Laird rarely expressed the reservations about U.S. policy that he felt. Phrases such as "I wanted to follow closely the guidelines you so convincingly established," and "under your guidance, all that was changed," and "in retrospect your decisions in 1969 constituted a true watershed" abound in his report.

p. 186   Swank cable on airport attack. January 25, 1971.

p. 187   Swank cable quoting Sirik Matak. "Resignation of Lon Nol," 01917432 April 71. Swank's reporting during Lon Nol's resignation and restoration was extremely cautious; the embassy had little idea what was happening.

p. 187   "The Nixon Doctrine in its purest form." Presidential news conference, November 12, 1976.

Chapter 13

p. 189   Swank profile. The New York Times, July 15, 1970.

p. 189   "Waves" and "sparks." Swank interview with the author, May 29–30, 1976. The author's assertions as to Swank's instructions and opinions in this and succeeding chapters derive mainly from this interview.

p. 190   Laird resistance gives way. Odeen, December 28, 1970.

p. 191   Mataxis as Martian. Khmer Republic, Issue 3. Phnom Penh, 1971.

p. 191   Mataxis on Cambodia as troika. Interview with the author, January 28, 1977.

p. 191   This and other information on the workings of the MEDTC through 1971 are derived from a report prepared for the Committee on Foreign Affairs of the House of Representatives by two members of its staff, John Sullivan and Robert Boyer. The Joint Chiefs objected strenuously to many of the criticisms that the report made; they applied pressure to the Committee leadership and, as a result, the report was never published. It is a valuable document. By contrast

General Mataxis's end-of-tour report, obtained under the Freedom of Information Act, contains nothing of any interest whatsoever.

p. 192   McCain cable complaining about Swank. OR 170106Z, April 1971.

p. 192   NSSM 99 problems. Laird and his Vietnamization staff discussed these concerns at their morning meetings. Odeen, February 3, March 26, April 19, June 1, 1971.

p. 193   Laird's attitudes and complaints. *Ibid.*

p. 193   Laird and Rogers. Odeen, June 1, 1971.

p. 193   Kissinger's June 7 memo. This called for a new Military Assistance Plan "including specific time-phase goals with alternatives as necessary to achieve accelerated training and logistics capabilities for FANK. . . . The issue of the appropriate number of U.S. personnel in Cambodia will be resolved in the context of the final decision on a military assistance plan."

p. 194   2,000 officers in MEDTC. Odeen, May 19, 1971.

p. 194   Memo to Laird. Prepared by Office of Systems Analysis, Office of the Secretary of Defense, May 1971.

p. 194   Laird complaint. Odeen, June 16, 1971.

p. 194   Laird "power curve." Odeen, June 10, 1971.

p. 194   JCS memo for 220,000 men. July 1, 1971.

p. 194   ISA memo. By Warren Nutter and Philip Odeen, July 2, 1971.

p. 194   JCS revised plan. JCSM-392-71.

p. 195   State's view of Mataxis's incompetence. Odeen, June 28, 1971.

p. 195   Swank's view. Interview with the author May 29–30, 1976.

p. 195   Kissinger memo. October 20, 1971, referring to SRG meeting of October 18, 1971.

p. 195   Swank as whorehouse keeper. Interview with William Harben, February 8, 1971.

p. 196   Amos' views. After Laird's Vietnamization meeting on August 20, 1970, Philip Odeen wrote that Amos "felt we ought to give them lots of military assistance and help build up a large military establishment. Mr. Laird indicated he hoped to talk to Colonel Amos before he left for Cambodia." Also interview with Amos, January 13, 1977.

p. 196   Piazza work. Piazza interview with the author, February 1, 1977.

p. 197   Mataxis' contempt for rules and for Swank. Interview with the author, January 28, 1977.

p. 198   *New York Times* story. September 20, 1971.

p. 199   *Newsweek* story. October 18, 1971.

p. 199   Swank cables. Phnom Penh 5204 and 5279, October 1971.

p. 199   McCain incident. Odeen, October 4, 1971.

p. 199   Swank's letter. *Newsweek*, November 22, 1971.

Chapter 14

p. 201   Australian complaint about children in army. See Senate Foreign Relations Committee Report, "Thailand, Laos, Cambodia and Vietnam: April 1973," June 11, 1973, p. 32. The investigators, Richard Moose and James Lowenstein, were told that there had been as many as 6,000 children under sixteen in the army and that the number was now about 4,500. They noted that "unit commanders like to recruit children because they can pocket their pay, and the children don't complain." After an Australian journalist wrote about the large number of children being trained by Australian troops in Vietnam, the Australian Government refused to handle any more such units

p. 201–4 Chenla II. This account is based on published sources and interviews with Cambodian officers and U.S. military attachés.

p. 204 Swank cables. *Washington Post*, December 17, 1971, and January 11, 1972, and interview with Swank, May 29–30, 1976.

p. 205 Kissinger on "advance information." Senate Armed Services Committee Hearing, *Transmittal of Documents from the National Security Council to the Chairman of the Joint Chiefs of Staff*, February 6, 20, 21, and March 7, 1974, Volume I, p. 52.

p. 205 Kissinger revisions of Laird's memos. J. Fred Buzhardt, interview with the author, February 17, 1978.

p. 205 Radford gave a full account of his activities to the Senate Armed Services Committee Hearings, *Transmittal of Documents*, Volume 2.

p. 206 Admiral Welander's account of his role. *Ibid.*

p. 206 Buzhardt statement. Buzhardt interview with the author, February 17, 1978.

p. 207 Ehrlichman notes. Impeachment Hearings, House Judiciary Committee, Hearings on Impeachment, 1974, Statement of Information, Appendix III, p. 214.

p. 207 Kissinger listening to Young's report. *Transmittal of Documents*, Part 2, pp. 48–49.

p. 208 Psychiatrist's report. This was contained in one of the papers generated by NSSM 152.

p. 208 Nixon statement on Cambodia. News Conference, December 10, 1970.

Chapter 15

p. 209 Mad Mullah. *The Memoirs of General Lord Ismay* (London: Heinemann, 1950; New York: Viking, 1960), Chapter 2.

p. 210 Eaker letter. January 1, 1945, cited in *The U.S. Army Air Forces in World War II*, Volume 3, p. 733.

p. 210 CIA report on North Vietnamese industry. Pentagon Papers 4:168, Quoted in Robert L. Gallucci, *Neither Peace Nor Honor, The Politics of American Military Policy in Vietnam*, Baltimore, 1975, p. 61.

p. 211 Tonnage of one B-52 squadron. In his "Report to the President" on his January 1971 trip to Paris, Bangkok, South Vietnam and CINCPAC, Laird wrote, "U.S. air support continues at a high level. In December 1970, for example, more than 17,000 attack sorties were flown in support of friendly forces in Indochina. The B-52 unit which I visited in Thailand drops more than 50% as much ordnance in one year as all U.S. air elements combined dropped in the Pacific theater in World War II."

p. 212   Air Force histories. These official histories, prepared by the Office of
Air Force History, were obtained, with substantial deletions, under the Freedom
of Information Act.
p. 212   Laird disparagement. *The Administration Emphasizes Air Power*, p.
92.
p. 212   "Bridging the gap." *Ibid.*, p. 93.
p. 212   Footnote on Koreans. Odeen, March 26, April 26, June 25, 1971.
p. 212   White House "contingency" argument. Odeen, February 2, 1970.
p. 212   Nutter's suggestion on sorties. Odeen, April 28, 1970.
p. 213   Laird's anger. Odeen, April 28, 1970.
p. 213   Banking system. Odeen, May 19, and June 20, 1971.
p. 213   Laird comment on "so much heat" and request to Odeen. Odeen, June
5, 1970.
p. 213   Kissinger on Thai troops. Odeen, June 5, 1970.
p. 213   Pursley comment. Odeen, June 10, 1970.
p. 213   Nixon to WASSAG. Odeen, June 16, 1970.
p. 214   Packard comment. Odeen June 17, 1970.
p. 214   JCS cable to Abrams. Limdis, Ivy Tree, 2835, June 17, 1970.
p. 214   Laird instruction on poststrike reports. Odeen, June 29, 1970.
p. 214   Pentagon statement. January 18, 1971.
p. 214   Laird statement. January 20, 1971.
p. 214   Rogers statement. News conference, January 29, 1971.
p. 214   *The New York Times.* January 22, 1971.
p. 215   Pilots' testimony. See for example that of Gerald J. Greven, *Bombing
in Cambodia*, pp. 276–323.
p. 215   Footnote. Memorandum for Record by Major Ronald E. Gardner,
February 20, 1971: Arclight strike in Cambodia, TS HOA/73/76.
p. 216   Mekong River convoys. This story is contained in *Aerial Protection of
Mekong River Convoys*, Project Checo Report, HQ PACAF, Directorate of Operations Analysis, Checo/Corona Harvest Division, October 1, 1971.
p. 216   Swank petroleum cable. Amemb 971310Z January 1971.
p. 217   Nixon "laying down" new "understanding," and "no limitations."
January 4 and February 17, 1971.
p. 217   Nixon on Laird. *RN: Memoirs*, p. 499.
p. 217   Laird public statement on air power, *Washington Post*, April 14, 1971.
p. 217   Laird on "roof of Capitol." Odeen, April 7, 1971.
p. 218   South Vietnamese Air Force in Cambodia. Thomas Thayer, "War
Without Fronts," p. 826.
p. 218   Footnote. Dr. Robert C. Seamans, Jr., Oral History Interview, K
239.0512-687.

Chapter 16

p. 220   Many of the economic facts and figures in this chapter are derived from
the Agency for International Development's draft "Termination Report on Eco-

nomic Assistance to Cambodia, Fiscal Years 1971–1975," September 1975. The draft was never completed or published. It was obtained from AID under the Freedom of Information Act.

p. 222   Plethora of Cambodian Government statistics. General Accounting Office Report to the Senate Refugee Subcommittee of the Judiciary Committee, "Problems in the Khmer Republic (Cambodia) Concerning War Victims, Civilian Health and War-Related Casualties," February 2, 1972.

p. 223   Chak Angre camp. *Ibid*, p. 24.

p. 223   "Low profile" toward refugees. The GAO report noted "According to the U.S. Ambassador to Cambodia, it has been the policy of the United States to not become involved with the problem of civilian war victims in Cambodia. At the time of our review in September 1971, the Ambassador did not consider the civilian war problem to be of such serious proportions as to require U.S. assistance." p. 9.

p. 223   Senate Refugee Subcommittee Report. "Refugee and Civilian War Casualty Problems in Indochina" September 28, 1970, p. 40.

p. 224   Lon Nol government refugee statistics. GAO report, p. 14.

p. 224   Swank assertion that no request had been made. GAO report, p. 9. Also William Sullivan, testimony to Senate Refugee Subcommittee, "Problems of War Victims in Indochina," Part II, May 9, 1972, p. 7.

p. 224   Hospital conditions. GAO report, pp. 45–53.

p. 225   Infant deaths. GAO report, p. 19.

p. 225   Provision of drugs. GAO report, p. 49, also Senate Refugee Subcommittee hearing, May 9, 1972, p. 24–25.

p. 225   Pheng Kanthel-Blackburn story. *Ibid.*, pp. 15–20.

p. 226   Kennedy-Corcoran-O'Connor exchange. *Ibid.*, pp. 20–21.

p. 227   Ministry of Defense demands for funds. Draft AID termination report.

p. 227   FANK Census. "Report on the Payment of Phantom Troops in The Cambodian Military Forces" General Accounting Office, July 3, 1973, Appendix 1, p. 2.

p. 227   Laird's auditors. *Ibid.*

p. 228   GAO conclusion. *Ibid.*

p. 228   Footnote on Harben report. Airgram, Phnom Penh A 34, "Racial Tensions Flare in Constituent Assembly: Biodata on Hoeur Lay Inn and Ung Mung," March 8, 1972.

p. 228   The quotations from Harben are taken from an unpublished paper he wrote on Cambodia and several interviews with him in 1976 and 1977.

p. 229   Swank on "their society." Interview with the author, May 29–30, 1976.

p. 233   Swank citing Diem. *Ibid.*

p. 233   Footnote. Pentagon Papers, US-GVN Relations, June 65–Fall 67, summary and analysis, p. 1.

p. 234   Shark analogy. Paper by W. F. Beazer, attached to draft AID termination report.

p. 234   Swank's statement on Harben paper. Interview with the author, May 29–30, 1977.

p. 235   Harben comment. Unpublished paper.

Chapter 17

p. 237 Nixon on Khmer Rouge. Nixon persisted in charging that the Khmer Communists were Vietnamese puppets, even when the two parties were publicly denouncing and fighting each other. His memoirs, published in 1978, perpetuated this fundamental misapprehension. See p. 883.

p. 237 1934 party document. Milton Osborne, "Kampuchea and Vietnam: A Historical Perspective." Pacific Community, April 1978, pp. 249–63.

p. 237 Links of the new party to the Viet Minh. See "Summary of Annotated Party History." A 1973 document captured during the 1970–75 war, released in 1978 by the CIA.

p. 237 Indochina Federation. These conflicting claims were repeated over and over again in their propaganda war during 1978.

p. 238–39 Revised party history. Speech by Prime Minister and Secretary of the Communist Party of Kampuchea, Pol Pot, September 28, 1977, BBC Summary of World Broadcasts, October 1, 4, and 5, 1977. This speech is essential to any historical study of the Cambodian revolution.

p. 239 Pol Pot's autobiography. Given to Yugoslav journalists visiting Phnom Penh in March 1978. Tanjug in Serbo-Croat, March 18, 1978; BBC Summary of World Broadcasts, March 20, 1978. Other details of his life can be found in "Communist Party Power in Kampuchea (Cambodia): Documents and Discussion," compiled and edited with an introduction by Timothy Michael Carney, Data Paper 106, Southeast Asia Program, Department of Asian Studies, Cornell University, Ithaca, N.Y., January 1977, p. 62.

p. 240 Hu Nim's dissertation. Ibid., pp. 14–16.

p. 241 Land holdings on Mekong banks. Ibid., p. 16.

p. 244 Party tactics in the sixties. Pol Pot speech, Radio Phnom Penh, September 28, 1977.

p. 245 Saloth Sar (Pol Pot) on Battambang revolt. Ibid.

p. 245 Treatment of Khmers Rouges. François Ponchaud, Cambodia: Year Zero, London 1978, p. 394.

p. 246 Party strength in 1970. State Department and CIA sources. See also Carney. Vietnamese leader's figures: Hoang Tung, interview with Nayan Chanda, Far Eastern Economic Review, April 21, 1978.

p. 249 Growth of Khmer Rouge. DIA Intelligence Appraisal, July 8, 1971.

p. 250 Colby recollection. Interview with the author, July 5, 1977.

p. 251 Khmer Rouge claim over arms supplies. Pol Pot speech, September 28, 1977.

p. 252 "Regrets for the Khmer Soul." Translated and reprinted by Carney, pp. 34–55.

p. 252 Collectivization not reform. Carney, op. cit., p. 18, 99fn.

p. 255 Sihanouk's life in Peking. Many of these details are derived either from published interviews with the Prince or from the author's interviews with Etienne Manac'h, February 18, 1976, and other officials of the Quai d'Orsay; and with Sihanouk's former Chef du Cabinet in Peking, Pung Peng Cheng, May 29, 1977, and his former press aide Nouth Choeumm, May 30, 1977.

Chaper 18

p. 259 Haldeman on *Time* magazine. *The Ends of Power*, p. 84.

p. 260 Richard Wilson. Published accounts and Wilson telephone interview with the author, November 7, 1978.

p. 260 Nixon's secret letters to Thieu. South Vietnamese officials released some of these letters during the final days of the war in April 1975. Nixon himself reproduces others in *RN: Memoirs*, pp. 737, 749–50.

p. 261 Secret State Department analysis. This was subsequently leaked to Senator Edward M. Kennedy and released by him.

p. 261 Nixon's secret aid commitment to Hanoi. The fullest account of this promise and of the way in which Kissinger tried to link it to a cease-fire in Cambodia is in Gareth Porter, "The Broken Promise to Hanoi," *The Nation*, April 30, 1977. See also *The New York Times*, February 2, 1976, and *International Bulletin*, February 13, 1976.

p. 262 Kissinger on "innumerable Cambodian factions." January 24, 1970, press conference, weekly compilation of Presidential documents, January 29, 1973, pp. 64–74.

p. 264 Sihanouk statements. Interview with Agence France Presse, Peking, January 31, 1973.

p. 264 Khmer Communist refusal to compromise. On February 12, 1978, for example, Phnom Penh Radio broadcast the confession of a captured Vietnamese soldier who claimed that in 1973 Vietnamese cadres were told that Cambodia must be forced to accept the Paris Agreement and "whether Cambodia agrees with us or not is not the problem, because Cambodia has a small population."

p. 267 Colby statement. Interview with the author, July 5, 1977.

p. 269 Negroponte on Cambodia. Telephone interview with the author, October 29, 1976.

p. 269 Bushnell on Swank. Interview with the author, July 4, 1977.

p. 269 Scowcroft on Swank. Interview with the author, February 16, 1978.

p. 270 Swank on Enders. Interview with the author, May 29–30, 1976.

p. 270 Cleland's end-of-tour report together with those of General Mataxis and Cleland's own successor, General William Palmer, were obtained, on appeal, under the Freedom of Information Act. Some material was deleted from them by the Defense Department.

p. 271 Berent. Interview with the author, March 28, 1977.

p. 271 Sosthene Fernandez. Interview with *The New York Times*, March 23, 1973.

p. 271 Embassy lack of maps and photographs. *U.S. Air Operations in Cambodia: April 1973*, staff report of the Senate Foreign Relations Committee, April 27, 1973, p. 6.

p. 272 Pilot complaints about maps. HAF-CHO (AR) 7101, *History of 8th Tactical Fighter Wing, April 1–June 30 1973*, Volume I, p. 57.

p. 272 Harben on Saang. Interview with the author, February 8, 1977.

p. 272 Pentagon referrals to Admiral McCain's office. *The New York Times*, March 28, 1973.

p. 272   Official maps of the bombing. Contained in *Air Operations in South-east Asia*, Volume I, *Project Corona Harvest V, 1 July 1972–12 August 1973*, "A Strategic Air Command Study on the Effectiveness of Air Power in South-east Asia."

p. 272   Air Force history on JCS increasing scope of bombing. *History of the United States Support Activities Group, Seventh Air Force, 13 February–31 March 1973*, p. 75.

p. 273   Sullivan and *Washington Post* quotations. *Washington Post*, March 28 and 30, 1973.

p. 273   History of the 43rd Strategic Wing, January–June 1973. *The Cambodian Campaign*, Narrative of Air Warfare over Cambodia, pp. 67–74.

p. 274   Sirik Matak interview. *The New York Times*, March 24, 1973.

p. 274   "Free Patriotic Khmers." William Harben, interview with the author, February 8, 1977.

p. 275   Kissinger briefing to Valeriani. April 9, 1973, memorandum circulated by NBC.

p. 275   William Harben. Interview with the author, February 8, 1977.

p. 275   Moose and Lowenstein on Lon Nol Government. "Thailand, Laos, Cambodia and Vietnam: April 1973," staff report of the Senate Foreign Relations Committee, June 11, 1973, pp. 21–22.

p. 275   The story of Moose and Lowenstein in Phnom Penh is partly continued in *U.S. Air Operations in Cambodia*. Also author's interviews with the principal officials involved.

p. 276   Enders' proposals. Cable Phnom Penh 2747, March 26, 1973.

p. 276   Enders' warning to State. Phnom Penh, 3341, April 10, 1973.

p. 277   Moose and Lowenstein report. *U.S. Air Operations in Cambodia*, p. 2.

p. 277   Swank. Interview with the author, May 29–30, 1976.

p. 277   Rogers' conversation with aide. Rogers' aide was Jonathan Fred Ladd, who was now back in Washington working at the State Department. Ladd interview with the author, May 17, 1976.

p. 278   The constitution and the bombing. See Gerhard Casper, "Constitutional Constraints on the Conduct of Foreign and Defense Policy: A Nonjudicial Model," *University of Chicago Law Review*, June 1976, pp. 487–88.

p. 278   McGovern remarks. *Congressional Record*, May 17, 1973, S 9371, quoted by Arthur M. Schlesinger, Jr., *op. cit.*, p. 196.

Chapter 19

p. 280   Sihanouk's views. Author's interviews with Etienne Manac'h, February 18, 1976, Pung Peng Cheng, May 29, 1976, Nouth Choeumm, April 19, 1977.

p. 281   Radio Phnom Penh broadcast on Vietnamese behavior. February 12, 1978.

p. 281   Cambodian diplomat's complaint. *Far Eastern Economic Review*, January 13, 1978.

p. 281 Chou En-lai's appeal to Manac'h. Manac'h interview with the author, February 18, 1976.

p. 282 The French officials were interviewed both in Paris and in Washington.

p. 282 David Bruce and film. David Bruce interview with the author, July 6, 1976.

p. 282 Administration claims of North Vietnamese troops in Cambodia. Hearings before Senate Appropriations Committee. See also statement by State Department spokesman, Charles W. Bray, *Washington Post*, April 24, 1973.

p. 283 Account of the House vote. *Congressional Quarterly*, "Weekly Report," May 12, 1973, p. 1170.

p. 283 Sullivan and Nguyen Co Thach talks. Porter in *The Nation*, April 30, 1977.

p. 283 Le Duc Tho's arguments. Porter, *loc. cit.*

p. 283 Sihanouk's statement on Washington's refusal. Reuter, from Algiers, June 4, 1973.

p. 283 Gwertzman quotations. *The New York Times*, June 30 and July 1, 1973.

p. 284 Steerman statement. Interview with the author, June 1, 1976.

p. 284 Bruce statement. Interview with the author, July 6, 1976.

p. 284 Reaction to Nixon veto. *Congressional Quarterly*, "Weekly Report," June 30, 1973, p. 1707.

p. 285 Nixon memoirs. *RN: Memoirs*, pp. 888–89.

p. 285 Footnote. *RN: Memoirs*, p. 883.

p. 285 Kissinger's assurances. On June 30, 1973, Bernard Gwertzman in *The New York Times* quoted "a senior official of the Nixon administration" as saying that the bombing compromise "would allow the United States to continue the 'extremely delicate' negotiations that are now going on to end the fighting there." These involved Sihanouk. "Until recently the administration had disparaged the importance of Sihanouk . . . and had tended to concentrate its efforts on getting Hanoi to use its influence towards an accord between the insurgents and the government in Phnom Penh."

p. 286 Chou En-lai to Magnuson, July 6, 1973.

p. 286 FUNK Congress decisions. Carney, *op. cit.*, p. 21.

p. 286 Officials' comments on Kissinger's "delicate negotiations." Doolin, interview June 14, 1976; Tom Enders, telephone interview, January 1977; Brent Scowcroft, interview February 16, 1978; David Bruce interview, July 6, 1976, Um Sim, *The New York Times*, August 15, 1973, and interview, January 20, 1976; Emory Swank interview, May 29–30, 1977.

p. 286 Doolin's testimony. To House Committee on Foreign Affairs, June 6, 1973.

p. 287 Knight letter. *Bombing in Cambodia*, p. 5.

p. 288 General Brown's testimony. *Ibid.*, pp. 496–505; his letter, pp. 508–9.

p. 288 Sihanouk's press conference. Senate Foreign Relations Committee, *Nomination of Henry A. Kissinger*, Hearings, Part I, pp. 33–36, also *Bombing in Cambodia*, pp. 391–94.

p. 289 Friedheim's about-turns. *The New York Times*, July 19 and 21, 1973.

p. 289 Laird and Wheeler's denials and Kissinger's opinion on falsification. *The New York Times*, July 19, 1973.

p. 289 Kissinger's statement to the Senate Foreign Relations Committee. *Nomination of Henry A. Kissinger,* Part I, p. 243.

p. 290 Hughes-Clements exchange. *Bombing in Cambodia,* p. 443.

p. 290 Laird's reply to Clements. *The New York Times,* August 10, 1973.

p. 291 The account of the Holtzman and Donald Dawson case is derived principally from the court records in the offices of Dawson's lawyers, Karpatkin, Pollet and Le Moult, of New York City; also from telephone interviews and correspondence with Dawson, an interview with Holtzman, and a telephone interview with Burt Neuborn.

p. 294 B-52 beacon on U. S. embassy, Phnom Penh. *History of the United States Support Activities Group, Seventh Air Force, April 1–June 30, 1973,* p. 112.

p. 294 David Opfer statement. *Far Eastern Economic Review,* August 20, 1973.

p. 294 Footnote on bombing error. *History of the United States Support Activities Group, Seventh Air Force, April 1–June 30, 1973,* p. 119.

p. 295 Sihanouk statement to *New York Times. The New York Times,* July 5, 1973.

p. 295 Sihanouk interview with T. D. Allman. Published widely. including in the *Bangkok Post,* September 29, 1973.

p. 296 Cambodian Communist criticisms of Vietnam. Radio Phnom Penh, May 17 and April 14, 1978.

p. 297 Enders' claim. Telephone interview, January 1977.

p. 297 *History of the 43rd Strategic Wing, January–June 1973.* "The Cambodia Campaign," Narrative of Air Warfare over Cambodia, pp. 67–74.

p. 297 End-of-tour report. Colonel Frederick W. Fowler, Chief of the Air Intelligence Division at MACV, South Vietnam, August 72–February 73, and Chief Targets Division USSAG-J2, Nakhom Phanom, Thailand, February–August 73.

p. 298 General Vogt's figures. Interview with the author, February 11, 1977, also speech to Rotary Club in Honolulu, December 4, 1973.

Chapter 20

p. 300 "Mr. Secretary or Dr. Secretary?" Kalb and Kalb, *op. cit.* p. 447.

p. 300 Haldeman-Nixon conversation. House Committee of the Judiciary, *Hearings on Impeachment of the President,* 1974, Appendix III, p. 40.

p. 301 Nixon on Kissinger. Nixon, *RN: Memoirs,* p. 433.

p. 301 Kissinger-Rogers-Rush. Haldeman and DiMona, *op. cit.,* pp. 175–77.

p. 301 Nixon explanation for taping system. Nixon, *RN: Memoirs,* p. 701.

p. 301 Haldeman explanation of taping system. Haldeman and DiMona, *op. cit.,* p. 195.

p. 302 Kissinger letter to Nixon. Nixon, *RN: Memoirs,* p. 715.

p. 302 Reston column on Kissinger and bombing of Hanoi. December 30, 1972.

p. 302 Haldeman on Kissinger and Reston column. Haldeman and DiMona, *op. cit.,* p. 95.

p. 302 Haldeman on Kissinger and the tapes. Haldeman and DiMona, *op. cit.*, pp. 210–11.

p. 302 Price on Kissinger. Raymond K. Price, Jr., *With Nixon* (New York: Viking, 1977), pp. 305–6.

p. 303 Kissinger-Woodward conversation. Bob Woodward and Carl Bernstein, *All the President's Men*, (New York: Simon and Schuster, 1974), pp. 313–16.

p. 304 Kissinger on irresponsibility of Chilean people. This remark has been widely quoted. It was originally cited in *The CIA and the Cult of Intelligence* (New York: Knopf, 1975), but was deleted by demand of the CIA before publication.

p. 305 Kissinger on CIA in Chile. Statement, October 9, 1973.

p. 305 Kissinger and the Middle East. For a short analysis, see Stanley Hoffmann "Who Can Salvage Peace?" *New York Review of Books*, August 17, 1978.

p. 306 Kissinger on "illegitimacy" of European governments. Address to Congressional Wives, March 11, 1974. *Daily Telegraph*, London, March 13, 1974.

p. 306 Kissinger and the Shah; Kissinger and the Italian neo-Fascists. House Select Committee on Intelligence, report, published by *The Village Voice*, February 16, 1976.

p. 306 Kissinger's talk with Jiri Hajek. *From Dubcek to Charter 77*, Vladimir Kusin, Q. Press, Edinburgh 1978, p. 33.

p. 308 Stanley Hoffman on détente. Hoffman, *Primacy or World Order* (New York: McGraw-Hill, 1978), p. 46.

p. 308 Moynihan on Sonnenfeldt on Kissinger. Daniel Patrick Moynihan with Suzanne Weaver, *A Dangerous Place* (Boston: Little, Brown, 1978), p. 3. Sonnenfeldt's denial, *Time*, December 18,1978.

Chapter 21

p. 310 Swank press conference. *Washington Post*, September 6, 1973.

p. 312 End-of-tour reports of Cleland and Palmer. The military information and descriptions in the following pages are from these reports unless otherwise noted.

p. 312 Sihanouk's complaint. *Far Eastern Economic Review*, January 7, 1974.

p. 314 Elizabeth Becker and brass sales. Cleland refers to the incident in his end-of-tour report.

p. 317 Fleas off dog with cancer. W. Beazer in draft AID termination report.

p. 317 Description of rich in Phnom Penh. *Baltimore Sun*, April 17, 1975, quoted by Hildebrand and Porter, *Cambodia: Starvation and Revolution*, p. 74.

p. 317 The descriptions of the economy and society on the following pages are largely from the AID termination report.

p. 319 Refugee children. *The New York Times*, July 29, 1974.

p. 319 Khmer Rouge performance. The end-of-tour reports of Generals Cleland and Palmer both contain interesting analyses of Communist strategy.

p. 321 State Department study of the Khmer Rouge. Kenneth Quinn, "The Khmer Krahom Program to Create a Communist Society in Southern Cambodia," U.S. Consulate Can Tho, Vietnam, Airgram, February 20, 1974. This paper was declassified in 1976. It was revised and published by Quinn as "Political Change in Wartime: The Khmer Krahom Revolution in Southern Cambodia 1970-74," *Naval War College Review*, Spring 1976.

   p. 321   Sihanouk as "cherry pit." Oriana Fallacci interview, *The New York Times Magazine*, August 12, 1973.

   p. 321   The Party's use of youth. Timothy Carney; *op. cit.*, pp. 30-33.

   p. 322   Khmer Rouge terror. *Baltimore Sun*, March 2, 1974. *Washington Post*, November 24, 1974, *New York Times*, March 9, 1974.

   p. 324   Vietnamese casualties. Senate Refugee Subcommittee report, *Relief and Rehabilitation of War Victims in Indochina: One Year After the Ceasefire*, January 27, 1974, p. 10.

   p. 324   Graham Martin's cable and the Kennedy-Kissinger exchange. *Congressional Record*, March 19 and April 2, 1974; Kennedy press release, May 27, 1974.

   p. 325   Nixon and Cambodia. *The New York Times*, February 3, 1974.

   p. 325   Dean's cable to Kissinger. April 22, 1974.

   p. 326   Dean's wager with Sek Sam Iet. This account is taken from the notes of an embassy official present at the meeting.

   p. 327   Congressional report on Dean. House Foreign Affairs Committee, staff report, *United States Aid to Indochina*, July 1974, p. 25.

   p. 327   The Kissinger-Dean relationship. This description derives from unattributable interviews with members of the State Department.

   p. 328   Dean proposal for meeting with Khieu Samphan. *The New York Times*, August 27 and September 8, 1974.

   p. 328   Dean's Congressional testimony. House International Relations Committee, *Cambodia Evacuation*, May 5, 1976.

   p. 329   Wiretap material. Senate Foreign Relations Committee, Hearings, *Dr. Kissinger's Role in Wiretapping*, published September 1974. Fulbright's statement, p. 59.

   p. 330   Judiciary Committee staff and members' attitudes. This account is based on interviews with and the records of members of the staff and the committee itself.

   p. 332   The debate on Article IV. House Judiciary Committee's "Debate on Articles of Impeachment," 1974, pp. 490-517.

   p. 333   Sihanouk on Nixon's resignation. ". . . Nixon himself started the Cambodian war, so he was bound to continue it. President Ford is free from those old obligations and can now bring peace to my country." *The New York Times*, August 25, 1974.

   p. 324   Dean's trip to Washington. This account is based on interviews with members of the U.S. embassy, State Department officials, members of Congress and their staff. Fraser statements, *The Vietnam-Cambodia Emergency 1975*, Parts I-IV, House Committee on International Relations, 1976, p. 291.

Chapter 22

   p. 325   The full text of the State Department's "Summary of Negotiating Efforts on Cambodia," March 4, 1975, read:

We have made continual and numerous private attempts, in addition to our numerous public declarations, to demonstrate in concrete and specific ways our readiness to see an early compromise settlement in Cambodia.

Throughout the negotiations that led to the Paris Agreement on Viet-Nam in January 1973, the United States repeatedly indicated its desire to see a cease-fire and political settlement in Cambodia as well as in Vietnam and Laos. In later discussions concerning the implementation of the Paris Agreement, the United States conveyed its ideas and its desire to promote a negotiated settlement between the Cambodian parties.

On many other occasions in 1971 and 1972 we made clear our interest in seeing an independent and neutral Cambodia established through negotiations and not through a battlefield victory.

A number of major efforts toward negotiation were made in 1973, efforts which were thwarted by the forced bombing halt in August of that year.

In October, 1974, we broached the idea of an international conference on Cambodia with two countries having relations with the side headed by Prince Sihanouk (GRUNK). We also discussed the elements of a peaceful settlement. We received no substantive response to these overtures.

In November, 1974, we again indicated with specificity our readiness to see a compromise settlement in Cambodia in which all elements could play a role to a government with relations with the GRUNK. Our interlocutors showed no interest in pursuing the subject.

In December 1974, we tried to facilitate a channel to representatives of the Khmer Communists through a neutralist country with relations with the GRUNK. Nothing came of this initiative.

In December 1974 and early January 1975, we concurred in an initiative to open a dialogue with Sihanouk in Peking. Sihanouk at first agreed to receive an emissary, but later refused.

In February, 1975, we tried to establish a direct contact with Sihanouk ourselves. We received no response.

Also in February 1975 we apprised certain friendly governments with clear interests and concerns in the region, and with access to governments supporting the GRUNK, of our efforts to move the conflict toward a negotiated solution and of the degree of flexibility in our approach. They could offer no help.

Unfortunately, none of these attempts have had any result. The reactions we have gotten so far suggest that negotiating prospects will be dim as long as the Cambodian Government's military position remains precarious.

We are continuing to pursue our long-stated objective of an early compromise settlement in Cambodia. In this process we are, and have been, guided by the following principles:

1. The United States will support any negotiations that the parties themselves are prepared to support.
2. The United States will accept any outcome from the negotiations that the parties themselves will accept.
3. As far as the United States is concerned, the personalities involved will not, themselves, constitute obstacles of any kind to a settlement.

p. 336   This account of the Martinique initiative is based principally on interviews with senior officials in the Quai d'Orsay including Etienne Manac'h, February 18, 1976, and Henry Froment Meurice, July 27, 1976, and with the then

Foreign Minister, Jean Sauvarnagues. Also interview with Brent Scowcroft, February 16, 1978, and telephone interview with Helmut Sonnenfeldt, October 12, 1978.

p. 336   Ceaucescu's initiative. Edith Lenart, *Far Eastern Economic Review*, July 15, 1974.

p. 337   Sihanouk on tiger and dog. *The New York Times*, August 25, 1974.

p. 337   Um Sim's principal overture to Mansfield was made on February 7, 1974. Mansfield interview with the author, May 17, 1976.

p. 338   Giscard's telegram to Sihanouk in Algiers and Sihanouk's reaction. *Le Point*, Paris, March 24, 1975.

p. 340   Chou En-lai on Kissinger. Sihanouk interview with Agence France Presse, February 27, 1975.

p. 340   Graham Martin's views on Cambodia. Telephone interview with the author, July 1977.

p. 340   Brent Scowcroft on Kissinger's attitude to Lon Nol's removal. Interview with the author, February 16, 1973.

p. 340   Schanberg on "embassy official" and Kissinger. *The New York Times*, December 15, 1974.

p. 341   Giscard's TV retraction. December 20, 1974, in response to a question put by Pierre Salinger of *L'Express*.

Chapter 23

p. 344   The final battle for Phnom Penh. This account is derived principally from General Palmer's end-of-tour report, reports of the military attaché's office in the U.S. embassy, Phnom Penh, other declassified documents, interviews with American and Cambodian officials and soldiers, and contemporary press reports.

p. 346   The closing of the Mekong and the airlift. These stories are recounted in detail in *History of the United States Support Activities Group/Seventh Air Force*, January 1–March 31, 1975.

p. 348   Rice consumption 1975. *The New York Times*, February 26, 1975, quoted in Hildebrand and Porter, *op. cit.*, p. 23.

p. 348   Dean's complaints. *History of the United States Support Activities Group/Seventh Air Force*, January 1–March 31, 1975, p. 146.

p. 348   Inspector General's report. *Cambodia: An Assessment of Humanitarian Needs and Relief Efforts*, March 12, 1975, reprinted in *Congressional Record*, March 20, 1975, p. S 4619, quoted in Hildebrand and Porter, *op. cit.*, p. 25.

p. 349   Schanberg report from Neak Luong. *The New York Times*, February 24, 1975.

p. 349   General Fish's statement. *Foreign Assistance and Related Agencies Appropriations for 1975*. Hearings before a subcommittee of the Committee on Appropriations, House of Representatives, February 3, 1975, p. 12, quoted in Hildebrand and Porter, *op. cit.*, p. 38.

p. 350   Philip Habib's statement. House Committee on International Relations, *The Vietnam-Cambodia Emergency 1975*, p. 287.

p. 350 Kissinger warning. *Washington Post*, February 26, 1975.

p. 351 Kissinger statement on "certain destruction." *Ibid.*

p. 351 Ford warning. *Ibid.*

p. 351 "The Kissinger Doctrine," Anthony Lewis, *The New York Times*, February 27, 1975.

p. 351 Cambodian newspaper articles. H. D. S. Greenway, *Washington Post*, March 20, 1975.

p. 352 Dean statement to Congressional delegation. In House Committee on International Relations, Hearings on *The Vietnam-Cambodian Emergency 1975*, p. 62.

p. 352 McCloskey statement. Senate Foreign Relations Committee, Subcommittee on Foreign Assistance and Economic Policy, Hearings on *Supplemental Assistance to Cambodia*, February 24, 1975, p. 64.

p. 353 The story of Sarsar Sdam was well known among relief officials in Cambodia. It is contained in internal memoranda to W. Howe, Program Director for Catholic Relief Services from his Field Operations staff, on August 19 and August 26, 1974.

p. 354 Khieu Samphan statement. *Le Monde Diplomatique*, November 1974.

p. 354 Journalists' song. Martin Woollacott, *The Guardian*, London, September 6, 1977.

p. 354 Sihanouk's *chef du cabinet*. Interview with the author, Pung Peng Cheng, May 27, 1976.

p. 354 Khmer Rouge decision to empty the cities. This was revealed in March 1978 to a Yugoslav journalist in Phnom Penh by Prime Minister and Party Secretary Pol Pot. The film was broadcast by Panorama, the BBC, London, May 15, 1978, and by CBS television June 7, 1978.

p. 355 Hospital conditions. U.S. AID draft termination report and General Palmer's end-of-tour report.

p. 355 Accounts of Khmer Rouge soldiers. U.S. military attaché's interview with the author.

p. 356 Dean's cable. Phnom Penh 5368, March 24, 1975.

p. 356 Major Alan Armstrong wrote two long internal embassy reports on the army at this time: "Analysis of the 7th Division, January 1975," January 29, 1975, and "FANK Morale—The Will to Resist," March 9, 1975.

p. 358 Final Assessment of the Military Situation in Cambodia. April 1975, U.S. Defense Attaché's Office study.

p. 359 Dean's outburst about "fighting to the last Cambodian." Made to Stewart Dalby of the *Financial Times*, London.

p. 359 Dean's dinner party. This account is based on interviews with several of the journalists present.

p. 360 Sihanouk's overture. This account is based on interviews with Pung Peng Cheng and French and American officials involved.

p. 363 Um Sim's outburst. *Washington Post*, April 12, 1975.

p. 363 Kissinger comment. Interview with Pierre Salinger, *L'Express*, Paris, April 21–27, 1975.

Chapter 24

p. 365   The account of the evacuation of Phnom Penh is based on reports by Jon Swain, *The Sunday Times*, London, May 11, 1975, and Sydney S. Schanberg, *The New York Times*, May 9, 1975.

p. 366   Ponchaud's reaction. François Ponchaud, *Cambodia: Year Zero*, p. 7.

p. 368   The author talked to refugees at the Aranya-prathet refugee camp on the Thai-Cambodian border in December 1975. See *The New York Review of Books*, March 4, 1976.

p. 369   Yugoslav reports. See, for example, Slavko Stanic, "Cambodia, Path Without Model," broadcast by Tanjug in Serbo-Croat, April 19–24, 1978.

p. 369   Scandinavian ambassadors' reactions and descriptions. Stockholm Radio, January 22, 1978; BBC Summary of World Broadcasts, January 24, 1978.

p. 369   "Absurd film . . . nightmare." *Ibid.*

p. 370   Footnote—Government food stocks. Khmer Report: Phnom Penh 5857; U.S. AID draft termination report, p. 16; confirmed in letter to author from Donnelly Sohlin, Acting AID Mission Director Phnom Penh, January 1975, dated January 3, 1978.

p. 370   U.S. government acknowledgment of need for airlift. Letter from Department of State to Representative Robert W. Edgar (Dem. Pa), August 13, 1975.

p. 372   "They wanted to swallow us . . ." Radio Phnom Penh, June 24, 1978.

p. 372   Hanoi's alleged plan. Radio Phnom Penh, May 10, 1978.

p. 372   Frank Snepp on spy rings. Snepp, *Decent Interval*, p. 340.

p. 372   North Vietnamese fear of U.S. retaliation. This was fully expressed in the memoirs of General Van Tien Dung, the commander of the final assault on Saigon, entitled "Great Spring Victory" broadcast on Hanoi Radio in April 1977. *Foreign Broadcast Information Service*, Volume IV, No. 110, Supp. 38 and No. 131, Supp. 42, June 7 and July 7, 1976.

p. 373   Mayaguez. The American container ship, S.S. *Mayaguez* was sailing from Saigon to Sattahip, Thailand, with a cargo of U.S. government matériel. By the time it steamed only 1.75 miles past the island of Poulo Wai on May 12 a full-scale island war was underway between the two new Communist governments of Vietnam and Cambodia. Nonetheless, no warning to shipping had been issued by Washington.

At 2:20 P.M. local time on May 12, shots were fired across the *Mayaguez'* bow by a Cambodian patrol boat and she was boarded. The radio operator sent out distress signals. President Ford was informed some four hours later. Reconnaissance planes from Thailand were ordered to search for the ship, and American naval vessels were dispatched to the area.

The National Security Council was convened, and Kissinger argued that much more was at stake than the seizure of an American ship. After the collapses of Lon Nol and Thieu, American credibility was more involved than ever. Throughout the crisis the Secretary insisted that for domestic and international reasons, and particularly to impress the North Koreans, the United States must use force. The White House publicly demanded the immediate release of the ship, and the Chinese government was asked to deliver a twenty-four-hour ultimatum from the U.S. government to the Cambodians.

Sideshow

At 5:24 P.M. on May 13, American planes spotted a fishing boat moving the crew of the *Mayaguez* to the island of Koh Tang. American marines in Thailand were readied for attack. Early on the fourteenth a fishing boat was seen leaving the island and heading for the mainland port of Kompong Som. The *Mayaguez* crew was sighted on deck. United States planes were ordered to try to prevent the crew being taken to the mainland. They strafed and gassed the boat, but it did not stop. (Several of the *Mayaguez*' sailors suffered permantent damage to their health and later sued the U.S. government.) After it reached Kompong Som, United States planes were ordered to sink all boats around Koh Tang. Seven were destroyed.

Only now, two days after the seizure of the *Mayaguez*, did the U.S. government ask the United Nations to use its machinery for settling international disputes to try to obtain the return of the ship. Kissinger then insisted that more force was required, and he demanded that B-52 strikes be mounted against Cambodia once more. On instructions from the White House the Joint Chiefs cabled CINCPAC a detailed plan that included the orders "Sink all Cambodian small craft in the target areas of Koh Tang, Poulo Wai, Kompong Som and Ream. In coordination with SACADVON, B-52 strikes against Kompong Som and Ream airfield, Guam-based B-52s and tankers will be utilized in above planning. . . ." In the end this order was countermanded and only tactical aircraft were used.

Although it was almost certain that the crew had been taken to the mainland twenty-three hours beforehand, at dawn on May 15, U. S. Marines were ordered to attack Koh Tang. Despite the provisions of the 1973 War Powers Act, which demands that the President consult with Congress before committing American troops to combat, leaders of Congress were informed after the instructions had been sent. The island was far more heavily defended than intelligence reports had indicated; the Marines were pinned down by fire and began to suffer casualties. Then Phnom Penh Radio promised to release the ship. Despite the conciliatory nature of the broadcast, Kissinger and Ford ordered Kompong Som to be bombed. Ford later conceded that this placed the *Mayaguez* crew at risk.

The *Mayaguez* crew was then spotted coming back toward the ship in a Thai fishing boat; at 10:08 A.M. on May 15 the men were picked up by the U.S. Navy. The news was flashed to the White House. After this news was received another wave of bombing attacks on the mainland took place.

In the attacks on Kompong Som the railroad yard, the port, the oil refinery and the airfield were virtually destroyed. At Ream naval base, 364 buildings were flattened. Nine Cambodian vessels were sunk at sea. In order to rescue the Marines on Koh Tang, the island was heavily bombarded. In making these attacks, the White House ignored the August 1973 ban on bombing Indochina as well as the 1973 War Powers Act. Several critics maintained that only minimal diplomatic attempts to secure the release of the crew were made, because Kissinger wished to display force. The principal purposes of the bombing seem to have been to punish the Cambodians and to reassert a concept of American bellicosity, which the collapse of Phnom Penh and Saigon was seen to have damaged.

As such, they were a great success. British newspapers were full of praise for the effort, and Senator Barry Goldwater declared "It was wonderful, it shows we've still got balls in this country." James Reston, apparently reflecting Kissinger's own attitude, exulted in *The New York Times:* "Uncle Sam just went out of Cambodia and slammed the door." *Newsweek* declared the operation "a daring show of nerve and steel . . . swift and tough—and it worked." C. L. Sulzberger declared in the *Times* that "Overnight, by resolute and skillful leadership in the *Mayaguez* crisis, President Ford has seemingly moved from the doldrums of Hooverdom toward the vigor of Harry Truman. He made up his mind; he consulted political leaders; he acted; and he succeeded. Small as the incident may later seem in history, a polluting stain is being erased from the previous American image of lassitude, uncertainty and pessimism." Senator Clifford Case said, "I don't want anyone saying that we liberals or doves would prevent the President from protecting American lives in a piracy attack." Kissinger himself warned that "the impact ought to be made clear that there are limits beyond which the United States cannot be pushed." President Ford later asserted that "it did not only ignite confidence in the White House . . . it had an electrifying reaction as far as the American people were concerned. It was a spark that set off a whole new sense of confidence for them, too."

Ever since, Ford has claimed the *Mayaguez* affair as his greatest foreign-policy triumph. It is not, perhaps, unfair to accept his assessment. One might, however, note that in "saving" the 40 American seamen, 41 American military men were killed, and 49 more were wounded. There are no reliable estimates of the number of Cambodians who died in the attack on Koh Tang or in the renewed bombing of the mainland; nor can one do more than speculate on the effects the attacks must have had on Khmer Rouge paranoia about their enemies.

Sources for this account include James Reston comment, *The New York Times,* May 16, 1975; *Newsweek* comment, *Newsweek,* May 26, 1975; Kissinger "there are limits," *The New York Times,* May 17, 1975; Senator Clifford Case "we liberals," *The New York Times,* May 26, 1975; President Ford's "electrifying reaction," Roy Rowan, *The Four Days of Mayaguez* (New York: Norton, 1975), p. 223. *History of the Pacific Air Forces, July 1, 1974–December 31, 1975,* "The Mayaguez Affair," pp. 426–69.

p. 373   Pung Peng Cheng's estimate, and statement on Khmer Rouge expectations. Interview with the author, May 29, 1976.

p. 373   Pol Pot's admission. Yugoslav television film.

p. 374   Pol Pot on "smashing spy organizations" and "the enemy secret agent network." Press conference in Peking, New China News Agency in English, October 3, 1977; BBC Summary, October 4, 1977.

p. 375   Pol Pot on lack of medicine and health problems. Radio Phnom Penh, July 30, 1976.

p. 375   Description of life in cooperatives. Ponchaud, *op. cit.,* pp. 87–107.

p. 377   Ponchaud on *Angka.* Ponchaud, *op. cit.,* pp. 126–27.

p. 377   Renunciation. Ponchaud, *op cit.,* p. 120.

p. 378   The account of Sihanouk's life since April 1975 is based on interviews with his aides Pung Peng Cheng and Nouth Cheoumm, interviews with Western diplomats in Peking, and published accounts.

p. 378   Sihanouk's song "Farewell Cambodia," Ponchaud, *op. cit.,* p. 171.

p. 378   Sihanouk on "cruel policy" of the Khmer Rouge. Associated Press, October 17, 1975.

p. 379 Sihanouk's reception in Phnom Penh. Interview with Sihanouk's press aide, Nouth Cheoumm, published in *Far Eastern Economic Review*, October 24, 1975.

p. 379 The author attended Sihanouk's Paris press conference.

p. 381 Pol Pot profile. Hanoi Radio, September 13, 1978.

pp. 382–83 Pol Pot on the revolution. Speech over Radio Phnom Penh, September 28, 1977 and press conference in Peking, New China News Agency, October 3, 1977.

p. 384 Phnom Penh on Vietnamese "ingratitude." Radio Phnom Penh, December 30, 1977.

p. 384 Cambodian explanation of breakdown of talks. Radio Phnom Penh, June 24, 1978.

p. 384 Vietnamese description of Cambodian attack. Hanoi Radio in English, January 12, 1978.

p. 385 Cambodian Foreign Minstry assurance on Thai-Cambodian border incident. Statement No. S/77/046 in response to Thai foreign ministry's complaint, 0305-8545, January 31, 1977.

p. 385 Hanoi on murder of Hanoi-Khmers. Hanoi Radio, February 12, 1978; Hanoi in Cambodian, February 15, 1978.

p. 386 Hanoi on resistance movements in Cambodia, Vietnam News Agency in English, June 21, 1978, and Hanoi in Cambodia in Cambodian, June 22, 1978.

p. 387 Hanoi on Cambodian attempt to distract attention. Hanoi Radio in English, February 21, 1978.

p. 387 Phnom Penh on Vietnamese hatred for Cambodians and desire to annex Cambodia. Radio Phnom Penh throughout 1977; for example, April 12, 1978.

p. 387 Phnom Penh on killing thirty Vietnamese. Radio Phnom Penh May 10, 1977.

p. 387 Vietnamese on China's intention to provoke a disease. Central Committee member and editor of the Party paper, Hoang Tung, in interview with Nayan Chanda, *Far Eastern Economic Review*, April 21, 1978.

p. 388 Vietnamese commentary on China and "the clique." Hanoi Radio, July 15, 1978.

Afterword

p. 394 David Frost interview with Richard Nixon. Printed in *The New York Times*, May 20, 1977.

p. 394 Kissinger interview with Theo Sommer, *Die Zeit*, No. 28 (July 2, 1976). From 1976 through 1978 the author of this book made repeated efforts, both in writing and through intermediaries, to talk to Dr. Kissinger. He was unsuccessful.

Bibliography

Caldwell, Malcolm, and Lek Tan, *Cambodia in the Southeast Asian War*. New York and London: Monthly Review Press, 1973.

Chester, Lewis, Hodgson, Godfrey, and Page, Bruce, *An American Melodrama*. New York: Viking, 1969. London: André Deutsch, 1969.

Debré, François, *Cambodge: La Révolution de la forêt*. Paris: Flammarion, 1976.

Dudman, Richard, *Forty Days with the Enemy*. New York: Liveright, 1971.

Evans, Rowland, Jr. and Novak, Robert D., *Nixon in the White House*. New York: Random House, 1971.

Gallucci, Robert L., *Neither Peace nor Honor*. Baltimore and London: Johns Hopkins University Press, 1975.

Haldeman, H. R., and DiMona, Joseph, *The Ends of Power*. New York: Times Books, 1978. London: Sidgwick and Jackson, 1978.

Hall, D. G. E., *A History of Southeast Asia*. London: Macmillan, 1964.

Hildebrand, George C., and Porter, Gareth, *Cambodia, Starvation and Revolution*. New York and London: Monthly Review Press, 1976.

Hoopes, Townsend, *The Devil and John Foster Dulles*. Boston: Little, Brown, 1973. London: Deutsch, 1974.

———, *The Limits of Intervention*. New York: David McKay, 1973.

Kalb, Marvin, and Kalb, Bernard, *Kissinger*. Boston: Little, Brown, 1974.

Kissinger, Henry A., *The Necessity for Choice*. London: Chatto and Windus, 1960.

———, *Nuclear Weapons and Foreign Policy*. New York: Norton, 1969.

———, *The Troubled Partnership*. New York: McGraw-Hill, 1975.

———, *The White House Years, 1968–72*. Boston: Little, Brown, 1979. London: Michael Joseph, 1979.

———, *A World Restored*. London: Weidenfeld and Nicolson, 1957.

Lukas, J. Anthony, *Nightmare: The Underside of the Nixon Years*. New York: Viking, 1976.

Meyer, Charles, *Derrière le sourire khmer*. Paris: Plon, 1971.

Morris, Roger, *Uncertain Greatness: Henry Kissinger and American Foreign Policy*. London: Quartet, 1977. New York: Harper and Row, 1977.

Nixon, Richard, *RN: The Memoirs of Richard Nixon*. New York: Grosset and Dunlap, 1978. London: Sidgwick and Jackson, 1978.

493

Sideshow

Ponchaud, François, *Cambodia: Year Zero*. New York: Holt, Rinehart and Winston, 1978. London: Penguin Press, 1978.

Porter, Gareth, *A Peace Denied*. Bloomington: Indiana University Press, 1975.

Rather, Dan, and Gates, Gary Paul, *The Palace Guard*. New York: Harper and Row, 1974.

Safire, William, *Before the Fall*. New York: Doubleday, 1975.

Schell, Jonathan, *The Time of Illusion*. New York: Knopf, 1976.

Schlesinger, Arthur, Jr., *The Imperial Presidency*. Boston: Houghton Mifflin, 1973.

Shawcross, William, *Quality of Mercy: Cambodia, Holocaust and Modern Conscience*. New York: Simon and Schuster, 1984. London: Deutsch, 1984.

Sihanouk, Norodom, *My War with the CIA*, as related to Wilfred Burchett. New York: Monthly Review Press, 1973. London: Penguin Press, 1973.

——, *War and Hope: The Case for Cambodia*. New York: Pantheon, 1980. London: Sidgwick and Jackson, 1980.

Snepp, Frank, *Decent Interval*. New York: Random House, 1977.

Szulc, Tad, *The Illusion of Peace*. New York: Viking, 1978.

Westmoreland, William C., *A Soldier Reports*. New York: Doubleday, 1976.

Wise, David, *The American Police State*. New York: Random House, 1976.

Background Information Relating to Southeast Asia and Vietnam, Senate Foreign Relations Committee, December 1974.

Bombing as a Policy Tool in Vietnam: Effectiveness: Staff study for the Senate Foreign Relations Committee, October 12, 1972.

Bombing in Cambodia, Hearings before the Senate Armed Services Committee, July and August 1973.

Cambodia: May 1970. Staff report of the Senate Foreign Relations Committee, June 7, 1970.

Cambodia: December 1970. Staff report of the Senate Foreign Relations Committee, December 16, 1970.

Communist Party Power in Kampuchea (Cambodia): Documents and Discussion, compiled and edited with an Introduction by Timothy Michael Carney, Data Paper 106, Southeast Asia Program, Department of Asian Studies, Cornell University, Ithaca, New York, 1977.

Dr. Kissinger's role in wiretapping. Hearings before the Senate Foreign Relations Committee, through 1975.

Evacuation and Temporary Care Afforded Indochinese Refugees—Operation New Life. Report by the Comptroller General, June 1, 1976.

Human Rights in Cambodia, Hearings before the Subcommittee on International Organizations of the House Committee on International Relations, May 3 and July 26, 1977.

Humanitarian Problems in Indochina, Hearings before the Refugees Subcommittee of the Senate Judiciary Committee, July 18, 1974.

Humanitarian Problems in South Vietnam and Cambodia: Two Years After the Ceasefire. Study mission report for the Refugees Subcommittee of the Senate Judiciary Committee, January 27, 1975.

Bibliography

Impeachment of Richard M. Nixon, President of the United States, Statements of Information, Hearings, and Report, by the House of Representatives Judiciary Committee, August 1974.

Intelligence Activities. Hearings before the Senate Committee to study Governmental Operations with Respect to Intelligence Activities, 1975, published 1976.

Military and Economic Situation in Cambodia. Staff survey report for the House Committee on Foreign Affairs, March 13, 1975.

Problems in the Khmer Republic (Cambodia) Concerning War Victims, Civilian Health, and War-Related Casualties. Comptroller General of the United States, February 2, 1972.

Problems of War Victims in Indochina, Part II: Cambodia and Laos, Hearing before the Refugees Subcommittee, Senate Judiciary Committee, May 9, 1972.

Refugee and Civilian War Casualty Problems in Indochina, Staff report of the Refugees Subcommittee, Senate Judiciary Committee, September 28, 1970.

Relief and Rehabilitation of War Victims in Indochina, Part I: Crisis in Cambodia, Hearing before the Refugees Subcommittee, Senate Judiciary Committee, April 16, 1973.

Relief and Rehabilitation of War Victims in Indochina: One Year After the Ceasefire. Study mission report for the Refugees Subcommittee, Senate Judiciary Committee, January 27, 1974.

Report on the Payment of Phantom Troops in the Cambodian Military Forces. Comptroller General of the United States, July 3, 1973.

Seizure of the *Mayaguez*. Hearings Before the Committee on International Relations, Parts I–III, May, June, July, 1975 and Part IV, October 4, 1976.

Supplemental Assistance to Cambodia. Hearings before Subcommittee of the Senate Foreign Relations Committee on S 663, February 24 and March 6, 1975.

Thailand, Laos and Cambodia: January 1972. Staff report for Subcommittee of the Senate Foreign Relations Committee, May 8, 1972.

Thailand, Laos, Cambodia, and Vietnam: April 1973. Staff report for a Subcommittee of the Senate Foreign Relations Committee, June 11, 1973.

The Vietnam Cambodia Emergency 1975, Part IV—Cambodia Evacuation: Testimony of Ambassador John Gunther Dean. Hearing before the Special Subcommittee on Investigations, House Committee on International Relations, May 5, 1976.

Transmittal of Documents from the National Security Council to the Chairman of the Joint Chiefs of Staff, Hearings before the Senate Armed Services Committee, February 6, 20, 21, March 7, 1974.

US Air Operations in Cambodia: April 1973. Staff report for Subcommittee of the Senate Foreign Relations Committee, April 27, 1973.

US Policy and Programs in Cambodia. Hearings before a Subcommittee of the House Foreign Affairs Committee, May 9, 10; June 6, 7, 1973.

U.S. Assistance to the Khmer Repbulic (Cambodia), Comptroller General of the United States, October 10, 1973.

United States Aid to Indochina, Staff report of the House Committee on Foreign Affairs, July 1974.

War Powers Legislation, 1973. Hearings before the Senate Foreign Relations Committee, April 11 and 12, 1973.

Index

Carney, Timothy, 252
Carswell, G. Harrold, 134
Carter, Jimmy, 80, 98–99, 393, 394
Carver, George, 137
Case, Clifford, 491*n*
Castro, Fidel, 370
Catholic Relief Services, 227, 318, 353
Ceaucescu, Nicolae, 336
Central Intelligence Agency (CIA), 54,
  64, 81, 112, 170, 201, 233, 248–
  249, 250–251, 314
  in Cambodian coup, 114–116, 118–
  122, 123, 125, 232
  Cambodian invasion and, 137–138
  "disinformation" from, 119, 122
  domestic dissidents and, 157, 158
  in Khmer Rouge, 236, 372
  Khmer Rouge evacuation policy
  and, 372
  Kissinger and, 99, 305, 306
  National Estimates Board of, 137
  Nixon and, 182
  Special National Intelligence
  Estimate of (SNIE), 173
  see also intelligence, U.S.
Chak Angre refugee camp (Phnom
  Penh), 223
Chams, invasion of, 39
Chantal, Madame, opium parlor of,
  193
Charner, Admiral, 43
Chau Seng, 243
Cheng Heng, 176, 204, 229, 275
Chenla, kingdom of, 38–39, 65
Chenla I, Operation, 202
Chenla II, battle of, 202–204, 229, 421
Chiao Kuan-hua, 338, 340
Chile, 98, 304–305, 329*n*, 351
China, dynastic, 38, 41, 43
China, People's Republic of, 24, 52,
  53, 90
  Cambodian independence supported
  by, 257, 387
  Cambodian peace efforts and, 336–
  343
  conference of revolutionary
  movements held by, 143–144

Cultural Revolution in, 67, 244, 257
  vs. "hegemonism," 390
  Khmer Rouge and, 48, 246, 247,
  257, 258, 336, 387–390, 405–406
  leadership changes in, 380, 381
  Lon Nol and, 124, 126, 143, 144,
  338–339
  Nixon and, 74–75, 85–86, 99, 260,
  304, 387, 415
  North Vietnam and, 115–116, 210,
  248, 257, 371, 406
  Sihanouk and, see Sihanouk, Prince
  Norodom
  Soviet relations with, 90, 338
Chinese-Cambodian Friendship
  Association, 245
Chinese merchants, 56, 57
Chinese People's Liberation Army,
  143, 162
Chou En-lai, 64, 124, 125, 144, 206,
  246, 257, 281–282, 286, 336, 338,
  339, 340, 378, 380, 381
Chou Ta-kuan, 40
Church, Frank, 164
Churchill, Winston, 66
CINCPAC, 136, 167, 272, 276
Civilian Irregular Defense Groups
  (CIDG), 64–65
Cleland, John, 15, 228, 229, 251, 270–
  271, 433–434, 446–447, 454
  on Cambodian army, 312–316
Clements, William, 290
Clifford, Clark, 80, 93, 106
Cochin China, 43–44
Colby, William, 54, 65, 122, 170, 182,
  250, 265, 307, 308, 443
Cold War, Kissinger and, 75–76
Columbia Eagle, 120*n*
Commodity Import Program, 221–222,
  225
Communist bloc:
  Cambodia and, 52–53, 61
  Vietnam outcome and, 87
"Communist Infrastructure in
  Cambodia," 249
Communists, 236–258
  Cambodian, see Democratic

Sideshow

Kissinger, Henry A. (*cont.*)
"house doves" and, 141–142
on intellectuals and policymakers,
77–78
international order and, 306, 308
interview with David Frost, 427, 442
irrationality and, 90–91, 372
Joint Chiefs and, 83, 92, 93, 195,
205–208, 418
Khmer Rouge and, 248, 325–326
Korean War as viewed by, 86
Laird and, 83, 96, 102, 103, 104,
105, 106, 107, 155, 178–180, 192–
193, 194, 205, 212*n*, 213
"linkage" concept of, 77, 306
Lon Nol and, 128, 161, 189, 261,
262, 327, 340, 409
loyalty to President of, 146, 156
memoirs of, 409–421
military and, 83, 104–105
as National Security Assistant, 79–
80, 98, 309
news leaks plugged by, 34–35, 105–
107, 108*n*, 155, 206–208
Nixon as seen by, 74–75, 79, 99–
100, 154, 302, 445
Nixon's relationship with, 82–83,
99–100, 102, 107, 156, 301–303,
309
Nixon's selection of, 79–80
Nixon's tapes and, 301–303
Nixon's views on, 100, 301, 302
NSC reorganization and, 80–84, 102
NSSMs and, 81–82, 84, 102, 178–
182, 192–193, 200, 230–235, 305
in Paris talks, 108, 109, 282
peace agreement and, 259, 260, 261–
262, 264, 324–325
Phnom Penh defense strategies and,
178–182, 190
Plumbers and, 206–208, 303
political outlook of, 76–79
press and, 33–35, 96–99, 155, 300,
328–330
right-wing threat as rationale of,
156, 157, 158
Rockefeller and, 74, 75, 78, 79

Rogers and, 83, 96, 102–103, 105,
107, 155–156, 157, 193, 300–301
Salzburg press conference of, 329–
330
secrecy justified by, 28
secrecy maintained by, 84, 95, 155,
289, 308
as Secretary of State, 300–309
"Shawcross's Documents" memo
and, 410, 420, 439
Sideshow and, 409–421, 422–457
Sihanouk and, 71*n*, 122, 125, 257–
258, 264, 283, 285, 288–289, 336,
360, 361, 390–391, 409.
Soviet Union and, 76, 77, 86, 305,
306, 307–308
staff relations of, 100
strategic concepts of, 75–76, 86
on U.S. objectives in Cambodia,
193–194
Vietnam policies of, 87–90, 104
Vietnam talks proposed by, 88
on war in Cambodia, 260, 261–262,
394–395, 409–421
wiretaps and, 35, 97, 105–107, 155,
303–304, 328–329
Kleindienst, Richard, 272*n*; 277
Knight, Hal, 30–32, 152, 287, 289, 414
Koh Kralor, siege of, 326–327
Koh Tang, U.S. attack on, 490*n*–491*n*
Komer, Robert, 72
Kompong Cham, town of, 126–127,
200, 250, 296, 312
Kompong Cham, province, 44, 149,
232
Kompong Seila, siege of, 356
Kompong Som (Sihanoukville), 57,
165, 179, 200, 369, 490*n*
see also Sihanoukville
Kompong Speu, town of, 249, 372
Kompong Thom, 200, 250, 264, 322,
407–408
relief of, 202–204
Korean War, 86–87, 147, 210, 293
Kossomak, Queen Mother, 118, 119,
127, 128
Kosygin, Alexei, 123, 143